Estonia

the Bradt Travel Guide

Neil Taylor

edition
7

www.bradtguides.com

Bradt Travel Guides Ltd, UK
The Globe Pequot Press Inc, USA

FINLAND

Tallinn: Twenty-five years ago a backwater, now a thriving European capital
pages 73–134

HELSINKI

N

Bradt

0   50km
0   30 miles

BALTIC SEA

Stockholm

Prangli

Naissaar

Vääna-Jõesuu

Maardu

Paldiski

TALLINN

Kihelkonna: Climb the tower to look across the whole of Saaremaa
pages 274–5

Keila

Vasalemma

Kohila

Riisipere

Rapla

Vormsi

Risti

Kärdla

Haapsalu

Märjamaa

Hiiumaa

Kopu

Käina

Matsalu Nature Reserve

West Estonian Archipelago Biosphere Reserve

Kassari

Emmaste

Lihula

Vändra

Muhu

Vilsandi

Orissaare

Virtsu

Saaremaa

Soomaa National Park

Kihelkonna

Audru

Pärnu

Kuressaare

Munalaid

Kilingi-Nõmme

Salme

Abruka

Kihnu

Mõisaküla

Jamaja

Mõntu

Häädemeeste

Nigula Nature Reserve

Sääre

Ikla

Ruhnu

Ainaži

Kuressaare: See a totally intact medieval fortress, unique in the Baltics
pages 261–71

Gulf of Riga

VENTSPILS

Pärnu: Relax with Estonians all through the summer at their smoothest and longest beach
pages 241–51

Gauja

LATVIA

Venta

Daugava

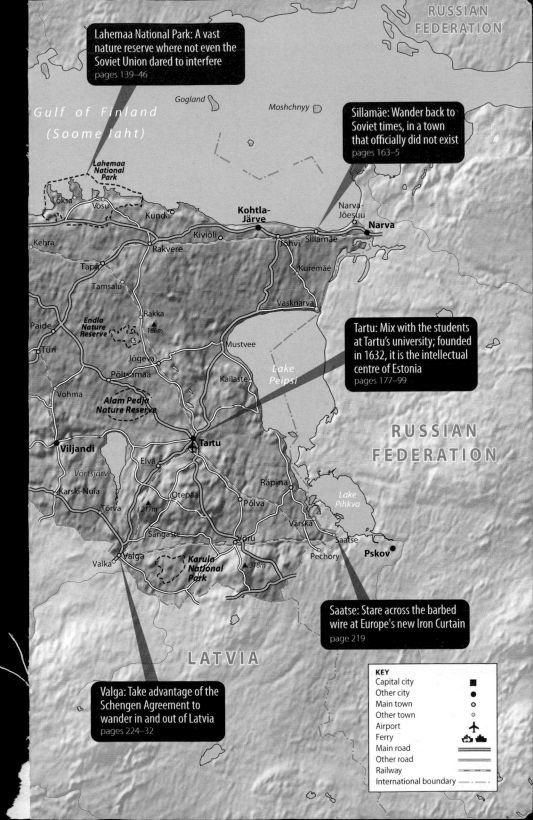

RUSSIAN FEDERATION

Lahemaa National Park: A vast nature reserve where not even the Soviet Union dared to interfere
pages 139–46

*Gulf of Finland
(Soome laht)*

Gogland

Moshchnyy

Sillamäe: Wander back to Soviet times, in a town that officially did not exist
pages 163–5

Lahemaa National Park

Loksa

Võsu

Kunda

Kehra

Rakvere

Kiviõli

Kohtla-Järve

Jõhvi

Sillamäe

Narva-Jõesuu

Narva

Tapa

Tamsalu

Kuremäe

Paide

Endla Nature Reserve

Rakka
166m

Vasknarva

Tartu: Mix with the students at Tartu's university; founded in 1632, it is the intellectual centre of Estonia
pages 177–99

Türi

Jõgeva

Mustvee

Põltsamaa

Kallaste

Lake Peipsi

Vohma

Alam Pedja Nature Reserve

Viljandi

Elva

Tartu

RUSSIAN FEDERATION

Võrtsjärv

Karski-Nuia

Otepää

Räpina

Lake Pihkva

Tõrva
217m

Põlva

Sangaste

Värska

Võru

Saatse

Valka

Valga

Karula National Park

318m

Pechory

Pskov

Saatse: Stare across the barbed wire at Europe's new Iron Curtain
page 219

LATVIA

Valga: Take advantage of the Schengen Agreement to wander in and out of Latvia
pages 224–32

KEY

Capital city	■
Other city	●
Main town	◉
Other town	○
Airport	✈
Ferry	🛳
Main road	
Other road	
Railway	
International boundary	

Estonia
Don't
miss...

Castles
Narva Castle used to be the outpost of the Swedish Empire; now Russians look enviously across the EU border
(S/KK) page 170

Seaplane Harbour
If what is explained at Seaplane Harbour had not happened, there would be no independent Estonia; 21st century technology brings to life early 20th century history
(W/Alamy) pages 114–15

The Western Islands

Older Estonians flock to Saaremaa Island for their holidays; here the calm of the 1930s still predominates

(SS) pages 260–78

National parks and nature reserves

Lahemaa National Park is where nature rules supreme, both by the sea and in the forest

(S/AG) pages 140–6

Rocca al Mare

Rocca al Mare represents Estonian country life as it used to be in the 1930s, self-sufficient, colourful and centred around the church

(TT/VE) pages 124–5

Estonia in colour

above left St Nicholas Church in Tallinn is now deconsecrated, but remains a centre for Estonian musical life, particularly for organ music (S/KK) page 106

top right Tallinn's medieval grandeur still dominates in the Old Town; no conqueror or modern architect has dared to touch it (TT/VE) page 78

above right There's no shortage of restaurants and cafés on the cobbled streets of Tallinn's Old Town (S/NK) page 78

below Architecturally, the Old Town has always remained the centre of Tallinn and is its main attraction (S/AK) page 78

top left Fighting last took place in Tallinn in the 16th century and this destruction at the St Birgitta's Convent, just outside Tallinn, was the result (S/EB) page 128

above left Set into a limestone cliff, Tallinn's modern art gallery is the first purpose-built museum in the city (SS) pages 118–19

above right St John's Church, one of Tallinn's few 19th-century buildings, dominates Freedom Square, where all major parades take place (S/A) page 112

below left Kiek in the Kok is the repository for Tallinn's military history; see here why so few armies dared risk battle in its surroundings (S/E) pages 102–3

below right Peter the Great did not live to see Kadriorg Palace completed, but his heirs certainly enjoyed it and now any visitor can too (S/VT) page 120

AUTHOR

Neil Taylor was from 1975 to 2005 Director of Regent Holidays, a British tour company that has specialised in travel to the Baltic states since they regained their independence in 1991. Now he writes and broadcasts on travel trade topics and is active in the British Guild of Travel Writers. He was previously on the boards of ABTA and AITO. In 2000 Neil was awarded the Lifetime Achievement Award by the British Guild of Travel Writers and in 2011 he was awarded the President of Estonia's medal for services to tourism.

AUTHOR'S STORY   *Neil Taylor*

Until 1992, Estonia was a vague concept in my life, somewhere that should still have been independent, but which had been swallowed up into the Soviet Union. I went for the first time then with little interest and with little knowledge. On that occasion, I was in Estonia for only four days, but I became addicted at once and am now there at least six times a year; I have a flat in Tallinn to prove my long-term loyalty. I am glad that I could pass on my enthusiasm to Bradt at a time when to other publishers it was simply 'The Baltics'. This, the seventh edition, is evidence of the commitment that Bradt has always shown to the book and to Estonia.

Updating this book makes me feel young again. I visit bars that have an unspoken upper age limit of 25. I am often to be seen in restaurants well after 23.00 and in clothes that should not have been brought into the 21st century. How convenient that no museum opens before 10.30 so that my curtains need only do so at 09.30. With Tallinn Old Town being Estonia's only serious hill, I am even kept fit.

I am happy to enjoy an easier life than most Bradt writers. Buses and trains run to time and are sufficiently comfortable for me to keep notes and to reach all of Estonia's borders. However, journeys in them do not provide enough time for me to master the 14 cases in the Estonian language. Perhaps I will reach six before the next edition. In the meantime, I must thank all the English-speaking Estonians who have endured my barrage of emails and frequent visits. We share the same enthusiasm and I am sure we will continue to do so.

PUBLISHER'S FOREWORD   *Hilary Bradt*

The first Bradt travel guide was written in 1974 by George and Hilary Bradt on a river barge floating down a tributary of the Amazon. In the 1980s and '90s the focus shifted away from hiking to broader-based guides to new destinations – usually the first to be published on these places. In the 21st century Bradt continues to publish these ground-breaking guides, along with others to established holiday destinations, incorporating in-depth information on culture and natural history alongside the nuts and bolts of where to stay and what to see.

* * *

After years of travelling to familiar places as a tour leader, I jumped at Neil Taylor's offer to spend a few days in Estonia. What a wonderful country! I loved the way the grim Soviet-style architecture near Tallinn airport gave way to this lovely medieval city; the vibrancy of the emerging Estonian culture, long suppressed; and the otherness of a place that was only a couple of hours away by air. That was nearly 20 years ago. Tourism is now firmly established, but the beauty and vibrancy remain: I can't wait to make a return trip with this new edition of *Estonia* in my pocket.

Seventh edition March 2014   First published 1995

Bradt Travel Guides Ltd, IDC House, The Vale, Chalfont St Peter, Bucks SL9 9RZ, England; www.bradtguides.com

Print edition published in the USA by The Globe Pequot Press Inc, PO Box 480, Guilford, Connecticut 06437-0480

Text copyright © 2014 Neil Taylor
Maps copyright © 2014 Bradt Travel Guides Ltd
Photographs copyright © 2014 Individual photographers (see below)
Project Managers: Claire Strange and Laura Pidgley
Cover research: Pepi Bluck, Perfect Picture

ISBN: 978 1 84162 487 7 (print)
e-ISBN: 978 1 84162 783 0 (epub)
e-ISBN: 978 1 84162 684 0 (mobi)

British Library Cataloguing in Publication Data
A catalogue record for this book is available from the British Library

Photographs Alamy: whyeyephotography.com/Alamy (W/Alamy); awl-images.com: Walter Bibikow (awl/WB); Shutterstock: Anilah (S/A), Anna Grigorjeva (S/AG), Andrey Kutsenko (S/AK), Ad Oculos (S/AO), Estea (S/E), Evgenia Bolyukh (S/EB), eans (S/EN), gadag (S/G), kolyvanov (S/K), KKulikov (S/KK), Nickolay Khoroshkov (S/NK), ragnisphoto (S/R), Veronika Trofer (S/VT), Vishnevskiy Vasily (S/VV), Zvonimir Atletic (S/ZA); SuperStock (SS); Visit Estonia (VE): Aivar Ruukel (AR/VE), EAS (EAS/VE), Jaak Nilson (JN/VE), Lembit Michelson (LM/VE), Sven Zacek (SZ/VE), Toomas Tuul (TT/VE)
Front cover Windmill at Angla, Saaremaa Island (awl/WB)
Back cover A view of Tallinn (JN/VE); Estonian folk clothes (VE)
Title page St Nicholas Church, Tallinn (S/KK); red squirrel (VE); Haapsalu (S/A)
Maps David McCutcheon FBCart.S

Typeset from the author's disc by Ian Spick, Bradt Travel Guides
Production managed by Jellyfish Print Solutions, printed in India
Digital conversion by the Firsty Group

CONTRIBUTORS

Michael Bourdeaux is an Honorary Canon of Rochester Cathedral and has made a lifelong study of religion in Russia and in other countries of the former communist bloc. In 1969 he founded Keston College, a study centre for his subject. His most recent book is *Gorbachev, Glasnost and the Gospel*, which also contains a study of the freedom movement in the churches in the Baltic states. Contact: www.keston.org.

Wiltraud Engländer has written a German guidebook on the natural history of the Canary Islands. She has travelled in Estonia extensively whilst working on a television series on the natural history of the Baltic countries. In 2004 she filmed singing birds all over Europe for a DVD on birdsongs.

Philip Gross is Professor of Creative Writing at Glamorgan University and won the 2009 T S Eliot Poetry Prize. His poem appears on page 39.

James Oates is a 20-year veteran of investment banking with such firms as JP Morgan, UBS, Lazard and Flemings and is the CEO of Cicero Capital, a specialist investment house based in Tallinn and operating across central Europe. He is a regular guest on the BBC business programmes as well as being frequently interviewed in different broadcast and other news media. For more information, see www.ciceroinvest.com.

Carol Pearson is a writer and journalist who lives in Cambridge. She is the granddaughter of August Maramaa, mayor of Viljandi. Her mother fled Estonia in 1944 when Soviet troops swept across the country; in 1947 she arrived in the UK as a refugee and met and married an Englishman.

Linda Reiss left Saaremaa for Sweden with her parents in 1944 when she was ten years old. Since 1965 she has worked as an artist in Bristol, England.

Maila Saar works for Estonian Holidays in Tallinn, specialising in tours for English-speaking groups. She has contributed to several English–Estonian dictionaries and written a guidebook to London for Estonian tourists.

Tina Tamman worked until 2005 as an analyst of the Estonian media at BBC Monitoring. Her book *The Last Ambassador* a biography of August Torma, Estonian ambassador to the UK from 1934 until 1971, was published in 2011.

Clare Thomson's mother is an Estonian who left Estonia in 1944. Clare's first book, *The Singing Revolution*, was about her first visit to Estonia, her mother's homeland, in 1989, and is the best-known record of events at that time. She has since divided her time between London, Belgium and the Baltics and has written a book about Ghent.

Acknowledgements

An erratic author always needs patient, long-suffering editors at the publisher's and Bradt have never let me down in this respect. For the current edition, I am grateful to Claire Strange and Laura Pidgley who have skilfully guided me throughout its writing, despite the nightmare of Estonian accents.

DEDICATION

To my wife Tiina who has now made Estonia a permanent part of my life.

FEEDBACK REQUEST AND UPDATES WEBSITE

At Bradt Travel Guides we're aware that guidebooks start to go out of date on the day they're published – and that you, our readers, are out there in the field doing research of your own. You'll find out before us when a fine new family-run hotel opens or a favourite restaurant changes hands and goes downhill. So why not write and tell us about your experiences? Contact us on ☎ 01753 893444 or e info@bradtguides.com. We will forward emails to the author who may post 'one-off updates' on the Bradt website at www.bradtupdates.com/Estonia. Alternatively you can add a review of the book to www.bradtguides.com or Amazon.

Contents

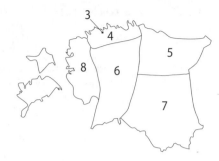

NOTE ABOUT MAPS

Some maps use grid lines to allow easy location of sites. Map grid references are listed in square brackets after listings in the text, with page number followed by grid number, eg: [74 C3]. Please note, in order to keep the maps legible, not all sites have been pinpointed on the maps. However, grid references have been nonetheless supplied to highlight their general location.

LIST OF MAPS

Introduction

In 1991 Estonia's independence was re-established and only 13 years later it joined NATO and the EU; in 2011 it joined the euro. Its journey from being an enforced Soviet backwater to an integral part of Europe had come to an end. Earlier editions of this book have shown how this journey would affect visitors as hotels became refurbished, museums revitalised and roads able to handle the increasing amount of traffic. Politically this edition is being published at a time when Estonia can be proud of what it has achieved and when greater optimism than ever before can be shown towards the future. The government has been in power for longer than almost all other European ones and relations with Russia seem finally to be improving as tourists from there pour in and as the Russian government slowly accepts Estonia as an equal rather than as a renegade. There might even be a border treaty between Estonia and Russia during the currency of this edition.

Since the publication of the previous edition of this book, Tallinn has been the European Capital of Culture, which has helped to extend its range of attractions. It now has its Seaplane Harbour Museum and a revitalised Television Tower. Although on a smaller scale, the cultural scene all over the country has become more welcoming and less introspective than used to be the case. Whether at Saatse, a few metres from the Russian border, or in Pärnu on the Western coast, formerly bland museums are now making serious efforts to reach out to both the local population and to foreign visitors. The star attraction in this field may remain the Transport Museum near Põlva, which entrances equally children, their parents and their grandparents but many others are making serious efforts to catch up. 'Catching up' is a phrase that will apply from 2014 to the railways as well, as schedules multiply and decaying rolling stock is removed. A particular pleasure in the summer of 2013 was to take one of Tallinn's new suburban trains. No longer will the buses have a monopoly on all major travel routes in Estonia.

My first visit to Estonia in 1992 was an adventure, travelling with a suitcase of soon to be useless Russian roubles and wondering where I might next get petrol for the car. The adventure has now gone, and I have no regrets about that. What gave me pleasure then, and still does, were the space, the sense of calm and the great cultural diversity that Estonia offers. Culture may be a provocative art exhibition, a quartet playing in a church or thousands singing at a song festival, but it will always be there, throughout the year and throughout the country. What has been added is colour and gastronomic diversity. Estonian towns were grey in 1992 and I was often relieved to see green weeds as the only contrast in decaying concrete slabs. Since then, painters, designers, restorers and landscape artists have all had their part to play in ensuring that a walk in any Estonian town is now a pleasure, in the town centre or in the suburbs, in a park or by the sea. When that walk is over, where to eat will no longer be a question of necessity, but of choice, and often of a large choice. Eating a Korean meal in Valga, 200m from the Latvian border, or a Chinese one in Narva, 500m from the Russian border, is an immediate pointer for overland travellers to the diversity the country now offers. Estonia may have a population of only 1.3 million but it is truly international throughout.

In 2012 half-Estonian, half-Russian writer Andrei Hvostov called his country 'the Estonian Republic of Unsaid Things' as he wrote about the secrecy of Soviet times continuing well after the collapse of that regime. He was happy to play the iconoclast, raising many issues dating back to World War II that others had been happier to ignore. There is a parallel with tourism here, given the many places in Estonia that deserve more visitors than they currently see. If visitors feel I have revealed most of what is wrongly 'unseen' in Estonia, I will be more than content.

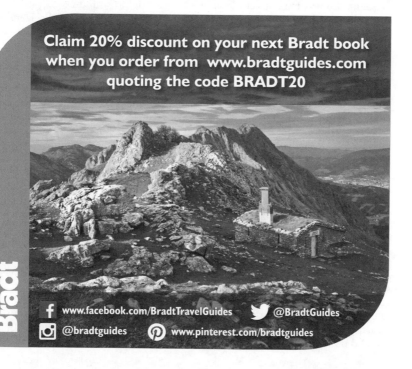

Part One

GENERAL INFORMATION

Location Northern Europe; borders with Russia and Latvia. Tallinn, the capital, is 85km from Helsinki, 320km from St Petersburg, and 1,800km from London.

Climate Winter temperatures range between –5 and 5°C although short spells of much colder weather also occur. Summer temperatures of 20°C are normal, though occasionally temperatures reach 30°C. There is no identifiable rainy season.

Status Parliamentary democracy

Population 1,286,540 (2012 census)

Life expectancy Men 65, women 75

Capital Tallinn (420,000 inhabitants)

Major towns Tartu (98,000), Narva (63,000), Kohtla-Järve (39,000), Pärnu (42,000)

Administrative divisions 15 counties (*maakond*), 193 townships (*vald*)

People Ethnic Estonian 68%, ethnic Russian 25%, other racial backgrounds 7%

Language Estonian, a member of the Finno-Ugric group

Religion Predominantly Lutheran, though all major faiths are represented in the population

Currency Euro divided into 100 cents

Exchange rates In January 2014 £1 bought €1.21 and US$1 bought €0.74

National airport/airline Tallinn/Estonian Air

International dialling code +372

Time GMT and BST +2hrs

Electricity 220 volts, 50Hz

Flag Horizontal blue–black–white

National anthem 'Mu isamaa, mu õnn ja rõõm' (My fatherland, my joy and happiness)

National flower Cornflower

National bird Barn swallow

Public holidays 1 January (New Year), 24 February (Independence Day), Good Friday, 1 May (May Day), 23 June (Victory Day), 24 June (Midsummer), 20 August (Re-Independence Day), 25 and 26 December (Christmas)

1

Background Information

GEOGRAPHY AND ENVIRONMENT *Wiltraud Engländer*

Estonia has the most varied nature of all the Baltic countries. The most northwestern part of the extensive east European plain, it protrudes into the Baltic Sea as a kind of peninsula. The Baltic Sea, in turn, has left its traces on Estonia in the formation of the landscape. Numerous bays, straits and islets enrich the coast. Its coastal terraces, sand dunes and beaches are still natural in many places and invite endless walks. Estonia's larger and smaller islands with their old windmills and fishermen's houses exhibit their own kind of rugged charm.

The northern and western regions were shaped by the glaciers of the Continental Ice Belt. Intensive erosion during several ice ages and the denuding effect of the sea left behind a rather flat landscape, with a mean height of only 50m. Estonians are nevertheless proud of their highest peak, Suur Munamägi, reaching 318m. Minerals embedded in northern Estonia's bedrock – oil-shale, phosphorite, limestone and the Cambrian blue clay – are now extracted for use in industry. Erratic rocks of different size are scattered all over Estonia, especially in the north. These rocks were transported from the Swedish coasts by great movements of ice.

Vast marshes and wild forest areas on the mainland form a wilderness which, although common all over Europe hundreds of years ago, now remains only in the Baltic countries. Many otherwise rare species have been preserved here in considerable numbers. Due to its location, Estonia is a melting pot for species diversity: eastern Russian, northern Scandinavian and even Arctic species as well as southern and western European species occur here together. For some of these species the Baltic Sea marks the border of their distribution.

The other side of the coin is less positive, however. Estonia's environment suffered considerably from 45 years of Soviet occupation. According to the European Commission, there were three major environmental problems in Estonia, the first being air pollution due to CO_2 emissions from the oil-shale power plants, which were among the worst polluters in Europe and the source of almost all the air pollution in Estonia. The two other major problems were waste management and water quality. In order to live up to EU standards, Estonia accelerated the building of new landfills and the construction of new treatment plants. It committed itself to fulfil the European demands on oil-shale pollution by the summer of 2009. Financial support was provided by the EU. Before its admission to the EU, Estonia joined international environmental conventions for the protection of the Baltic Sea and assistance from Western countries is beginning to ensure that this valuable ecosystem has a future. Following accession to the EU, the country experienced increased consumption of energy and natural resources and greater waste production. However, Estonia avoided a repetition of the failures of Western countries made in the face of increasing environmental pressure under similar circumstances.

The remains of the Soviet regime are still obvious. The Baltic countries served as food suppliers during the Soviet era, and more land came under the plough than is needed at present. Now these areas are abandoned and the land is overgrown by herbs, wild flowers, junipers and bushes, and will soon turn into secondary forest. As a new member of the EU its agriculture is moving forward to a more effective but also more intensive form. The future will show how this will influence the landscape.

Luckily, as a side effect of the ineffective economy, large areas of biological importance remained more or less intact, and many species that are rare in western Europe have been preserved in relatively good condition. The occupation of border areas, especially along the coast, was an important factor in environmental preservation, since military areas were completely out of bounds and the landscape was preserved in its natural state. After the liberation many of these areas were turned into nature reserves and are now some of the country's most valuable wild areas.

For details of Estonia's climate, see page 51.

NATURAL HISTORY AND CONSERVATION *Wiltraud Engländer*

THE BALTIC SEA The Baltic Sea has played a key role in the history of Estonia. As a main travel route it was important not only for trading, but also for its wealth in **fish**, an important resource for the people living on its shores. The fish are a mixture of species of freshwater and marine origin. The salinity of the Baltic surface water is only five to seven parts per thousand. Due to decreasing salinity from south to north, the number of species varies from 40 in the south to 20 in the Gulf of Finland and the Gulf of Bothnia.

In the open sea there are three main marine species: herring, sprat and cod. Herring and sprat are the most important commercial fish species for Estonia. Smelt, sea trout, eel, vimba and salmon migrate between fresh water and the sea. There is also a tradition here of catching lampreys during their migration upriver. Freshwater fish are found in the coastal areas, but rarely penetrate into the open sea. Perch, roach, pike, pike-perch, ide, bream, silver bream and ruff are also common in inland water bodies.

The Baltic Sea is a sanctuary for the **grey seal**; their breeding numbers in Estonia are greater than in Finland or Sweden. The most important nursing colonies for the whole Baltic are the coasts of the western islands. By the end of winter the pups are born at the edge of the ice or on the rocky shores of the islands west of Saaremaa. Pup mortality is high due to pollution, lack of food and injuries. The worst enemies of grey seals are fishermen, who hold them responsible for depleting the fish stocks. In fact, industrial overfishing has been taking a serious toll on the fish stocks for many years, with a consequent effect on the availability of fish for both seals and man.

The **ringed seal** has declined to one-tenth of its historical population during the last century, mainly due to overhunting. Heavy pollution in Riga Bay, leading to sterility in females, has, together with other factors, kept the reproduction rate low so that the population is not able to recover. The nursing areas are on the edge of the ice. Mothers give birth in early spring. They maintain breathing holes sheltered by ice floes, where the pups are hidden during their first weeks. In May ringed seals become more social: they gather in groups to change their fur and bask in the sun.

COASTS AND ISLANDS Estonia is a land of islands. About 1,500 small and large islands are scattered along the shore of the mainland to the west and north of the country, taking up one-tenth of its area. The largest and most attractive islands are Saaremaa, Hiiumaa, Muhu and Vormsi. The rocky, stony or sandy coasts allow a great variety of natural habitats. Together with the relatively undisturbed coasts in the northwest they are an important stronghold for breeding and migrating birds.

In the north of Estonia the rocky shelf of the continent shows on the surface. Steep and brittle limestone clint cliffs developed in the Ordovician period, 500 million years ago. These limestone formations are so special to Estonians that limestone has been declared the 'national rock'. The most outstanding clint cliffs are found near Ontika and are 56m high. Between Ontika and Toila, the Valaste Juga waterfall with its 20m height might not be the world's most impressive cataract, but it is Estonia's highest and worth seeing. Some smaller Silurian clint cliffs can be visited on the northern shore of Saaremaa near Panga and Muhu.

A special type of habitat is the stony alvars on the shores of western Estonia and the islands of Saaremaa and Hiiumaa. The limestone bedrock with its thin topsoil and fragile plant communities is unique. Between the grey pebbles small plants struggle to find a hold. When the soil turns a bit richer junipers start to grow. In the past grazing kept the juniper bushes down; nowadays they are threatening the fragile vegetation by simply overgrowing it.

When the glaciers retreated from Estonia after the Ice Age, the land started rising when relieved of the pressure. This process is still continuing; today the coast is rising at an average of 2mm per year and new coastal meadows are permanently developing. The new land, used by man from the start, has evolved into a new type of landscape: wooded meadows, a habitat that holds the highest number of plant species per square metre in the whole of Europe. Carpets of flowers change their colours successively and in early summer several species of orchids grow among hundred-year-old oaks. The reintroduction of grazing is now being encouraged, since vegetation that is not grazed or mowed will be quickly overgrown by reeds or bushes and the diversity and richness of species would be lost forever.

LAKES AND RIVERS In the central and southern parts of Estonia the Continental Ice Belt carved valleys and deposited large amounts of gravel. The result is the lovely landscape of the Haanja, Otepää and Karula heights with their hills, valleys and lakes. There are some 1,450 natural and manmade lakes in Estonia, the largest being Lake Peipsi (Europe's fifth-largest lake) and Võrtsjärv.

Of the more than 7,000 rivers, streams and drainage ditches, nine are over 100km in length. The north Estonian rivers flowing into the Gulf of Finland form scenic waterfalls as they spill over the edge of the clint cliffs. The rivers of south Estonia, such as the Võhandu, Ahja and Piusa, have carved picturesque valleys with high outcrops of red sandstone.

Many rivers in Estonia are still unregulated or their courses have been modified only to a moderate extent, and thus a remarkable amount of floodplain has been preserved in more or less natural condition. Inland waterways are, however, sometimes badly overgrown due to too many fertilisers being swept into the water.

ANCIENT PEAT BOGS One-fifth of the country's territory is covered by marshes. The majority of these began as lakes that were gradually turned into quagmires by the spreading shoreline vegetation, although about a third was formed by the paludification of mineral land. Starting from nutrient-rich fens and evolving through the transitional marshes, the development of a swamp finds its final form in a raised marsh or bog, an amazingly autonomous and resilient ecosystem. A bog consists mainly of peat mosses that get all the minerals they need from precipitation and dust particles. Peat mosses grow annually at a rate of 1–1.5mm. It has taken thousands of years for the bogs in Estonia to develop peat deposits with an average thickness of 5–7m. The thickest peat layer (17m) is recorded in Vällämäe bog in the southeast. The oldest marshes are about 10,000 years old. In several parts of Estonia peat bogs are heavily exploited, but the country still has the most extensive living peat bogs in Europe.

WILD FORESTS Almost half of Estonia's territory is covered by forest and woodland. Estonia is located on the border where the coniferous Euro-Siberian taiga meets the northern part of Europe's deciduous forests. Scots pine is the most common tree, followed by silver birch and downy birch, Norway spruce, grey and common alder and aspen. Botanists distinguish 23 different forest types. On sandy soils dry pine forest is most common, whilst other forest types include temperate spruce forests, hardwood–spruce mixed forests and dry heath pine forests. Where the soil is moist there can be found transitional swampy forests, bog pine forests, fen birch forests or swampy black alder forests. A speciality on the poor soils of the seaside is alvar forest.

The largest patch of forest can be found in northeast and mid-Estonia, from the northern coast to the Latvian border. On Hiiumaa and in the northeast, large tracts of primeval forests have been preserved. Estonia's forests are managed less intensely than those in western Europe and their drainage has been less efficient. Biological diversity in the forests is therefore often higher than elsewhere.

In autumn, thousands of people go to the woods to gather berries and mushrooms; mushrooms are even exported. Usually there are two peaks of mushroom growth: late summer and mid-autumn, depending on the weather, especially on rainfall.

Due to their inaccessibility, peat bogs and forests are a vital stronghold for many species. Most of Estonia's mammals and many bird species live in these habitats.

WILDLIFE

Mammals Many European species extinct in other countries can still be found in Estonia. There are around 100–200 wolves, 1,000 lynx and 600 bears living in Estonia. When hunting dropped off in the mid-1990s, **wolf** numbers rose to about 500. Recently, however, the government has offered a cash reward for every wolf killed. Protection versus control of the large predators is a very sensitive political issue, leading to serious conflict about their management. In a recent poll to establish the number of wolves the public would accept as appropriate, it was found that the currently maintained number of between 100 and 200 wolves was generally accepted as the best. Unlike in other countries, Estonians are willing to live together with wolves, as long as there are not too many, so the country might play an important role in the survival of wolves within Europe.

Brown bears are an attraction to hunters from the West, having been hunted to extinction in most other European countries. The government regulates the 'sport' by issuing licences. In autumn the shy bears come to feed in the oat fields, and with luck can be observed at several places in the evening.

Roe deer are the most abundant mammal species and they can often be seen in fields and along forest borders in the early mornings. Wild **boars** are very common, too, and traces of them can be seen in many forested areas. Conversely, **elk** are elusive and shy, although signs of their feeding activities can be seen at transitional zones of forest and wetland. They browse branches of shrubs and small trees and thus cut them back quite severely. **Foxes** can sometimes be seen crossing the road or fields. **Raccoon dogs** and **badgers**, although rather common, will hardly be seen. They are nocturnal animals and spend most of the day in their dens, which the two species occasionally share and also use for hibernation. The raccoon dog is a new species in the Baltics. It has immigrated from the East and is now spreading further to Western countries.

European **beavers** leave their traces everywhere in the forests and wetlands. Their lodges and dams can reach an impressive size. Nevertheless they are shy and difficult to see. The last evening light may offer possibilities for a sighting. Spring is also a good time, for after the ice melts the beavers are busy felling trees for fresh food. The region's **otters** and **pine martens** are more elusive creatures, and far more difficult to spot.

Estonia was one of the last strongholds of the very rare and extremely threatened European **mink**. In other parts of Europe this species has been largely replaced by the introduced American mink, which is bigger and more aggressive and thus has an advantage in competition. The situation is alarming, since in just a few years the remaining populations have shrunk drastically in numbers, and only a few hundred individuals are left in the wild. In an attempt to save the species, the islands of Saaremaa and Hiiumaa were cleared of the competing American mink. Initiated by Tallinn Zoo, an ambitious reintroduction project was started in 2000. Several dozen European mink were released on both islands that year with the aim that a self-supporting population would establish itself. With a backup of 200 animals breeding in captivity, a species that would otherwise have disappeared is now likely to survive for ever. European mink in captivity can be visited in Tallinn Zoo.

Several species of **dormouse** live in the forests, but they are almost impossible to encounter. The most secretive animal of Estonia's forests is the extremely rare and elusive **flying squirrel**. It is a symbol for large and natural virgin forest, yet only about 200 of them live in the east of Estonia. Even the scientists who study them see one only about once a year.

Amphibians and reptiles

The wealth of wetlands and ditches in Estonia favours a rich amphibian life. During the Soviet era, due to intensified agriculture, amphibians had a rather hard time. Now, with the Baltic's economy still down at a low level and fewer fertilisers used in subsistence farming, amphibians are recovering fast. The night concerts of **frogs** and **toads** sometimes sound like a scene from the tropical rainforest. They spawn in shallow ditches and beaver ponds which are warmed by the sun and create the best conditions for the developing tadpoles. Brown frogs spawn at the water, but then move away to the surroundings in summer, whereas several species of green frogs stay close to the water all summer. The common toad and the common **newt** are quite widespread, while others – the crested newt, the green toad, the natterjack or the pool frog – are rather rare and are consequently under protection. Amphibians hibernate underwater, but only when there is a thick layer of ice are they safe from predators such as otter and mink.

Three species of **lizard** and two species of **snake** make up Estonia's reptiles. The common lizard and the common viper prefer moist environments. The grass snake is most abundant in more open habitats, although it is often preyed upon by white storks. All Estonian reptiles have been included in a local list of protected species.

Birds

A total of 333 bird species have been found in Estonia, two-thirds of them breeding on the coast or in the forest and wetlands. Birdlife is at its peak from the end of April to the beginning of July. In spring, vast areas of coastal meadows

1

in the west are flooded by the melting snow in the rivers. These wet areas offer plentiful food to breeding greylag geese and a new colony of barnacle geese which has established itself here. These areas are also favoured for breeding and feeding by wader species such as dunlin, avocet, lapwing and black-tailed godwit and by the rare great snipes for their splendid displays. The coasts are scattered with boulders of various sizes. Many small stones are turned by turnstones in search of food. In spring the black-and-white oystercatchers perform their noisy territorial ceremonies and search for mussels and worms to feed their chicks. Between gravel and stranded material, sandwich and Caspian terns hide their nests. Eider ducks rely on their camouflaged plumage for protection when they sit motionless on the nest. The coast is also home to the white-tailed eagle, Europe's biggest and rarest eagle species. About 40 pairs now breed in Estonia, ten pairs alone on Saaremaa. On the coast of Estonia's islands even birds from Sweden and Finland find a refuge during winter.

Old forests with trees more than 200 years old are a necessity for the shy black stork to build its nests. The many dead trees are still home for the white-backed woodpecker, a species extremely rare in the rest of Europe. Black woodpeckers and three-toed woodpeckers are the more exceptional of the six woodpecker species in Estonia. Another European rarity, the capercaillie, still exhibits its scenic early-morning displays in Estonian forests. Rather inconspicuous, on the other hand, are half a dozen owl species. The Ural owl, long-eared owl and Tengmalm's owl are more abundant; the huge eagle owl is rather rare. The lesser spotted eagle can be called a true 'Baltic eagle'. It can often be seen sitting on posts, whereas the golden eagle will rarely be encountered.

Wetlands and peat bogs are the breeding grounds for the common crane. In spring the pairs fly over the plains calling loudly and searching for a secret spot for their nests; they are very shy and should not be disturbed. Wetlands are perfect breeding habitats for many wader species, such as golden plover, wood sandpiper, lapwing, curlew and whimbrel.

The symbolic bird of rural areas, the white stork, is a new species here. It bred in Estonia for the first time in 1841. During the decades the numbers rose and there are now about 2,000 pairs breeding on trees and artificial platforms.

Estonia is not only important for many breeding birds, but is also a vital stepping stone along the East Atlantic flyway. Like a funnel, the shape of the Baltic coast determines birds' migration routes. Millions of birds of 39 different species pass through Estonia in spring and autumn along the northern coast, along the coasts of Lake Peipsi and over the mainland of west Estonia. In winter and early spring thousands of long-tailed ducks, scaups, common scoters, velvet scoters and black-throated divers congregate in Riga Bay and Väinameri. They winter in the ice-free areas before they leave in an impressive mass migration. Large flocks of Bewick's swans and up to 100,000 barnacle geese come from Britain and the Netherlands in early spring to stop near Matsalu and Saaremaa Island. After a few weeks they fly off again to their Siberian and Scandinavian breeding grounds. During their moult migration in July and August up to 200,000 common scoters pass through Estonia. By August the first breeding birds start their autumn migration to the south: 30,000 common cranes use Estonia as a resting ground. They feed on the coastal meadows together with large flocks of greylag geese. During mild winters the autumn migration for some species can last up to December.

Good birdwatching localities along the coast are Vilsandi Island west of Saaremaa, Saareküla on the southeast coast of Saaremaa, Käina Bay on Hiiumaa and the Hiiumaa Islets, and Matsalu Bay. All these areas are recognised as Important Bird

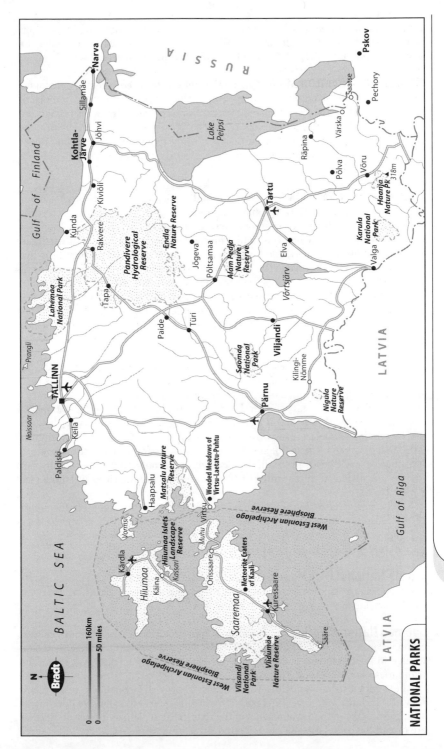

Areas of European or global importance. In the last century bird-ringing stations were founded along the Baltic coasts. The bird station in Puhtu co-ordinates the work of ornithologists monitoring millions of migrating birds every year.

NATURE CONSERVATION AREAS During the 1990s Estonia enlarged its percentage of protected areas from 3% to almost 10% of its territory. The most important areas are the islands of Saaremaa and Hiiumaa, and the nature reserves of Matsalu, Nigula and Endla. Estonia also has an impressive percentage of areas with the highest protection status within Europe, with only Finland having slightly more. There are 210 plant and 300 animal species in Estonia that are endangered or rare and need special protection.

Lahemaa National Park

The beautiful and varied Lahemaa National Park is situated in the very north of Estonia. The northern part of the park is formed by a rugged coastline with four promontories, some marvellous bays and a couple of islands, the biggest of which is Mohni. The southern part is made up of karstland and mires. Within the park 200 bird species nest, whilst elk and brown bear live there but are rarely observed. The decreasing population of the pearl oyster finds a last stronghold in the rivers of the park. There are many places of architectural and historical value worth visiting; some of them operate as museums or offer visitor services. There are 12 nature trails introducing different landscapes of the park. Guided tours are available by pre-arrangement. The visitor centre is located at Palmse (see page 143).

Vilsandi National Park

The northwestern coast of Saaremaa Island, from Atla up to the Harilaid Peninsula, the bigger island of Vilsandi and the adjacent smaller 160 islands and islets are included in Vilsandi National Park. One-third of the country's protected plant species can be found here and are safeguarded in the botanical–zoological reserve. The region is also designated an Important Bird Area, hosting 247 breeding bird species, of which the most numerous is the eider duck with over 8,000 breeding pairs. The national park is an important stopover area for migratory birds like barnacle geese and Steller's eider. Vilsandi is open to the public daily, but visitors are advised to pre-arrange their visit with the headquarters in Loona (see pages 265–6).

The islands of Saaremaa and Hiiumaa and several islets around them form part of the Biosphere Reserve of the West-Estonian Archipelago. This relatively large area has a special conservation objective as a representative example of a natural or only minimally disturbed ecosystem.

Karula National Park

East of Valga, in the southeast of Estonia, the picturesque landscape is protected as a national park. The rounded moraine hills have been left by glaciers and are interspersed with more than 30 lakes.

Soomaa National Park

Soomaa National Park protects the largest area of central Estonian mires. Four large bogs, Kuresoo, Valgeraba, Ördi and Kikepera, are located in the catchment of the longest river in the country – the River Pärnu. Its tributaries separate several bog areas.

The wooded meadows of the River Halliste, formerly a botanical reserve, are now also included in the national park. This area is subject to extensive flooding in spring especially in the lower reaches of the river. Several plant and bird species that are rare in the rest of Estonia can be found here.

Matsalu Nature Reserve The reserve is located on the west coast of the mainland and includes the shallow Matsalu Bay and its surrounding coastal areas. The spectacular floodplains on the mouth of the rivers are important for specific plant communities and many wader species. Matsalu is also famous for its wooded meadows, which are managed landscapes of great botanical value. The coastal meadows, as well as being used as pastures, are excellent feeding areas for waders and barnacle geese. Fifty islands along the shore are important for many plant species and breeding birds. Around the bay extensive reed beds grow. The bird-ringing centre in Penijõe near Matsalu co-ordinates the marking of more than 100,000 birds each year throughout the country. Guided tours as well as boat trips to the reed-bed area are available by arrangement with the headquarters in Lihula. Around Matsalu and on the coast of Haeska there are several towers for birdwatching, and visitors are encouraged to report on their sightings.

Viidumäe Nature Reserve On the western part of the island of Saaremaa an area is designated for the protection of rare plants, and communities of spring mires and pine stands with oak undergrowth. Guided tours can be arranged at the headquarters in Viidu (see page 274).

Nigula Nature Reserve The reserve is located in the very southwest of Estonia. Attempts are being made to create a bigger reserve that also includes the Latvian region of northern Vidzeme. On the Estonian side of the border the reserve embraces a vast peat-bog area with over 370 large pools and five forested islands. It is rich in plant and bird species, especially birds of tundra and peat-bog habitats which breed here. On the coast at Kabli there is a trapping site for bird ringing. There is a 3.2km trail on boards through the bog. The headquarters of the reserve is in Vanajärve, where visits may be pre-arranged (see page 252).

Endla Nature Reserve The area of Endla Raba consists of a sophisticated peat-bog ecosystem with many pools. The rivers that form the water resources of the Pandivere region separate different bogs. The peat layer is on average 3–4m thick and occasionally even 7m. All bird species of wet and wooded areas can be observed here. There is a 1.4km board trail through the bog passing two watchtowers. Pre-arranged guided tours are available on request at the headquarters in Tooma.

Alam-Pedja Nature Reserve North of the large Emajõgi River, in the Võrtsjärv Basin, lies a vast lowland that collects all the flowing waters from the surrounding elevations. The Alam-Pedja Nature Reserve is situated in the northeastern part of this basin. Rainwater from a huge catchment area is carried down by numerous rivers and brooks. The only outflow by the Suur-Emajõgi River is very slow due to the extremely shallow gradient. The rivers of Alam-Pedja and the area north of it are part of the Pandivere Hydrological Reserve.

The nature reserve is among the biggest in Estonia. The density of the human population is especially low here, almost comparable to the density of wolf, bear and lynx in the area. Otters are abundant although it is almost impossible to see them. More likely you could come across one of the hundred or so beavers. Alam-Pedja is known as the largest and most densely populated nesting site of the great snipe in the Baltic countries.

A nature trail starts at Selli and leads over 4km of trail and boardwalk to Sillaotsa. To reach the semi-arch trail, turn off southwest towards Palupõhja at the Laeva cross along the road from Tartu to Tallinn. From Sillaotsa it is 1km along

1

the road back to Selli. For a boat trip on the waterways of the Alam-Pedja Nature Reserve you should bring your own boat. A starting point could be in Põltsamaa. Mind the dams!

Haanja Nature Park The park is located in the highest part of Estonia, the upland of Haanja. You can admire the highest peak in Estonia and the whole Baltic, the Suur Munamägi (318m), and the deepest lake in Estonia, the Rõuge Suurjärv (38m). At the top of the mountain peak there is a watchtower. Haanja Nature Park has a number of picturesque valleys and lakes as well as places of historical and archaeological interest.

Other reserves Numerous reserves are designated for nature conservation as well as recreation. There are 13 landscape reserves, mainly in the northeast and southeast; 25 mire reserves, mainly in the north and east but also south of Matsalu; two ornithological reserves on Saaremaa and Hiiumaa; two botanical reserves protecting the wooded meadows around Vilsandi National Park and south of Karula National Park; six botanical–zoological reserves, mainly south of Matsalu; and one geological reserve at the meteorite craters of Kaali on Saaremaa. One of the prettiest reserves is the landscape reserve of the Hiiumaa islets. The islets are of different geological origin and maintain various plant and animal communities. Visits to the islets should be pre-arranged with the headquarters in Salinõmme, near Suuremõisa.

HISTORY

ANCIENT HISTORY Evidence of settlements on the current territory of Estonia goes back about 7,000 years. From 5000BC, until the late Bronze Age around 1000BC, there was clearly extensive farming, fishing and hunting. Much archaeological work remains to be done throughout the country but excavations at Kunda on the north coast, halfway between Tallinn and the Russian border, have produced several thousand artefacts made from bone and stone. Similar, smaller discoveries have been made in the valley of the Emajõgi River near Tartu, and also beside the Pärnu River, indicating the importance of fishing at that time and the lack of urban development. The first signs of artistic development, such as designs on axe-heads and on pottery, date from around 2000BC, while hill forts, cattle rearing and simple agricultural settlements also date from this time. Sadly, both the Baltic Germans and the Russians neglected archaeology on political grounds as it suited them to portray the Estonians as savages waiting to be civilised. Only since 1990 has evidence of the diversity of Estonian society prior to 1200BC emerged, thanks to the growing number of excavations.

As Estonia has no sources of metal, the few bronze tools dating from this period came from what is now Poland. The Roman Empire never reached Estonia, but the trading links it established brought iron tools and jewellery, although the poverty of Estonia is clearly shown by the small number of such objects found in tombs and by the fact that so few were robbed. The Roman author Tacitus refers to the 'Aestii' tribes in his writings but this term refers to the whole Baltic area beyond Germany. It was another thousand years before the term became limited to its current usage.

From around AD800, Estonia enjoyed a relatively peaceful Viking invasion. The Vikings were mainly interested in trading routes to Kiev and Istanbul and needed to avoid the Mediterranean in view of the Saracen pirates. Novgorod in Russia was also expanding rapidly as an *entrepôt* between East and West and Estonia was to benefit from this transit traffic; the Estonians exported furs, timber and honey whilst importing metal. Minimal written material remains from this period but the thousands of Arabic, German and Byzantine coins which can be seen in museums all over Estonia show the extent of the trade. Skirmishes with Russia were frequent in the 12th century, but Estonian historians proudly point out that 13 Russian attacks were repelled between 1030 and 1192. In the 12th century, for the first and last time in the country's history, Estonian pirates frequently raided Denmark and Sweden. It would be 700 years before Estonia again controlled its coastline.

CENTURIES OF OCCUPATION From around AD1200, Estonian history was dominated by the constant struggle against invaders, forcing the country to look east, south or west, depending on who the occupying power was. For the next 500 years, the country's fate was in the hands of the Danes, Germans and Swedes. From 1721 until 1991, the Germans and the Russians sometimes shared control, sometimes fought over it, but never, except between 1920 and 1939, relinquished it. Different enemies would even repeat the same battles. In 1227 the German crusaders finally defeated the Danes on Saaremaa Island. Seven hundred years later, in 1944, Saaremaa saw the last and most bitter battle between the Nazi German and Soviet forces.

In 1201, the German Bishop Albert, having established a diocese in Riga, subdued the Latvian countryside in the following few years and then turned his attention to Estonia. After three years of bitter fighting between 1208 and 1211, the Teutonic Knights subdued Estonia. The Germans were sufficiently concerned about possible renewed Estonian resistance and attacks from Russia that they formed an alliance with the Danes. In 1219, a small Danish force landed on the Estonian coast and built a fortress to secure their new base. The Estonians called this settlement Tallinn – meaning Danish castle (or city) – and the name was never changed. Half-hearted attempts were made by the Danes to broaden the territory under their control, but none succeeded.

Bishop Albert died in 1229 and the initial crusading fervour of the Teutonic Knights was soon to fade, together with their three traditional vows of poverty, chastity and obedience. They ran the country as autonomous feudal barons, with no central authority. Religious domination gave way to economic domination. Estonians in the countryside were reduced to vassal status working the estates, although in the towns they had greater freedom to operate small businesses. One major revolt took place during the two centuries of German occupation. It began on St George's Day (23 April) 1343, when in a single evening 1,200 Germans were massacred, and finished two years later, by which time a tenth of the Estonian population had been killed, reducing it from 150,000 to 135,000. Fighting took place throughout the country and when it was finally over, the Danish king Valdemar IV was more than happy to sell Tallinn and the surrounding countryside to the Teutonic Knights. They could keep control relatively easily; the Estonians lacked size and national leadership, the Swedes had to struggle to maintain control of Finland, the Russians were defending their eastern borders against the Mongolians and the Lithuanians were conquering the Ukraine. Therefore, until the middle of the 16th century, Estonia was to remain a German colony. No major rebellion ever took place again.

If the aim of Estonia's invaders was usually economic, a religious excuse could always be found. Ivan the Terrible, coveting the port of Narva to support his foreign trade, justified his invasion in 1558 on the grounds that the Germans had abandoned Christianity and were burning Russian icons. Viljandi and Tartu fell soon afterwards. Three years later, the Swedes seized Tallinn to prevent further Russian expansion. The remains of the bastions they built in Tallinn, Narva and

Pärnu can still be seen. They were never used in subsequent battles, which usually took place in the countryside.

The 1570s saw constant warfare in Estonia between the Swedes and the Russians, which finally came to an end in 1582 with a Swedish victory following their seizure of Narva. The population by then had fallen to 100,000. Although the Germans had lost formal sovereignty, and were not to regain it until 1941, they maintained their economic grip on the country. The nominal justice system stayed in their hands, as did the local police forces. Ironically, the Swedes allowed the Baltic Germans, as they came to be known, to impose a far harsher regime on the local Estonian peasants than was ever allowed in Sweden itself. However, as it was distanced from this day-to-day control, the Swedish occupation is still regarded as the most tolerable in Estonian history. During the recent Soviet period, it was often surreptitiously described as a 'golden era'.

THE RISE OF THE ESTONIAN LANGUAGE Tartu University was established in 1632 by King Gustav II who had appointed his former tutor, Johan Skytte, as provincial governor in Estonia three years before. Skytte had previously been Chancellor of Uppsala University. In his opening speech at the university, he expressed the hope that not only the nobility but also some poor peasants should be able to benefit from education there. However, as he was never able to confront the Germans on serfdom, his ideal could not be put into practice. During the Swedish period, the Estonian language was studied seriously for the first time and the inauguration of printing presses in Tartu and Tallinn in the 1630s led to the production of grammars, hymns and biblical stories in Estonian. Because so few Estonians were granted an education by their German masters, these books were all produced by Swedes. In 1697, the Swedes announced a policy of universal education in Estonia but their defeat a few years later by the Russians prevented this from being put into practice.

END OF SWEDISH RULE Swedish rule came to an end for a variety of reasons. First, severe famine struck Estonia three years in succession from 1695 to 1697, killing 70,000 people or about 20% of the population. Second, the Swedish crown had repeatedly tried to curtail the power of the Baltic-German landlords and third, Peter the Great, like many previous and subsequent Russian leaders, envied the ice-free Baltic ports. His first attack on the Swedish empire, at Narva in northeast Estonia, ended in humiliating defeat at the hands of the 18-year-old Swedish king, Charles XII. However, with the founding of St Petersburg in 1703 as a secure base for a further attack, he then formed an alliance with Poland and could successfully pursue the Great Northern War which was in due course to lead to the total conquest of the Baltics. This war would devastate Estonia to an extent it would never witness again. The general in charge of this scorched earth campaign for Peter the Great was proudly able to report to him that: 'There is nothing left to destroy; not a cock crows from Lake Peipsi to the Gulf of Riga.' Only Tallinn was spared, primarily because Peter the Great enjoyed being there, but also because he realised its value as a military and naval base. Tartu and all other major Estonian towns were not. Even Tallinn survived only in an architectural sense. In 1710, plague struck, killing 70% of its population of 10,000.

Peter the Great soon realised how best to use the Baltic Germans; being eager to learn from abroad, he had no inhibitions about using foreigners to help his administration. The Germans kept order amongst the Estonian peasantry and collected taxes, whilst the Russian army and navy provided national security. This *modus vivendi* was to suit both sides for the next hundred years. In the bigoted words of one traveller at the end of the 18th century, 'Estonian men go cheaper than niggers in the American colonies, a manservant can be bought for 30 roubles, a maidservant for ten roubles and a child for four roubles.'

A hundred years after Peter the Great, the Russian army was still using 'foreign' commanders. The defeat of Napoleon owes a lot to Barclay de Tolly, a Baltic German with Scots roots. Before tackling Napoleon, he had successfully fought against the Turks, Swedes and Poles. He mastered the techniques of what would now be called guerrilla warfare and organising retreats, or 'strategic withdrawals', which were really traps for the enemy. Marshall Kutuzov is generally given the credit for defeating Napoleon but it is probably more due to Barclay de Tolly that Estonia would stay in Russia's hands for another hundred years.

Napoleon's invasion of Russia in 1812 finally ended the close relationship between the Russian tsars and the Baltic Germans. The latter found the increasing taxes needed for the war, together with the abolition of serfdom in 1816, an unwarranted intrusion into their traditional lifestyle and both were resisted strongly. By keeping control of land totally in their own hands, they were able to forestall the economic and political aspirations of the Estonian population for a few more decades, quite a feat considering that there were only about 200 Baltic-German families and 800,000 Estonian peasants. Catherine the Great had toured the Baltics in 1764 and had been struck by the mistreatment of the local peasantry. However, no serious action was taken until the accession of Alexander I in 1801. The Russians, unlike the Baltic Germans, were afraid that some of the ideas spread across western Europe by the French Revolution might reach Estonia and that concessions in advance would be the best tactic to resist them. The Baltic Germans turned out to be correct for another 40 years. The development of a textile industry and of distilleries on their estates greatly increased their incomes. Their complacency became apparent from their lifestyle; their manor houses became more opulent and their sojourns to the spring Tallinn season stretched from February ever further into March. Whatever was fashionable in London, Paris or St Petersburg quickly reached Tallinn. One British visitor in 1844 complained that 'only the Germans could have formed such a state of society. It is a machine, with everything for show and nothing for reality.'

PEASANT UPRISINGS Reality had in fact already intruded into the countryside three years earlier when the first serious peasant uprising occurred in 1841; rumours had circulated that the tsarist government was willing to allocate land in central Asia to peasants from the Baltics, who then went in increasing numbers to the governor-general's office in Riga to make their claims. The news that these rumours were false led to disturbances in many parts of Estonia; the uprisings were ruthlessly suppressed and resulted in the first of too many series of banishments to Siberia that were to tarnish Estonian history for the next 110 years. Yet lessons were drawn from this, together with the shortage of labour brought about by the Crimean War, forcing the introduction of legislation allowing peasants to buy land and curtailing the still excessive powers that landlords had over them. For the next 80 years, developments for Estonia were positive. By 1900, for instance, 40% of privately owned land was in Estonian hands and, in 1890, Russian civil servants took over the administration of justice from the German landlords.

Hope for Estonia was not now restricted to the countryside. The increasing industrialisation led to an Estonian middle class in the towns not willing to be docile appendages to the German factory owners. The population in the towns was still very small in the mid 19th century – Tallinn had 20,000 inhabitants and

Tartu 14,000 – but what was significant was that by then Estonians had become the majority and Germans the minority. The arrival of the railway in 1870 would greatly increase urban activity and hence the population as well. By 1897 Tallinn had 64,000 inhabitants of whom only 10,000 were Baltic Germans. Its port had started to compete with Riga and it exported grain and vodka, both relatively new products from the Estonian countryside. From 1877 anyone who paid taxes was entitled to be placed on the electoral register, so for the first time Estonians were able to take part in local administration.

THE NATIONAL AWAKENING The second half of the 19th century is normally described in Estonia as the period of 'National Awakening'. No specific event brought it about, and no specific organisation would ever lead it, but trends in both town and country radicalised the Estonian population into demanding what would eventually lead to full-scale independence. The intellectual ferment came from Tartu University, the practical and financial support from Tallinn, but the individual activists from all over the country. Their reputations are as strong now as during their lifetimes and, as they could be presented as anti-tsarist and anti-capitalist, their works could be openly published and studied during the Soviet period. They quarrelled and competed bitterly but this did not matter in the long term as they succeeded in propagating the concept of an Estonian culture with a long and serious tradition. One of the first Estonians to receive a university education was Friedrich Robert Faehlmann who became a lecturer in the medical faculty at Tartu University and in 1838 founded a 'Learned Estonian Society'. Yet it used a German name, Gelehrte Estnische Gesellschaft, rather than an Estonian one, and all its written and oral proceedings were in German.

Johan Voldemar Jannsen founded the first Estonian newspaper in Pärnu before moving to Tartu, where in 1864 he established what is still the best-known paper in Estonia, *Eesti Postimees*. He covered rural issues extensively and so produced a paper that could be both popular and populist. Ironically, his name had been Germanised as it was felt that an Estonian name was inappropriate for his first job as a sexton. He took the middle name Voldemar as this was the name of his Baltic-German landlord. His daughter Lydia Koidula was to become equally famous as a poet and playwright. One of the regular contributors to *Postimees*, Carl Robert Jakobson, left in 1878 to found his own paper, *Sakala*. Jakobson had spent many years in St Petersburg and felt that Estonians should collaborate with Russian radicals to overthrow German economic dominance. Having made a lot of money from writing school textbooks, he bought a farm in Vandra, central Estonia, and started to write extensively on agriculture.

Increasing literacy helped to spread the ideas of these authors. As Lutheranism was the primary religion, the clergy taught reading to spread knowledge of the Bible whereas the Catholic and Orthodox tradition had been to limit access of the Bible to the clergy. By the mid 1880s, 85% of the population could read, and by the turn of the century the circulation of *Postimees* had increased from an initial 3,000 to 10,000. About 35 books were published each year in Estonian in the 1850s, reaching 250 by the 1890s. The first Song Festival was held in Tartu in 1869, with 800 singers and an audience of 15,000.

RUSSIFICATION OF THE BALTICS The founding of the German Empire in 1871, following the Prussian defeat of the French, caused considerable panic in St Petersburg in view of German power in the Baltics and their many officials at the tsarist court. The subsequent 'Russification' of the Baltic provinces was as much

Edward VII, King of England from 1901–10, was notorious for interfering in his country's foreign policy. His Danish wife, Queen Alexandra, if unable to keep him away from a succession of mistresses, was at least able to prevent him from becoming too close to his cousins on the German throne. She, being Danish, could not forgive the loss to Prussia 40 years earlier of Schleswig-Holstein so was happy to help foster closer relations with the Russian Empire. The 1905 uprisings in many Russian towns delayed earlier plans for a royal visit. The two days the royal couple in the end spent in Tallinn harbour in June 1908 was a compromise between the need for such a visit to take place and the dangers that could ensue from further disturbances in either Tallinn or St Petersburg.

The fast-rising Labour Party in Britain objected to the visit on the grounds that it would give undeserved support to the tsarist regime. The party leader, Keir Hardie, said the visit would 'condone the atrocities of the Tsar such as executing political prisoners and sending suspects to Siberia without trial'. Ramsay Macdonald, who would become the first Labour prime minister in 1924, said the king 'should not hobnob with a blood-stained creature'. The king wanted to show his anger at Keir Hardie's remarks by banning him from a Buckingham Palace garden party, but was finally persuaded to change his mind. However 59 MPs voted in parliament against the visit taking place.

Tallinn, or Reval as it was then known, was considered safe enough for the Tsar and his entourage to cross and then to board his yacht the *Standart*. It went out into the bay to await the arrival of the British party on the *Victoria and Albert*. On the first evening, a flotilla of smaller boats, with Estonian, German and Russian choirs, entertained the royal parties. Earlier in the day, the local (Russian) police had stripped naked every member of the choir, both male and female, to check that they were not carrying guns or bombs. The *New York Times* reported that 'the singing of the Estonians was a particular pleasure, as their melodies floated over the moonlit waters'. The next day was largely taken up with social activity on both yachts, the king and the Tsar speaking in English to each other as they carefully ensured that their time on each yacht was equally divided. The king did not bring any cabinet minister with him, feeling that had he done so, he would have been 'like a prisoner handcuffed to a warder, whilst conversing with a relative through a grille'. Nonetheless, some political discussion took place. At the request of the Rothschild family, the king took up with the Russian prime minister Pyotr Stolypin the treatment Jews had been receiving in Russia. Stolypin promised improvements but it is unlikely that he took any action.

The Russians were surprised at what they regarded as casual behaviour by the British. They could not believe that government officials such as the ambassador sat down in the presence of their sovereign, since they themselves were required to stand hour after hour. They had not expected King Edward to be so well versed in Russian affairs, both domestic and international; though in fact he had simply applied himself a few hours earlier to a very thorough brief provided by the ambassador.

It would be another 98 years before a British sovereign came again to Tallinn, in 2006. Queen Elizabeth II had no qualms about walking in the town centre and her Labour government gave the visit its full support. Her visit was of course 100% in Estonian hands.

a religious campaign as a linguistic one. Lutheranism was seen as a threat to the Orthodox Church and hence to the power of the Russian state. Tartu University went through this process of 'Russification' in 1889, resulting in the dismissal of most of its German-speaking staff and the reintroduction of the Russian name for the town, Yuriev. As Russian also became compulsory in schools and in the civil service, this helped to marginalise the role of the Baltic Germans, few of whom could speak Russian. Ironically, a move which in St Petersburg had the aim of increasing central control had the opposite effect in Estonia. To most Estonians, the Germans had been their masters and any reduction in their powers was to be welcomed. Estonians were hardly independent in the late 19th century, but at least they saw their culture respected and an ever greater scope for using their own language. The tsarist Russians would never interfere in day-to-day life whereas such interference had been the hallmark of the Germans for hundreds of years.

The Bloody Sunday massacre in St Petersburg on 9 January 1905 led to dissent throughout the Russian Empire, including Estonia. A powerful communist underground movement had been operating in Tallinn for two to three years under Mikhail Kalinin, who was later to be a member of both Lenin's and Stalin's Politburo. Knowledge of the military ineptitude, which had led to Russia's defeat at the hands of the Japanese later in 1905, spread quickly and gave confidence to demonstrators both in town and country. Many of the manor houses that belonged to Baltic Germans were attacked and burnt down. Yet these demonstrations and attacks lacked real focus; in Latvia they were clearly social rather than nationalistic. Various groups in Estonia would have liked to monopolise them but none succeeded. The nationalist groupings that did form at this time were to be as divided as their successors in the late 1980s, and over the same gradualist/putschist issues. Tallinn saw a cruel imitation of Bloody Sunday on 16 October 1905 when 60 demonstrators were killed in Market Square. Further cruelty was to follow as the tsarist army re-established control throughout the country; 500 alleged conspirators were executed and several thousand banished to Siberia. Konstantin Päts, the future president, fled abroad and was sentenced to death in his absence. He was, however, allowed to return in 1910 when he re-established his newspaper, *Teataja*.

The start of World War I strained but did not break the relationship between the Baltic Germans and the Russians. The former still enjoyed greater autonomy than they would have done as part of the German Empire and a lifestyle that could not be re-established elsewhere. Taxes increased and many trading routes were blocked, but at the start of the war Estonia suffered little in comparison with most of Europe. No Estonian army units equivalent to the Latvian Riflemen (who became fervent supporters of the Bolsheviks) were formed at this stage. This move only came about in February 1917 as a reaction to the Russian Revolution, a time when such a unit could be genuinely autonomous. It was also a time when the issue of independence could again be raised. A unique event in Estonian history took place on 26 March when a demonstration of 40,000 flag-waving Estonians marched through the streets of St Petersburg. It had an immediate effect with the granting of autonomy to Estonia and the appointment of an Estonian, Jaan Poska, as governor, who was at the time mayor of Tallinn. A full government was quickly established and, in October, Konstantin Päts became its provisional head. It was fortunately in place just before the October Revolution broke out in St Petersburg since, whilst considerable autonomy, if not full independence, might well have been acceptable to a Kerenski regime in Russia, it was certainly not to the Bolsheviks. Within a few days of coming to power, the Bolsheviks dissolved the Estonian National Assembly but an underground Committee of Elders was able to continue its work and, crucially, could send delegations abroad to present Estonia's case to Western governments.

INDEPENDENCE 1918–40 Independence was to come very suddenly to Estonia, as it would do again in 1991; on this first occasion, however, it was initially to last just one day, 24 February 1918, which is still celebrated as Estonian Independence Day. It is easy to forget the continuing strength of the German army in early 1918. It had advanced through the Baltic area in 1917 and, taking advantage of the weakness of the new Soviet state, was able to seize much of Estonia early in 1918. Under the Treaty of Brest-Litovsk, which the Soviet government had been forced to sign with the Germans on 3 March 1918, the island of Saaremaa was ceded to the Germans and they were granted the right to maintain police forces throughout the country. In all but name, the Germans occupied the whole country, imposed their language on it and arrested many Estonians linked with the independence movement. Konstantin Päts was imprisoned in Lithuania. So during the course of 1918, the Estonian independence movement had three powerful opponents, the Germans, the White Russians and the Bolsheviks. Yet it found immediate support amongst the Western allies, and the delegations sent abroad were able to secure *de facto* recognition from the British, the French and the Italians. Despite the armistice of November 1918, the German army was not initially disarmed in the Baltics and it took British intervention to lead, if not directly, to a lasting Estonian independence. On 19 November, the German government gave *de facto* recognition to the Estonian government, several of whose members they had just released from prison.

November and December 1918 were critical months for Estonia; the Soviet army nearly reached Tallinn and 75% of the country fell into their hands. With the appointment of General Laidoner, however, a counter-attack began in the New Year and by the first anniversary of the Declaration of Independence on 24 February the whole country was back in Estonian hands. General Laidoner was to remain chief of staff until his arrest by the Soviet authorities in 1940.

A British fleet of three cruisers and nine destroyers finally reached Tallinn on 12 December 1918. A larger fleet was originally envisaged, but the mission was almost called off when a mine off Hiiumaa Island sank one of the cruisers on 4 December. The Estonians hoped that British land forces would follow but this was not to be, although extensive and immediate supplies of arms and ammunition were given. The British navy fought and defeated the Soviet Russians in Tallinn harbour over Christmas 1918. Regular military supplies, plus coal, wheat and oil were all delivered to Estonia from Britain in early 1919 and appeals from the White Russian armies that Estonian forces should be brought under their control were ignored. Many naval battles were fought between the British and Soviet forces during 1919 and British losses amounted to a cruiser, two destroyers, a submarine and eight torpedo boats. According to a Soviet history of Estonia produced in 1953, 'British and American imperialists had assigned ten million pounds for the purpose of suppressing the revolution in Estonia.' Christmas 1919 brought reports in the British press about possible warfare between Latvia and Estonia over their mutual border and these were taken sufficiently seriously that even the prime minister, Lloyd George, became involved in discussions. He personally ordered a mission to be sent under Sir Stephen Tallents to attempt to resolve the issue. The dispute was in fact comparatively minor and centred largely on one small town, called Valga in Estonian and Valka in Latvian. After six months of bitter negotiations, Tallents was able to obtain agreement from both sides for a border running through the town.

The Tartu Treaty Long negotiations were also needed with the new Soviet authorities before the Tartu Treaty was finally signed on 2 February 1920. These negotiations took place against a background of constant fighting, which ended only with the signing of an armistice on 3 January 1920. The fighting still involved White Russian forces, as hostile to potential Estonian independence as were the Bolsheviks. The most crucial provisions of the treaty were the recognition of the Estonian state by Soviet Russia and a clearly designated frontier. It was because of this diplomatic recognition that in 1940 the USSR was forced to claim that Estonia had voluntarily joined the union. The frontier is now a source of dispute between Russia and Estonia as the Russian Federation maintains control of about 5% of what had been Estonian territory between 1920 and 1940. Most current maps of Estonia printed there indicate the border as agreed by the Tartu Treaty. Although in the late 1990s the Estonians publicly agreed to the border imposed by Russia, it would be the autumn of 2013 before President Putin gave his agreement to the signing of a border treaty.

The 1920 constitution granted universal suffrage, a secret ballot and elections based on proportional representation. The parliament 'Riigikogu' had 100 members but no single political party, or even a stable coalition, was ever able to maintain power for more than a few months. Between 1919 and 1933, Estonia had 20 governments, mostly of a centre-right disposition with the agrarian parties being the strongest. Nonetheless, a state pension scheme and compulsory education were immediately introduced and the estates of the Baltic Germans were expropriated.

Estonia was finally recognised by Britain and France on 26 January 1921, but recognition by the United States did not follow until July 1922, although membership of the League of Nations had been granted in September 1921. An early foreign policy objective was the founding of a Baltic League, to link the three new republics with Poland and the Scandinavian countries in a defence union against the USSR, but this foundered on apathy in Scandinavia and hostility in Lithuania, whose capital Vilnius had been seized by the Poles in 1920. The need for it seemed less important when the USSR started to sign individual non-aggression pacts with the three Baltic states in the late 1920s. Estonia was the last to sign, in May 1932. Ironically, these agreements were supposed to last until December 1945. The three did finally form a 'Little Baltic Entente' in 1934 but it was totally ineffective in formulating a common foreign policy towards Nazi Germany or Soviet Russia.

On 1 December 1924 a Communist Party-attempted putsch was quickly suppressed, as it did not lead to a mass uprising. Soviet writers had to admit that tactics which had been very effective in tsarist times were no longer appropriate, and if insurrection were to succeed at all in Estonia, far greater work amongst the industrial population would be needed. That one of the first economic measures of the new government in 1920 had been the seizure of the estates owned by the Baltic Germans and the distribution of the land to the local peasants, ensured that rural support for any communist movement was likely to be minimal.

League of Freedom Fighters Estonia was to suffer, as did all European countries, from the aftermath of the 1929 Wall Street crash. Imports and exports in 1932 were less than half of the 1929 figure. This provided fertile ground for the establishment of the fascist 'League of Freedom Fighters', known as VAPS. Based initially amongst ex-servicemen, this organisation soon extended its support amongst the civilian population. It had fertile ground on which to grow. Anyone with unrealistic expectations of an independent Estonia and unrealised ambitions was drawn into this seemingly patriotic movement. Its first aim was to strengthen the hand of the presidency at the expense of the Riigikogu (parliament). Following a successful referendum, which the VAPS organised in October 1933, a new constitution was inaugurated in January 1934 giving the president largely dictatorial powers. VAPS hoped that the leader of the Estonian army in the war against the Bolsheviks, General Laidoner, would stand for them as president in the subsequent elections but he wished to distance himself from an organisation so clearly imitating the German Nazis. These elections never took place, since on 12 March 1934 one of the four candidates, acting prime minister Konstantin Päts, staged a *coup d'état* and proclaimed a state of emergency as a pretext for cancelling the elections. He dissolved VAPS, arrested 500 of their members and banned all other political organisations. He therefore beat VAPS at their own game and granted himself all the powers they would have given General Laidoner. Päts shrewdly appointed Laidoner as commander-in-chief and, with his loyalty assured, was then able in October 1934 to dissolve the Riigikogu. Päts replaced it with a tame two-chamber National Assembly, one chamber to be elected in the traditional way on the basis of personal majorities and one to be filled with his own appointees and those of the chambers of commerce. The first chamber had 80 seats against the 100 in the former Riigikogu and, as 50 of the candidates were returned unopposed, the success of the government was not in doubt.

The economic success that Päts was to bring about assured him of political stability. He guaranteed minimum prices for butter and eggs and offered subsidies to farmers who brought virgin lands under cultivation. Estonia became self-sufficient in barley, hay, wheat and rye. Subsidies were also offered to industries using Estonian raw materials, such as the oil-shale along the north coast. Tariffs on imports protected these fledgling factories. Unemployment fell to such a low level in 1937 that Polish labourers were brought in during the summer to help with the harvest. Päts was lucky too; economic conditions improved throughout Europe from 1934 and the policy of subsidies had begun under the previous government. He nonetheless did claim personal credit for this turnaround in Estonia's fortunes.

By 1938 Päts felt able to promote the idea of a new constitution which would curtail many of his powers. It claimed to strike a middle road between the 1920 constitution that had given minimal powers to the president and the authoritarian 1934 one that did the same towards the legislature. The president still had far more powers than his opposite numbers in say France or the United States, but more political debate was still possible in Estonia at that time than in most other countries of eastern or central Europe. The British newspaper the *Manchester Guardian* was able to write that these constitutional changes 'came quietly, amid general rejoicing; all will wish that other dictatorial interludes will end as happily'. Päts's local opponents saw them as window-dressing to enable him to maintain his arbitrary rule. The first election under this constitution was held in February 1938. Political parties were still banned, but many individuals totally opposed to Konstantin Päts stood and won seats. These included Jaan Tõnisson, a former prime minister, and Neeme Ruus, who would become secretary of the Communist Party two years later following the incorporation of Estonia into the USSR. Dissident voices were, however, much in the minority and during these final two years there was little co-ordinated opposition to Päts. He continued to rely on the support of the farmers and the Tallinn business elite. With 70% of the population living in the countryside, this was a logical move, but by forbidding active trade unions, he antagonised industrial workers and exposed them to the approaches of the underground communist movement.

Few could have predicted in February 1938 that independent Estonia was only to exist for a further two years. Diplomatically it rode a skilful tightrope between Nazi Germany and Soviet Russia and confidence exudes from all the books and brochures published at the time. Despite the outbreak of World War II, the Estonian Tourist Board still promoted holidays in Tallinn as an adjunct to the Olympic Games due to take place in Helsinki in June 1940. Yet the signing of the Ribbentrop–Molotov Pact in August 1939 sealed its fate, together with that of Latvia and Lithuania. The published section of the pact largely concerned trade. Germany would buy more coal and oil from the USSR (anticipating wartime difficulties from other sources) and the Soviets would buy German machinery. Under the secret protocols, Estonia, Finland and Latvia were to come under the Soviet field of influence, and most of Poland and Lithuania under Germany's. In September 1939, the USSR quickly took advantage of these secret protocols, knowing that with western Europe at war there would be little reaction. A mutual assistance pact was imposed on Estonia under which Soviet army, navy and airforce bases were set up around the country. These were used as springboards for the Soviet invasion of Finland. In October 1939, the Baltic Germans were summoned 'home', even though most had not lived in Germany for generations. A possible countervailing force to the USSR was therefore removed and increased Estonia's vulnerability.

SOVIET DOMINATION On 18 June 1940, the same day France fell to Germany, Estonia fell to the USSR. This date was chosen deliberately to minimise the chance of British or American protests. The standard Soviet history of Estonia admits as much in writing that 'the switch-over was facilitated by the international situation, with the imperialist powers involved in a war and consequently unable to render military aid to the Estonian bourgeoisie'. Andrei Zhdanov from the Soviet Politburo arrived in Tallinn the following day to finalise the takeover. Demonstrations were organised to 'welcome' him although trainloads of Russian speakers from outside the city had to be brought in to ensure satisfactory numbers. By 6 August, Estonia had become a Soviet republic. On 30 July, all the leading members of the former government had been arrested and taken to Russia. Konstantin Päts and General Laidoner would both die there, still in captivity, during the 1950s.

The Soviet system was rapidly imposed on all fields of life. By the end of August, 90% of private companies had been nationalised and any private property of more than $130m^2$ was expropriated. The kroon was withdrawn from circulation in September and replaced, at a disadvantageous exchange rate, by the Soviet rouble. From September, religious education in schools was forbidden and the faculty of theology at Tartu University was closed. Christmas was made a working day. The dismissal of senior Estonians culminated with a purge on 14 June 1941, during which around 10,000 people were dragged from their homes without warning on this one single day and deported to Siberia. At most, only a few hundred would ever see their homeland again, and then only after the death of Stalin in 1953. All contact with the outside world suddenly stopped; in theory, Estonians could now travel freely to Vladivostok but they could not send a letter or take a boat to Helsinki or Stockholm. Only in agriculture was change handled with more subtlety and less speed. Large estates were seized and the land distributed to peasants. Most independent farmers were able to keep their holdings, although much of the produce had to be sold at fixed prices to the co-operatives. English was replaced as the first foreign language taught in schools by either Russian or German. Newspapers were obliged to take a very pro-German line in covering the war, so joyfully reported the bombing of Britain, and German advances into the Balkans.

WORLD WAR II Despite constant warnings from their agents all over the world and from the British government, the USSR was totally unprepared for the German invasion on 22 June 1941. Lithuania and Latvia fell within days as there was no more than minimal resistance from either the Soviet army or the local population. Following the 14 June purge, which had been as ruthlessly carried out there as in Estonia, it is not surprising that the Germans, coming so soon afterwards, were seen as liberators in the three Baltic states.

They occupied Estonia more slowly, as their aim was to concentrate on reaching Leningrad, and only in Tartu was there serious fighting. The mainland was entirely in German hands by the end of August; as Soviet forces on the islands were totally cut off from their supplies, they were no further threat and the Germans waited until October before occupying them.

Alfred Rosenberg, the commissioner for the 'Ostland' (the civilian occupation regime), had been born in Tallinn and it is perhaps for this reason that he classified Estonians as Aryans rather than as Slavs; yet the Germans made no effort to win serious support amongst the local population. The nationalisation that had been introduced by the Soviets was simply taken over and run by Germans. Higher quantities of grain than the Soviets ever demanded were requisitioned from the farmers and rations for Estonians were about half those granted to Germans. The Gestapo was less active than the NKVD had been, probably because all likely dissenters had already been deported or killed and the Jewish population of Estonia was minute compared with that in Latvia or Lithuania. Estonians who under other circumstances might have volunteered for service to fight the Russians, were only conscripted at the last minute as a desperate measure when the Germans were in defeat. Only in 1944 was the national anthem again played and could the Estonian flag be raised, but by then it was far too late. The Russians started their re-invasion with bombing raids on Tallinn, Tartu and Narva; as so often in Estonian history, Narva became a battleground. In July and August there was fighting in much of eastern Estonia. On the western coast over 70,000 Estonians took the chance to flee to Sweden; 30,000 others were later to withdraw to Germany as the German army continued its retreat. By the end of the war, 10% of the Estonian population of one million had fled abroad.

On 17 September 1944 the German forces received orders from Berlin to retreat from Estonia within the next ten days. On this very same day a new Estonian government was formed in Tallinn under Otto Tief who had been a minister in several governments during the 1920s but was untarnished by close links to Konstantin Päts or to either occupying power. Tragically, this government was to last for only five days. On reoccupying Tallinn on 22 September, the Soviet authorities immediately dissolved it and the leaders were arrested. However, that this government existed is very important for understanding contemporary Estonian–Russian relations. The Russians always refer to the 'liberation' of Estonia at this time. The Estonians point out that the Russians arrested not Germans, but Estonians and tore down an Estonian flag from Tall Hermann Tower, not a German one. To stress the legitimacy of his government, Otto Tief even managed to produce two copies of the *State Gazette* during his short time in power.

SOVIET OCCUPATION The 45 years from 1944 until 1989, although recent, are the hardest period of Estonian history to describe. The Soviet authorities invited some British journalists to Tallinn in October 1944 but then felt it necessary to censor their reports. No Westerners were subsequently permitted entry into Estonia until 1960. From then until the early 1980s they usually had to stay in Tallinn and

The German occupation came as liberation for the Estonian people. The regime was far less despotic and there was no comparison between it and the horrible terror which, under the Soviet regime, held everyone in its grasp the whole time and controlled the smallest details of life.

Among the German soldiers and officers there were cultivated people with whom one could talk, whose attitude was friendly, and who knew how to evade the more severe orders; they were human, whereas the representatives of the Soviets all seemed to be barbarians. One will never forget those round heads, with a line of hair at the back cut in a straight line by the regimental razor. A form of haircut which they all had and which showed in this small detail the rule of iron under which they were living.

They were good children, these Russians, and they had good hearts, but real conversation was impossible with them and they had no general ideas. Their judgements were falsified by the perfect flowering of Soviet technique and its coarse-grained materialism, so that everything they said had a colossal a priori basis, as stupid as it was narrow. Any form of controversy was thus discouraged from the start. What purpose could it have served?

One can never sufficiently stress the width of the gulf made by the Eastern schism. These Russian Christians, having been separated from us for so many centuries, no longer have the same reactions as ourselves in anything, not even in religion. For centuries they have looked on us as enemies and as the worst type of heretics, and they take no interest in what we may have in common. Instead they merely notice that our customs are different, and see in this a mark of a different faith. Even those who practised their religion were far away from us.

The Russians automatically carried out the orders of their leaders, no matter how savage, and this absolute obedience made these good children terribly dangerous, given the calibre of the Politburo leadership. They were without conscience, personality or human dignity, being just slaves.

The Estonians could now breathe again. They did not care greatly for the Germans. They had known the yoke of the Baltic barons and their arrogance; indeed their grandparents still remembered the beatings they had received from them. Nevertheless the contrast was great, and furthermore the German soldiers were not the barons; one could live alongside them and the peasant was allowed to keep his land.

From A Priest in Russia and the Baltic *by Charles Bourgeois, published in 1953. Despite writing in a positive manner about the German occupation, Bourgeois was in fact imprisoned by them for two years from 1942 to 1944.*

were not allowed a stay longer than four nights. (Longer stays could have led to undue close contacts with the local population.) Much was written within the exile community both in Sweden and in the USSR but neither source could be trusted. Whilst Estonians are quite willing to discuss their experiences during the Soviet era, little has been written about it and in the 1990s museums rarely wanted to include items from this period in their collections. Estonians who had successful careers under Soviet tutelage understandably did not wish to remind others of this. Those who suffered were usually too modest to launch into print. Equally understandably,

Russian historians are not yet ready to take a dispassionate look at how their empire was run and then lost. From around 2000, the situation slowly began to change as generations were growing up with no knowledge of this period; they had to be educated about it. Museums and art galleries started to add Soviet rooms.

Whatever regime came to power in Estonia at the end of the war, they had a desperate situation to remedy. The tenth of the population who had fled or been killed represented a crucial cross-section of Estonian society. All the major factories had been destroyed, as had half the livestock in the countryside.

It was little consolation that the situation in the surrounding republics of Russia and Latvia, indeed throughout eastern Europe, was even worse. It was in agriculture that the new Soviet regime was first to make its mark. The lessons of over-rapid collectivisation had been learnt from the experiences of the early 1930s and farmers could initially keep their smallholdings. Larger farms that had not been seized either during the first occupation in 1940 or by the Germans were divided or given to the new Russian settlers brought into Estonia. However, as the farmers had no independent outlets for their produce, the introduction of the *kolkhoz*, the collective farms, did not in practice greatly affect their day-to-day lives. The first was set up on Saaremaa Island in 1947 and inevitably was named after Viktor Kingissepp, the revolutionary activist who had lived on the island and who was executed for terrorist activities in 1924. By March 1949 over 500 collectives had been established, rising to nearly 3,000 by June of that year. The process was complete in a macabre sense too. March 1949 saw as brutal a deportation as that of June 1941 when many farmers were sent to Siberia on the flimsiest of pretexts, usually a failure to devote sufficient energy to the *kolkhoz*. The aim of these deportations was to accelerate the collectivisation of agriculture. Purges, however, were just as rampant within the Communist Party; they hit the higher ranks of the Estonian Communist Party throughout the eight years from reoccupation in 1945 until the death of Stalin in 1953. This was despite the fact that ethnic Estonians never formed more than 40% of its membership, so nervous was the Kremlin of possible divided loyalties. Mirroring similar purges throughout eastern Europe at the time, party secretary Nicholas Karotamm was one of many senior members of the still small Estonian Communist Party to be dismissed for such colourful crimes as 'rightist opportunism' and 'promoting peaceful co-existence with class-hostile elements'. Those who survived the purges were often referred to as 'Yestonians' since the long periods they had spent in Russia marked their accents and lifestyles.

The development of heavy industry along the northeastern coast by the Soviet Union was to lead to environmental and ethnic disputes that are still unresolved today. The modest, pre-war, oil-shale exploitation at Kohtla-Järve was rapidly expanded so that by 1948 the gas produced from it could meet all the needs of Leningrad (only in 1953 was Tallinn partially supplied). Phosphate and uranium mines, chemical plants and paper mills were all also developed and expanded in this area. The extra workforce required was mostly brought in from Russia so the area became, and still is, largely Russian speaking. However one must not forget the 30,000 German prisoners of war who were kept in Estonia until 1949. The construction of the initial Tallinn harbour buildings, of Tallinn airport and of the higway to Narva was largely their work. Over 200,000 Russians were moved into Estonia between 1945 and 1953, with the result that the number of ethnic Estonians, who had represented about 95% of the national population before the war, fell to 70%.

The results of a policy of architectural schizophrenia carried out in the 1950s can still be seen all over Estonia. On the one hand, restoration started at St Nicholas

Church in Tallinn and at Narva Castle. In fact St Nicholas became a training centre for this work. These projects were extended to the bastions in Narva and to Nun's Tower on Tallinn's city wall. Yet at the same time, another St Nicholas Church in Pärnu was blown up, as was Peter the Great's house in Narva, the Stone Bridge in Tartu and Tallinn Synagogue. All these buildings were badly damaged in World War II, but could have been restored if political considerations had not dictated otherwise. From the 1960s the Soviet policy became much more positive with over 200 full-time restorers being employed in Estonia. Work began on Narva Town Hall and in Kiek in de Kök in Tallinn. Listed buildings and protected zones would follow in the 1970s.

Forest Brothers The Soviet authorities could impose their will with relative ease on the open countryside and in the towns. This did, however, leave the forests, which they were unable to control until well into the 1950s. These forests provided a relatively safe haven for an extensive underground guerrilla movement that could move swiftly and safely to attack vulnerable targets. The movement became known as the 'Forest Brothers' and, although neither organisation would ever be aware of the other, the techniques they used in Estonia came to be used with equal effect by the Vietcong in Indo-China. The Forest Brothers were a Baltic-wide phenomenon but it was impossible for co-operation to be established between the three countries of Estonia, Latvia and Lithuania. Russians might control villages by day, but rarely by night. Intelligence was so good that attacks could be launched on arms depots, on convoys and on isolated individuals with minimal chances of a successful reprisal. Over-ambitiousness and the very occasional betrayal were the main problems the movement initially faced. Once the Western powers made clear their lack of interest in the former Baltic states, it was futile to hope for the imminent overthrow of the Soviet regime, but the Forest Brothers could maintain morale and a commitment to Estonian culture at a time when the future looked particularly bleak. Eventually the Soviet authorities were able to curtail the activities of the Brothers.

The March 1949 deportations, when 22,000 Estonians were taken to Siberia, created a climate in which only the most courageous could continue resistance. By 1950, the Baltic Sea was too well patrolled for boats to have any chance of reaching Finland or Sweden. Internal passports, ration books and job allocation made a partisan existence ever more precarious. The development of the timber industry led to forest patrols, and the collectivisation of agriculture reduced the possible hiding places in barns and outhouses. Anger and bitterness drove those who did remain in the movement to acts of ever greater daring. Banks were robbed and senior officials who had been implicated in the deportations were murdered. Isolated acts of resistance would continue throughout the occupation but from the mid-1950s it would be hard to justify the term 'movement' any more. One of the most famous Brothers, Kalev Arro, disguised himself as a vagrant for 20 years before being killed in a shoot-out in 1974. Another, August Sabe, lived as a fisherman and drowned in September 1978 whilst trying to escape from security forces. The Estonian community abroad marked his death as that of the last Forest Brother when the news reached them the following year. The Soviet authorities had planned to celebrate the arrest of 'this dangerous criminal' but realised just in time that such publicity could only be counter-productive. The greatest tribute to the Forest Brothers comes ironically in Soviet histories of Estonia: that frequent mention has to be made about 'bandit' activity in the late 1940s shows how powerful they were.

By the 1970s, 'banditry' had given way to dissidence, and resistance moved from countryside to town. The increasing range of consumer goods and higher real wages for minimal work led to an apathetic acceptance of the Soviet regime on the farms. In the towns, the intellectual thaw introduced by Khrushchev and the minimal contacts that again became possible with foreigners and the Estonian diaspora gave cause for hope in the 1960s.

The Soviet invasion of Czechoslovakia in August 1968 caused great concern in Estonia but fortunately stagnation rather than further repression followed. It was well known that the Estonian SSR enjoyed a higher standard of living than any other of the republics and, if the local population detested the 'import' of Russian workers and pensioners, it was at least comforting to know that they were abandoning home in Russia for the hint of Western life that Estonia could still offer. This differential in living standards would remain until the demise of the USSR. Estonia always had better goods in the shops, better housing and a more dependable social infrastructure than any of the other republics, including its Baltic neighbours. Yet, as access to Finnish television increased in the 1970s and 1980s, cynicism towards the USSR was bound to strengthen as the local population took the lifestyle portrayed in American soap operas as the standard to which they should aspire.

OPENING UP TO THE WEST Although only a minute percentage of the population was allowed to use it, the re-establishment of the ferry service to Helsinki in 1965 also gave cause for hope. In that first year, 9,000 Finns came over, rising to 95,000 by 1977. (In 2000 the comparable figure was 2.5 million.) For many tourists, this trip was just a 'booze cruise', and for the Soviet regime it was an easy foreign currency earner. But it enabled some exiled Estonians to return home for brief visits and to show the country that it was not completely forgotten abroad. Some of the foreign currency would illegally 'trickle down' to the local population to enable them to enjoy Western goods not seen since 1939. Latvia and Lithuania would have to wait another 20 years for a similar international link. The boat used for this link from 1980 was called the *Georg Ots* after a famous Estonian singer who died in 1975. In 1986 it would be used as Gorbachev's headquarters at the Reykjavik summit. It now plies between Kaliningrad and St Petersburg transporting Russians unable to get transit visas through the Baltic countries.

Courageous public attacks on the most vulnerable aspects of Soviet policy took place regularly in the 1970s and early 1980s. Estonians suffered long prison sentences for writing to Kurt Waldheim, the UN Secretary-General, to complain about Soviet rule, for protesting against the expulsion of Alexander Solzhenitsyn from the USSR in 1974, for demanding Soviet implementation of the 1975 Helsinki Agreement and for publicising the dangers of pollution from industry along the northeast coast. In 1979 Estonian dissidents combined with Latvian and Lithuanian groups to demand the publication in full of the Ribbentrop–Molotov Pact and also that the three Baltic republics should be declared nuclear-free zones. Yet prison sentences were lower than they had been in the 1950s and 1960s. 'Only' five to six years was now the norm rather than 25 under Stalin and ten under Khrushchev. Arrests would always ensure publicity in the West and increasing protests from abroad towards any Soviet institution.

The holding of some of the events of the 1980 Olympic Games in Tallinn gave the city its first exposure to the outside world since 1940. For thousands of residents drafted in to work in the tourism and service industries, it was also their first contact with foreigners. For three weeks, English suddenly became a living language and Tallinn a cosmopolitan city. If direct dialling abroad, foreign newspapers and wide menus in cafés disappeared as quickly as they had been introduced, at least the yachting harbour at Pirita and a restored Old Town remained. The Soviet Union was, however, entering a period of deep stagnation. Leonid Brezhnev finally died in November 1982 after two years of critical illness, and his successor Yuri Andropov was to live for little more than a year. Konstantin Chernenko was in similar ill health and he died in March 1985. Only then did Mikhail Gorbachev become general secretary and the policies he launched were to lead to the dissolution of the USSR, although this was hardly his aim. In 1983, probably unbeknown outside Estonia itself, Arnold Rüütel was elected as chairman of the Estonian Supreme Soviet. At the time, this body was powerless and irrelevant but he was to turn it into the main body co-ordinating the drive to independence. Eighteen years later, in 2001, he would be elected president of Estonia, which by then had been independent for ten years.

Two even more crucial issues had first to be tackled: the proposed new port at Muuga to the east of Tallinn and the proposed new phosphate mine at Rakvere, further east towards Narva. Both would require the immigration of at least 10,000 Russians, and both were ecologically unsound. The phosphate mine would have been lethal, polluting both Lake Peipsi and the Pärnu River. The Chernobyl nuclear disaster, which took place in April 1986, further strengthened Estonian concerns about large-scale Soviet industrial development. In 1987 there were major clashes, fortunately all peaceful, between the Soviet authorities and many different groups of protesters. That year was also to see many 'firsts' – protest banners in English, public argument with Gorbachev during his visit to Tallinn, references in the press to public opinion, and finally the complete abandonment of both projects. The environment was a perfect issue to choose since it could not be branded as 'capitalistic' or 'nationalistic' and the reaction to Chernobyl in the West forced Moscow to face it. Yet as progress on this environmental issue moved so quickly, 1987 also brought out into the open the Ribbentrop–Molotov Pact, which could not avoid the sovereignty issue. On 23 August, the anniversary of its signing in 1939, about 2,000 people gathered in Hirve Park to demand the publication of the 'secret' protocols which had allowed the USSR to absorb the three Baltic states.

The year 1988 was to be one of autonomy, a word that frightened the Kremlin but that could not justify a military reaction. As with most radical Estonian movements, it began in Tartu University, where a dozen well-known academics published an economics discussion paper in September 1987. (Tactically it was still unwise to attempt publication in the capital.) Its main points were that the republics should be largely self-regulating in the economics field and should be able to trade independently with each other and with the outside world. A convertible rouble would have to be the mainstay of such an economic policy. A greater role was foreseen for the private sector although this was not yet specified, again for tactical reasons. The initial public debate could therefore centre on the obsessive over-centralisation of the Soviet system whilst the real agenda of nationalism and a capitalist economy could remain hidden until it was safe to bring it out completely into the open. Limited economic autonomy was formally granted in 1988 but implementation was difficult, given the threat it posed to the jobs of those supposed to publicise and carry out these policies. Many previous taboos were broken in 1988. The 1941 and 1949 deportations could be condemned in the press, 24 February (the former national day) discreetly celebrated and, more important than anything else, the Estonian flag could be publicly displayed. Karl Vaino who had been the inert general secretary of the Estonian Communist Party for the previous ten years, was finally dismissed by Moscow in June. In the same year, by subtle, gradual and often obtuse manoeuvres, Estonia was to achieve independence without a single violent death and without the trade blockades that Lithuania had to endure. (Latvia was to follow a similar gradualist course.) The last militant outburst took place on 2 February 1988 when a demonstration in Tartu was brutally dispersed by the Soviet police. Fortunately, this was the last police outburst too. The most famous, and the happiest, demonstration in Estonia's history took place in September 1988 when 250,000 people, a quarter of the adult population of the country, packed the Song Festival ground in Tallinn and for the first time the word 'independence' came into the public domain.

The gradualist vein continued in 1989 and 1990 but it was a lonely task for Estonia. Whilst most Western countries had never given diplomatic recognition to the Soviet takeover of the Baltic states, they were not yet willing to provoke Moscow by re-establishing embassies in any of the three capitals. Many Western newspapers warned the Baltic states of the dangers of 'secession'. A stable Soviet Union under Mikhail Gorbachev, a leader to whom the West immediately warmed, was a far more crucial goal but this was a leader who could not, and still does not, understand the background to Baltic demands for independence. To him, it simply reflected 'narrow-mindedness'. On 15 February 1991 Gorbachev wrote in a letter to several Western leaders: 'The speeches of a few unbalanced individuals who manage to climb onto high rostrums do not provide any clue to their deeply held opinions. I hope that reason will prevail, although irrational and extreme nationalist fervour, with fascist overtones, can be very vociferous, especially in Lithuania.' A few months later, these 'unbalanced individuals' would be presidents and prime ministers in their newly independent countries. In a phone call around this time to Margaret Thatcher, he said 'we consider Lithuania as one of our Soviet republics. We will approach the problem in this context.'

Gorbachev was perhaps right in projecting a future for a USSR with greater political and economic autonomy for the republics and this might have suited many of the non-Baltic ones quite well. They could not look back to a relatively prosperous period of 20 years between 1920 and 1940, the renewal of which was bound to be the aspiration of all three Baltic republics. They could also observe many positive aspects of Soviet rule which did not apply in the Baltics.

In 1989, Estonian was again recognised as the official language, there were further moves towards economic autonomy, and the Ribbentrop–Molotov Pact was published in full by *Pravda* in Moscow. It therefore became impossible for the Soviet government to maintain its claim that Estonia had 'voluntarily' joined the USSR in 1940. The 50th anniversary of the pact on 23 August was marked by a rare and very effective symbol of Baltic co-operation – a human chain of two million people that stretched from Vilnius to Tallinn. The following year saw contested elections and the increasing marginalisation of the Russian-speaking community, but it did not see Estonian support for the Lithuanian declaration of independence on 11 March. Continuing the gradualist approach, Estonians now talked about a 'period of transition' and of practical measures that could accompany it rather than full independence, which could still not realistically be implemented. Certain issues, such as conscription into the Soviet army, were deliberately fudged to avoid possible clashes. Joint ventures with Western companies began and were tactfully presented as being in the spirit of perestroika. Closer links were established with the nascent regime of Boris Yeltsin in the Russian Federation, who was just as eager to see the end of Gorbachev's Soviet Union.

The year 1991 began ominously. The outbreak of the Gulf War in January gave Moscow scope for increased military activity in the Baltics which it was hoped would not be noticed in the West. Thirteen civilians were killed in Vilnius defending the Television Tower and four in Riga defending the radio station.

A visit by Boris Yeltsin to Tallinn, in which he proposed mutual recognition of the Russian Federation and the three Baltic states, helped to prevent similar violence in Estonia, as did a smoother relationship between the fledgling Estonian government and the local Soviet commanders. A referendum held on 3 March gave substantial support for the independence movement, with 64% voting in favour and 17% voting against. As the Russian-speaking minority in Estonia is about 30% of the population, this showed considerable support amongst them for a break from the USSR. The early summer brought increased tension in all three countries. Negotiations were deliberately stalled by Moscow on the pretext that the proposed Union Treaty should take priority; shop prices rose and supplies dwindled. The Estonian government was divided on the Narva issue – whether or not to grant special status to this border town which had a tiny Estonian population. The only positive development was increasing Western interest in the Baltics, which reduced the likelihood of further military action. There was no doubt that independence would be re-established, but it would probably take longer and be a more painful process than was at first foreseen. Lennart Meri was already establishing himself as the international face of Estonia and took the title of foreign minister. Being 193cm tall, and fluent in English, French and German, he forced his way into many international functions, to the fury of any Soviet representatives there.

INDEPENDENCE The pattern of 24 February 1918, when Estonia enjoyed just one day of independence, could easily have been repeateded on 20 August 1991. With hindsight, we know that the attempted coup in Moscow against Gorbachev could not have succeeded but, given the willingness of the Soviet military to fight in the Baltics earlier in 1991, further similarly frenzied activity was quite possible. On 20 August, it was the second day of the coup and its outcome remained uncertain. Yet the Estonian Supreme Council bravely met in the parliament building in Toompea and issued a declaration that proclaimed independence and sought diplomatic recognition. The building was at that time surrounded by Soviet troops rushed in from Pskov, the nearest Russian town to the Estonian border. Diplomatic recognition was granted within days by over 40 countries and only a week later, on 29 August, the first embassy was reopened in Tallinn by the Swedes. In the meantime, on 24 August, Lenin had been removed from his pedestal and the Russian government under Boris Yeltsin made clear its support for the new Estonian government. On 14 September, US secretary of state James Baker visited Tallinn. Continued independence was now assured.

Looking back now after almost 25 years of independence it is only the first year that can really be described as dramatic. The handover of Soviet assets, the withdrawal of the Soviet military, the status of ethnic Russians and the designation of the border with the new Russian Federation caused much friction, but fortunately no violence. Lennart Meri, who in August 1991 was preparing to lead a government in exile should the coup have succeeded, was elected president in October 1992 of what was by then a very stable Estonia. He would be re-elected in 1996. By late 1992 a pattern was set which has continued uninterrupted since then. Estonia had turned immediately westwards, and both small and large private companies were established, some 100% Estonian, others joint ventures. Air and sea transport links to Scandinavia and Germany were rapidly expanded, Western consumer goods poured in, followed by a similar flood of Western tourists and the Estonian diaspora. The country's transition from a Soviet republic to a completely independent economic structure was marked by the reintroduction of the kroon as the national currency on 20 June 1992. It was tied to the German mark at the rate of

In 1990, up to half a million people, one-third of the population of Estonia, gathered together in Tallinn to sing the first Estonian programme since the war. The streets and trams were filled with men and women in regional national dress. Crowds reserved places on the pavements in advance to watch the choral procession as it passed through the centre of town and along the coastal road to 'Song Square' stadium. It took at least three hours for the dizzying display of 28,000 singers to pass, a seemingly endless stream of men balancing shining brass instruments and women wearing colourful striped skirts, tartan bodices and white blouses fastened with large silver brooches. The ancient conductor, Gustav Ernesaks, came by in a horse-drawn carriage acknowledging the cheers with a wave and a nod of his head. (He died in 1994 and in 2004 a statue of him was unveiled in the Song Festival grounds.) 'Viva Latvia!' was the cry welcoming a group of Estonians from the southern neighbour and a roar of applause greeted a group of dark, long-nosed Georgian men in crimson suits; but it was the Lithuanians, still suffering from the Russian blockade, who won the loudest cheer.

School groups bore banners displaying not the post-war number system but their old, historical names. A choir from a Russian-language school expressed its loyalty to Estonia by wearing costumes of blue, black and white. There was no applause for the choir from the 'Friendship Society', the Soviet organisation which had monopolised foreign cultural relations for years and which was to be liquidated a few months later. 'Horrible,' said one almost sympathetic onlooker, 'to be singing in that choir today.'

In 1990, for the first time since the war, there were no communist portraits or slogans, and previously banned religious and patriotic songs were sung instead of the 'red' ones that had always been added to the programme. These included 'Eesti Vabaks' (Estonian Freedom), which would have led to a one-way ticket to Siberia in previous years for anyone who dared to sing it. Looking down from the sunlit hilltop, over the flood of people towards the giant but remote half-moon-shaped stadium, I heard the song chanted over and over again. It was the only moment resembling anything like a protest in an otherwise relaxed and rather unemotional gathering.

Small shacks set up around the perimeters of the grounds sold ice cream, chocolate, sausages and tomatoes, while hard-currency stalls supplied Czechoslovakian beer to Estonian émigrés and the tiny minority of local Estonians who had any *valuta* (foreign currency). It was not very fair on the majority. People wandered aimlessly about the grounds during the concert. Others sat on plastic bags and made boat-shaped sun hats out of newspapers. Small Estonian children collecting beer cans urged Western consumers to drink up fast. An elderly woman went up and kicked two young Estonian men as they lay sprawled out on the grass reading newspapers as the Estonian national anthem was being sung. Later an Estonian friend said: 'Surely in a democratic society they should be allowed to do what they want?'

From The Singing Revolution: A Political Journey Through the Baltic States *by Clare Thomson, 1991.*

MAJOR DATES IN ESTONIAN HISTORY

1219	June: King Valdemar II of Denmark occupies Estonia
1237	First mention of the Tallinn almshouse
1248	Lubeck law adopted for Tallinn as it joins the Hanseatic League
1343–45	St George's Rebellion against Danish rule
1346	Denmark sells Estonia to the Teutonic Knights
1348	Twenty-nine gravestones exported from Tallinn to Lübeck, the first record of such business
1525	First book printed in Estonian
1632	Opening of Tartu University
1710	Treaty of Nystadt brings Estonia into Tsarist Empire
1739	Earliest publication of the Bible in Estonian
1814	John Quincy Adams, later US President, spends three weeks in Tallinn
1816	Abolition of serfdom in the tsarist Baltic provinces (this occurred in Russia in 1861)
1864	First publication of an Estonian daily newspaper, *Postimees*
1869	First Estonian Song Festival held at Tartu
1872	Strike at Kreenholm factory
1905	Uprisings in Tallinn follow those in St Petersburg
1908	British king Edward VII meets Tsar Nicholas II in Tallinn harbour
1918	24 February: proclamation of independence. The very next day German troops seize Tallinn. They withdraw on 11 November. 12 December: British fleet arrives in Tallinn
1920	2 February: signing of the Tartu Peace Treaty between Estonia and the USSR
1921	1 January: Estonia joins Eastern European time, one hour behind St Petersburg and Moscow time 1 July: wearing of Soviet military uniforms is banned 19 July: flights from Tallinn to Stockholm begin
1924	1 December: a communist putsch attempt is crushed
1928	1 January: kroon is introduced as the national currency 3 July: first steamer service to the UK starts
1933	11 August: proclamation of state of emergency
1934	12 March: ban on all political parties 27 November: study of English language made compulsory in all secondary schools
1936	February: import of all Soviet printed matter forbidden
1937	1 June: the first British-built submarine is delivered to the Estonian navy
1939	23 August: signing of Ribbentrop–Molotov Pact which places Estonia in the Soviet field of influence 28 September: Estonia forced to sign a Mutual Assistance Pact with the USSR which allows 25,000 Soviet troops to be stationed in Estonia
1940	16 June: Soviet occupation begins
1941	14 June: deportations to Siberia 28 August: German troops occupy Tallinn

1944	17 September: German troops retreat from Tallinn. Formation of Estonian provisional government, dissolved five days later with arrival of Soviet troops.
1949	March: further deportations to Siberia
1950	Population of Tallinn reaches 200,000
1964	12 March: President Urho Kekkonen of Finland spends three days in Estonia, the first foreign leader to visit the then Soviet republic since the war
1965	Twice-weekly ferry service to Helsinki opens: to be Estonia's only direct link outside the USSR until 1989
1980	19 July: opening of Olympic Games sailing and yachting events at Pirita outside Tallinn
1989	24 February: Estonian flag is raised on Tall Hermann Tower 23 August: human chain of two million people linking Vilnius with Tallinn to commemorate 50th anniversary of Ribbentrop–Molotov Pact
1991	20 August: following failed coup in Moscow, Estonia declares re-establishment of independence. Recognised by Moscow on 24 August.
1992	20 June: reintroduction of kroon as Estonian national currency 5 October: election of Lennart Meri as president of Estonia
1994	31 August: withdrawal of last Russian troops from Estonia 28 September: sinking of the *Estonia en route* from Tallinn to Stockholm with the loss of 850 lives
1996	20 September: re-election of Lennart Meri as president of Estonia
1998	March: accession talks with EU begin
2000	Erki Nool wins a gold medal in the decathlon at the Sydney Olympics
2001	12 May: Dave Benton and Tanel Padar win the Eurovision Song Contest with 'Everybody' 8 October: Arnold Rüütel inaugurated as president of Estonia
2003	Launch of Skype, an Estonian invention 14 September: with 67% of participants in favour, Estonia votes in a referendum to join the EU
2004	2 April: Estonia joins NATO 1 May: Estonia joins the EU
2006	14 March: death of Lennart Meri 24 September: Toomas Hendrik Ilves defeats Arnold Rüütel in the presidential election 19 October: visit by Queen Elizabeth II and the Duke of Edinburgh to Tallinn
2007	21 Dec: Estonia joins the Schengen group so all border controls with Latvia are lifted
2011	Estonia joins the euro, after 19 years with its own currency Tallinn is joint European Capital of Culture with Turku in Finland
2018	Estonia to hold the presidency of the EU Council

1DM to 8EEK and then to the euro at a rate of €1 to 15.65EEK. With each passing currency crisis across the border in Russia, the Estonians were perhaps entitled to feel ever more detached from their Soviet past. The annual rate of inflation in 1993 and 1994 was around 25%, but since then has usually been down to 3–4%.

Whilst there was great optimism in those early years, it was a tough adjustment for many older people used to the Soviet system of a regular salary and regular prices and no risk of unemployment. Mart Laar, the prime minister at the time, made no secret of the fact that there would be short-term pain for long-term gain. When Margaret Thatcher died in April 2013, he reminisced about this period and what he felt he had learnt from her. 'What I picked up from her was decisiveness,' he said. 'If you want to do something, do it. Do not just stand there trembling.' In Latvia and in Lithuania there was probably more 'trembling' at this time, and their adjustment certainly took much longer as a result.

The sinking of the ferry *Estonia* in September 1994 showed how in tragedy as much as in success Estonia had joined the West. A press conference was held at which Prime Minister Mart Laar spoke, and then answered questions, in fluent English. Given the transformation already in place, the world's press could descend on Tallinn within hours, book into a hotel, plug in their computers, transmit their films and file their copy with almost the same ease as they could from within their home countries. The possible causes of the tragedy were immediately subject to extensive public analysis and formal enquiries were established.

Even the early tourists in 1993 found it hard to believe what a 'normal' country they were visiting. Many did not need visas, and those who did bought them on arrival in a few minutes. Gone were currency and customs forms, hour-long airport check-ins, police registration and black-market exchange rates; in were credit cards, telephone cards, piped music, Chinese restaurants, Irish bars, and British newspapers available on the day of publication.

PREPARING FOR THE EU For many Estonians, there was a euphoric unreality about independence. It came so unexpectedly, and after such a seemingly entrenched Soviet occupation, that its instant success had sometimes to give rise to concern. A collapse on the Tallinn stock market in 1997 was a useful warning about the uncertainties of the business world, and unemployment, resulting from bankruptcies and business failures, served a similar function. Whilst few Estonians regret the demise of the USSR emotionally, there are many older people who have suffered economically and some now regret the loss of former cultural links. Pensioners need the financial support of the next generation and miss the collective facilities that the old regime provided. Members of the ethnic Russian community, concentrated along the northern coast from Tallinn to Narva, feel cut off from their relatives across the border. The middle-aged and young amongst them must retrain and learn Estonian, otherwise there is little future for them.

For most Estonian young people, however, the Soviet Union – and even Russia – is now a very abstract concept. They are unlikely to go to Russia and they are certainly not learning the language any more, given that English offers so many more opportunities. They travel, but always westwards and usually just for a short period of time. Estonian salaries are now sufficiently high, given the low cost of living, to keep young people at home. Unemployment has not been a serious issue since independence and those in their twenties and thirties are very career-orientated so will often change jobs. Yet salaries are still not high enough to persuade sufficient couples to start families early and the population fell by about 10,000 a year from 1991 until 2011. Although births now exceed deaths, the pull of higher salaries abroad remains. As in many western European countries, women feel obliged to put a career before a family and social pressures to 'settle down' are absent. The appointment in 2003 of a Minister for Population (a poet with four daughters) showed the government's concern about this falling population and there is now increasing financial support for those willing to start a family. These measures are ensuring that the population is unlikely to fall further. If salaries continue to rise ahead of inflation, so do the consumer pressures to spend, spend, spend. In the 1990s a derelict factory greeted tourists on the way into Tallinn from the airport. By 2004 it was two competing shopping centres.

When in 2001 Lennart Meri handed over the presidency after his two terms to Arnold Rüütel, he said that 'Estonia is now a normal, boring country.' Only someone who had lived there between 1940 and 1990 could understand what a positive statement this was.

When Estonia won the Eurovision Song Contest in 2001, it was as unexpected as independence had been in 1991 and was probably greeted with equal acclaim. Larger and jealous competitors doubted Estonia's ability to host the event the following year, but it was a great success and several million fewer people would confuse the Baltics and the Balkans as a result. Full use of the programme was made to promote Estonia as a serious tourism destination.

Membership of the European Union and NATO became early goals of Estonian foreign policy and these were both achieved without difficulty in spring 2004. No attempt was made by Estonia to work with its Baltic neighbours in this endeavour. In fact, the reverse was the case, as Estonia rarely hid its contempt for what it saw as economic backwardness in Latvia and Lithuania. The country's most famous foreign minister during the 1990s, Toomas Hendrik Ilves, who was to become president in 2006, liked to point out that the only link between the three Baltic countries had been the Soviet and German occupations. He also described Estonia as a Nordic rather than as a Baltic country.

EU standards were imposed years before 2004, probably at a more rigorous level than in many countries that were already members. If a café or a factory closed, this would rarely be as a result of bankruptcy but usually because the owners did not think it worthwhile to meet these standards. As working hours' directives came to be observed, tourists no longer ran the risk of a coach driver trying to fit two shifts into one day, but equally they could not drink milk straight from the farm. Estonian diplomats abroad lobbied hard in all EU capitals and proved that they could understand and implement all the legislation pouring out of Brussels.

If on occasion Estonians or others feel frustrated at the lack of resources available in certain fields, they can always be comforted by looking across the Russian border for confirmation of the progress made since 1991. The election of Arnold Rüütel, a graduate of an agricultural college rather than of Tartu University, as president in 2001 was a reaction of the 'have-nots' in contemporary Estonia, many of who live in the countryside. It was perhaps a warning that not every Estonian can afford a car and a Mediterranean holiday. Probably the 'have-lesses' would have been a fairer description given the affluence found in so many villages now.

Autumn 2003 saw a 67% 'yes' vote for joining the EU, which can be interpreted as a greater pro-business vote than the 2001 election displayed. Autumn 2006 saw a closely fought presidential election between the incumbent Arnold Rüütel standing again and Toomas Hendrik Ilves, who narrowly defeated him. Ilves bought a farm in southern Estonia several years before the election and frequently invited journalists there for interviews. He could thus encroach on Rüütel's territory without sacrificing his firm support from the business and intellectual communities in Tallinn and Tartu. He has consistently used his perfect English to maintain Estonia's high international profile. He is a frequent attender at cyber conferences abroad, warning others of the constant dangers posed by Russia in the field. Fortuitous timing ensured that the first foreign visitors to be impressed by him were Queen Elizabeth II and the Duke of Edinburgh whose state visit took place a week after his inauguration.

Estonia was hit less by the international financial crisis of 2008–09 than were most of its neighbours (see below). It had not suffered greatly from wild consumer spending and government reserves were stronger. Clearly property markets tumbled and the travel industry was initially hit badly but this was partly because of so many airlines cancelling flights to Tallinn. For the first time in its history since 1991, unemployment was an issue that the government and individuals were forced to face, but in no way to the extent that it hit Greece and Spain. The same prime minister and the same president were in power in 2007 and in 2013. With Vladimir Putin in control in Russia, governmental relations would never become warm, but the swarms of Russian tourists who started to visit Estonia from 2011 were a sign of considerably improved people to people links. Estonia's enthusiasm for the euro remains undiminished and partly because of its success, Latvia is joining it in 2014 and Lithuania in 2015.

ECONOMY *James Oates*

Estonia – 'the little country that could' – still stands out. Over the course of not quite 25 years of re-independence, it has moved from being part of one of the least open economies to becoming one of the most open in the world. Starting with one of the most bureaucratic it has established one of the most flexible regulatory regimes. From being one of the most backward industrial economies it has become a global leader in the use of information technology. In this transformation it has been able to achieve high rates of economic growth, low inflation and a transformation in the living standards of most Estonians. Although the crash of 2008 hit Estonia hard, the government's continued fiscal discipline and well-educated and flexible labour force got Estonia through the crisis – to the point where the country is now one of the strongest economies in the European Union and increasingly well integrated with its Nordic neighbours.

Estonia is noticeably catching up with Finland: the city of Tallinn – with nearly half the Estonian population – already has a GDP per capita that is the same level as the average for Finland, and the gap between Russia and the Commonwealth of Independent States (CIS) and Estonia, who so recently shared the same state, continues to grow wider every year.

Even before the restoration of Estonian freedom and independence in 1991, key economists and political leaders were considering how the hidebound and desperately impoverished economy of Soviet Estonia might best be transformed. The Soviet rouble, by the advent of *de facto* Estonian independence in 1991, was already essentially worthless. Thus it was that the newly reformed Bank of Estonia first put into place the conditions for monetary reform and a new currency. The decision was taken to tie the currency to the German mark – now the euro – and to back each note or coin issued fully with reserves. In this the Bank of Estonia was undoubtedly helped by the recovery of the pre-war gold reserves that had been sent to the Bank of England and other central banks in 1939. The Estonian kroon was a powerful success, and it was with very mixed feelings that Estonians exchanged kroons for euros when the country entered the eurozone in January 2011. Yet membership of the single currency has brought significant benefits to the country, and removed the risk of a destabilising devaluation of the kroon.

Perhaps the key to Estonian economic success has been clarity. Through all of the various governments since the restoration of independence, there has been a consistency of economic policy. In tax, for example, after the first government under Prime Minister Mart Laar established a single, flat tax rate of 26%, the rate of tax has been reduced to 21%. There are no exceptions and it makes for a very simple tax code and very little tax avoidance. In fact Estonians can fill out their tax return on a single sheet of A4 paper, although these days 95% fill out the form over the internet.

The commercial code was simplified, and all aspects of doing business were speeded up, based on electronic models, not paper ones. In recent years corporation tax for reinvested profits in Estonia has been set at 0%, which has made Estonia an increasingly attractive base for operations throughout the Nordic area. Simple business procedures and very simple taxes have continued to attract large flows of foreign direct investment.

Meanwhile successive governments have maintained a disciplined approach to government expenditure. In the Constitution of the Republic, the government is forbidden from running a deficit budget. In the mid-1990s, the government therefore borrowed hardly any money. Although some local governments, such as the City of Tallinn, did tap the financial markets from time to time, the Republic of Estonia only raised a credit to create a benchmark for the country. Unsurprisingly that benchmark was quite high for such a small country; from the first rating in 1997 Estonia has been rated as investment grade by the rating agencies.

It has not just been the policies of the government and the Bank of Estonia that have driven Estonian economic growth. One of the major strengths of the Estonian economy is the quality of its labour force. Estonia has a highly skilled population. Indeed it is estimated that over half the population is involved at any one time with further education at graduate or postgraduate level. Rates of literacy, numeracy and language skills are generally substantially above the European Union average.

In addition to a general commitment to education, the country has embraced new technology to a degree almost unmatched anywhere else. The use of integrated wireless technology is amongst the highest in the world, and second only to Estonia's Nordic neighbours Finland, Sweden and Norway. The government has implemented a radical agenda for e-government, an area in which the country is now a global pioneer and is integrating its e-government platform with its neighbours. Investors have taken note, and there is now an entire culture of entrepreneurship across the gamut of information technology businesses. The general use of technology in such areas as banking has created a hugely techno-literate society and substantially reduced costs.

From the days of decaying Soviet heavy industry, Estonia has been transformed into a largely service-driven economy. However, one area has not changed since the Soviet occupation – indeed it has not changed for centuries: the importance of the harbours. The port of Tallinn, despite ongoing political tension between Estonia and the Russian Federation, has increased its shipments almost every year. Russian and Ukrainian grain, coal, oil and metals are exported, while a variety of international products are imported for onward shipment to Russia and beyond. More and more of these cargoes are people, for Tallinn has become an increasingly attractive destination for cruise ships and the Tallinn–Helsinki ferry route is one of the busiest in the world. Tourism is another part of the economy that has boomed, and many Swedish and Finnish visitors come to the spas on Estonia's west coast. Indeed there are many Swedish- and Finnish-owned holiday homes across the country.

From a very unpromising start, Estonia has become one of the most open and liberal economies in the world. Indeed it is increasingly held as a model for the whole process of transition. It is now a full member of the European Union, the eurozone and the Organisation for Economic Co-operation and Development (OECD) – the 'rich club' of industrialised nations – and is one of the few countries that obeys the rules of all the organisations it has joined. Estonia continues to stand out as an economic leader; as former Prime Minister Mart Laar has said, Estonia has become 'the little country that could'.

PEOPLE

In the first independence period, from 1920 to 1940, ethnic Estonians made up over 90% of the population of 1,100,000. Estonia lost nearly 20% of its population between 1941 and 1945. Many of those deported to Siberia died there or *en route*. Military and civilian casualties were high during the fighting and then many fled as refugees to Sweden before the return of the Soviet army in 1944. By 1945 the population had dropped to 900,000 and although it would increase again to 1,400,000 by 1989, only 60% were then ethnic Estonians. Most of the remainder were Russian immigrants allocated as workers to the new factories along the northeast coast. The census carried out in 2012 reported a worrying drop in the population to 1,286,000, caused by later marriage and a very high divorce rate. (Primary schools around the country are closing because of this lower birth rate.) Ethnic Estonians represent 65% of this number and Russians 28%. Ukrainians and Belarussians make up most of the remainder. It is expected that the population will stay at around 1,300,000 in 2014 and the years following.

LANGUAGE

Estonian is a Finno-Ugric language so has little in common with most other European languages. It is most closely linked to Finnish. Anyone over 35 or so will have had to learn Russian at school in Soviet times so it must still be regarded as the second language for the older generation, although Estonians are reluctant to speak it. English will soon replace Russian in this role for younger people since it is the common language for most tourists and business visitors, and is widely spoken in hotels and shops. Younger people in the towns always speak some English but for travellers in the countryside, where foreigners are few and far between, a knowledge of even a few Estonian words can be invaluable. In the northeast of the country, Russian is extensively spoken and very few native Estonian speakers live there. For basic Estonian words and phrases, see pages 291–3.

RELIGION *Michael Bourdeaux*

All too often, visitors take the Alexander Nevsky Cathedral in Tallinn, its onion domes dominating the city on the Toompea Hill, as a symbol of the city. In reality it symbolises 2½ centuries of Russian domination, now fading into the past. Yet as the main church of the Russian people, or nearly 30% of the population, the Russian Orthodox Church is by a large margin the most significant presence in Estonia after the Lutheran Church. Estonia became Christian far later than the heartland of Europe and more than two centuries after the Slavic lands around Kiev and Novgorod. Although the Swedish bishop Eskil of Lund consecrated Fulco as the first bishop of Estonia in 1165, the main period of Christianisation, enforced by

Estonia, September 1994
Five Aeroflot sky-tubs by the lumpy runway
sport blue and white paint now: ESTONIAN AIR
Like gulls with a storm in the offing
they face the same way as the wind.

There are trains cut in half at the border
like worms; an independent engine
pulls out from the platform while its rolling stock
stays Russian. lines have to be drawn

like today: PAKA (bye for now
not quite like adieu) flyposts most walls
with a Red Army helipad cap, a walrus neck
that seems an easy target from behind.

Like kids with their parents' cameras
there are families posed edgily outside
the place people tried not to mention,
with a name plate saying anything but KGB.

The barracks is a film set waiting
for a new producer and a cast of thousands.
The windows are kicked out from the inside,
bunk rooms trashed. Here's half a skip of uniforms.

Round the base, there's been a fly-buzz of types
in leather jackets all this last year,
men in a small way of business but expanding
and with foreign friends. Out there in the bay

ochre hulks have faced home up the Gulf of Finland
for months as if waiting the word
(the Moscow–Tallinn post goes quicker
these days via London.)

Beneath the stained ziggurat
of the Olympic pride yachting complex
a sharp Finnish hydrofoil suns its wings.
A car ferry trots out in the team's new colours

and is not yet anybody's news.

From The Wasting Game by Philip Gross, 1998.

German overlords, was the 13th century. German domination remained complete,
which brought Estonia into the Reformation, accomplished between 1523 and 1525
without conflict, leaving Lutheranism as the state church.

There were Christian schools in the villages as well as in the towns. Christian literacy was far more advanced than in Russia, with the first translation of the New Testament appearing in 1686, as compared with 1825 in Russia. However, the years 1710–1918 saw two centuries of Russian domination during which the Protestant Church, by its very nature alien to the Russian tradition, could not freely develop and it became more conservative than its German counterpart. A Russian law of 1832 reduced the evangelical faith to that of a 'tolerated religion', while 20% of Russian immigrants considered the Orthodox Church to be the state religion. German influence had, however, been so strong that even as late as 1939, with 200 years of Russian colonisation now in the past, 49 of the 227 clergy were German.

As part of the Tsarist Empire, Estonia benefited from the 1905 reforms which allowed freedom of conscience to a limited degree and there was an awakening of the Lutheran Church fostered by the clergy. Independence from Russia in 1919 following the upheaval of the revolution guaranteed religious liberty and permitted the Lutheran Church to establish a new framework for Church government, with a synod being responsible for the election of bishops.

A decree of 1925 proclaimed the separation of Church and state, but Christian teaching continued in schools and the faculty of theology at Tartu University was responsible for the training of the clergy. There is an interesting statistic for 1934: 78% of the population declared themselves Lutheran, and 19% Orthodox, even though the Russian population had been reduced to below 10% during these years of independence. Apart from the obvious fact that many of the Lutherans must have had nominal adherence only, the Orthodox Church had clearly made significant gains amongst Estonian people. (No 'wavering' believer of non-Russian nationality would be likely to claim to be Orthodox.)

The Soviet occupation of 1940 and annexation at the end of World War II was a disaster for believers, just as for Estonia as a whole. Communist atheism would now devastate the Church, as it had already done in Russia and Ukraine. Approximately two-thirds of all clergy were murdered, deported to Siberia or banned from office. No sure statistics are available, but the Orthodox Church now became a political tool and was given significant privileges, with the obvious aim of imposing Moscow's influence on a recalcitrant but cowed population. This probably led to a decline of allegiance to Orthodoxy among Estonians, but the Orthodox hierarchy gained notably in influence.

The most significant religious figure in Estonia in the communist period was the Bishop of Tallinn, Alexi. He was appointed in 1961 at the astonishingly young age of 32. With the surname Ridiger, his father was of the old German aristocracy, but his mother was pure Russian and he grew up bilingual. His appointment can only have meant that the Soviets saw him as a man who would help render the Russian status as overlord in Estonia as acceptable to the people. He did, however, protect his own churches and the Pühtitsa Convent at Kuremäe remained one of the few female monastic institutions in the Soviet Union that never seemed seriously threatened. After his translocation to the diocese of Leningrad, he eventually became Patriarch Alexi II of Moscow. In the 1980s he was a leading figure in the Conference of European Churches.

In broader outline however, Estonia was subjected to the same Stalinist 1929 Law on Religious Associations that controlled and brutalised Church–state relations throughout Soviet territory. Protestants could preach (with censorship) in a limited number of open churches, the Orthodox could celebrate the liturgy, but beyond that virtually no feature of normal Christian life was possible. It was not legal to teach children, or to undertake parish activities or charitable work. The training of the Lutheran clergy was virtually impossible, though when circumstances improved there was a correspondence course, while Orthodox candidates could attend a seminary in Russia.

The ban on religious literature was virtually complete. Every school and university held its compulsory classes in atheism, though students often did not take them very seriously. The Soviets attempted to replace Christian rituals of baptism and confirmation by 'new Soviet traditions' as the press called them, but these efforts collapsed long before the end of communism.

By the 1970s, less than 10% of the population professed any belief in God, but this statistic is almost certainly warped by intimidation; admitting to such a belief could, and often did, lead to dismissal. Long before the lifting of communist oppression and the abolition of the old law under Gorbachev in 1990, the Lutheran Church was beginning to become more engaged with society again. There was the remarkable example of Pastor Harri Mõtsnik. He committed an unforgivable sin against communism in 1970 when, at the age of 42, he gave up a legal career to become a Lutheran pastor. His sermons became manifestos of religious and even national liberation. In one he said:

> Freedom is not an illusion, but an experience of reality. It is a vital need. It is not out of place to remember the valiant men and women who have chosen the noble path of self-sacrifice rather than self-interest and furthering their own careers; they have chosen the struggle for freedom as the only way of hope for the Estonian people, setting on one side the fear which they surely experience within and in face of the totalitarian regime which confronts them. Truth is their guide along the way.

Needless to say, the KGB mercilessly harassed Mõtsnik, so much so that his health eventually gave way. Overall Estonian Lutherans played nothing like the role in throwing off the yoke of communism that Catholics did in Lithuania, but neither should their influence be discounted.

In the Soviet period the Orthodox Church was an instrument of Russification – one might almost say Sovietisation. Linguistically and culturally the dominance was complete, despite the original tradition that the Orthodox liturgy would use the language of the people. However, at the same time Russian Orthodoxy provided a haven for genuine religious belief, perhaps more readily available than in many parts of Russia itself, and enjoyed by perhaps some 30,000 people or more, including many Estonians as well as Russians.

After 1991 a split was inevitable between the Russian Orthodox Church as such and a revival of genuine Estonian Orthodoxy. As early as the mid 19th century, significant numbers of Estonian peasants came to see the Orthodox Church as closer to their spiritual needs than the Lutheranism of their landlords. The inter-war years saw the establishment (partly for political reasons in the climate of the time) of an independent ('autocephalous') Estonian Apostolic Orthodox Church, as it was called, which was of course summarily abolished by the Soviets in 1945. Renewed independence brought about a revived conflict between the Russian and Estonian elements in the local Orthodox Church and the split was formalised in 1997, when the Estonian Orthodox Church reconstituted itself under the Archbishop of Helsinki.

Any visitor to Tallinn can experience the splendour of Russian Orthodox worship at the Alexander Nevsky Cathedral and can go on to witness the Estonian variant in the other Orthodox church in the Old Town. Of course, there are many places in the countryside where there is only one Orthodox church and it is likely to cater for both Russians and Estonians. Some 54 of the 85 parishes have declared independence from Russia, but divisions are not neat.

CULTURE

PAINTING Estonian cultural activity, like so much else from the 13th to the 19th century, was dominated by the Baltic Germans. It is possible to mention many names from that time such as Hermen Rode, who painted the altarpiece in St Nicholas Church (see page 106), and Bernt Notke, famous for his *Danse Macabre* in the same church, but it is unlikely that either artist ever came to Tallinn. They were committed to Lübeck.

Johann Köler (1826–99) rose to become a professor of art in St Petersburg but he was born of peasant stock in Estonia and frequently returned there. It is also the subject of most of his paintings and, most important of all, Estonian was his first language. Not surprisingly, the history of art in Estonia really starts with him. He was also the first of a generation that did not need to feel the obligation of presenting a picture as a photographer then would. He could play with light, and bring his emotions into his work. For the last 30 years of his life, the two professions of painting and photography worked apart and he could take advantage of it in both his portraits and in his landscapes. Whilst his academic post meant he had to paint high-society portraits, and altar frescoes such as that in Charles's Church (see pages 99–100) his major work would be amongst the peasants in his native countryside. Köler remains respected in Estonia: in 2008 one of his pictures sold for EEK2.7 million (€175,000) the highest price ever realised for a painting in Tallinn.

Köler travelled abroad frequently and this was a trend that his successors followed. France would be the main point of attraction, followed by Italy, Germany and then Russia. When Estonia became independent in 1920 contact with Russia largely ceased, but it would increase with western Europe.

From the next generation, two artists stand out, **Ants Laikmaa** (1866–1942) and **Kristjan Raud** (1865–1943). They were brought up at a time when Estonia could look forward if not to independence then at least to greater autonomy. The year 1903 would see the first exhibition in Tallinn devoted exclusively to Estonian art and therefore largely to the pictures of these two. Both would travel extensively, but always with the aim of returning to Estonia and settling there. They took on board the slogan of the main nationalist movement of the time, Noor Eesti (Young Estonia): 'Let us remain Estonian, but let us also become European.'

Laikmaa is often compared to the Welsh artist Augustus John, both in his style of painting and in the wide variety of women in his private life. His choice of landscapes however was much narrower; they are nearly all from western Estonia, the area around Haapsalu where he would settle towards the end of his life (see page 240). The lack of formalism in his work shows how much had changed in Estonian art within one generation. The influence of all the different artistic schools prevalent in France when he was there can be seen in much of his work. Raud worked largely with charcoal and pencil, painting very little. He is best remembered for the drawings he did of Kalevipoeg, the Estonian mythological hero.

The 1903 exhibition coincided with Laikmaa setting up an art school in Tallinn and with Raud doing the same in Tartu. Their pupils who survived World War I would absorb one or several of the current French passions, mainly Impressionism, Expressionism and Fauvism. Many would teach at the Pallas Art School in Tartu, which was sadly destroyed in World War II.

The leading artist during the early independence period was **Konrad Mägi** (1876–1925) who portrayed nature in a very positive way. His flowers would always be in bloom, his skies sunny and his lakes deep blue. Darkness only penetrated his very late work, reflecting perhaps his final illness as well as his knowledge of the paintings of Edvard Munch. He was also unusual in not being politically active, which set him apart from most of his famous contemporaries.

Artists born early in the 20th century would face a terrible dilemma in 1941 and again in 1944. Some would retreat with the Soviet army to be forcibly settled in the artistic colony in Yaroslavl. Others would throw their hand in with the Germans and flee to Germany or Sweden in 1944. In both cases, Estonian art would suffer terribly. **Eerik Haamer** (1908–94) was never able, in his Swedish exile, to re-establish his pre-war reputation in Estonia. The Soviets allowed exhibitions of his work from the 1970s but he was not tempted back and these of course could not help him elsewhere. Fame only returned in the last few years of his life, when he could return after independence had been restored. **Karin Luts** (1904–93) suffered a similar fate, being known throughout Estonia in 1944 and yet dying unknown in Sweden 50 years later. She would write extensive diaries about her loneliness and failure to interest Swedes in her work. The empty bottles she drew as still lifes are perhaps an appropriate metaphor of her unfulfilled existence once she had left home. Despite close family links in Estonia, she never returned there.

Those who stayed behind had different issues to contend with. From 1945–55 Socialist Realism, imposed from Moscow, took over. As with the blocks of flats that were rising then all over eastern Europe, the paintings had no individuality and could have come from Albania or East Germany just as easily as from Estonia. A sufficient selection of these can be seen at the Estonian Art Museum (KUMU) (see pages 118–19). There are pictures of Lenin and Stalin and of intensely active factories. Serious artists, like serious writers, would hide much of their work at this time, whether it was contemporary or dated from the independence period before the war. Several artists such as **Paul Kondas** (1900–85) painted in secret throughout their lives and only became known after their deaths, following the downfall of the USSR. A gallery in Viljandi, where Kondas lived, is now devoted to his work (see page 203).

Perhaps the most fortunate artist from the Soviet period is **Evald Okas** (1915–2011). To be safe from the Germans, he was taken to Yaroslavl in 1941 together with nine other trusted Estonian artists including Adamson-Eric (see below) who would stay there until the end of the war. The others returned to what was then Soviet Estonia but he continued his studies at the Moscow Academy before returning home. By the 1950s he had won two privileges denied to all other Estonian painters. He could draw nudes (always women) and travelled all over the world. He was undoubtedly talented, but many Estonians regretted the political focus of his works, such as the 1947 ceiling in the Concert Hall (see page 111) or the mural painted in 1987 at the Maarjamäe Palace where in both cases 100% political correctness is glaringly obvious. However his bookplates are totally different and independence came just in time for him to reinvent himself in a non-political environment. Shortly before his death, he said he avoided computers but liked to follow other artistic trends. The museum in Haapsalu (see pages 239–40) named after him, concentrates on his later output.

The thaw after Stalin's death was dramatic. Interestingly, Soviet sources were quite happy to admit this. *Soviet Estonia*, a book published in 1980, acknowledges that 'revolutionary subject matter' prevailed immediately after the war, and then 'In the late 1950s, the creative attitude began to be rehabilitated and painting became

There must have been a natural culture lying dormant in these people. The two cultures, which have forced themselves on Estonia, are bad ones. The Russian culture, exact in the niceties of greeting ladies, kissing hands and flashing looks under eyelashes, had coarse, brutal and unpleasant foundations. The Baltic Germans, clicking their heels with military precision, and bowing stiffly from the hips, have for the last decades deteriorated so swiftly into a decadence which can still be read in the lines under their eyes. It is inevitable that both should have made an impression on the Estonians. Hands are still occasionally kissed but not very often now. Hats are lifted effusively and hands are shaken at every possible opportunity. One hears less, however, the clicking of heels. There seems to be in the Estonian an undercurrent of sensitiveness which very rarely errs. Graciousness, a facile politeness blended with the simple directness of their peasant ancestry, are the formidable points of the modern Estonian character.

Yet they are nevertheless a pleasure-loving people. They work hard for six hours a day, enjoy themselves fourteen hours and sleep four. They drink hard, but who blames them when they produce such excellent vodka. They have definite ideas on food and the majority of it is good. They like to be well-dressed, and the young women will sacrifice nourishment for it. They have homes, but these appear to be chiefly *pied-à-terre*, in which to eat dinner and to sleep. Perhaps it is because they do not know the joys of open fires.

From Baltic Corner by Ronald Seth, published in 1938.

more diverse.' More important than the 'creative attitude' were the people who were then rehabilitated.

Adamson-Eric (1902–68), although part of the Yaroslavl group, was banished from the art world in 1949 and had to work in a factory. Yet in 1966 a booklet on Soviet Estonian art said that his paintings 'are ever gaining in brilliancy'. To Westerners, Estonian art might well not have seemed diverse in the 1960s and 1970s, but to those from elsewhere in the USSR, it certainly was. Pop art arrived in the 1960s and from 1965 it became possible to watch Finnish television, so applied artists could immediately be stimulated by what they saw. Painters from then on would never turn back to political themes.

Richard Uutmaa (1905–77) was an artist who managed to ignore the Soviet system and it ignored him. He is now best known for his seascapes, and the sympathetic portrayal of fishermen that many include, but the bookplates and prints he produced in the Soviet period gained Estonia international recognition.

Jüri Arrak (b1936) was lucky that only ten years (the 1960s) of the Soviet system really harmed his work. Instead of painting publicly then, he worked in a metal factory and then as a taxi driver in St Petersburg, both jobs providing themes for his later work and for that which he produced at the time but had to hide. In 1970 he was allowed his first solo exhibition. Given its mixture of Pop art, Surrealism and Cubism, he was lucky that it was permitted to be held as it probably would not have been elsewhere in the USSR. His 'Soviet' paintings show hints of his religious leanings, which finally burst forth in the altarpiece he painted in 1990 for Halliste church (see page 254). George and the Dragon is a theme he started in Soviet times and continues to the present day. One of these pictures is on the cover of

Peter I Barta's book *The Fall of the Iron Curtain and the Culture of Europe*, 2013.

It is impossible to generalise about the artistic reaction to the downfall of the Soviet Union, except to say that it encouraged individualism. Estonian artists were no longer a community and fought each other in what quickly became a totally business environment. They now have websites rather than patrons or censors. Many in fact became commercial artists, turning to advertising, graphic design and interior decorating to make a living. Some are now using a computer screen rather than a paintbrush. They are being joined by many exiles returning to finish their lives in Estonia.

SCULPTURE The most casual of visitors to Estonia will be aware of the role that sculpture plays in contemporary society. No square can be redeveloped, no monument erected, without one of Estonia's famous practitioners in this field being involved. It has followed a similar path to that of painting, literature and architecture in being closely linked to the political background current at the time. Two sculptors whose lives closely overlapped with each other, **August Weizenberg** (1837–1921) and **Amandus Adamson** (1855–1929) were the first who could be called Estonian and much of their work survived both world wars although several pieces by Adamson commemorating the liberation of Estonia in 1918–20 were destroyed in Soviet times and were copied later.

As his father died when he was nine, Weizenberg had no formal school education and his first contact with art being was an apprentice to a cabinetmaker. During his twenties he travelled around Europe studying and working but in 1873 he settled in Rome. He lived there for the next 17 years, although he frequently travelled back to Estonia and signed all his work 'A W Estonus'. He explained that it was the proximity to Carrara marble that kept him in Italy. His first exhibition, and therefore the first exhibition of Estonian sculpture, was held in Tallinn in 1878. Following that, his fame in his home country (although still a Russian province at the time) was assured. His most famous work is the statue of Linda, the mythical heroine, which stands on Toompea close to the parliament building in Tallinn.

Adamson also lost his father early, at the age of seven, and after a few years at an orphanage he ran away to sea at the age of 14. After being sent back to Tallinn from St Petersburg he too started work in a furniture workshop. When he was 18 he returned legally to St Petersburg to study and would spend much of his working life there. Unlike Weizenberg, who worked only in marble, Adamson was happy to experiment with other materials, particularly wood that he had got to know so well through his first job. During World War I there was no chance of his regular clients being able to afford his work so in 1917 he returned to his small house in Paldiski (see pages 136–7), the port close to Tallinn. This led to a sudden downturn in his finances and it would only be in the last few years of his life that local councils could afford to commission statues and memorials from him. Sadly Paldiski itself was not rich enough to do so, and Adamson was too poor to give them one. He was buried, as he wished, beside the Liberation Memorial he made for Pärnu Cemetery (see page 251).

Enn Roos (1908–90) is the sculptor best known from the Soviet era because of his publicly displayed formal work. Sadly for his subsequent reputation, he has been linked above all with just one statue, the notorious *Bronze Soldier*, or the 'liberation monument' commissioned at the end of World War II and which stood in central Tallinn until April 2007 when it was moved by the government (see page 79). He was head of sculpture from 1962–77 at what is now the Estonian Academy of Art. Hopefully as time passes his animal sculptures, largely in terracotta, will be better remembered. One public monument on display is his bronze lynx outside Tallinn Zoo.

Much more radical was **Ülo Õun** (1940–88) whose abstract work would be perfectly acceptable now but who often had difficulties during his life, which probably contributed to his suicide just before Estonian re-independence when all his work could have been exhibited openly. Visitors to Tartu cannot help but notice his *Father and Son* (see page 195) erected only after his death on one of the city's main streets.

The two contemporary giants, in every sense of the word, in modern sculpture are **Mati Karmin** and **Tauno Kangro**. There cannot now be a town in Estonia without a statue or memorial by Mati Karmin (*www.karmin.ee*) who was born in 1959. The statues of Jaan Tõnisson and Juri Lotman in Tartu, the memorial to Charles Leroux in Tallinn, and the memorial to the victims of the Estonia disaster on Hiiumaa are among many described later in this text. Karmin has also made furniture and much else from the disused mine shells abandoned by the Soviet army on Naissaar Island when they left in 1994.

Tauno Kangro (*www.skulptuuristuudio.ee*) was born in 1966 and will not be really happy until his 14m-high statue of the mythical hero Kalevipoeg is commissioned to soar from the water in the bay beside Tallinn harbour. The idea is that this will be the first and the last image of Tallinn that cruise passengers will have. In principle, the town council agreed to it in 2008, but no action has been taken since then. However Kangro already has another major monument to his name, the statue of an aurochs that dominates Rakvere (see pages 153–7). Specialists in granite and bronze assure him that his statues will last 700 years.

LITERATURE Estonians have always taken literature very seriously, and over the last two centuries the flow of writing has reflected the main traditions found in other European countries. However, few of the important character-defining novels from the last hundred years have been translated into English. This is unfortunate because Estonia's literature reveals a great deal about Estonians' preoccupations and *Weltanschauung* ('view of life').

Estonia's lively tradition of writing and reading goes back a long way: the Estonian word for book (*raamat*) has its roots in an Old Slavonic word, which suggests that Estonians' first contacts with books occurred due to Orthodox missionaries. Nevertheless, despite the early arrival of Danish and German culture in the 12th and 13th centuries, it took a while for the first book to be published in the Estonian language. The Lutheran catechism was published in 1525, to be followed by the first full translation of the Bible in 1739. In the meantime, the first Estonian-language primer arrived in peasant schools in the 17th century.

The flowering of Estonian literature had to wait until the time of the National Awakening in the mid-1800s. Suddenly there were plays, novels, short stories, poetry, recorded folklore and journalism in Estonian – in addition to the existing literature in German. The major figure was **Friedrich Reinhold Kreutzwald** (1803–82), who recorded Estonian folklore and produced the national epic *Kalevipoeg*, the story of the mythical founder of the Estonian nation. **Johann Voldemar Jannsen** (1819–90) was the publisher of *Postimees*, the first Estonian-language newspaper and the organiser of the first Estonian Song Festival held in 1869 in Tartu; his daughter **Lydia Koidula** (1843–86) is now probably better remembered than her father, perhaps because her portrait was on the 100 kroon note that circulated between 1992 and the introduction of the euro in 2011.

By the turn of the century, the country had very high literacy rates, although the overwhelming majority of the population lived on farms. It is not uncommon to hear elderly people recalling memories of the family sitting around a table in a candle-lit farmhouse while their grandfather read aloud from one of the first Estonian-language newspapers that hit the stands in the middle of last century. Literature came into its own during the inter-war independence period. One of the key themes is the farm boy who is bright and smart and can outwit the devil – that is, the Germans or the Russians, depending on who was overlord at the time. The other important theme is the Estonian sense of fairness and a stubbornness about what they think is right and just. The most famous novel in this genre is *Truth and Justice* by **Anton Hansen Tammsaare** (1878–1940) who dominated Estonian literature during the first period of independence and fortunately for him, died in March 1940 just before it came to an end. As *Truth and Justice* has five volumes, it has not yet been translated into English but a revised translation of his last novel *The Misadventures of the New Satan* was published in 2011. This weaves a supernatural element into his regular village theme.

During the Soviet occupation, it was without doubt **Jaan Kross** (1920–2007) who kept hope alive, even though he had been imprisoned by the Germans and then kept for seven years in a labour camp by the Soviets, largely without supplies of paper. He was highly skilled in manipulating Soviet censors, often disguising contemporary themes by setting his novels in early times, which fooled officialdom but not his genuine readers. In this respect he can be compared with the Albanian author Ismail Kadare. Kross's later works cover the recently ended Soviet occupation and the period leading to the re-establishment of independence. In 2003, he completed his autobiography, which is still available only in Estonian. Many of his novels, however, have been translated into English, *The Czar's Madman* being his best-known one. He might well have won a Nobel Prize had he written in a more widely known language.

Poetry has always been popular in Estonia. Many poets are now active, but only one, **Jaan Kaplinski** (b1941), has had much of his work translated into English.

MUSIC While Estonia's glacier-flattened landscape may be relatively unvaried, it makes up for it with a remarkable variety of music. This is a place where music makes revolutions, and revolutions happen in music. The calibre of the different forms of music is clear, from the huge song festivals complete with choirs that number tens of thousands to the silences interspersed with the sound of a small tinkling bell that you hear in the profound music created by contemporary composer Arvo Pärt.

Estonians have always liked to sing. There is a long folk music tradition, and in recent centuries a passion for choirs has been prevalent. The **Song Festival** tradition dates as a national event from 1869 in Tartu, which brought together Estonian singers from across the country. The tradition expanded and eventually moved from Tartu to Tallinn. The modern festival has performers numbering 30,000 with audiences up to 100,000. In 1990, the first non-Soviet flavoured Song Festival was enjoyed by some 300,000 people waving the previously banned blue, black and white Estonian flag and singing with hope in their hearts (see box, page 31). The festival now takes place every five years.

Such large song festivals may seem Soviet in size, but the atmosphere is more like a county fair that has become national. For many people, it is a particularly special event, since even the smallest choirs from tiny places like Kaansoo (translated as 'leech-swamp'!) can compete with other choirs in the regional competitions, which select the best performers for the festival.

The festivals are held in specially constructed Song Festival grounds (*laulu väljak*), situated just to the east of Tallinn centre, on the edge of the bay (close to

Pirita). The festival grounds are worth a visit in their own right, because the size of the choral event cannot really be grasped without seeing the song bowl. The most recent Song Festival was held in July 2009 and was as well attended as all the previous ones. The next one is due in 2014.

Between song festivals, the grounds provide a venue for other major events. A national Estonian youth song and dance festival is held in the years between the major song festivals, while rock concerts, especially international tours, also use the festival grounds, including in recent years Robbie Williams, Elton John and Madonna. A more folksy gathering is held at the annual beer festival, Õlle Summer, in July. The music ranges from folk to rock, with an emphasis on singing and dancing.

Tallinn is an impressive medieval city, and the medieval music played there is of a high standard. It is worth catching the **Hortus Musicus ensemble**, led by Andres Mustonen. They look medieval, play medieval and choose the best medieval venues (no shortage in Tallinn).

The avant-garde composer, **Arvo Pärt** (b1935), is Estonia's most well-known contemporary composer. His music has been described as an antidote to the neurotic age, depicting a simple but striking world, almost akin to the apparently simple but actually complex structure of a crystal. Pärt started his career in Estonia but in 1980 was forced to emigrate since the Soviet authorities deemed his music unacceptable. He moved to Berlin but has now returned to Estonia. One of the chief performers of his music is the world-class Estonian Philharmonic Chamber Choir (Kammerkoor). Under the direction firstly of Tõnu Kaljuste and now of Paul Hillier, they have premiered many of Pärt's works.

But Pärt is not the only creator of Estonian contemporary classical music. **Veljo Tormis** has used ancient Estonian and Finno-Ugric songs to produce some of the most amazing sounds, while other modern Estonian composers whose music is frequently performed in Estonia include **Lepo Sumera** and **Erkki-Sven Tüür**. Lepo Sumera died of a heart attack in 2000, aged only 50.

Estonia's more traditional classical composers, whose works are still performed, include **Eduard Tubin** (1905–82), who wrote an impressive collection of symphonic works and Estonia's first ballet *Kratt* ('Goblin'). *Kratt* was being performed in March 1944 when the Russians bombed Tallinn, hitting the Estonia Theatre. Survivors tell of the blaze in Tallinn's residential area and people in evening dress fleeing the burning theatre, as a background to the surreal sight of the main character, the 'kratt', running through the burning, snowy streets, his cape flowing. A museum devoted to Tubin's work opened in the castle at Alatskivi in 2012 (see page 176). Also part of Estonia's classical music history is **Rudolf Tobias** (1873–1918), the composer of *Jonah's Mission* (see pages 285–6).

Music performances are not restricted to summer events and Tallinn. There are a number of major annual festivals throughout the country and throughout the year, including the **Jazz Festival**, the **Viljandi Folk Music Festival** and the **International Organ Festival** held in atmospheric Estonian churches, as well as classical music outdoor performances in various small Estonian towns. Opera and operetta are popular and well subscribed, and there is an impressive frequency of classical music concerts and ballet. There is also a thriving local rock scene, which includes bands like **Ice Edge** (Jäääär) whose name even Estonians find hard to pronounce.

After creditable performances in every Eurovision Song Contest since the re-establishment of independence (always making it into the top ten), Estonia finally won in 2001. An energetic performance of the song 'Everybody' by the unlikely duo of Tanel Padar (local blond boy with cheeky punk looks) and Dave

Benton (black Aruban-born Dutch, but now resident in Estonia) enthralled first the Estonian public and then the Eurovision jury. The May 2002 contest was therefore held in Tallinn. Estonia has sadly come nowhere near winning since.

The challenge remains to get Estonian art known outside the country. The author Jaan Kross has been translated all over Europe. The music of Arvo Pärt is played worldwide and more recently the software application Skype, which was written by Estonia-based developers, has become equally well known. Yet even in Latvia and Finland, only a specialist would be able to name a single Estonian artist. The €175,000 mentioned above as the price paid for a Köler painting caused a sensation in Estonia. If it were noted at all abroad, it would have been simply as an indication of how long the path ahead is for Estonian art to be taken seriously at an international level.

2

Practical Information

WHEN TO VISIT

Estonia is warmer than many of its neighbours, thanks to the influence of the Gulf Stream. Harsh days do come each winter when temperatures can fall to −12°C (10°F), but such bitter weather rarely lasts for more than a few days. January 2012 was an exception, when temperatures dropped throughout the country for several days down to − 30°C (− 20°F). In the summer, occasional heatwaves have brought temperatures of 30°C (90°F), but around 20°C (65–75°F) is much more common.

In December and January, with 18 hours of darkness, the days are so short that sightseeing outdoors offers little pleasure. October and March are excellent months with 12 hours of daylight, lower hotel prices and few other visitors. October offers autumn colours throughout the country and March the chance to enjoy snow-covered forests, the frozen sea and more sunshine than in any other month. The frozen sea often makes access to the smaller islands easier in winter than in summer since roadways are marked on the ice. Estonia follows the Scandinavian tradition of dealing with snow on the main roads immediately, so driving is rarely a problem in winter. All major roads are quickly cleared, even on Saaremaa and Hiiumaa islands.

In May and September there is little risk of cold weather and all outdoor facilities are open. By midsummer at the end of June, daylight lasts 18 hours, so July, the school holiday period in Sweden and Finland, is a very popular month for tourists. Fortunately for British visitors, August is no longer peak season so is ideal for those tied to school holidays. Throughout the year, rain tends to come in unexpected short sharp outbursts; always take an umbrella or a coat!

HIGHLIGHTS AND SUGGESTED ITINERARIES

Tallinn is of course bound to be part of any Estonian itinerary, but it should never be *the* itinerary, even for those with only a few days to spare. The islands are totally unlike each other, as are many of the mainland towns. What bonds them is the ease of travel and the sense of space that greets visitors throughout the country. Frequent buses and wide roads make for easy access everywhere.

A LONG WEEKEND (IN TALLINN)

Day 1   Ideally this should be spent entirely in the Old Town. A walking route is suggested in the Tallinn section (see pages 99–115).

Day 2   Prangli Island, Pirita Harbour, Maarjamäe Museum and Kadriorg Park

Day 3   Rocca al Mare in the morning; Seaplane Harbour Museum after lunch.

Day 4   Full-day excursion to Lahemaa National Park

ONE WEEK BY BUS
Day 1   Tallinn Old Town
Day 2   Morning bus to Narva (about three hours). Afternoon in Narva to visit the castle.
Day 3   Morning walk along the ramparts. Afternoon bus to Tartu (about three hours).
Day 4   In Tartu to visit the university and the Estonian Folk Museum
Day 5   Morning bus to Viljandi (about two hours) to visit Castle Park and Kondas Museum. Late afternoon bus to Pärnu (about two hours).
Day 6   Morning in Pärnu to visit the churches. Afternoon bus to Haapsalu (about one hour) to visit the castle and Railway Museum.
Day 7   Return to Tallinn (about two hours)

TWO WEEKS BY BUS
Day 1   Tallinn Old Town
Day 2   Tallinn: Prangli Island, Pirita, Maarjamäe Museum, Kadriorg Park and Palace, Kumu Art Museum
Day 3   Morning bus to Palmse in Lahemaa National Park (about two hours). Afternoon at Palmse before overnight at Vihula.
Day 4   Tour Lahemaa National Park from Vihula
Day 5   Morning bus to Rakvere (about two hours). Afternoon in Rakvere.
Day 6   Morning bus to Narva (about three hours). Afternoon in Narva.
Day 7   In Narva and Narva-Jõesuu
Day 8   Morning bus to Tartu (about three hours). Afternoon in Tartu.
Day 9   Whole day in Tartu
Day 10 Morning bus to Pärnu (about three hours)
Day 11 Morning bus to Kuressaare (about three hours including ferry crossing). Afternoon in Kuressaare.
Day 12 Whole day by bus around Sõrve Peninsula with a stop at Sääre
Day 13 Morning bus to Haapsalu (approximately three hours including ferry crossing)
Day 14 Return to Tallinn

TWO WEEKS BY CAR
Day 1   Tallinn Old Town
Day 2   Around Tallinn: Paldiski, Rocca al Mare Open Air Museum
Day 3   Lahemaa National Park with overnight at Palmse or Vihula
Day 4   Morning in Lahemaa. Afternoon via Kohtla-Järve, Jõhvi and Pühtitsa Convent to Narva.
Day 5   Narva and Narva-Jõesuu
Day 6   Via Iisaku, Lake Peipsi and Alatskivi to Tartu
Day 7   Tartu
Day 8   Põlva, Värska, Saatse, Obinitsa, Võru
Day 9   Valga, Tõrva, Viljandi, Pärnu
Day 10 Ferry to Saaremaa Island and drive to Kuressaare
Day 11 Tour around the Sõrve Peninsula
Day 12 Tour around main island to include Vilsandi Nature Reserve, Panga Cliffs, the Angla Windmills and Karja Church
Day 13 Ferry back to mainland and drive to Haapsalu
Day 14 Return to Tallinn

TOURIST INFORMATION

Every town in Estonia has a centrally located tourist office with a wide range of leaflets on local attractions and from other parts of Estonia. They also sell maps, cards and guidebooks. Their postcard prices are often lower than those charged in neighbouring shops. Some can book hotels, guides and arrange car hire but most will refer such enquiries direct to suppliers or to local travel agents. Because of very tight budgets, they are unable to post or fax material, but they can of course email information. It goes without saying that the staff always speak good English. There are no tourist offices at the land borders or at Tallinn airport, but there is one at Tallinn harbour. The main tourist offices are as follows:

Haapsalu Karja 15; ☎ 473 3248
Hiiumaa Hiiu 1; ☎ 462 2233
Jõhvi Rakvere 13a; ☎ 337 0568
Kolka (Lake Peipsi) Suur tee 25; m 5563 9398
Kuressaare Tallinna 2; ☎ 453 3120
Narva Peetri plats 3; ☎ 59 9137
Otepää Tartu mnt 1; ☎ 766 1200
Paide Keskväljak 8; ☎ 385 0400
Pärnu Uus 2; ☎ 447 3000

Põlva Kesk 42; ☎ 799 4089
Rakvere Laada 14; ☎ 324 2734
Tallinn (centre) Niguliste 2; ☎ 645 7777
Tartu (town hall) Raekoda; ☎ 744 2111
Valga Kesk 11; ☎ 766 1699
Värska Pikk 12; ☎ 796 4782
Viljandi Vabaduse 6; ☎ 433 0442
Võru Jüri tn 12; ☎ 782 1881

The email address of most offices is the name of the town@visitestonia.com. Therefore the address for the Haapsalu office is haapsalu@visitestonia.com.

However, the Kolka address is info@peipsimaa.ee and the Värska one is tik@verska.ee.

TOUR OPERATORS

The tour operators who have extensive experience in handling individual and group tours on a year-round basis to Estonia include:

AUSTRALIA
Well-connected Tours 67 Ferguson St, Forestville, NSW 2087; ☎02 9975 2355; e info@wctravel.com.au; www.wellconnectedtravel.com.au. Group tours to Scandinavia & the Baltic countries.

CANADA
Valhalla Travel & Tours 131 Queensway South, Keswick, Ontario L4P 1Z8; ☎800 265 0459; e info@valhallatravel.com; www.valhallatravel.com. Valhalla has regular group tours to the 3 Baltic countries & to Finland. They also operate individual programmes.

UK
Baltic Holidays 5 Wood Rd, Manchester M16 9RB; ☎0845 070 5711/0161 860 5248; in the USA: ☎401 429 6614; info@balticholidays.com;

www.balticholidays.com. Offers a wide range of individual & group tours to all 3 Baltic countries. See advert on page 50.
Baltic Travel 1 Lyric Sq, London W6 0NB; ☎020 8233 2875; e info@baltictravelcompany.com; www.baltictravelcompany.com. Individual travel through the 3 Baltic countries.
Explore Worldwide Nelson Hse, 55 Victoria Rd, Farnborough, Hants GU14 7PA; ☎0845 2914541; e res@explore.co.uk; www.explore.co.uk. Small group soft adventure tours arranged during the summer through the 3 Baltic countries.
Kirker Holidays 4 Waterloo Court, 10 Theed St, London SE1 8ST; ☎020 7593 2283; e travel@kirkerholidays.co.uk; www.kirkerholidays.com. Deluxe short breaks in Tallinn & at Pädaste Manor.
Martin Randall Travel Voysey Hse, Barley Mow Passage, London W4 4GF; ☎020 8742 3355;

e info@martinrandall.co.uk; www.martinrandall.
com. Extensive programme of group tours to
Estonia & to the 3 Baltic countries for those
interested in art, architecture & music.
Naturetrek Cheriton Mill, Cheriton, Alresford,
Hants SO24 0NG; ✆01962 733051; e info@
naturetrek.co.uk; www.naturetrek.co.uk.
Birdwatching tours to Estonia.
Operas Abroad 80–83 London Lane, London
EC1A 9ET; ✆020 7511 9018; e info@operasabroad.
com; www.operasabroad.com. Individual & group
travel arrangements, including tickets, for music
festivals & performances throughout Estonia.
Regent Holidays ✆020 7666 1244; e regent@
regent-holidays.co.uk; www.regent-holidays.
co.uk. Operate an extensive programme of group
tours, w/end breaks & individual arrangements to
Estonia & its islands. Cycling tours of Saaremaa.
Combinations are also possible with Finland, St
Petersburg & the neighbouring Baltic countries.

See advert on page 70.
The Travelling Naturalist PO Box 3141,
Dorchester, Dorset DT1 2XD; ✆01305 267994;
e info@naturalist.co.uk; www.naturalist.co.uk.
Birdwatching & botanical tours.
Vamos Travel Pure Offices 54, Plato CI,
Leamington Spa, Warwickshire CV34 6WE;
✆01926 330223; e info@vamostravel.com; www.
vamostravel.com. Multi-adventure breaks &
incentive holidays.

USA
Amest Travel 16 Ocean Parkway #19, New York
11218; ✆ 718 972 2217; e info@amest.com;
www.amest.com. Group tours with different
themes in the Baltic region.
Vytis Tours 40–24 235th St, Douglaston, New
York 11363; ✆800 778 9847, 718 423 6161;
e vyttours@earthlink.net; www.vytistours.com.
Individual & group tours to all 3 Baltic states.

IN ESTONIA The following is a selection of local operators in Tallinn who work with
tour operators abroad. They can also make arrangements on the spot throughout
Estonia for visitors who have not prebooked. Their public offices all close on Sunday
and on Estonian national holidays. Outside Tallinn, tourist offices often do this
work in their own town, or will refer enquiries to a nearby local travel agent. There
are no hotel booking agencies at Tallinn airport.

Estonian Holidays Vana Viru 6; ✆627 0500;
e holidays@holidays.ee; www.holidays.ee, www.
estonianholidays.com
Estravel American Express Travel Suur-Karja

15, 10140 Tallinn; ✆626 6233; e incoming.team@
estravel.ee; www.estravel.ee
Via Hansa Rüütli 13; ✆627 7870; e tallinn@
viahansa.com; www.viahansa.com

RED TAPE

In 2007, Estonia and its Baltic neighbours joined the Schengen group of EU
countries so there are now no border controls between them and no visas are
needed for travellers from the UK, other EU countries, Australia, Canada, New
Zealand and the USA. For those who do need a Schengen visa, it is now valid in
the three Baltic countries. The website of the Ministry of Foreign Affairs is www.
vm.ee and it lists Estonian embassies around the world which can issue visas to
people entering the Schengen area through Estonia. It also lists foreign embassies
based in Tallinn.

Travellers from all countries wanting to combine a visit to Estonia with one to
Russia must ensure that their travel agent has prebooked their accommodation in
Russia and obtained the necessary Russian visa. Attempting to do this in Estonia is
both time-consuming and expensive. Whilst there is always talk about simplifying
entry procedures to Russia from Estonia, the Russian authorities in fact make
obtaining visas more complicated and more expensive every year. In Britain,
particularly in the summer, at least a month should be allowed for obtaining a
Russian visa, if exorbitant express fees are to be avoided.

From 1965 until 1988, Estonia's sole link with the West was a twice-weekly ferry to Helsinki, yet it had daily flights to most of the then capitals of other Soviet republics. Now the situation is completely reversed, with minimal links east and an ever-increasing range of links to the West. Ferries go hourly to Helsinki and there are direct flights from Tallinn to most European countries. Bus routes link Estonia with Russia and with Latvia and some buses continue through Lithuania and Poland to western Europe. Trains operate daily from Tallinn to St Petersburg and to Moscow.

BY AIR

International flights Estonian Air (*www.estonian-air.com*) is the national carrier but Air Baltic (*www.airbaltic.com*), Finnair (*www.finnair.com*), LOT (*www.lot.com*), Lufthansa (*www.lufthansa.com*) and SAS (*www.flysas.com*) are active at Tallinn airport too. Estonian Air is partially owned by SAS so can sell through-tickets using both carriers to destinations they do not serve directly. It is therefore possible to fly to say the UK via Stockholm or Copenhagen booked entirely through Estonian Air. This offers twice-daily links to Heathrow, Birmingham and Manchester. After a gap of many years, Estonian Air were allowed by the Russian authorities to restart a service to St Petersburg in autumn 2009. Other routes they operate that are likely to be of interest to tourists are to Moscow and Vilnius.

Air Baltic is Estonian Air's main competitor, offering six flights a day between Riga and Tallinn to feed their extensive international network from Riga. The year 2009 saw the opening of Tartu airport (*www.tartu-airport.ee*) to regular passenger flights for the first time since the Soviet era. Varying services have operated since then to Helsinki, Riga, Stockholm and Tallinn.

Helsinki is often used as a gateway for travel to Estonia; Finnair have six flights a day between Helsinki and Tallinn so there will always be connections with their onward flights to Europe, America and Asia. In Britain they fly to London and Manchester.

For many years, Estonia was the only EU country to which Ryanair did not fly, but they finally joined the fray in 2011, several years after easyJet. In 2013 Ryanair flew to Stansted and easyJet to Gatwick and one or other usually has a flight from Manchester or Liverpool, sometimes from Glasgow too.

Particularly good rates apply between October and April, with of course the exception of Christmas/New Year.

BY FERRY

From/to Helsinki During 2007 and 2008, the ferry company Tallink (*www.tallink. com*) took over several of its competitors, including Siljaline, so its name is now Tallink Silja, but Eckerö (*www.eckeroline.ee*) and Vikingline (*www.vikkingline. com*) remain. Ferries take about two hours so it is therefore quite possible to visit Helsinki for the day. There are also overnight services with cabins that allow about seven hours for sleep. Ferries should be avoided from Helsinki on Friday afternoon and evening and returning on Sunday evening when they are very crowded with sometimes rowdy Finnish tourists. Travel during the middle of the day is usually cheaper and more congenial. Reductions are available for pensioners, sometimes defined as those aged 60 and over, sometimes as those aged 65 and over.

Catamarans are operated by Lindaline (*www.lindaline.fi*) from a separate pier beside the Linnahall, which is even closer to the Old Town and to extensive public transport. They take about 90 minutes to cross to Helsinki, but do not operate in stormy weather or when ice is seen as a threat.

From/to Stockholm Ferries to Stockholm take 16 hours and usually operate overnight. There are also car ferries from Paldiski to Kappelskär, a port 90km from Stockholm. They are operated by DFDS (*www.dfdsseaways.us*) and by Tallink Silja (*www.tallink.com*)

The Port of Tallinn website (*www.portoftallinn.com*) gives full details of all services from/to Helsinki and from/to Stockholm.

BY TRAIN Rail services within Estonia and to/from the neighbouring countries consistently declined from independence until 2005 and were of little use either to business travellers or to tourists. However there was then a sudden turnaround.

In 2005 a faster service to Tartu was introduced twice a day, with a first-class carriage, and the station at Rakvere reopened. In 2006, the Latvians announced plans to restore a service from Riga to Valga, which could then offer onward connections to Tartu and Tallinn. In early 2007 faster trains started to operate between Tallinn and Viljandi. The Narva–Tallinn route was reopened in 2008. The year 2010 saw the return of trains between Tallinn and St Petersburg. Formerly moribund stations came to full life again and early 2014 saw a considerable increase in the frequency of trains on the main routes and also new rolling stock. Details of fares and schedules are on www.edel.ee.

There is a daily service from Tallinn to Moscow, which takes 18 hours, and which is operated by Gotravel (*www.gotravel.ee*), the company that runs the Schnelli Hotel next to the station in Tallinn. Tickets for this train can and should be prebooked abroad since the Russian visa will specify dates of entry and exit.

BY BUS This is the easiest and cheapest way to reach Estonia from Russia and Latvia. Public buses always have priority over other traffic at the Russian border so delays there are minimal, but they are long enough to provide a respite for smokers.

The years 2012–13 saw a great change in the bus services operating in and out of Estonia. The company Luxexpress (*www.luxexpress.eu*) drove out its former competitors Eurolines and Hansabuss and only Ecolines (*www.ecolines.net*) is left with minimal services to and from Estonia. The Ecolines website is hardly inviting as it promotes the service of a stewardess 'who controls discipline and order on board' with no explanation as to why a steward cannot do this equally well or why such a service should be necessary at all. However, Luxexpress is reliable and offers four different levels of comfort on its buses from/to St Petersburg and to Riga: Lux Simple, Express, Lounge and Special with fares on the Special service costing twice the price of the Simple one. Wi-Fi is available on all buses and they all take about 4½ hours between Tallinn and Riga, with a short stop *en route* at Pärnu, where it is also possible to join the service. About ten buses a day operate between Tallinn and Riga, but as each bus is a different class, it is necessary to check the cost and facilities on the website before booking.

BY CAR Car drivers in the 1990s often had to face delays of several hours crossing each of the borders (eg: Poland, Lithuania, Latvia) between Germany and Estonia. Now that all the relevant countries are in Schengen, the borders are completely open. However, police do stop cars from time to time to check that drivers have all the correct documentation. The car ferries from Helsinki and Stockholm are convenient but expensive. Car-hire rates are competitive in Estonia but in the short summer season it is normally essential to prebook. Travellers to Saaremaa or Hiiumaa can make considerable savings by asking their travel agents to arrange car hire separately on the islands and travelling by bus to and from Tallinn. This also avoids the difficulty of prebooking the car ferries from the mainland. Drop-off charges are high for cars picked up in one Baltic country and left in another so it is more economical to hire a new car in each country and to travel by bus in between.

HEALTH *with Dr Felicity Nicholson*

No inoculations are required for Estonia as health standards are very high throughout the country. Still, travellers here as anywhere should be up to date with tetanus, diphtheria and polio, which now come as an all-in-one vaccine (Revaxis) that lasts for ten years. Hepatitis A vaccine may be recommended for longer-stay travellers or those visiting more remote parts of the country. Depending on what you are doing you may also be advised to be protected against hepatitis B and rabies.

Travellers planning to visit more rural parts of Estonia from late spring to autumn should take ample supplies of insect repellent, and are advised to take precautions against tick-borne encephalitis. Around 200 cases are reported each year. The worst-affected areas are Pärnumaa and Läänemaa (west), Ida-Virumaa (east), Saaremaa Island (west) and Põlvamaa and Tartumaa (southeast). As the name suggests, this disease is spread by the bites of ticks that live in long grass and the branches of overhanging trees. Wearing hats, tucking long trousers into boots, and applying tick repellents can all help. It is important to check for ticks each time you have been for a long walk. This is more easily done by someone else. If you find a tick then slowly remove it by using special tweezers, taking care not to squeeze the mouthparts. There is an effective vaccine available in the UK for adults aged 16 and over (Ticovac) and for children from one to 15 years of age (Ticovac junior). Two doses of vaccine should ideally be given about a month apart but can be given two weeks apart if time is short. A third dose should be given five to 12 months later if the traveller is at continued risk. Taking the preventive measures described above is also very important. Go as soon as possible to a doctor if you have been bitten by a tick (especially if you have not been vaccinated) as tick immunoglobulin may be needed for treatment. This is usually available in Estonia.

Vaccination against hepatitis B can take six months to become effective. As the disease is most likely to be picked up through unprotected sex or through inadequately sterilised needles, using condoms and taking an emergency medical kit that contains these sterile needles, sutures, etc will go a long way to preventing exposure. However, Engerix, one of the hepatitis B vaccines is licensed for a shorter course, which can be taken over 21 days if there is no time to do the full course. This course can only be used for those aged 16 or over. Hepatitis B vaccine is always recommended when working in medical settings and also with children.

RABIES Rabies vaccination is essential for anyone likely to be in close contact with animals or for those who are going to be more than 24 hours from medical help. Rabies is spread through the infected bite, scratch or lick over an open wound from any warm-blooded animal. Dogs are the most likely source in Estonia. If you are bitten or scratched wash the wound immediately with soap and water, apply an antiseptic and go straight for medical help. If you have received the pre-exposure course of three doses then you should still follow the above procedures, but you must tell them what vaccinations you have had. You will no longer need Rabies Immunoglobulin (RIG), a human blood product in limited supply that costs around US$800 a dose. You will still need two further doses of vaccine but this should be relatively easy to come by.

TRAVEL CLINICS AND HEALTH INFORMATION A full list of current travel clinic websites worldwide is available on www.istm.org/. For other journey preparation information, consult www.nathnac.org/ds/map_world.aspx. Information about various medications may be found on www.netdoctor.co.uk/travel.

HEALTH IN ESTONIA Tap water is safe to drink throughout Estonia; however, you may still prefer to drink bottled water, as the mineral content can be an irritant until you get used to it. Local hospitals offer a high standard of treatment for any emergencies. Most Western brands of medicine are available throughout the country. There is a reciprocal healthcare agreement with Britain. UK residents should produce a European Health Insurance Card (EHIC). Application form T7 is available from post offices or online at www.ehic.org.uk. However, not all treatment is free and you may have to pay part of the costs of any doctor or dental treatment, home visits, prescriptions or in-patient hospital treatment. Therefore, it is wise to have good insurance when you travel.

SAFETY

Walking plays a major part of any tour in Estonia. Both in the towns and in the countryside many sites can only be reached and appreciated in this way. Whilst roads

---

NOTES FOR TRAVELLERS WITH A DISABILITY

Gordon Rattray, www.able-travel.com

Some of Estonia's older buildings are difficult for people with mobility problems to access, as entrances are often stepped and narrow, and altering these features is a costly undertaking. However, newer constructions and many public buildings are better designed, and the situation is constantly improving. Depending on your ability, and with some research and effort, a visit to this country is quite feasible.

GETTING THERE Arrivals Assistance with an aisle chair will be provided at Tallinn airport and there is a toilet for travellers with disabilities in the building. Arrivals by sea will find Tallinn port also fairly accessible, with lifts, sliding doors, disabled toilets and disabled parking.

GETTING AROUND Although some railway stations have ramps and access, this is not a general rule. Trains do not have disabled toilets and some platforms are so low that wheelchair travellers will need to be lifted into the carriage. In Tallinn, several new buses, trams and trolley buses with low floors have recently been introduced, and their routes are marked in yellow on English-language timetables (*http:// soiduplaan.tallinn.ee*). The City Tour bus service (m *53 429 968;* e *info@citytour.ee; www.citytour.ee*) also has accessible vehicles.
    These two Tallinn taxi companies cater for wheelchairs:

Toiran 673 1933; m 522 7477; e toiran@hot.ee. The dispatchers do not speak good English, so it may be better to write an email.
Tulika Takso 612 0040; e info@tulika.ee. This service must be ordered at least 1 day in advance.

HEALTH Doctors will know about everyday illnesses, but, as with anywhere, you must understand and be able to explain your own particular medical requirements.

---

are usually well maintained, pavements rarely are, so be constantly on the lookout for pot-holes, ill-fitting manhole covers and loose paving slabs or cobbles. In winter, falling or dripping icicles are a further hazard but the accompanying sunshine that usually gives rise to this provides ample compensation. Town streets are well lit at night, important in midwinter when there are only six to seven hours of daylight. Crime is less of a problem than in many other European countries and is very rare outside Tallinn.

Passports and unneeded valuables should be left in hotels; take the obvious precautions of dressing modestly and not flaunting money. Car theft is a problem at night so always use the guarded car park that most hotels have.

WOMEN TRAVELLERS

Estonian women might still have to do the majority of domestic chores at home, but at work and on the street they are equal. They can go to bars together, dress as they want and, with the high rate of divorce now prevalent, many live on their own, or often as a single parent. Women are in no more or less danger than men; pickpockets in tourist areas are opportunists on the lookout for anybody of either sex who they can take advantage of. Whether you are male or female, you are equally as vulnerable if you leave a bar after a few too many at 03.00.

If possible, take all necessary medication and equipment with you. It is advisable to pack this in your hand luggage during flights in case your main luggage is lost in transit.

INSURANCE Specialised travel insurance can be purchased in the UK from **Age Concern** (\0800 169 2700; www.ageconcern.org.uk), who have no upper age limit, and **Free Spirit** (\0845 230 5000; www.free-spirit.com), who cater for people with pre-existing medical conditions. Most insurance companies will insure travellers who have a disability, but it is essential that they are made aware of your disability.

SECURITY The usual security precautions detailed above apply, but it is also worthwhile remembering that, if you have mobility problems, you may be more vulnerable than others.

FURTHER INFORMATION Good starting points for trip research are the **Estonian Chamber of Disabled People** (\661 6629, 661 6628; e epikoda@epikoda.ee; www.epikoda.ee) and the **Estonian Tourist Board** (\627 9770; e tourism@eas.ee; www.visitestonia.com).

For Tallinn, an excellent online resource providing detailed information (including photos) on all aspects of accessibility is http://liikumisvabadus.invainfo.ee. This site is available in English and is constantly updated. **Tallinn City Board of Disabled People** (\655 4160; e tiia@tallinnakoda.ee) provides advice for people with disabilities. **Tallinn Tourist Information Centre** (\645 7777; e turismiinfo@tallinnlv.ee; www.tourism.tallinn.ee) can give general information.

BOOKS Bradt Travel Guides' title *Access Africa: Safaris for People with Limited Mobility* is aimed at safari-goers, but is packed with advice and resources that will be useful for all adventure travellers with disabilities.

GAY AND LESBIAN TRAVELLERS

Visitors to Tallinn may be surprised at how limited the gay scene is. Whilst the legal restraints faced by the gay community in Soviet times have all of course been abolished, the hostility has still not been totally eradicated. As a result, open affection outside the few gay clubs is very unusual and visitors are advised to avoid this.

TRAVELLING WITH CHILDREN

Estonia is much more child friendly since joining the EU. Facilities on buses and at building entrances have been installed for people with disabilities and these are equally helpful for pushchairs. Restaurants in the suburbs of Tallinn, and in the smaller towns, often have play areas for children as the lower rents there enable the owners to provide them. Tallinn Old Town, with its narrow, steep and cobbled streets, will remain difficult for small children, but elsewhere the flat landscape, the space and the mild summer climate make Estonia an easy destination for travel with children.

MONEY

Estonia joined the euro in 2011 so visitors are unlikely to see references to kroon, the currency that circulated from 1992 until then. Given the low costs in Estonia, it is best not to accept notes of a higher value than 20 euros. Exchange bureaux tend to charge absurdly high rates of commission. Banks are only open Monday–Friday and some on Saturday morning and where possible should be used to exchange money. Good exchange rates are offered by banks for sterling, Russian roubles, US and Australian dollars. However there are no banks at Tallinn airport or at the harbour, only exchange bureaux, so it is important to arrive with some euros.

There are plenty of ATM machines in the larger towns, but not many in the smaller ones. Credit and debit cards are now widely used throughout the country and are a safe alternative to large amounts of cash. Passport numbers are sometimes requested when purchases are made with credit cards, so take a photocopy of the information page from your passport to avoid carrying around the passport itself.

BUDGETING

Other sections give indications of fares and food costs and there is nothing unusual about them.

Litre bottle water	€1	Mars bar	€1
0.5 litre beer	€2.50	Postcard	€0.80
Loaf of bread	€1	T-shirt	€10
Street snack	€1.50	Litre of petrol	€1.40

GETTING AROUND

BY AIR Avies Air (*www.avies.ee*) provides domestic flights between Tallinn and the islands of Hiiumaa and Saaremaa. As these now operate twice a day and are heavily subsidised by the Estonian government, the 30 to 45-minute flight is an attractive alternative to a four-hour bus/ferry journey. At the time of writing the airfare was not much higher than the bus fare. The price to Kärdla on Hiiumaa was €17 as opposed to €13 for the bus and to Kuressaare was €25 rather than €17. Flights between Pärnu, and the islands of Ruhnu and Saaremaa are much more unpredictable. The website of Kuressaare airport on Saaremaa (*www.eeke.ee*) always has up-to-date information.

BY TRAIN During the currency of this guidebook, readers will see a great improvement in rail services, which started in 2013. Services will be increased, stations reopened and journey times reduced. New rolling stock will have access for the disabled. The Tallinn–Tartu service is the one most likely to be used by tourists, with fast trains taking two hours, but in 2014 similar services are expected to Rakvere and Narva. Details are on www.edel.ee.

There are no complicated fare structures akin to those Western Europeans now know well, so tickets are bought on the train or in a ticket office just before departure. First-class, when available, is worth the small supplement charged. In this case, it is worth buying the ticket at the station as there is a 10% saving. For further details see individual towns and cities.

BY BUS Domestic bus tickets can be prebooked but, apart from services to the islands during the summer, and on Friday evenings, this is rarely necessary. An extensive network operates from Tallinn to all major cities and also cross-country. Most of the nature reserves are on bus routes with a sufficiently frequent service to plan a half- or full-day trip based on them. For the longest distances, fares are no higher than €13. There is competition on the main routes from Tallinn so fares to Pärnu and to Tartu vary from €7 to €12. Few timetables are printed but services are clearly posted in bus stations. All companies use the same bus stations and *en route* stops. Do check timings before booking as sometimes an express service leaving later may arrive earlier than a service with many *en route* stops. There is an excellent website for Estonian bus services, www.tpilet.ee. It lists connections as well as direct routes and all fares. Bookings can made online a week ahead of travel. Sometimes there is a slight reduction in the fare for doing this. The four letters õ, ä, ö, ü come at the end of the alphabet so Jõhvi will be listed after Juuru but before Järva. Pärnu will be listed after Porva but before Pääskula. Those over 60 and under 26 are entitled to a 10% reduction, which for pensioners increases to 50% for Tuesday to Thursday travel.

BY BICYCLE Estonia is a very flat country, with Suur Munamägi, the highest 'mountain', being only 318m. The weather is often appropriate for cycling, with temperatures during much of the tourist season fluctuating only between 10–20˚C. Main roads should normally be avoided as there are no cycle tracks and the scenery is not particularly varied. Longer distances can be covered by bus (dismantled cycles are accepted in the hold) and then local excursions carried out from each country town or within one of the national parks. The islands of Saaremaa and Hiiumaa are ideal for cyclists as motor traffic is minimal and sightseeing stops come every few kilometres. The suggested itineraries given on page 52 are suitable for cyclists as well as for motorists. **City Bike** (✆ 683 6383; e *mail@citybike.ee; www.citybike.ee*) arranges group tours of Tallinn and around Estonia.

BY CAR It is not necessary to buy an international driving licence for Estonia although you must carry the original vehicle registration document (V5). Speed limits are strictly enforced and are usually 90km/h on the open road and 50km/h in built-up areas. Changes are clearly indicated.

The definition of drinking and driving is so tough that it is not worth drinking alcohol at all before driving. Do also bear in mind that the effects of evening drinking may not have worn off by the following morning.

Roads are generally straight, wide and well maintained; driving is often a pleasure in Estonia as the traffic is minimal. Petrol/gas costs about €1.40 a litre so is similar to the UK price.

Car hire Estonian tour operators (see pages 53–4) can arrange car hire through their partners abroad, both self-drive and with a driver. Cars can be delivered to Tallinn airport and to the harbour. Rates have tended to fall over the last few years because of competition and the effects of the recession, but remain higher in the summer.

Whilst drop-off is possible in Latvia or Lithuania, the expense of this is rarely worthwhile, so it is best to cross the border by bus and then hire another car, or plan a circular trip returning to Tallinn. Because of the high demand during the short summer season, it is very difficult to hire on the spot, but out of peak season these firms can help at the last minute. The following are the main organisations for car hire:

🚗 **Avis** Liivalaia 13; ☎ 667 1500; www.avis.ee
🚗 **Hertz** Tallinn airport; ☎ 605 8923; www.hertz.ee

🚗 **Sixt** Tallinn airport; ☎ 605 8148; www.sixt.ee
🚗 **Tulikarent** Tihase 34; ☎ 612 0001; www.tulika.ee

BY TAXI Taxis in Tallinn (see page 81) have a poor reputation. Outside the capital, though, dishonesty is very rare. Many journeys will come within the flag-fall rate of €3. Taxis are always available at the main bus stations but do not wait at border crossings. There are also ranks at obvious central locations away from the bus station, as in Tartu or Haapsalu.

MAPS For details of maps and atlases available in Estonia and overseas and where to buy them, see page 298.

ACCOMMODATION

Tallinn now has a wide range of hotels from two- to four-star and is beginning to offer bed and breakfast and hostel accommodation as well. Tourists staying in hotels will normally book these through tour operators before they arrive but details of hostel and bed and breakfast accommodation can be obtained from the tourist board office near Town Hall Square in Tallinn, although it keeps office hours so cannot help visitors who arrive in the evening. There are also no facilities for booking hotels at the airport, bus station or harbour.

Pärnu and Kuressaare also have a wide range of hotels but the choice is much more limited in other centres such as Haapsalu, Tartu and Viljandi. Several small towns such as Otepää, Paide and Rakvere have a good choice of three-star hotels and this standard is being developed in the national parks. The northeast has seen great hotel development since around 2006 so it is now possible to stay comfortably in Narva and Sillamäe, which was previously not the case. There are also a number of manor houses, such as Vihula in Lahemaa National Park, that are opening up as hotels and conference centres.

Three- and four-star hotels charge rather less than similar hotels in western Europe and two-star hotels are much cheaper. In the higher categories in Tallinn, rooms tend to cost £50–80/US$80–130 a night for a twin; about £10/US$15 less in Pärnu. Two-star hotels in the capital charge about £25/US$40 for a twin and elsewhere charges rarely exceed £15–20/US$25–35. Rates always include a buffet breakfast. There are few hostels outside Tallinn as the two-star hotels that exist in even the smallest towns cater for this market. As many two-star hotels are renovated into three-star ones, they tend to be replaced by more basic hostels, which are installing en suite facilities to warrant a two-star description.

Farmhouse accommodation is rarely sold to foreigners as access requires a car and few families speak any language apart from Estonian and Russian. Bed and breakfast is beginning in Tallinn but, given the cramped accommodation most Estonians have to accept, few families have spare rooms to let in this way. Camping has never been particularly popular in Estonia as many town dwellers have tiny country cottages to which they can retreat most weekends. The possibility of sudden storms also reduces the chance of an enjoyable stay. Sites are, however, now being established beside Lake Peipsi on the Russian border and at Lake Vagula at Võru. Others will soon be available at Viljandi and in Lahemaa National Park. The websites of the local tourist boards should have up-to-date details; otherwise they can be emailed for this information.

The Estonian spelling of hotel is *hotell*. In email and website addresses, some will use the Estonian spelling and some the English one. Policy can change on this but hopefully all addresses quoted in the book are correct as of spring 2014. (There is a similar situation with museums as the Estonian spelling is *muuseum*.)

Note that hotel prices fluctuate in Estonia over the course of the year; however, the figures below give a rough indication of likely charges during mid season, for a twin room with breakfast.

$$$$$	€200+
$$$$	€150–200
$$$	€100–150
$$	€70–100
$	€40–70

EATING AND DRINKING

The cost of eating out in Tallinn leapt in 2007–08 but then dropped rapidly during 2009 and 2010. It has increased slowly since then, but the introduction of the euro in 2011 did not have the inflationary effect that some of its opponents feared. Be very careful when ordering wine not to overpay and if the restaurant has house wine at say €20, stick to beer which will always be good value.

Prices listed below give an indication of costs for three courses without wine.

$$$$	more than €60
$$$	€40–60
$$	€20–40
$	less than €20

RESTAURANT OPENING TIMES Tallinn restaurants usually open at 12.00 and close around 23.00, staying open through the afternoon. Cafés open at 10.00 since Estonians do not breakfast out and, as it is included in hotel room prices, there is no incentive for tourists to find it elsewhere. Cafés close around 18.00, except for those that become bars in the evening, when they will stay open until midnight at least. Opening hours are similar elsewhere in Estonia, although sometimes smaller restaurants may operate reduced hours.

Our information on Estonian eating habits dates back to the middle of the 19th century when standards of nutrition started to improve as a result of land reforms. At that time, the main meal was supper, consisting of porridge or soup served with bread and salted herring. Meat was a delicacy, usually served only on Thursday and Sunday.

Meat became more common early in the 20th century and a basic hot meal would consist of pork slices, potatoes and a sauce. Bread remained a major item of food, being considered sacred, and even stale bread was never thrown away. Rye bread was the most common and wholemeal rye is still one of the most popular kinds, with black bread also often being eaten. Black and white puddings can be regarded as the most well-known national dish, with pork fat, onions and spices being added, together with blood for the black pudding. Sweet dishes were prepared only for festive occasions, with honey an essential ingredient. Beer has always been a popular drink and there are now breweries all over the country.

Between 1918 and 1940, traditional food gradually gave way to more sophisticated cooking. Foodstuffs began to be imported and exported, with Estonian ham and butter being greatly appreciated in Britain. Spices were now a regular adjunct to most Estonian dishes and coffee became a popular drink. Estonians drink it black, but cafés will serve it with milk for foreigners.

With the range of foreign restaurants now opening in Estonia, it is rare to find the traditional dishes such as black pudding or baked potatoes with pork and sauerkraut outside the home environment. Only at Christmas and on Shrove Tuesday will restaurants return to their Estonian roots and serve these dishes, or perhaps bean soup followed by smoked pork. Cafés are easy to find in all towns and villages and they serve a wide range of cakes – fruitcake, chocolate cake and curd cake – often with whipped cream. Bakers like to celebrate Shrove Tuesday with an ever-wider range of buns and cakes.

Although Estonia has a long coastline, fish is rarely eaten as a main course, but rather as an hors d'oeuvre, smoked or salted. 'Tallinn sprats' are small raw sprats preserved in brine and spices. Fish can also be mixed with cooked vegetable salads and a sour cream dressing. Wild mushrooms are the most popular ingredient for such salads. In the countryside, stewed turnips are staple fare but potatoes and meat remain crucial. Vegetarianism is hardly known in Estonia. The bias towards savoury food is perhaps best summarised in an old Estonian saying: 'Better a salty morsel than a square meal of sweet.'

As the tax on alcohol is so low in Estonia, it is often tempting in a café to enjoy a glass of Vana Tallinn, Estonia's national liqueur. The recipe of spices used to make it is, of course, a secret but Drambuie is probably the nearest in taste to it of Western liqueurs. The close contact with western Europe has brought wine to Estonia but its price is still too high for most local people and beer remains the main alcoholic drink.

PUBLIC HOLIDAYS

1 January (New Year)	23 June (Victory Day)
24 February (Independence Day)	24 June (Midsummer)
Good Friday	20 August (Re-Independence Day)
1 May (May Day)	25 and 26 December (Christmas)

SHOPPING

Wooden toys, bowls, spoons, candlesticks and tablemats are sold extensively in Tallinn and in Kuressaare on Saaremaa Island. Tallinn porcelain is not promoted as much as it should be, although it is of a high, delicate standard. The few shops that do sell it will wrap it properly so that it survives a journey abroad. Hand-knitted sweaters and gloves and knitted socks are available in all sizes as shops need to cater for tall Swedes and Danes just as much as for the shorter local population.

Independence brought an immediate passion for Western pop music but this has now passed, so CDs are available of folk music and orchestral music from contemporary composers such as Arvo Pärt or earlier ones such as Rudolf Tobias. The Song Festival in July 2004 led, as expected, to the production of many choral CDs, and this happened again after the July 2009 festival.

Duty on tobacco and alcohol increased during 2009, but cigarettes can be bought for less at any kiosk than at so-called duty-free shops. Most tourists return with a bottle of Vana Tallinn (Old Tallinn), a sweet liqueur guaranteed to enhance a dull fruit salad or a bland portion of vanilla ice cream. With Estonia now in the EU, tourists travelling home to other EU countries can take back as much drink as they wish, provided it is for their personal use. British visitors are, however, still restricted to 200 cigarettes or 250g of smoking tobacco.

For a more precise memory of a visit to Estonia, there are many extensively illustrated photographic books with English texts (see also pages 294–8).

Every Estonian town has a large department store in the centre selling these and other articles, but they are surrounded by smaller specialist shops with wider selections. Shops keep long hours to attract business and many are open on Sundays. There is an extensive open-air market along the streets near the Viru Gate in Tallinn. Stallholders are active year-round, however bitter the weather might be in winter.

ARTS AND ENTERTAINMENT

Informal music festivals take place throughout the country during the summer. Most famous are the **Old Town Days** in Tallinn in early June, the **Classical Music Festival** in Pärnu in early July, the **Tartu Accordion Festival** in mid-July, the **Folk Music Festival** in Viljandi in late July and the **White Lady Days** in Haapsalu in August. Over the next few years, further more serious events are likely to be arranged during the winter.

The opening of the Jõhvi Concert Hall in October 2005 was an instant success in a part of Estonia that had for years been culturally neglected. Its programmes and those for all other classical music concerts can be checked on the website www.concert.ee.

In early July 2009 the most recent Song Festival took place in Tallinn and in the end around 150,000 people (10% of the Estonian population) attended. The festival takes place every five years so the next one is in 2014. For the few seats available at the Song Festival grounds, used for all big events, tickets can be bought in advance through tour operators but standing room is open to all on a first-come, first-served basis.

There is no shortage of cultural activities in all major towns and tickets for concerts, ballet and theatre can normally be bought on the day without difficulty. Prices by Western standards are low – €15 will buy an excellent seat. In Tallinn, the Estonian Theatre and the Estonian Concert Hall are conveniently situated beside each other.

OUTDOOR ACTIVITIES

Well-organised outdoor activities are available in most national parks. There is no specific listing for location and costs of these activities or of accommodation possibilities but websites for the parks are helpful for this (links to websites can be found on the Tourist Board's excellent website, *www.visitestonia.com*). Fortunately, away from the northeast coast, Estonia suffers little from pollution. Strict regulation will ensure that this continues. Ecotourism is taken seriously and is now enjoyed by many local visitors and tourists from abroad. Full information can be obtained from the **Ecotourism Initiative** (\ *444 3779;* e *info@ecotourism.ee; www.ecotourism.ee*).

MUSEUMS

Museums usually only open from 10.30/11.00 to 17.00 and close at least one day a week; many close on both Monday and Tuesday. Most museums close completely

PHOTOGRAPHIC TIPS   *Ariadne Van Zandbergen*

EQUIPMENT Although with some thought and an eye for composition you can take reasonable photos with a 'point-and-shoot' camera, you need an SLR camera if you are at all serious about photography. Modern SLRs tend to be very clever, with automatic programmes for almost every possible situation, but remember that these programmes are limited in the sense that the camera cannot think, but only makes calculations. Every starting amateur photographer should read a photographic manual for beginners and get to grips with such basics as the relationship between aperture and shutter speed.

Digital SLRs come in different formats, which refer to the size of the sensor. The format of the future is the full-size sensor, but at present all full-size sensor cameras are in the higher price bracket. Different lenses are designed to accommodate the camera sensor sizes.

Always buy the best lens you can afford. The lens determines the quality of your photo more than the camera body. Fixed fast lenses are ideal, but very costly. A zoom lens makes it easier to change composition without changing lenses the whole time. If you carry only one lens with a full-size sensor camera, a 28–70mm or similar zoom should be ideal. This corresponds to a 17–55mm or similar for a camera with a smaller sensor. For a second lens, a lightweight telephoto zoom will be excellent for candid shots and varying your composition. Wildlife photography will be very frustrating if you don't have at least a 300mm lens. For a small loss of quality, tele-converters are a cheap and compact way to increase your focal length: a 300mm lens with a 1.4x converter becomes 420mm, and with a 2x it becomes 600mm. Note, however, that 1.4x and 2x tele-converters reduce the speed of your lens.

For wildlife photography from a vehicle, a solid beanbag, which you can make yourself very cheaply, will be necessary to avoid blurred images, and is more useful than a tripod. A clamp with a tripod head screwed onto it can be attached to the vehicle as well. Modern dedicated flash units are easy to use; aside from the obvious need to flash when you photograph at night, you can improve a lot of photos in difficult 'high contrast' or very dull light with some fill-in flash. It pays to have a proper flash unit as opposed to a built-in camera flash.

on 23 and 24 June and 20 August and early on 22 June, so travellers interested in them should avoid these dates for a visit to Estonia.

Policies vary at Christmas, New Year and Easter so the websites of individual museums need to be checked carefully. By 2013, more museums were beginning to realise the commercial stupidity of closing on days when visitors are most likely to come so in future this should be less of a problem than it used to be. Visitors to Tallinn who plan to include several of the more expensive museums in their itinerary would be well advised to buy a Tallinn Card (see page 82), which includes all admission charges.

MEDIA AND COMMUNICATIONS

LOCAL PUBLICATIONS *Tallinn In Your Pocket* appears every two months. As there is a cover price for it, it is a full, critical and often hilarious listing of hotels, restaurants, museums and shops. Its readers are assumed to be awake 24 hours a

The resolution of digital cameras is improving the whole time and even the most basic digital SLRs are more than adequate for ordinary prints and enlargements. For professional reproduction, cameras with a resolution up to 24 megapixels are available.

Memory space is important. The number of pictures you can fit on a memory card depends on the quality you choose. Calculate in advance how many pictures you can fit on a card and either take enough cards to last for your trip, or take a storage drive onto which you can download the content. A laptop gives the advantage that you can see your pictures properly at the end of each day and edit and delete rejects, but a storage device is lighter and less bulky.

Bear in mind that digital camera batteries, computers and other storage devices need charging, so make sure you have all the chargers, cables and converters with you. Most hotels have charging points, but do enquire about this in advance.

LIGHT The most striking outdoor photographs are often taken during the hour or two of 'golden light', after dawn and before sunset. Shooting in low light may enforce the use of very low shutter speeds, in which case a tripod might be required to avoid camera shake. Some top digital SLR's now give good results with minimal grain when shooting at very high ISO settings which makes low light photography a lot easier and reduces the need of a tripod in many situations.

With careful handling, side lighting and back lighting can produce stunning effects, especially in soft light and at sunrise or sunset. Generally, however, it is best to shoot with the sun behind you. When photographing animals or people in the harsh midday sun, images taken in light but even shade are likely to be more effective than those taken in direct sunlight or patchy shade, since the latter conditions create too much contrast.

Ariadne Van Zandbergen is a professional travel and wildlife photographer specialising in Africa. She runs The Africa Image Library. For photo requests, visit www. africaimagelibrary.com or contact her by email at e info@africaimagelibrary.com.

day. It is as comprehensive on nightlife as it is on breakfast cafés. Each issue has a supplement on another small town in Estonia. *Tartu In Your Pocket* and *Pärnu In Your Pocket* are published annually each spring. The website www.inyourpocket. com has the complete text of each issue on it. There are other free publications that try to copy the *In Your Pocket formula*, but as their editorial content is paid for entirely by advertising, the bias in it is clear.

INTERNET Internet facilities are available free of charge in all public libraries, and in smaller towns this may be the only option. These libraries are usually open 09.00–17.00 on weekdays and on Saturday mornings. It is very rare for hotels to charge for Wi-Fi and it is available free in many public areas too. An increasing number of hotels have a computer in the lobby that guests can use without payment. Given the increasing use of personal computers from around 2010, internet cafés had by 2012 largely disappeared in Estonia.

TELEPHONE The international dialling code for Estonia is +372 and there are no dialing codes within the country. There is no set format for telephone numbers.

BUSINESS

Since independence, Estonia has enjoyed a remarkably stable business environment. A banking crisis in 1994 and the collapse of the Russian economy in autumn 1998 left their mark but the country suffered much less than Latvia and Lithuania when faced with similar difficulties. There was a parallel situation in 2009, with its southern neighbours being hit much harder by the worldwide economic downturn. Estonia has no desire to work with its Baltic neighbours, as it sees itself as a Nordic country, modelled on Finland and Sweden. Trading relations with Britain have been particularly good, as they had been before the war, and tourists arriving in 1993 were surprised to see Mars bars, Scotch whisky and copies of *The Guardian* throughout the country, soon to be followed by books, cars and management consultants. This was just two years after Estonia had been a reluctant part of the Soviet Union. The market of 1.3 million native consumers is of course a small one but it is enhanced by an equal number of tourists each year, many of whom consume luxury goods.

In the 1980s Estonia pioneered devolved management, in so far as this was possible in the Soviet era, so could adapt more easily to Western markets than many of the neighbouring republics. A policy of encouraging foreign investment introduced immediately after the re-establishment of independence has been firmly maintained since then and will probably not be changed. The liberal visa policy, low rates of taxation and the harmonisation of the legal framework to meet EU requirements have all helped to attract foreign investors. Whilst some Estonians may regret the increasing shareholdings taken in their banks by Swedish ones, and certainly used the difficulties in 2009 to air these objections, others will see this as the ultimate accolade and a sure sign of long-term security. Some will hope in due course to use Estonia as a springboard into Russia, seeing its role as similar to the one that Hong Kong used to play towards China. Few regret Estonia's adoption of the euro in January 2011, with Latvia following in 2014 and Lithuania likely to do so in 2015.

Business negotiations in Estonia have never suffered from the time-wasting rituals encountered in many developing countries. Small talk is not encouraged, nor is lavish entertaining. Blunt speaking is the order of the day since time costs money in Estonia, just as much as it does abroad. If time is tight, meetings can easily take place in the evenings and at weekends. Partners of Estonian Air offer two- and three-night business packages to Tallinn.

Enterprise Estonia (*www.eas.ee*) works actively abroad and is represented in most embassies. In some countries, such as Finland and Germany, it has a separate office.

BUYING PROPERTY

Many foreigners have done this happily, even though procedures rely on trust much more than they would in western Europe. Lawyers have a minimal role and are usually only involved when they supervise the exchange of documents in a neutral capacity, checking that both parties have behaved correctly. The introductions and negotiations are done between two estate agents who represent each side. Buyers of flats will need to push them for detail on service agreements and earlier structural problems. Make sure you meet the neighbours as well before making any commitment, to establish the history of the building. Surveys are not always provided or suggested but should be undertaken by foreigners to show serious interest in the property.

The fall in property prices that started in 2008 and accelerated through 2009 was a great boon to foreign buyers. Prices did increase a little from 2010 and there has been a gradual increase each year since then. However a wide range of property across the country is always on the market.

TRAVELLING POSITIVELY

As Estonia is a fully Western country, visitors will not see grinding poverty or serious begging. Charities do operate in Estonia, although far less than in Britain and the US, since there is still the feeling lingering from Soviet times that the state will handle any problem and also few people have built up sufficient savings to be able to abandon paid work for the voluntary sector.

I like to be extravagant outside Tallinn, where whatever I spend will go further and is needed more. Crafts are tasteful, so there is no problem in supporting local artists who work in wood, wool and glass. Small museums need encouragement too, however frustrating their environment and sometimes their staff may be. Do not give away any old clothes or equipment. The need for these disappeared in the mid-1990s!

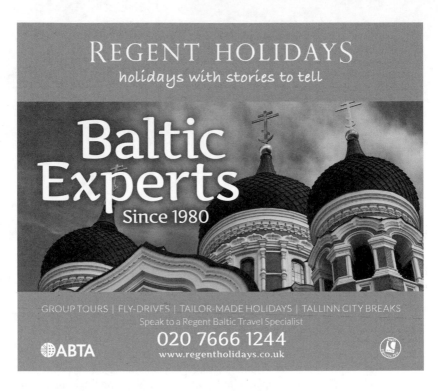

Part Two

THE GUIDE

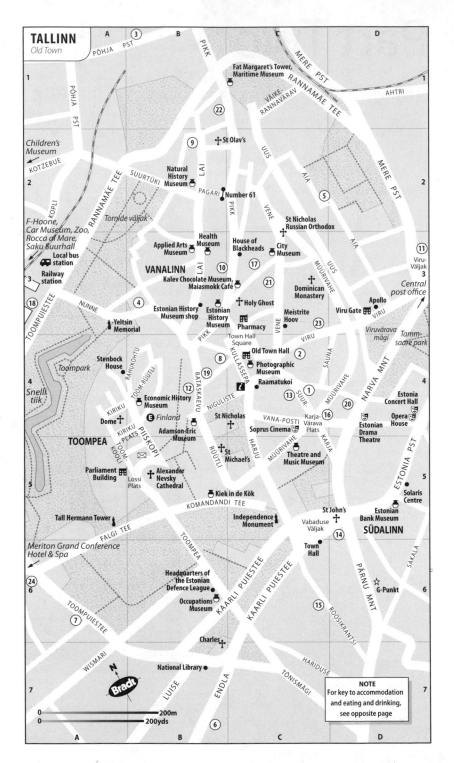

TALLINN
Old Town

A · ③ · B · PIKK · C · MERE PST · D

PÕHJA PST

1

Fat Margaret's Tower,
Maritime Museum

VÄIKE-
RANNAVÄRAV
RANNAMÄE TEE
AHTRI

MERE PST

Children's
Museum

PÕHJA PST

KOTZEBUE

②②

LAI

⑨ ✝ St Olav's

UUS

AIA

SUURTÜKI

2

Natural
History
Museum
PAGARI ✝ Number 61

⑤

KOPLI

F-Hoone,
Car Museum, Zoo,
Rocca al Mare,
Saku Suurhall

RANNAMÄE TEE

Tornide väljak

PIKK

VENE

St Nicholas
Russian Orthodox

AIA

⑪
Viru-
Väljak

3

Local bus
station

Applied Arts
Museum

Health
Museum

House of
Blackheads

⑰

City
Museum

MÜÜRIVAHE

UUS

Central
post office

Railway
station

VANALINN

LAI

⑩

Kalev Chocolate Museum,
Maiasmokk Café

②①

Dominican
Monastery

Apollo

Viru Gate ⑪ VIRU

Viruvärava

⑱

NUNNE

④

Estonian History
Museum shop

Estonian
History
Museum

✝ Holy Ghost

Meistrite
Hoov

②③

Tamm-
saare park

TOOMPUIESTEE

Yeltsin
Memorial

Pharmacy

VENE

VIRU

Viruvärava
mägi

Toompark

RAHUKOHTU

Stenbock
House

TOOM-RÜÜTLI

Town Hall
Square

Old Town Hall

②

SAUNA

Estonia
Concert Hall

4

Snelli
tiik

KIRIKU

RATASKAEVU

Economic History
Museum

⑧

KULLASSEPA

Photographic
Museum

MÜÜRIVAHE

NARVA MNT

4

⑫

⑲

Raamatukoi

②⓪

Opera
House

Dome

KIRIKU
PLATS

TOOMPEA

KIRIKU
KOOL

PIISKOPI

Finland

Adamson-Eric
Museum

NIGULISTE

St Nicholas

⑬ SUUR ①

VANA-POSTI

Soprus Cinema

Karja-
Värava
Plats

⑯

Estonian
Drama
Theatre

Estonian
Drama
Theatre

Parliament
Building

TOOM-
KOOLI

Lossi
Plats

Alexander
Nevsky
Cathedral

RÜÜTLI

✝ St
Michael's

HARJU

MÜÜRIVAHE

Theatre and
Music Museum

KARJA

ESTONIA PST

5

Kiek in de Kök

KOMANDANDI TEE

St John's ✝

Estonian
Bank Museum

Solaris
Centre

Tall Hermann Tower

Independence
Monument

Vabaduse
Väljak

⑭

SÜDALINN

SAKALA

FALGI TEE

TOOMPEA

Meriton Grand Conference
Hotel & Spa

Town
Hall

PÄRNU MNT

G-Punkt

6

②④

Headquarters of
the Estonian
Defence League

KAARLI PUIESTEE

KAARLI PUIESTEE

⑮

ROOSIKRANTSI

Occupations
Museum

⑦

TOOMPUIESTEE

WISMARI

Charles ✝

HARIDUSE

LUISE

National Library

ENDLA

TÕNISMÄGI

7

Bracht

0 ___ 200m
0 ___ 200yds

⑥

NOTE
For key to accommodation
and eating and drinking,
see opposite page

A · B · C · D

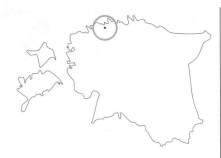

3

Tallinn

Whether approached by air, land or sea, Tallinn is immediately identifiable as a capital that looks to the West rather than to the East. The departure board at the airport lists London, Copenhagen and Stockholm but rarely St Petersburg. The boats that fill the harbour, be they massive ferries or small yachts, head for Finland and Sweden, not Russia. The traffic jams that are beginning to block the main streets are caused by Volkswagens, Land Rovers and Saabs, not by Ladas. Links with the West are celebrated; those with Russia are commemorated. In May 1998, Tallinn celebrated its 750th anniversary since on 15 May 1248 it adopted Lübeck Town Law, which united most members of the Hanseatic League. A month later, as on every 14 June, flags were lowered in memory of those deported to the Soviet Union on 14 June 1941. In 2011, Tallinn was one of the Cultural Capitals of Europe, a status only on offer to towns in the EU.

Immediately after independence was regained in 1991, Western goods started pouring into the shops, and Russian ones are now very hard to find. There is a similar reluctance to buy from most of the other former Soviet republics apart of course from their Baltic neighbours and recently from Georgia, with whom Estonia has formed a close bond since the Russian–Georgian war of 2008. Tallinn's travel agents offer the same tempting prices for holidays in Turkey, Greece and Italy that are available in western Europe, but nobody is interested in St Petersburg or the Crimea. Architecturally, with the exception of the Alexander Nevsky Cathedral, it is the Germans, Swedes and Danes who have left their imposing mark on the churches and fortifications of the Old Town.

Tallinn was always ready to defend itself but in the end hardly ever did so.

Tallinn

3

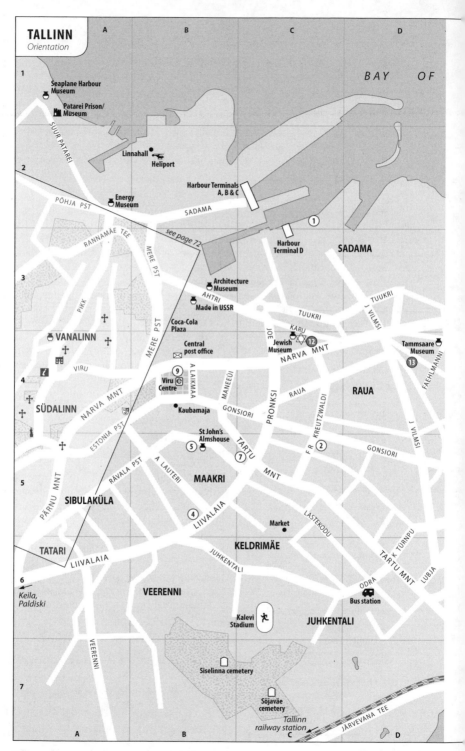

A   B   C   D

1

BAY   OF

Seaplane Harbour Museum

Patarei Prison/ Museum

SUUR PATAREI

Linnahall
Heliport

2

Harbour Terminals A, B & C

PÕHJA PST

Energy Museum

SADAMA

see page 72

RANNAMÄE TEE

MERE PST

Harbour Terminal D

SADAMA

①

3

Architecture Museum

AHTRI

Made in USSR

PIKK

TUUKRI

J TUUKRI

J VILMSI

VANALINN

Coca-Cola Plaza

Central post office

JOE

KARU

Jewish Museum

⑫

NARVA MNT

Tammsaare Museum

⑬

VIRU

i

⑨

Viru Centre

A LAIKMAA

MANEEUI

PRONKSI

RAUA

RAUA

FAEHLMANNI

4

SÜDALINN

NARVA MNT

Kaubamaja

GONSIORI

F. R. KREUTZWALDI

②

GONSIORI

J VILMSI

ESTONIA PST

St John's Almshouse

⑤

TARTU

⑦

MNT

5

RAVALA PST

A LAUTERI

MAAKRI

LIIVALAIA

PÄRNU MNT

SIBULAKÜLA

④

Market

LASTEKODU

TARTU K TÜRNPU

TARTU MNT

LUBJA

TATARI

LIIVALAIA

KELDRIMÄE

JUHKENTALI

6

Keila, Paldiski

VEERENNI

ODRA

Bus station

Kalevi Stadium

JUHKENTALI

VEERENNI

7

Siselinna cemetery

Sõjaväe cemetery

Tallinn railway station

JÄRVEVANA TEE

A   B   C   D

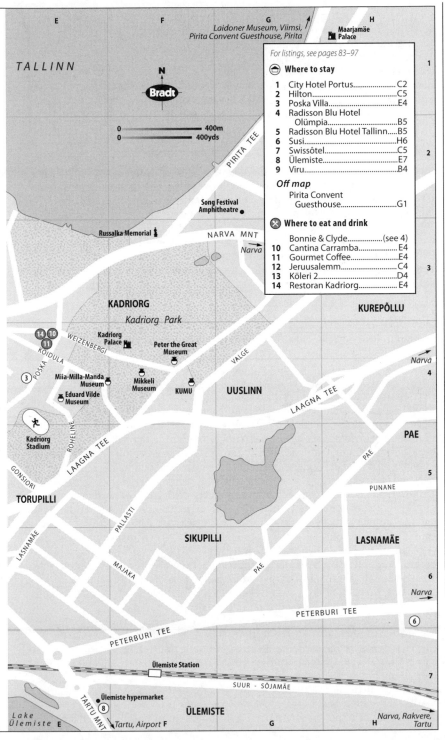

TALLINN

N
Bradt

Laidoner Museum, Viimsi,
Pirita Convent Guesthouse, Pirita

Maarjamäe
Palace

For listings, see pages 83–97

Where to stay

1 City Hotel Portus......................C2
2 Hilton.....................................C5
3 Poska Villa..............................E4
4 Radisson Blu Hotel
   Olümpia................................B5
5 Radisson Blu Hotel Tallinn.....B5
6 Susi.......................................H6
7 Swissôtel...............................C5
8 Ülemiste................................E7
9 Viru.......................................B4

Off map
   Pirita Convent
   Guesthouse..........................G1

Where to eat and drink

   Bonnie & Clyde.................(see 4)
10 Cantina Carramba................. E4
11 Gourmet Coffee.....................E4
12 Jeruusalemm......................... C4
13 Köleri 2.................................D4
14 Restoran Kadriorg................. E4

0 _____ 400m
0 _____ 400yds

PIRITA TEE

Song Festival
Amphitheatre

Russalka Memorial

NARVA MNT

Narva

KADRIORG

Kadriorg Park

KUREPÕLLU

14 10
11

WEIZENBERGI

Kadriorg
Palace

Peter the Great
Museum

VALGE

Narva

KOIDULA

POSKA

3

Miia-Milla-Manda
Museum

Mikkeli
Museum

KUMU

UUSLINN

LAAGNA TEE

Eduard Vilde
Museum

ROHELINE

Kadriorg
Stadium

LAAGNA TEE

PAE

GONSIORI

PUNANE

5

TORUPILLI

PALLASTI

SIKUPILLI

LASNAMÄE

LASNAMÄE

MAJAKA

PAE

6

PETERBURI TEE

Narva

6

PETERBURI TEE

Ülemiste Station

SUUR - SÕJAMÄE

7

Lake
Ülemiste E

TARTU MNT

Ülemiste hypermarket

8

Tartu, Airport F

ÜLEMISTE

G

Narva, Rakvere,
Tartu

H

Only for 16 years, between 1561 and 1577, were its fortifications put to the test, when the Swedes, Danes and Russians all attacked the city. The nearest it came to what might have been a major battle was at the conclusion of the Northern War in 1710, but plague had reduced the population from 10,000 to 2,000 so the Swedes offered little resistance to the army of Peter the Great. Tallinn has suffered many occupations but, apart from a Soviet bombing raid in 1944, the city has not been physically harmed as no battles were ever fought there. Its fate was always determined elsewhere, in the 14th just as much as in the 20th century.

The division in Tallinn between what is now the Old Town on the hill (Toompea) and the newer town around the port has survived political administrations of every hue. It has divided God from Mammon, tsarist and Soviet governors from their reluctant Estonian subjects, and now the Estonian parliament from bankers, merchants and manufacturers who thrive on whatever coalition happens to be in power. Tallinn has no Capitol Hill or Whitehall. The parliament building is one of the most modest in the Old Town, dwarfed by the town walls and surrounding churches. When fully restored, the Old Town will be an outstanding permanent monument to Gothic and Baroque architecture, and a suitable backcloth to formal political and religious activity. Outside its formidable wall, contemporary Tallinn will change rapidly according to the demands of the new business ethos. For those arriving by sea, tower blocks now identify Tallinn just as much as the silhouette of the Old Town.

HISTORY

Written records on Tallinn date only from the 12th century although it is clear that a small port existed earlier.

As wood was the only building material used before then, archaeological evidence is sparse. There is the further problem that German and Russian historians were always eager to concentrate on their 'achievements' in later periods and as a result to suggest that little worthy of record happened before their arrival. Research since 1990 in Estonia, coupled with earlier work undertaken in Scandinavia, is now producing evidence of sophisticated trading links across the Baltics from at least the 9th century, and Tallinn is likely to have played a role in this. There are many examples of Estonian jewellery from this time now exhibited in Sweden, to which they had been exported.

In 1219 the Danes occupied Tallinn and much of what is now northern Estonia, on the pretext of spreading Christianity. The name Tallinn dates from this time and in Estonian actually means 'Danish city' (or castle). Although this name was chosen to suggest only temporary occupation, it has been maintained. The first German merchants settled in 1228 and they were to maintain their economic domination until 1939, even during the long periods of Swedish and tsarist rule. Their elaborate coats of arms, displayed in the Dome and Niguliste churches, were a formal expression of this power. When, for instance, the Swedes surrendered to the Russians in 1710, the capitulation documents confirmed that German would remain the official language of commerce. Reval, the German name for Tallinn, is sometimes seen in English publications; it probably comes from Revala, the old Estonian name for the surrounding area. A more colourful explanation is that it comes from the two German words *reh* and *fall*, meaning the falling of the deer as they attempt to escape the Danish occupation.

Tallinn's intense fortifications are inevitably the first visual impression the town makes on a visitor. Much of what we now see dates from the 14th century as the Teutonic Knights quickly saw the value of limestone in building city defences, particularly as it could be quarried from what is now Harjumägi Park, above Freedom Square. Since this is the period when crossbows were giving way to cannons, the walls and their towers became progressively taller and thicker during the 15th and 16th centuries. Kiek in de Kök (see pages 120–1) and Fat Margaret (see page 110) are the best examples of this development with their walls at least 2m thick and sometimes double this. The ground floor was the magazine for ammunition and the top floor served as an open observation tower. Guns were stored on the two or three intermediary floors. The 15th century would see the start of buttresses and also stone piping to protect and store fresh water during a siege. Bastion tunnels were added during the 17th century.

Although Tallinn had no close source for metal, documentary references point to its use in building from the 15th century and many examples from the 16th and 17th centuries are extant. These are not only in windows but also in locks, waterspouts, piping and above all in weather vanes. Iron and copper were the metals largely used, which explains why contemporary designers are still keen to use them.

Peter the Great visited Tallinn on 11 different occasions, so crucial was the city

TALLINN BEFORE WORLD WAR II

Tallinn fascinated me; it is like plenty of other cities with an old part on top of a hill and a new part down below. If that was all I had wanted, I need have gone no further from London than Lincoln. But it was the general atmosphere and the people which so struck me. Here was none of the wealthy prosperity of Stockholm nor the studied modernity of Helsinki. Instead I was seeing a melange that I had met nowhere else with a ferocious grasp at gaiety that was as far removed from the natural happiness of Latindom as from the unbending stolidity of Saxonhood and Scandinavia.

On top of the Tallinn hill, I was in a quarter that might almost have been an English cathedral close. The nobility used to live there, but now it houses government ministries whose gentlemen staff might almost have been English themselves, so perfectly do they speak our tongue. Up and down all Estonia there are plenty of similar gentlemen politely eager to show their hospitality to the stranger and to make a guest welcome to their land.

Coming downhill again, the streets were not the decorous promenades of cultured Finland. Here and there will be a chattering group of girls in what they think are the latest fashions of the Western world and then there could be a couple of old men in huge shabby coats that were probably first worn in Russian days now 20 years past. Everywhere there were students. In a land as new as prairie Canada one rather wonders how on earth they are going to find employment for all these anxious scholars.

By accident I found myself at what the guidebook calls the 'unimpressive Swedish Church of St Michael'. The architecture was indeed unimpressive – I only recall a lot of whitewash – but the congregation was the reverse. These people were so terribly and so whole-heartedly earnest. As the preacher droned on, even I of an alien creed could appreciate their attentiveness. There was no apparent oratory, no gestures, no ritual, nothing but the Word of God and they were following every word with an almost fierce eagerness. There is nothing indifferentist about Estonia.

From Keepers of the Baltic Gates *by John Gibbons, written in autumn 1938.*

Tallinn HISTORY

3

as an ice-free port to his empire. In 1711 he joined Christmas celebrations in Town Hall Square. He would later comment 'If Tallinn had been mine in 1702, I would not have established my residence and the capital city of European Russia on the low-lying land of the Neva River, but I would have done so here.' He instigated the permanent expansion of Tallinn beyond the city walls by building Kadriorg Palace near the coast about 3km from the Old Town. Tallinn was then to enjoy 200 years of peace and increasing prosperity.

Architecturally, the Old Town has always remained the centre of Tallinn and its main attraction. Gert Walter, a Baltic German who settled in East Germany and could therefore return to Tallinn during the Soviet period, describes the Old Town as having 0.5% of the surface area of Tallinn but giving it its entire magic. In 1814, the future US president John Quincy Adams came to Tallinn, when he was the first US minister accredited to St Petersburg. He walked around the city walls in 47 minutes and wrote that he felt transported back to the 12th century. By the end of the Crimean War in 1855, it became evident that the city walls and towers could no longer have any military relevance, and they were handed over to the city authorities. Sadly some were destroyed at that time and it was only from the 1890s that their architectural value became appreciated. Fortunately 27 of the original 46 towers have remained intact.

The completion of the railway link with St Petersburg in 1870 turned Tallinn into a major city. The port was enlarged to handle the increasing volume of goods that could now be brought there and factories were established to take advantage of the larger markets. In the 20th century, most events that would determine Estonia's future took place in Tallinn. Independence was declared there in 1918 and in 1991; German occupations were imposed there also in 1918 and again in 1941. The Soviets came in 1940 and then chased the Germans out in 1944. In the 20th century, the Russians and Germans between them occupied Tallinn seven times, and the country has been independent three times, although it has to be admitted that independence on the first occasion in 1918 lasted for only one day. Britain can claim considerable credit for ensuring that the next period of independence would last much longer – 20 years. Intervention by the Royal Navy during 1918–19 in the Gulf of Finland near Tallinn ensured that neither the Bolsheviks nor the Germans were able to conquer Estonia at that time.

The port always adapted to the political circumstances in which it found itself. During the first independence period from 1920 to 1940 it exported large quantities of timber and dairy products to Britain as the market to the new Soviet Union was lost. Passenger services linked it with all its Baltic neighbours. From 1945 until 1990 it would suffer a moribund 45 years with little international trade being allowed. Sections of the harbour area were closed to the public as a military area and regeneration of this area is still continuing. The twice-weekly ferry service that operated for Finnish visitors from the 1960s rapidly increased to a boat an hour during the 1990s as the notorious 'vodka tourists' poured in, together with some other visitors who had broader interests. Whilst 2.5 million passengers a year come to Tallinn on this route, the port has to battle hard with Russian, Latvian and Lithuanian ports for the transit traffic in goods from Russia and central Asia. Another battle, in which Tallinn has been tremendously successful, is first to encourage cruise ships to berth here, and then to extend their stay. After being rigidly controlled in St Petersburg, passengers enjoy the easy-going mixture of excursions and free time in the Old Town.

Between 1945 and 1990 the city's population doubled in size to 500,000, about 30% of the total population of Estonia. Since then, Tallinn's population, like that of the whole country, has dropped considerably as couples delay starting families and living on one's own becomes more popular. It is now approximately 420,000. The year 2002 was the first since 1990 when more births than deaths were registered and since then the populations of both the town and the country have remained static.

On 26 April 2007 a traffic island in central Tallinn suddenly became a major international news item. Until then, it had been the site of the **Bronze Soldier**, a monument erected in 1945 by the Soviet Union to commemorate their 'liberation' of Tallinn on 22 September 1944. Many formal ceremonies took place there in Soviet times, and after the restoration of independence in 1991 Soviet veterans tended to place wreaths there both on 9 May each year to commemorate the end of the war, and on 22 September. It was thought, too, that a number of bodies had been buried there in 1944 but they had never been identified. These were finally excavated at the time the monument was moved.

The Estonian government planned from early 2007 to move the monument to a military cemetery where, amongst others, some British sailors from the 1918–20 campaign were buried. There were two reasons for this decision. First, what had become a noisy traffic island was no place for a war memorial; and second, its prominence in the town centre was seen as an insult to Estonian sovereignty. Estonia could not forgive Soviet vandalism which led to the destruction of nearly all of the monuments to the fighting in 1918–20, but the government in no way wanted to emulate this behaviour. (Latvia and Lithuania did not have to face this issue since the equivalent monuments in Riga, Vilnius and Kaunas are a long way from the town centre.)

A DESCRIPTION OF TALLINN IN 1984   *Kate Wharton*

I spent last week in one of the saddest cities in the world, Tallinn in Estonia, famed for its medieval and 18th-century architecture. Extraordinarily, this tiny backwater of the Soviet Empire has been in the news recently as its people were warned by the voice of *Pravda*, Moscow's main daily newspaper at the time, that they were not Soviet enough. Suddenly the secrets of this benighted land began to emerge. So, last week, determined to find out about the real Estonia, I became the first Western journalist in the country for many, many months, and certainly the first since Estonia came back into the news.

At issue in Estonia is the enforced Russification of their land and the disappearance of their language and all their customs. The blue, black and white flag of independent Estonia was banished in 1944. Today the Russian flag is everywhere. So is the huge figure of 40, accompanied by a hammer and sickle, to remind everyone that the yoke has been in place for 40 years and is intended to be there in excess of 40 x 40. Already more than half the population, 52%, is Russian rather than Estonian and by 1987, when the vast military harbour outside Tallinn is finished, the proportion will rise to 65%.

About 65,000 Estonians fled to the West in 1944. Thousands more were deported to remote parts of the Soviet Union and most of the present-day dissidents now rot in Russian labour camps. As Ernst Jaakson, Estonian Consul-General in New York, told me: 'There is hardly an Estonian family in existence that has not been separated from its loved ones or nearest relatives as a result of the Soviet occupation.'

Published in The Mail on Sunday, *2 September 1984.*

It has still not been established why on 26 April 2007 several hundred young Russian-speaking males went on the rampage in the streets near the monument, looting the shops and waving their stolen goods at press photographers and television crews. Their behaviour was an acute embarrassment to most Russian speakers in Estonia who either accepted the government view or, if not, would certainly not have wanted their views represented in this way. Many ethnic Russians, disgusted at the behaviour of this small minority, came to express their regrets the following morning to the shopkeepers who had been hit.

The Russian government banned the transmission of pictures from the demonstrations and cut a lot of railway transit traffic through Estonia, even though it was largely members of the Russian-speaking community who worked on the railways. Cyber attacks were launched on Estonia, which for two days seriously harmed communications between Estonia and the outside world, and on the basis of misreporting in the Russian press, many Russian tourists cancelled their holidays in Estonia. President Putin asked them to visit Kaliningrad instead; perhaps some did so, but by Christmas the number of Russian visitors to Tallinn was not much lower than the 2006 figure. In the eyes of most ordinary Russians, the issue, like the soldiers formerly scattered across a traffic island, had been properly buried.

In 2011 Tallinn was the European Capital of Culture, appropriate as the euro was adopted as the national currency that year. The Seaplane Harbour (see page 114) and the rebuilt Television Tower were the two major projects linked to it. Ironically, 2011 would see a large increase in the number of Russian tourists; from then Tallinn really took on a role of presenting Europe to Russians, who found the experience to be totally positive. With Tallinn's increasing multi-culturalism – it elected its first black councillor in the autumn of 2013 – and its architectural and gastronomic diversity, this role makes complete sense and hopefully offers a model for what could and should happen across the border. About 100,000 Russian tourists came to Tallinn over the 2013/14 New Year period, an amazing endorsement from a neighbour whose government had still not signed a border treaty with Estonia.

GETTING THERE

TALLINN AIRPORT The airport is only 3–4km from the town centre. The current terminal was originally built for the Olympics in 1980 and was then completely rebuilt in 1999 to cater for the increasing number of flights expected from abroad. A further extension was built between 2006 and 2008. On 29 March 2009 the airport was renamed after **Lennart Meri**, Estonia's first president after the restoration of independence. It would have been his 80th birthday. The earlier 1950s terminal is now used as a conference centre and private restaurant, so can cater for groups meeting at the start or finish of their programmes. Whilst the technical equipment is totally up to date, the décor has been deliberately left as it was.

The deadline for check-in is only 40 minutes before take-off but this cut-off time is strictly enforced, even for passengers with hand luggage only. However, this is the time at which passengers must reach the check-in desk, not merely join the queue, so during early morning and early evening peak times passengers should allow an hour to ensure they meet this deadline. The exception is in business class where of course there are no queues for check-in.

The airport promotes itself as the 'cosiest' in Europe and it certainly has a more homely feel and a less ruthlessly commercial one than others. There is an art gallery with changing exhibitions by contemporary young painters, a library where passengers are encouraged to exchange books, and free Wi-Fi everywhere. Those who are willing to pay for access to the airport lounge, or have the cost included in their ticket, will be pleasantly surprised by its quietness, large size and the terrace, which is an extra pleasure in the summer. Luggage comes quickly to the carousel after a plane's arrival.

A local bus (number 2) operates from the airport to Viru Square [74 D3] every 20 minutes, Monday to Friday, from around 06.00 to 23.30. There are fewer services at the weekend. It is still not a dedicated service to the airport, continuing to an outlying suburb. It stops *en route* into town at the bus station [74 D6] which is useful for those simply wanting to transit in Tallinn. The fare is €1.60 if paid in cash to the driver, free for those with a Tallinn Card (see page 82) and €1.10 for those who buy a Tallinn travel card.

Passengers arriving on flights after 23.00 should prebook a transfer through their travel agent as not many taxis serve the airport at that time. Taxis are plentiful earlier in the day and are metered. The fare into the town is likely to be about €8–10.

Exchange rates offered at the airport are very poor, so money should be exchanged in town at banks.

There is no tourist office or hotel booking agency at the airport and, as Tallinn hotels are fully booked at certain times of the year, reservations should always be made well beforehand. Flight arrival and departure information is available on www.tallinn-airport.ee.

GETTING AROUND

LOCAL BUSES/TRAMS AND TROLLEYBUSES Many tourists to Tallinn rarely take either a bus or a taxi during their stay, as the Old Town is very close to most of the hotels and the steep narrow roads conveniently restrict traffic to pedestrians only. However, by restricting themselves to this area, visitors miss everything that is cheaply and easily accessible by bus outside the Old Town. There are competing bus companies so exact routes and numbers change from time to time but services are frequent and the public transport map *Tallinn Ühistranspordi kaart*, published by Regio, is updated and reprinted frequently. Some stops have maps but not all do and the names of the stops listed in the timetables are unlikely to mean much to visitors.

Tourists who buy the Tallinn Card (see page 82) travel free of charge on all three forms of transport. Others must either pay the driver €1.60 in cash or buy a travel card. Good bus services operate to Pirita and Rocca al Mare and also to the cheaper suburban hotels. Tram enthusiasts will be pleased at the number of places relevant to tourists which their routes pass. A tram is one of the ways to reach Kadriorg Park [75 F3], with its palace and modern art gallery. The park is the terminus for routes 1 and 3.

LEAVING TALLINN The long-distance bus station (Autobussijaam) [74 D6] is on Lastekodu, off the Tartu road which leads to the airport. The enquiry number is 680 0900 but do not expect English to be spoken. Thankfully, the website, www.tpilet.ee, is in English and some services can be booked online. It gives prices for each bus and the reduced price, if available, for students and pensioners. By travelling midweek from Tuesday to Thursday, pensioners can often get a 50% reduction in their fare. There are no printed timetables but all services are listed on a large departure board showing arrival times and also buses for the return journey. As a bus or taxi takes only a few minutes from the town centre, it is advisable to go a day ahead to book a specific bus and to check timings, if the booking cannot be done online. Whilst in the winter and midweek it may often be easy to catch a bus without prebooking, around the holiday periods and on less frequent services it is essential. Remember to book on an express and not a slower bus for the longer journeys. Prices are fairly low – €15 to Saaremaa and Hiiumaa islands (including the ferry), Narva or Võru, or €10 to the nearer towns of Pärnu or Tartu. A ticket has to be bought for each sector travelled, so a stop between Tallinn and Narva at Lahemaa National Park will require two tickets, not one. Stops of ten minutes are made at least every two hours, which allows time for a cigarette, use of the toilets and purchase of refreshments. Smoking is not allowed on buses.

On most routes, the first bus leaves around 06.00 and the last one around 21.00. To Tartu, they operate every half-hour, and the journey takes two hours. To Narva (three hours) the service is hourly. Buses go every two hours to Pärnu and Viljandi and the journey time in both cases is around two hours. Buses to Kuressaare, the capital of Saaremaa, operate six times a day and a space on the ferry is always guaranteed. Every town in Estonia, plus many villages such as those in Lahemaa National Park, has a bus service from Tallinn, so it is not usually necessary to change *en route*.

TOURIST INFORMATION

A variety of free maps and listings brochures are available at most hotels, but their layout and content is of course dictated by the advertisers who support them. A useful bimonthly publication is *Tallinn In Your Pocket* which is amusing, critical and accurate, so well worth its modest cost. It covers hotels, restaurants, museums and forthcoming events. The entire content is available free online at www. inyourpocket.com. For **local tour operators** see page 54.

TALLINN TOURIST BOARD The tourist board has a shopfront office on the corner of Kullassepa and Niguliste [72 C4] which sells a small range of books, maps and cards, although Raamatukoi's stock, on the opposite corner, is much more extensive. They always have up-to-date editions of *Tallinn In Your Pocket*. There is also a large reference folder with timetables for ferries to Finland, buses out of Tallinn and local railways.

This office, like all other tourist offices around Estonia, has a website: www.tourism. tallinn.ee. Visiting these sites before departure will save a lot of time on arrival.

THE TALLINN CARD Sold at the tourist board office and in many hotels, the Tallinn Card will suit visitors keen to visit a number of museums and the outlying attractions. The cost includes a sightseeing tour, cycling tour, use of public transport and admission to all museums. It can also save money at some shops and restaurants. For those active in the evenings it also includes admission to the Hollywood nightclub. Full details of what is included can be seen on www.tallinn.ee/tallinncard. In 2013 the cost was €24 for 24 hours, €32 for 48 hours and €40 for 72 hours. It therefore becomes excellent value for those staying longer and eager to have a busy sightseeing programme. An active tourist spending three days in Tallinn would certainly spend much more than €40 on transport, admission charges and tours.

WHERE TO STAY

Tallinn now has about 60 hotels but they are often fully booked at weekends, during trade fairs and in the peak summer season. With the influx of Russian tourists that began in 2010, hotels are now full during the first ten days of January when the New

Year leads into the Russian Christmas, and the first ten days in May, when several still-observed Soviet holidays coincide with new Russian ones. Prebooking is therefore always advisable. Specialist travel agents abroad often have access to lower prices than those quoted by the hotels directly, and they may also have allocations at several hotels specifically reserved for them. The year 2009 was, however, the first poor year for hotels, even during the summer, so prices dropped to their 2003 levels. By 2013 they were increasing again, as tourists from Asia were added to the regular number of European visitors.

No new hotels of any size opened between 2009 and 2014, but it was announced in mid-2013 that the first Hilton in the Baltics would open in Tallinn in 2015. The company will take over the current Reval Park Hotel & Casino (*www.parkhotel.ee*) & have assured punters that gambling will continue to be its main *raison d'être*.

The recommendations that follow are obviously rather arbitrary and omission of a hotel should in general be taken as resulting from lack of space rather than necessarily as a criticism. It can be assumed in all cases that the rooms in the hotels mentioned below have private facilities, that the hotel accepts credit cards, and that it has a restaurant and bar. However most hotels have a wide variety of rooms so it is important to check what sort of room is being booked. Many hotels have saunas that guests can use free of charge. Baths are rare in Estonian hotels, even in four-star establishments, so should be specifically requested. However, this problem is slowly being addressed: the **Savoy Boutique Hotel** that opened in 2006, the **Telegraaf** that opened in 2008, and the **Meriton Spa** that opened in 2009 have very few rooms without them. Wi-Fi is never a problem: all hotels offer it free of charge.

The word 'hotel' in Estonian has a double 'l' in the spelling. Some use this in their email and web addresses, whilst others adopt the English spelling with one 'l'. Some change their practice from one to the other, so do check with both spellings if one does not work.

PRICES In luxury hotels expect to pay around €200 a night, in first class €140 and in tourist class €80 for a twin/double, although there is little difference when the room is used as a single.

The more expensive hotels sometimes reduce prices at weekends and in July–August, the local holiday season, whereas the cheaper hotels usually increase them then. The highest rates are charged over Russian and Finnish holidays when hotels in all classes get fully booked. Quoted rates usually include a full buffet breakfast.

Rock-bottom accommodation is hard to find in Tallinn, as is bed and breakfast. There is neither the wherewithal nor the will to make Tallinn backpacker friendly. Most Estonian families do not have a dining room, let alone a spare bedroom, so cannot rent out rooms. In Tallinn run-down buildings, which elsewhere might be converted to hostels, are quickly transformed into offices or exclusive private houses. The increasing number of small hotels that are opening are again unlikely to stimulate demand for inferior accommodation at a not much lower price. The *Tallinn In Your Pocket* website (*www.inyourpocket.com*) always has an up-to-date list of hostels and agencies for arranging long stays in private houses.

See the price codes table given on page 63. For location of listings see maps, pages 72 and 74–5.

LUXURY

⌂ **Schlössle** (27 rooms) Pühavaimu 13/15; ✆699 7700; e sch@schlossle-hotels.com; www.schlossle-hotels.com. A town house owned by many successful Baltic Germans over the years, it was converted during the mid-1990s into Tallinn's first truly luxurious hotel & senior government ministers from abroad often stay here. It still maintains the air of a gracious private residence. There is a small conference centre, but it seems incongruous. The hotel is a setting for constant but unostentatious indulgence, for champagne rather than wine & until the 2007 smoking ban, for cigars rather than for cigarettes. The restaurant, like all the best ones in Tallinn, is in a cellar & has an extensive menu. For those able to abandon this indulgence, the hotel is within walking distance of all the attractions in the Old Town. **$$$$**

⌂ **Telegraaf** (86 rooms) Vene 9; ☏ 600 0600; e info@telegraafhotel.com; www.telegraafhotel. com. When it opened in Apr 2007, it became Tallinn's largest 5-star hotel. Uniquely for the Old Town, it offers a swimming pool, AC, spa rooms & an underground car park, so maintains the intimacy of a boutique hotel whilst offering the facilities of one 2 or 3 times its size. The building dates from the late 19th century, when it was a post & telegram centre, & this façade has been preserved, as has the main staircase inside. Most rooms have baths, rather than just showers, & all have a servery from the corridor, which enables food & drink to be delivered without the staff having to enter the room. Tallinn residents come here regularly for the Tchaikovsky restaurant, given that Estonians have always enjoyed Russian cuisine, if rarely anything else Russian. The music here is always live & is provided by a classical trio on piano, violin & cello. **$$$$**

⌂ **Three Sisters** (23 rooms) Pikk 71; ☏ 630 6300; e info@threesistershotel.com; www. threesistershotel.com. Perhaps because it is so luxurious, the hotel does not bother with an Estonian name as no Estonian could afford to stay here. Housing the Queen & the Duke of Edinburgh in Oct 2006 will ensure its reputation for years to come. It has several similarities to the Schlössle (see above). Both buildings have a history of over 500 years & both can claim famous rather than notorious owners. Here a library is the dominating public room & a member of staff escorts guests into the lift for the 1-floor journey down to the restaurant. Having so few rooms, one even with a piano, the atmosphere of a 19th-century town house can still be maintained. Computers & plenty of other 21st-century paraphernalia are available if needed, but it seems a pity to let modernity intrude. Estonians who wish to impress their friends on the cheap come for lunch here & linger

over a £5/US$8/€7 club sandwich. Foreigners come in the evening for pumpkin soup, pork with chanterelle mushrooms & a particular rarity in Estonia, homemade ice cream. **$$$$**

⌂ **Radisson Blu Hotel Tallinn** (280 rooms) Rävala 3; ☏ 682 3000; e info.tallinn@radissonblu. com; www.radissonblu.com/hotel-tallinn. All the main central Tallinn hotels that opened during the 1990s were conversions of existing buildings. In 2000, the Radisson broke away from that tradition by building from scratch & constructing what was until early 2006 the tallest building in Tallinn (it was subsequently overtaken by Swissôtel). This gave it the advantage of not having to make any compromises & a purpose-built formula was worked out to appeal to both business & leisure travellers. It has often pioneered what other hotels are then forced to copy, such as free Wi-Fi for all guests & proper facilities for the disabled. Another novelty was a special low-level check-in for small children, with toys around should there be any delay. Lounge 24, a rooftop café, gives excellent photo opportunities towards both the Old Town & the new financial area that is growing up (literally) in the immediate vicinity of the hotel. For tourists wanting a more unusual photo, Tallinn Central Prison is easily visible from here. Cultured guests will appreciate the paintings in the lobby area by Kaido Ole, one of Estonia's best-known contemporary artists. The restaurant & Lounge 24 have been priced to cater for local patrons too, so are not as high as might have been expected in a 4-star hotel. **$$$$**

⌂ **St Petersbourg** (27 rooms) Rataskaevu 7; ☏ 628 6500; e stp@schlossle-hotels.com; www. schlossle-hotels.com. The St Petersbourg is under the same management as the deluxe Schlössle Hotel (see pages 83–4) & suits those who want a comfortable Old Town address plus some luxury. It may well be the oldest hotel in Tallinn, as it has had this role under every single regime of the 20th century. Its location near to many famous clubs & restaurants appeals to visitors who can dispense with sleep for much of the night. Those who cannot should request a room on the top floor. It is one of the very few hotels in Tallinn to offer a babysitting service. **$$$$**

⌂ **Savoy Boutique Hotel** (44 rooms) Suur-Karja 17–19; ☏ 680 6688; e savoy@tallinnhotels.ee;

www.tallinnhotels.ee/savoy-boutique-hotel-tallinn. The Old Town location & baths in nearly all of the rooms will appeal to older tourists wanting a leisurely stay. This should however be midweek as nearby bars become rowdy at w/ends. Unusual facilities here include free landline phone calls throughout Estonia, wooden shutters to keep out the early-morning summer sun, AC & handmade iron curtain rails. The charger for laptops & mobiles has cleverly been put into the safe, so that they can be left securely in the rooms. Its bar/café has unusual features too. It is decorated with mini tiles & those who like to sit at the bar do so in armchairs, not on stools. The contrast could not be greater with the stag bars 100m away at the other end of Suur-Karja. **$$$$**

🏠 **Barons** (33 rooms) Suur-Karja 7; 📞 699 9700; e barons@baronshotel.ee; www.baronshotel. ee. For every bank that closes in Tallinn a new hotel opens, but in this case it is on the same site. 13 different banks in fact occupied the building during the 20th century. Some doors as a result do seem excessively secure. Visitors will find it hard to believe that Barons opened in 2003 rather than 1903, since the panelling, the minute lift, the sombre colour schemes & the illustrations of Tallinn are all from the earlier date. So is the name of the road: 'karja' means 'to herd', as cattle used to be led to pasture along it. Whenever renovation is carried out, more & more decoration from the early 20th century comes to light. The view from many rooms & from the restaurant over the Old Town will again keep the 21st century away. It is also being kept away in the basement, which is a cigar lounge standing up to non-smoking pressures elsewhere. For once it is sensible to go upstairs to eat in Tallinn, rather than downstairs, as the restaurant here is on the 1st floor, a proper distance from the cigars. Try to avoid Fri & Sat nights here, when the hotel is an oasis of quiet against a backdrop of raucous behaviour in the surrounding bars. No rooms have baths but the suites have jacuzzis. **$$$**

🏠 **Cru Hotel** (15 rooms) Viru 8; 📞 611 7600; e cruhotel@cruhotel.eu; www.viruinn.ee.cruhotel. eu. It is perhaps surprising that this was the first hotel to convert an old town house as carefully as possible into a boutique hotel. It opened in May 2006 with beams providing constant obstruction, such is the eagerness to preserve rather than to convert. Access is difficult for both the old & the very young, given the number of stairs & the

length of the corridors. Needless to say, there is no lift. The positive side of this scenario is that the fit & the middle-aged will enjoy an escape from all-too-modern Viru Street back into the 19th century, & the assurance that no families or rowdy youngsters will disturb them there. Good soundproofing ensures their isolation. Regular visitors will remember the former name of this hotel, Viru Inn. **$$$**

🏠 **Domina PK Ilmarine** (105 rooms) Pohja 23; 📞 614 0900; www.pkhotels.eu. This hotel is located in what was once Estonia's major machine-tool factory from the tsarist period until World War II, a business so well regarded during the country's first period of independence that both the president & the prime minister invested in it. During Soviet times it became a hearing-aid factory but today the building has been converted into a surprisingly modern hotel. Its location outside the Old Town gives it more space, with large bedrooms & public areas, as well as ample parking space for coaches & private cars. A children's playground is very close. Part of the hotel is allocated to flats for long-stay guests. **$$$**

🏠 **Kalev Spa** (100 rooms) Aia 18; 📞 649 3300; e kalevspa@kalevspa.ee; www.kalevspa.ee. Around 2000, Estonians suddenly discovered that they needed to keep healthy, so spas & gyms sprung up around the country, particularly on the coast. This spa hotel, which opened in early 2006, was the first one in a town centre, so its facilities, including a very welcome swimming pool, are geared as much to residents as to visitors from outside. Their use is free to hotel guests. The restaurant overlooks the pool, which may make overindulgent guests feel guilty. **$$$**

🏠 **Merchant's House** (37 rooms) Dunkri 4–6; 📞 697 7500; e info@merchantshousehotel.com; www.merchantshousehotel.com. In summer 2005, a formula that had worked so well in Riga at the Gutenbergs Hotel finally reached Tallinn. Woodwork & frescoes dating from the 14th–16th centuries have been integrated into a hotel that will satisfy even the most fastidious customer. Rooms vary in size & shape, as do the corridors, but short detours to reach them are a small price to pay for such a special environment. Given the round-the-clock activity on Dunkri, it is good that only 3 of the rooms face it, & that the library, which also does, is so well soundproofed. The 'winter' restaurant is among the cellars of the basement, the 'summer' one in the courtyard on to which most rooms face. Tallinn's first ice bar is on the ground floor &, on a similar theme, it is worth mentioning that all rooms have AC, an important asset for several weeks during the summer. The temptations at the ice bar can be viewed on their website, www.icebar.ee. Tallinn's only vegetarian restaurant, Urban (*www.urbanrestoran.ee*), opened here in Nov 2013. **$$$**

🏠 **Meriton Grand Conference & Spa Hotel** (465 rooms) Paldiski mnt 4; 667 7111; e hotel@ meritonhotels.com; www.meritonhotels.com. When the Tervise Paradiis opened in Pärnu a few years ago (see pages 244–5), few people could have thought that any other hotel in Estonia would equal or surpass it in the range of treatments offered, but that has now happened here. Having the largest swimming pool in Estonia (free to guests during the morning) & a variety of watersports to accompany it, Tallinn has brought the coast to its centre. With its conference facilities & array of different restaurants the hotel will probably succeed in keeping many guests within its ample glass doors for their entire stay. Those wanting to keep fit will find many different challenges in the gym. Each floor is named after a different Estonian village & its designs are part of the carpets & curtains. Most rooms have baths; only 10% have showers. Trpl rather than dbl glazing ensures that no sound whatsoever can penetrate from outside the building. Chinese food has always been a disappointment in Tallinn but at long last there is a restaurant here rightly patronised by as many locals as guests at the hotel. **$$$**

🏠 **Nordic Forum** (270 rooms) Viru Väljak 3; 622 2900; e forum@nordichotels.eu; www. nordichotels.eu. Being situated just outside the Old Town, this hotel offers the space that those inside cannot. Having opened in 2007 as a completely new building, it has all the modern amenities that other older ones cannot necessarily manage, so there is full AC, soundproofing & access for the disabled. Walking for tourists to the main sites & for business visitors to the financial centre are equally convenient. Of particular appeal is the large rooftop swimming pool. Those who can afford it should book one of the corner rooms with their extensive views & large private saunas. See advert on inside back cover.**$$$**

🏠 **Old Town Maestro** (23 rooms) Suur-Karja 10; 626 2000; e maestro@maestrohotel.ee;

www.maestrohotel.ee. This small hotel now has its midweek regulars who want straightforward furnishings, peace & quiet & yet an Old Town location. Sadly Suur-Karja becomes a very different street at the w/end & needs to be avoided then. Rooms are much bigger than might be expected from a converted town house but the lift is much smaller – it can take only 1 person with a case at a time. The road is traffic-free but that does mean wheeling cases along the cobbles on arrival & departure. The reception area doubles up as a bar, which adds to the family atmosphere. The sauna & the business centre are, surprisingly, side by side on the top floor. Photographers should bring their cameras for the unusual views over the town. **$$$**

🏠 **Palace** (87 rooms) Vabaduse Väljak; 640 7300; e palace@tallinnhotels.ee; www. tallinnhotels.ee. The hotel brochure claims it has offered 'excellent service since 1937' & this is definitely true. Although many other hotels now match its facilities, Estonians are very loyal to it as the hotel was one of the few links from the first independence period that remained throughout the Soviet era. Embassies were briefly set up in the hotel in 1991 before foreign legations could reclaim their pre-war buildings. It is now equally conveniently situated for tourists interested in the Old Town & business visitors needing the government ministries. In 1997 President Meri opened a Presidential Suite, which will doubtless remain one of the most expensive in Tallinn at €350 per night, but the remaining 86 rooms are more modestly priced. **$$$**

🏠 **Radisson Blu Hotel Olümpia** (400 rooms) Liivalaia 33; 631 5333; e olumpia. tallinn@radissonblu.com; www.radissonblu. com/olumpiahotel-tallinn. Built originally for the Olympic Games in 1980, this hotel is now the firm favourite of foreign business visitors to Tallinn & is regularly upgraded. In recent years it has been concentrating on more family facilities, with play areas for children. Guests are often joined by the local expat community, which has a particular affinity for the 1960s music played in the Bonnie & Clyde nightclub. At w/ends & during the summer, rates drop to attract tourists paying their own way. Tour operators can obtain further discounts if bookings are also made at other Radisson hotels in the Baltics &/or in St Petersburg. All rooms are now at least of 4-star standard & the reception staff work very quickly during the arrival & departure 'rush hours'. The restaurant on the top floor offers excellent views of the Old Town & many rooms do so as well. With the gym high up too, the same views will reward anyone working out. $$$

🏠 **Santa Barbara** (53 rooms) Roosikrantsi 2a; ☎640 7300; e reservations@stbarbara.ee; www. stbarbara.ee. The austere limestone façade from the turn of the century hides a very professional operation. Both children & pets are welcome, & the soundproofing can handle any noise either may make. AC had not arrived by 2013 so upstairs rooms could get hot in midsummer. There is a car park at the rear. The cellar restaurant is completely German, with not the slightest intrusion from Estonia or anywhere else. The hotel has 53 rooms so staff get to know all the guests, many of whom are now regulars. $$$

🏠 **Swissôtel** (238 rooms) Tornimäe 3; ☎624 0000; e tallinn@swissotel.com; www.swissotel. com/hotels/tallinn. It was not surprising that in 2007, just before the credit crunch, the Radisson should have a competitor arising over the road; what is surprising is that it had taken 8 years for another chain to embark on this competition. (After a further 8 years, in 2015, Hilton would come to Tallinn.) It redefined 'international' in Estonia, since it looked east as well as west. All staff have to speak Russian as well as English & all the sales material is in 3 languages. Rooms start on the 12th floor & continue to the 29th, with executive ones being on floors 27–29. There are no sgl rooms as such, just dbls with separate baths & showers. Only a few twins have just a shower. Amongst the novelties in each room are espresso machines, ironing boards & fresh flowers. Adaptors are not needed as all rooms are equipped with 3-pin sockets to meet the needs of European, British & American plugs. There are 3 further plugs in the safe, for recharging laptops & mobiles. $$$

🏠 **Ülemiste** (128 rooms) Lennujaama tee 2; ☎603 2600; e sales@ylemistehotel.ee; www. ylemistehotel.ee. Being beside the airport, this hotel inevitably appeals to travellers with early or late flights, & as a new building it caters well for the disabled. The regular airport bus stops outside the hotel & takes about 10–15 mins from there into the town centre. As the hotel has 128 rooms, it can cater for large groups & has the parking space for both coaches & private cars. Space is the theme, too, in the entrance, the lobby & in the rooms. It is worth paying extra for top-floor rooms with a view over the lake. Tourists from the EU eager to take advantage of Estonia's shopping opportunities will find the location next to a major shopping centre very convenient. Prices charged there (in Rimi for alcohol, tobacco & chocolate & in Jysk for linen, handiwork & kitchen tools) are much lower than those charged in the town centre or in the shops at the airport. For those prepared to take the risk, some vacant rooms are sold at half-price after 23.00. $$$

🏠 **Vana Wiru** (80 rooms) Viru 11; ☎669 1500; e hotel@vanawiru.ee; www.vanawiru.ee. Viru Street is always full of tourists but most will not know of the existence of this hotel as its entrance is at the back. Its vast marble lobby suggests luxury but in fact the 80 rooms are of a standard size & mostly with showers rather than baths. Few have good views but with a location beside the city wall, one can forgive anything. Groups will like the convenient coach park right beside the entrance. The hotel is part of the Baltic Hotel group which also includes the Imperial (see page 88) & the Promenaadi in Haapsalu (see page 235). $$$

🏠 **Viru** (500 rooms) Viru Väljak 4; ☎630 1390; e viru.reservation@sok.fi; www.viru.ee, www. sokoshotels.fi. When built in 1972 for Intourist, the hotel was Tallinn's first skyscraper. Being the centre of the tourism trade for much of the Soviet era, during the 1990s the enormous Viru initially found it hard to redefine its role in the face of competition & ever-rising standards. By 2000 it had finally undergone a complete renovation & can now serve both business clients & fastidious tourists. Particularly since its takeover by the Sokos group, it has become very biased towards Finnish clients, some of whom can provide unwanted liveliness late on Fri & Sat evenings. Its location is excellent for the Old Town & of course for the Virukeskus, the shopping centre now part of the same complex. Tourists determined to have a bath rather than shower are more likely to succeed here. Throughout 2006, it negotiated with the town council for permission to build further, but these plans met fierce resistance as they would have intruded on one of the very few open spaces in central Tallinn. In view of the credit crunch, the hotel is probably now glad that these plans were not realised. In 2011, it opened the KGB Museum on the 23rd floor. See page 198 for further details. In 2012 a rooftop cinema followed, active from mid-May until the end of August. $$$

🏠 **Von Stackelberg** (52 rooms) Toompuiestee 23; 📞 660 0700; e vsh@uniquestay.com; www. uniquestay.com. In early 2009 this new name appeared on what had been for several years the Uniquestay, but many of the best features were retained, including Uniquestay management, & the hotel has been upgraded. In 2014 it will add a further building & a garden, a welcome & rare extra in Tallinn hotels. This will have 9 rooms & will add underground parking to the facilities offered in the hotel. The von Stackelbergs were for generations a famous Baltic-German family & this was their Tallinn house. All rooms have tea-/coffee-making facilities & a computer. Most have a bath too. Half are standard & half are Zen, with all the therapeutic furniture that goes with such a designation. However the Spa Centre goes even further, with literally top-to-toe treatment available so some guests understandably spend more time there than sightseeing in Tallinn. Uniquestay also run Vihula Manor in Lahemaa National Park (see pages 140–1) & booking both hotels together makes an attractive 'town & country' package. Much of the food served at the hotel restaurant La Bohème comes from the farm at Vihula. See advert on page 152. **$$$**

TOURIST CLASS

🏠 **City Hotel Portus** (107 rooms) Uus Sadama 23; 📞 680 6600; e portus@tallinnhotels.ee; www. portus.ee. Regular visitors to Tallinn will remember this hotel as the Saku, named after the brewery & which provided a glass of beer at check-in. If the ambience is slightly more sober now, this is undoubtedly a hotel for the young & lively. Rooms have their numbers painted on them, so that guests with uncertain late-night vision can still hopefully find the right one. It is in the port, so convenient for those also visiting Helsinki. The beer store has been converted into a children's playroom but the corridors are still painted red, orange & yellow. The Italian restaurant offers a surprisingly good meal with which to start or finish a stay in Tallinn. Bus number 20 stops outside the door, which is convenient for those who do not want to take the 15min walk into town or risk being ripped off by the notorious taxi drivers based at the port. **$$**

🏠 **Imperial** (32 rooms) Nunne 14; 📞 627 4800; e imperial@baltichotelgroup.com; www.imperial. ee. Like the Konventa Seta in Riga, this hotel is

built into the town wall, which is therefore being preserved as part of it. Although on one of the few real roads in the Old Town, the location is quiet. Rooms vary greatly in size & protruding beams sometimes add more of a medieval ambience than some guests would wish. Its restaurant is known for including cheese in all its dishes, even in the final cup of coffee. **$$**

🏠 **Kreutzwald** (84 rooms) Endla 23; 📞 666 4800; e reserv.kwh@uhotelsgroup.com; www. kreutzwaldhotel.com. The bland location of the hotel on one of the main roads leading from the town centre should not put anyone off from entering. There are then many incentives for staying put including flat-screen computers in every room, the hallmark of the Unique Group that took over the hotel in 2006. The basement is now the life & soul of the place, with a gym, several saunas, a massage centre & Nipernaadi, an Estonian restaurant. A map on the wall shows the many areas of Estonia from which its food is sourced. A ground-floor café/restaurant caters for those wanting a lighter meal or just a drink. Given the gastronomic desert that surrounds the hotel, the variety offered by the 2 hotel restaurants is a godsend. Car drivers will appreciate the on-site parking available, a rare privilege so close to the Old Town. See advert on page 152. **$$**

🏠 **L'Ermitage** (91 rooms) Toompuiestee 19; 📞 699 6400; e reservations@lermitagehotel.ee; www.lermitagehotel.ee. Despite being located on a main road, this hotel is in many respects quieter than others as it is so well soundproofed; late-night revellers do not get this far from the Old Town as they would actually have to walk for 10mins. They would also object to the hotel being totally non-smoking & twin beds rather than dbls being the norm. Half the rooms have showers, & the other half baths. It appeals to groups, as coaches can stop directly in front & it is not big enough to make it impersonal. Hopefully this stays the case when a new wing with 31 rooms opens early in 2014. Those on their own are rewarded with the views of the town wall from the sgl rooms on the 6th floor. **$$**

🏠 **Meriton Old Town Garden Hotel** (50 rooms) Lai 24/Pikk 29; 📞 667 7111; e reservations@meritonhotels.com; www. meritonhotels.com. The hotel stretches between 2 main streets in Tallinn Old Town & the garden provides a courtyard in the middle. Apart from here, the hotel is totally non-smoking. 9 of the rooms are basic economy, with bunk beds, but the others are all fully furnished & incorporated into the largely wooden fabric of the old building. Even though this building has a lift from the ground to the 3rd floor, the hotel is best suited to the short & to the fit. The standard rooms all have tea- & coffee-making facilities in the room. Clients in the standard rooms can use the swimming pool & gym of the Meriton Grand (see page 86). The location could not be better for sightseers & its restaurant Eesti Söögituba (Estonian Dining Room) really lives up to that name, with not a single foreign dish on the menu, & whilst there is a wine list, it would certainly be more sensible to drink beer here. $$

🏠 **Meriton Old Town Hotel** (40 rooms) Lai 49; 📞 614 1300; e reservations@meritonhotels.com; www.meritonhotels.com. Those who normally shun 2- or 3-star hotels may well accept such a standard here, given that most rooms have views over the Old Town, of St Olav's Church or towards the harbour. There is also the added appeal of the hotel being built into the city wall. Being on the edge of the Old Town, the place is quiet yet with a reasonably central location, within walking distance of many museums & shops. It is worth paying the slightly higher costs for the rooms on the 4th floor, with their larger size, baths rather than showers & above all for the views. The basement rooms make up for the total lack of a view with the skilfully implanted use of the old city wall. The Russian restaurant, like its Estonian opposite number in the Meriton Garden Hotel, is 100% Russian, except that the staff will speak English if necessary. $$

🏠 **Pirita Convent Guesthouse** [off map, page 75] (21 rooms) Merivälja 18; 📞 605 5000; e pirita@osss.ee; www.osss.ee. For anyone determined to have quiet at night, this is undoubtedly the place to go for. Ideal guests are those who have dinner here & then go to their rooms. The yachting harbour of Pirita is 3km northeast of the town & the ruined convent with this new guesthouse is set well back from the main road. Prices, too, are provincial rather than Tallinn. Tourists with a car will be happy with the space here & others will be pleased that after 500 years a religious order is finally active on the site again. $$

🏠 **Shnelli** (124 rooms) Toompuiestee 37; 📞 631 0100; e reservations@gohotels.ee; www.gohotels. ee. As part of the much-needed renovation of the

railway station, this hotel opened beside it in 2005. It is a straightforward 3-star hotel with the 'green' rooms facing the park below the Old Town & the 'blue' hopefully facing a sea & sky which display this colour, but which also overlook the platforms of the railway stations. The former obviously cost rather more. The railway theme predominates and is even reflected in the design of the corridor carpets. A covered walkway links the hotel to the station & its restaurant. As with stations everywhere now, the trains are less important than the shops to which most of the space has been let. The restaurant is much cheaper than any similar one in the Old Town, & particularly at w/ends offers a pleasantly quiet place to dine. There is little risk of being disturbed by trains using the station, even when services on the major routes double in 2014. Sgl visitors hoping to change their status whilst in Tallinn may want to take advantage of the rooms only let to 2 people after midnight for €32, subject to availability. Make sure you get there before 04.00, when prices revert to normal. $$

🏠 **Susi** (100 rooms) Peterburi 48; 📞 630 3300; e susi@susi.ee; www.susi.ee. An estate agent would probably describe the location as 'unprepossessing' since it is surrounded by factories & a petrol station & is on the wide St Petersburg motorway. It is literally the high point of Tallinn, at 55m above sea level. On 14 May 1343, the St George's Night rebellion took place here. It had started further north on 23 Apr & this was the nearest point to Tallinn that Estonian forces would reach. Over 10,000 were killed in a desperate attempt to overthrow the Teutonic Knights. A plaque in the hotel lobby commemorates the battle, as does the park on the other side of the road where there are several further monuments. The hotel is more comfortable & more modern than the other tourist-class hotels outside the centre & is easily accessible by tram. The pictures displayed on its staircase put many of Tallinn's museums to shame. There are oils, lithographs & watercolours showing contemporary & historical Tallinn; other pictures are of country scenes. They are well lit & sensibly framed & of course can be seen 24hrs a day. Should the lift break down, this gallery is more than adequate compensation. The hotel suits many groups as parking is easy, as is access to the airport & the Tartu road. $$

🏠 **Poska Villa** (8 rooms) Poska 15; 📞 601 3601; e poskavilla@venu.ee; www.hot.ee/poskavilla. For those who prefer simplicity in the quiet ambience of Kadriorg to the pace & sophistication of central Tallinn, this villa with its garden is ideal. The tram into town is about 10 mins' walk away, some buses are closer, but probably more enticing is Kadriorg Park with its palace, formal & informal gardens, museums & KUMU. **$**

APARTMENT RENTAL This option is becoming popular for both tourists and business visitors, particularly as letting companies are flexible on the length of stay, so even a few days is quite possible. Much of Estonia is reachable as a day trip from Tallinn so an apartment can be used as a base for exploration elsewhere. Two specialist companies are active in this field:

🏠 **Old House** Rataskaevu 16; 🕿 641 1464; e apartments@oldhouse.ee; www.oldhouse.ee

🏠 **Tallinn City Apartments** Pärnu mnt 10; 🕿 525 5321; e welcometotallinn@gmail.com; www.tca.ee. See advert on page 70.

✖ WHERE TO EAT AND DRINK

There is now such a choice of restaurants in Tallinn that it is invidious to attempt a shortlist. Every major nation is represented and more unusual ones include Argentina, Georgia, Lithuania and Scotland. Hawaiian and Thai food appeared for the first time in 2000, Czech and Arabic food followed in 2002 and by 2003 Russian food had also staged a comeback, having been completely rejected in the years immediately following independence. By late 2005 they had been joined by African, Armenian and Cuban restaurants. Then 2006 saw the first regional restaurant, a Tuscan one rather than just 'Italian', so perhaps Provençal and Sichuan restaurants will in due course follow. After the Russian war with Georgia in 2008, Estonians showed their hostility to Russia by eating in the Georgian restaurants that then sprang up. At the time of writing in late 2013, nobody has opened a revivalist Soviet restaurant, though the success of such ventures in Riga and in former East Berlin must in due course tempt some members of the Russian-speaking community in Tallinn. The new Soviet Life exhibition (see page 112) is a likely venue for the first one here.

The one surprising lack early in 2013 was a totally vegetarian restaurant, but this was remedied in the **Merchant's House Hotel** (see pages 85–6) in November 2013 with the opening there of the Urban vegetarian restaurant. Readers of earlier editions of this book may miss Eesti Maja, Sisalik and Toscana on their return to Tallinn after a few years but they will find an ample choice to replace them.

By 2010 'Estonian' restaurants were opening, which had little to do with the cuisine this might have signified during the first period of independence. It simply referred to the use of locally sourced materials, rather than to any tradition.

A welcome trend that accelerated from 2008 is for restaurants to open away from the Old Town. This was first in Kadriorg, near the palace and then from 2011 in Kalamaja, behind the railway station in an area that no tourist would previously have dreamt of visiting.

Quite a number are listed below and the minor inconvenience in reaching them will be more than compensated by greater space, lower prices and often original décor. I have yet to find a restaurant that bans piped music from its public areas, although this can be arranged in private rooms. I would be delighted to hear from any readers who do. A dark entrance, down poorly maintained stairs in a side street, is usually an indication that good food and value lie ahead. Bright lights at street level should be avoided.

The cost of wine varies enormously between restaurants, and is often as high as in Britain or the USA. Sticking to beer saves a lot of money – and it is, after all, an

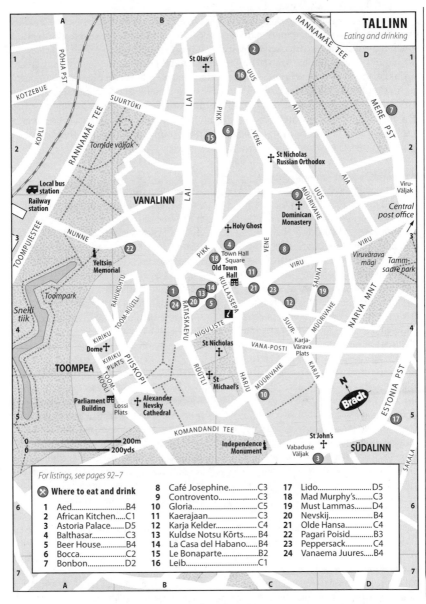

TALLINN
Eating and drinking

For listings, see pages 92–7

⊗ **Where to eat and drink**

1	Aed.........................B4
2	African Kitchen.....C1
3	Astoria Palace.......D5
4	Balthasar................C3
5	Beer House............B4
6	Bocca......................C2
7	Bonbon...................D2

8	Café Josephine..............C3
9	Controvento...................C3
10	Gloria..............................C5
11	Kaerajaan........................C3
12	Karja Kelder....................C4
13	Kuldse Notsu Kõrts.......B4
14	La Casa del Habano......B4
15	Le Bonaparte.................B2
16	Leib..................................C1

17	Lido............................D5
18	Mad Murphy's.........C3
19	Must Lammas.........D4
20	Nevskij......................B4
21	Olde Hansa.............C4
22	Pagari Poisid...........B3
23	Peppersack..............C4
24	Vanaema Juures.....B4

Estonian national drink. A small beer is 0.3 litres and a large one is 0.5 litres. On Old Town Square and in the immediate vicinity, reckon to pay about €4 for a small beer and €6 for a large one. Elsewhere €2.50 and €4 are the more normal charges. Excluding drink, expect to pay about €12 for a two-course lunch and €35 for a three-course dinner. At lunchtime many restaurants have a dish of the day – *päevapraad* – and in late 2013 it was possible to pay €4.50 for a substantial portion of meat and vegetables. This Estonian word is often not translated, presumably in the hope that foreigners will instead pay three times as much for similar dishes on the main menu.

Most of the following restaurants have been open for several years and are popular with tourists, expats and local residents. I have, however, deliberately included some that are not well known abroad and which cannot afford to advertise. Apologies in advance to the many other excellent restaurants that, with more space, would also have been included. Websites are listed so that menu planning can begin abroad and not just at the table. Restaurants are usually good at keeping these up to date, and for those in a rush it is possible to prebook not only a table but also the meal. Eating in hotels is popular in Tallinn and some of their restaurants are covered in the hotel descriptions. For information on restaurant opening times see page 63 and for location of listings see maps on pages 72, 74–5 and 91.

LUXURY

✕ **Bocca** Olevimägi 9; ☎641 2610; www. bocca.ee. A passer-by on the pavement here who happened to notice the plain glass windows with the 2 canvas panels behind them would not believe that during 2003 Bocca got more publicity abroad than all other Tallinn restaurants put together. Publicity has rightly continued, if not at quite such a frantic pace. Only the cars parked outside suggest considerable opulence inside. Critics liked the modern minimalist layout against the medieval backdrop of very solid limestone. They liked the changing lighting schemes – & the fact that plenty of modest pasta dishes were available if octopus & veal seemed unnecessarily extravagant. The glitterati have long since moved on, but standards here have stayed the same. $$$$

✕ **Gloria** Müürivahe 2; ☎640 6800; www. gloria.ee. The restaurant's publicity proudly mentions that it opened in 1937, but oddly its décor suggests that it is at least 40–50 years older. Electric light seems a recent intrusion & it is unlikely any 20th-century accountant would have been in favour of the amount of space & types of materials used. If an example of glass or porcelain from that time by chance does not appear on the table, look for it in the display cases in the foyer. Corks & corkscrews are also exhibited in this way. Private alcoves are the norm for dining here, although a larger room caters for parties who need to be together. A band plays most evenings, so don't forget to dress for the dance floor. The menu is short but sufficient & the service is what is to be expected in a restaurant of this type. All the ingredients are top quality but more imagination & variety is needed in the sauces. Prices for the food & wine are astronomical by Tallinn standards, but not for other drinks, so make the most here of cocktails & coffee & savour the Estonia/Russia of 1900. $$$$

✕ **Kaerajaan** Raekoja plats 17; ☎615 5400; www.kaerajaan.ee. Opening a classy restaurant in 2008 based on Estonian food proved a number of points. Firstly, Estonians did not need to be ashamed of their own dishes; secondly, the credit crunch would not deter serious eaters in Tallinn; & thirdly, a location with a view over Town Hall Square has to succeed. Allow a long evening here & do not worry about the high cost. It will be worthwhile & the experience will be genuinely Estonian. $$$$

FIRST CLASS

✕ **Balthasar** Raekoja plats 11; ☎627 6400; www.balthasar.ee. Garlic dominates every course here, even the ice cream, but above all in the salads. Whilst other dishes do appear on the menu, they tend to be as appetising to a meat-eater as a vegetarian option in a steakhouse. The restaurant took over the top floor of the former pharmacy (see page 107) & has kept as many of the original wooden furnishings as was practical. With the restaurant's views over the Town Hall Square it is tempting to linger here, but it also offers a quiet respite over lunch between morning & afternoon sightseeing tours. The range of short drinks at the bar can be equally tempting at other times of day. $$$

✕ **Controvento** Katariina käik; ☎644 0470; www.controvento.ee. What is unique about this restaurant (& a rare occurrence in Tallinn) is that it could keep the review written when it first opened in 1992. It has the same menu, décor & probably many of the same clients, who want no-nonsense home cooking in an Italian bistro with no attempts to emulate culinary fads. Prices have had to increase somewhat but they remain modest in comparison with the competition in the Old Town. $$$

✕ **Gourmet Coffee** Koidula 13a; ☎661 3035; www.barista.ee. Despite its name, few people actually come here just for coffee or even just for tea. Many will drink neither, having a light meal with beer or wine. Situated in Kadriorg, it is unusual in mixing locals & tourists, but both welcome the play area for children & the leisurely atmosphere. Those who do ask for coffee will greatly please the staff: they are happy to show off their knowledge on this topic & to meet customers who appreciate it. $$$

✕ **Kadriorg** Weizenbergi 18; ☎601 3636; www.restorankadriorg.ee. People-watching from restaurants in the town centre tends to involve horror at misbehaving foreigners or concern for the rushing Estonians. The location of this restaurant, on a 1st floor above the tram stop for Kadriorg Park & Palace, gives views of a totally different kind. The passers-by here have time, grace & are relaxed. Raucous stag parties would never make it this far, nor would anyone counting their time in minutes rather than in hours. The kitchen faces inwards & is totally surrounded by glass, so diners can see what goes into each dish. The food is Italian & the wine list is longer than the menu. Priorities here are clearly Italian too. $$$

✕ **Leib** Uus 31; ☎611 9026; www.leibresto. ee. Only in Estonia could a successful restaurant call itself Leib, which means 'black bread'. Many restaurants opened in 2012 & 2013 with an Estonian theme, but this is probably the only one to restrict itself to Estonian ingredients. It is fortunate that this allows for such a wide range of poultry, meat & fish, not to mention the crucial herbs. Wines of course have to come from various countries, & they certainly have varying prices, but it seems a pity not just to stick to beer at €3 for half a litre. $$$

✕ **Nevskij** Rataskaevu 7; ☎628 6565; www. hotelstpetersbourg.com/nevskij-restaurant. Estonians understandably hate everything Soviet but here they are transported back to the tsarist regime, with the furnishings & service as much as with the food. Vodka is the only bond between the 19th & the 21st centuries. Such is the congenial ambience that not only are Estonians willing to speak Russian here, they are happy to give the food its due, & stay all evening. If communism left a bad taste, revived tsarism does not. $$$

✕ **Olde** Hansa Vanaturg 1; ☎627 9020; www. oldehansa.com. Ignore the silly name & even sillier costumes worn by the staff but enjoy the candles (there is no electric light) & the genuinely Estonian live music. Some tables are for 2 but don't venture in for a quiet, intimate evening. This is really a party venue so come as a group & with a very empty stomach. Portions are enormous, even for soup & ice cream. $$$

MODERATE

✕ **Aed** (Garden) Rataskaevu 8; ☎626 9088; www.restoranaed. This is not a totally vegetarian restaurant, even though 'aed' means 'garden', but it is the next best thing. The vegetables & the sauces are what diners remember here, considering the general lack of quality of both elsewhere in Tallinn. Its opening during the bitter winter of early 2006 made this an even more effective selling point. If the courtyard at the back were a little bigger, one could imagine all the herbs used growing there in pots. The large TV screens do not show football matches, or shrieking old rock stars, but a constantly changing selection of classical paintings. The restaurant is small for the Old Town, but this might be a plus as it keeps out loud stag groups. $$

✕ **African Kitchen** Uus 34; ☎644 2555; www. africankitchen.ee. Cheap & cheerful, this restaurant also has a lot to offer. Beer at €3 a half-litre & serious main courses for under €10 were certainly unusual elsewhere in the Old Town in 2013. Even more unusual is the dedicated, so isolated, smoking room. The menu is diverse, & the website to the point. There's also an equal spread across the continent with 1 cocktail (& only 1) from each of 25 different African countries & all at the same price. Come here with a group or be willing to become part of one. This is not the place for dining à deux. Live music is played, with no extra costs, every Fri & Sat evening. $$

✕ **Beer House** Dunkri 5; ☎627 6524; www. beerhouse.ee. This should really be called Bierhaus, so German is the architecture, food & of course the beer. A wine list & pizza will be brought if requested, but it makes much better sense to have one of the 7 different beers brewed on site together with grotesque quantities of roast meat. Then imagine you are in Munich before ordering some apple pie or chocolate cake. Live music only comes late in the evening, as it would do in Germany. $$

✕ **Cantina Carramba** Weizenbergi 20a; ☎601 3431; www.carramba.ee. Opening in Kadriorg outside the town centre in 2004 was certainly a gamble, but it has definitely paid off, as the subsequent arrival over the next 10 years of other restaurants in the area has proved. The variety of Mexican food, not to mention its low cost, is certainly worth the 10min tram ride it may take to get here. Onion rings in beer dough is one of the many original dishes served. The menu displays little pepper symbols alongside many of the dishes, so you can see how hot they are; 1 pepper indicates medium whereas 3 is really hot. As it is open during the day, an afternoon visit to the palace or KUMU can be followed by an early supper here. When ordering, do bear in mind that although the cuisine is Mexican, the portion sizes served are very American. $$

✕ **F-Hoone** Telliskivi 60a; ☎ 680 1114. It takes great *chutzpah* to open a restaurant in a former factory, behind a block of flats, beside a petrol station in an area still littered with Soviet debris, & very much on the wrong side of the tracks, even if you take a top chef from the Old Town. However 2012 proved that this formula can work in Tallinn & perhaps will pave the way for further gentrification in this area. The use of spices, the diversity of the menu & its prices will more than compensate for the dreary tram ride to get there, or for the price of a quicker taxi. There is a large play area for children. $$

✕ **Jeruusalemm** Karu 16; ☎ 664 4370; www.jeruusalemm.ee. Eating in a synagogue seems slightly inappropriate but, now that it has been possible since 2007, such behaviour perhaps causes less concern. Drinking here is tempting too, since the wine is so modestly marked up. For many tourists & locals, this will be the first experience of a Jewish environment & the restaurant, together with the adjacent shop, has been set up with this in mind. Always phone first before coming as it is sometimes closed for private functions. $$

✕ **Köleri 2** Köleri 2; ☎ 600 5688. The restaurant takes it name from the address. Although on the edge of the town centre, where concrete blocks give way to Kadriorg's opulent houses, the restaurant shows its suburban status in the best of many ways, with parking spaces, a large play area for children & galettes so large they can easily be divided into 3 portions rather than 2. However those who have had an active day in Kadriorg Park might just manage a galette to themselves. Wallets can stretch to an ice cream too, but stomachs may not. $$

✕ **Kuldse Notsu Körts (The Golden Pig)** Dunkri 8; ☎ 628 6567; www.schlossle-hotels.com, www.hotelstpetersbourg.com. Although this restaurant belongs to the luxury St Petersbourg Hotel next door, the 2 establishments have nothing in common. This country restaurant, with low ceilings & long wooden tables, seems pleasantly incongruous in the middle of the Old Town. However, this is precisely its appeal. It offers varied Estonian fare – thick mushroom soups, pork in innumerable guises & apples in almost as many. Drink apple juice or beer rather than wine. $$

✕ **Le Bonaparte** Pikk 45; ☎ 646 4444; www.bonaparte.ee. The formal restaurant at the back & the easy-going café at the front are both French through & through. The décor is very domestic & totally unpretentious. The care & flair all go into the food, which is still too rare in Tallinn, whether it is a simple cake in the café or an elaborate pâté at the start of a serious meal. Other unusual touches are the individual towels in the toilets & coat-warmers for visitors in winter. Prices in both the restaurant & the café are fortunately very Estonian. Those who want a French picnic can buy a range of cheeses & bread at the counter. Bonaparte also provides the catering at KUMU (see pages 118–19), the national art gallery $$

✕ **Must Lammas (The Black Sheep)** Sauna 2; ☎ 644 2031; www.mustlammas.ee. For years this Georgian restaurant was called Exit but it changed its name in early 2001. Luckily little else has changed. All guests are greeted with portions of firewater & strips of salted beef as the menus are handed out. Eat meat, meat & more meat all evening, topped, if you did not have lunch, with some ice cream drenched in brandy. Start with stuffed vine leaves & move on to beef & pork stews. $$

✕ **Peppersack** Viru tänav 2; ☎ 646 6800; www.peppersack.ee. Johan Peppersack was one of Tallinn's best mayors when Estonia was ruled by the Swedes in the 16th & 17th centuries. He fought the occupiers for money & for autonomy with a tenacity that no other mayor could equal in the subsequent 400 years. He would not have tolerated the mess Polish restorers, local Estonians & the Soviet occupiers got into when they tried & failed to restore the building in time for the 1980 Olympics. The compromise between Polish Baroque & the former Gothic is still there. Perhaps it is better to look at the live entertainment, which can feature fencers, troubadours or martial artists. (Check the website if it matters which.) The menu is extensive but many find it easiest just to order one of the feasts at a fixed price which includes 3 courses & drink. Several of these are fish-based & one is vegetarian. $$

✕ Vanaema Juures (Grandma's Place)

Rataskaevu 10/12; ☎631 3928; www.vonkrahl.ee. This is probably Tallinn's most famous restaurant but not even a visit from Hillary Clinton has gone to its head. The valid & repeated descriptions of it – good home cooking, a traditional décor & a cosy atmosphere – degenerate into cliché but few would dispute them. The furnishings & photographs from the previous independence period (1918–40), together with discreet music from that time, deter the young & raucous, but others will immediately appreciate the originality of total Estonian surroundings. When in 2010 Grandma started to feel her age, she wisely teamed up with the von Krahl Theatre next door & with the Aed restaurant as well. Until then she had refused to set up a website. $$

BUDGET

✕ Café Josephine Vene 16 (Masters' Courtyard); ☎641 8291; www.pierre.ee. Tallinn is not famous for its pastries, but those with a sweet tooth are most likely to be satisfied here. A small interior expands across the courtyard during the summer, when a talented classical musician will entertain with a violin or cello. Its savouries added to its pastries make a welcome light meal, both at midday & during the evening. $

✕ Karja Kelder Väike-Karja 1; ☎644 1008; www.karjakelder.ee. Estonians of a certain age remember this place with a tinge of nostalgia from Soviet times, when the décor was as reminiscent of the 1930s as the management dared to make it. The décor has stayed & the prices have got conveniently stuck in the 1990s, but the menu has broadened across the Atlantic & towards the Pacific. For foreigners it is best at lunchtime when locals haven't the time to wander down the stairs into the basement, or even better during the afternoon. $

✕ Lido Solaris Centre Estonia pst 9; ☎609 3364; www.solaris.ee. This enormous self-service restaurant (it seats 300) is a close copy of the well-known Vērmanītis restaurant in Riga. Hearty portions of any dish are guaranteed, as is a country décor & plenty of space for children to run around. There is no need to economise in Tallinn but if needs must, this is the place to do so. $

✕ Pagari Poisid (Bakers' Boys) Nunne 11. Being just off the tourist beat, although opposite the Imperial Hotel, very few non-locals walk the 450m from Town Hall Square to experience a wide choice of both savoury & sweet snacks at provincial rather than Tallinn prices. Even in midsummer it is not too crowded, thanks to the locals largely taking their purchases with them. $

ENTERTAINMENT AND NIGHTLIFE

On regaining independence, Tallinn immediately rebelled against the limited and formal entertainment that had previously been available. Out went dance bands, string quartets and folk dancing; in came discos, striptease and jazz. Private enterprise immediately seized the Finnish market that came every weekend laden with money and determined to spend it – not necessarily in the most sensible of ways; vodka at a quarter of the price it is at home is bound to lead to grief. Above all, the night went on until breakfast. No club now dares to close before 02.00. Admission fees are rare so it is common to sample quite a few different places in one evening. Now that Tallinn has a large middle class, the clientele is very mixed in most clubs as Estonians no longer feel excluded from them. None are yet typecast, but go for smart-casual dress. Anything torn or ill fitting is frowned on in Estonia. Better to be out of date than out of figure.

OPERA AND CONCERTS The **Estonian National Opera** [72 D4] (*www.opera.ee*) has performances three or four times a week. Specialist tour operators can prebook tickets as the programme is fixed about six months in advance. Given the inevitable government cutbacks in this field, it is remarkable how up to date the building now is following its 1998–2005 reconstruction, with the stage lighting being particularly impressive. Unlike Riga, Estonia's opera rarely attracts world-famous performers – and indeed some Estonian performers, especially in this field, have been attracted abroad by the much higher fees paid there. The fact that about 30% of the opera's tickets year-round are sold to non-Estonians shows the high standard that it offers, as well as the very reasonable prices charged. Even after the Opera House reopened in 2005 following its restoration, the highest ticket price was usually €30, which it still is eight years later, and many cost much less. Performances are always in the original language; 20% or so are of contemporary Estonian works, with the remainder being popular classics. The opera is closed in July and August.

Classical concerts are held in the **Old Town Hall** [72 C4], the **Estonia Concert Hall** [72 D4], the **House of Blackheads** [72 C3] and in **St Nicholas Church** [72 C4], all of these venues being in the Old Town. In most cases tickets are sold only on the day or the day before the concert so there is no need (or possibility) to prebook from abroad. Whilst some performances take place in midsummer, music-lovers are well advised to come at other times of year when the choice is wider and the standard higher.

Young people congregate at **Saku Suurhall** [off map, 72 A3], the concert hall opposite the zoo, near Rocca al Mar, where live music is staged most evenings. Performers are always local. Sometimes this is replaced by family shows and sometimes by Russian plays not genteel enough for the main Russian Theatre. The website (*www.sakusuurhall.ee*) is only in Estonian ('Pileti hind' are the ticket prices and 'Jäähalli' is the ice-skating rink).

CINEMA Films are always subtitled and never dubbed so tourists can see films missed at home without any problem. The **Sõprus Cinema** [72 C4] (*www.kino. ee*) in the Old Town at Vana-Posti 8 is easily accessible from many hotels. It is now part of a Baltic chain called Cinamon, which is the name used for the complexes that have opened in Vilnius and Kaunas. Younger people flock to **Coca-Cola Plaza** [74 B3] (*www.superkinod.ee*), a combination of 11 separate cinemas and a shopping mall. It is situated behind the central post office on Viru Square and therefore is close to many hotels.

A rooftop cinema above the Viru Hotel (*www.rooftopcinema.eu*; see page 87) opened in 2012. The 150 sheltered seats are a little more expensive than the 250 that are not. Films are always shown in their original language with Estonian subtitles, and are not dubbed. The **Solaris Centre** [72 D5] (*www.solaris.ee*), which opened in autumn 2009, has both a cinema complex and a concert hall that also hosts conferences. Its arrival has helped to reduce admission prices elsewhere and the environment, with its roof garden, restaurants and stylish shops, adds to the appeal of going there. The previous building on this site, the Sakala Centre, had a life of only 21 years, since it was built in 1985, and one of its towers has been retained in the Solaris Centre. Its link with the then Russian ruler of Estonia, Karl Vaino, led to its nickname 'Karl's Cathedral' and probably to its relatively quick demise and transformation into a totally non-Soviet building with no hint of its former role as the site of compulsory mass meetings.

NIGHTCLUBS Tallinn prides itself on its nightlife and some tour operators promote it extensively. It has tended to attract some people who should really have kept their vomiting and urinating back home in Britain and Finland. However there has been a pleasant and continuous tendency since the autumn of 2007: the drop in the number of stag groups plaguing the Old Town.

Fortunately, nightclubs do not go in and out of favour as quickly in Tallinn as they do elsewhere and many clubs that were thriving six or seven years ago still do so now. Many do not charge an entrance fee, particularly midweek, so if you find you have stumbled into somewhere not to your taste, it won't cost much – or anything – to move on. The clubs listed below are all totally different, and this is deliberate. *Tallinn In Your Pocket* (*www.inyourpocket.com*) keeps very up to date on this topic as it is published six times a year and not being dependent on advertising can be objective. To whet your appetite, check their website before leaving home.

☆ **Astoria Palace** [72 C6] Vabaduse väljak 5 (Freedom Square); www.astoria.ee. It is rare for a nightclub to boast that it opened in 1926 rather than in 2006, but the Astoria rightly does so & is happy to promote its link with dance-hall days. The music played does not usually go back that far, but do not be surprised to relive the 1960s & 1970s here, in both Soviet & Western styles. The website warns visitors that it has no weapons deposit, so guns must presumably be left at home. With luck this deters the sort of guest who might otherwise have brought one.

☆ **Bonbon** [72 D2] Mere pst 6e; ╲ 661 6080; www.bonbon.ee. Considering the style of clientele who are regulars here, it is amazing that its location has remained for years in one of Tallinn's sleeziest areas near to the port. Door staff clearly have a sense for who belongs & who does not, & often late on Sat it is closed to all, such is its popularity.

☆ **Bonnie & Clyde** [74 B5] Olümpia Hotel, Liivalaia 33. As this club is safely ensconced in a 4-star hotel, it is never a mistake to suggest a date here. Do, however, dress up properly, 1st to get in & 2nd not to lower the tone. If you are under 25, you may well not want to try unless you can be sure of being taken for at least 30. If you are 45, do not worry; nearly everybody else is too.

☆ **La Casa del Habano** [91 B4] Dunkri 2; www.havanas.ee. For those who hate nightlife but for business reasons have to pretend otherwise, Tallinn's first cigar lounge provides the perfect answer. La Casa has a licensed smoking room so there's no need to stand outside on the street before lighting up. To impress, insist on a Cuban cigar, but the miserly can also order Danish & Dutch ones. Sit at the window during the evening & see all of single Tallinn go by. As the lounge is also open during the day, come back then for a different view of families & cruise passengers.

☆ **Mad Murphy's** [91 C3] Mündi 2. Yes, the old aluminium Guinness advertisements are corny, yes the music can be dated & yes, because of the location on Town Hall Square it can get very crowded in summer, but nonetheless a visit to Tallinn is not complete without a look-in at Murphy's. Expats regularly congregated here, even before fish & chips came on to the menu. In the summer, spilling on to the square is normal so relative peace can alternate with Irish liveliness.

GAY TALLINN Tallinn's gay scene is surprisingly limited. Previously there had been gay clubs in the Old Town but by 2013 they had all moved out, mostly to Tatari, an area just to the south of Freedom Square, perhaps because of increasing rents in their former premises. However it may equally well be because they can now openly rent larger buildings and gone are the days when it was necessary to ring a bell to gain admission. The website www.gaymap.ee provides a full listing of facilities around Estonia.

☆ **G-Punkt** [72 D6] Pärnu mnt 23; www.gpunkt. ee. This club is perhaps the most daring in Tallinn, with an extensive facebook presence & clear support from the Russian-speaking community. Not to be undermined by other sorts of clubs in Tallinn, it stays open until 06.00 every night, except for Mon when it is closed.

☆ **Ring Club** [74 C6] Juhkentali 11; www. ringclub.ee. Women & striptease are strictly segregated here but do check the explicit & detailed English-language website before setting off. Juhkentali is close to the bus station & is hardly the most salubrious road in Tallinn, which perhaps suits the risqué approach of this club & the gloomy underground surroundings in which its activities take place.

☆ **X-Baar** [91 C4] Tatari 1; www.xbaar.ee. The move of X-Baar from cramped small premises on an Old Town lane to a 3-storey building with a terrace on a major road says it all on the coming- out of the Tallinn gay scene. It has further to go but what a contrast to the increasing persecution of gays being instigated by the Russian government just over the border.

SHOPPING

From Monday to Friday most shops open 10.00–18.00 and on Saturday they close earlier, usually around 16.00. On Sundays they stay closed. However those in the Old Town of interest to tourists open in the summer 10.00–19.00 seven days a week. Supermarkets open every day, usually 09.00–21.00. Only the smallest shops now refuse credit cards.

BOOKS AND POSTCARDS Postcards are best bought at the **post office** [72 B5] at the top of the Old Town (*Lossi plats 4, beside the Alexander Nevsky Cathedral*), although sadly it is closed at weekends. Here they cost about half the price charged by the sellers on the street. This post office also sells a wide selection of stamps for collectors.

Raamatukoi [72 C4] (*Harju 1, opposite the tourist office*) and **Apollo** [72 D3] (*Viru 23*) are the best sources for travel books in English on Tallinn, Estonia and the neighbouring Baltic countries. They usually stock a wide selection of Bradt guides and also paperback fiction in English. As with the post office, their charges for postcards are much lower than those of street-sellers. Apollo also has a branch in the Solaris Centre [72 D5] (page 111) where many fairly new travel books are heavily discounted, a rare practice in the Estonian book trade. The **Estonian History Museum** has opened a shop not in the museum itself, but behind it on the corner of Börsi Käik and Lai [72 B3]. It sells souvenirs based on its collections and also probably every book published in English about any aspect of Estonian history.

OTHER PURCHASES It is hard to support ethnic cleansing, but with the purchase of souvenirs it can probably be justified at **Meistrite Hoov** (Masters' Courtyard) at Vene 6 [72 C3] where a condition of trading is that anything sold is produced in Estonia. There is nothing wrong with Russian wooden dolls, Lithuanian amber and Chinese papercuts, but Tallinn Old Town is not the place where they should be promoted, as they all too often are. Come here for a range of small outlets selling locally produced beeswax candles, honey, woollen sweaters, juniper butter knives, hand-painted ceramics and glass. Renovation, which started in 2002, was largely complete by 2013.

For chocolate it is important to go to the **Kalev** shop at Lai 1 [72 B3], rather than to their other shops in the Old Town since prices here are much lower.

Those who shop for necessity rather than for pleasure usually call in at the hypermarket **Ülemiste** [75 E7], beside the hotel of the same name a few hundred metres from the airport. It sells a wide range of souvenirs, cheap household goods, black bread and vodka which can be picked up just before checking in for a flight. Shopaholics, however, for years have gone to the **Viru Centre** [74 B4], a shopping complex beside the hotel of the same name and now linked to Tallinn's largest department store, **Kaubamaja**. Its multi-lingual website (*www.virukeskus. com*) gives full details of all the shops it houses. Being completely enclosed, and with the bus station in the basement, the outside weather is irrelevant year-round. In autumn 2009 strong competition for the Viru Centre arrived with the **Solaris Centre** [72 D5] (page 111), already mentioned in the context of its concert hall and cinema. Some shops are in both centres, others only in one.

Tourists tend to concentrate on the Old Town but many modern buildings are of interest too. The main sights in the Old Town can be covered in one day but more time would be needed for other visits. See the suggestions for a day-long walking tour as well as a day tour of Pirita and Kadriorg. Several sights outside Tallinn warrant half a day on their own.

A WALKING TOUR THROUGH TALLINN The tour starts at the final Soviet architectural legacy to Estonia, the **National Library** [72 B7] (*Eesti Rahvusraamatukogu; www. nlib.ee*) which was begun in 1986 and completed in 1993. It is situated at the intersection of Endla and Tõnismägi close to the Kreutzwald and Santa Barbara hotels. Its predecessor was opened in 1918 in the parliament building on Toompea and had 2,000 books, a number that only increased to 6,000 during the 1930s.

After World War II, the history of the library mirrored that of the country as a whole. Its bleakest period was until 1953 when most of the collection comprised Russian books translated into Estonian. On Stalin's death, the library was renamed after one of Estonia's most famous authors, Friedrich Kreutzwald, a clear sign of a more liberal climate. By 1967 funds were specifically allocated for books in the Estonian language and in 1988, shortly before this new building was supposed to open, it was renamed the National Library and the formerly restricted sections were opened to all.

The design seems to symbolise glasnost: light streams in through many massive windows, and large open shelves display a wide cross-section of the two million books stored there. In the entrance hall, prints are displayed by the early 20th-century artist Eduard Wiiralt. Sadly these are not lit as well as they should be. The building will remain a grandiose memorial to massive public sector investment. Yet it was almost not completed. The fading Soviet government was not eager to continue funding projects outside Russia and the new Estonian one was faced with bills it could not pay. On 28 June 1989, between four and five thousand volunteers joined the building works under the slogan 'Dig a grave for Stalinism'. The director, Ivi Eenmaa, later to become mayor of Tallinn, single-handedly fought Moscow and then each new Estonian government for adequate funds and was finally able to open the library on 22 February 1993, two days before National Day.

On the traffic island opposite the entrance to the library was the site of the *Bronze Soldier* (see page 45). Now it is a garden although pro-Soviet demonstrations still take place here on 9 May, the former 'Victory Day', which commemorates the end of World War II, and on 22 September, the day in 1944 when Soviet forces reoccupied Tallinn.

In its almost Episcopalian simplicity, **Charles Church** (Kaarli Kirik) [72 B7] is the perfect antidote to what is to come later in the walk. It is a massive and austere late 19th-century limestone building which seats 1,500 people. At a time when Russian rule was becoming more oppressive, its size discreetly symbolised Estonian nationalism. The name comes from the wooden church originally built here in the late 17th century, during the reign of the Swedish king Charles XI. The architect was Otto Pius Hippius, who also built Sangaste Castle (see page 212) and the Alexander Church in Narva (see page 171). The church took 20 years to build, being completed in 1882, as it was dependent on voluntary contributions. This can be seen from the different limestones used, bought as and when money became available. Partly to save costs, and partly to give the church a medieval appearance, the limestone was not covered with plaster. It opened without heating, gas lighting being seen as a priority in 1896. Only in 1923 was money found for it. In contrast to the time it took for the building, the large altar fresco was completed in ten days in 1879 by the well-known artist Johann Köler. He gave his services free of charge, as did the architect Hippius. Many other works by Köler are displayed in KUMU, the Estonian Modern Art Museum [74 F4] (see pages 118–19).

On leaving the church, turn right into Kaarli and then take the first road on the left, Toompea. On the corner is the entrance to the **Occupations Museum** [72 B6] (see pages 123–4).

The first building on the left, just on Toompea, is the **Headquarters of the Estonian Defence League** [72 B6], which dates from 1918 when most of Estonia's forces were volunteers. The plaque on the wall is to its founder Johannes Orasmaa who died in Kirov prison in 1943, having been arrested on the same day in 1940 as General Laidoner (see page 121). Orasmaa was a great skier, and he encouraged his troops to take up this sport, so that they could be equally agile militarily when the need came. Continuing up the hill, the next statue on the left is to Admiral Johan Pitka, who worked actively with the British navy in 1918–20. As with General Laidoner, he was awarded a KCMG by the British. In 1940 he fled to Finland,

TALLIN IN 1960   *Michael Bordeaux*

For 15 years after World War II, Tallinn was a closed city, nestling amongst the forest of defensive (offensive) weaponry trained on the NATO countries. Suddenly in 1960 it was opened to Western visitors. I was lucky enough to have been a student at Moscow University at the time, so in May 1960 I was perhaps the first British visitor. Diplomats kept away until independence in 1991 because according to the bureaucrats a visit would have implied recognition of the Soviet occupation. I not only went there by train from Leningrad but stayed illegally in a private house for the first and only time during the 25 years that I knew the Soviet Union. Far from being worried that I would bring trouble on their heads, the occupants barred the exit and refused to let me out until I had agreed to stay for three nights, having found my photograph displayed on their wall!

How did this come about? In 1958 the Soviet authorities allowed a few handpicked theological students to study abroad. One from Riga and one (Pastor Kaide Rätsep) from Tallinn arrived at Wycliffe Hall, Oxford, while I was there. As I was a graduate in Russian, we gravitated towards each other. The next year, the door suddenly opened to me to study in Moscow as a member of the first-ever exchange programme with the USSR and I met Pastor Rätsep there when he was in transit to London. I promised I would call on his family if ever the opportunity arose.

It did. On arriving in Tallinn, I took a suburban train to the (as it still is) upmarket suburb of Nomme with its large wooden houses among the trees, looking more like Scandinavia than the Soviet Union. Maps of any practical use were unobtainable, being considered items of military intelligence, so I had to ask my way to the Rätseps' house. A rare Russian speaker eventually pointed me down one of the many paths cut into sand and I found a two-storey house separated from its neighbours by a wooden fence and a strip of pine trees. I knocked on the bright green door. A man with grey hair put his head out of an upstairs window before coming down. We had no common language, but I mentioned the name of the person who turned out to be his son. He invited me in, and there on the wall was the photograph of the Wycliffe Hall student body of 1958.

returning to Estonia in 1944 to fight the Russians, although he was by then 72 years old. He probably died fighting, but it is possible that he committed suicide to avoid capture by the Soviet forces. To the right is **Deer Park**, so named in the 1930s when deer did graze here. It was founded in 1865 as an arboretum and dendrology garden when the moat around the town walls was no longer needed. It still has this function, but is best remembered for all the political meetings held here by dissidents as Estonia worked towards independence in the late 1980s.

At the first crossroads, note the simple monument to 20 August 1991, the date Estonia declared independence during the failed Moscow coup. Had it been necessary, Estonians were ready to use the walls and towers to defend the Old Town from possible Soviet attack but the quick collapse of the coup and the immediate recognition by the USSR of Estonian independence prevented this.

To the left of the monument just below the hill is an entrance to the **Bastion Tunnels** [72 B6]. Tours do not, however, start here but at Kiek in de Kök [72 B5] (see pages 120–1) where tickets are bought. The public was first admitted in March 2007 and entry is possible only as part of a group tour. This starts with a brief film on the history of Tallinn and then continues with a train ride along

He simply would not allow me to leave and I somehow understood that I must await the return of his daughter-in-law. I was anticipating a conversation of a few words, knowing how elementary Kaide's knowledge of English had been when he arrived in Oxford. On the contrary, Enid Rätsep was bilingual, having been born in free Estonia of an English mother. The family at home had always spoken English, a tradition not entirely dead in 1960. Their 12-year-old daughter spoke it quite well. Later I would meet Enid's brother who sang me Harry Lauder songs while marching me through the streets of medieval Tallinn. Thirty years later I reflected on whether this might have been a preview of the Singing Revolution. I could hardly believe I was in the Soviet Union. Lampshades and bedspreads were of British pre-war manufacture. I slept in Kaide's study with a bookcase of German and English theology behind my pillow.

All of us, as if by common agreement, steered clear of the topic of the Soviet occupation but the family thoroughly organised my time for the next three days. After eight months in drab winter Moscow, the elan of ancient Tallinn in its bright spring colours took me into a new world. A visit on Sunday to Kaide's Lutheran church, Charles Church, left mixed impressions. Strangely, the family did not want to accompany me. This huge church was about half full, with 40% of the congregation younger people, a far higher proportion than one saw in Russia. I tried to see the pastor after the service, but the corridor was blocked by dozens of young people waiting outside his door. None of these, to my surprise, would speak to me, although most must have known Russian. I surmised they were waiting for religious instruction, illegal under the Soviet system at the time, and were unwilling for a foreigner (or a Russian if they took me for one) to intrude.

On my final day, having purchased an air ticket to Riga, I was waiting on the tarmac beside a small aeroplane. An official came up, took me inside and told me my intended flight was illegal for a foreigner. 'Our rules are less strict than yours in Britain for Soviet citizens,' he said. 'When I was there, I was prevented from visiting many places. You can go where you like, but not always by your chosen route. Visit Riga by all means, but you must do so by train via Leningrad.'

one of the tunnels, before a walk through several others. The tunnels date from the 17th century, and were built in the expectation of a long Russian siege. Their construction lasted several decades and even now not all the tunnels have been explored or even located. They were never used for fighting in the Northern War, as the Swedes were finally defeated in 1709 by Peter the Great several hundred miles away at Poltava, now in Ukraine, and the other battles all took place a long distance from Tallinn. The Russians never needed them either, and they were handed over to Tallinn municipality in 1857. They were, in fact, only of real use for two days, 9 and 10 March 1944, when local people used them as air-raid shelters during the Soviet bombing campaign.

The Soviets in turn prepared them for further invasions, in this case nuclear ones, which again never materialised and they installed the thick metal doors as protection against chemical attacks. They installed electricity, a water supply and a telephone system, much of which remains. There is no artificial ventilation, with all the air coming from ducts leading to the surface. In the 1980s they functioned as a sculpture warehouse and the homeless made considerable use of them in the 1990s. Much of the equipment abandoned by the Soviets in 1991 was stolen in a still-unsolved robbery that took place on Christmas Day 2004.

Up the small hill is a bronze statue of Linda, mother of the mythological Estonian hero Kalevipoeg, whose tears in theory formed Lake Ülemiste. It was produced in 1880 by August Weizenberg (1837–1921), who maintained close links with the Estonian nationalist movement, even though he lived for 18 years in Rome and 14 years in St Petersburg. A marble bust of this statue, also by Weizenberg, is in KUMU (which he made in Italy using Carrara marble).

A plaque on the house to the right, on the corner of Komandandi, commemorates its use by Gannibal, the black slave who rose to be a senior adviser to Peter the Great and who was briefly in charge of the Reval (Tallinn) garrison. He is perhaps better remembered as the great-grandfather of the poet Alexander Pushkin. Gannibal did not stay in Reval long, finding its racism towards him an unwelcome contrast to cosmopolitan St Petersburg. Nowadays, he might find the complete opposite.

Straight ahead is a monument that dates from the 15th century, **Pikk Hermann** (Tall Hermann Tower) [72 A5], which has withstood numerous invasions and remains intact. Measuring nearly 50m in height and supported by foundations 15m deep, the first Estonian flag was flown from here in 1884, 34 years before the country was to become independent. Subsequent conquerors always marked their success by raising a flag here. A German guidebook printed in 1942 lists 12 major dates in Tallinn's history, the last being 28 August 1941 when the German flag was raised over Pikk Hermann. The Estonian flag was flown for four days between 18 and 22 September 1944, after the Germans had left but before the Soviets returned. During the Soviet occupation, the Estonian SSR flag was flown, but the Estonian national flag returned during the perestroika period on 23 February 1989. It is raised at sunrise and lowered at sunset, except at midsummer when it is not lowered at all on the night of 23/24 June. The blue in the flag represents the sky, black the soil, and white the aspirations of the Estonian people. The monument is open to the public on just one day a year, 23 April, the day in 1919 when the first session of the Estonian Constituent Assembly took place.

Turn right down the hill (Komandandi) to **Kiek in de Kök** [72 B5] (Peep in the Kitchen; see pages 120–1). The reason for the name becomes obvious as you climb the 45m to the sixth floor of the tower and have a view into more and more houses; only the steeples of St Nicholas and St Olav are higher. From its initial construction in the 15th century until completion in the late 17th century, the tower grew in height and width with walls and floors as thick as 4m, but ironically, after a Russian attack in 1577, it never saw military action again. The last time it was prepared for war was in the 1850s when the Russians feared a British invasion during the Crimean War. The neighbouring Neitsitorn Virgin's Tower, like most in the city wall, dates from the late 14th century and was continually enlarged during the 15th century. From around 1800 when its defensive potential declined, it was converted into a barracks, but during much of the 20th century famous artists were allowed to live there. It became a popular café towards the end of the Soviet period, but following a closure of nearly two decades, it returned to this function in the summer of 2013, and offers the chance to walk along part of the city wall.

On leaving Kiek in de Kök turn back up the hill and turn right into Toompea, which ends in the square between the Parliament building and the **Alexander Nevsky Cathedral** [72 B5]. The juxtaposition of these two buildings appropriately contrasts official Estonian and Russian architecture. One is simple, small and functional, the other elaborate, and deliberately powerful. Ironically, the tsarist power the latter represented was to last only a further 17 years after its construction. Entering the cathedral represents a symbolic departure from Estonia. No-one speaks Estonian and no books are sold in Estonian. It is a Russian architectural outpost dominating the Tallinn skyline and was built between 1894 and 1900, at a time when the Russian Empire was determined to stifle the burgeoning nationalistic movements in Estonia. It was provocatively named after Alexander Nevsky, since he had conquered much of Estonia in the late 13th century. The icons, the mosaics and the 15-ton bell were all imported from St Petersburg. Occasionally plans are discussed, as they were in the 1930s, for the removal of the cathedral as it is so architecturally and politically incompatible with everything else in Toompea, but it is unlikely that any government would risk the inevitable hostility that would arise amongst the Russian-speaking population of Tallinn. (Had this action been taken, it would have followed the example of Warsaw, where an Alexander Nevsky Cathedral built under similar circumstances was torn down in the 1920s.) In the garden area at the side of the cathedral is a unique building in the Old Town, a public toilet, so it is invariably busy during the summer and around the Russian Christmas early in January.

The **Parliament building** [72 A5], most of which dates from 1921, is one of very few in the Old Town to have seen frequent reconstruction, the last one resulting from a fire in 1917 which may have been started by the Bolsheviks. The façade is a simple classicist one, and all the stone and wooden materials are local. Earlier buildings on this site had usually served as a governor's residence although, in the late 19th century, the building became a prison. One of its most famous prisoners was the Estonian short-story writer Friedebert Tuglas (1886–1971), who became involved in anti-tsarist political activity around the time of the 1905 uprisings. He wrote a story called *The Sea* here, in a room from which he could just about get a view of the coastline. Ironically publication of his work would be banned in the early Soviet era after World War II, although he was rehabilitated in 1955 and was able to enjoy considerable fame at the end of his life. The earliest fort was built on this site in 1227 and the northern and western walls date from this time.

The most famous room within the building is the White Hall, with a balcony overlooking the square. The current décor, with white cornices and a yellow ceiling, dates from 1935. From 1922 there had been a more elaborate neoclassicist design, including ceiling mirrors and elaborate panelling. The carpet was a gift from Tajikistan in the 1980s when it was a custom for the Soviet republics to present official gifts to each other. It took eight men to carry it into the building. The current

Parliamentary Chamber was rebuilt in 1998 and members of the public can attend debates there, but no interpretation from Estonian is provided. There are 101 members of Parliament, often representing as many as ten different parties. Visitors are forbidden to enter 'with cold steel, firearms and pungent-smelling substances'. Apart from the annual opening of the building on 23 April, it is normally necessary to arrange visits in advance. The Parliament website (*www.riigikogu.ee*) gives further information on this.

Continue up the hill along Toomkooli with the post office on your right. By the end of 2014, this street should be completely restored, the first one to be back to its 1920s glory. Straight ahead, on Kiriku Square, is the **Dome Church** (Toomkirik) [72 A4], sometimes called St Mary's Cathedral. Work started soon after the Danish invasion in the early 13th century and the first church was consecrated by King Waldemar II in 1240. It was slowly enlarged over the next four centuries as funds became available but much of the interior was destroyed in the fire of 1684, which devastated the whole of the Old Town. The Swedish king Charles XI imposed a special tax for the rebuilding of Tallinn and within two years the church had been largely restored. The Baroque spire was added in 1778 so in all the church has an architectural history of more than 600 years. The altarpiece, painted in 1866, is the work of the Baltic-German artist Eduard von Gebhardt (1838–1925) who was born in Estonia but spent most of his life in Germany (other examples of his work are all there). The organ, probably the most powerful in Estonia, was made in Frankfurt an der Oder in 1913 so is the last to have been imported from Germany before World War I.

The Dome Church was the religious centre for the main families of the Tallinn Baltic-German community; their coats of arms cover the church walls and their tombstones cover the floor, although a few are of Swedish origin. At the back of the church are two tombstones commemorating the butchers' and the shoemakers' guilds. The most impressive tomb, which is beside the altar, is that of the French mercenary Pontus de la Gardie (1520–85), who served in the Swedish army in many battles with the Russians. In the north aisle is a monument to Samuel Greig (1736–88), a Scots admiral who served in the tsarist navy from 1763 until his death. The inscription expresses the sorrow of Catherine II at his death, probably genuine as he was thought to have been one of her lovers. She sent her personal physician, another Scot, Dr John Rogerson, to try to save his life. Like many Scots predecessors and successors, Greig had a distinguished career in this navy. He helped to destroy the Turkish fleet at the Battle of Chesme in 1770 and to build up Kronstadt into a major naval base. Next to this monument is one to Adam von Krusenstern, the Baltic German who led the first Russian expedition to sail around the world, in 1803. Note the two globes, both of which omit New Zealand.

In 2011, the tower was opened to visitors who can manage a hundred or so narrow steps. (An extra charge is payable to climb it, but it is included in the Tallinn Card.) At the top, apart from the view, there is a photography exhibition to enjoy, comparing the views in 1892 and 2010. The greatest difference is the one looking south, now dominated by the Russian cathedral which had not yet been built when the earlier picture was taken.

Turning left out of the church, the building that dominates the opposite side of Kiriku plats was the Estonian Art Museum until late 2005. Although it looks as though it was built as an art gallery, it was first used in the 19th century as the headquarters of the Estonian Knighthood, a major business guild. During the first independence period (1920–40) it was the Foreign Ministry and for much of the Soviet period it served as the National Library. The Art Museum reopened in

February 2006 in its new premises in Kadriorg Park [75 F3] (see pages 118–19). In 2013 the building was being used by students of the Estonian Academy of Art, whilst the main Academy building was being renovated.

To the left of this building is a largely unrestored street, Kiriku, and what looks like an abandoned garage has incongruously been turned into the **Economic History Museum** (*www.muuseum.mkm.ee*) [72 B4]. This covers Tallinn's industrial history from the late 19th century until the 1990s, but the topic really deserves more space and more graphics and an extension into the 21st century. The most telling photographs are those from shops during the Soviet era. The near-empty shelves tell all and there is no need for a caption.

To the right of the former art museum, on the other side of Kohtu, is the **Finnish Embassy**, an early 19th-century building which was the winter family house of the von Uexküll family until World War I. Like many prominent Baltic Germans, they had a manor house in the countryside (Vigala) where they spent the summer, but both properties were lost during the land reform that followed the establishment of Estonian independence. The building was bought by Konstantin Päts, later to become prime minister and then president of Estonia. He, however, could not afford to keep it for himself so he sold it to the Finnish government, who in turn rented some of it back to him, using the rest of the building as their embassy. As with all other embassy buildings, in the summer of 1940 it was seized by the Soviet authorities, but was returned to the Finns on the restoration of Estonian independence.

Next to the embassy is a large limestone building typical of the late 19th century, when this material was easily mined in what is now the Tallinn suburb of Lasnamäe. It was the town house of the Ungern-Sternberg family (see pages 281–2), probably best described as notorious rather than famous. The architect was Martin Gropius, known to many visitors to Berlin for the building that carries his name and whose great-nephew was Walter Gropius of Bauhaus fame. The building was acquired by the Estonian Literary Society in 1910, an organisation founded in 1842 but whose remit went well beyond literature, encompassing all fields of science and which by 1910 had 625 members. From the beginning, its members were encouraged to donate objects for a museum that would open here in 1911, so very soon after the society took over the building. This collection is now in the History Museum (see pages 119–20). Inevitably, the society was disbanded by the Soviets in 1940 but its successor, the **Estonian Academy of Sciences**, has been there since the restoration of independence.

Take Toom Rüütli, the road to the left of the former art museum building, where after 150m you will come to the **main viewing point** across Tallinn. From here there are views of the Old Town and harbour, and look out for the Song Festival grounds and the Soviet-built suburbs in the distance. It is usually crowded during the tourist season so try the viewing point along Rahukohtu, Court Street, the next turning to the left. The main building on the left-hand side of the street here is **Stenbock House** [72 B4], used since 2000 as the residence and office of the prime minister. Although normally closed to the public, free concerts sometimes take place here in the courtyard. The plaque on the wall commemorates all the members of Parliament killed after the first Soviet occupation in 1940. Towards the end of the tsarist period, during the first period of independence and during the Soviet regime, the building was used as a court, hence the name of the street. Built as a court in the late 18th century, the government could not afford to maintain it and the Stenbock family took it over as a residence. A staircase leads down from the Rahukohtu viewpoint through **Shnelli Park** [72 A4] to the railway station, and Stenbock House is in fact best viewed from there. If this route is taken, it is possible to return via Nunne to the Old Town and to see a monument to Boris Yeltsin on the wall of the park, which was unveiled in his widow's presence in August 2013. It reflects the help he gave to Estonian independence when he was working towards the break-up of the Soviet Union near the end of the Gorbachev era, and in particular for his dramatic intervention in August 1991 which prevented the Soviet old guard from staging a successful coup against Gorbachev. Relations would later worsen between him and the Estonian government and attempts to finalise a border treaty, which started in 1993, had still not reached a conclusion 20 years later.

To reach the lower town, return along Piiskopi towards the Russian cathedral and then walk down the steps of **Lühike Jalg** ('Short Leg') [72 B5], rather a misnomer as there are in fact about 100 steps. Stop at the top for a brief respite in one of the tempting cafés or souvenir shops, before continuing the walk. Just at the descent, look to the left along **Pikk Jalg** ('Long Leg') [72 B4]. The façade that commands one of the best views over Tallinn is modelled on the main building of Tartu University.

On the right at the end of Lühike Jalg is the **Adamson-Eric Museum** [72 B4] (see pages 115–16). Continuing down the hill, the steps become a road that continues to a junction. To the left is Rataskaevu and to the right, Rüütli, both of which house some of Tallinn's best-preserved old houses. Ahead is **St Nicholas Church** (Niguliste) [72 C4], unusual (in Tallinn) in the fact that it was a military installation as well as a church, with ample hiding places and secret exits to the city walls. In common though with other churches, it was first built in the 13th century and then expanded over the next 400 years. The original spire dated from 1696 and, being outside the town walls, the church was spared from the 1684 fire. It was, however, badly damaged during the Soviet air raid on Tallinn of 9 March 1944 and the spire was only restored in 1984. Fortunately the carvings, chandeliers and pictures, many dating from the 16th century, had been removed before the raid. They are all now on display again and are particularly valuable given that so much similar work was either destroyed in the 1684 fire or suffered from neglect in more recent times. In fact, there was a considerable risk after the war that the building would either be abandoned as a ruin or even be destroyed, but in the end the interior of the church was slowly restored during the Soviet period from 1953 onwards. A small exhibition describes this work with captions in English. St Nicholas has kept its role as a museum and concert hall so has not been reconsecrated. The life of St Nicholas is portrayed in the altarpiece, measuring over 6m wide and painted in Lübeck by Hermen Rode between 1478 and 1482. From the same period, and also from Lübeck, is the *Dance of Death*, probably an original copy of part of the similar frieze by Bernt Notke, which was in Lübeck's Marienkirche. Note the one very modern addition to the building: a stained-glass window by the contemporary artist, Rait Prääts, whose glass can also be seen at the National Library.

On leaving the church, turn right to see the memorial to the writer Eduard Vilde (1865–1933) [72 C4]. The illustrations depict scenes from his novels and plays. The two stones represent an open book. Between 1918 and 1920 he served as Estonian ambassador in Copenhagen and Berlin, convincing both governments that an independent Estonia was here to stay. **Tallinn Tourist Information Centre** [72 C4] is on the other side of the road. Proceed down the steps to Harju and then turn right again. Until 2006, this former bomb site had deliberately been left as it was after the Soviet raid of 9 March 1944, but was then converted into a memorial garden, with a skating rink in winter. In June 2002 a referendum was held in Tallinn about the future of this site. Only 2% of the population turned out to vote, but 87% of them wanted to keep the site as a memorial and not let it fall into the hands of developers.

The most famous building on the site before the war was the Golden Lion Hotel where Graham Greene stayed. He began to plan *Our Man in Tallinn* there but after the Soviet occupation he felt that Havana would make a more appropriate background for the story, as a town still accessible to outsiders, which Tallinn no longer was.

On the corner of Harju and Kuninga is the bookshop **Raamatukoi** [72 C4], which sells both new and secondhand books in foreign languages on Estonia. On the Kuninga side, note the plaque to the writer Juhan Smuul (1922–71), who lived here, as the building belongs to the Writers' Union. He also lived on the island of Muhu (see page 277). Despite winning both Stalin and Lenin prizes and being chairman of the Writers' Union, Smuul was a genuinely popular writer at the time which is why the plaque has not been removed. However he is no longer studied at school, so his name is not known to many younger people. Jaan Kross (1920–2007), Estonia's most famous 20th-century writer, lived in this complex until a few months before his death, remaining fit enough to reach his fourth-floor flat without a lift. (In Soviet times, only buildings with five floors or more had lifts installed.) Kullassepa, with the tourist office on the left, leads into **Raekoja plats**, or Town Hall Square [72 C4]. Just before reaching the square, it is worth turning right for a few minutes into the small alley, Raekoja. The building on the right, which now houses the **Photographic Museum** [72 C4] (see page 124), was the town's main prison until the early 19th century.

Town Hall Square is similar to many in northern Germany as it was the commercial centre for the Baltic Germans. In the 16th century, the Germans accounted for about 1,500 of Tallinn's total population of around 5,000. They maintained all positions of authority, ruling from the Town Hall and the surrounding buildings. The square was the centre for all major events in the town, both happy and tragic. Carnivals, weddings and Christmas have all been regularly celebrated here and the Tallinn Old Days Festival, held each year in early June, recreates the carnival atmosphere with its musical and artistic events. What was possibly the world's first Christmas tree was displayed here in 1441. Yet the square was also the site for frequent executions and floggings, its grimmest day being in 1806 when 72 peasants were executed following a failed uprising. Nowadays it is hard to imagine such a background as work and punishment have given way to total relaxation. Cafés surround the square and spread into it during the summer. Since 2001, a Christmas market has taken place here throughout December and continues into January to cover the Russian Christmas two weeks after ours.

One of the few buildings on the square that has kept its original function is the **pharmacy**, which dates from 1422. Tour guides often like to point out that this is 70 years before Columbus discovered America. Probably it is the oldest one in Europe apart from Dubrovnik's. The coat of arms of the Burchart family, who ran the pharmacy for 400 years, can be seen over the entrance. Amongst the medicines they dispensed, which are unlikely to find contemporary favour, were fish eyes, lamb's wool and ground rubies, but patients were at least offered these potions with a glass of hot wine to help digestion. In 1725 Peter the Great summoned Burchart to St Petersburg, but he died before Burchart could reach him. In 2000 the pharmacy was extensively refurbished.

The **Town Hall** [72 C4] (see pages 126–7) is the only late Gothic building still intact in Estonia, dating largely from the 15th century. The exterior and the interior are equally impressive. Across the square, opposite the Town Hall, are several short streets that lead to Pikk. One of these is Saiakäik, the smallest street in Tallinn. Walk along here and turn right to the junction of Pikk and Pühavaimu for the

Holy Ghost Church [72 C3]. That it does not face due east suggests that there was already a complex street layout by 1300 when building began. It was the first church to hold services in Estonian and the first extracts from the catechism in the Estonian language were printed for use here in 1535. The 1684 fire destroyed much of the interior and the original spire. The next spire was for many years the oldest in Tallinn, dating from 1688. It was badly damaged in a fire in 2002 but was quickly replaced. On the north wall inside the church, the large wooden clock (carved by Christian Ackermann from Königsberg) dates back to the same period. The folding altar carved in 1483 by the Lübeck artist Bernt Notke, who also painted the *Danse Macabre* in the Niguliste Church, was spared from the fire.

The galleries on each side of the church have a sequence of paintings mostly depicting a number of biblical scenes. These date from the mid 17th century, and have no text with them as it would be nearly another hundred years before a Bible was published (in 1739) in Estonian. It is thought that they are the work of several different artists although no specific one has yet been identified. For many years, the topics on each picture could hardly be identified but thanks largely to a donation by the British Headley Trust, they were restored between 1998 and 2003. To commemorate Queen Elizabeth II's visit to the church in October 2006, a booklet was produced that illustrates each of the 50 panels and links them to the relevant biblical quotations.

Only the organ is modern, dating from 1929; it is one of the few in Tallinn's churches built by an Estonian and not imported from Germany. To the left of the altar, the white ensign and the plaque below it commemorate the British sailors who gave their lives between 1918 and 1920 fighting the Bolsheviks. A replica of this plaque was unveiled at Portsmouth Cathedral by Prince Andrew in December 2005.

Cross Pikk for the Ajaloomuuseum, the **Estonian History Museum** [72 B3] (see pages 119–20). The building is as impressive as any of the contents, and was perhaps more so until the extensive renovation work that took place here in connection with Tallinn being European Capital of Culture in 2011. Dating from 1410, it was the headquarters of the Great Guild and has changed little since. Visitors who arrive when the museum is shut can at least be consoled by the sight of the 15th-century doorknockers. As you turn left into Pikk, the new Russian Embassy is on the left and on the right is **Maiasmokk** [91 C3], a café that has deliberately stayed old-fashioned both in décor and in prices. The name translates appropriately as 'sweet tooth'. The café is thought to be the origin of an Estonian definition of communism as being 'marzipan every day'. In summer 2004 the **Kalev Chocolate Museum** began to move here from its earlier site near the factory in the suburbs, but nearly ten years later it was still not complete. For now it only has a small exhibition on the ground floor concerning the production of marzipan and is really an extension to the shop, rather than the other way round. In due course further floors should cover the whole 200-year history of the company.

Pikk has two of the few *Jugendstil* buildings in Tallinn, both designed by Jacques Rosenbaum, the only architect of note to practise in this field in Estonia, whereas it attracted a whole school of architects in Riga. Rosenbaum left Estonia in the mid-1920s for Berlin, where he would have a much more successful career working for the senior Nazis, Fritz Todt and Albert Speer. Number 18, next to Maiasmokk, has a flamboyant Egyptian theme; number 25 on the corner of Hobusepea is more modest and is now part of the Russian Embassy. Some may see an unwanted extension of this embassy at Pikk 29a where the **Russian Museum of Tallinn** (*www.vemu.ee*) opened in autumn 2012. Others will see it as a natural reflection of improved relations at the grass-roots level between ethic Estonians and ethnic Russians. The museum does not have a permanent collection but displays changing exhibitions, all centred on modern Russian art.

Pikk 26 is the **House of Blackheads** (*www.mustpeademaja.ee*), open to visitors during the summer and for concerts all year round. This association, catering for unmarried successful young businessmen, only existed in Estonia and Latvia, so Riga has a similar building. The black head of St Maurice is above the door but below the stone arch. The exterior is largely as it was when built in the 16th century. The association was almost as long-living, only fleeing into exile in 1939, but it had thrived for the previous 400 years under the Swedish and Russian empires, and continued to do so during Estonia's first period of independence. The silver survived World War II and is now displayed in Niguliste Church (see page 106).

The interior dates largely from the early 20th century, though some Soviet intervention, mainly the dark varnish, is visible around the entrance. It was a cultural centre at that time. The White Hall is used for state banquests and Queen Elizabeth II was entertained here in 2006. It was designed by the well-known Riga architect Wilhelm Neumann (1849–1919) responsible for the Riga Stock Exchange and for the Latvian National Art Museum and the glass is the work of his colleague Ernst Tode, who worked on these buildings too.

Number 61 [72 B2], built across Pagari, and probably the blandest building in the Old Town, was the KGB headquarters in Soviet times, and now houses the Interior Ministry. Unlike its opposite number in Vilnius, it has not been opened to the public. Next on the left is **St Olav's Church** (Oleviste) [72 B2] named after the king of Norway and now a Baptist church. When first built in 1267, its 140m-high steeple made it one of the tallest buildings in the world. This steeple caught fire in 1820, having been struck by lightning, and its replacement 'only' reaches 120m. It is still, however, a major feature of the Tallinn skyline. It is open daily during the summer and photographers should make the climb in the morning, when the sun will shine from behind the tower on to the Old Town. Much of the interior of the church was destroyed in the subsequent fire, as it had been in an earlier one in 1625. The rebuilding, completed in 1840, provides a contrast to most other churches in Tallinn for its plain interior. Tsar Nicholas I donated a large bell in 1850 and his generosity is noted in an inscription written, with no trace of irony, in German. The organ dates from this time but the chandeliers are earlier and have been donated from other buildings.

A few metres further down on the right is **Fat Margaret's Tower** [72 C1], which houses the **Maritime Museum** (Meremuuseum) (see page 122). Outside is a plaque unveiled by Prince Andrew in May 1998 which commemorates British naval involvement in the battles between Estonian forces and the Bolsheviks from 1918 to 1920. The tower was built between 1510 and 1529. Some walls are as much as 6m thick. In 1830 it became a prison but after being stormed in 1917 it was left as a ruin for the next 60 years. Polish restorers, famous throughout the former Soviet bloc, finally came to the rescue in 1978. Climb to the roof for very photogenic views of St Olav's and the town gates. A café opened here in the summer of 2013.

Turn right out of the museum and leave the Old Town on Suur Rannavärara, the continuation of Pikk. On the right is the monument *Broken Line* dedicated to those who died in the *Estonia* tragedy, when the boat of this name sank in September 1994. It can be interpreted in a number of ways, perhaps symbolising the boat breaking into two or the total divide between life and death. Cross Põhja Puiestee to the disused power station. Built in the late 1920s, it then had some claim to *Jugendstil* influence but many subsequent alterations have completely removed any hint of beauty and style.

Return into the Old Town and walk behind Fat Margaret along Uus. Number 31 is the **Scottish Club**, in fact a restaurant open to all, and which has the best-maintained lawn in Estonia. Turn right into Olevimägi and then left into Vene. On the left is a smaller, but no less Russian version of the Alexander Nevsky Cathedral, **St Nicholas Russian Orthodox Church** [72 C3]. Again no concessions are made to Estonia; everything is written, spoken and sung in Russian. It dates from the early 19th century. On the right at number 17 is the **City Museum** (Linnamuuseum) [72 C3] (see page 117). As with the History Museum, the building is as of much interest as the contents. Having escaped the fires that ravished so many buildings in the Old Town, this 14th-century merchant's house still has examples of 16th-century wooden panelling, windows and furniture. On the right are the ruins of the **Dominican Monastery** [72 C3], founded in 1246 but destroyed during the Reformation in 1524 when the monks were forced to flee. Extensive archaeological excavations were carried out between 1954 and 1968 when the ruins were first opened to the public. Take a torch and wear sturdy shoes as the surviving ambulatories are poorly lit. Of most interest are the stone carvings by the 16th-century Dutch sculptor Arent Passer. Chamber-music concerts take place here during the summer. On leaving the monastery, turn left into Vene and left again into Katariina Käik. Gravestones from the monastery are lined up along the left-hand wall. This tiny alleyway is where local expats used to buy their souvenirs of Tallinn, as few tourists found it. However, cruise passengers now come here, so locals have moved on to Meistrite Hoov, a courtyard off Vene. Turn right at the end into Müürivahe, which runs below the city wall. Elderly Russians have stalls here, selling woollen sweaters, gloves and socks both in midsummer and midwinter. The walk ends at the junction with Viru Street. To the left is the 15th-century **Viru Gate** [72 D3], as formidable as the fortifications seen at the start of the walk. To the right is McDonald's; will it also last five centuries?

ELSEWHERE IN TALLINN Visitors with more time can see many other museums. One old favourite, the Fire-Fighting Museum, housed on Vana Viru in a former fire station opposite the Viru Hotel, sadly closed in late 2006 to make way for shops likely to be of interest only to male travellers. However, this is the only museum that has closed in Tallinn recently and rapacious commercial developers have been kept away from the others. In the Old Town, on Lai, are the **Applied Arts Museum** [72 B3] (see page 116) at number 17 and the **Health Museum** [72 B3] at numbers 28–30.

Close to the Applied Arts Museum is the **Natural History Museum** at Lai 29 [72 B2], much of which is in fact contemporary rather than historical. Whilst there is an impressive collection of stuffed animals, of far greater interest is the collection of photographs of the Estonian countryside, all well lit and well labelled in English. The collection was renovated in 2013 and with all its warnings, some might be deterred from ever visiting the countryside again. If you should ever find yourself between a sow and her piglets, having suffered a viper bite, or face to face with a brown bear, hopefully you will remember the hints provided here.

Despite its name, the **Theatre and Music Museum** [72 C5] (see page 126) at Müürivahe 12, only covers music of a rather different kind from that played on the opposite side of the road in the Hollywood nightclub.

A walk from the Viru Gate along either Pärnu mnt or Estonia pst, and then along Kaarli pst back to the National Library, passes the main buildings that remain from the end of the tsarist period and the first independence period, from 1900 until 1940. *Jugendstil*, neo-Classicism and functionalism are all represented here and it is to be hoped that developers do not get permission to make drastic changes. The **Estonia National Theatre** [72 D4] was in fact designed by a Finnish architect, Armas Lindgren, and opened in 1913, although the rebuilding that followed the bombing of Tallinn in 1944 was carried out under the Estonian architect Alar Kotli. The ceiling was the work of Evald Okas (see page 43) who was in charge of two other artists and a team of German prisoners of war. They had to complete it by November 1947, in time for the 30th anniversary of the Russian Revolution, and yet give the impression that it was just by one artist. Quite a lot of eggs, both whites and yolks, must have gone into the tempera, given the extent of this painting. Okas slipped in a self-portrait here, and also one by Gustav Ernesaks (see page 31), the conductor who kept song festivals as Estonian as he could during the Soviet era.

The money for the original building was raised by private subscription and the tsarist authorities attempted to block the project. They did briefly succeed in preventing the Estonian language from being used in any production. In 1918 the Estonian National Assembly met here.

On the opposite side of Estonia pst from the theatre is the **Estonian Bank Museum** [72 D5] (see page 119). Behind the bank is the **Solaris Centre** [72 D5], which has cinemas, a conference centre/concert hall and a wide range of restaurants and shops.

On **Vabaduse Väljak** (Freedom Square) [72 C5], the Palace Hotel and the Town Hall beside it both date from the 1930s. In 1939, what is now the Town Hall housed the offices of the American legation, and the future president J F Kennedy spent a few nights there. The size and the imposing nature of similar buildings along Pärnu mnt testify to the confidence of the regime at the time. Behind them are a number of functionalist buildings that survived the 1944 bombing raid. A statute of Peter the Great stood in this square from 1910 to 1923. It was commissioned to celebrate 200 years of tsarist rule as Peter conquered Tallinn in 1710. Designs were suggested by Estonia's most famous sculptors and it was thought the commission might go to Amandus Adamson (see page 45), whose works include the Russalka Monument (see page 131) and the statue of Lydia Koidula in Pärnu (see page 248), or to August Weizenberg (see page 45) responsible for the statue of Linda near the Parliament building, but proposals from both of them were rejected. One by the French sculptor Leopold Bernstamm was accepted instead, hardly a surprising decision given that he was known to be a favourite of Tsar Nicholas II. The square was then named Peter Square. The statue, brought from Paris, weighed 5 tons and the granite base brought from Finland weighed 50 tons. With Estonia's independence assured from 1920, the statue would clearly have to be removed and the square renamed. This happened in 1923 when the name became Freedom Square and the statue was eventually moved to a site in Kadriorg Park, close to what is now the Peter the First House Museum. The statue was, however, considerably reduced in size, with the metal from one leg being used to mint Estonia's new coinage in 1928. The remnants of the statue disappeared during World War II and were never subsequently found. In Soviet times the square of course had to be renamed again, this time as Victory Square, and statues commemorating revolution heroes from the early 20th century were erected in the park beside it. The return to the name Freedom Square was in fact tolerated by the Soviet authorities in 1989, so did not need to await independence in 1991.

If the Soviets were clear what they wanted from the square, the Estonians were not, either during the first period of independence or since 1991. However, after what has amounted in total to over 30 years of quarrelling, decisions were finally taken in 2007 and the results could be seen from 21 August 2009, the 18th

3

anniversary of the re-establishment of independence. On this day, the redesigned square was reopened by President Ilves. As the cars that used to be parked there are now housed underground, cynics asked out loud whether a president should really open a car park. The square is dominated by the **Monument to the Estonian War of Independence** which was fought between 1918 and 1920. This is on the hillside overlooking the square and replaces a statue of Viktor Kingissepp, an ardent revolutionary who attempted to overthrow the Estonian government in 1922. The monument is a pillar 28m tall, made of Czech glass and topped by a cross. It is seen at its best after dark, when it is illuminated.

The building of **St John's Church** [72 D5], at the eastern side of the square, represents one of the last battles in Tallinn between the Upper Town and the Lower Town. Because relations between the two Lutheran communities were so bad in the second half of the 19th century they each built separate churches 500m apart, Charles Church [72 B7] (see pages 99–100) being the centre of worship for the Upper Town. St John's is described as being neo-Gothic and the Tallinn city architect Christoph August Gabler is given credit for it, but it lacks coherence and gives the impression of being designed by a committee. It was threatened with demolition both in the 1930s and in the 1950s and was damaged in 2008 by the construction works for the underground car park. Its future is now secure but it does not blend well with either the surrounding Functionalism or with the more modern monuments. The interior is very plain, with no coats of arms, and simple stained glass. The organ installed in August 2009 comes from Germany and replaces an earlier German one that dated from 1913. The church has twinning links with two communities in England: St Nicholas Church in Chislehurst and St John's in Shirley, Surrey.

Until 2003, the walk from Viru Gate across Viru Square gave an appropriately unflattering picture of the construction that took place between 1960 and 1980. Looking towards the harbour, there are still many buildings dating from the time when this area was a closed naval base, but gradually these are being torn down. Only two are being preserved, because they date from around 1910. They are the **Architectural Museum** [74 B3] (see pages 116–17) and the former grain elevator building at Rotermanni 4 which became a Soviet military museum in summer 2009, but which broadened its remit in 2013 to take on the name **Soviet Life**. This new museum exhibits trucks, cars, bicycles, signs, films and anything else the Soviet army and civilans left behind in 1994. Because of constant shortages, people made articles that in the West would always be bought, such as a lawnmower and even a car. Examples of both are shown here. One map of Estonia from 1979 is interesting as it marks the one trip that older people look back on with pleasure, the ferry from Tartu to Pskov. Compare the pictures here of empty shops with the shop from 1938 rebuilt at Rocca al Mare (see pages 124–5). As the building has no heating, the museum is only open in the summer. Unusual souvenirs in the gift shop include gas masks that would have been worn had there been an attack from the West. Between this museum and Viru Square a market called **Rotermanni** opened in 2009 with the clever website address www.flavoursofestonia.com. Come here for fresh organic fruit and vegetables and a good selection of cheeses, all produced in Estonia. The market expands on Sundays to include handicrafts but is closed completely on Mondays.

Looking back towards Narva maantee, the **Viru Hotel** [74 B4] stood out for 30 years as the only tall building in the area. It was the inevitable result of conflicting Soviet policies in the early 1970s; on the one hand, tourists needed to be admitted to Tallinn to boost the country's international image; on the other, they must not be allowed serious contact with the local population. An isolated tower block was obviously the answer, and until 1980, when some of the Olympic Games was held in Tallinn, the Viru was the only hotel for foreigners. Many probably only saw Tallinn from the bar on the 22nd floor. From 2011, the top of the hotel has offered a new attraction, the **KGB Museum** (*www.sokoshotels.fi*). Admission is on a group tour basis only and tickets can be bought at the hotel reception. Given the popularity of these tours, it is advisable to book one at least a day in advance. The KGB fled in rather a hurry in August 1991 so left much of their listening equipment and did not even clean out their ashtrays. Before then, little escaped their attention, and certainly not any behaviour, or better still misbehaviour, by a foreigner that could be exploited.

Estonians console themselves with the knowledge that the Viru Hotel did at least spare them a 'Stalinist cathedral', which was one proposal for this location, or an enormous memorial to Mikhail Kalinin, which was another. Kalinin, a member of Lenin's Politburo, lived in Tallinn for three years between 1901 and 1904 whilst he was banished from St Petersburg. A Soviet guidebook published in 1987 blames the lack of 'artistic and economic means' for the failure of both projects. One published a year or two later might have given the true reason: the intense local opposition. A more modest statue of Kalinin was instead erected on Tower Square, a park between the Old Town and the railway station.

Behind the Viru Hotel is a department store built in the 1960s, **Kaubamaja** [74 B4]. In the Soviet period it was crudely divided between a shop for the local population and one for foreigners. Both were flagships in their different ways. The local shop was better supplied than most in St Petersburg and Moscow and the notorious 'Berioshka', which took only precious valuta (hard foreign currencies) in exchange for vodka, wooden dolls and fur hats, was the only Soviet shop that thousands of tourists would ever enter.

This area was completely transformed in 2004 when a shopping centre opened on what had previously been the square, with a bus station underground and a walkway to link it to the original Kaubamaja. The exterior of the Viru Hotel was brightened up and extended. If, in the old days, some people never left the hotel, perhaps today they will never leave the square. There are about 70 different shops and ten different restaurants. Tallinn had known out-of-town shopping malls for a few years before 2004, but this was the first one in the centre. It is clearly a success and not just patronised by Finnish tourists.

Before the war, the main Tallinn synagogue stood on the site that Kaubamaja now occupies. Although badly damaged during the war, it could have been rebuilt but the Soviets used this damage as a pretext for removing it. A completely new **synagogue** [74 C4] (*www.ejc.ee*) was opened in May 2007 on Karu, about a kilometre from the former site and close to the harbour. Its extensive use of glass, unusual in synagogues, symbolises the openness the Jewish community wants to show to other Estonians. It has seating for 200. Inevitably most of the funding came from abroad, but many Estonians contributed what they could. The architects and builders were all local, but they travelled to Israel to understand Jewish culture and the operation of a synagogue. The Estonian Jewish community currently has about 2,500 members, many from other parts of the former Soviet Union.

Next to it, in a building that still houses the Jewish School, is the **Jewish Museum** [74 C4] (*www.eja.pri.ee*). A remarkable quantity of papers, artefacts and photographs has survived from pre-war Estonia and the museum also covers the struggles involved in reviving the community during Soviet times. The complete catalogue can be downloaded from the website. Being within the Pale of Settlement, Tallinn and Estonia never had a large Jewish community, in contrast to Latvia and Lithuania, but the 4,000 members of it in the 1930s were very active around the whole country.

Tourists rarely used to venture 'beyond the tracks', in other words behind the railway station, but this changed in 2012 with the developments at **Patarei** [74 A1], reached after a ten-minute walk along Suur-Patarei, close to the Pöhja tram stop between the station and Linnahall. This coastal walk was one of the projects developed for Tallinn's year in 2011 as European Capital of Culture. Alternatively, take the number 3 bus from Laikmaa, the street beside the Viru Centre, to the Kalamaja bus stop. To most Estonians, Patarei simply means 'prison', which is what this former tsarist fortress was from 1919 to 2002. It had previously been built as a barracks in 1840 and also as a fortress at a time when Tallinn seemed more threatened from the sea than overland. Both the German and Soviet occupiers were happy to continue its use in this way and many prominent dissidents from the Soviet era were held there. Probably the most famous was the writer Jaan Kross (see page 47). In 2006, when visitors were first granted access, they saw the hurriedly abandoned remains of what the Estonians took over from the Russians and which were hardly improved during the 1990s. They therefore walked up broken staircases, saw loose electric wires, rusting bedsteads and pealing photographs of former pornographic beauties. Not even shattered glass was cleared, let alone any weeds growing in the courtyards. Guides talk of vague plans for concerts, cafés and even a 'prison experience', based on what the Latvians have made a major attraction in the former prison at Liepaja, but these are likely to be a few years off. Little in fact has happened here between 2006 and 2014. Keep an eye on the website www. patarei.org for any developments.

Since the spring of 2012, one of the highlights of a visit to Tallinn has been the complex next to Patarei Prison, the **Seaplane Harbour** [74 A1] (✆ 6200 550; www. lennussadam.eu), which opened in May that year. The basic structure of the hangars dates from 1916, when they were commissioned by the tsarist Russian government from a Danish company, Denmark being neutral in WorldWar I. Such was the strength of the concrete with which it was constructed, that the building survived intact for the next hundred years and was happily exploited by each new army of occupation throughout the 20th century. An attempt to sell it towards the end of the Soviet regime in 1990 led to a long-running ownership dispute which culminated in 2000 with the president himself, Lennart Meri at the time, taking direct action by demanding access and being turned away in Russian by a security guard who spoke no Estonian. This led a few years later to the Estonian government legally re-acquiring the site; instead of it being restricted to senior Soviet military officials and their boorish bodyguards, it was to become a centre welcoming people of all ages and all backgrounds. Not having a Soviet history, it opens every day, offers access to the disabled and creates in side halls a range of children's activities that do not clash with the major exhibits.

There is an instant impression of 3D on entering the building, as it is necessary to look up, ahead and down at the same time to guage the true effect of the collection. A walk begins on a bridge above most of the collection, in the air as it were, looking down on the boats at surface level and the submarines below it, with planes directly ahead and on both sides. Chinese tour groups feel let down by the small size of Kadriorg Palace but they certainly feel happy here, given the size of the hangars and of the exhibits. They are presumably as surprised as others are at the sight of the earliest Estonian submarine, built in wood in 1854 and which became the prototype for others then produced in St Petersburg. Of simpler build, but crucial for centuries to Estonia, were the canoes dug from a single tree trunk that are exhibited here. When they became unusable each winter as ice froze both rivers and the sea, ice yachts would take over. Panels and film cover many aspects of Estonian naval history, including a visit paid to Tallinn by Charles Lindbergh in 1933 when he was researching flight routes between the USA and the Soviet Union. The centre of the exhibition is the submarine *Lembit,* which after several unhappy moves around Tallinn harbour, is now suitably ensconsed here.

Lembit and a second submarine called *Kalev* were originally commissioned by the Estonian navy in 1936 from the shipyards in Barrow-in-Furness in northern England. *Kalev* was sunk in October 1941, by which time both had been taken over by the Soviet navy and removed from Tallinn to avoid them falling into German hands. The *Lembit* saw service throughout the war, being mainly used to attack German cargo ships *en route* to Sweden. Its torpedoes had a range of 12km and it could sink below the surface for up to 24 hours. Its speed reached 60km/h. It remained in service until 1955, after which it was used for training. The Soviets made no attempt to conceal its British background so many of the original features remain. In fact, it was they who first made it into a museum in 1985, in recognition of its use during the war.

Outside the harbour, still in the water, is the ice-breaker *Suur Tõll.* Having been delivered to the tsarist navy in 1914 from the Stettin shipyards in Germany, *Suur Tõll* would inevitably have a complicated history over the next eight years, being based in Tallinn all that time. The Finns and Estonians who operated it wanted to prevent its fall into either White Russian or Boleshevik hands. Under the Tartu Treaty signed between the USSR and Estonia in February 1920, it was finally given to the Estonians. It could break ice a metre thick when launched, and it was still doing so with the same equipment in the 1980s. Visitors can see the engines, the living quarters and the two separate kitchens from which food for the officers and for the men was prepared.

MUSEUMS AND OTHER SITES Most Tallinn museums close at least one day a week – usually Monday or Tuesday – and some close on both days but newer ones, such as the Seaplane Harbour, open seven days a week. The major national holidays, 24 February, 23 and 24 June and 20 August used to be an excuse for them to close, but each year more now open on these days. However, as 23 and 24 June are the midsummer holiday, on those days museums are more likely to remain closed.

Opening hours in the summer, May–September, are usually an hour or so longer than at other times of year and some museums such as KUMU, that close on both Monday and Tuesday in the winter, close only on Monday in the summer. The ones that foreigners usually visit do of course charge more to take advantage of this, so around €5–6. Others charge €2–3. There are reductions for students and senior citizens. They are all free of charge to holders of the **Tallinn Card** (see page 82), so those planning a number of museum visits would be well advised to buy the card. Most museums have free admission once a month, though the day chosen will vary from museum to museum. Note that in Estonian the word 'muuseum' uses a double u and website addresses for museums, unlike hotels, always use the Estonian spelling. Several state museums share the site www.ekm.ee and several city ones appear on the site www.linnamuuseum.ee.

Adamson-Eric Museum [72 B4] (*Lühike Jalg 3;* ⟍ *644 5838; www.ekm.ee*) Adamson-Eric (1902–68) was without doubt the most famous Estonian artist who worked during both the independence period and the Soviet era. This house has no links with him, although before being used as a museum it did have workshops for coppersmiths. The museum opened in 1983 and the collection is based on around 1,000 works bequeathed by his widow. These cover his whole life in both painting and applied art. Gifts from abroad have been added to the collection. Labels are in English. Adamson-Eric's parents were able to pay for long periods of study during the 1920s in both Paris and Berlin. Elements of Fauvism and Cubism can be seen in many of his pictures but he was equally drawn to the Bauhaus and worked closely with Walter Gropius, George Grosz and Otto Dix. On his return to Estonia he first specialised in portraits, then added landscapes and broadened into applied arts. In this field, his work became as diverse as his painting. Around 1930, he began with tapestries and textiles and then added ceramics and metalwork to his range. Shortly before the war, he diversified even more, starting to work with leather and to design stage sets. He retreated with the Soviet army in 1941 and managed to maintain his artistic integrity despite the stringent demands of Soviet officialdom. With the inevitable lack of materials for applied art at this time, he concentrated again on painting. In 1949, the political tide finally turned against him and he was expelled from the Communist Party, forced to give up his posts and sent into factory work. Although released in 1953 on Stalin's death, his health had deteriorated and he suffered a stroke in 1955. His reaction was simply to learn to paint as well with his left hand as he had previously done with his right! His health slowly improved and he was able to add porcelain painting and tile design to his work in the field of applied art. He remained active until shortly before his death in 1968. Several of his paintings that were in western Europe during the Soviet era have now been given to the museum.

Applied Arts Museum [72 B3] (*Lai 17;* ☎ *641 1927; www.etdm.ee/en/*) This museum was founded in 1980, and the bleak concrete staircase certainly shows this. The exhibits, however, could not be more of a contrast. They are all from the 1950s onwards, as earlier work was largely destroyed in World War II. The third floor (second to British visitors) exhibits work up to 1970, so concentrates on wood and on textiles. The second floor continues from then until the present day, so unlike with many other creative fields, there was no sudden change in 1991. Here there is much more work in glass and in china. In all fields the collections are extensive and show the Estonian dedication to pottery, weaving, glassmaking and woodwork that has surmounted all political regimes. The ground floor is used for temporary exhibitions, so it is worth checking the website to see what is currently on show.

Architecture Museum [74 B3] (*Ahtri 2;* ☎ *625 7000; www.arhitektuurimuuseum. ee*) As a limestone building dating from 1908, this is one of the very few left from the time when the whole area around the harbour was industrial. Still often called Rotermann Salt Storage after its first owner and role, it now stands out against a background of office development and some plots of land still abandoned. As a sensitive security zone in Soviet times, little rebuilding took place in this area then, but the pace of activity since 1991 has certainly made up for it. Evening opening in the summer often enables tourists to add a visit here to one of the Old Town in the afternoon.

The building was renovated in 1995 with the aim of housing such a museum. The basement houses the permanent exhibition, which covers all styles of architecture prevalent in Estonia during the 20th century. The ground floor shows plans of some of the buildings from which Tallinn was fortunately spared. The display concentrates on the work of local architects, also on the materials that they preferred: limestone, dolomite and oak. Higher floors have changing exhibitions, but again these are always on an architectural theme. The bookshop here is the best source of English-language material on architecture and a considerable quantity has, and continues to be, published in Estonia.

Car Museum [off map, 72 A3] (*Paldiski mnt 135;* ☏ *514 1444; www.automuuseum.ee*) Until the summer of 2013, car enthusiasts in Estonia could only see one or two vehicles in different museums around the country, or they had to go to Riga's Car Museum. Fortunately this situation has now finally changed and a former warehouse beside the zoo houses an impeccably restored collection of both Western cars from the immediate post-war period and Soviet ones from throughout their occupation. Older visitors from the USA, Britain and Germany will recognise the Cadillac coupé with tailfins, the Austin Healey and the Opel Kapitän. They might also recognise the various Ladas on show, mostly modelled on the Fiat 124, since these were sold in the West in the 1970s and 1980s and were the only cars available for most Soviet citizens, and then only after a long wait, with probably good connections as well. The Chaika used by senior Estonian communists on their formal outings is also on display.

Children's Museum [off map, 72 A2] (*Kotzebue 16;* ☏ *641 3491; www.linnamuuseum.ee/lastemuuseum/en/*) Opened in 1985 as a memorial to one of Lenin's closest colleagues, Mikhail Kalinin, the museum even then had a small collection of toys. Kalinin is now forgotten and toys have taken over completely. The collection of dolls and dolls houses goes back as far as the 18th century, but there are also board games, teddy bears and general toys from 1900 onwards since this is one of the few elements of Estonian life where some items were unaffected by the changing political environment. The Teletubbies are a recent addition.

City Museum [72 C3] (*Vene 17;* ☏ *644 6553; www.linnamuuseum.ee*) The ground floor is taken up with a model of Tallinn in 1825 and it is remarkable how close this is to the town today. The Alexander Nevsky Cathedral is the only major addition and there is the section of Harju Street destroyed by Russian bombing in 1944. Many of the exhibits would now be regarded as politically incorrect in the West as they concentrate on the accoutrements of the rich; life below stairs and outside the guilds and churches is ignored. Part of the museum is quite understandably called the 'Treasury', given the quantity of tapestries, silverware, pewter and porcelain displayed there. Nonetheless, the collection shows the breadth of industry and culture that developed in Tallinn from 1860 onwards. The arrival in 1870 of the railway from St Petersburg led to an increase in the population from 30,000 to 160,000 by 1917. One anniversary the Estonians were forced to celebrate in 1910 was the 200th anniversary of the Russian conquest. On the top floor films of pre-war and Soviet Estonia, of the 1944 bombing, the 1980 Olympics and the 1989 demonstrations that would in due course lead to independence are shown. Allow at least an hour to see all of these. A room of Soviet posters has also been added, together with an early 20th-century kitchen. In the portraits of Tallinn's mayors, note that the first Estonian one, Voldemar Lender, only took office in 1906. The café on the top floor is unusual in offering only homemade food and so is worth visiting on its own. This museum is well labelled in English and the postcard sets they sell are excellent value.

Eduard Vilde Museum [74 E4] (*Roheline 3;* ☏ *601 3181; www.linnamuuseum.ee/vilde*) On leaving the Mikkeli Museum (see page 123) turn left to pass the park library and then turn left again and after 200m or so you will come to this splendidly isolated house where Estonia's most prolific writer spent the final six years of his life, between 1927 and 1933. It is modestly furnished, and characteristic of how many middle-class Estonians lived at the time. There is a monument to his work beside the Niguliste Church (see page 106) and a 'joke sculpture' in Tartu (see page 188) of him talking with Oscar Wilde; they never met in real life.

Estonian Art Museum (Eesti Kunstimuuseum; KUMU) [75 F4] (*Weizenbergi 34/Valge 1;* ☎ *644 9139; www.kumu.ee*) It is not surprising that the Queen's visit to Tallinn in October 2006 centred on KUMU as finally the capital city boasted a museum devoted almost entirely to work by Estonians. KUMU is an abbreviation of the Estonian word Kunstimuuseum – Art Museum – but it is in fact much more than that. 'Arts Centre' would probably be the best description as KUMU is just as eager to encourage new art as it is to promote its long-standing collection. The aim is to devote about half its space to exhibitions rather than to permanent displays.

This is also one of the very few buildings in the Baltics constructed specifically for a collection. Normally it has been the other way around, with collections having to fit into a building that happens to be available. This was in fact the fate of this collection for many years, when it was housed in the Estonian Knighthood building opposite the Dome Church at the top of Toompea. However, from 1993, when a competition was announced for a new art gallery to be housed in Kadriorg Park, Estonians knew that in due course their art would be displayed in suitable surroundings, with appropriate space and light. The winner of the competition was the Finnish architect Pekka Vapaavuori, and as Tallinners have lived happily for a century with a theatre designed by a Finn, there was little objection to expertise being drawn again from across the water. Construction only in fact started in 2002 and KUMU finally opened in February 2006.

A few of the paintings shown have been in state hands since 1920. Many had to be hidden during the war and the Soviet occupation. Of course much of what might have been here was destroyed during World War II or shortly afterwards. It is fortunate that so much diverse art was preserved, often at great risk to the artists and their collectors.

Those with a political interest in Estonia will probably want to visit the fourth floor first, where art produced during the Soviet era is displayed. Artists working at that time had the same dilemmas as their colleagues in the music and literary fields. It was possible to acquiesce totally to the demands of Moscow or, with subtle scheming, to maintain some artistic and Estonian integrity. Hence the name of this gallery is 'Difficult Choices'. The demands of Moscow did change considerably between 1945 and 1990 and the work shown here reflects this. The abstract sculpture *Pegasus* by Edgar Viies (b1931), produced in 1963, could not have been displayed publicly much earlier and might well have faced disapproval again during the stagnant period of the early 1980s. (It was originally produced for a restaurant on Harju that carried this name.) From a distance, the industrial landscapes of Lepo Mikko (1911–78) might seem to be purely political, but closer inspection will reveal a wide range of human expressions and varied use of colour. Some of the art shown from the 1950s, like the blocks of flats in the vicinity of KUMU, could have been produced anywhere from East Berlin to Vladivostok. There were understandable objections to showing such work here, but future generations of Estonians need to be aware of what happened in their country during the 1950s, the toughest decade of the Soviet era.

Earlier Estonian art is shown on the third floor, most of it dating from the late 19th century until 1940. Gregor von Bochmann (1850–1930) is often regarded as the first real Estonian artist even though he spent most of his life in Germany. He painted Estonian peasants and their meagre surroundings, which differentiates him from earlier Baltic Germans who only painted each other or idealised rural scenes. Konrad Mägi (1878–1925) is probably the artist best known outside Estonia and perhaps that is why his paintings still command higher prices than those of any other Estonian painter. He was one of the founders of the Pallas School of Art in Tartu (a hotel with this name now stands on the site), which encouraged diversity and travel amongst its pupils, and so was immediately closed down by the Soviet authorities in 1940. Impressionism had a great influence on his work. France was also to influence one of his best students, Karl Pärsimägi (1902–42), whose political involvement there was to lead to his death in Auschwitz after he was caught trying to help French Jews.

The second floor is reserved for temporary exhibitions, which in the summer will always have an Estonian theme. In the auditorium on the first floor (ground floor for British readers) KUMU aims to branch out into other cultural fields, so it will hold film shows, concerts and performances. The second floor also has a restaurant which overlooks Kadriorg Park and which is open in the evenings. The museum is fully accessible to the disabled.

Estonian Bank Museum [72 D5] (*Estonia pst 11;* \ *668 0760; www.muuseum. eestipank.ee; admission free*) Entering this building creates the immediate feeling of being in Riga, with its curling stairwell and stained-glass windows. The first room has wax figures of the eight famous Estonians who featured on the kroon banknotes used between 1992 and 2010 and exhibits linked to them. Best known abroad was the chess player Paul Keres (1916–75) on the 5 kroon note and an electronic chessboard here displays his most famous games. The one woman out of the eight, and certainly not a token one, was the author Lydia Koidula (1843–86). She featured on the 100 kroon note, which was often called a 'Koidula' in colloquial speech. A separate display covers the banknotes and coins issued by the pre-war Estonian government and by the different German and Russian occupiers and also the role played by the bank before and after the introduction of the euro.

Estonian History Museum [72 B3] (*Pikk 17;* \ *641 1630; www ajaloomuuseum. ee*). This should be visited as much for the building as for its display. It dates from 1410, when it was the headquarters of the Great Guild and the basic structure has changed little since then. Visitors who arrive when the museum is shut can see the 15th-century doorknockers, but it is worth going indoors for the woodwork alone. In the 18th and 19th centuries, the building had several functions and these are described in the basement display. From 1750 it was an auction house for art and for property and from 1872 it was the stock exchange, which is commemorated in the name of the lane beside the building, Börsi Käik. After the fire at St Olav's (see page 109) in 1820, the congregation met here for 20 years. In 1896 it was the venue for the first film show in Estonia.

The interior was completely redesigned in 2011 to celebrate Tallinn as European Capital of Culture and the collection now operates under the slogan 'Spirit of Survival: 11,000 Years of Estonian History'. 'Survival' is the theme of a time capsule, also in the basement, which brings to life the many horrors and the few amusing absurdities of the Soviet regime. Exhibits are well labelled in English and concentrate mainly on archaeology and costumes.

For much of the 19th century it was the only museum in Tallinn, opening in 1822 and having initially been based on a haphazard collection brought together by the town pharmacist Johann Burkhard (1776–1838). He affectionately called it 'mon faible' (my weakness) as an admission of there being no theme to it. He began it with an opium pipe and then added a wide range of curiosities from the Middle East, India and China.

Of more contemporary interest are the coin collection and a section on the founding of the local Freemasons in the late 1770s. They were later banned by Alexander I in 1822. The museum shop, around the corner in Börsi Käik, has a wide selection of tasteful souvenirs and a comprehensive selection of books and brochures in English on Estonian history. A visitor walking along this lane to the shop will literally 'cover' this long period of history which is marked by events noted on slabs of stone across it. A few project Estonia's future and the last one looks forward in 2418 to the celebration of 'it's' 500th anniversary of independence. At least that gives 400 years, surely plenty of time for correcting the punctuation.

The website should be checked for the pictures of communist statues *in situ* and then being pulled down.

Kadriorg Palace (Foreign Art Museum) [75 F4] (*Weizenbergi 37;* ☎ *606 6400; www.ekm.ee*) The Great Hall is the artistic centre of the building. The triumphal decoration of the ceiling here celebrates Peter the Great's victory over the Swedes in the Northern War and is loosely based on Rembrandt's *Diana and Actaeon*. The hunter being torn apart by his dogs can be seen to symbolise the Swedish king Charles XII being let down by his army. The painting collection is mainly Flemish and Baltic German and is based on what was left behind in their manor houses by the Baltic Germans when Hitler 'called them home' in the autumn of 1939. Many rooms have been restored to their original 1930s layout, when President Päts lived here. The Danzig-Baroque library is the most elaborate room and was only completed in 1939, a year before the Soviet takeover. It was designed by Olev Siinmaa (see page 244) the architect most famous for his work in Pärnu. Note the wooden engravings of Old Tallinn below the ceiling. The furniture throughout dates from that time and not from any earlier period since the Russian royal family took furniture with them as they travelled between their palaces and 'borrowed' extensively from the local nobility.

Kiek in de Kök [72 B5] (*Komandandi 2;* ☎ *644 6686; www.linnamuuseum.ee*) The permanent exhibition here is spread over three floors and covers the defences of Tallinn, as its walls were slowly built and enlarged. The last time it was prepared for use was in the 1850s when there was the likelihood of a British invasion during the Crimean War. It also goes back before the 13th century occupations to show how vibrant a fortification existed here before Estonia was conquered. This aspect of local history is now beginning to receive the coverage that it deserves in a number of museums. Given that museums were previously in German or Russian hands, they were happy to lend credibility to the idea that 'civilisation' only arrived with them.

Turning to the Middle Ages, note on the top floor the model of the 'Plague Doctor' with a waxed tunic and cape impregnated with herbs. He carries a cane with which to touch patients so that he can reduce any risk of infection to himself. Photographers should take advantage of the embrasures for shots of the upper town. The staff are usually happy to open the windows for this. Lower floors show modern art, with no link to the museum theme. In 2011 the exhibition was completely redesigned, with extensive audio-visual input added. There is also a café on the top floor, with excellent views of the Tallinn Old Town fortifications.

Tours to the Bastion tunnels (see page 101) start here and tickets are sold at the museum kiosk.

Laidoner Museum [off map, 75 G1](*Mõisa 1 Viimsi;* ✆ *621 7410; www.laidoner.ee*) This building served as the office of General Laidoner who was chief of staff during the Independence War and then for much of the 1920–40 period. He was arrested in 1940 by the Soviet occupation forces and imprisoned by the Russians until his death on 13 March 1953. It is some consolation to Estonians that he outlived Stalin by a week. As far as possible, the building has been restored to the state in which he would have known it. The most moving exhibit here is a French–Russian dictionary given to him during his imprisonment in 1944; he used several pages of it to compose his political testament. It ends, in English, with the words 'Estonia, with all thy faults, I love thee still. Johan Laidoner'. Considering how jealous Stalin was of his reputation, it is remarkable how many items associated with him and with this house have survived. Many friends clearly took risks in hiding some of the material exhibited here. During Soviet times, the KGB took over the building in order to break the links with Estonian independence completely.

The museum was greatly expanded in 2001. With the help of the Imperial War Museum in London, there is now a British Room, covering the navy's role in helping to establish Estonian independence in 1918–20. It is expected that many more exhibits will soon come from Britain. This would be appropriate in view of General Laidoner's often quoted remark: 'Without the arrival of the British fleet in Tallinn in December 1918, Estonia and the other Bolshevik states would have found themselves in the hands of the Bolsheviks.' The Poles have likewise opened a room in honour of Marshal Pilsudski who played a similar role to Laidoner in ensuring his country's independence from Russia.

Further expansion took place in connection with the celebrations in 2008 of the 90th anniversary of Estonian independence. A recent gallery covers the theme of 'Estonia in the Cold War' when, as in World War II, Estonians found themselves on opposing sides.

Maarjamäe Palace [75 H1] (*Pirita 56;* ✆ *601 4535; www.ajaloomuuseum.ee*) Although few labels are in English and the one available guidebook is now badly out of date, this is without doubt the best museum in Tallinn. It is definitely worth the journey towards Pirita needed to get here. (Take bus 1, 34a, 38 or 58 from the Viru Centre to the Maarjamäe Palace.) New rooms are constantly being added, exhibits are generously displayed, layout is sensibly planned and there is the complete absence of benign neglect that seems to permeate so many other Tallinn museums. The 90th anniversary of independence, celebrated in 2008, was an added incentive for this museum to extend its collection and doubtless the 100th anniversary will be even more so.

It covers Estonian history from the mid 19th century until the present day. It amply contrasts the lifestyles of the rich and poor and shows the diversity of industrial products and international contacts that the country enjoyed during the first period of independence between the two world wars. It even had a thriving tourist board whose brochures displayed here sold Estonia as 'The Cheapest and Most Interesting Country in Europe'. One room is devoted to the life of Konstantin Päts, Estonia's president between the two world wars. It features portraits both of his close political associates and of his political opponents. That their dates of death are nearly all between 1940 and 1942 shows the brutality of the Soviet regime. The portraits are all by Ants Laikmaa (see page 42), the most famous portrait painter of the 1930s.

3

On more contemporary themes, the anti-Soviet guerrilla movement and the return to independence are covered movingly but not bombastically. Amongst new themes covered in rooms opened since 2000 are the battle for Tallinn in early 1918 and the German occupation from 1941–44. The role of Estonians living in St Petersburg is often forgotten, but the museum covers a demonstration held there by 40,000 of them in March 1917, which played a crucial role in the build-up to independence.

An extension in 2006 added a gallery explaining the campaigns of the mid-1980s against the commercial exploitation of phosphate. By mid-1987 the local Estonian-language press was daringly expressing opposition to this mining, on obvious environmental grounds. There were public displays on 1 May at Tartu University, knowledge of which would reach the outside world through Radio Free Europe, thanks to a broadcast by Toomas Hendrik Ilves who was working there at the time. He is of course now (2014) President of Estonia. The next stage was to carry placards in English, with the slogan 'Phosphate, No Thanks' so that photographs could be seen abroad. Over the next year, the success of these demonstrations led to open defiance of Moscow on many more issues.

What to do with the conference room at the museum is clearly a subject of embarrassment. Its wall mural, *People's Friendship*, was completed in 1987 by Evald Okas, one of the most famous artists of the Soviet period (see page 43), so it just preceded perestroika and then independence. This was when the building was still the Museum of Revolution. Visitors who wander into the conference room will find it totally curtained, but there is no objection from the staff if visitors draw back the curtains in order to view it. Earlier it had been Baskerville Hall in a Soviet film made in 1981 of *The Hound of the Baskervilles*, with the London scenes being filmed in Tallinn.

At the back of the palace are some Soviet statues too big (and too boring) to drag to the Occupations Museum (see pages 123–4) in the town centre. Some of them are still standing; others have been left sideways to gather moss and slowly to decay.

Maritime Museum [72 C1] (*Pikk 70;* ✆ *641 1408; www.meremuuseum.ee*) This museum remained, in late 2013, in something of a time warp, and the higher floors are too reminiscent of most Tallinn museums from the mid-1990s when minor work was done to take account of the new era of Estonian independence. They badly need fresh signage, lighting and some more up-to-date exhibits. The ground floor, however, gives rise to hope as by 2013 it had been completely renovated, showing an exhibition of sailors' lives and what they found in the ports they visited, which included West Hartlepool in England, Brooklyn in the USA and Singpaore. Of the souvenirs displayed here from what they brought back, silk fans are to be expected, but rocking chairs and milk jugs advertising Johnny Walker probably are not.

The tower was built between 1510 and 1529. Some walls are as much as 6m thick. In 1830 it became a prison but after being stormed in 1917, it was left as a ruin for the next 60 years. Polish restorers, famous throughout the former Soviet bloc, finally came to the rescue in 1978.

The upper floors cover shipbuilding, cartography, port construction and fish breeding. There is an exhibit on the *Estonia*, which sank off the Finnish coast on 28 September 1994 with the loss of 850 lives. The roof, which has been home to a café since 2013, gives excellent views of Tallinn in each century: to the north are the skyscrapers from the financial district which of course all date from after the Soviet collapse in 1991, and to the east and south, the towers of the old city wall.

Miia-Milla-Manda [75 E4] (*Koidula 21a;* \ *601 7057; www.linnamuuseum. ee/miiamillamanda*) Opening in late September 2009, it lost the race with Ilon's Wonderland in Haapsalu (see pages 238–9), which opened earlier that summer, to be the first museum dedicated to young children. That museum is fine for exhibits, but does not give children the chance to play. Here, both indoors and out, children aged three to 11 have an enormous supervised play area for practising household tasks, art and games. The building, in Kadriorg Park, was a sports centre in Soviet times and soon degenerated into a blot on the landscape. Now it can call for attention like any of the other more famous buildings here. The name comes from a children's story written in the 1930s.

Mikkeli Museum [75 F4] (*Weizenbergi 28;* \ *606 6400; www.ekm.ee*) Johannes Mikkel, born in 1907, spent his whole working life, right up to his death in 2006, buying and selling art. He was able to start buying during Estonia's first independence period when departing Baltic Germans and Russian nobles felt they had to abandon enormous quantities of paintings, porcelain and prints. He was allowed to trade during the Soviet period, and he enhanced his collection with items bought in the Caucasus and central Asia. There is no predominant theme, but the quality and taste of every item stands out, even though doubts began to be expressed after his death about the alleged provenance of works he ascribed to Dürer and to Rembrandt. Do not miss the small room on the top floor, which now has pictures by Estonia's three most famous 20th-century artists, Konrad Mägi, Ants Laikmaa and Evald Okas (see pages 42 and 43). Visitors to Vilnius can perhaps compare Mikkel with Kaziz Varnelis who was equally skilled and equally tasteful in what he decided to buy. Folders in English are available in every room with descriptions of all major exhibits, and modern lighting ensures that each item can be viewed as effectively as possible.

National Library [72 B7] (*Tõnismägi, 2;* \ *630 7611; www.nlib.ee*) As this library mainly serves local residents rather than visitors, opening hours are in fact shorter during the summer. In July and August it is open 12.00–19.00 Monday–Friday whereas during other months it is open for these hours on Saturday as well as 10.00–20.00 during the week. Day tickets can be bought in the entrance hall (free to Tallinn Card holders, see page 82). There is a comprehensive secondhand bookshop here and also a large cafeteria with prices welcomingly different from those in the Old Town. The gallery behind the hall is decorated with prints by one of Estonia's most famous early 20th-century artists, Eduard Wiiralt, although sadly this area is not well lit. However, do make the effort, as this is the most comprehensive collection of his work. To encourage regular use, the library has several music rooms, shops, a café and even piped music. On a bitter winter's day, tourists may wish to await a change in the weather amongst the many English-language books and journals now available there. As one of Estonia's many adaptations to entry into the EU, there are also large French, German and Scandinavian reading rooms. Normally, however, visitors should head straight for the eighth floor to view two contrasting Tallinns. To the north and east is the Tallinn of the posters – the spires, turrets and golden domes. In the other direction is a part of the town best seen at this distance, consisting of abandoned factories and fading tower blocks, with minimal intrusion of any colour. This area is still changing too slowly.

Occupations Museum [72 B6] (*Toompea 8;* \ *668 0250; www.okupatsioon.ee*) This museum could only be built thanks to funds provided by an Estonian American,

Olga Ritos, who fled abroad in 1944 after her father and uncle had been killed by the Soviets. When the museum was formally opened in 2003 by her and Prime Minister Juhan Parts, they cut not a ribbon but barbed wire. The pathetically inadequate clothing of the prison camps is perhaps the most moving exhibit, though the sight of small cases into which thousands of Estonians had to pack belongings for their Siberian exile must run a close second. A red star and a swastika are always shown side by side as in Estonian eyes the Russians and the Germans were equally guilty. Do allow plenty of time to watch the films, all of which are in English, as they bring to life the drama and terror of both occupations as well as the occasional lighter sides of life that were possible under them.

There are also display cases showing day-to-day life in Estonia under Soviet rule. It seems hard to believe that most Estonians knew nothing else until 1991. The cellars are now being used to exhibit statues from Soviet times, which had all been pulled down when Estonian independence was restored in 1991. One is of Viktor Kingissepp (1888–1922) who was executed after attempting a *coup d'état* in Tallinn in 1922. His statue had a life in public of only one year, being unveiled on 26 March 1988 in the capital of Saaremaa Island that still bore his name; in the following year its Estonian name of Kuressaare was restored and the statue was taken down. Another statue is of Mikhail Kalinin (1875–1946), a close colleague of Stalin, whose death was commemorated by giving his name to the former German capital of East Prussia, Königsberg. One name is, however, missing. A statue of Stalin that had survived since 1956 could not be included; being 4m high, there was no way it could be brought into the museum for display. It has been dumped, together with a Lenin statue of a similar size, at the back of the Maarjamaë Palace (see page 121).

Photographic Museum [72 C4] (*Raekoja tn 4/6;* \644 8768; *www.linnamuuseum. ee*) Estonia has always had a strong photographic tradition and this museum displays not only cameras produced in the country but photographs from the 19th century and early 20th. The earliest photographs date from 1840. We tend to think of business cards with photos as fairly new but the museum displays one printed in 1859. April Fool pictures created with cameras started a little later, in the 1890s, and canals in Pisa and leaning towers in Venice also date from then. The Minox camera was produced commercially in Riga from 1938, but the first ones were made in Tallinn in 1936, with several prototypes being displayed here. It is fortunate that many pictures from the first independence period have survived. One British custom has been taken over by Estonian photographers: everybody says 'cheese' in English for a photograph and it is also the name of the local photographic journal. The basement is a gallery for the display and sale of contemporary photographs.

Rocca al Mare Open Air Museum [off map, 72 A3](*Vabaõhumuuseum tee 12;* \654 9100; *www.ekm.ee*) This deserves half a day to itself, ideally in balmy summer weather. It is open daily except at Christmas and New Year. Take the 21 bus from the railway station and also take a sweater as protection against the wind on the many non-balmy days. A winter excursion on a sunny day is worthwhile to get some impression of what most Estonians used to endure month in, month out, every winter. Visitors at midsummer on 23 June can enjoy the all-night celebrations held here. Just beyond the entrance is a modern exhibit for young people of a small door with a latch, to prepare them for these in so many of the buildings.

The name (in Italian) means 'cliff beside the sea' and was given by the original owner of the estate when it was bought in 1863. The museum was founded in 1957 and opened to the public in 1964. It was the first such museum in the USSR and irrereverent visitors at the time pointed out that it not only provided food for thought but food to eat as well. The descriptive panels throughout are in English. It now consists of around 70 buildings and when complete should have a hundred. The aim is to show all aspects of Estonian rural architecture, with houses of both rich and poor. Most date from the 19th century but one of the chapels was built in 1699. The whole of Estonia is represented – windmills are from the island of Saaremaa but in contrast there are fishermen's cottages from Lake Peipsi on the Russian border. Even the poorest families managed to afford a sauna since to Estonians it is as crucial to living as a cooking pot.

The interiors have all been appropriately furnished with kitchen utensils, weaving looms and chests of drawers. Amongst the more unusual buildings is a tabernacle from the Herrnhut movement, a strict offshoot of the Lutheran Church. Future plans include the restoration of a Swedish cottage – about 8,000 Swedes lived in Estonia before World War II. There is already a Swedish church here, brought from the formerly Swedish-speaking village of Sutlepa. The exterior is 17th century and the interior 19th century. Inside there is a permanent exhibition of drawings from all the other Swedish churches in Estonia. A recent addition has been of a 1938 shop, which could never have been shown in Soviet times, given the range of goods that it offered on a year-round basis. Take a look in the store at the sack of sugar marked 'Tate & Lyle. British Refined Granulated Sugar'.

In bad weather, finish your tour at the Kolu Tavern. Kolu is a village between Tallinn and Tartu. The tavern still has two separate bars, one originally for the gentry and one for the peasants. It serves filling, hot food such as pea soup and mashed potatoes with bacon, but do not expect any concessions to the 21st century; it remains firmly in the 19th, although a more conventional restaurant will in due course be built for more fastidious diners.

St John's Almshouse [74 B5] (*Tartu Rd;* ☎ *644 6553; www.linnamuuseum.ee*) This museum is built over part of the pavement near the junction of Tartu mnt and Rävala pst and it opened in 2005. The foundations of the building date from the early 13th century, as does the neighbouring cemetery, but neither were discovered until 2001 during a road-widening project on Tartu mnt. Luckily it was possible to implement this scheme whilst granting access to these foundations, which are now protected and covered. The museum exhibits a wide range of finds from the site, including several skeletons. The original building was destroyed in the Livonian Russian–Swedish war towards the end of the 16th century but those that followed were all used as hospitals and as centres for the elderly. The last one was pulled down in the 1960s.

There is a separate, constantly running film show about Kivisilla, which was regarded as a suburb of Tallinn until as late as the 19th century. With its many small factories and workshops, it could not be more different from the skyscrapers for offices and hotels that arise all around today.

Tammsaare Museum [74 D4] (*Koidula 12a;* ☎ *601 3111; www.linnamuuseum.ee*) The interior of this museum was completely redesigned in 2006, with background information now displayed in each room in English although there are no labels in English for individual items. Anton Hansen Tammsaare (1878–1940) spent the last eight years of his life here, so the flat gives an idea of how a middle-class Estonian lived at that time and shows the contrast to what would follow under the Soviet occupation. Although he was by far Estonia's most famous author of the period, he had to write feverishly to stay in credit, partly because his wife was never the only woman to whom he felt attached. It is sad that his works were initially not translated into English after the Soviet occupation, so the books sold here date from then. In 2009 however, *The Misadventures of the New Satan*, his last novel, was published in English and there are plans to translate parts of his five-volume *Truth and Justice*. Perhaps to make up for this lack of books, there are tasteful and reasonably priced souvenirs such as key rings and mugs for sale at prices about a quarter of what might be charged in the Old Town. Some downstairs rooms are now used for modern art exhibitions, which provide a much-needed splash of colour to the sombre atmosphere upstairs.

Theatre and Music Museum [72 C5] (*Müürivahe 12;* \ *644 6407; www.tmm.ee*) Despite its name, this museum deals only with music. A violin-maker's workshop has been reconstructed and the display covers most instruments of the orchestra, all of which have been made at sometime or another in Estonia. The production of violins and pianos has a long and distinguished history in Tallinn, both of models and of instruments actually to be played. One violin model uses hair from a one-year-old child. New instruments continue to be added to the collection, the most modern being a harpsichord from 2002. Another recent development is the naming of the tower above the museum after the composer Arvo Pärt; its walls carry formal and informal pictures of him.

Very few labels are in English, but fortunately this does not matter too much given the self-explanatory nature of the exhibits. On the stairs are usually exhibited pictures of Vladimir Sapoznin (1906–96), who began his career at the age of five in a circus and retired only when he was 80. He was sufficiently well known at the age of nine to be brought to the attention of Tsar Nicholas II, who gave him a set of tin soldiers. Whatever Estonia's political background, he whistled, sang in five different languages, played at least ten instruments, and popularised step dancing. In short, he brought constant musical happiness. Sadly he is now largely forgotten and few recordings or films remain to show his brilliance to subsequent generations.

Town Hall [72 C4] (*Raekoja plats 1;* \ *645 7900; www.tallinn.ee/raekoda;* ☺ *different parts of the Town Hall open during the summer to visitors – these vary every year so it is important to check the website for current information*) This was the administrative and judicial centre of the town and the extensive range of woodwork and paintings in the Council Chamber mainly reflects judicial themes. Six centuries of Tallinn's history have been determined in this room and it is only since 1991 that its use has changed to a purely ceremonial role, with visitors allowed to tour and concerts taking place here. For much of this time, there were clearly ample funds in the public Treasury, as is shown by the opulence of the candelabra, the money chests and the size of the wine cellars. One of the carvings of David and Goliath on the magistrates' bench is often taken to symbolise the relationship between Tallinn Council and its nominal masters on Toompea in the Old Town. The Council Chamber has always been heated, unlike the neighbouring Citizens' Hall. Dancing, eating and drinking at winter receptions tended to be particularly vigorous to compensate for this.

The original weathervane on the top of the spire, known as Old Thomas, was destroyed in the 1944 raid (see page 102) but the rest of the building was spared. German architects, artists and craftsmen were employed for the Town Hall and all documents were written only in German, even during the long periods of Swedish and Russian rule. Only the tapestries have a non-German origin, being Flemish. The originals are not displayed any more, because of their fragile condition, but two exact copies woven over a six-month period in 2003 by the British company Hines of Oxford now hang in the Citizens' Hall. Both are over 8m long and show scenes from the legend of King Solomon.

A permanent exhibition opened in summer 2004 in the attic behind the clock. Its main exhibit is a model of Tallinn as it was in 1825, but more important is the fact that this attic has been cleared. Restoration that started in 1952 finally came to an end 52 years later. It generated 273 tons of debris, much of which had been stored here. Some of the smaller, more valuable finds in wood, earthenware and textiles are now on display alongside the model. It is sometimes possible to climb up the spire; the view from the top offers excellent shots of the Old Town for photographers but the steps are steep and in poor condition so this is only to be recommended for the fit and the determined.

All state visitors sign the Town Hall register, so Nicholas II did in 1902, but when he returned in 1908 to meet the British king Edward VII, this had to be in the bay as Tallinn was not considered safe enough for the royal meeting (see box, page 17). Mikhail Gorbachev signed in 1987, but realises there is no wish to see him return. Queen Elizabeth II has signed as has the Dalai Lama and Vaclav Havel, amongst many who would never have been allowed to Tallinn in Soviet times.

Zoo [off map, 72 A3](*Paldiski mnt 145;* ✆ *694 3300; www.tallinnzoo.ee*) When it was established at its present location in 1983, cynics claimed it was to compensate for the ban on travel abroad applied to most Estonians, giving them the chance to see animals they would never experience in their natural environment. In common with the human population, the density here is low, so cages are large and there is ample space between them. Being open every day of the year, it attracts family groups and younger children should be taken to a special section of the zoo catering for them, where they can feed and touch animals. Renting a cart for a euro to take them to that section will certainly enhance the pleasure of their visit. Do read the English-language website before a visit, which puts those of many other Tallinn attractions to shame with its helpful history and background to the current collection. A visit here can be combined with one to the Car Museum about 200m away at Paldiski mnt 135 (see page 117) and also to Rocca al Mare (see pages 124–5), as the 21 bus continues there from the zoo stop.

EXCURSIONS FROM TALLINN

PRANGLI ISLAND The journey by boat from the Viimsi Peninsula, to the northeast of Tallinn, may only take an hour, but the contrast provides another world. There are tracks rather than roads, wood remains the most important building material, and the Soviets allowed it to continue as a fishing community and therefore did not plague it with concrete and unexploded mines. The population was by then 300, although had been 500 before the war. It is now 100, although this increases in the summer when Tallinn residents come to spend the holidays here. In allowing it to continue as a fishing community, the Soviets followed a policy instigated by Peter the Great, who realised it could not have a military role in defending Tallinn, unlike Naissaar.

On a warm day, the seashore feels like the Albanian coast, with empty beaches, pine trees and never a hint of rushing. Juniper and ash are the other woods that grow here extensively and cod is the principal fish. Seal hunting was extensive before it was banned in 1980, ironically the same year a seal became the Olympic mascot for the Games held that year in Moscow and in Tallinn.

Included in a tour is a visit to a memorial to Estonians who were genuinely fortunate to have been bombed by the Luftwaffe on 24 August 1941. They were on a boat called *Eestirand* which had originally been built in Dunbarton, Scotland, for herring fishing. It was bought by an Estonian company in the 1930s so was seized by the Soviet occupiers in 1940. By mid-August 1941, the German army was approaching Tallinn from all sides and Soviet forces had to organise a hurried retreat to Leningrad by sea. The *Eestirand* was part of a convoy and was filled with over 3,000 men conscripted into the Soviet army. Some 2,700 of them managed to reach Prangli, some by swimming and some on the boat which could just about be manoeuvred towards the shore. They were all thus spared from the siege of Leningrad and three years in the Red Army. The 230 who were 'rescued' by other boats in the flotilla were the unlucky ones, suffering just this fate. The *Eestirand* was left as a wreck by the Germans and after the Soviets returned in 1944, it was soon scrapped. The *Lembit* submarine, now housed beside the Seaplane Harbour (see pages 114–15) was also part of this convoy. At the memorial there are some graves of the bodies washed ashore of those killed by the bombing.

As there is no public transport on the island, or from Tallinn to Leppneeme village, the harbour for boats to Prangli, a small group tour is the best way to see it. Full details of these are available on www.tallinndaytrip.com.

PIRITA, VIIMSI AND KADRIORG Pirita, now served by several buses from central Tallinn, was built as the Olympic village for the yachting and sailing events of the 1980 Olympics. For a precious three weeks, Tallinn briefly became an international city. An array of consumer goods, Western newspapers and direct international telephone dialling suddenly appeared in the city and left as quickly as they came when the Games were over. Only the buildings have remained and they are so obviously of Soviet design that the harbour hardly seems to belong to modern Estonia. On returning to Pirita, visitors of Estonian origin may wish to take the 34 bus for 2km inland to **Metsakalmistu**, the Forest Cemetery. Most famous Estonians are buried in this pine forest, including the writer A H Tammsaare, the poet Lydia Koidula, the chess player Paul Keres and more recently, Lennart Meri, president from 1992 to 2001. Since independence, the body of Konstantin Päts, president until the Soviet occupation, has been returned and he is now buried here together with his immediate family. He died in a Soviet psychiatric hospital in 1956. The body of General Laidoner, however, still lies in a communal grave in Vladimir Prison where he died in March 1953, despite strong pressure from the Estonian government for it to be formally identified and returned. Laidoner was commander-in-chief for much of the pre-war period and his former house on the Viimsi Peninsula, about 5km from Pirita, is now the Laidoner Museum (see page 121).

The walk back to the centre of Tallinn is 3–4km. Cross the main road from the harbour to the site of **St Birgitta's Convent**. Although the convent is included in most sightseeing tours, walking here can be a precarious experience as the surroundings of the ruins are so badly maintained. The convent lasted intact for only 170 years, from 1407 until the siege of 1577 when it was largely destroyed by troops of Ivan IV in the Livonian wars. The outline of the main body of the church, the western gable together with the vestry, cloister and refectories, is clear. Minor restoration and excavation work started in 1960 and was brought to a close only in 2001. The new convent on the north side was completed in 2000 and part of the building is used as a hotel (see page 89).

Continuing towards Tallinn, the buildings along the coast all date from the late 1970s, when they were built for the 1980 Olympic Games. Being the 'Moscow

Olympics' most events took place in the Russian capital that year, but Tallinn competed successfully against Leningrad and Sochi for the sailing events; the Olympic flame burnt on this site from 20 to 30 July 1980. Soviet publications from then report on the 'enthusiastic participation of 200,000 volunteers' who ensured that the project was completed on time – in fact a full month ahead of the start of the Games. One pensioner apparently worked here without pay for 5,025 hours and earned 22 gold badges as a result. The road from Tallinn was widened into a dual carriageway as part of the preparations for the Olympics, and the site of the Games now functions as a yacht harbour and a hotel complex.

Close to the Tallinn side of the harbour, shortly after the road rejoins the coast, there are two monuments between the road and the sea. Stop here for the views across the bay of both old Tallinn and the new financial centre. One of the monuments was unveiled on 12 September 1989, the 100th anniversary of the tragic parachute jump undertaken by Charles Leroux. He had 238 successful jumps behind him but on this occasion was blown out to sea and drowned. The monument is the work of one of Estonia's most renowned contemporary sculptors, Mati Karmin (see page 46), who was born in 1959, his career spanning both the Soviet and the independence periods. Amongst his other works are the *Kissing Students* in Tartu Town Hall Square, and the memorial on Hiiumaa Island to those killed on the *Estonia* in September 1994 (see page 279). The smaller memorial is to the British motor-racing driver Michael Park, co-driver to the Estonian Markko Martin. Park was killed in a crash in Wales in September 2005, which Martin survived, although he gave up driving as a result.

Staying on the land side of the main road, after 800m is the **Maarjamägi Soviet War Memorial**. It could hardly be anything else, given its size and the military themes of the bronze statues. The Estonians carry out minimal maintenance here but, as with all Soviet war memorials, they are not removed and Russians congregate on the days of the old Soviet holidays such as May Day and 7 November. On other occasions, bored teenagers hang around drinking and smoking. The text is particularly offensive to Estonians as the monument is dedicated to 'Fighters for Soviet Power'. It was only completed in 1975. A Soviet guidebook excuses this long delay by claiming 'at last Estonian artists had enough skill and adequate economic means to complete such an ensemble'. The obelisk dates from 1960 and commemorates the hurried departure from Tallinn of the Bolshevik fleet in 1918 when German forces occupied the town. A Soviet text published in 1982 explains its location:

It is not easy today to solve the problem of how to fit a monument or a memorial ensemble within city limits. The flow of transport, and the tense busy life of a big city make the setting up of monuments on squares and central streets of a city very difficult. That is why monuments are usually erected in quiet corners of public gardens in parks where the atmosphere is conducive to a meditative mood and allows one to leisurely absorb the artistic image of the monument.

It is a pity this text was forgotten during the *Bronze Soldier* dispute (see page 45). Inland from the memorial, a German cemetery has now been reconsecrated and is being properly maintained with the support of the German government. References here are to 'defensive battles' as the most appropriate way of describing resistance to the Soviet forces.

An even more dominant landmark from the Soviet era is the **TV Tower** (*www.teletorn.ee*), similar to many imposed on eastern European cities. This one was built between 1975 and 1980 opening just in time for the Olympic sailing events taking place in Tallinn. It had a dramatic role to play in August 1991, when Estonians were able to defend it against Soviet troops and prevented it being used for the transmission of Moscow-generated propaganda. It stayed quaintly Soviet until 2007 with kopek coins still being needed for the telescopes. It was then wisely closed for a complete renovation, reopening in the spring of 2012. The daring visitor can take an 'edge walk' at the top, firmly buckled of course, but still only for the fighting fit with no fear of heights. Others will be content with the view across Tallinn and at ground level with an extensive exhibition on its history.

A few hundred metres further along this road is **Maarjamäe Palace** [75 H1], which has probably had one of the most turbulent ownership histories of any site in Tallinn. Maarjamäe means 'Mary's Hill' but the German name, Streitiberg ('Hill of Strife'), was for many centuries more appropriate. The only consolation is that the blood shed here spared Tallinn itself from many battles. The final one took place in the early 18th century as Russia seized the Baltics from the Swedes during the Northern War (see page 14). To set the seal on his conquest, Peter the Great established Kadriorg Park as a summer residence, so many of the St Petersburg nobility felt obliged to follow suit. Those who could not immediately afford the luxury of a suitable building subsidised it with a factory, so lime kilns and sugar refineries adjoined the manor houses. The sugar was sold in Riga and St Petersburg and the plant was run on British coal. A fire in 1868 destroyed much of the factory and it was never rebuilt. In the 1870s, when the estate was bought by Count Anatoli Orlov-Davydov from St Petersburg, the rebuilding he ordered came to deserve the title 'palace'. Terraces, a gateway decorated with copper eagles, and the Gothic tower gave it an almost regal air. The Dutch consulate bought it in the 1920s, when the Orlov-Davydovs emigrated to France, and continued its use as a summer residence. It was to lose its appeal in this role when in 1926 the road to Pirita was built across the grounds, cutting off the manor house from direct and private access to the sea. However, the road brought with it commercial potential realised in a hotel and restaurant called the Riviera Palace. In 1937 the Estonian air force took it over as a training school and they are sadly responsible for the dreary façade at the front of the building. From 1940 until 1975, when Maarjamäe became a museum, the Soviet military used, but did not abuse it. During the 1980s, Polish restorers finally brought the building back to its turn-of-the-century glory, turning their attention to the chandeliers, fireplaces, parquet floors and ceilings.

It is ironic that one of the last Soviet legacies to Tallinn should be the perfect surroundings for a museum that chronicles Estonian independence. A further legacy can be seen at the back of the building – remnants of Soviet statues too bulky to drag to the Occupation Museum in the town centre. However, a relatively intact Lenin was standing up in the summer of 2013 looking down on all his fallen successors, including Stalin.

Continuing towards the town centre is one of the few late 1950s constructions of which Estonians can be fiercely proud – the **Song Festival Amphitheatre** [74 G2] (*www.lauluvaljak.ee*). It has the massive grandeur to be expected from that time but is not wasteful of materials and does not dominate the surrounding area. What decided the Soviets to build it then remains uncertain. It could be seen as a sign of liberalism, akin to the broader scope being allowed in literature and in painting, or equally as a sign of Soviet confidence that they were fully in control of Estonia so could allow song festivals with equanimity. The parabola provides cover for 5,000 singers and up to 20,000 more have often taken part. The most famous recent festival took place in 1989, when the previously banned national anthem, the 'Song of Estonia', was sung by an audience of around 300,000 people, 20% of the entire population of the country. The most unpleasant year was in 1950, with frequent changes in the programme, the addition of Russian songs, and the arrest of several senior participants. The dullest was undoubtedly 1985, reflecting the stagnation of the USSR at that time.

In winter, the steep slope at the back of the parabola provides Tallinn's only ski- and toboggan-run. Note the plaques at the top of the slope that commemorate each of the song festivals held every five years since 1869. The 2004 festival was commemorated by a statue at the top of the auditorium of Gustav Ernesaks (1908– 93), who did more than anyone else to keep the Estonian element alive in the song festivals held during Soviet times. The tower was opened to the public in 2000, and gives photographers good shots of the Old Town and the port combined. On its walls, it has an exhibition covering many of the festivals held here so to some extent it duplicates what is now shown at the Tartu Song Festival Museum (see page 198).

Returning to the shoreline, at the junction of the roads to Pirita and to Narva, note the **Russalka (Mermaid) Memorial** [74 F3], which commemorates the sinking of a battleship with this name in 1893. It depicts an angel looking out to sea. In 2005 replica gas lamps were erected around the monument. The sculptor, Amandus Adamson, is one of Estonia's most famous, and perhaps because of this monument he was granted official respect in the Soviet period, as a memorial bronze bust of him stands in Kadriorg Park. Do not be surprised to see Russian-speaking wedding couples laying flowers here every Saturday. This is a favoured place to be in Tallinn around midnight on New Year's Eve. The rich living across the bay in Viimsi like to rival each other in the scale of their firework displays and all can be seen from here. Equally those organised by the municipality in Tallinn are almost as impressive and are launched at the same time. This area becomes the best venue to see them all.

Inland, the vista is now dominated by **KUMU** [75 F4], which well deserves all four capital letters, given the size of the building. It looks down from the hill at the eastern end of Kadriorg Park. This is the Eesti Kunstimuuseum, the Estonian Art Museum, which opened in February 2006 (see pages 118–19).

Just before KUMU is **Peter I House Museum**. It was bought for him in 1713, when he began to plan Kadriorg Palace and could be assured that the Swedes would no longer be a threat to his power in Estonia. It is furnished as he would have known it, so modestly and with a practical bent. This was one of the first buildings to be renovated in 1944 after the Soviet return to Tallinn. However much the regime professed to hate its tsarist predecessors, Peter was always accorded great respect. However ostentatious the palaces that he built, where he actually lived was always much simpler. The house was maintained better under the communists than it had been under several of Peter's successors. It would not be until 1804, when Alexander I was on the throne, that the Russian royal family again took an interest in Tallinn and restored this building.

The park is the next stage of the walk and one corner is just behind the Russalka Memorial. The park, and **Kadriorg Palace** [75 F4], which forms its centrepiece, was built immediately following Peter the Great's first visit to Tallinn in 1718 with his Italian architect Niccolo Michetti. Sadly it was not completed by 1725 when Peter the Great died and no subsequent tsar ever showed the commitment that he did. In fact Catherine I never came to Tallinn again after his death. Perhaps the description often given of the palace as a 'mini-Versailles' is fair, as what was carried out does show some French and Italian influence. A fire destroyed much of the interior in 1750 and it was subsequently never again used by the Russian royal family. Kadriorg Palace became the official residence of the Estonian presidents, but now houses the Foreign Art Museum (see page 120).

Kadriorg Park is a year-round joy for local people and tourists alike. In winter the combination of sun and snow amidst the trees and sculptures offers a peaceful contrast to the hectic commercial life of Tallinn just a few hundred metres away. Spring brings out the blossom of the cherry and ash trees, summer the swans, the squirrels and the fountains and autumn the blends of gold and red as the trees shed their leaves. In 2004 serious work started to restore the formal gardens that used to surround the palace. By late 2013, most of this had been completed, as had a thorough restoration of the palace itself, although one or two Soviet buildings still needed to be removed.

A hundred metres back towards town, on Weizenbergi opposite the main entrance to Kadriorg Palace, the **Mikkeli Museum** [75 F4] (see page 123) is worth visiting. This building was the palace kitchen but in 1997 was opened to house the collection of Estonia's most generous private art collector, Johannes Mikkel, who donated it to the nation.

On leaving the museum and turning left, a slight detour can first be made to the far side of the lake behind the Mikkeli building. The splendidly isolated house at Roheline 3 is the **Eduard Vilde Museum** [75 E4] (see pages 117–18) where Estonia's most prolific writer, both at home and in exile all over Europe, spent the final six years of his life between 1927 and 1933. Typically for most established Estonians at that time, the furnishings are simple and there are many empty spaces.

Return to Weizenbergi to continue back into town. At the corner of Poska on the left, house number 20a has some Baroque imitation of the palace although it was built only in 1939. Weizenbergi lasts a further 300m or so before joining Narva mnt. Every house is probably now owned, or was before World War II, by a famous Estonian. Ladas or small Toyotas may be parked in the street, but considerable wealth is discreetly hidden behind the lace curtains.

The turn-of-the-century, four-storey houses display hints of *Jugendstil*, whilst the wooden ones are characteristic of middle-class suburbs throughout Estonia. On a neighbouring street, Koidula, one of the largest wooden houses belonged to Estonia's most famous author, A H Tammsaare (1878–1940). In his honour it is now the **Tammsaare Museum** [74 D4] (see pages 125–6). At the junction of Weizenbergi and Narva mnt there is a taxi rank and bus stop. A large Methodist church has recently been built on the far side; otherwise from here back to the Viru Gate along Narva mnt is an area of constant change, now dominated by Tallinn University whose main building here was completed in 2012.

NAISSAAR ISLAND If Tallinn is cutting edge, dynamic and every other cliché associated with the capitals of the EU accession countries, the island of Naissaar is the complete opposite. Most of its website (*www.naissaar.eu*) is only in Estonian and its boat schedules remain a state secret until the start of services in the early summer. The electricity supply, usually limited to two hours in the morning and a further two in the evening, impose a firm schedule for getting up and going to bed. However, it is worth making sacrifices, at least for a day trip, to see the legacies of not only those who lived there but also those who succeeded in occupying the island for several years or those who, like the British, just stayed a few months. It is advisable to prebook a guide, if only to be sure of avoiding areas where there could still be unexploded mines, the worst of several Soviet legacies.

History Naissaar has had to reinvent itself several times during the 250 years since it began to be regularly inhabited. The name means 'women's island' but there is no clear reason why, only fanciful and largely unprintable legends. Ironically, it has in fact been male dominated for most of its occupation, with women having far less importance than on the mainland. Arabic coins from the 8th century have been found here, but as yet there is no knowledge of how these might have been brought to Naissaar or even about communities that must have lived there over the next thousand years. The early Swedish-speaking settlers who came in the mid 18th century were fishermen who traded their catches and spruce in Tallinn for the agricultural goods that the sandy windswept terrain on the island did not allow them to grow. Many had in fact lived in Finland and they came to escape the tsarist seizure of Finland from the Swedes, even though Estonia was of course also in the Russian Empire by then. However neither the Russians nor any Baltic-German landlords attempted to exert any control over the island and it was also spared the plague. These factors encouraged a community to settle there and a population of 200–300 did so; the number of inhabitants was to stay at this figure until the start of World War II. A Swedish primary school was established in 1874 and an Estonian one in 1925.

The island was always cut off for several weeks at a time in winter, when the ice was too thick for boats to secure a passage but too thin for horses, and later cars, to cross it. The few affluent islanders were invariably pilots who guided foreign trading ships into Tallinn harbour. Captains unwilling to pay the fees could find their boats shipwrecked around Naissaar and the cargoes that were salvaged could provide more income than the pilot's fee would have done. Piracy was certainly more lucrative than fishing, the main occupation on the island.

The British navy occupied the island for a few months in 1854 as part of its attempt to prevent supplies reaching Russia during the Crimean War. This was only partially successful, as the German port of Königsberg, the capital of East Prussia, was able to profit greatly from this situation. The naval personnel, on the island for several months, taught the local people how to play cricket, but the game did not catch on.

If you were asked where in the world has the densest railway network, Naissaar is hardly going to spring to mind as the answer, but it might well be correct in view of the activity in this field shown between 1910 and 1913. In that short time, the island was criss-crossed with narrow-gauge railways to move timber and peat. Forty kilometres of track were laid, 2km for every square kilometre of land. Naval defences were also built at that time. The Soviet authorities used most of these rail tracks and recently several have been restored; some lines are pulled by a steam engine and on others visitors propel themselves on a draisine, a type of bicycle fixed to the tracks. As more of the network is restored, this will become the best way to see the island, as it is just too large for walking to be realistic.

Each Russian regime was marked with deportations. The first took place in 1730, when the Russians built a fort on the island to defend it from possible Swedish attacks. This made sense at the time, in the wake of the Northern War, which the Russians had recently won after 20 years of battles. In fact, the Swedes would never attempt to invade again. The next deportation came towards the end of the tsarist regime, in 1914, as part of the defence against the Germans. This excuse was to be used twice again, in 1940 and then in 1944. However from 1944 onwards, it became clear that Estonians would never be allowed to return to Naissaar, partly because the northern tip of the island is only 35km from the Finnish coast and with the danger of unexploded mines they could not even do so in 1991 in the aftermath of independence being restored. It was not until 1994 that Naissaar became Estonian again. In the meantime it had been home to 3,000 Soviet soldiers who laid 10,000 mines to protect the USSR from a NATO invasion that never came. Ice floes often moved these mines and set them off. Some of those that have been defused are used by the sculptor Mati Karmin (see page 46) for his work.

Naissaar today The port where boats arrive has the railway going in several different directions, the island administrative centre and a café. Visitors are likely to stay in the village of **Männiku**, about 2km from the port. The houses look reasonably modern but very un-Soviet with the use of light woods and extensive glass. This is because they were all prefabricated in Finland and were part of the reparations demanded by the Soviet Union at the end of World War II. The larger Soviet buildings, including the factory that produced the mines, have all been abandoned now, but a schoolroom has been converted into an amusing museum. Much has been left as the Russians abandoned it, with posters proclaiming perestroika, unread books by Lenin, enormous radiograms and even some ballot boxes. Two waxworks of Soviet marines have been added, one asleep and one on the toilet. In 2006 some photographs were added of the German occupation here between 1942 and 1944.

In the 1990s the village of **Lõunaküla** at the southern end of the island was completely abandoned, although it had been the administration centre in the 1930s. Not a single house remains from that time, as Soviet soldiers destroyed the last one – for firewood – in 1978. The shell of the church, built in 1934 by the Swedish Lutherans, has remained, since the building was used firstly for storing hay and then as a sports hall. Proper restoration began in 2009 and was completed in 2012.

The memorial in the cemetery to the British soldiers who gave their lives in this area during the Crimean War was first erected in 1927 but was of course destroyed in Soviet times. Many of those buried here in fact died at sea. The cemetery was built near the shore and away from the church in deference to the French Catholics, who could not be buried on Lutheran ground.

Lõunaküla suddenly sprang to life in 2006 when Estonia's most famous conductor, Tõnu Kaljuste, started to sponsor a series of concerts here during July and August. These were a great success and so became an annual event. The website www.nargenfestival.ee gives full details of the programmes as they become available. A package is offered including the connecting ferry each way and a ride on the narrow-gauge railway.

4

Around Tallinn

HARJUMAA COUNTY

This county ('Maakond' in Estonian) surrounds Tallinn and offers totally contrasting attractions to those in the capital. Few tourists find them, although access is often easy with extensive local bus and train services, or with a hired car. The name means 'flat lands' and in a way no more need be said, but it does not hint at the variety of natural scenery or at the diversity of architecture. The county stretches from the Baltic coast south of **Paldiski** in the west to the **Lahemaa National Park** in the east. It is probably easiest to cover the western and southern area in day trips from Tallinn, although there are small hotels in all the towns described. Staying in Lahemaa is strongly recommended.

EXCURSIONS IN HARJUMAA COUNTY Two museums, although not close together nor even in a town, warrant a visit for the eccentric nature of their collections. The **Freedom Fighting Museum (Vabadusvõitlejate Muuseum)** (↳ *676 6197; www. hot.ee/vvmuuseum*) is in Lagedi, about 10km from central Tallinn and halfway between the Narva and Tartu roads. No English is spoken here and there is none on the website, so it is essential to take an interpreter and also to book a visit in advance as the museum does not have fixed opening hours. A locked drawbridge and several snarling dogs greet visitors who arrive unannounced. Criminals have been tempted on several occasions by the range of weapons displayed here so this security is understandable.

The original house was brought here from Narva-Jõessu and reassembled by Voldemar Päts, brother of the pre-war president Konstantin Päts. He was head of the Tallinn Art School and then Minister of Education from 1936–40. He escaped to Austria in 1944, then moved to Sweden before finally settling in Canada. Not surprisingly, the house was burnt down by the Soviets, but as the family in Canada had kept all the plans, it could be rebuilt in its original format during the 1990s. Some 46 trees that had grown on the site in the meantime were removed before this work started.

Most of the vehicles exhibited outside are those used by the Germans and Estonians to resist the Soviet forces in 1944, but some more modern Soviet ones, abandoned in 1994, are also here. Indoors is an extraordinary range of small arms and military equipment all of which must have been kept illegally in Soviet times. When government finances are tight, the Estonian military has been known to comment enviously on the range of arms kept here. The collection is being enlarged all the time, such is the interest in the cause shown by the families of former members of the Estonian resistance. One room is devoted to Alfons Rebane, the most decorated Estonian soldier in World War II, who was undoubtedly happy with much Nazi ideology. After the

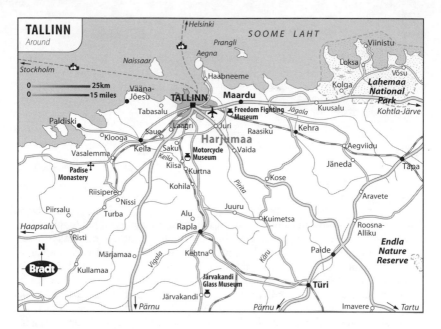

war, he worked in the UK for British intelligence before retiring to Germany. On one wall of this room is a large picture of 'Hitler The Saviour' and a copy of *Mein Kampf* is displayed. Rebane was reburied with honours in Estonia in 1999, but this gave rise to considerable controversy abroad, understandably amongst Jewish groups, who could not accept his close links to Nazi Germany. However the museum owner makes it clear that he regards Germany and Russia as equal enemies, particularly as his father was killed by the Germans.

The **Motorcycle Museum** (℄ *508 7150; www.unic-moto.ee/muuseum*) is in Kurtna to the south of Tallinn. The nearest station, on the line to Rapla, is at Kiisa, about 2km to the west. Dissidence took many forms in the USSR. Brave literary challenges to censorship, public religious worship and circulating books smuggled in from Finland were regular practices. Other Estonians carefully collected pre-war items as memories of a time when the country was independent but disguised these passions by adding Soviet items. This was the tactic adopted here. The museum only opened in 2002 but the collection was started by its owner in 1978, when pre-war motorcycles were still in use 40 years after their manufacture. The 50 machines regularly displayed here include names that will be well known to enthusiasts, such as AJS, Harley-Davidson and Saxonette, and the earliest bike is an FN from Belgium which dates from 1912. JAWA was the best Soviet brand and one, Vihur, was manufactured in Estonia. Examples of both are exhibited here, together with motorcycles from Czechoslovakia and Hungary. Real devotees in this field can also examine oilcans, posters, engines and magazines.

Paldiski

History Since independence, an uneasy quiet has descended on this former Soviet naval base situated 40km west of Tallinn, which has now become a passenger and cargo port. Peter the Great inspected the site personally in 1715 before authorising the building of a harbour, which was originally planned as the largest in the Russian Empire. He didn't live to see its completion, which was not until 1768, as financial problems had led to frequent delays. Much of the labour was supplied by prisoners; so many died of ill treatment that Paldiski became known as the 'second Siberia'. Their efforts were largely wasted as Paldiski was to have little importance over the next hundred years. This would change suddenly with the arrival of the railway in 1870; it became known as the Orange Railway because of the exotic fruits (amongst many other items) that it brought from the West into Russia. The restored station building dates from then and there are plans for a hostel to open in the upstairs rooms. For now, it provides a pleasant café.

In 1912 Paldiski was grand enough to host a meeting between Tsar Nicholas II and Kaiser Wilhelm II from Germany. Two years later they would be at war.

In September 1939 the USSR imposed a mutual assistance pact on Estonia under which Paldiski was seized as a naval base. In May 1940, shortly before the full occupation of the country, all Estonians were expelled from the town, a practice that would be repeated all too often from 1945 in many other towns and villages along the coast. The two islands in the harbour, Suur (Big) Pakri and Vaike (Small) Pakri housed a Swedish-speaking community, each with a school and church. The combined population was around 350 until 1940, when they also were all expelled. In Paldiski the Soviet military built a completely closed zone from which Estonians were totally excluded throughout their rule. It is now clear that atomic weapons were tested in the harbour in the 1970s and 1980s. The two Pakri islands became bombing ranges so have not been re-inhabited.

The Soviet military did not even leave Paldiski in 1991; it would be a further three years before they finally did so. A population of around 4,000 was left (it had been 16,000 during the occupation) with only 10% of them speaking Estonian. The remainder were Russian-speaking civilians. A curtain behind a window, an occasional light or even the sight of an occasional human being, was the only sign that life had not totally died out here. Paldiski was by then the largest Soviet blot on the Estonian landscape; only the dustbins, brightly coloured and modelled on penguins with their beaks open, provided relief from piles of rubble, barbed wire and ransacked blocks of flats. It would be around 2000 that improvements really started, with the opening and then expansion of both the cargo port and the car-ferry service to Sweden. At last the slogan 'A Town with a Future' in Paldiski's English-language brochure was no longer a joke in very bad taste. This was also the year when the town's hotel and main restaurant opened, the **Valge Laev** (White Ship) (*Rae 38;* ✆ *604 5039*), and it remains the best place to have lunch or a snack whilst touring the town.

Getting there and around Unusually for Estonia, a regular **train** service operates between here and Tallinn, with 12 services a day, the journey lasting a little over one hour. However, individual tourists would be well advised to take a **car and guide** for a half-day excursion as several *en route* stops can be made and Paldiski itself is too large to walk around. Guides are booked not in Paldiski, but at the museum in Keila (see below); they can meet visitors either at Paldiski station or at Keila station. A local and regularly updated map of Paldiski is on sale in kiosks in the town but is not available elsewhere. Estonians are more than happy to see the back of the Russian sailors but have yet to find a new role for this harbour. A daily car-ferry service to Kappelskär in Sweden started in summer 2000 and the switching of some cargo services from Tallinn is slowly under way.

What to see and do The 18th-century **St George's Church** was a ruin in Soviet times but now has windows and a roof again. It was Orthodox, but looks Lutheran because its domes are still missing. The 19th-century **St Nicholas Church** was granted this name by the Tsar when the congregation requested permission to use it. The building was to an extent looked after in Soviet times, in that it was converted into a cinema, although it also suffered use as a warehouse and rubbish dump. Gravestones were uprooted to provide material for the extension that the cinema required. The altar painting from the 1880s amazingly survived throughout the 20th century. Recent restoration at the church has been strongly supported by Finnish army veterans, some of whom worked on the site. Services and concerts now take place here regularly.

The most famous Estonian to have lived in Paldiski was the sculptor Amandus Adamson (see page 45). His house was given to the state by his daughter in 2005 and opened as the **Amandus Adamson Studio Museum** (*www.amandusadamson. eu*) on 12 November (his birthday) 2010. He lived there from 1918 until his death in 1929 and his family kept it through the Soviet period. They managed to retain quite a range of documents and furniture belonging to Adamson. His sculpture is exhibited largely in KUMU (see pages 118–19) in Tallinn but a 3D film of most of his works is shown here. A sculpture garden is planned for the currently vacant plot of land next to the house.

The **Town Hall** is an 18th-century limestone building which was formerly a naval college. Its best-known pupil was Admiral Pitka (see pages 100–1). Walking along the cliffs still gives an idea of what Peter the Great designed, but as the port expands, less land is available for this. However, the **lighthouse** and the surrounding area remains completely open for tourists. The lighthouse at 54m high is the tallest in Estonia, just beating those on Hiiumaa Island.

A stop should be made between Paldiski and Keila at **Klooga**. Shortly after independence, a monument was erected in the forest here to commemorate the massacre of 2,000 Jews on 19 September 1944, just before the German withdrawal. Members of the small Estonian Jewish community who could not escape in 1941 had already been killed by then; these victims were largely from other eastern European countries.

Keila is a railway junction from which trains originating in Tallinn continue either to Paldiski or to Riisipere, where the former line to Haapsalu now terminates. This ensures a regular train service to Tallinn, although there are also **bus routes**.

Of most interest here is the **Harjumaa Museum** (*Linnuse 9;* \ *678 1668; www. muuseum.harju.ee*) and this is where to arrange for a car and guide for travel around the county and in particular to Paldiski. Most museums have a specifically Soviet room but here the whole 20th century is blended together to show which household items survived the political changes. Porcelain and hairdryers had the longest shelf life in those days. However two activities described here could only be linked to the open 1930s. One is fishing and the other is smuggling. Estonian fishermen made a fortune taking alcohol into Finland, which followed the American policy of trying to ban alcohol sales after World War I, and they nominally maintained this until 1938. On the other hand, Keila was a centre for temperance and this is covered too. More conventional displays cover the extensive fighting that took place in the county in both world wars, but from which Tallinn was largely spared.

The museum is housed in an early 19th-century manor house but close to its entrance are the remains of a castle that once stood here. It was built in the 14th century but was then largely destroyed in the Livonian War at the end of the 16th century. Some excavations from here are housed in the museum.

St Michael's Church (*www.eelk.ee/keila*) dates from the 14th century and its size reflects the affluence of the town at the time. Most of the interior was destroyed

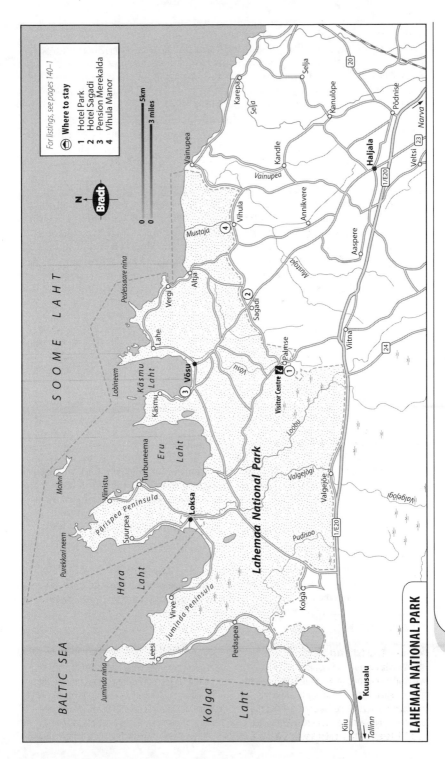

LAHEMAA NATIONAL PARK

For listings, see pages 140–1

Where to stay
1 Hotel Park
2 Hotel Sagadi
3 Pension Merekalda
4 Vihula Manor

Bradt

N

0   5km
0   3 miles

BALTIC SEA

SOOME LAHT

Purekkari neem

Mohni

Jumindana nina

Pedassaare nina

Lobineem

Käsmu Laht

Eru Laht

Turbuneema

Suurpea Peninsula

Pärispea Peninsula

Viinistu

Juminda Peninsula

Leesi

Virve

Pedaspea

Kiiu

Tallinn

Kuusalu

Kolga Laht

Hara Laht

Loksa

Kolga

Pudisoo

Valgejõgi

Valgejõe

1/E20

Loobu

Võsu

Visitor Centre

Palmse

Vitna

24

Sagadi

Vergi

Lahe

Käsmu

Võsu

Altja

Mustoja

Vihula

Vainupea

Vainupea

Annikvere

Aspere

Kandle

Karepa

Selja

Selja

Selja

Kanulõpe

Põdnise

Veltsi

23

Haljala

1/E20

Mustoja

20

Narva

Vitna

Lahemaa National Park

at the same time as the castle, in the late 16th century. What we now see here, in particular the altar and the pulpit, dates from the 17th century, so from Swedish times. However, the congregation remained sufficiently affluent through the 19th and early 20th centuries to support constant renovation. In fact it is only since 1990 that the church has had to face major financial problems but fortunately money was still found in 2004 to erect a cross on the spire.

The ring crosses in the cemetery around the church are further evidence of the high standard of living enjoyed even by peasants here under Swedish rule. Correspondingly, the private family vaults also in the cemetery, such as those of the von Stackelberg family, also show how rich many of the Baltic-German farmers became in the 19th century.

Lahemaa National Park Situated along the north coast of Estonia, about 100km from Tallinn *en route* to Narva, Lahemaa National Park and the buildings within it show both the Baltic-German and the Soviet occupations at their most benevolent. The von der Pahlen family, which owned Palmse Mansion, the architectural high point of a visit to the park, contributed to Estonia for two centuries with their administrative, commercial and academic activities. Whilst to the west the Soviets would blight the outskirts of Tallinn with shoddy tower blocks and to the east ransack the coast with oil-shale exploitation, Lahemaa, the Land of Bays, was given the status of a protected national park in 1971 and great efforts were made to support and enhance the wildlife of the area. Similar support was given to restoration of the manor houses and fishing villages. The boundaries of the park stretch for 40km along the coast and include several islands. Most Estonians, and all foreigners, were forbidden to enter the park because of its proximity to the coast but this did at least prevent any tourist and industrial development. Building work is now restricted to the minimum necessary to grant access to visitors and to provide for their stay. For details of flora and fauna, see pages 6–8.

Getting there and around Given the distances between major sites, hiring a **car** or joining a **group tour** is the best way to travel around the park. See page 54 for local tour operators who organise such programmes from Tallinn. Cyclists can bring their bikes on the public buses that link the villages of Võsu, Käsmu and Palmse with Tallinn and Rakvere. **City bike** (*www.citybike.ee*) has group tours from Tallinn, providing transport to the park and then a tour around it. Within a full day, it is possible to cover some sights and then return to Tallinn but now that Vihula Manor has opened in the park, a more leisurely visit with a stay there can be recommended.

Many of the buses going east from Tallinn to Narva stop at Viitna and Haljala. The service to Vihula goes from Rakvere, which has frequent services all over Estonia. A limited **bus service** operates within the park, but stops are always conveniently situated close to the manor houses or in the village centres. For location of listings see map, page 139.

 Where to stay and eat

🏠 **Vihula Manor** (44 rooms) ☏ 326 4100; www.vihulamanor.com. Few hotels are opened by a foreign minister, but Vihula received this accolade in Jun 2009. Perhaps the fact that the owner is Danish & the operators are British led to this interest at the highest level in Estonia. It

deliberately offers what Tallinn (& St Petersburg) cannot: an outside environment controlled 100% by nature but a luxurious one inside conducive equally to idleness or to wellness. (A complete range of spa treatment is available.) Rooms are scattered across various buildings in the complex, some of which have alarming names such as Pigeon House & Laundry House, but 3–4-star accommodation is assured throughout, in many cases with views towards the wood or over a pond. The estate as visitors now see it dates from the early 19th century, when Baltic-German influence was at its greatest, so local wood & limestone predominate. Gaudy gold & marble is notable for its complete absence & good taste for its presence. The estate was bought by the von Schubert family in 1810, taking over from a family whose production of 14 children led to bankruptcy. Thevon Schuberts sensibly had far fewer children, & like many other Baltic-German families, made money from distilling. Some of the production was of course locally consumed, but most of it went to the very burgeoning market in St Petersburg. The hotel website details the many disagreeable tenants who imposed themselves here during the 2 world wars, & then during the Soviet era, but now hopefully even their ghosts have been banished. As the hotel is run by Uniquestay, who operate the von Stackelberg & the Kreuzberg in Tallinn (see page 88), extra touches are tea-/coffee-making facilities in every room, & some Zen rooms with jacuzzis & computers. Packages are available combining stays at the von Stackelberg with time here. Nature is wonderfully slow in Vihula, with the streams meandering rather than rushing & tall trees ensuring that breezes rustle rather than high winds blow. The immediate surroundings, which include a beach 2km away, should therefore be enjoyed on foot or by bicycle but the rest of the park, plus Rakvere, are best visited by car. These surroundings include an increasing area devoted to farming & horticulture, with the products of course being served in the hotel. See advert on page 152. **$$$$**

🏠 **Hotel Park** (27 rooms) Palmse; ☏ 322 3626; e info@phpalmse.ee; www.phpalmse.ee. This hotel was built in 1995 in the former distillery to Palmse Manor House. The rooms are simply furnished in wood, as is the dining room & the beer cellar. Being off the road, quiet is assured & there are plenty of short walks in the lovely grounds of the manor. Strangely, it does not accept credit cards & as there are no ATMs nearby, visitors will need to bring with them whatever money they are likely to need to cover their stay. **$$**

🏠 **Hotel Sagadi** (28 rooms) Sagadi; ☏ 676 7888; e sagadihotell@rmk.ee; www.sagadi.ee. This hotel was completely rebuilt & extended during 2006, with all facilities upgraded so it changed from a hostel to a hotel. It is worth paying the little extra for a ground-floor room with windows on to the courtyard. The hotel is on the left-hand side of the main entrance to the estate, where the Forestry Museum used to be. A local bus stops outside the manor & the hotel has a reasonably priced taxi service. **$$**

🏠 **Pension Merekalda** (8 rooms) Neeme 2, Käsmu; ☏ 323 8451; e info@merekalda.ee; www.merekalda.ee. This guesthouse is a cluster of buildings beside the bay just outside the village. Some rooms are large enough for families, & the grounds provide an ample lawn for children & gentle access to the hotel's own beach. Outside school holidays, it is a very quiet location. Whilst B&B is provided, other meals are not, so a car is essential to reach shops & restaurants. **$**

What to see and do

Touring the park Leave the St Petersburg highway from Tallinn to Narva at Viitna and then drive through Palmse, Sagadi, Vihula, Kunda, Altja, Võsu, Käsmu and Kolga before returning to the main road 18km further west. Drivers starting from the east or south will come off the main road at Rakvere or Viru-Nigula and begin the tour at Kunda. **Viitna** is best known for its coaching inn, which dates from 1791. Like so many buildings in Estonia, it was destroyed at some stage in its history by fire; what is surprising is that the fire here was in 1989. Let us hope that it is the last serious fire to blight Estonian architecture. The inn appeals most in midwinter with its open fire and substantial portions of food, but at all times of year offers a good respite from the dull drive between Tallinn and the Russian border at Narva. It is no longer a hotel, but in the days of horse-drawn transport it served this function, being a day's ride from Tallinn. The inn was clearly divided into two sections so that masters and servants would not eat together. One side is now a post office and the other a self-service restaurant and souvenir shop, both with prices much lower than those charged in Tallinn.

Palmse Manor The manor is 6km off the main road, the perfect distance to ensure easy access but equally to ensure a totally calm natural environment. It is without doubt the most impressive manor house in Estonia and the 15 years of restoration between 1971 and 1986 have left a lasting and appropriate memorial to the von der Pahlen family. They were diverse in their brilliance, some entering Russian government service, some succeeding in business and some running this estate. Among those still remembered are Peter Ludvig von der Pahlen (1745–1826) who, as Governor of St Petersburg, was one of the plotters involved in the assassination of Tsar Paul 1 in 1801, and Alexander von der Pahlen (1819–95) who initiated the bulding of the St Petersburg–Tallinn railway. The main building and the surrounding gardens were begun in 1697 but the Northern War between Sweden and Russia halted construction. It was completed in 1740 and then work started on the other buildings. The family lived here until 1923, when the estate was nationalised in accordance with the Land Law of 1919. The land was then divided amongst ten families and the house became a convalescent home; after World War II the Soviet administration converted it into a pioneer camp for young people. The other buildings had all been left to decline and by 1972, when restoration began, were in such poor condition that it was necessary to consult drawings and photographs from the turn of the century to see their original format.

Different histories like to typecast both the architecture of the manor house and the landscaping of the gardens. The former has been labelled French, Dutch and Italian, the latter English and Chinese. None of these labels is helpful, as the von der Pahlens wanted a tasteful, solid and modest environment both indoors and outdoors and used largely local materials. They had no desire or need for ostentation as they all had highly successful careers. They distilled as profitably as they ran the Baltic Railway Company; their paintings are as worthy as their botanical research.

Apart from one episode in 1805, their 200-year rule passed without peasant unrest and the famous Estonian writer of the 19th century, Friederich Reinhold Kreutzwald, puts this down to the relationship between the family and their farmers being similar to that between parents and children. They shunned military activity and the only sign of Prussian patriotism is the name they gave in 1871 to one of the paths through the wood – Parisian Way – following the defeat of the French by the Prussian army the previous year.

Apart from one chair in the main bedroom, and the chandelier in the reception, none of the furniture is original but the items that have been collected from all over Estonia are similar to those the family would have used. The chairs in the concert hall have all been recently produced, but follow the original designs. The late 19th-century music box is still in working order and plays 24 different pieces, mainly dance music. The drawings and charts on the first floor are by the 20th-century artist Olev Soans (1925–95) although many are modelled on 19th-century originals. On the balustrade are two monograms, one from the von der Pahlen family in 1785 and one added 200 years later to commemorate the restoration in 1985. The tiled stoves throughout the house are original, as are the two granite obelisks that guard the entrance. In 2004 the basement wine cellars were reopened and they give considerable space for the display of 19th-century kitchenware and furniture. These were extended in 2006 to include a small bar and shop selling local fruit wines and grape wines with the manor house brand. Another addition, surprising for the 21st century, was a smoking room.

To the left of the main building is a small wooden one, which looks like a small chapel. It has the German name *Kavalierhaus*, which defies translation into English but was where the younger people congregated. Now it would be a computer centre by day and a disco by night but, in the early 19th century, sedate dancing could take place for much of the day. Its current use is as a discreet **souvenir shop**. To the right of the main building is the former bathhouse, which has now been converted into a **café**. It is called Isabella, after Isabella von der Pahlen (1846–1915) who surprising married into the notorious Ungern-Sternberg family (see pages 281–2).

In the former stables in front of the café, there is now a **transport museum** with an exhibition of cars, bicycles and motorbikes, some of which date back to the 1930s. The most notable items are a fire engine sent from Viljandi to Tallinn in March 1944 to help deal with the aftermath of the Soviet bombing, and the Zil that belonged to Alexandra Kollontai, a close associate of Lenin in the run-up to the 1917 revolution but who was then exiled into the diplomatic corps by Stalin. She died of natural causes in 1952, when she was still working as an adviser in the Foreign Ministry.

Behind the transport museum, an agricultural museum is being developed, with labourers' cottages and farming tools on display. In 2013, the one ticket for Palmse Manor granted admission to all the other collections on the estate.

Further left is the orchard and the greenhouse, testimony to several generations of botanists in the family. Sadly the greenhouse no longer cultivates the grapes, plums, apricots and pineapples that used to enhance the family meals. The distillery has been converted into a **hotel** (see page 141) and although it serves a wide range of Estonian spirits, none are now produced within the confines of the park. The former stables are now an **information centre** for the whole park and the shop there sells a wider range of maps and guides than does the souvenir shop. There are two particularly useful leaflets, 'Viru Bog Nature Trail' and 'Lahemaa Birds'. They also show a film of the park that lasts about 15 minutes and which shows more of the wildlife and nature than any visitor would be able to cover. A walk along the lakeside is worthwhile, if only for the view back to the main house, but it can then be extended by taking one of the many different trails through the woods. Of sociological rather than architectural interest is the monument to the von der Pahlens erected in 1933 by the ten families who took over their land, which clearly shows the affection with which they were still regarded a decade after their departure. More impressive, although untouched by humans, are the erratic boulders, the massive lumps of granite that cluster in several places in the woods.

Sagadi Sagadi is a 6km drive from Palmse and its manor house is very different. Local writers prefer it to Palmse, making comparisons with the chateaux on the Loire and even with the Garden of Eden. Travellers arriving with such expectations will definitely be disappointed, but those with a more open mind will see how a typical Baltic-German family lived and ruled. The land was owned by the von Fock family from the 17th century, but the current building, and those immediately surrounding it, date largely from the 1750s. Construction was not therefore hindered by the Northern War, which halted work at Palmse. The façade was rebuilt in 1795, with the addition of the balcony. The von Focks had a variety of business careers, largely in shipbuilding and in forestry, but none reached the eminence of the von der Pahlens. The family lived in the building until 1939 although, following the Land Law of 1919, the estates were nationalised and the main building became a primary school. It kept this function until 1970, and soon afterwards full restoration of the whole estate began. Some of the furniture is original but, as at Palmse, many pieces have been brought from other houses that were not restored. The carpet in the banqueting hall is from Aubusson in France and belonged to President Konstantin Päts.

Allow time for a leisurely walk in the park behind the house. It contains what is probably Estonia's tallest oak tree (about 33m in height) and also exhibitions of contemporary sculpture.

The **Forestry Museum** was extended in 2006 and moved into new premises in the former stables, to the right of the entrance gates. Most trees that grow in Estonia are displayed here, including ash, birch, grey alder and Scots pine. There is also an extensively provided shop which sells a wide range of goods all hand-produced in Estonia. Baskets made from pine chips are amongst the more unusual souvenirs. Prices here are much lower than in Tallinn. On the left-hand side the outhouses have now been converted into a **hotel** (see page 141).

Altja The fishing village of Altja is 8km from Sagadi. It has never been much more than a hamlet but it suffered under the Soviet regime when fishing, its sole livelihood, was banned and the population dropped from around 120 to merely 20. Subsistence farming was hardly a substitute as only potatoes could grow in the sandy soil and the grazing lands supported only a minimal number of cattle or oxen. Fishing is now being revived and the excellent **inn**, which tourist groups use for lunch, provides employment during the summer. The mashed potatoes, with a diversity of ingredients always added, are the highlight of a meal here. Although outsiders, even Estonians, were not allowed access to the coast at that time, restoration of the wooden buildings started in 1971. The inn dates from the early 19th century and, for most of its life, women were not admitted except on 25 March, Lady Day. Most of the buildings are not in fact inhabited but are net sheds for storing boats and fishing equipment. There are several walks along the coast, and paths have been cleared between the erratic boulders. Given the isolation and, in the winter, the desolation of this village, it is hard to picture it a hundred years ago as an affluent port where the fishermen and boatbuilders could enjoy coffee and wine.

Käsmu The village of Käsmu is a further 8km along the coast. When built in the early 19th century, it was often known as 'millionaire's village', such were the profits made from salt smuggling. In the 1920s smuggling shifted to alcohol when Finland attempted to impose prohibition. Finland gave up this aim in April 1932 and Käsmu suffered considerably. A macabre end to this traditional role came in June 1940 when many likely victims of Soviet hostility were smuggled out of Estonia before the whole country was occupied.

Käsmu is clearly no ordinary fishing village and this early prosperity shows signs of returning as affluent Tallinn businessmen buy up the former captains' houses. The main building is the **Maritime Museum** (*www.kasmu.ee*), which previously served as a navigation college during the first period of independence and then as a coastguard station in the Soviet period. The large watchtower next to the building dates from the latter, when swimming was banned after 21.00, such was the supposed risk that escapes to Finland might be made under the cover of darkness. The museum has two unique features in that there is no admission charge and it is open at any time. The owner, Aarne Vaik, spent 20 years collecting material surreptitiously for the museum when there was no chance of displaying it. At present the collection concentrates on the 1920s and 1930s but it will be extended through World War II and the Soviet period. A natural history section to cover sea fauna and flora is also being planned. One item of particular interest to British tourists is the £1 note from 1919; with all local currencies at that time being so insecure, sterling was the only acceptable currency for maritime insurance.

Beside the village church is the **Baron Dellingshausen Memorial**, perhaps unique in being built by him to feign his death. He was implicated in the failed plot to kill Tsar Alexander II in 1881 and fled to Germany leaving this memorial as a safeguard against the police looking for him. The false tomb was soon discovered but the baron was able to die of natural causes in the safe environment of Potsdam. The building now houses a photographic exhibition of local people at work and at home, all the pictures having been taken in 1999.

Kolga Kolga is 30km west of Käsmu so can be visited on the way back to Tallinn. The estate was originally a monastery, but in 1581 the Swedish king gave it to his French army commander Pontus de la Gardie as a reward for his military prowess. He himself hardly used it as he was drowned in the Narva River four years later in 1585, but the property stayed in his family until the mid 17th century when Christina de la Gardie married the Swedish admiral Otto Stenbock. The 'Stenbock era' was to last until 1940 when the family returned to Sweden at the time of the Soviet occupation but few senior members of the family ever really used it. Eric Stenbock, who spent a year here in 1886–87, was perhaps the most colourful member of the family who did. He had hoped to marry and settle in the house, but having failed in that endeavour, he returned to Sweden. He was, however, remembered for the quantity of opium he smoked during that year and for the games of charades that he arranged for local children. From 1940, the estate was inevitably allowed to degenerate and only in 1980 did maintenance and restoration begin. Much remains to be done but a visit is still worthwhile as it is easy to picture how impressive the whole area must have been. The classical columns surmounted by the Stenbock coat of arms were built at the turn of the 19th century when the family was at its most prosperous, thanks to its successful distilling and farming. It is to be hoped that such prosperity quickly returns to the area. At the time of writing in late 2013 the future of the manor was uncertain, but there is a small museum in the outhouse that displays some of the furniture from the main building and which gives a history of the estate.

Viinistu Visitors who turned up here during the 1990s would have found a village that modern Estonia had completely ignored. Thanks though to a former manager of Abba, the continuingly successful Swedish pop group, it has suddenly become mainstream.

Jaan Manitski, who was born here in 1943, could chart his family links to the area stretching back 400 years, so when the family fled to Sweden in 1944, they always hoped to return. He did so in 1989 when, having made a fortune, he decided that money was no longer of great importance to him. He compared it to cow dung: something useful in small doses but which stinks in larger quantities. His first work in Viinistu was growing mushrooms; he then had a short spell as Estonian foreign minister where he caused havoc in the accounts department by leaving without bothering to claim his last month's salary. He is now part-owner of Estonia's major daily paper *Eesti Päevaleht* but what he will definitely be remembered for is the **Viinistu Art Museum**, which opened in 2003.

Until 2006, visitors here were rewarded with the best collection of 20th-century Estonian art in the whole country, and in particular with works by Konrad Mägi (see page 43) and Eduard Viiralt. With the opening of KUMU in Tallinn (pages 118–19), this is no longer the case, but it should not deter anyone from including the museum in their visit to Lahemaa. The collection is being constantly extended and several rooms are devoted to temporary exhibitions, some of which will

4

undoubtedly shock more sensitive visitors, who may prefer to limit their viewing to the permanent collection. Further exhibitions are held in a former warehouse, about a hundred metres along the coast. In 2005, a **hotel** opened next door to the main building and in every subsequent year there has been an extension to the exhibition facilities. These were joined by a chapel in 2013, with a relaxing view out to sea.

Space has been cleared for outdoor concerts. The website www.viinistu.ee (in Estonian) has the necessary current information. Rich Estonians who patronise the arts are very rare; as more business people enjoy the success that Jaan Manitski did, let us hope they follow in his footsteps.

OTHER ATTRACTIONS IN HARJUMAA COUNTY

Jäneda Readers of *An Estonian Childhood* by Tania Alexander, and H G Wells enthusiasts, will need no further incentive to come to this house, about an hour's train journey or bus ride from Tallinn. Although there is a railway station called Jäneda about 2km from the house, it is often quicker to take a suburban train to the last stop on the line at Aegviidu and then to arrange transport from there, as it is only 6km away. New electric trains were introduced on to this route in the summer of 2013 so it is now a very comfortable journey.

The building dates from 1913 when it replaced an earlier one destroyed in a fire. It was modelled on the Red House in Bexley Heath, just outside London. In its early days, when still in the Russian Empire, it usually provided respite for those escaping from the Bolsheviks in Petrograd, later to be Leningrad and now St Petersburg. A British naval attaché, Dennis Garstin, composed the following ditty, anglicising the name Jäneda to Yendel:

> At Yendel girls begin the day in optimistic negligée
> Followed hot-footed, after ten, by the pyjama-radiant me.
> I'm always sad in Petrograd.
> My nicer thoughts meander back, back to Yendel.
> Oh to be in Yendel for eternity.

He was only one of many men to be seduced by Jäneda in several senses of the word. Maxim Gorky and H G Wells were amongst these others. Wells in fact completed his autobiography here in 1934 with the words: 'I am finishing this autobiography in a peaceful and friendly house at a small lake in Estonia.' However, the owner of the estate had himself been murdered in the grounds in 1919. He was the father of Tania Alexander. The house she describes, and to which Wells refers – Kallijärv – is not this main one but a smaller one about a kilometre away beside the lake.

In 1928, an **agricultural school** was founded in the main and adjoining buildings by Konstantin Päts, who would later become president of Estonia. In Soviet times, Arnold Rüütel, president of Estonia from 2001 to 2006, studied here and agriculture has remained his major interest. Its second most famous pupil was the writer Juhan Smuul (see page 277). The school continues to this day and some of its students work in a **hotel** which has been opened on this site (✆ 384 9750; e info@ janedaturism.ee; www.janedaturism.ee). The hotel and the surrounding buildings make a congenial backcloth for parties and works outings.

The **museum** in the main building covers the history of the estate between 1920 and 1940, with many documents fortunately being saved from then. It also covers the Soviet period of the agricultural college, with the appropriate array of red banners and portraits of Lenin and Stalin. As in so many institutes in Soviet times, the Stalin memorabilia were only hidden after 1956 and were never destroyed, though few can have imagined that they would later be brought out for ridicule rather than for devotion.

Padise Monastery

Padise Monastery (*Padise; www.padiseklooster.ee*) Some 48km south of Tallinn and 18km south of Keila *en route* to Haapsalu, the Padise Monastery ruins dominate the surrounding countryside. The first stone building dates from the early 14th century, when it became a Cistercian foundation. This order is known for its simple lifestyle so there are no elaborate statues or tombs here and the location was deliberately distant from towns. However they were experts at underfloor heating. They ate fish but not meat, so were surrounded by ponds and in the 14th century the seashore was much closer than it is now. There is recent evidence of an earlier wooden settlement and some artefacts from it are on display. Bitter fighting took place in this area between Sweden and Russia in the late 16th century during the Livonian War when it became a fortress and the monks were forced to leave. In 1580 it took a 13-week siege by the Swedes to remove the Russian troops. Monks would never return and it then became a private manor house; in 1766 lightning destroyed much of the interior and it was never rebuilt. It would stay in ruins until 1937 when limited restoration began, which was continued from the 1950s under the Soviet regime and is still under way.

RAPLAMAA AND JÄRVAMAA COUNTIES

RAPLA, TÜRI, PAIDE AND IMAVERE Combining a visit to these towns and the surrounding villages makes a congenial tour of a day or two. Alternatively, the area can be visited *en route* from Tallinn to Tartu.

Getting there and around Both Paide and Türi enjoy a frequent **bus** service north to Tallinn and south to Tartu and Viljandi. There are also east–west services that stop in both towns *en route* from Narva to Pärnu. Rapla has a less frequent bus service but is almost unique in Estonia in having a good **train** service from Tallinn. The station is in fact about 2km from the town centre but local buses meet each train. **Car hire** is a sensible option for travelling in this area, as some of the places recommended away from these three towns are not on major bus routes.

Where to stay and eat Rapla has no hotels, but plenty of guesthouses and several pubs with rooms. One of the nearest to the town centre is Jõe (*Jõe 31a;* ☏ *489 4600;* e *info@joe.ee; www.joe.ee;* **$**), famous as one of the first guesthouses in Estonia to have a website. 'Jõe' means river in Estonian, which perfectly describes the location of the building.

A new restaurant **Roheline Ait** (Green Granary) (*Tallinna mnt 15a;* ☏ *603 1015; www.rohelineait.ee;* **$$**) took Rapla and then Estonia by storm in 2013, charging for meals what Tallinners expected to pay for a snack. Fans of live folk music should come in the evening whereas those who prefer a quieter environment should come during the day.

Hotel accommodation in Paide is much cheaper than in Tallinn or Tartu and as both are little more than an hour's drive away it is possible to stay in Paide and still have a full day for sightseeing in either city. Although it's a very modern town-centre hotel, **Nelja Kuninga** (Four Kings) (*Pärnu 6;* ☏ *385 0882;* e *neli.kuningat@neti.ee; www.nelikuningat.ee;* **$**) reverts back with its name to 1343, the date of the first major uprising of Estonian peasants against their still relatively new masters, the Teutonic Knights. The four Estonian elders chosen to represent their community in negotiations were imprisoned in Paide Castle and then murdered, so were subsequently honoured with the title of king. The restaurant is called the Golden Crown. Clients expecting regal standards will be disappointed; those happy with a standard three-star hotel will be pleased, particularly when comparing the prices with Tallinn. Paide also has a guesthouse, **Toru** (*Pikk 42*; \ *385 0385*; $), which is about five minutes' walk from the town centre.

Rapla There can be few if any other towns in northern Europe where an archaeological dig produced two contemporary 11th-century coins, a penny minted in England under William the Conqueror and a dirhem produced under Emir Daisam in Azerbaijan. Yet Rapla was already sufficiently cosmopolitan then for many traders to stay. The region then went into decline for 700 years until Catherine II took the area seriously again. By the late 19th century, it had become sufficiently grand for German chancellor Bismarck to pay several private visits. He was a university friend of the local Baltic-German landlord, Alexander Keyserling, whose manor house Raikküla is a few kilometres outside the town. The main oak tree there has been named 'Bismarck Tree' as the two of them used to sit and chat underneath it.

Rapla has always been at the forefront of Estonian nationalism, from the St George's Day Rebellion in 1343, through peasant uprisings in the 1850s and the anti-tsarist movement in 1905, to support for the Forest Brothers in their guerrilla warfare against Soviet forces after World War II. Estonians are proud of two separate achievements of Rapla, one in tsarist times and one in Soviet times. Despite the size of the town, neither a Russian Orthodox church nor a statue of Lenin was ever allowed to grace the landscape. The long-term links the town is happy to mention are those with Britain. It enjoyed several centuries of timber and flax trading with Scotland and the design of early iron crosses found in the cemetery suggests that the first Christian influences might have come from there rather than through the Teutonic Knights. In the 19th century, to free themselves from German or Russian names given by their landlords, several Estonian families took British place names instead. Bristol, Glasgow and London still, as a result, feature in the local telephone book.

From an architectural point of view, the Soviet era seems to have largely passed the whole town by. This makes a short stop here particularly attractive and, for those with more time, there are many manor houses within the county that are now sufficiently restored to warrant a visit. The county also represents a microcosm of Estonian history. The Antarctic explorer, Adam Johann von Krusenstern, was born in 1770 in Hagudi, 10km to the north of Rapla on the Tallinn road. The 19th-century playwright, August Kotzebue, came from Jarlepa, to the northeast of Rapla. Otto Tief, prime minister for just one day in 1944 before he was deported to Siberia, came from Alu, a village just outside Rapla, which has one of the best-preserved 19th-century manor houses. Although Lennart Meri, president from 1992 to 2001, had no links with Rapla, the community is pleased that he made up for this by marrying a Rapla girl. Jüri Rumm is not a name to be found on any book jacket or in any political history of Estonia, but his fame as a 19th-century horse thief has given him legendary status and a recent film will ensure this renown continues. His cover job was as a servant at Kehtna Manor, 10km south of Rapla, but he only really came to life after dark. Monuments, museums and houses throughout the county commemorate these and many other famous Estonians linked to the area.

The town of Rapla is famous for its two-tower **Mary Magdalene Church**. This church is unique in another respect – since the early 18th century, it has never been destroyed or burnt down. Fortunately the pulpit being built at that time could be kept in Tallinn until the end of the Northern War in 1720. The rebuilding at the beginning of the 20th century came about simply through the wishes of the local people and as a result of their affluence. The font and the altar date from the previous building. The church seats 900 in all: 500 downstairs and 400 upstairs. The congregation dropped to around 200 in 1949 when public displays of religion required the greatest courage. It increased in the 1980s to around 500 and then to 1,000 at independence.

At no time in the Soviet era could Christmas trees have been taken into the building, but during more liberal times, the pine trees outside the church were sometimes decorated in late December. The plaques beside the altar note the landowners who contributed to the cost of the building. The peasants who actually built the church scrawled their names under the supporting arches. The organ, installed in 1939, was probably the last pre-war one built in an Estonian church that survives. (One built in 1940 for St Peter's Church in Narva was destroyed during the fighting in 1944.)

The **Järvakandi Glass Museum** (*www.klaasimuuseum.ee*) is 18km south of Rapla and perhaps because of its relative isolation, provides on its website a virtual tour of all its exhibits. It is however well worth the effort of seeing them in the original, and for those who would like to try their hand at glass-blowing, that is possible too. The exhibits go back several centuries, but it is the contemporary ones that are really of interest and they show how predominant Estonia is in this field. The house belonged in the 19th century to a foreman at the factory. One room has now been redesigned to look as it did in the 1920s. Sheet glass used to be produced in Järvakandi, but after a botched privatisation in the early 1990s, that business was lost and has not been recovered.

The **church at Juuru**, 12km east of Rapla, has its origins more in politics than in religion. It was largely rebuilt in 1895 with Baltic-German money, to help reduce the spread of Russian Orthodoxy. This was the time when the Alexander Nevsky Cathedral was built in Tallinn, so where the Lutheran Baltic Germans could fight back, they did so. Much of the interior is earlier, the pulpit being by the 17th-century Tallinn woodcarver Christian Ackermann, whose work can also be seen in Rapla, Türi and in the Dome Church in Tallinn. Panels are based on those in the Holy Ghost Church in Tallinn. The cemetery dates from 1690, just before the plague when burials in town had to be banned on health grounds. The stone crosses have inscriptions in Estonian.

The **Mahtra Peasants Museum** (*www.mahtramuuseum.ee*), also in Juuru, covers an uprising that took place near here in 1858 against the corvée which the Russians were still trying to collect from local peasants. In the end it was suppressed, but only after bitter fighting and the use of considerable Russian reinforcements. The museum describes the fighting with the help both of models and of memorabilia, which include the manacles in which the leader of the rebellion, Hans Tertsius, was held before being sent to Siberia. The museum opened in 1970; as the revolt was more economic than nationalistic, it had a useful role to play in the Soviet presentation of Estonian history.

Mahtra War is one of the most famous novels by Eduard Vilde, written as a newspaper serial in the 1890s for the *Postimees* newspaper. The racy style that such a work needed to bring in the readers each week has ensured the continued publication of the novel, and hence the interest in this uprising. The museum, however, covers more than just the battles. There is a good 'upstairs, downstairs' contrast between day-to-day life at the manor and in the cottages at that time.

4

A kilometre outside Juuru is **Atla Manor**, the centre for earthenware production in Estonia. Their products are available in shops throughout Estonia, and a selection can be seen on www.keraamika.ee, but are obviously cheaper here. As usual in Estonia, there is no hard sell.

Märjamaa is to the west of Rapla so can be easily visited *en route* to Pärnu. The church is unusual in many respects. Its walls are 2m thick although they were never actually used in defence. On the northern side there are no windows, although the variety of designs on the south side makes up for this. Most of the building dates from the end of the 17th century. Retreating Russians bombed and totally destroyed the interior in 1941 when they thought, wrongly, that Germans had taken it over as a base. An altar by Christian Ackermann was one of many valuable pieces destroyed. Basic restoration started in 1960 and thanks to help from the Finnish town of Vihanti, more work has been done since the re-establishment of independence. The altar painting of Christ, the Virgin Mary and John the Baptist is very modern, having been completed in 2003.

Türi If a visitor to Estonia could visit only a single church, **St Martin's** in Türi would probably be the one to choose. It is very conscious of its central location in the country so it brings together architectural and artistic trends from throughout Estonia and from a range of periods. The walls therefore combine brick, granite and limestone. They date from the late 13th century, whereas the polychrome rooster was put on top of the tower in 1999. In between, there are the 16th-century wooden carvings by Christian Ackermann around the altar and the pulpit and then the 19th-century tower. The stained glass by the contemporary artist Dolores Hoffmann will surely be treasured for many centuries to come. One window illustrates the birth of Christ and was used in 2003 by the Estonian Post Office as the subject of their Christmas stamp. The whole church appeared on a stamp in 1995. Considering the wartime damage elsewhere in the town and in the surrounding county, it is remarkable how the church survived. Türi is twinned with Sherborne in Britain.

In 1937 a radio transmission tower was erected with British help. It was nearly 200m high, but was destroyed by the Russians as they retreated from the Germans in 1941. It was not replaced after the war.

Elsewhere, Türi appeals to two probably conflicting groups of people – railway enthusiasts and horticulturalists. When Estonia had a serious commitment to a railway system, it was centred on Türi, and railway workshops still operate there. They will doubtless be busy again from 2014 with the expanding services across Estonia. The **town museum** (*www.tyri.ee/muuseum*), which covers its history until 1940, concentrates on the 19th-century industrialisation. Unlike other town museums, in 2013 it had not yet shown exhibits covering Soviet times. As this building was a paper mill, the process of pulping is explained. It has a lot of material on the railway system, particularly bearing in mind that the collection only started in 1995. It is possible that in due course there will be a dedicated railway museum here, but this will depend on what happens to the material currently housed at Lavassaare (see pages 254–5). Türi would seem to be a logical home for it. The town website (*www.turism.tyri.ee*) is always kept up to date so will record any progress on this. The railway station was blown up by the Russians as they retreated in 1941, as was much else in Türi, but they rebuilt it soon after their return in 1944. It was extensively modernised in 2007 to reflect the increasing seriousness of rail travel in Estonia. In 2013 there were five trains a day to Tallinn and three to Viljandi. A first-class fare to Tallinn of €8 or €4.50 in economy is very good value. The café in the station is the place to eat in Türi, with pictures on the wall of trains from all over the world, including the UK. There is a proper waiting room and ticket office so further train services can to be expected in the near future.

Garden fairs take place throughout May in Türi but there is clearly collective pressure on the entire population to take horticulture seriously. They do, after all, have the space and the time necessary for this. A visit anytime during the summer will show the results of this activity.

The **Broadcasting Museum** (*www.rhmuuseum.ee*) opened here in 2001, in the same new building that houses the town museum and the tourist information office. The first Estonian radio broadcasts were made from here, in view of its central location, and the opening of the museum was a celebration of the 75th anniversary of this. Visitors are greeted by music from the 1930s. The technical equipment and the sets that reached the consumer from the 1920s until the present day are all shown, for both radio and television. These of course were imported from all over the world in the 1920s and 1930s but came only from within the Soviet Union after that. There are also unusual behind-the-scenes views of film studios, hospitals and mines, all from Soviet times.

Paide Halfway between Tallinn and Tartu, Paide makes a pleasantly quiet interlude between Estonia's two busiest cities. It uses a heart as its logo, given its position in the centre of Estonia. Abroad it is best known as the birthplace of the composer Arvo Pärt, born here in 1935. Paide means 'limestone' in Estonian and the German name for the town, Weissenstein, means the same. A visitor in 1923 enjoyed the peaceful atmosphere, ascribing it to the fact that the town 'had neither communists, nor capitalists, only *petits bourgeois*'. He would not be disappointed were he to return now, since the architecture of the 19th-century Town Hall Square has remained largely intact and the octagonal tower **Pikk Hermann**, blown up by the retreating Soviet army in 1941, has now been fully restored. It was first built in the 13th century. Our 1923 visitor would certainly be bemused here, now that it has become the **Wittenstein Time Centre** (*www.wittenstein.ee*). This is a kind of interior *son et lumiere* based on Estonia's history where sound and film, plus a few conventional exhibits and a modern lift, gives the visitor a 90-minute experience of life in Estonia from cavemen to the present day. Wittenstein is an earlier German word for 'limestone'.

The tower is surrounded by castle ruins, now used as an open-air display of modern sculpture. It has been in this condition since the early 17th century, but was bitterly fought over before that between the Russians, Swedes and Poles. There were no subsequent attempts to restore it.

The **Church of the Holy Cross** in the town centre has also suffered tremendous damage but has always been rebuilt. The present structure dates largely from the mid 19th century, with some internal work added in the early 20th century. It is a mystery why the tower is in the middle and not at the west end of the church. Much restoration still needs to be done to the interior, as it was totally neglected during Soviet times.

The original collection of the **Järvamaa Museum** (*www.jarvamaamuuseum. ee*) dates from 1905 and the museum has been in this building for 45 years, but was extensively refurbished in autumn 2000. One of the founders was the mayor at that time, Oskar Brasche, who had inherited a chemist's shop originally founded in 1796. He donated the complete interior of this shop to the museum. Another room portrays farming life in the late 19th century, when the abolition of serfdom made peasants largely self-reliant. The local wood was made into jugs, plates and chests, leather into shoes, and flax or wool into clothes. The use of metal was limited to knives, chisels and axes. With schools teaching in Estonian from 1835 onwards, they would all be literate. Another room shows how a more fortunate family spent their ample leisure time, in this case singing around the piano, all dressed to the nines. Like several recently restored museums, Paide no longer sees the need to eradicate the Soviet period. The 'Golden Sixties' are portrayed with smiling farmers receiving their prizes. A sitting room has been recreated so realistically that even the regulation bowl of coarsely wrapped boiled sweets has not been forgotten.

Imavere As with Paide and Põltsamaa (see pages 206–7), Imavere makes a good break on the otherwise chronically dull drive from Tallinn to Tartu. The dairy industry was the backbone of the Estonian economy during the first independence period from 1920 to 1940. Many people living in Britain at that time remembered Estonia simply as the place where their butter came from and some still have the tins to prove it. The **Estonian Dairy Museum** (*www.piimandusmuuseum.ee*) shows how this came about as a mixture of government policy and private initiative. Although some exhibits deal with dairy farming as far back as 1850, the museum concentrates on those crucial 20 years and the exhibition stops at 1940. By then there were about 300 dairies in Estonia, mostly operated on a co-operative basis. In 1938, 15 million kilos of butter were exported, 57% to the UK and 39% to Germany so only 4% went elsewhere.

This is very much a family museum with lots of activities linked both closely and distantly with the dairy industry for the amusement of children. A large outdoor playground with swings is open whenever the museum is. Of course in the old days, children would help with the churning of butter and several pictures illustrate this.

because U are unique

top   Singing festivals, such as the Student Song
           and Dance Festival, have been the backbone
           of Estonian culture since the mid 19th century
           (LM/VE) pages 47–8

above left   The Seto national minority, who live in
               southeast Estonia, continue with their
               independent style of dress
               (JN/VE) pages 223–4

above right Tallinn's Rotermanni market sells local
               handicrafts as well as organic fruit and
               vegetables (VE) page 112

right   Tourists and locals happily mingle
           in Tallinn's Town Hall Square
           (LM/VE) page 107

above

Rakvere Castle is set on one of Estonia's few hills, which were always put to use as a refuge from the dangers of the surrounding countryside (TT/VE) page 156

left

At Sangaste Castle a trace of southern England unexpectedly appears, with its 19th-century heritage largely intact (SS) pages 212–13

left

Kuressaare Castle on Saaremaa Island has remained intact for centuries, still looking as threatening as it always has done (S/G) page 267

below

Scotland makes its only appearance in Estonia, with Alatskivi Castle, a faithful model of Balmoral (EAS/VE) page 175

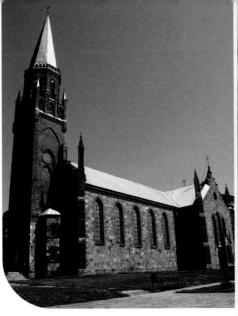

above left   St Paul's Church, Viljandi was built in the late 19th century to serve the increasing population of the town (S/K) page 203

above right   St Catherine's Church, Pärnu, is named after the Russian Empress who was on the throne when the church was built in the late 18th century (JN/VE) page 249

right   The Alexander Nevsky Cathedral, Tallinn, was built overlooking the town as a symbol of Tsarist power, just 17 years before the regime collapsed (S/EN) page 103

below   Inside the wooden Ruhnu Church (TT/VE) page 281

above   Lahemaa National Park was the first one to be created in the former USSR; it dates from 1971 (S/AG) pages 140–6

left   Soomaa National Park, along the western coast, is a series of wetlands often prone to flooding (AR/VE) page 10

below   Abruka is an island with a population now down to 30, but where moths and butterflies continue to thrive (S/AO) pages 278–9

above left Vilsandi National Park on Saaremaa is one of the main centres in Estonia for studying migratory birds (VE) page 274

above right Most of Haapsalu's buildings date from the late 19th century when the town was the favoured seaside resort of the Russian artistocracy (S/A) pages 233–40

right The Kaali Craters on Saaremaa were formed by a meteorite crashing 3,000 years ago (VE) page 276

below Altja is now a fishing village, but was formerly the centre for smuggling alcohol to Finland during prohibition there (TT/VE) page 144

above left Although extinct in other parts of the world, there are around 1,000 lynx in Estonia (SZ/VE) page 6

above right Due to rising numbers of wolves, the Estonian government now offers cash rewards for each wolf killed (SZ/VE) page 6

left European beavers leave their traces everywhere in the forests and wetlands (SZ/VE) page 7

below left Roe deer are Estonia's most common mammal, often seen in fields and forest borders (SZ/VE) page 6

below right Squirrels flitter amongst the red and gold of Kadriorg Park in autumn (VE) page 132

above   Extremely rare in the rest of Europe, white-backed woodpeckers can be seen on Estonia's many dead trees (SS) page 8

above right   Estonia is home to half a dozen owl species, including the ural owl (SZ/VE) page 8

right   The symbolic bird of rural areas, the white stork is a new species in Estonia (S/ZA) page 8

below   Estonia's coast is home to the white-tailed eagle, Europe's largest and rarest eagle species (S/R) page 8

Saaremaa is one of Estonia's most attractive islands: its rocky, stony and sandy coastline allows a great variety of natural habitats (VE & LM/VE) pages 260–78

5

North and Northeast Estonia

This area of Estonia has been largely ignored by tourists since independence, or at best raced through *en route* to St Petersburg. There are a number of reasons for this. During the Soviet occupation, many Russian settlers moved in and some towns still remain 90% Russian-speaking; their interests and commitments have therefore been eastwards rather than westwards. Decent hotels have been few and far between and industrial pollution severely harmed much of the coastal area. The larger hotels at **Lake Peipsi** were used to receiving allocated Soviet trade-union groups so never needed to promote themselves and could not adapt to the more fastidious requirements of middle-class Western tourists. However, since 1996 a determined effort has been made to tackle these problems and to spread the economic blessings of tourism that the rest of Estonia has enjoyed. The urban environments are now clean and strict controls ensure the maintenance of the national parks and the water flowing into Lake Peipsi. Visiting the area in 2003 was a very different experience from going in 2001, and from 2009 the changes were even more dramatic. There are many new hotels, attractions are being built and some museums are actually touting for visitors, rather than seeing them as a tiresome intrusion. The concert hotel in Jõhvi and the spa hotels along the coast attract visitors from throughout Estonia, and increasingly from abroad too. Apart from in Narva, there are few restaurants of note, so most visitors eat in their hotels. Estonia's entry into the Schengen Agreement greatly simplified entry visas for Russians and the tough economic situation elsewhere made the large increase in tourists from the St Petersburg area very welcome.

RAKVERE

Rakvere is just off the main Tallinn–Narva–St Petersburg highway, about 100km from both Tallinn and Narva. Compared with most towns in Estonia, it has had a remarkably peaceful history, benefiting from membership of the Hanseatic League from 1300. It has stayed a quiet, but affluent county town, largely undisturbed by the changing political regimes. The local motto is 'full of might' and evidence for this started to appear around 2000, even if the mayor's claim at the time that 'Rakvere will be New York' remains far-fetched for a town with a population of 18,000. However, to publicise the town since then, the castle and theatre have been renovated, the town has commissioned one of the largest pieces of sculpture in the country, and in 2003 it hosted a 19-hour reading in full of the national epic *Kalevipoeg* to celebrate the 200th anniversary of the birth of its writer, Friedrich Reinhold Kreutzwald. A total of 126 volunteers were needed to read the 20,000 verses involved.

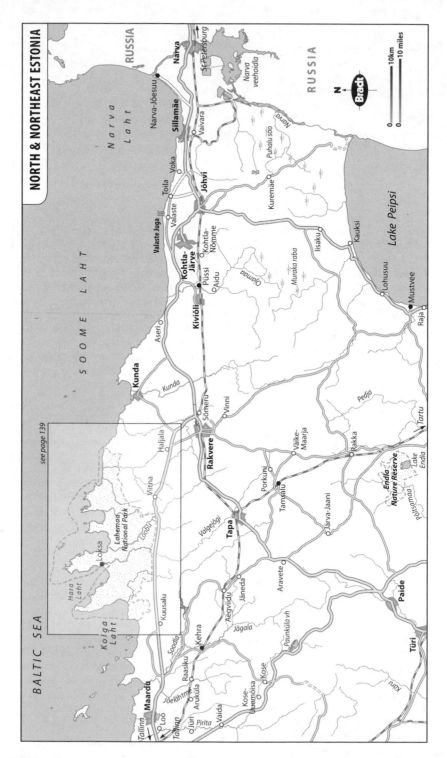

NORTH & NORTHEAST ESTONIA

They had considered reading the 5,000 pages of the EU Association Agreement, but partly because this would have taken a week and partly no doubt because of the boring nature of the material, it didn't take place. That such an idea was even considered shows the new spirit of irreverence that has broken out in Rakvere after a decade of torpor through the 1990s. It also results from close co-operation between the local authority and the business community, both of which are bubbling with ideas to provide facilities which many towns five times its size would die for. The first decade of the 21st century saw a new theatre, a private airport, a spa centre, a completely redesigned central square, the completion of repairs to the castle and a New Year's Eve firework display that puts every other city in the Baltics to shame. Its only major lack in 2013 was a special restaurant; there is a good choice of places to snack, but none really stand out. Fortunately Vihula is not too far away.

The Russians bombed Rakvere around the railway station in 1944, but otherwise the only violence in Rakvere's history took place in 1574; a quarrel broke out between German and Scottish mercenaries, both serving in the Swedish army against the Russians. The Germans slaughtered most of the Scots and the few who survived that onslaught were taken prisoner by the Russians and then immediately killed. The German name for the town, Wesenberg, probably stems from an old German word for aurochs, a type of bison, prevalent here when the Teutonic Knights first arrived in the 13th century.

GETTING THERE AND AROUND Considering the town's population of only 18,000, it is remarkably well served by buses to all parts of Estonia. In particular it is worth noting the **buses** that operate from here to several villages in Lahemaa National Park and to Vihula Manor, which enable visitors without a car to explore that area. Buses going south pass the Pandivere and Endla reserves. Buses to the east serve Kohtla-Järve, Narva and St Petersburg. Rakvere is also on the main railway line between Tallinn and St Petersburg. Passenger **trains** stopped serving the station in 2001 but the service was renewed in 2007, when the station had been completely rebuilt. From 2012, the revived train services to St Petersburg stopped here and from 2014 there will be an enhanced domestic service to Tallinn and to Narva. The fare is about €4 to both Tallinn and to Narva. The journey takes 90 minutes to Tallinn and two hours to Narva. The town is dominated by the castle but is small enough to **walk** between its attractions.

TOURIST INFORMATION The tourist office is close to the bus station at Laada 14 but the entrance is on Adoffi (\ *324 2734*; e *rakvere@visitestonia.com; www.visitestonia. com/rakvere*). For many years, it did not have a shopfront but was on the first floor of this block. In 2005 it finally moved downstairs, reflecting the change of approach taken by the local authority to tourism.

 WHERE TO STAY AND EAT Rakvere is a convenient base for exploring the nearby manor houses and castles, as well as Lahemaa National Park (see pages 140–6). Equally it is easy to reach on day trips from either Tallinn or Lahemaa.

⌂ **Aqva Hotel** (120 rooms) Parkali 4; \ 326 0000; e info@aqvahotels.ee; www. aqvahotels.ee. The opening of this hotel in 2008 shows as little else can how Rakvere constantly punches above its weight. Where else in a town of 18,000 people could a hotel of this size & sophistication succeed as soon as it opened? Not only that, it had to build a large extension 2 years later. Recession seems to be a word unknown in Rakvere. This hotel is a full wellness centre, & not just a spa. It therefore has both wet & dry treatments & a full-size swimming pool. The staff

5

are from all over east Asia & the clients from all over Estonia, with an increasing interest from Russians. In fact its highest room rates are around 7 Jan, the Russian Christmas. Perhaps for them there is a smoking room, but it is totally insulated from the rest of the hotel, as regulations now demand. Estonia, like many countries in east Asia, has space for generous hotel lobbies & this is taken to an extreme here. Fountains would look cramped, so water cascades down walls. Families have not only rooms designed for them but also the Pirate Restaurant, with an extensive games centre on this theme right beside the eating area, so children can be watched the whole time. **$$$**

⌂ **Katariina** (24 rooms) Pikk 3; 322 3943; e info@katariina.ee; www.katariina.ee. The opening of this hotel in 2002, & the rebuilding of the neighbouring shops on Pikk, showed that Rakvere was serious in wanting tourists to stay, as they now had a congenial environment to spend an evening. Improvements in the neighbourhood continue year by year. The hotel foyer is an art gallery too, an outlet for local painters, & local bands play in the restaurant each Fri & Sat evening. **$$**

⌂ **Villa Theresa** (18 rooms) Tammiku 9; 322 3699; e villatheresa@hot.ee or info@ villatheresa.ee; www.villatheresa.ee. This small family-run hotel has been carved out of an opening in a wood on the outskirts of the town; now it is perfectly quiet but this was not the case in Dec 1918 when the Bolsheviks used it for executions. It is about 1km from the bus station & main shopping centre. One of the rooms has been adapted for those with disabilities. All rooms are named after German towns. One, Preetz, near Kiel, is where the former owner was born. **$$**

⌂ **Wesenbergh** (37 rooms) Tallinna 25; 322 3480; e info@wesenbergh.ee; www.wesenbergh. ee. Centrally located in a building now 100 years old, but which was fully restored in 1998, & renovated again in 2013, its large rooms suit the business community who are its backbone throughout the winter. Some describe it as 'the end of civilisation' in view of their contempt for anything further east towards the Russian border & the consistently high level of 'Western' service here. **$$**

WHAT TO SEE AND DO The castle (*www.svm.ee*) dates originally from the 14th century but neglect and looting are more responsible for its current ruined state than any specific attack. It has in fact been a ruin since the 17th century and even basic maintenance was not undertaken before 1975. It is now beyond repair, but in 2002 an extensive renovation programme was begun and by 2004 it had more or less become a theme park, with a Livonian dining hall and a chamber of horrors. Further renovation was completed in 2013. The conventional exhibits expected in a castle are few and far between. It now offers indoor and outdoor performances during the summer, and groups are welcome 24 hours a day. Details of these performances can be checked on the castle website. The squeamish would do well to take a virtual tour on this site before committing themselves to the 'real' thing.

The 750th anniversary of the founding of Rakvere in 1252 was marked by the commission in 2002 of a statue of an aurochs (very large, extinct type of cattle) by Tauno Kangro (b1966), whose work is always provocative and always larger than life, particularly where the depiction of sexual organs is concerned. This aurochs is no exception, as it weighs seven tons, is 7m long and has a distance of 3m between its two horns. The plinth lists all the donors who contributed, and also gives a history of the castle in the languages of its many occupiers – Danish, German, Polish, Russian and Swedish. The Danes introduced stone buildings into Estonia in the 13th century. Before that, they were all of wood.

For Estonians, the theatre (*Kreutzwaldi 2a; www.rakvereteater.ee*) in Rakvere is just as famous as the castle. Building started in 1927, when fundraising began under the auspices of Jacob Livv, brother of the writer Juhan Liiv (see page 176), but it was only completed early in 1940, just before the Soviet invasion. Its formal opening took place on 24 February, Independence Day, the last time for 50 years when it could be celebrated. It had a particularly unhappy time during the 1950s and 1960s when alcohol or excessive dissidence (or in some cases both) curtailed the careers of many potentially brilliant actors and directors. Although somewhat greater artistic freedom was granted later on, the building fell into decay and cynics wondered whether it would become a totally open-air theatre, so bad was the state of the roof. That is now well in the past and instead of being an artistic graveyard it has become an artistic cradle and centre. The completely renovated building reopened in 2005 and attracts 60,000 visitors from all over the country every year. 'Transitory Men' has been the symbol of this theatre since its foundation and 'the men' are now represented by two sculptured figures in front of the entrance. In early July each year, the theatre's appeal becomes international when performers come from all over Europe to participate in *Baltoscanda*, a wide-ranging drama festival. In the spirit of current Rakvere, expect to be provoked and even shocked by what is offered. The dedicated website, www. baltoscandal.ee, gives details of upcoming performances.

The **Holy Trinity Church** on Pikk dates from the 15th century but has been destroyed and rebuilt so often since then that the exterior all seems very modern. Inside, however, is woodwork by Elert Thiele, a 17th-century woodcarver best known for the frieze in Tallinn Old Town Hall. His pupil Christian Ackermann would become far more famous than he did, and the pulpit here is Ackermann's work. Ackermann is better known of course for his pulpit and altar in the Dom Church in Tallinn. The organ was built by the three Kriis brothers in 1925, as nearly any organ of note built in Estonia between 1880 and 1940 came from their workshop in Võru. The church is eager to welcome foreign visitors. In 2012 it became possible to climb up the spire, and leaflets were printed in English. In 2013 it opened a café.

The **secondary school** on Vabaduse Tänev (Freedom Street) is an unexpected masterpiece of Estonian functionalist architecture and was fortunately completed just before the first Soviet invasion in 1940. It was unique at the time in building classrooms for specific subjects and in allocating space specifically for a gymnasium. Its special status continued to be recognised in the 1960s during the Soviet period when a swimming pool was added. For many years the **Rakvere Exhibition House** (*Tallinna 3; www.svm.ee*) did not do the town justice but recent additions in the archaeological section, models of former burial mounds and a new section on the manor houses of the surrounding county now make a visit worthwhile. Even more tempting for most will be the vodka bar, justified as the museum has extended its collection to include an exhibition on the history of legal and illegal distilling in Estonia.

Significance should not be read into the police decision to open the **Estonian Police Museum** (*3a Tallinna; www.politseimuuseum.ee*) in Rakvere in 2013 but it follows the practice developed at the castle of bringing activity, noise and colour into an environment more used to glass cases and static models. For those who have longed to solve a hostage crisis, control riots or be at the centre of a road accident, this is the place to come. A playroom offers an introduction to traffic issues for young children.

The value of a visit to the **Citizens' Home Museum** (*Pikk 50; www.svm.ee*) has never been in doubt. It has been owned and inhabited since the late 18th century by a number of successful small businessmen, each of whom added tastefully to the furnishings, upholstery and kitchenware. The museum opened in 1983 and ever since then donations from local people have helped to broaden the collection. Recent additions include workshops of a tailor and of a cobbler and many photographs from 1920–40.

Some 25km south of Rakvere is the **Väike-Maarja Museum** (*Pikk 10; www.v-maarja.ee*) in the village of the same name. It is unique in Estonia in its concentration on the Soviet period. This is because it was the most successful collective farm in Estonia and made its director Boris Gavronski famous all over the USSR. He came in 1967 and stayed until its end in 1990. Between 1979 and 1987 he increased monthly wages from the already high 250 roubles a month to the enormous 350 a month. A few exhibits are from earlier times and a 19th-century schoolroom has been recreated. As Väike-Maarja is on the Rakvere–Tartu road, it is easy to reach by bus from either town.

For those travelling by car, it is worth making a small detour to the northeast on the way back to Rakvere by visiting **Porkuni**, a castle tower dating from the 15th century which houses the **Limestone Museum** (*www.porkuni.ee*). The museum opens only in the summer so do check the website for further details. Many of the exhibits are of interest only to professional geologists, but plenty of others show how important Estonia's national stone has been in its history. The other buildings date from the 1870s and since the 1930s have housed a school for the deaf.

TAPA

Tapa owes everything to the development of the railways in the 19th century. What was formerly a little village had the good fortune to find itself at the junction of the Tallinn–St Petersburg and Tallinn–Tartu railways, which opened in 1870 and 1876 respectively. It then also became a major agricultural distribution centre, earning the nickname 'sausage town' from its importance in the meat trade. Most of the Estonian bacon exported to Britain before the war was packaged here. Tapa suffered widespread destruction by the Soviets during their retreat in 1941 and bombardment before their return in 1944, which explains the empty feeling of the town centre. Tapa unfortunately means 'to kill' in Estonian.

More recently the Russians bequeathed an enormous military and air-force base, which can be seen from the Paide road. For those in a car, a short diversion is worthwhile to see it in its full horror. Although different, the destruction here by the departing soldiers was as ruthless as that carried out by their grandfathers 50 years earlier. Anything with possible resale value was removed so no single thread of copper wire or a single piece of wood remains. Stolen petrol too bulky to take was poured into the ground, ruining the water supply and potential civilisation for several years afterwards. Only water supplies more than 150m below ground could be regarded as safe. With the uncertainties that have constantly surrounded Estonian railways privatisation in the early years of the 21st century, the town now has to look to diversification into small-scale manufacturing and into agriculture to ensure its future. It has, however, no plans to abandon its coat of arms, a silver letter 'T' on a red background, symbolising the railway junction.

GETTING THERE AND AROUND The train takes about an hour to Tallinn, 90 minutes to Tartu and 45 minutes to Rakvere. In 2013 there were six trains a day to Tallinn, three a day to Tartu and one a day to Narva but considerable increases in rail services are expected in 2014. For timetables and fares see www.edel.ee. **Buses** also serve these three towns, as well as Rapla and Paide. Buses leave from the railway station, which is appropriately located right in the town centre.

WHAT TO SEE AND DO The **Orthodox church** (1904) and the **Methodist church** (1920) are both close to the station and show the divided ethnic loyalties of the town. Both are still well supported, financially and with good congregations. The **museum** (*www.tapamuuseum.ee*), in Pikk, about a kilometre from the station, dates only from 1991, but has built up a remarkably diverse collection in that time and is constantly expanding. Unusually for Estonia, it is run entirely by volunteers. The railway theme of course predominates, with pictures, timetables, uniforms, ticket printers, gas lamps and even candle lights. There is also a banknote display covering 1920–40, ceramics and glassworks. Hopefully the departure of the Soviet military and the town's current transition can soon be covered.

Visits to the railway workshops can be arranged for specialist groups, where a great deal of current and abandoned rolling stock can be seen from public areas, exhibits include a Russian L-1361 steam engine built in 1950 and displayed here since 1975.

KOHTLA-JÄRVE

If any Estonian town aiming to attract tourists is likely to fall victim to music-hall jokes, it must be Kohtla-Järve. Its comprehensive English-language brochure admits that it has no ancient history or beauty, but hopes that visitors will realise that it has great potential. It then proclaims the rather ambiguous slogan that 'Kohtla-Järve is mostly open to the winds of change'. A small town before World War II, it was rapidly developed in Soviet times as an industrial centre with the expansion of the oil-shale mines. A new chemicals plant was established to use the raw materials that the oil-shale provides. Kohtla-Järve is now the fourth-largest town in the country, after Tallinn, Tartu and Narva. By the late 1980s, the town had become a byword for industrial pollution, and much early political activity in Estonia against the Moscow authorities was aimed at bringing this to the attention of the international community. This pollution has now been controlled, but the city buildings and the health of older residents will remain scarred for many years to come.

Such political activity did not come from the Russians, who moved into the area to work in the mines and factories, but from ethnic Estonians now living elsewhere. Most Russians in Estonia were happy at least to acquiesce in the moves towards independence; only in Kohtla-Järve were there serious attacks on, for instance, the increasing use of the Estonian language from 1988.

The artificial hills surrounding the town comprise the layers of limestone that divide the beds of oil-shale and which are surplus to the requirements of the cement industry. They have been converted into artificial ski slopes and hang-gliding centres, since the few natural hills in Estonia are a good 150km to the south and this area is assured of regular, substantial snowfalls throughout the winter. They even have ski lifts and illumination so that they can be used in the evenings.

The period 2013–15 will see considerable development in the 'heritage triangle' of Kohtla-Järve, Kivõli and Aidu. The mining museum at Kohtla-Järve, described below, paved the way for tourism in this area and then Kivõli followed with the ski runs. In September 2013, Aidu opened a rowing course more than 2km long,

AN UNFORTUNATE DISCOVERY

A local legend ascribes the discovery of oil-shale as a fuel to a peasant who built a sauna from what he took to be a reliable stone. When planning a relaxing evening in front of his new stove, he was horrified to see it engulfed in the flames he had just generated. He suffered, but, in the long term, Estonia would benefit from the discovery of 'combustible stone', which is the literal translation of the Estonian word for oil-shale.

which had been carved out of a former oil-shale quarry. Five million cubic metres of earth were moved for this. The quarry had been set up in 1964 under the typical procedures from that time, a unanimous vote by the local collective farm. It should not be long before a new generation votes with its oars and with its wallets to enjoy itself here and perhaps even to buy a country cottage.

GETTING THERE AND AROUND Local **buses** regularly serve Tallinn, Rakvere, Jõhvi, Sillamäe and Narva. Tallinn is about a two-hour journey, Narva about one hour. At Jõhvi it is possible to change to buses going to Tartu, Valga and Võru. By 2014, there should be a serious **train** service linking the area with Tallinn to the west and Narva to the east. As with most Estonian towns, Kohtla-Järve is small enough to **walk** around.

 WHERE TO STAY AND EAT

Alex (10 rooms) Kalevi 3; ☎ 339 6230; e alex@alex.ee; www.alex.ee. A small modern hotel is most welcome in Kohtla-Järve, though some may feel there is overkill on the facilities offered to attract local people in as well. There are 9 billiard tables & a casino that closes only from 07.00–09.00. However, these can easily be avoided by guests wanting a conventional stay, as can presumably the 'drug-shop', which the website offers as a nearby facility. The restaurant is pleasantly normal, being the only place to eat in the town centre. **$$**

WHAT TO SEE AND DO From around 2000, Kohtla-Järve and the surrounding towns really began to try to present themselves internationally. Earlier visitors to the **Museum of Oil Shale** (*www.pkm.ee*) were amused to see a Soviet exhibition that had not changed since the early 1980s with a beaming Leonid Brezhnev, ever-rising production figures and workers who never strike. The local government was of course sensible to close it down and rebuild the exhibition in modern surroundings in 2000 – it is now in the Town Hall – even if the result is more predictable. For those not interested in the technical side, several dramatic paintings and sculptures are also on display.

The functionalist **secondary school** is very similar to that in Rakvere, although built by a different architect. The large, rounded projection can be compared to that on the Ranna Hotel in Pärnu. The **Orthodox church** may well be unique in its functionalist design. The lack of any onion motifs or other similarities to what is normally expected in the design of Orthodox churches is clearly a reflection of anti-Russian feeling at the time it was built. The museum and the church are both on Jarvekula, the main street through the town. The school is on Spordi, a cross street to Jarvekula and close to the museum.

Even those who can only make a 'virtual' visit to the **Kohtla Mining Museum** (*Kohtla-Nõmme, about 5km southwest of Kohtla-Järve; www.kaevanduspark.ee*) will instantly see what progress has been made in the last few years. This was a working mine from 1937 until 2000. It is probably the only museum in Estonia to open seven days a week on a year-round basis. Those who take the trouble to go, and visitors do so from all over Estonia, are rewarded with travel on the underground railways, the obligation to wear protective clothing and, perhaps less enticing, the chance to eat a miner's meal.

Life outside the museum buildings is equally active, with the former slag heaps now converted into tracks for skiing, orienteering and motorcycling to ensure year-round use. The visitor centre above ground expands each year as more exhibits relevant to mining are discovered and in 2013 it opened a **hostel** for those happy with simple accommodation.

The village of Toila is situated on the coast 10km to the north of Jõhvi. Such is the intensity of feeling towards the pre-war president Konstantin Päts that the site of his summer house **Oru Castle**, although now destroyed, is still a centre of interest to local tourists.

The palatial building was originally constructed at the turn of the 20th century by a St Petersburg businessman hoping to present it to the Tsar in return for a title. The garden layout, which still remains, was designed by Georg Kuphaldt, best known for his work in central Riga in conjunction with the 700th anniversary celebrations held there in 1901. Until he was expelled from Riga to Germany in 1915, he was the most sought-after landscape gardener in the Russian Empire. The Estonian government bought it as a summer residence for the president in 1935 but it was destroyed by the retreating Soviet army in 1941. Only the terrace, the entrance gates, the long gravel drive encompassed by willow trees and steps to the garden remain, although a series of underground passages is also gradually being reopened. Yet the surroundings are of such unusual natural beauty that it is easy to forget the absence of the palace. The Püha River cuts a dramatically deep course through the estate to the sea, with a botanical garden formed on either side. Sheer cliffs stretch along the coast for several kilometres. An outdoor concert centre was completed in 1995 with seating for several thousand and only the absence of cheap accommodation prevents more visitors from coming.

In 2006, the servants' quarters, the only part of the complex not to have been destroyed, were partially reopened as a museum commemorating President Päts. It also has a model of the castle as it looked in the 1930s and pictures taken at that time. The remaining areas clearly show their recent past as a Soviet pioneer camp.

It is possible to drive along parts of the **coast** from the Russian border at Narva-Jõesuu to Saka Manor House north of Kohtla-Järve, and where the main road turns inland, paths and cycle tracks remain. The most dramatic section is between Toila and Saka. This was made a protected area in 1939, and the Soviet restrictions on access to the coast in Estonia prevented any development after that. Halfway between Toila and Saka is the **waterfall** at Valaste, which looks natural but in fact was engineered in the 1970s. Its drop of around 25m makes it the deepest waterfall in the Baltic states. It is at its best in midwinter, when it completely freezes. Wedding couples have their picture taken with the waterfall as a background and fix a lock to the bridge as a symbol of hope for their marriage to last. The 24-hour café here has facilities for the disabled and a much wider menu than one might expect at such an isolated location.

GETTING THERE AND AWAY Buses run several times a day from Jõhvi and **taxis** for this short journey are not expensive. A **driver/guide** is worthwhile for Toila and the neighbouring area. This can be arranged as part of a tour or on the spot at the tourist office in Jõhvi.

 ## WHERE TO STAY

Toila Sanatoorium (150 rooms) Ranna 12; 334 2900; e info@toilaspa.ee; www.toilaspa. ee. So international does this hotel want to be that its website was in 4 languages & its prices were quoted in euros as early as 2002, 9 years before Estonia adopted the euro. Probably people will meet here whose paths would never cross elsewhere. Russians come on sentimental grounds, thinking it is still home. Finns come because the basic costs & those for treatments are so much lower than those at home, or elsewhere in Estonia. Estonians use it as a base for work or pleasure over the whole northeast. It can be recommended to Westerners for similar reasons. It offers enough on site for taking it easy, but is a useful base from which to drive, walk or cycle along the coast & to explore inland as well. If the accommodation is somewhat dated now, the treatments offered are certainly not. Transfers are arranged to Tallinn. $$$

✕ WHERE TO EAT AND DRINK

✕ **Fregatt** Pikk 18; ☏ 336 9647; www.fregatt.ee. This is a good restaurant in Toila, which has attracted a middle-aged clientele with its dependable steak, generous Irish coffee, prices about a 3rd of what they would be in Tallinn & the music of Roy Orbison. They are quite willing to turn off the music altogether, or to substitute contemporary Estonian music. $

JÕHVI

Jõhvi is the capital of Ida Viru, the eastern county of Estonia. At first glance, it is tempting to write it off as a Soviet leftover, best driven through at the fastest speed possible. Certainly other towns in the area still have a completely Russian feel but Jõhvi is clearly trying to promote co-existence. This must be its future, with a population one-third Estonian and two-thirds Russian. The town is re-establishing an Estonian identity, without trying to hide a Russian past of half a century. This is seen in the variety of shops recently established and the enormous rebuilding programme under way in the town centre. The development of exports, such as dairy products, is still geared to Russia. However, a reasonable hotel and a new concert hall now provide an excellent pretext for staying.

GETTING THERE AND AROUND The bus station is close to the Town Hall, the Concert Hall and the Wironia Hotel. Perhaps because the local population is poorer here than elsewhere in Estonia, fewer people have cars so the public transport system is much more extensive. Direct services operate frequently all over the country, with hourly **buses** to Tallinn, Kohtla-Järve, Narva, Rakvere and Kuremäe and a service four times a day south to Tartu and Võru. The buses from Tallinn and Tartu to St Petersburg stop *en route* in Jõhvi. The journey to Tallinn takes two hours 30 minutes, to Narva it is about one hour. A passenger train service was restored in 2008, but offering just a morning train to Tallinn and an evening train to Narva. This service will probably be increased in 2014. **Walking** is the best way to get around the town centre.

TOURIST INFORMATION The tourist information office is at Rakvere 13a (☏ *337 0568; www.johvi.ee*).

WHERE TO STAY AND EAT

🏠 **Wironia** (21 rooms) Rakvere 7; ☏ 336 4200; e info@wironia.ee; www.wironia. ee. This hotel opened in autumn 2004 so finally Jõhvi got a normal, town-centre hotel. Despite its small size, it has a large restaurant & conference facilities. However, it really needed some renovation by 2013, as Jõhvi deserves higher standards. $$

WHAT TO SEE AND DO Architecturally, the **Town Hall**, which dominates the centre, can only be Estonian with its mixture of Functionalism and Classicism. Some neighbouring Soviet horrors can therefore be forgiven. The nearby **St Michael's Lutheran Church** has also survived the frequent changes in secular regimes and managed to win support from all of them despite the execution of two vicars, one in 1918 and one in 1941. This latter fact gives it the macabre distinction of being the only church in Estonia with two martyrs. The Soviets in a small way redeemed themselves by keeping the church open and by rebuilding the organ in the early 1950s. This organ (the first of six produced in Soviet Estonia) was destroyed by the installation of central heating in the 1980s. In 1984, the Soviets also rebuilt the tower, which had been destroyed by the Germans in 1943. A Swedish congregation presented a new organ in 1996.

As the church was as much a castle as a place of worship, it has a complex array of tunnels and hiding places. The pulpit has frequently been repainted, but the design is the original early 18th-century Baroque. The altar is modern, but the six steps that lead up to it disguise a cover for an extended cellar, which over many centuries housed supplies and hid troops. Now it hosts the church museum, and an audio-guide is available to give further background to the history of the church. As more excavations are carried out, further 17th and 18th-century woodwork is being revealed and some 19th-century Bibles have been discovered.

The **Concert Hall** (✆ *334 2000; www.concert.ee/johvi-111*) opened in 2005 and although the population of the town is only 16,000, a hundred concerts a year take place here and most of the 900 seats in the auditorium are filled, perhaps because the maximum price is often only €10 even when international musicians perform. There is also a smaller hall seating 160 for chamber music and for films. Previously there was no central focus to Jõhvi; it offered nothing in the cultural field. Now people flock in from miles around to this concert hall. It complements the three others run by Eesti Kontsert in Tallinn, Tartu and Pärnu. Given that the population of Estonia is only 1.3 million, this shows the excellent provision now made in the cultural field, which inevitably had to be neglected in the early days of independence.

KUREMÄE

Tourists who appreciate the Golden Ring around Moscow should travel the 25km southeast from Jõhvi to visit the largest Russian Orthodox church outside Tallinn. **Pühtitsa Convent** (✆ *337 0715*), in the centre of Kuremäe, was completed in 1910 and seats 1,200 people; services are often full with most members of the congregation travelling long distances to attend. Six smaller churches, a museum and a formal garden were added later to the complex, which is surrounded by a brick wall. Remarkably, the community of around 150 nuns and the buildings themselves were unharmed through all the changes in regime of the last 100 years. The museum chronicles this remarkably peaceful story. The surrounding land, which the nuns cultivate, produces enough to support the community and to cater for visitors, and the sale of tasteful souvenirs is beginning to ensure maintenance of the buildings. Note the cemetery just outside the compound. Wrought-iron crosses are frequently seen in northern Estonia but it is rare to find such a large number of fine examples in one single cemetery.

SILLAMÄE

At long last it is possible to picture Sillamäe as it was in the 19th century when Tchaikovsky was just one of many Russian musicians and artists who came here during the summer. Natural colour is returning with its trees and flowers and the pastel decoration on the larger buildings has now recovered from 40 years of pollution. The wide stone steps down to the seafront are clearly modelled on the Crimea. On a hot summer's day it might be possible to think one is in Odessa. Architecturally, it is possible to use the word 'Stalinist' in a positive sense as the neo-classicist buildings in the town centre all date from the early 1950s, although one has to mention that many were constructed by German prisoners of war held in the Soviet Union until 1955. Because it was the Soviet scientific and military elite who came to live here, the standard of architecture is much higher than might otherwise be expected. Two buildings from that time, the **cultural centre** and the **cinema**, have preservation orders on them. Marx and Lenin look down on the audience from beside the stage in the cultural centre. The foyer in the cinema is as large as the auditorium, and full of chandeliers and broad pillars. It has kept the Soviet name Rodina (Motherland). When it opened in 1955, it offered six showings a day to cater for the many shift workers in the town; this was of course well before television became widespread in the USSR. Both buildings are usually open every day, and then in the evenings as well if performances are taking place. The basement of the cultural centre was built as a bomb shelter and it may be converted into a 'nuclear' museum describing all the top secret activities that took place in Sillamäe during the Soviet era.

It was the construction in 1928 of an oil-shale processing plant and its massive expansion after the war that led to the horrendous pollution of the 1970s and 1980s. As uranium was processed here for the Soviet military, the town was closed, even to most Estonians, and it was removed from maps. The mining of uranium stopped in the 1950s but the processing of supplies then imported from East Germany continued until the 1970s. During this time, 100,000 tons of uranium were produced but then the plant started to diversify. Uranium production stopped in 1990. Adjusting suddenly to environmental concerns, to the free market and to Estonian as a working language has been very difficult for the plant and for the town, but from around 2000 progress could clearly be seen. The port is being developed, training colleges are being established and, although Russian grandees from St Petersburg are unlikely to return, there is no reason why tourism should not be promoted. The plant was privatised in 1997 and then sold to the American company Molycorp in 2011, who have given it the name Molycorp Silmet. As a result, within 20 years a town that officially did not exist is now being promoted worldwide in English on a website. In 2012 the plant won the Company of the Year award given by Estonia's business paper *Äripäev* and also Exporter of the Year award given by the Ministry of Economic Affairs. Sillamäe therefore looks likely to stay on the map metaphorically as well as literally.

The population of Sillamäe is Russian-speaking, although all signs are in Estonian. A few road names that would not be acceptable elsewhere in the country have been kept here, such as one that commemorates the spaceman Yuri Gagarin.

The **Town Hall** stands out as not being an obviously Soviet building, even though it dates from 1949. The Lutheran tower gives a slight medieval feel to it, although the vases with palm trees that line the entrance steps bring it back to southern Russia. (These trees are kept during the winter in glasshouses, so are firmly protected from the northern winter.)

GETTING THERE AND AROUND The location of the **bus** station outside the town, about 1.5km from the centre, is a legacy of Soviet times, and this is where all the long-distance services stop. Several local routes do serve the town and port although it is possible to **walk** to most places of interest. Walk into town as quickly as possible, since the buildings *en route* reflect the worst that the Brezhnev and Khrushchev eras of Soviet history can provide. The railway station on the line from Jõhvi to Narva is in Vaivara so a visit to both places can start or finish there. The harbour hopes to become a major cargo terminal in the next few years, competing with Tallinn for transit traffic from Russia. Hopefully this will not lead to the demise of the small fishing industry that was revived as the town reopened to the outside world. A passenger ferry operated to Kotka in Finland during 2006 and 2007 but this is unlikely to be reinstated unless permission is granted to cross Russian waters, which would greatly reduced the travelling time and hence the costs of operation.

 WHERE TO STAY AND EAT

🏠 **Krunk** (21 rooms) Kesk 23; ✆392 9030; e admin@krunk.ee; www.krunk.ee. This hotel was most welcome when it opened in 2001, since at the time Narva had no hotel worthy of the name so most visitors commuted from Sillamäe. The façade blends into the 1950s neo-Classicism that characterises this part of the town, but inside it offers the full panoply of conference facilities, satellite TV, internet connections in every room & a restaurant with a wide menu. All this had been taken for granted for years elsewhere in Estonia, but not in the northeast. Its picture on the website gives a good architectural introduction to the town. The website is a technological experience in its own right, with a virtual tour throughout the hotel accompanied by Russian music. **$$**

WHAT TO SEE AND DO

Sillamäe Museum (*Kajaka 17a; www.sillamae-muuseum.ee but only in Russian & Estonian*) This museum gives a vivid and extensive picture of the town in Soviet times. It even has a 'red' room festooned with banners, tapestries and statues. Ration coupons from the late 1980s show how tough life had then become, but elegant samovars give a more positive picture. Some exhibits go back to the 1930s and some of those from the 1950s are not all that different from what a British museum of that era would show – television sets with doors, wind-up gramophones and radiograms with legs. One room is completely apolitical, showing the geology of the area and the rare metals that have been found there, but its collection of stones come from all over the former Soviet Union. The Visit Estonia website makes the astonishing admission that only Russian is spoken in the museum, a further instance of the time warp which it represents.

Vaivara If the existence of Sillamäe had to be denied throughout the Soviet period, so did equally the history of the area for the preceding three centuries. To a Soviet patriot, the Swedish defeat of Peter the Great in 1700 had to be concealed just as carefully as that of the Soviet armies in 1918 and 1941, when they fled in the face of the German army. Equally no Soviet or contemporary Russian textbook admits to the strong resistance the Soviet army faced, which blocked their advance into Estonia for six months in 1944. This now has been put to rights at the Vaivara **Blue Mountains Museum** (*www.muuseum.vaivaravald.ee*) 4km south of Sillamäe. Inevitably the collection is strongest in memorabilia from WWII, both in the building and outside, but few non-Estonians will leave here without having had to change a number of preconceptions.

NARVA

Narva could only be a border town. It is dominated by its fortress which always defended it, until the 20th century brought aerial bombardment. The Narva River now separates the town from Ivangorod in Russia, and ever-larger border control stations on both sides reinforce this. During the first period of independence, between 1920 and 1940, the frontier was about 8km further east but most Estonians are now reconciled to this new border, although in 2013 it had still not been formally agreed between the two governments. At times of tension in Russia,

5

such as during the currency crisis of autumn 1998, the clear division that the river provides between the two countries is probably welcomed in Tallinn.

When Estonia joined the EU and NATO in 2004, this welcome spread well beyond Tallinn. Local residents have to be more ambivalent as the population is almost entirely Russian-speaking and, of the 14 schools in the town, only one teaches in Estonian. Perhaps this ambivalence is best shown in the statue of Lenin that is still on display in the castle grounds: although hardly in a prominent position, he looks firmly eastwards across the Narva River to Russia. He has presumably abandoned any hope of his ideology returning to the land behind him. Were he able to turn round, he would find a large McDonald's and a German pub serving Irish beer. He would not have been happy to know that, in a petition circulated in September 1998 over the river in Ivangorod, the local population asked to rejoin Estonia.

A rushed visit to Narva can be made in a few hours, as a break *en route* from Tallinn to St Petersburg, but it is worth spending the night there to allow for time to visit the town properly. A visit can be extended to include the seaside resort of Narva-Jõesuu.

HISTORY Narva's history goes back as far as that of Tallinn, as both cities were built up following the Danish occupation in the 13th century and the two cities would witness many successes and defeats in parallel as conquerors and defenders quite rightly saw both as equally important. Close trading links with Britain were established in the late 16th century, during the reign of Ivan the Terrible when large quantities of fur and flax were exported, but Narva would then lose its importance for Russian goods when it fell into Swedish hands. Both cities would look back to the 150-year Swedish era of the late 16th and 17th centuries as the most benevolent occupation and the most successful commercial era, prior to independence.

The architectural legacy of that era in Narva is now restricted to a few buildings as so much was lost in World War II and in subsequent development. Peter the Great realised the potential of Narva as a harbour, just as he did with Tallinn, and developed it accordingly. In 1700 he lost a battle with the Swedes there but four years later he was able to seize the town and, like the rest of Estonia, Narva would stay in Russian hands until the beginning of the 20th century. The fighting then was as ferocious as it would be in both world wars. No town has suffered as extensively and as consistently as Narva when rival occupying powers have fought to control Estonia. During World War I, Narva's role on the eastern front can be compared to that of Verdun in the west.

In the 19th century Narva quickly developed into a major industrial centre. This was in due course to centre around the **Kreenholm Manufacture**, a strange translation that stuck through all regimes until 2000, when the then Swedish owners changed it to Krenholm Textiles (at the same time taking out one 'e' from Kreenholm to give the name a more Western flavour). It was established in the 1850s and was soon to employ 10,000 workers. Its founder was one of the most successful industrialists amongst the Baltic Germans, Baron Ludwig Knop. His constant presence in any new industrial development gave rise to the ditty: 'In any church there is the pope, in any plant there is the Knop.'

In 1870 the opening of the St Petersburg–Narva–Tallinn railway provided a great stimulus to the business but then, in 1872, Kreenholm was the site of one of the first strikes in tsarist Russia, with workers protesting against the 14-hour day imposed by management. Workers were again active in the 1905 and 1917 uprisings. Kreenholm's textile production, however, survived under all regimes, winning in the Soviet era the Order of Lenin and the Order of the October Revolution. In 1994, the factory was sold to the Swedish company Boras Walfveri and by 1999 was profitable, selling largely to western Europe, with Estonian management and a Russian-speaking workforce. Some of the lessons learnt came from the first independence period of 1920–40, when the border with the Soviet Union was as closed to trade as is the current one with Russia. At that time the labour force dropped from 10,000 to 2,500. In 2003 the factory had to start laying off workers again in order to compete with factories in Asia, but in 2006 its workforce consisted of 3,400 employees. It went bankrupt in 2010, and there is now minimal activity on the site.

The end of World War I would see many battles in the vicinity of Narva but not actually in the town itself. The success of the Estonian forces in driving back the Bolsheviks enabled them to impose a harsh territorial settlement on the nascent Soviet Union in the Tartu Treaty signed in February 1920. In contrast, from January to July 1944, Narva suffered one of the most intense bombardments of World War II as Soviet forces retook it with great difficulty from the Germans. It became known as 'Women's City' since so few men survived the battle and the women had been evacuated as the fighting started. (Even with massive post-war immigration, by 1960 the population was 70% female and 30% male.) Much of the town was destroyed, although it is now felt that more could have been restored had the Soviet government wanted to do so. This was in fact considered in the late 1940s, but such plans were later turned down to prevent nostalgia for a pre-Soviet era. Warsaw could have provided a model and the town is now seeking foreign investment to make whatever amends are possible in one or two streets. The renovation project around the Old Town Hall, completed in 2012, shows what can be done. The paving on the square has been restored and the former stock exchange has been rebuilt as a university.

The Soviet era saw a return to massive industrial expansion with the construction of a hydro-electric power station and several furniture plants, using the locally mined oil-shale, but with disastrous effects on the local environment. The resort of **Narva-Jõesuu** (see page 172), protected from this pollution, appealed to the nomenklatura and to the trade unions, so its continued future as a health centre and summer beach resort was assured.

The early 1990s, when independence was restored, was an uncertain period in Narva as most of the population found themselves stateless in a foreign country, being of Russian origin and unable to speak Estonian. Whilst Narva remains poor by Estonian standards, the dire conditions over the river in Ivangorod and the surrounding countryside reconcile the local population to being cut off from their former neighbours. Each year more can meet the language requirements for Estonian citizenship, and potentially new industrial developments will hopefully reduce unemployment.

Estonia's accession into the EU caused great problems for the Russian-speaking community in Narva as border controls on both sides became even tougher than they had been for the previous 12 years. However an increasing number of Russian tourists each year manage to obtain Schengen visas and therefore come to Estonia. It is perhaps significant that all the signs to the border are bilingual, not in Estonian and Russian but in Estonian and English. One English word now current in Estonia – 'secondhand' – has more poignancy in Narva than elsewhere. It describes a shop full of goods that no serious dealer would handle so is really a sheltered flea market.

GETTING THERE AND AROUND Narva is very well served by local and express **buses**. When travelling to Tallinn or Tartu, it is important to book an express rather than a much slower bus that stops *en route*. There are frequent services to Narva-Jõesuu on the coast. Three Tallinn–St Petersburg buses a day stop at Narva and there are also buses that start in Narva and then cross the border into Russia. These scheduled buses always have priority at the border, so are not subjected to the hours of delay that private coaches and cars often have to endure. Allowing for the border stops, the bus takes about five hours to St Petersburg and costs €20. Travel to Tallinn takes nearly four hours and the cost is around €12. By 2014 there will be a considerable number of train services to Narva, internationally to St Petersburg and to Moscow, and domestically to Rakvere and to Tallinn.

The bus and train stations are side by side and like many of the town's sites, are within walking distance of the Narva Hotel. There are frequent local buses from there to other parts of the town. Maps at the stop show the different routes available. The train station was built in the 1950s with stone taken from one of the churches in Narva destroyed when the town was rebuilt after the war. Note the memorial beside the bus station to Estonians deported to Siberia by the Soviet occupiers with the dates in 1941 and 1949 when these took place.

TOURIST INFORMATION The tourist office is at Peetri Plats 3 (\ *359 9137*; e *narva@ visitestonia.com; www.tourism.narva.ee*). Help from the EU in 2005 has stimulated a wide range of well-produced leaflets in English on Narva and on the surrounding county of Ida-Virumaa, which includes Jõhvi and Sillamäe.

WHERE TO STAY Tourists coming from, or travelling on to, St Petersburg would be well advised to have a night in Narva. Leaving early or arriving late will allow a full day in St Petersburg, whilst avoiding its hotel and meal prices. In 2005 three new hotels opened in Narva, including the Narva Hotel and the Inger, both listed below; it is surprising that the third-largest town in Estonia had to wait so long for accommodation to be available. None, however, have opened since. For location of listings see map, opposite.

Narva Hotel (51 rooms) Pushkini 6; \359 9600; e hotell@narvahotell.ee; www. narvahotell.ee. Determined to put the Soviet past behind it, the Narva has many signs in English & current copies of the *Financial Times* spread liberally across the tables in the reception area. The only element in the hotel geared to Russian guests is that a whole floor is dedicated to rooms for smokers. Having opened in 2005, it is fully equipped to receive disabled guests. Several rooms have views across the river to Russia & of the 2 castles. The management takes a politically neutral stance on them: the cost is the same as for those facing Estonia. Being quite large, it can take groups as well as individuals. The restaurant serves a number of Russian dishes, but the description in English always precedes the Russian one. **$$$**

Central (20 rooms) Lavretsovi 5; \359 1333; e centralhotel@hot.ee; www.centralhotel. ee. A converted late 19th-century town house on a side street off Pushkini, it used to be the mayor's residence. Today it prides itself on the total lack of entertainment offered, guaranteeing peace &

quiet. The police station opposite provides further reassurance. **$$**

Inger (83 rooms) Pushkini 28; \688 1100; e hotel@inger.ee; www.inger.ee. This hotel has adopted a totally different strategy from that of the Narva. Perhaps it is not deliberate but the hotel clearly appeals to what the Germans would call the 'Ostalgie' market, blending the words for 'East' & for 'nostalgia'. The 1980s USSR has been recreated here. The occasional foreign guest can speak in English, but Estonians should not waste their breath trying to be understood in their language. Nobody can talk in any language at all over dinner as the music is so loud & the dancing such a perverse attraction – overdressed & over-perfumed women dance together as their men are far too drunk even to stand up, let alone to lead them into a tango. **$$**

Laagna (30 rooms, 15 cottages & camping) \392 5900; e info@laagna.ee; www.laagna.ee. This hotel is 12km from Narva, but is popular for its isolated location beside a lake near a village of the same name. It is sufficiently far from the main

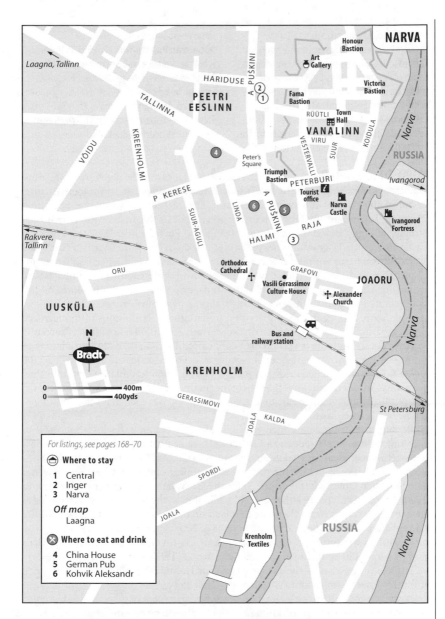

Honour Bastion

Laagna, Tallinn

HARIDUSE

Art Gallery

Victoria Bastion

PEETRI EESLINN

TALLINNA

A PUŠKINI

Fama Bastion

RÜÜTLI

Town Hall

VANALINN

VIRU

RUSSIA

Narva

VÕIDU

KRENHOLMI

Peter's Square

VESTERVALLI

SUUR

KOIDULA

Ivangorod

P KERESE

Triumph Bastion

PETERBURI

SUUR-AGULI

LINDA

6

A PUŠKINI

Tourist office

Narva Castle

Ivangorod Fortress

HALMI

5

RAJA

Rakvere, Tallinn

3

ORU

Orthodox Cathedral

GRAFOVI

JOAORU

UUSKÜLA

Vasili Gerassimov Culture House

Alexander Church

N

Bradt

Bus and railway station

0   400m
0   400yds

KRENHOLM

GERASSIMOVI

St Petersburg

JOALA

KALDA

For listings, see pages 168–70

🛏 **Where to stay**

1 Central
2 Inger
3 Narva

Off map
  Laagna

😋 **Where to eat and drink**

4 China House
5 German Pub
6 Kohvik Aleksandr

SPORDI

JOALA

Krenholm Textiles

RUSSIA

Narva

Tallinn road to be spared any traffic noise. It is also possible to camp nearby or to bring a caravan. The sea is a 3km walk or cycle ride. The hotel also runs a riding school. **$$**

✕ **WHERE TO EAT AND DRINK** Around Peter's Square (Peetri Plats) there are plenty of cafés where substantial meals can be had for little more than €8. Expect more leisurely service than elsewhere in Estonia. The castle has an excellent restaurant but it only serves prebooked groups. Tourists racing from Tallinn to St Petersburg often have lunch there *en route*. The restaurants in the Narva and Inger hotels are often used by local people but for a lighter meal there are a few other options.

China House Tallinna 6b; ✆357 5099; www.china24.ee. Narva's first Chinese restaurant opened in 2006, a welcome & necessary addition to the city's eating options. By 2008 they had added Thai & Indian food to the repertoire. It is difficult to find, being situated in a courtyard behind Tallinn 6, but the precarious walk will be rewarded with variety, enormous portions & prices half of those in Tallinn (& probably a tenth of those in St Petersburg). $

German Pub Pushkini 10; ✆353 1548. This is both restaurant & pub & serves Guinness & Murphy's as well as the predictable German & Estonian brands. $

Kohvik Aleksandr Pushkini 13; ✆357 3150. This café has had good standards for many years. It serves meals, snacks & drinks all day. $

WHAT TO SEE AND DO Dominating the town, Narva Castle dates from the 13th century and amazingly, for the first hundred years, survived as a wooden structure. Some of the current brickwork dates from the 14th century, but the 50m-high **Herman Tower** and the final extensions were built in the 16th century. This final strengthening followed the building of Ivangorod Fortress over the river. No other castle in Estonia is as well preserved, except perhaps for Kuressaare on Saaremaa Island. It is a town within a town, and when necessary could be self-sufficient for months on end. Allow at least two hours for walking around the ramparts and exploring the museum. Inevitably, the **museum** (*www.narvamuuseum.ee*) has concentrated on military history but soon should have more material on the Soviet period. Some rooms are usually devoted to temporary exhibitions of modern art. These are listed in a sort of English on the website. Extensive renovation is currently in progress so sometimes certain areas are closed to visitors. Guides are happy to point out the contrasting neglect of Ivangorod Fortress. Just to the north of the castle is the modern road bridge to Russia, built in 1966 to replace what until then was only a wooden structure. It has become totally inadequate as a border crossing, but it is likely to be many years before agreement will be reached on the building of a new one further north.

Beyond the bridge, now incorporated into a riverside park, are nine massive bastions built by the Swedes as a further defence against the Russians. This is now a peaceful area, ideal for a walk on a summer's evening. In fact one of the bastions here is called 'Peace'. Whilst the name may be appropriate now, it certainly was not in 1700 when Charles XII defeated Peter the Great here, only to suffer a reverse in 1704. There was no peace either in 1944 when it took the Soviet army six months to defeat the Germans here. The steps that lead up to the town from the riverside are named after Adolf Hahn, a dynamic mayor of Narva in the late 19th century who also planned the future of Narva-Jõesuu as a spa town. He insisted that gardens and parks should be included in urban expansion. This area was under renovation in 2013 so future visitors should see it much as Hahn laid it out and as it remained until the Soviet bombardments began in March 1944.

As the castle ramparts are open all day, photographers may well wish to return on several occasions to record different views. The range of subterranean passages built as part of the fortifications by the Swedes beneath the park are still waiting to be fully excavated but there are plans to open some of them to visitors in 2015. It is worth walking south of the castle as well as north. In 2000, the statue of the Swedish lion returned to Narva. The original was unveiled by the then king of Sweden in 1936 but it was subsequently destroyed by the Soviet authorities who could not accept any commemoration of a Russian defeat. The year 2000 was the 300th anniversary of the Swedish victory at Narva over Peter the Great.

With the **Krenholm factory** ceasing production in 2010, there are no longer tours of the complex, but the outside of the building, which suffered little damage in the war, is best viewed from the pedestrian bridge which is one of the border crossings to Russia. This vantage point also offers good views of the river for photographers. With fishermen rather than armed guards along each shore, the border seems very tame for what is now 'fortress Europe'.

Returning into the town along Pushkini, note one of the few other large buildings that survived the war, the **Vasili Gerassimov Culture House**. The interior was repaired during 2001 and returned to being an enormous centre for plays, films and concerts. Gerassimov was one of the leaders of the strike at Kreenholm in 1872. The 17th-century **Town Hall**, of Baroque design, was restored in the early 1960s. An account written in 1938 describes the doorway as 'typical of Swedish Narva' but sadly it is now unique in this context. Interior restoration is now under way and visitors should go up to the first floor (second floor for Americans) to see the model of Narva in the 17th century, so when it was part of the Swedish Empire. It is hardly surprising that the Swedes considered making it the capital every fifth year. The local Soviet administration met here between 1917 and 1919 before the Russians were driven out by Estonian forces. November 2012 saw the reopening of the former stock exchange building.

One other building of note also escaped serious damage in the war, the **Orthodox cathedral**, where even the iconostasis is intact. The foundation stone was laid by Tsar Alexander III in 1890. It is located beside Krenholm and was designed by the same architect, Pavel Alish. The modern buildings surrounding it were deliberately constructed to block views of the church and to reduce its former dominance of the area. The **Lutheran Alexander Church** was completed in 1884 and is named after Tsar Alexander II who had been assassinated in St Petersburg in 1881. He had been a frequent visitor to Narva. Following considerable wartime damage, some repairs started in 1956, even though the church was then deconsecrated and used as a warehouse for the rest of the Soviet period. Serious reconstruction was only begun in 2006 and was completed in 2008. The Estonian Post Office issued a commemorative stamp in 2009 for the 125th anniversary of the original opening of the church.

Take the lift up the tower for the widest view of Ivangorod it is possible to have in Estonia. It is an uninviting mixture of pylons and blocks of flats, so probably best seen at this distance. Walk down through the collection of photographs of all the churches pulled down in the 1950s in Estonia.

The church is the largest in Estonia and can hold 5,000 people, with half standing and half seated. The architect, Otto Pius Hippius, is probably best known for the Charles Church in Tallinn (see pages 99–100) and Sangaste Castle (see pages 212–13). In 1867 he had entered, against 50 others, the competition to build a new cathedral for Berlin but in the end none of the entries were accepted. If Hippius had won, the church we now see in Narva would have been in Berlin. The stained glass is all contemporary, by the artist Dolores Hoffmann whose work can be seen in many churches all over Estonia.

The massive new Russian consulate is situated beside the Lutheran church. Its procedures are as strict and its prices as high as those of any other Russian consulate, so there is no point in asking about a quick trip across the river to Ivangorod.

The **Art Gallery** (*Vestervalli 21; www.narvamuuseum.ee*) was opened in 1991 in a former 19th-century army storehouse. The permanent collection is based on a bequest made around 1900 by the Lavretsov family, who had been successful merchants in Narva for several generations. It specialises in 19th-century Russian art, bought by the family as it was produced. Paintings were added in the 1920s and 1930s but little happened to the collection during the Soviet period, when much of it was dispersed to St Petersburg and Tallinn. Now the gallery is equally important for its contemporary art exhibitions. The website gives details of these along with the opening hours.

NARVA-JÕESUU

The road to the resort town of Narva-Jõesuu follows the river from Narva for 14km. In the summer this trip can be done by boat; contact the tourist office in Narva for details. On leaving the town, the road passes several memorials and cemeteries. As in other parts of Estonia, the Soviet ones have remained, even including a tank that commemorates the 1944 invasion, but those dedicated to independence fighters in 1918 have had to be restored as have others erected in memory of those deported in 1941 and 1949. There is also a cemetery for the many German soldiers killed in 1944. Pine forests, the widening of the river and soil turning to sand announce the approach to the resort.

Legend has it that during the 17th century it was given the German name of Hungerburg by German sailors unable to find any food in the vicinity. During the 19th century, though, it prospered and was as popular as Haapsalu and Pärnu with the St Petersburg aristocracy. This continued into the first period of independence when it was equally as popular with the Tallinn elite. Neglected and run-down until around 2011, it then hurriedly started to emulate the rest of Estonia in eliminating Soviet buildings and restoring the wooden villas in cases where this was possible.

The beach is about 13km long so is never crowded. There are no high-rises. On hot days in July, it could almost be Mediterranean.

GETTING THERE See under *Getting there and around* for Narva, pages 167–8. Local bus 31 from the Narva town centre takes 40 minutes between the two towns and long-distance buses also link the two.

 WHERE TO STAY In contrast with other towns in this area, there has been little new building or upgrading since the mid-1990s, apart from the Meresuu listed below. However this may well change as the town starts to make a real effort to attract Russians from across the border and not just Russian speakers within Estonia.

🏠 **Meresuu Spa & Hotel** (109 rooms) Aia 48a; 📞357 9600; e sales@meresuu.ee; www.meresuu.ee. This hotel represents an oasis of luxury beside the beach & away from the town. It concentrates on serving families, unusual in hotels of this high standard, so all the rooms are non-smoking. The pools & saunas are free of charge to hotel guests all day. **$$$$**

LAKE PEIPSI

Estonia's largest lake, and at 3,600km² one of the largest in Europe, now forms the border with Russia so it faces an uncertain future. In tsarist times, the Estonian side provided refuge for the Old Believers, persecuted in larger cities from the 17th century until the end of the tsarist era in the 20th century for their disaffection with the Orthodox Church; they were allowed to live in relative peace in the isolated border lands. They maintain customs abandoned by the 'modern' Church but even within this community there are differences in their degree of 'oldness'. At Mustvee, for instance, the church has electricity, but at Raja only beeswax candles are used. Men and women are always kept apart in their services. Nowadays it forms a sort of refuge for a new generation of Old Believers, who cannot cope with the pace and new direction of contemporary Estonia. More information on the Old Believers in Estonia is available on the website www.starover.ee. There are now about 15,000 Old Believers in Estonia. In Soviet times, the Estonian side supported fishing and a large number of trade-union holiday centres.

The villages here tend to divide themselves into Estonian- and Russian-speaking and this is reflected in the architecture too. Russian communities are much more open whereas Estonians want their privacy. If you see a hedge, the house behind it will belong to an Estonian-speaking family. From the border at the Narva River around to Raja, south of Mustvee, the villages are 'Russian'. From Kasepää southwards, they are Estonian. The 2,000 population of Mustvee is equally divided. A recent census found 1,000 Estonian speakers and 1,000 Russian speakers but it did not say which they use amongst themselves. Mustvee means 'black water', and it describes the colour of the river as it reaches the lake after passing through several swamps.

Fishermen must now be careful not to stray across the border in the middle of the lake and are having to survive on a limited catch. They also run allotments growing cucumbers and onions. The structures of the old collectives have remained although these are now voluntary associations of fishermen who realise they can make more money this way than by attempting to operate totally on their own. The fresh yellow paint on many of their houses, which matches the dandelions that grow in profusion here, proves the point.

For tourists, the opening in the summer of 2013 of the **visitor centre** at Kolkja (*Suur Tee 25;* m *5563 9398; info@peipsimaa.ee; www.peipsimaa.ee*) has been an invaluable asset to the region, since it encourages visitors to explore the whole lakeside area and not just concentrate on one village. One room offers an introduction to the different fish that can be caught in the lake. Its handicraft shop has a comprehensive selection of the linen and wooden items produced in the area.

Like most of the museums and attractions in the area, the centre is only open 1 June to 31 August and prebooking is essential for visitors planning to come at other times.

BATHING IN PRE-WAR ESTONIA

Where the pine forest comes right down to the edge of the shore, it is possible to bathe without costumes, the women on the right, the men on the left. This is a custom which has been inaugurated at most Estonian seaside resorts. I was told an amusing story by an English woman writer, whom I met later in the summer. She and her son found themselves at Narva-Jõesuu on their way back from a visit to Finland. They went down to the beach armed with costumes and towels, and sat down on a bench wondering if it were permissible to undress on the beach. They did not know the regulations and were all the more chary because they could distinguish a policeman hovering in the distance. As they sat there in uncertainty, two young men came along and sitting on the next bench a few yards away, took off all their clothes and ran down to the sea nonchalantly naked. After that, there was no further need for scruples at all. It is of no use, a woman who has wandered on to the wrong part of the beach, complaining to the authorities of the indecent behaviour of the men. It is their own fault if they go there and are shocked. [Nude bathing was apparently common in pre-war Estonia although this is no longer the case.]

Extract from Travels in Estonia *by Ronald Seth, published in 1939.*

GETTING THERE AND AROUND As in other poorer parts of Estonia, good public transport makes up for the lack of cars. Several **buses** a day run from Tartu to the lake and along the shore to Mustvee. Others link Mustvee with the northeastern towns of Jõhvi and Narva and there is also a route along the lake to Mustvee, inland to Rakvere and then to Tallinn. Tartu–St Petersburg buses stop at Mustvee. One main road runs largely alongside the lake, with the villages being settlements stretched out on either side. South of Kallaste it turns inland to Alatskivi and then to Tartu.

WHERE TO STAY As the area still really caters only for local tourists who have their own summer houses here or rent rooms from friends, there is little commercial accommodation.

Aarde Villa (8 rooms; Aarde Villais; ☎776 4290; e info@aardevilla.ee; www.aardevilla.ee) Opened in 2002 at the village of Sääritsa, Aarde Villa is about 10km south of Raja, off the main road but directly beside the lake. It was once a border-guard station & guests can climb up the former lookout tower. There are extensive gardens with facilities for both adults & children & for those who like to catch their own supper, fishing expeditions are organised on the lake. **$**

Nina Kordon (8 rooms; ☎5336 4685

e info@ninakordon.ee; www.ninakordon.ee) Housed in a former school, the Nina Kordon was a welcome addition in 2012. After Estonian re-independence, it also was a border-guard station during the 1990s. Luckily none of this history is evident from the refurbishment which has created as far as is practical a 1920s residential environment. As the village of Nina is not on the main lake road but on a separate one from Alakskivi, the location is particularly quiet. This hotel opens in the winter for ice fishing. **$**

VILLAGES AROUND THE LAKE

Mustvee The small towns along the lake such as Lohusuu and Mustvee have Lutheran churches for the local Estonian population and Orthodox ones for the Old Believers. A hundred years ago there were seven **churches** in Mustvee and today there are still four in use, despite the small population. The Orthodox is the oldest, dating from the 1860s; the Lutheran and Baptist ones were both built in the 1870s, and the current Old Believers one was completed in 1930, although they had had a church here since 1795. The new church was built entirely from local wood; the plaster covering was to give the impression of a stone building and therefore one that could rival the other churches. The church could, and often did, accommodate 1,000 people for a service. The Soviets did not close it after the war and 700 people courageously declared their allegiance to the church in 1946. None of the churches have regular opening hours so the best opportunity of seeing the interiors is around the time of a service.

The **Town Museum** at Narva mnt 22 consists entirely of exhibits gathered together by local children over the last 20 years. These vary widely and include helmets abandoned in both the world wars, samovars, lanterns and banknotes from all the different regimes of the 20th century.

Raja The Old Believers church at Raja was destroyed in the war, as there was considerable fighting in this area in 1944, and only the campanile remains. Worship now takes place in the **icon-painting school** where there is a regular exhibition of recent work. This school was founded in 1880 and has continued its work through all changes of regime in Tallinn and Moscow.

Hopes that Russians would return in large numbers for holidays were dashed by the 1998 financial crisis there. Increasingly strict visa regulations following Estonia's entry into the EU in 2004 have been a further disincentive. For Russian speakers happy to relive Soviet holidays from the 1960s, the trade-union centres provide spartan but adequate accommodation and a base for exploring the small lakeside villages. Beaches, though, are few and far between; the best is at Kauksi on the north shore of the lake. Even in summer, an eerie quiet pervades much of the coast and foreigners may be stared at, given that they are so rare. It is hard to think of a greater contrast to Tallinn with its 24-hour activity.

Tiheda Since 2012, the **Samovars Museum** has been open here – 4km south of Raja – with some of them dating back to 1700. This is hardly surprising given the sturdiness of their construction and the crucial role they played in family life. There are also silver and bronze holders for the glasses from which tea was taken. Cups are rare in these communities.

Iisaku A convenient trip can be made 12km inland to the village of Iisaku to see one of the liveliest small museums in Estonia; it already puts to shame many in Tallinn and Tartu. Housed in a former school, the **Iisaku Museum** (*Tartn mnt 58; www.iisakumuuseum.ee*) expands month by month and, with clear labels in English, it already offers an extensive introduction to the natural history of the area and to life in the countryside since the early 19th century. Many of the exhibits were contributed by local schoolchildren and they are still encouraged to look for more. Rarely for Estonia, the museum opens at 10.00 during the summer and at 09.00 during the winter instead of the more usual 10.30 or 11.00 and is open daily from 1 June to 30 September. A Soviet room and a costume collection were added in 2004–05. More recently a schoolroom and a teacher's flat from around 1900 have been built. Many contemporary teachers are envious of the facilities available then! The website has vivid illustrations of many exhibits, but the text is still only in Estonian.

Kallaste About 25km south of Mustvee is the largest village on the lake, Kallaste. Perhaps if relations with Russia improve it may become a large tourist centre as it offers beaches and a potential yachting harbour, although at present no hotel. The walk through the village offers two unusual sights – a series of redstone caves along the shore and two buildings in the centre, the Town Hall and the Agricultural College. Both feature classical pillars, not what would have been expected from the early 1950s when they were built. An equally unexpected architectural monument, **Alatskivi Castle** (*www.alatskiviloss.ee*), can be seen 8km south of Kallaste. The original owner, Arved von Nolcken, produced his own design, following a long visit to Britain in 1875. He engaged Russian bricklayers and builders from Latvia; only the carpenters were local Estonians. Even the tiles for the stoves were brought from Riga. He took as his model for the gables and towers the royal palace at Balmoral, in Scotland, which in turn was based on 16th-century Scottish castles. The tall entrance hall with fireplaces, extending upwards through two floors, is presumably based on a Robert Adam design.

The drive was originally lined with lime trees, which added an English, rather than a Scottish, element. The building was completed in 1885 but was only used as a serious residence until von Nolcken's death in 1909. His son used it as a hunting lodge, and then during the first independence period it was first a school and then a border-guard station. The Soviets ran a collective farm from it. Only in 2003 did serious reconstruction begin; by 2005 a secure roof had been completed. A **restaurant** followed, now one of the best known in the country and if prices are close to Tallinn ones, the ambiance and varied menu make this quite justified. The full menu is on the Castle website noted above. In 2011 the **Eduard Tubin Museum** opened at the castle. Tubin (1905–82) was a composer of remarkable diversity, covering symphonies, piano and violin works, and songs. He worked in Tartu until leaving for Sweden in 1944, but from 1961, when he became a Swedish citizen, he regularly returned to Estonia, which ensured that much of his work continued to be performed through the Soviet era. Many of his original manuscripts are on display, there is fortunately much remaining on film of him, and recordings of all his major compositions can be heard here. A very active Tubin Society (*www.tubinsociety. com*) keeps his works well known on a worldwide basis.

The cellars contain a museum of life as it was led in Tartu county manors in the 19th century. Waxworks show the staff carrying out their different tasks, and furniture similar to what would have been here originally has been brought together to complete the picture. The upper floor of the castle now offers **accommodation**, which obviously has to be exclusively suites in a property of this nature. There are just four suites and, again, the Castle website (*www.alatskiviloss.ee*) gives full details.

Kolkja Two roads go south from Alatskivi; the main one turns inland to Tartu and the other goes eastwards back to the shore of Lake Peipsi. The next village along the lake, after 8km, is Kolkja, where an **Old Believers Museum** (*www.hot.ee/ kolkjamuuseum*) opened in 1998. It shows their costumes, their religious artefacts and, above all, their simple standard of living that is so apparent when driving along this shoreline. The simple fish-and-onion **restaurant** (*745 3445; www.hot. ee/kolkjarestoran;* **$$**) in the village can be recommended. It does not serve coffee, only tea, and sugar is never added. Sweet things can, however, be eaten as part of the meal.

Rupse Taking the Tartu road, the next village after 3km is Rupse, the location of the **Liiv Museum** (*www.muusa.ee*). Juhan Liiv (1864–1913) is one of Estonia's most famous poets, and he grew up on this farm. Most of his life he suffered from schizophrenia and travelled listlessly around the country on trains until he was thrown off for not paying, and not being able to afford the fare. Sadly, he destroyed much of the poetry he wrote but enough remains to ensure his continuing reputation; some of his drafts are here. Visitors can also see the room he shared with his very conventional brother (who became mayor of Rakvere) and the outside sauna that was also used for roasting meat and washing down corpses. A Liiv Prize is awarded to a young poet every year and they leave a handwritten copy here of the winning poem. The museum opened in 1962 and expanded considerably in the late 1980s towards the end of the Soviet era.

6

Central Estonia

TARTU

Unlike Tallinn or Pärnu, Tartu is not a town of instant charm. Arriving by any of the dreary approach roads does not suggest the imminence of a famous university town or of one where Estonia gained its statehood. Yet intellectually and architecturally it is the centre of Estonia. Its university cultivates an Oxbridge/Ivy League tradition but has combined it with the radicalism of Berkeley or the London School of Economics. Estonia's most famous scientists studied and taught here and its most famous patriots, whether in opposition to the Tsar, the pre-war president Konstantin Päts or the Soviet regime, likewise spent their formative years in Tartu. The 200km distance from Tallinn suited both sides. Political activists could be more daring and the government could feign liberalism, safe in the knowledge that its detractors would not be a threat to the capital. With independence and democracy now safe in Estonia, Tartu will have to take up new causes. It introduced parking meters to the country in 1992 but a more lasting testimony to the first period of renewed independence must be in the offing.

It is only since about 2000 that Tartu started to take tourism seriously. Museums were moved from gloomy suburban locations to properly adapted buildings in the town centre. In contrast, the National Museum will leave Tartu altogether in 2016 for a new purpose-built site at Raadi Manor House, 3km away, but this is understandable given the breadth of the collection. Hotels also started to open in the town and to promote themselves vigorously. Pedestrian precincts appeared and so did signs in English. In 2003, the squalid bus station and the equally run-down Hotel Tartu beside it were modernised. The year 2007 saw the opening of the 200-room Dorpat Hotel and the conference centre beside it opened in 2008. A serious train service to Tallinn was resumed in 2005, although it was not until 2012 that the railway station was properly rebuilt. A greatly increased train service both to Tallinn and south to Latvia is expected in 2014. Tartu airport reopened with flights to Stockholm and to Riga in 2009.

The celebration in October 2007 of the 375th anniversary of the founding of the university, which was attended by Queen Silvia of Sweden, was a great incentive for renovation in the Old Town. To be a successful second city, Tartu will need to be a business centre as well as an academic one and must compete with Tallinn as a base for Estonian and international companies. In tourism it will need to operate seven days a week during the summer. For many shops to close early on Saturday and all day on Sunday, and for several museums to close all day on Monday and Tuesday sends out a disturbing message of indifference to Tartu's increasing number of domestic and international visitors.

Tartu now has a diverse programme of festivals that take place all year round except in July and August (when the hotels fill up anyway). If it matters whether you

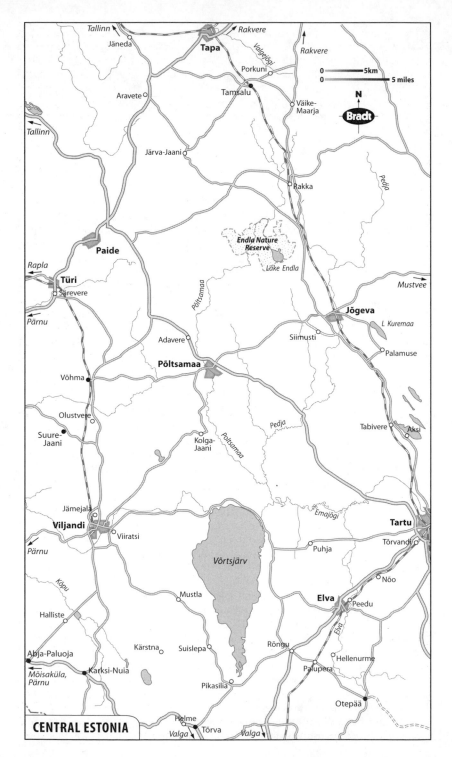

CENTRAL ESTONIA

turn up for the cross-country ski marathon, the break-dancing finals or student rag week, check their dates on www.kultuuriaken.tartu.ee before contacting your tour operator. This site also gives the programme at the Vanemuine Theatre, which spills out on to the Town Hall Square (weather permitting) during the summer. One thing unites all these programmes: even if they were not designed as such, they are a perfect deterrent to stag parties, which stay firmly in Tallinn as a result.

A full day is needed to cover the town centre and the university, and a further half day to visit a selection of the museums. The parks beside the river offer relaxing walks and concerts in the summer.

HISTORY The university was founded in 1632 but the town dates back much further than this. Its location at the crossroads of the north–south link from St Petersburg to Riga and the east–west one from Tallinn to Pskov has given it written records since 1030. Until recently the Emajõgi River also had a serious role in trade.

Although Tallinn was always spared fighting within the city, Tartu sadly was not, and during the 16th century it was the constant battleground between the Russians, the Baltic Germans, the Poles and the Swedes. Three more recent calamities hit the town – its destruction by Peter the Great's armies in 1708, a fire in 1775, and then World War II, when both the Russian retreat in 1941 and their return in 1944 caused considerable damage.

As the earlier town was largely built of wood, what the visitor now sees dates only from the late 18th century onwards. The major buildings, such as the Town Hall and the Stone Bridge, were built specifically on the instructions of Catherine the Great. The bridge was destroyed by Soviet bombing in 1944, but it is hoped that in due course funds can be raised to rebuild it.

In the small streets around the Town Hall Square the 20th century is not obtrusive, and the 21st is only allowed to develop over the river. It is easy to visualise a thriving market town, which was its role for many centuries.

The town's future outside the university will depend largely on relations with Latvia and Russia. If trade continues to decrease with these two countries and EU membership stimulates more contact with the West, Tartu's location to the east will make it less competitive than towns along the coast. However from 2012 onwards, there has been a considerable increase in tourists from both Russia and Latvia.

Tartu University (*www.ut.ee*) The importance of the university can be seen in the determination of each new conqueror to make their mark on it immediately. Conversely, bands of lecturers sometimes moved the university to temporary safety when the town of Tartu was threatened.

When it first opened in 1632, it was the second university in the Swedish Empire, Uppsala being the first. It is thought that there was only one ethnically Estonian student in the university at that time. Twenty years later, because of the Russo-Swedish war, it moved to Tallinn for ten years and when the Russians attacked again in 1700, it moved to Pärnu. Most of the faculties were housed in Pärnu fortress, just above the gunpowder cellar. Before Pärnu fell to the Russian armies, the archives for these turbulent 70 years were taken to Stockholm and many of the academic staff, being Swedish, returned with them. The issues these archives cover have a very modern ring to them. The possibility of war with Russia is mentioned, as is the constant need to remind students to be loyal to the Swedish king. There are also concerns that scientific discoveries should not threaten theological teaching. Far more worrying for many of the staff, however, were the lack of pay, difficult landladies, leaking roofs and disputes with the military over room allocations.

Peter the Great had originally planned to reopen the university either in Pärnu or in Tartu but the founding of the Academy of Science in St Petersburg in 1724 put paid to this. Both Pärnu and Tartu submitted plans to refound the university on various occasions during the 18th century, but these were unsuccessful; it would only reopen nearly a hundred years later in 1802, as a reaction to the French Revolution. The tsarist authorities panicked at the ideas that students sent to study in western Europe were bringing back with them and from 1798 such studies were banned. In the best Tartu tradition, however, the result was that such ideas simply reached Estonian students more quickly than they otherwise would have done as the teaching staff were unwilling to acquiesce in the reverent approach that the Russians and the Baltic Germans had wanted.

The university now had a comparatively stable century ahead of it. Funding from the state was adequate and provided for all the main buildings that were needed on its reopening. Even a botanical garden was included. It was lucky that the Napoleonic Wars started only after the completion of Tartu University otherwise funds would never have been found for it. The town was to grow with the university, the population increasing from 3,500 in 1802 to 8,500 in 1826. The teaching staff were drawn from all over Europe, with the majority having a German background as this was to be the language of instruction. If one member of the staff deserves special mention, it must be Karl Morgenstern (1770–1852) who ran the library for 37 years from 1802 until 1839. By joining the book exchange association of the major German universities, he ensured that Tartu became a mainstream European university. He also collected toys and until 2003 his former house was the Toy Museum now on Lutsu (see page 199). His successors, German and Russian, expanded this work so that by 1917 there were 180 exchange partners including several in Japan and the United States. Morgenstern was also accomplished at what would now be called public relations and persuaded many wealthy patrons to donate books and antiquities to the library and to the classical museum that he founded.

The period of peace between the Napoleonic Wars and the Crimean War again ensured immense financial support for the university, equalling that given to Moscow. The building of the railway links to Tallinn and St Petersburg in the 1870s and then to Riga in 1887 brought considerable expansion to the university, the number of students increasing from 600 in 1865 to 1,700 in 1889. The year 1889 also marked the start of greater control from St Petersburg and, with the use of Russian as the language of instruction, the Russian name for Tartu, Jurjev, replaced the German name of Dorpat at the university. The Estonian name Tartu was used only after independence in 1919, when Estonian also became the language of instruction. The Ministry of Education took direct control of academic appointments, so much of the autonomy previously enjoyed by the university was withdrawn and many of the German-speaking staff left. One embittered historian wrote that 'the bright flame of German science went out because it was smothered by barbaric Slavic hands'. The two protagonists for the soul of Tartu University during the 19th century, the Baltic Germans and the Russians, clearly saw the battleground as simply between themselves. The occasional Estonians who managed to enter were expected to integrate and put their peasant background behind them.

The German army seized Tartu on 24 February 1918, and on 7 March decreed that tuition in German instead of Russian would be instituted with effect from 20 March. After protest, this deadline was extended by a further two weeks. The university reopened in full at the end of April 1918 with a complement of 60 staff, 30 of whom had been recruited from German universities. This would however be the shortest 'interregnum' in the history of the university. Following the armistice of November 1918, the German military had to withdraw. In the meantime, many academics left with the retreating Bolshevik forces to found a university in exile at Voronezh. Most of the artefacts and books they took with them have remained there, even though the Soviet government agreed their return under the Tartu Treaty of 1920.

The new Estonian government wisely took its time before reopening the university in December 1919, with the prime minister Jaan Tönisson carrying out the formal ceremony. To begin with, about half the lectures were given in Russian and half in Estonian, but Estonian quickly became the predominant language. The new country immediately had at its service an internationally respected university. Former staff members happily came back from exile to work there and were soon joined by many foreign experts; by 1930, the teaching staff had reached 400. For 20 years, the university was pleasantly normal, teaching local students in their national language.

From 1940 to 1945 the situation became vicious. The Russians dismissed and deported many of the leading faculty members; the Germans treated the replacements they appointed even worse in 1941, when several were sent to concentration camps. In 1944, most senior members not sympathetic to the Russians had just enough time to flee to Sweden. Only 22% of the staff *en poste* in early 1940 were still there in the autumn of 1944. On all three occasions, the occupiers had detailed plans for running the university, cynically realising that it had to be neutered if they were to control Estonia effectively. The Soviet regime did make large funds available immediately on their re-occupation to rebuild the university, following the destruction much of the town had suffered during the war.

TARTU IN 1941   *Ants Oras*

The Red Soldiers marching in the streets to the tune of one of the four or five songs they seemed to know were a very neglected, listless lot. A large proportion of them were illiterate. Soon after the occupation, delousing stations were set up for them, an establishment with which we were made familiar for the first time. The Red Commanders, as the officers were still called, dressed more smartly but they were obviously unaccustomed to living in a 'bourgeois' environment, even after its Sovietisation. Having been assigned some of the best living quarters in our town, they found themselves out of their depth in dealing with such gadgets as bath taps, lavatory chains or electric lights. In one flat, a Soviet officer used his bathroom as a pigsty in which he reared a large sow. In spite of protests from inmates of the floor below, he refused to see the inappropriateness of his conduct. The Red wives adapted themselves more easily to their new surroundings, however. Being well provided with money, they stormed our shops, always buying the most expensive articles, although their taste was more gaudy than ours. Though they generally avoided red, of which they must have had a surfeit at home, their dresses looked exotic in their many-coloured richness. Their make-up was very marked and most of our perfumes were too subtle for them. An unexpected feature was their religiousness. The Orthodox churches were crowded with women fresh from Soviet Russia, whereas the men stayed away.

Ants Oras was a lecturer at Tartu University who fled to Sweden in 1944.

Constant expansion was planned throughout the Soviet era with student numbers doubling from 3,500 in 1950 to 7,000 in 1978. A computer centre was established in 1976 and a history of the university published in 1982 talked proudly of 'modern methods of management' being used in the running of the university. The 350th anniversary in 1982 was fervently and formally celebrated with a massive budget provided for further new buildings.

Anyone now prominent in Estonian public life was educated at Tartu under the Soviet system but the academic rigour of the courses and the subtlety of the teaching in most cases made the political background irrelevant. What was missing was contact outside the USSR; Tartu was a closed city so initially Westerners could not travel there at all and later only for the day from Tallinn.

Undergraduates had no chance to be taught languages by native speakers

A STUDENT IN SOVIET ESTONIA   *Tina Tamman*

I was a university student in Soviet Estonia for five years, which was then the standard length of studies. I was offered no choice of subjects, but I was happy at the time and remember this period fondly. In independent Estonia it is no longer fashionable or even acceptable to praise the Soviet period but I certainly benefited from the system.

The university had an excellent library, which opened at 08.00 and closed at 22.00, seven days a week. When I came to write a thesis in my final year, on the American writer William Saroyan, there was nothing available in Estonia and all the books and reviews had to be ordered from a library in Moscow. This service was quick, efficient and free of charge.

I benefited, too, from sharing a room at the university hostel, at first with ten other girls but after a few months I managed to transfer to a smaller room which I shared with only three others. Inevitably this brought the four of us very close, and we liked this. We learnt to be considerate. We had lots of parties with loud singing when there was something to celebrate and quiet periods when one of us had to study. From those parties, I still remember the Armenian brandy and the enormous piles of aubergine sandwiches: Bulgarian tinned aubergine pâté was the cheapest sandwich filler in those days.

Bedclothes in the hostel were changed once a fortnight. This did not, however, get rid of the bedbugs, which were widely believed to have been brought in by some Russians. I remember once waking up in the morning to see a dead bedbug on my pillow; I had apparently squashed it in my sleep. There was warm water in the showers, which worked most evenings, and there were lockable shower cubicles. In the communal washrooms, the water was icy cold, particularly in winter, and everybody washed in full view of each other. The toilets were often blocked and the communal kitchens filthy. Everyone took turns to clean the kitchens – some better than others! Quite a lot of cooking and eating was done in groups. The most popular dish was sautéed potatoes, which required only potatoes and cooking fat. Meat was beyond the reach of most students.

We did not pay for the hostel and most students received a grant of 35 roubles a month, which just about paid for the food; help was needed from parents for anything beyond this basic level. In contemporary Estonia the grant system has been largely abolished, and student loans introduced.

Although I was reading English, this involved studying Marxism–Leninism and a host of related subjects. Even physical education was compulsory. I was excused or to keep up to date with Western research. One of the first tasks of the new administration from 1989 was to 'internationalise' the university again without allowing its Estonian identity to suffer. Lecturers from many EU countries, rather than from just one, ensure this necessary diversity.

Wandering amongst the students and perusing the noticeboards, it is hard to realise that the current transformation took less than eight years. Reading the English-language brochures or browsing the website shows immediately what has been achieved. Until 2005, Tartu was Estonia's only university but then faced competition from Tallinn. Both have managed to do well since then, largely by attracting foreign students who are taught in English. The low fees, the intellectual rigour of the courses and the stability of Estonia appeal to the many students who cannot enjoy such facilities at home.

from Russian as I had done very well in it at secondary school. The strangest subject was 'safety in factory work', although none of us was expected to work in a factory. About a hundred of us would dutifully copy down what the lecturer told us; I remember him particularly drawing a lathe on the blackboard. I had never seen one in real life and have not done so since.

English studies were arranged in small groups of around 12 students. It was very formal, with an awesome English grammar book written by a Russian and published in Russia. All our language teachers were Estonians who had never been to England. Our literature teacher was an English communist who emigrated to the USSR, and then married an Estonian poetess. Literature for him ended before World War II and we were never taught anything about post-war writing.

There was no shortage of activities in Tartu. The town had an excellent theatre, as it still does, combining drama, opera and ballet. There were coffee-shops of the German and Austrian kind where we could linger. We could not afford butter on bread or sugar in coffee but we would talk long into the night, sometimes able to stretch to a glass of Hungarian wine.

By contrast, in the autumn we would be sent to a collective farm to work. This was hardly fun as it rained often, the potato fields became soggy and the potatoes heavy. The work was at the expense of our university studies and may well account for the fact that I never really mastered the basics of Latin.

We were guaranteed a job at the end of our university course regardless of our exam results. Since I had been reading English, I was offered a job as an English teacher, as were the other 25 of us. Take it or leave it, but sign on the dotted line for the minimum of two years – that was the principle. It is a day I still remember well. It was well organised and, with hindsight, even reassuring, but so demoralising at the time. I refused to sign at first but was told that I had no option, although I was not interested in a teaching career.

It has been reassuring in the years since that many of the students with whom I read English and shared accommodation have had very satisfactory careers as teachers after all. They did not seem enthusiastic at the time but later grew to like their teaching jobs.

Independence has changed a lot in people's attitudes; present-day pupils are willing to learn and their parents are even willing to pay for extra lessons. It is a far cry from the days when nobody in Estonia wanted to learn English because there was nothing one could do with one's language skills.

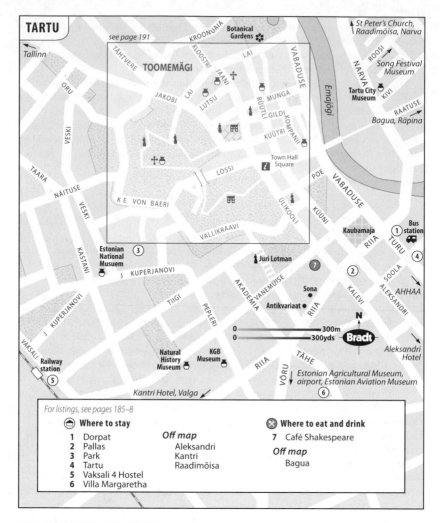

TARTU

see page 191

Tallinn

Botanical Gardens ✿

KROONUAIA

St Peter's Church,
Raadimõisa, Narva

TAHTVERE

TOOMEMÄGI

KLOOSTRI

LAI

JAANI

VABADUSE

NARVA

ROOSI

Song Festival
Museum

ORU

JAKOBI

LAI

LUTSU

RUUTLI

MUNGA

Emajõgi

Tartu City
Museum

KIVI

RAATUSE

GILDI

KOMPANII

Bagua, Räpina

VESKI

KÜÜTRI

TAARA

+✠

LOSSI

Town Hall
Square

POE

VABADUSE

NÄITUSE

VESKI

K E VON BAERI

ÜLIKOOLI

KÜÜNI

VALLIKRAAVI

Kaubamaja

Bus
station

RIIA

TURU

KASTANI

Estonian
National
Musuem

3

J KUPERJANOVI

Juri Lotman

7

2

SOOLA

AHHAA

AKADEMIA

VANEMUISE

Sona

KALEVI

ALEKSANDRI

TIIGI

PEPLERI

Antikvariaat

RIIA

N

0   300m
0   300yds

Bradt

Aleksandri
Hotel

J KUPERJANOVI

VAKSALI

Railway
station

5

Natural
History
Museum

KGB
Museum

RIIA

TÄHE

VÕRU

Estonian Agricultural Museum,
airport, Estonian Aviation Museum

Kantri Hotel, Valga

6

For listings, see pages 185–8

🛏 **Where to stay**

1 Dorpat
2 Pallas
3 Park
4 Tartu
5 Vaksali 4 Hostel
6 Villa Margaretha

Off map
    Aleksandri
    Kantri
    Raadimõisa

❌ **Where to eat and drink**

7 Café Shakespeare

Off map
    Bagua

GETTING THERE AND AWAY

By bus Tartu is well served by buses to all major towns in Estonia. They run every half-hour to Tallinn and most are non-stop, taking about 2½ hours. Buses operate several times a day to Rakvere, Narva, Võru, Valga, Viljandi and Pärnu. An increasing number of these can be booked online at www.tpilet.ee.

Expect to pay about €11 to Tallinn, but those aged 60 and over will pay half if they travel Tuesday–Thursday on buses run by the SEBE company. Ecolines and Luxexpress each operate two buses a day to Riga.

By train The railway station building had to be closed for several years as an environmental hazard, but it reopened in 2012. There are two fast trains a day to Tallinn (three on Fridays and Sundays) and this is undoubtedly the most comfortable way to travel between the two cities, and the most dependable. This service is scheduled to become more frequent in 2014. The journey takes a little over two hours. In 2013 the first-class fare was €13 and economy €9, with a 10% reduction on tickets bought in advance at the station. Services started that year to Koidula, on the Russian border, and to the Puisa Caves nearby. There are also trains to Valga on the Latvian border, which connect with trains to Riga and probably during the currency of this book there will be a direct service between Tartu and Riga.

By air Tartu airport [off map, page 184](☏ *730 9210; www.tartu-airport.ee*) opened in summer 2009 for passenger flights. The airport is 8km to the south of the city. The website gives details of the airport bus that operates to the city centre and of taxi companies and their fares. In 2013 Flybe operated five times a week between Helsinki and Tartu. In earlier years there had been flights to Riga and to Stockholm, which hopefully will return.

By ferry, boat and barge Sightseeing boat trips operate along the Emajõgi River in the summer. Some are short trips within the town, and others go to Lake Peipsi. Full details of all boat and ferry services are on www setoline.ee. Negotiations started with the Russians in 2001 to resume what had been a very popular trip in Soviet times – a boat from Tartu to Pskov – but after years of waiting for the Russians to deal with the visa issue, the Estonians gave up pursuing the matter. In 2006 the first rebuilt Peipsi barge took to the river again from a landing stage on the east side of the river at Ujula 96. In the 19th century, hundreds of these barges linked the rivers and lakes of Estonia and inland Russia and were easily identifiable with their large square sails. None survived World War II, but a sufficient number of plans and drawings were left to enable modern craftsmen to start building them again. When not in use, the barges can be visited at their landing stage. The website www.lodi.ee gives a full history of these boats and details of tours being operated on the Emajõgi.

GETTING AROUND There is an extensive **bus** network within Tartu and to the suburbs. Locally produced city maps show the routes, but these maps are also displayed, together with timetables, at most bus stops. Individual tickets can be bought from drivers for €1, but they are cheaper at kiosks, which also sell day tickets for €2.50 and books of ten tickets for €6.40. Full details of routes, timetables and fares are on www.sebe.ee/en/tartu-city-transport.

TOURIST INFORMATION The tourist board have an office/shop conveniently located in the **Town Hall** [191 C2](*Raekoja Plats 14;* ☏ *744 2111;* e *info@visittartu.com; www. visittartu.com or www.tartu.ee*). It sells a wide range of postcards, small souvenirs and maps for the whole of Estonia as well as on Tartu specifically. Their office also has a computer which visitors can use free of charge. *Tartu In Your Pocket* is published every six months and is the best source of information on opening hours, exhibitions and new restaurants. It can also be consulted online at www.inyourpocket.com. A local site with some English on it, www.kultuuriaken.tartu.ee is the best source for concert and theatre programmes. The word in the address means 'cultural window'. The most detailed history in English of Tartu and its buildings, to which the author of this book was a contributor, is *Millenary Tartu*, which was republished in 2013. For location of listings see maps, pages 184 and 191.

 WHERE TO STAY

🏠 **Antonius** (16 rooms) Ülikooli 15; ☏ 737 0377; e sales@hotelantonius.ee. In late 2008, 5-star luxury finally reached Tartu with the opening of this hotel directly opposite the main

entrance to the university. The Estonian president came soon afterwards to give it his personal stamp of approval. It is in an 18th-century building, which was difficult to adapt to the 21st. It has had many different uses, including as a bank & as a police station. Its age is left deliberately apparent in every room, as is clear from the old furniture, the brick or limestone walls & some bathrooms being reached by what would have been a door opening a safe. It may even be necessary in some rooms to stoop below wooden beams. The computer in the lounge is the only concession to modern taste. Being run by the same team who brought luxury to Pärnu with the Ammende Villa (see page 244), appropriately similar standards were imposed here too. 2 back rooms bear no relation to standards in the others, so only accept them with a massive discount. $$$$

🏠 **Barclay** (49 rooms) Ulikooli 8; ☎744 7100; e barclay@barclay.ee; www.barclay.ee. This hotel opened in 1996 & has always had a deliberately dated, perhaps even sombre air about it, but for many this is precisely its appeal. Its surroundings are quiet & so are the guests, who accept the leisurely pace of service in the restaurant as they are unlikely to be in a hurry. The restaurant, Neljapäev (Friday), was considerably upgraded in 2013 & has become well known for its fish dishes. The building was previously the Soviet military HQ, under the command of Dzhokhar Dudayev, who would later become president of the breakaway republic of Chechnya. As he was very sympathetic towards the Baltic independence movements, a plaque at the entrance commemorates him. This was placed here after he was assassinated by the Russians in 1996. $$$

🏠 **London** (60 rooms) Rüütli 9; ☎730 5555; e london@londonhotel.ee; www.londonhotel.ee. This is a very conventional, in the best sense of the word, business hotel in the town centre opened in 2003. Rooms are large, as is the reception area, which even boasts a fountain. The staff at the front desk are consistently helpful. It provides an excellent location in winter, with everything else on the doorstep, but in the summer, life on the streets might last a bit too long for comfort. Rooms on the top floor have AC, which can be important in midsummer. The hotel wisely replaced its restaurant in 2013; the new Polpo (www.polpo.ee) does true justice to the range of modern Estonian cuisine. $$$

🏠 **Pallas** (61 rooms) Riia 4; ☎730 1200; e pallas@pallas.ee; www.pallas.ee. This hotel is under the same management as the London. Pallas is the name of a famous art college that was

located on this site before the war, but which was destroyed in 1944. The hotel is a completely new building, above a department store but worth the ascent to the 2nd floor. The lobby & the rooms are all decorated with paintings from its former pupils. The 'star' works of art, by the director of the school, Ado Vabbe, are understandably exhibited in the suites. It is a short walk to the old town, but close to the bus station & a number of specialist shops. $$$

🏠 **Aleksandri** (41 rooms) Aleksandri 42; ☎736 6659; e aleksandri@aleksandri.ee; www.aleksandri.ee. This guesthouse is about 15 mins' walk from the town centre. Rooms are large & the road is quiet, even if some of the guests are not, & its website must be the noisiest of all the Tartu hotels who add music to the visuals. It appeals to families & to sports groups in equal measure. Unusually for Estonia, b/fast is not included in the room price, but is available next door in the rather incongruous surroundings of the Õlle Tare beer hall. $$

🏠 **Dorpat** (205 rooms) Soola 6; ☎733 7180; e info@dorpat.ee; www.dorpat.ee. The opening of this enormous hotel in 2007, followed by a conference building in 2008, shows Tartu's confidence in a future as a year-round business centre. Its 3-star rating, plus its location beside the bus station, will certainly ensure a stream of tourists through the summer. Many rooms have views & the whole 3rd floor is dedicated to those allergic to carpets, so the rooms & corridors are furnished only in wood. The spa centre visitors will now take for granted in a hotel of this size, but probably not the salt chamber which can cater for 8 people at once. Prices are so reasonable that visitors are unlikely to complain about the soundproofing, the lack of AC in standard rooms, or about the curtains not quite thick enough to keep out the summer light. Many locals & tourists from other hotels come into the restaurant for the set-price business lunch. $$

🏠 **Kantri** (27 rooms) Riia 195; ☎738 3044; e info@kantri.ee; www.kantri.ee. Located 5km south from the town centre, this hotel cultivates a manor-house feel with its small number of rooms & ample surroundings, although it is in fact a completely new building. It was the 1st hotel in Tartu to take groups when foreigners started to arrive in the early 1990s & its attractive prices still entice them. However a coach or a car is essential for anyone staying here as there is minimal public transport in the vicinity. **$$**

🏠 **Park** (19 rooms) Vallikraavi 23; ✆742 7000; e info@parkhotell.ee; www.parkhotell.ee. Situated in University Park, this 2-3-star hotel attracts regular visitors with its quiet location & a real fire in the b/fast room. It had the misfortune to open in 1940 but in Mar 1964 welcomed a guest whose visit to Tartu will never be forgotten by those old enough to remember it. Finnish president Kekkonen was the first Westerner to see Tartu after the war & he spoke Estonian throughout his stay, to the consternation of his hosts – most of whom spoke very little, or none. (His skiing was equally proficient & therefore alarming to his local minders.) He formulated a speech that did not directly offend the Russians, but with its many references to Estonia & its minimal ones to the USSR, made clear where his sympathies lay. Many Estonian exiles felt he had sold out to the USSR, but an equal number of others, & certainly Estonians who had stayed in the country, were pleased to see any possible links with the outside world, however controlled they would be from Moscow. Less welcome guests at the hotel 2 years later were Jean-Paul Sartre & Simone de Beauvoir, rewarded for their loyalty to the USSR by a trip to Estonia & to Lithuania, an unheard-of privilege for Westerners at the time. Simone found the hotel 'très elegant', the rooms 'modernes et gaies' & was relieved at the absence of a minder at the end of the corridor, highly unusual in the USSR. The best suite in the new hotel, renovated in 2000, is named after President Kekkonen & at only €100, is luxury at a bargain price. Regular visitors like the quiet location & the lack of any evening entertainment. It is a hilly walk of 15mins to the town centre but after a snowfall or during a long summer evening, this can be very congenial. In Soviet times of course it was a way of ensuring no casual contact took place between any visitors to the university & local students. **$$**

🏠 **Raadimõisa** (40 rooms) Mõisavärava 1; ✆733 8050; e info@raadihotell.ee; www.raadihotell.ee. In a sense, this hotel opened 10 years too early, as its location will only be convenient when the National Museum opens over the road in the former Raadi Manor House in 2016. It is just on the edge of the city, about 2.5km from the centre. However its rooms are all spacious, several have parquet floors for those

allergic to carpets, & access by coach is easy, which certainly doesn't apply to any of the hotels in the Old Town. **$$**

🏠 **Tartu** (74 rooms) Soola 3; ✆731 4300; e info@tartuhotell.ee; www.tartuhotell.ee. Visitors who knew this hotel in the 1990s will be very pleasantly surprised by all the improvements that have taken place since then. It took a long time to rid the building of its Soviet legacy but that has now happened. It is now a proper 3-star hotel, with many rooms being converted for family use. It will suit families in other ways too. There is plenty of parking space for those with cars, & for others it is beside the bus station, beside AHHAA (see page 196) & within walking distance of the town centre. **$$**

🏠 **Villa Margaretha** (17 rooms) Tähe 11–13; ✆731 1820; e info@margaretha.ee; www.margaretha.ee. The building is about 100 years old, so blends Art Nouveau & Art Deco. Visitors who come must therefore accept narrow staircases rather than lifts & less light than would now be seen as normal, plus the lack of soundproofing. As a former military social centre, it has had a history which should perhaps simply be described as 'colourful' but one tragic day here in Feb 1919 remains etched in the history of Tartu. Julius Kuperanov, one of the bravest commanders in the Independence War, was laid to rest here for a night after dying of his wounds in battle but before he was buried. His tomb would become a centre for resistance during the Soviet period, when brave students would rally there & leave flowers. Given the peace that now rules in this hotel, set a kilometre or so away from both business & academic life, it seems hard to believe that the building had a very different role throughout the 20th century. **$$**

🏠 **Vaksali 4 Hostel** (27 rooms) Vaksali 4; ✆744 1610; e info@hostel4.ee; www.hostel4.ee. Rooms here are small, facilities are shared & no b/fast is served, with guests making their own in the kitchen, but given the prices charged this is no cause for complaint. With rail services due to Increase in 2014, the railway station being beside the hostel will be an increasing bonus for travellers arriving from elsewhere in Estonia. As several buses serve the station, the hostel is well connected to all parts of the town, including the centre, which is otherwise a 20min walk away. **$**

✕ WHERE TO EAT AND DRINK When this book first came out in 1999, writing on Tartu restaurants and cafés was disappointingly straightforward: anything reasonable was automatically included. By early 2004, an entire listings magazine could have been devoted to this topic and it became worthwhile for Tartu to have its own *In Your Pocket* so it was no longer a mere supplement to the Tallinn one. Tartu does not have nor need the variety that Tallinn offers, but there is now sufficient choice that anyone staying for several days need never return to an earlier venue, although this is likely to be a pleasure. Pretentious luxury has not yet come to Tartu, but good cooking from anywhere famous for its food certainly has done. Restaurants and cafés are more 'stable' in Tartu than in Tallinn, perhaps because Tartu simply follows success and ignores failure. They should always be a pleasant surprise in comparison with Tallinn. The really parsimonious should, during the week, check the website www.paevapraed.ee which lists the daily lunchtime specials at all the Tartu restaurants that serve them. At the weekend, few do, so the site then becomes more important in tracking them down. For the location of listings see maps, pages 184 and 191.

✕ Eduard Vilde Vallikraavi 4; ☎773 43400; www.vilde.ee. You do not have to be under 30 to be admitted here, but it probably helps. There's an excellent range of cakes & open sandwiches, unusually fresh coffee, gentle service & academic décor as well as loud music. Note the griffin logo around the walls, this mythological winged lion being the protector of publishers. The terrace seems to be the refuge of every smoker in Tartu, so avoid this if it bothers you. The café was first named after Peter Ernst Wilde (1732–85), a doctor, veterinary surgeon & publisher who printed the first medical textbooks in Estonian here & won the rare privilege of being allowed to publish uncensored. With a change of ownership in 2009, it took the name of the writer Eduard Vilde (1865–1933). There is a restaurant upstairs, & literary pundits can test their wits by trying to identify all the Irish & Estonian writers portrayed on the walls. Groups can book, at no extra cost, a side-room to the restaurant which is music-free. At the front of the building, a bronze sculpture pictures an imagined meeting between Oscar Wilde & Eduard Vilde, perhaps similar *enfants terribles* with similar names. This was unveiled in 1999 to commemorate the centenary of Oscar Wilde's death in 1900. In 2004, the Tartu city government presented a copy of this statue to Galway, in Ireland. $$$

✕ Bagua Pikk 40; ☎740 2509. It is not necessary to cross the river to find Chinese food, but as the Old Town is packed either with tourists or with students, it may make sense to take the 15min walk to get here. Prices are of course lower than in the town centre & with portions double what you might expect, this is the place to tuck in & still make savings. The staff are willing to turn off the music when asked, which is often. $$

✕ Café Shakespeare Vanemuise 6; ☎744 0140; www.shakespeare.ee. Not surprisingly, this is situated in the Vanemuise Theatre. Following the Western pattern, theatres are now eager to encourage visitors to come at times when there are no performances, just as much as when there are. The exterior is drab, but the varying exhibitions & the equally varied menu make up for this. Quite a lot of ad hoc entertainment is provided by the actors who double as waiters here – Vanemuise was, after all, the god of song in Estonian mythology. Being in 'theatreland' the restaurant/café is open until midnight during the week & 02.00 on Fri & Sat, but is just as popular at lunchtime. Tell the staff if you are in a rush, otherwise they will assume you want a leisurely meal, in line with most students & artists. $$

✕ Crepp Rüütli 16; ☎742 2133; www.crepp.ee. France finally came to Tartu in 2005, when this opened as a café. A restaurant was added upstairs in 2009. All the pictures on the wall are of France & even French newspapers are available. It almost seems a surprise that the French spelling 'crêpe' is not used in the name. The menu is in fact more extensive than the name suggests, but always with a French bias, so expect a baguette rather than black bread. If sightseeing has been tiring, the armchairs here will be an added bonus. $$

✕ Neljas Aste (The Fourth Instance) Lossi 17; ☎742 5574; www.neljasaste.ee. It is an encouraging comment on the lack of crime in Estonia that space could be found in the law courts to open a restaurant. It is one of many setting up just outside the Old Town, near hotels & offices but able to offer much lower prices, particularly for strong drinks. The dishes here have provocative names but innocent ingredients: Dictatorship of the Proletariat is simply a herring salad. Note the restaurant closes at 19.00 so is really geared to lunch & snacks through the day. $$

✕ **Pierre Chocolaterie** Raekoja Plats (Town Hall Sq) 12; ☎730 4680; www.pierre.ee. Despite its name, visitors & locals come here as much for meals as for coffee breaks. In fact its attraction, as with many eateries in Tartu, is that locals who could not afford to eat out in Tallinn can certainly do so in Tartu. Day trippers could sensibly eat a large savoury main dish here & then buy a small box of chocolates for the train or bus journey back to Tallinn. $$

✕ **Püssirohukelder** (Gunpowder Cellar) Lossi 28; ☎730 3555; www.pyss.ee. Catherine the Great ordered this building in the 1760s but ever since 1825 it has been thought more sensible to keep beer, rather than gunpowder here, & always in enormous quantities. For much of the 1990s this was a grand, medieval restaurant built sufficiently deep below the city walls to ensure that mobile phones would not work here. Although it made no attempt to hide the brickwork when it reopened in 2001 as a very lively pub & disco, the age range of the clientele has dropped at least one generation. Its publicity material proclaims that 'it always survives wild party nights'. Perhaps this is because they call a large glass a 'men's beer' & a smaller glass a 'women's beer'. It is also proud of its 11m-high roof, which perhaps makes it the tallest pub in the world, & so perhaps the most expensive to heat as well. The menu is limited, though reasonably priced, & vegetarians are as unwanted as ever, but who need worry about food in such surroundings? The website address says it all. $$

✕ **Tsink Plekk Pang** Küütri 6; ☎730 3415; www.pang.ee. Whilst Chinese food in Tallinn still has to make its mark, it came instantly at a high level when this restaurant opened in 2002. It also brought Indian, Japanese & Thai food to Tartu at the same time. It has all the qualities that in the context of Chinese food assure quality – noise, a bland décor & brusque service. Perhaps more for local Chinese than for Estonians, a smoking room opened in 2009. $$

✕ **Ülikooli Kohvik** (University Café) Ülikooli 20; ☎737 5405; www.kohvik.ut.ee. Gentrification hit the 1st floor of this former student dive with a bang in 2005. Out went the local students & prices geared to them & in came a genteel café with an English-language website for those twice their age & with 4 times their income. On the ground floor, the 2 mix somewhat uneasily, as a self-service restaurant has survived there. Quality, if not prices, does stretch downstairs, but older people will probably prefer the calmer atmosphere upstairs. $$

✕ **Werner** Ülikooli 11; ☎744 1274; www.werner. ee. Although located in the heart of the student area, this is a café where nobody need be ashamed to admit their age. The 19th-century prints of Tartu on the walls provide an ambience for looking backwards rather than forwards. Buillon with pie followed by salmon pancakes make an excellent lunch. Chess sets are provided free of charge for those who wish to linger. There is a formal restaurant upstairs, equally dated in the best sense of the word & the 2 parts of the business are kept well apart. $$

✕ **Pagari Pood** Raekoja Plats (Town Hall Sq) 2. An ideal fast-food outlet, being right in the town centre, but with ultra-provincial prices & a sufficient range of pies & cakes to satisfy the tourist desperate not to waste a lunch hour with leisurely eating. $

✕ **Rotund** Toomemagi. Located at the top of University Hill, the restaurant is an appropriate reward for the steep walk from the town. In summer it spreads out of its tight, octagonal surroundings into the park, but not being open late in the evenings spares it from wilder students. The food is basic but cheap & elaborate sauces help to enliven it. A good place to seek refuge from a sudden Baltic storm. $

SHOPPING Tartu prices have to be geared to academics rather than to the business community or foreign tourists so are considerably cheaper than those in Tallinn or in Pärnu. Most souvenir shops are along Rüütli or on Town Hall Square. A craft centre, **St Anthony's Guild** [191 B1], is situated behind Lutsu mnt and it is possible to watch everything that is sold there being made. The bookshop **Apollo** [map page 184](*Kaubamaja shopping centre, Riia 1; www.apollo.ee;*

⊕ *09.00–21.00 Mon–Sat, 09.00–18.00 Sun*) has a wide selection of travel books on Estonia in English. Academic books in English are available at **Krisotomus** [191 D2] on Town Hall Square (*Raekoja Plats 11; www.kriso.ee;* ⊕ *10.00–18.00 Mon–Fri*). Two secondhand bookshops with a wide range of publications in English are next door to each other on Riia. They are **Sõna** at Riia 5 and **Antikvariaat** [both map page 184] at Riia 7. Both are open 10.00–18.00 Monday to Saturday.

OTHER PRACTICALITIES
Changing money The **Tavid** currency exchange office [191 D2] at Rüütli 2 (*www. tavid.ee*) is open 09.00–19.00 Monday to Sunday and offers competitive rates for over 50 currencies, and its list shows how extensively Estonians now travel on their holidays. Their website gives the exchange rates offered in their Tallinn offices, but usually the Tartu ones are the same or very similar. Fortunately this office does not have the €200 minimum exchange for good rates, which is charged in Tallinn. The several banks in the town centre also give competitive rates.

WHAT TO SEE AND DO
A walk around Tartu A tour should start at the **Town Hall Square** [191 D2], which one might think is an apolitical name. However neither the Germans, who called it Adolf-Hitler Platz, nor the Russians who called it Soviet Square, clearly thought so. With one's back to the river, looking towards the Town Hall, not a hint of either of these former regimes can now be seen.

The concrete bridge across the river is a replacement for the first stone bridge in the Baltics – a gift to the town from Catherine II following the fire of 1775 – that used to cross the river here. It was destroyed in World War II by the Russians as they advanced on the town in 1944, but it is hoped in due course to rebuild the bridge in its original design.

What is now parkland on both sides of the river was a built-up area until the battles of 1944. The damage was so great that the Soviets simply cleared the site, but fortunately they never planned to redevelop it. There are four statues of note in this park, along Vabaduse pst to the left of Town Hall Square. The first is of the writer Oskar Luts (1887–1953) (see page 207) who spent much of his life in Tartu. The second is of Friedrich Reinhold Kreutzwald (1802–83) (see page 46) but those further along are of far greater interest. The first is of the mythical Estonian hero Kalevipoeg, the subject of Kreutzwald's most famous book. This is a copy of a statue cast in 1928 by Amandus Adamson (see page 45) which the Soviets removed, not so much because of this figure, but because of the dates 1918–20 which were on the original plinth and which commemorated the War of Independence. The next statue in fact dates from Soviet times but, given its theme, causes no dissent now. It was presented by the town in Armenia then known as Leninakan but which has since had its original name of Gyumri restored. It commemorates the Armenian writer Khachatur Abovian (1805–48) who studied in Tartu and married an Estonian. As a proponent of vernacular literature, he would have many followers in Estonia. The Armenian community in Estonia gathers here every 24 April, when they commemorate Genocide Memorial Day.

Return to the square and walk towards the Town Hall. To the right is the north side of the square, which has a number of well-preserved, late 18th-century buildings whereas those on the south side are largely 20th century. Number 18 is famous on two counts: it belonged to the family of General Barclay who successfully repulsed Napoleon, and it leans to one side because it was built on swampy foundations. It is now the **Art Museum** [191 D2](see page 196).

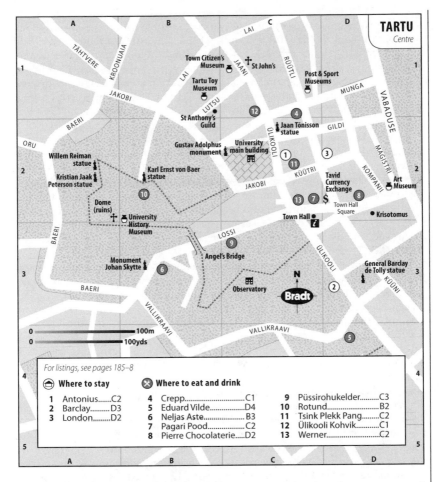

A B C D

TÄHTVERE

KROONUAIA

JAKOBI

BAERI

ORU

LAI

LUTSU

JAANI

LAI

ROOTLI

MUNGA

VABADUSE

Town Citizen's Museum

St John's

Tartu Toy Museum

Post & Sport Museums

St Anthony's Guild

12

Jaan Tõnisson statue

4

GILDI

MAGISTRI

Gustav Adolphus monument

University main building

ÜLIKOOLI

1

3

Willem Reiman statue

Karl Ernst von Baer statue

11

KÜÜTRI

KOMPANII

Kristjan Jaak Peterson statue

10

JAKOBI

Tavid Currency Exchange

Art Museum

BAERI

Dome (ruins)

University History Museum

13 **7** $

8

Town Hall Square

Krisotomus

Town Hall **i**

LOSSI

9

Monument Johan Skytte

6

Angel's Bridge

ÜLIKOOLI

General Barclay de Tolly statue

BAERI

VALLIKRAAVI

N

Observatory

Bradt

KÜÜNI

2

0 ————— 100m
0 ————— 100yds

VALLIKRAAVI

5

A B C D

For listings, see pages 185–8

Where to stay

1 Antonius......C2
2 Barclay.........D3
3 London.........D2

Where to eat and drink

4 Crepp..........................C1
5 Eduard Vilde................D4
6 Neljas Aste....................B3
7 Pagari Pood..................C2
8 Pierre Chocolaterie.....D2

9 Püssirohukelder..........C3
10 Rotund.........................B2
11 Tsink Plekk Pang.........C2
12 Ülikooli Kohvik............C1
13 Werner..........................C2

Although the **Town Hall** [191 C2], a former market, gives the impression of careful planning and its façade has survived in total from its construction in 1789, there was much dispute about its size, use and layout. A suitable design for the fountains at the front of the Town Hall was only resolved in October 1998. The one chosen, of an embracing young couple, clearly breaks with the more staid tradition of earlier Estonian sculpture.

Leave the square behind the Town Hall to the right, noting the large wall painting on the building at the corner of Lossi and Ülikooli, which pictures the university in the 1860s. A short walk along Ülikooli brings the main university into view [191 C2]. Look first however to the left, at the building on the corner of Jacobi and Ülikooli which displays a modern montage – photographs of staff members in 2007. The façade may well seem familiar to visitors recently in Tallinn; it was copied in Tallinn Old Town by the main building overlooking Pikk Jalg ('Long Leg'). The architect, Johann Wilhelm Krause, later became famous in Estonia, but this was his first major work, completed in 1809. He had previously enjoyed a very varied career. From 1778 to 1781 he studied theology in Leipzig but failed to graduate. He then spent a year as a British mercenary in the USA. It would be the late 1790s before he settled down in the Baltics to art and architecture.

The building now houses the main student assembly hall, the administration, and the **Museum of Classical Antiquity** [191 C2]. Posters in the entrance hall advertise all the concerts and plays taking place in the university. The collection in the museum is far more extensive than its name suggests. Whilst there are original Greek works and many plaster cast copies as well, the museum also has on display two Egyptian mummies and several hundred Russian icons, many recently seized from smugglers. There is one of four death masks of the German philosopher Immanuel Kant, which was presented to Karl Morgenstern, the founder of the collection. The museum first opened in 1803, just a year after tuition began again at the university. The **Assembly Hall** [191 C2] is acoustically one of the best concert halls in Estonia; Liszt and Schumann performed here in the 19th century and were followed more recently by every favourite Soviet pianist and violinist. It had to be rebuilt following a fire in 1965 which was caused by badly maintained electric wiring. Any important event in the university takes place here but the one that deserves particular mention was its reopening in December 1919 in Estonian hands and with Estonian established as the language of tuition, replacing German and Russian.

In the attic above the Assembly Hall, one of five original **student lock-ups** remains. These were based on models from Göttingen and Heidelberg and date from the early 19th century when German influence was at its strongest. Specific sentences were laid down for any of the misdemeanours students were likely to commit. Insulting a cloakroom attendant warranted five days, insulting a woman only four. (Female students were not accepted at the university until 1915.) Smoking on university premises and returning library books late were regarded equally, both leading to a two-day sentence, but swearing was four times as evil since it carried an eight-day sentence. The austere furniture and surroundings are no worse than many students at liberty would have endured in their lodgings. The graffiti on the walls testifies to the wide range of talent amongst those detained here. The incorrect Latin, however, was bequeathed by Soviet restorers after the 1965 fire.

Coming out of the university building and turning left along Jaani, look out for the statue of **Jaan Tõnisson** [191 C2] at the junction with Gildi, erected in 2001. Tõnisson had many senior political posts in the 1920s and was also editor of Estonia's most famous newspaper, *Postimees*. The local offices of the newspaper are opposite the statue. A hundred metres further down Jaani is **St John's Church** [191 C1] (Jaani Kirk) where restoration was completed in summer 2005. Visitors in the early 1990s found it difficult to imagine that it had once been one of the most imposing brick Gothic buildings in the Baltics, with 2,000 terracotta statues adorning both the inside and outside walls. The orginal church probably dates from the 13th century although we currently have little idea of its format then with few references in documents and no pictures. Archaeological excavations currently in hand should soon give us a clearer idea. By the 17th century the church certainly had its current layout, but much of the fabric was destroyed in 1708 during the Great Northern War, when the Russians and Swedes were fighting for control over the eastern Baltics. Many different architects worked on the building during the 19th century, including Wilhelm Bockslaff (1858–1945) who is best known for designing the Art Academy and the Great Guild in Riga. The building was badly damaged in August 1944 as the Germans retreated in the face of the Soviet armies. The church was neglected for most of the Soviet era, with much of the nave collapsing in 1952. There was even a threat to tear it down but then it was realised that the Niguliste Church in Tallinn might provide a suitable model, so the plan was to reopen it as a concert hall. Rebuilding work for this project finally started in 1989 under Polish supervision. Polish restorers had a worldwide reputation at the time in view of what they had achieved in Warsaw. Estonians took over in 1991 with the aim of restoring the church to its original state with about half of the original 2,000 terracotta statues on display. In 1997, the Christmas service was celebrated for the first time since World War II as the roof was completed that year. The copper steeple and the bells followed in 1999. A single window was commissioned in 2000 from Urmo Raus, an Estonian stained-glass designer who was then settled in France (and today lives and works in the Netherlands). This window has now been withdrawn; some people disliked the abstract design, others the fact that the artist no longer lived in Estonia and they wanted the work to be done locally. Visitors will therefore now see totally plain glass with frames of stainless steel.

Opposite the church on Jaani there was for many years a nondescript office building with a warning sign in Estonian and English – Varise Misohtlik, 'Liable to Fall Down'. This was a transit prison in 1941 and 1949 for those due to be transported to Siberia, and about 100 executions took place here in each of those years. In Soviet times it became a sobering-up station but as independent Estonia did not believe in such institutions, it again became a prison, but one from which it was all too easy to escape. It closed in 1999 and the building has now been transformed into luxury flats. In the neighbouring small streets are several stone and wooden houses that survive from the 19th century; fortunately these are being restored and not torn down. Crossing Lutsu the next building of note on the left-hand side is number 16, the **Town Citizen's Museum,** [191 C1] a recreation of a town house from 1830, where a middle-class family would have lived. At the time, they would have been German, or possibly Russian, but certainly not Estonian.

To continue the tour, return to the back of the university building where there is a statue of the Swedish king **Gustav Adolphus,** [191 C2] the founder of the university in 1632. The statue is new because the earlier one was removed during the Soviet era. This one was unveiled in 1992, during the first royal visit to Estonia following the restoration of independence, by King Carl Gustav of Sweden. The Swedish royal family offered to replace the statue in 1982 for the 350th anniversary celebrations but the offer was rejected. This did not prevent rebellious students from restoring the king in snow each subsequent winter.

A stiff ten-minute walk now follows to reach the monuments at the top of the hill behind the university. A walk in this area shows the university at its most serious and at its most carefree. Three memorial statues immediately stand out, one of **Karl Ernst von Baer** [191 B2] (1792–1876) who is seated with a book open in his lap. As the founder of embryology, he is Tartu's most famous scientist and also equally famous as an explorer. He was one of very few Baltic Germans to integrate with Estonians and to learn the language. This seriousness does not prevent students using his statue as a site for wild fraternity and sorority parties, with dancing and bonfires. Because he also taught in St Petersburg and in Königsberg, his work was praised in Soviet times. The Russians now claim him and refer to him frequently in histories of 'Kaliningrad'.

The second statue is of Estonia's first poet, **Kristian Jaak Peterson** [191 A2] (1801–22), who is standing, clasping a stick. It is claimed that he walked from Riga to Tartu to study here, such was his enthusiasm. He died of tuberculosis at the age of 21, but despite hardly reaching adulthood, he proved that poetry and serious prose need not be written only in German. His work covers a wide range of topics, including religion, music and the natural world, but he was sadly ahead of his time. Ironically, one year after his death, some poetry he wrote in German was published in Leipzig, but it was another hundred years before his poems in Estonian appeared. Since 1995, his birthday, 14 March, has been celebrated as

'Mother Tongue Day' and on this day in 2006 President Meri died; he was a great supporter of this cause. Next to Peterson is a statue of **Willem Reiman** [191 A2] (1861–1917) who was to Estonian history what Peterson was to the language. He was the first lecturer at the university to give history an Estonian, rather than a German or a Russian, perspective. Later he would be well known for his work in the temperance movement and had he lived into the independence era, he would undoubtedly have campaigned for Estonian prohibition, following the American and Finnish example of the time.

Behind the Peterson statue is **Kissing Hill**, a surprisingly open area for lovers to congregate; the tougher male students traditionally show their affection by carrying their girlfriends here from **Angel's Bridge** [191 B3], a distance of about 200m. This bridge was built as a memorial to **Georg Friedrich Parrot** (1767–1852), the first chancellor of the university when it reopened in 1802.

The hill is dominated by the **Tartu University History Museum** [191 B2] (*www.ajaloomuuseum.ut.ee*), housed in the shell of the former St Peter and St Paul Cathedral which had been originally built in the 13th century. When completed it was the tallest church in Estonia and, from pictures that survive, one of the most imposing Gothic ones in the Baltics. Wars and fires soon took their toll, and by the early 17th century the entire interior had been destroyed. Much of what remained was looted and the site even degenerated into a rubbish dump. In 1807 the choir was restored and rebuilt as the university library, a role it would maintain until 1985 when the present museum opened. Extensive renovation was carried out both in the first independence period and during the Soviet occupation and has continued more recently. In 2005 the tower was opened to visitors ready for a stiff climb. In the summer the view is restricted to that of church steeples rising through the trees, which block the view of anything else.

The museum was established here in 1982, when the library moved out. The top floor is still called Morgenstern Hall after Karl Morgenstern (see page 180) the first university librarian. The collections now cover all the scientific and medical fields in which Tartu showed particular expertise and most rooms have labels in English. A range of artists have painted all the highlights of the 19th century, while photographers have played the same role in this century. Perhaps the most interesting person covered is Ernst von Bergmann (1836–1907) who was professor of surgery here during the 1870s. He was the first medic to wash his hands before operating, rather than just afterwards, and was also the first one to wear a white coat in the theatre.

One large map shows the worldwide extent of the Tartu diaspora. The role of the Jewish community is documented in a chart which covers the period from 1865, when Jews were first allowed to live in Tartu, through to the 1890s, during which time the quota, which restricted the number of Jewish students, rose from 5% to 20%. This quota was abolished only in 1916. Jewish studies were banned by the Russians in 1940 and the few Jewish staff that remained at the time of the German invasion the following year were all arrested and murdered.

Following renovation in 2012, an expanded collection has been shown, including gifts from Soviet times, which were always exchanged when delegations from other republics visited the university. A coffee machine from that time has a sign on it saying that 'Groups of Veterans from the Great Fatherland War (the Soviet name for World War II) are exempted from queuing'.

About 200 metres east of the History Museum is the **Observatory** [191 C3] (*www.ajaloomuuseum.ut.ee/observatory*), which was built shortly after the reopening of the university in the early 19th century and was designed by Johann

Wilhelm Krause, the architect of the main university building. Until World War I it was probably the best in Europe, having registered 120,000 different stars. A small exhibition inside covers the history of the observatory and displays several telescopes. This exhibition has hardly changed since it first opened in the 1890s, so shows the best of 19th-century astronomy and telescopes that were actually used then. Several came from England and Germany. The most famous exhibit is the Frauhofer refractor which came here in 1824 and which was the first telescope through which distances in the solar system could be judged. However newer displays, largely interactive, cover the Soviet space programme and the developments brought to astonomy by electronics. The observatory had remained in use until 1964, when a new one opened outside Tartu at Toravere. The Estonian flag flies from this roof 24 hours a day; unlike the flag on Hermann Tower in Tallinn, it is not lowered at sunset.

There are several routes back to the town from the university. The quickest is along Lossi to the back of the Town Hall. The nearby Barclay plats should not be missed. In its centre is the statue of **General Barclay de Tolly** [191 D3], who successfully fought Napoleon. The statue was paid for by his troops. At the far side of the square, on Küüni, is a sculpture titled *Father and Son* which sounds innocent enough but in fact shows them both naked, with the small son built up to the height of his father. It is the work of Ülo Õun (1940–88) whose short career was entirely in the Soviet period and who tragically committed suicide just before the time when he could have expressed himself with the freedom that he so desperately needed. This work could of course only be exhibited after the Soviet era.

A longer route back goes along Vallikravi, Struve and Vanemuise and passes the University Library. In front of the library is a fountain/sculpture completed in 2007 in memory of **Juri Lotman** [map page 184] (1922–93), probably the most famous academic based in Tartu during the Soviet period. Semiotics was his field and probably only those who understand its meaning will be able to interpret this work of art. As a Jew, Lotman could not pursue his studies in Leningrad in the early 1950s, when Stalin launched his anti-Semitic campaign of 'cosmopolitanism' so he came to Tartu and stayed there for the rest of his life. Although respected worldwide, he was not allowed to leave the Soviet Union until the late 1980s.

St Peter's Church [off map, page 184] is worth a separate walk on its own, or can be combined with a visit to the Town Museum. Cross the river at the lower end of Town Hall Square, walk across the park on the other side to Narva mnt. Turn left and continue for about a kilometre. This enormous Gothic church has always had a role to play in Tartu politics, whatever the surrounding government. The architect Viktor Schröter also designed the façades of the Marinsky Theatre in St Petersburg and the National Opera in Kiev. It was consecrated in 1884 with seating for 1,500. Only three spires were complete by then, the other two following in 1903. The two-storey choir is similar to that in the Alexander Church in Narva. Services only took place in Estonian and the building of such a large Lutheran church was a deliberate snub to the Russian Orthodox Church, which had been actively proselytising in Estonia in the late 19th century. The altarpiece is by Johann Köler (see page 42), often seen as Estonia's first artist. It had a thriving congregation during the first period of Estonian independence and a resilient one in Soviet times, when it often acted as a kind of refuge for dissidents.

Museums Two museums, the Classical Antiquities and the University History, have been described in the walk above. Tartu has 14 others; the nine likely to interest foreign visitors are described here. All are usually open from 11.00 to 18.00,

6

Wednesday to Sunday (closed Monday and Tuesday), and are also closed on 23–24 June and 20 August but tour operators can make arrangements for group visits on closed days. As opening hours can change from year to year, and sometimes at short notice as well, it is important to check them on the website. In 2013, admission was free to all Tartu museums on the last Friday of the month. There is no equivalent to the Tallinn Card to cover admission fees and public transport. Four of the museums (Citizen's Home, KGB, Song Festival and Tartu City) are run by the city government and share the same website address: www.linnamuuseum.tartu.ee.

AHHAA [off map, page 184] (*Sadama 1;* ☎ *745 6789; www.ahhaa.ee*) Tartu has for many years been conscious of its somewhat stuffy image, perhaps in tune with its academic status. The opening of this science centre which puts the young firmly before the old, should help to change this. It is possible to walk around here, but most of the visitors will be climbing, leaping or perhaps merely staring at their distorted figures in the Hall of Mirrors. However for those who insist on viewing static displays, there is a real Sputnik satellite from Soviet times, animal skeletons and a towering ant hill, fortunately well encased in glass. To reinforce its contemporary image, it is open year-round and has a daily programme of films and displays; the website gives details of these. In good weather, the roof on the neighbouring Tasku shopping centre gives a good view towards the Old Town.

Art Museum [191 D2] (*Raekoja Plats 18;* ☎ *744 1080; www.tartmus.ee*) This is largely used as an art gallery for Tartu artists who made their name during the first independence period when, thanks to the local Pallas Art College, Tartu was the national centre for painting. Each member of the college, about 120 people in all, was supposed to give at least one of their paintings to found the collection. The original plan was to open it in 1938 to celebrate the 20th anniversary of independence, but in the end it only opened in late 1940, under the first Soviet occupation. A remarkably large number of women attended the college, including Karin Luts (1904–93), Estonia's most famous woman artist, whose work reflects the time spent in France and Italy. She went to Sweden in exile in 1944 but somehow never managed to regain her fame there. Several paintings by Konrad Mägi (1878–1925) are exhibited here. The work of an earlier artist displayed here, Georg Friedrich Schlater (1804–70), should also be noted. He was born in Tilsit, now Sovietsk, and grew up in Riga but spent his entire adult life in Tartu. He concentrated on lithographs of the city in the era just before photography took over, so has left an extensive architectural record of Tartu before the arrival of industry and railways. Later he would turn to portraits and photography.

Estonian Agricultural Museum [off map, page 184] (☎ *741 2397; www.epm. ee*) This museum is at Ülemurme, 6km south of Tartu, but buses going to Põlva and Võru all stop here. As its name implies, it is by far the largest museum in the country on this theme and even determined city dwellers should be interested by the diversity of its collection. It is far from being a collection of rusty tools, an all-too-common occurrence in this field. It has machinery, models, space, diagrams and effective lighting to show what has and what has not succeeded in Estonia over the last 200 years. Bee-keeping and flax processing are amongst the many topics covered and there is plenty of activity for families such as baking bread and churning butter. It is fortunate that so much survived the war, including tractors imported from America in the 1930s. Visitors are welcome to picnic in the grounds.

Estonian Aviation Museum [off map, page 184] (*Lange Village, 16km south of Tartu;* m *502 6712; www.lennundusmuuseum.ee*) This is one of the fastest-expanding museums in Estonia; it opened in 2002 when it was called the Tartu Aviation Museum but it rightly became 'Estonian' in 2008, given the size the collection had by then reached. All the aircraft are parked outside on fields that belong to the museum owner's family. Tartu was a major military centre in Soviet times (which is why foreigners could only visit it for the day under constant Intourist supervision) but was already active in this field before World War I and during the first period of independence. Most of the 13 aircraft currently on show are military ones abandoned by the Soviet and Polish air forces plus a few passenger aircraft from the 1990s. None is operational. The long-term hope is to increase the collection to 30–40. Indoors is a museum with 400 model aircraft.

Estonian National Museum [map page 184] (*Kuperjanovi 9;* ⬉ *742 1311; www.erm.ee*) This museum should serve as a model for others in Estonia; it is sad that more foreign tourists do not visit. Layout, lighting and description have all been properly thought out and, given the paucity of English-language books about Estonia, this is the best introduction to take their place. The 19th century is particularly well documented and temporary exhibitions enhance what is shown in the main collections. The museum covers not only Estonians, but also other nationals who have lived there such as the Baltic Germans, the Russians and the Swedes. Recent additions include a room on the Soviet period and photographs of many of the country's manor houses. Note in particular the pictures of bomb damage of 1941, of the final shopping queues in 1991 at the end of the Soviet era and the montage of Stalin on a gallows daringly put together in 1941. Do open the drawers upstairs to see the displays of gloves woven in all areas of the country. The total collection of beer tankards made from birch wood amounts to 3,000 but of course only a few can be exhibited at any one time.

The museum has a café in the entrance with some of the lowest prices in Estonia. Take the stairs at the back of the café up one floor to an exhibition of dolls. These were all made by the exile community in the USA during the Soviet occupation and represent the costumes of each region in Estonia, the idea being that future generations should have this bond with their parents' homeland.

Opposite the museum is the largest fraternity house of the university; such organisations were banned in the Soviet period but have enjoyed a revival since then. The university assures visitors that in this building 'old strict discipline has given way to modern liberty and the best man is not one who drinks most beer but the one who does it best and shows most sociability'. The railway station is a walk of around 300m from the museum so visitors coming for the day from Tallinn can end their tour here. (They cannot start it here as the museum only opens at 11.00 and the train arrives at 10.00.) In 2016 the museum will move to new larger premises at Raadi Manor House, on the outskirts of the town to the east. This is in fact where the museum was housed before the war. It then became a secret Soviet military base.

Estonian Postal Museum [191 C1] (*Rüütli 15;* ⬉ *730 0775; www.erm.ee*) This collection, previously run by the Post Office, came under the auspices of the National Museum in 2009. It does not limit itself to stamps. Postmarks are of equal significance in the political history of Estonia, as were the interventions of censors for almost all previous regimes. There are also maps of the routes taken by postal carriages before the advent of the railways. Note the stamps issued in Otepää from

22 July to 12 August 1941, when the Russians had fled and the Germans had not yet had time to impose their own postal system. The museum would have been much bigger had not much of the collection been taken in Soviet times by the Communications Museum in Leningrad. Of recent interest are the displays of packets intercepted which contained drugs; criminals clearly hoped this was a safer illegal activity than conventional smuggling. The shop here has a varied selection of postcards for sale at prices lower than elsewhere in Tartu plus of course sets of stamps recently issued by the Post Office.

The KGB Museum [map page 184] (*Riia 15b;* ✎ *746 1914; www.linnamuuseum. tartu.ee*) This museum opened in 2003 in its former local headquarters, although the entrance is in fact on Pepleri. The exhibition has really come about through the efforts of Enn Tarto who as a dissident had three different spells in prison during the Soviet era, totalling 15 years in all. Despite this, he was fortunately able to be an active parliamentarian during the 1990s. Visitors can see the cells as victims knew them and also an exhibition of Estonian resistance during the Soviet era.

Song Festival Museum [off map, page 184] (*Jaama 14;* ✎ *746 1020; www. tartu.ee/linnamuuseum*) This building is as important as its contents, since it was the headquarters of the Vanemuine Society from 1870 to 1903. The society was founded in 1865 to promote performances by choirs in Estonian and this led to the first Song Festival in 1869, which was held in Tartu. From 1896, they would all be held in Tallinn. In 1870, the open-air stage at the back of the building hosted the first performance of a play in Estonian, *The Cousin from Saaremaa*, written by Lydia Koidula. It was particularly well received since the audience had expected it to be in German, as all previous plays had been, and they were delighted with the change. Another change would take a further six years, as it was 1876 before women actors were allowed on stage. A major female role in the 1870 production was therefore taken by Harry Jannsen, Lydia Koidula's brother. The museum has pictures and mementoes from each festival, but the 20th-century ones are of most interest, since it is possible to hear recordings and see performances from each one. Those in the 1950s and 1970s suffered most from Soviet interference. The 1960 one is best remembered from the courageous impromptu singing of 'My Country is my Pride and Joy'. Given the enthusiasm that this raised, the Soviets did not dare to ban it again. The song festivals held abroad by exiles at that time are also covered.

Sport Museum [191 C1] (*Rüütli 15;* ✎ *730 0750; www.spordimuuseum.ee*) This museum opened in 1963 and, given Soviet support for this activity, much of the material was collected then. The current building opened in 2001 and is shared with the Estonian Postal Museum. A collection had in fact been started in 1934 so photos, medals and sportswear go back to the beginning of the 20th century. Many of the early posters are in German and the first sportsman of note who grew up in Estonia was the Baltic-German wrestler Georg Hackenschmidt (1877–1968) who became well-known in Britain before World War I and then settled in south London after World War II. Now he is equally remembered for the books he wrote about wrestling. Understandably the collection concentrates on Estonian Olympic champions, in their own right from 1920 to 1936 and again from 1992, but ethnic Estonians who won medals for the Soviet Union from 1948 to 1988 are also honoured. Estonian teams trained very hard for the 1940 Games, scheduled to take place in Helsinki. Paul Keres, best remembered as a chess player, is shown here in 1975, playing tennis in Vancouver a few days before he died of a heart attack. Enough gold medals have been won to dedicate a room to them without needing to show silver and bronze ones as well. The museum is updated after every Olympic Games; on display from the London ones of 2012 is the torch carried by the president's wife, Evelin Ilves.

Tartu City Museum [map page 184] (*Narva mnt;* \ *746 1911; www.tartu.ee/linnamuuseum*) The building that now houses the museum dates from 1790 when Tartu's architecture was at its height; after the fire of 1775 buildings were in stone, and were made to last and to impress. The architect Johann Walter, who also designed the Town Hall, was clearly briefed to make this the most lavish private residence in Tartu and to base the design on the contemporary French style of Louis XVI. However, it did not stay long in private hands and the next two centuries would see it being used as a printing press, a school, a hostel and then finally a cultural centre during the Soviet period. For the first ten years after the restoration of Estonian independence, this museum was housed in totally inadequate premises near to the university, but in 2001 it finally moved here, to a building that can do justice to the collection. The museum is fully equipped for those with disabilities.

The highpoints here are the model of Tartu in 1940, before any bombing, and the actual table at which the Tartu Treaty was signed. It was by this treaty, signed in 1920, that the Soviet Union recognised Estonian independence and its borders. Earlier exhibits cover 14th-century painted glass cups, and clocks, silver and textiles from the Swedish period in the 17th century, and the coin collection – around 7,000 in all – is the most extensive in Estonia. Films from the first period of independence and from the Soviet era are shown regularly.

Tartu Toy Museum [191 B1] (*Lutsu 8;* \ *746 1777; www.mm.ee*) The museum opened in 1994 although the building now occupied dates from 1770. Its collection, based entirely on voluntary donations, is mainly traditional, but modern toys are being added. In political terms, this is a classless museum with the porcelain dolls of the rich claiming the same space as the rag dolls and wooden horses of the peasants. The products of craftsmen and of the large factories are given equal space. It is hoped to extend the collection of board games and mechanical toys as more gifts are received. Some board games continued in the Soviet era but with different names and flags. That era also had the sexual divisions of the West with cars, trains and weapons for boys and dolls for girls. The dolls and their 'houses' come from all over the world. There was a drop in local production after 1990 when the appeal of international toys not previously available in Estonia drew customers away. In 2007 an extension opened to cover puppet theatres and films. Tasteful wooden toys are sold in the museum shop and a playroom is available for children.

VILJANDI

Both history and geography have been cruel to Viljandi. No major military conflict has passed the town by and major fires in 1682, 1765, 1894 and 1905 caused just as much damage. The lack of a large river and more recently of a railway junction has denied the town the prosperity it could otherwise have enjoyed. Being founded in the 12th century, its history is in fact older than that of Tallinn. Fortunately, much of its rich architectural legacy has survived, so a walk around the town centre offers a cross-section of most Estonian styles and materials. The foreign conquerors – the Germans, Poles, Swedes and Russians – also all left their mark. Probably Viljandi's richest period was in the late 18th century when a population of just a thousand

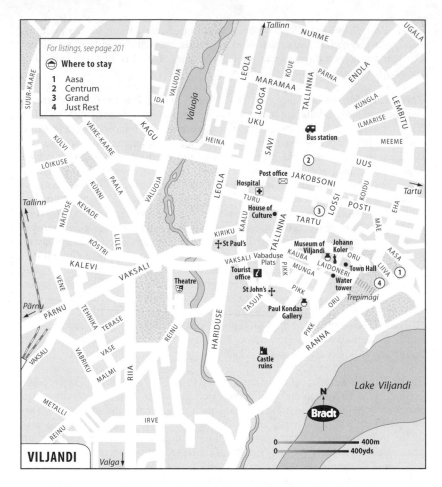

supported three goldsmiths and two wigmakers. It is now best known in Estonia for various athletics competitions that take place there, some in the town and some around the lake. A full music programme, much of it centred on the open-air concert hall in the castle, is offered during the summer.

GETTING THERE AND AWAY Express **buses** run hourly to Tallinn, and slower services also run hourly to Pärnu and Tartu. Journey times are around two hours in each case. The Pärnu buses serve Kaansoo, the entrance to Soomaa National Park. About three or four services a day run to Valga and Narva. A **train** operates three times a day to Tallinn and the €3 extra charged for first class is well worth paying. Extra services, and faster trains, are likely to operate from 2014. The railway station is about a 1.5km from the town centre, the bus station a kilometre or so in a different direction. The **tourist office** (*Vabaduse Plats 6*) has details of the extensive local bus routes.

WHERE TO STAY AND EAT Through the 1990s tourists just lunched in Viljandi but did not stay, as there was no suitable hotel. In 1999 the Centrum opened, followed in 2002 by the Grand. For location of listings see map, above.

Grand (49 rooms) Lossi 29; ☎ 435 5800; e info@ghv.ee; www.ghv.ee. Tourists using the swimming pool, the gym or the beauty salon here will find it hard to believe that during World War II this was a concentration camp disguised as a hospital & that during most of the Soviet period it was an art college. It had a short spell as the Hotel Viljandi in the 1980s & early 1990s. Only from 1938 to 1940 had it been a 'grand' hotel & its public areas are clearly modelled on that time. It reopened in 2002 & has stayed fairly, if not very, grand ever since. **$$$**

Aasa Guesthouse (7 rooms) Aasa 6; ☎ 434 5188; e info@aasakylalistemaja.ee; www. aasakylalistemaja.ee. Although about 1km from the town centre, the lakeside location is appealing. The interior is totally English, with doilies on the tables, individually sewn curtains & pillowcases, flower-patterned wallpaper & photos that could be of the English countryside. Big wardrobes in all

the bedrooms add to this feeling. However there is a sauna on the 3rd floor with a good view of the lake. **$$**

Centrum (27 rooms) Tallinna 24; ☎ 435 1100; e bron@centrum.ee; www.centrum.ee. Individual tourists will appreciate the location beside the bus station in the town centre. The ground-floor entrance could be larger & more inviting but, once on the 1st & 2nd floors, there is ample space & comfort. Some rooms are allocated for those with disabilities. **$$**

Just Rest (26 rooms) Ranna 6; ☎ 520 6772; e info@justrest.eu; www.justrest.eu. This is Estonia's first automatic hostel, a concept probably better known in North America than in Europe. Bookings are confirmed by a pincode that opens the door to the hotel & to the room booked. Prices do not include b/fast, but this is available in the café which is part of the building. The food served in the café is Estonian too. **$**

WHAT TO SEE From 1 June to 31 August, the tourist office organises a walk around Viljandi every day at 13.00, at a cost of €1 per person, which passes many of the sites mentioned below.

The town is dominated by the ruins of the **castle**, which dates from the early 13th century. Three hundred years later it had become, in appearance, the best-defended fortress in Estonia, with two surrounding walls, but every new invader could in the end seize it. When the Swedes conquered the town in 1620, they decided it was no longer worth rebuilding, and over the next 250 years much of the stonework was looted. Only in the late 19th century did the Baltic Germans revive interest in the castle and they ensured the preservation of the basic structure that can still be seen. The excavations they began, and the creation of the surrounding park, continued during both the first independence period and the Soviet occupation.

The 21st-century unofficial logo for Viljandi is undoubtedly the strawberry. There were eight concrete ones built around the town in 2007. For the reason, see below under the Paul Kondas Gallery.

The most famous Estonian born in Viljandi county (although not actually in the town) was **General Johann Laidoner** (see page 121), Estonia's prominent military leader during the first period of independence. The main square here was named after him in 1934, during his lifetime. The Soviets of course changed this, naming the square after Jaan Tomp, a revolutionary who was executed in November 1924 for being involved in an attempted military coup against the Estonian government.

The **Museum of Viljandi** (*Laidoner plats 10;* ☎ *433 3316; www.muuseum-viljandimaa.ee*), situated on General Laidoner Square, was completely rebuilt during 1998 and 1999. One room is dedicated to natural history, one to archaeology and one to local jewellery. There is also an accordion collection. Of most interest to foreign tourists is the model of the castle with illustrations of recent excavations. Note too the 19th-century prints on the wall in this room. The original archaeology section dates from 1878 but the museum was closed during most of the first independence period because of the Baltic-German bias of much of the material assembled during the late 19th century. The Germans reopened it in 1942 during their three-year occupation and it was maintained, largely as an archaeological collection, during the Soviet period. Carvings and fragments from the castle form part of this collection. Fortunately, the later material that both the Germans and the Soviets found offensive was hidden and can once again be displayed. These include 19th-century photographs and documents from the many Estonian literary organisations active at that time. Models of the town at different periods are on show, together with one of the castle before it fell into decline. A second floor added to the museum in 2002 covers village life from tsarist times until the end of the Soviet period. It has models of collective farms and also documents relating to the Estonian army in 1918. Householders with three or four rooms had to give passing soldiers one pair of underwear; those with five rooms two pairs and two pairs of slippers; and those with six or more rooms three pairs and three pairs of slippers. The building itself is of stone, one of the few dating from the late 18th century. Until 1940 it was used as a chemist's shop.

The statue of the working artist in the park behind the museum is of **Johann Köler** (1826–99) (see page 42), the first painter of Estonian ethnic origin to be internationally recognised and who was born into a poor farmer's family living just outside Viljandi. The extreme poverty of the family can be judged by the fact that their house did not even have a chimney. However, in due course he was able to rise to be a professor of art at the St Petersburg Academy, although most of the themes for his paintings would always come from Estonia. Several examples of his work can be seen at KUMU, the Estonian Art Museum in Tallinn (see pages 118–19). This statue dates from 1976, the 150th anniversary of his birth.

A hundred metres from the museum towards the lake is the **Water Tower**, which, until its reopening for tourists in 2001, had been abandoned since 1960. It has a 30m-high red-brick base topped by an octagonal wooden roof. It was one of the many projects instigated by Otto von Engelhardt, mayor between 1898 and 1917. Had it not been for the national fame acquired by his successor August Maramaa (see box, pages 204–5) he would still be remembered today, as are many other mayors who were active towards the end of the tsarist era. The tower now offers the best views over the town and lake, and also an exhibition of pictures chosen to represent different periods in the history of Viljandi.

The white-painted **Town Hall** now stands out to the left, and even more so in May when its surrounding rose garden is in bloom. Although elements of an earlier late 18th-century building remain, when it was a private residence, what we now see dates from 1931, including the clock bought from AEG in Germany. Its Baroque façade is a reminder of its original format. There are 158 steps at the side of the Town Hall, which lead down to the lake. The hillside is therefore called **Trepimägi** (Steps Hill). The higher ones cross where the 2m-thick city wall used to run and remnants of it can still be seen here and also close to the Grand Hotel at Lossi 29. The villas at the side of the steps were the most prestigious in the town during the first period of independence, but many have been subsequently neglected. The steps themselves, however, were restored in 1991. An annual running race around the lake takes place on 1 May each year and the statue at the bottom of the steps commemorates Hubert Pärnakivi (1932–93) who won the race 11 times.

The building now known as **St John's Church** dates from the late 18th century, as revealed by the hints of Baroque in its design. Several previous churches had been built on the site but they were all completely destroyed. It remained in use as a church at the beginning of the Soviet occupation but from the mid-1950s was used as a granary. The chandeliers and wooden furnishings were all dispersed to other churches that remained open. Nonetheless, extensive archaeological excavations were carried out during this period and it was restored during the 1980s with the aim of being reopened as a concert hall. The foundations of earlier churches can be seen in the basement. In 1989, at the end of the Soviet era, permission was granted for the building to return to the church and the first service was held at Christmas 1991. It was reconsecrated in time for Christmas the following year. Between the church and the castle is a statue of General Laidoner (see page 121) on his horse which was unveiled in 2004, probably the first equestrian statue to be erected in Estonia since 1991. Both the president and the prime minister attended the unveiling, such is the respect in which General Laidoner is held.

The former vicarage of St John's Church is now the **Paul Kondas Gallery** (*Pikk 8;* 433 3968; *www.kondas.ee*), which makes amends for this artist (1900–85) whose work was never publicly exhibited during his lifetime. It opened in 2003. Kondas was a teacher for all his working life and only took up painting seriously in his retirement when he was very much a recluse, respected openly abroad but not recognised officially at home. Frivolity and colour are the hallmarks of his work, but in some topics such as theft from government offices and nudity he went well beyond what could be officially sanctioned in Soviet times. He was also skilled at allegory. A painting nominally about the bombing of Dresden clearly shows Tallinn after Soviet air raids in 1944. All the 26 works displayed in this gallery were painted after his 50th birthday. His most famous painting *The Strawberry Eaters* dates from 1965 and explains the use of the strawberry as an unofficial logo for Viljandi. The eight concrete strawberries built around the town in 2007 all point to this gallery.

It started to expand in 2006, to include works by other contemporaries whose paintings were also banned during the Soviet era. One of these, Hugo Sturm (1891–1979), only started to paint in the late 1950s, when he was released from Siberia. He had been sent there for his role as a Forest Brother, the resistance movement active in the immediate aftermath of World War II.

St Paul's Church dates from the expansion of Viljandi in the late 19th century, before which St John's Church alone could serve people of the town and the surrounding countryside. (Between 1825 and 1867, the population increased from 1,000 to 3,000.) Baron Ungern Sternberg, famous mainly in Hiiumaa, also owned some land here, which he donated for the construction of this church. It was built between 1861 and 1866 under the supervision of two architects, Franz Block and Matthias von Holst, whose neo-Gothic design was to be used again in Riga where they both later practised. The church remained open during the Soviet period and the German organ, installed in 1866, was extensively restored in 1966.

There are many 19th- and 20th-century stone buildings in the town worthy of note. Tallinn 16, dating from the 1850s, is an opulent former private house with an elaborate Italian façade. Tallinn 6 was built 20 years later and was famous as the office of *Sakala*, one of the first newspapers printed in Estonian. The secondary school at Uueveski 3, like St Paul's Church, is late 19th-century neo-Gothic. The office building at Tartu 5 was completed in 1939 and is unusual for the quantity of glass used. Tallinna 5, now the **House of Culture**, is one of the few totally Soviet buildings in Viljandi. It can almost be described as Stalinist.

Most wooden houses were destroyed by fire, but a few remain. The former German clubhouse called 'Casino' at Posti 11 was built in 1843 to serve the large Baltic-German population but miraculously survived all the subsequent changes in regime. A much more modest, and slightly earlier, house is at Posti 2. Note here the cornices and the decorations on the front door. Posti 23 is plainer still but is revered by Estonians as the house of one of their most famous but impoverished playwrights, August Kitzberg, who lived at this address in the 1890s.

Carol Pearson

Just inside the front doors of Viljandi Town Hall is a full-size mural of August Maramaa (1881–1941). Unveiled in 1996 – the 55th anniversary of his death – it shows an elderly, rather frail man still proud but leaning on a stick and peering uncertainly across the staircase. Throughout the Soviet years, Maramaa had been excised from Viljandi's history and his formal reinstatement as an honorary citizen was widely welcomed. But this is not quite the image of August Maramaa that most people remember.

Maramaa was elected mayor of Viljandi in 1919 and the town, as we see it today, grew up in the space of just 20 years and evolved largely around his personal vision. 'I want to develop Viljandi into a perfect town in a free nation,' he said, 'the pulsating centre of prospering business and manufacturing life.'

But in 1919 this vision was still some way off. Estonia was a newly independent country and Maramaa had to deal with the realities of post-tsarist Estonia. The population of the town had increased as people moved off the land; schools, houses and hospitals were needed; unemployment was rising steadily and so was poverty. Maramaa began with a number of job creation schemes that put unemployed people to work paving roads and excavating around the lake and at the site of the ancient castle. Two new schools and a hospital were built, followed in 1932 by a home for the elderly and a children's home. Maramaa's town council also set about modernising the layout of the town, creating an industrial zone and a shopping centre.

Mayor Maramaa felt strongly about environmental matters and in 1928 he set up a department of 'Cleanliness and Beauty'. The streets in the centre of the town had to be cleaned twice a day, it was decided, and snow cleared within three days. During 1929, school children helped to plant 20,000 pine trees around the town. Special attention was also paid to Lake Viljandi since Maramaa's long-term aim was to turn the town into an inland health spa, modelled on Swedish resorts he had visited. Trees were planted; the shoreline was repaired; a swimming pool, restaurant and tennis courts were built.

August Maramaa was born near Tartu in 1881. He studied at Tartu University and moved to Viljandi in 1906 after being sacked as a teacher from a school in Vastemoisa for alleged 'revolutionary activities' – probably efforts to gain Estonian independence from tsarist Russia. He became mayor of Viljandi in 1919 and held the post for two years until he was elected to the Riigikogu (Estonian Parliament) as a Social Democratic and Labour Party MP. He continued as a town councillor over this period and became mayor for the second time in 1927.

During this time, Maramaa became a wealthy man though most of his income came from Estonian-language textbooks and from a series of children's stories called *Maret and Jüri*. These were published at a time when Estonian schools had stopped teaching Russian and were desperate for books in their own language. In 1906, Maramaa married Anna Roosen (also a teacher) and he used his wealth to build an impressive family home at 8 Uuveski Te, on the outskirts of Viljandi. His first son, Ulö, was born in 1910. My own mother, Linda, was his youngest child and born in 1923.

Around Viljandi, Maramaa was a fearsome figure, well known for overseeing the details of each project. He would start his working day by walking round the town with a juniper stick in his hand, checking everything was in order. When the Grand Hotel was built on the corner of Lossi Street in 1937, at least one senior engineer resigned because Maramaa wanted to do everything himself. Records show that he ordered the window glass, decided on the door panels and personally inspected all the finished work. When it opened, the hotel was called EVE, which was short for Esimene Viljandi Esinduslokaal (the First Best Place of Viljandi). When the Grand Hotel reopened in 2002, its literature still carried the EVE logo.

In 1939, Maramaa refused to stand for re-election. He claimed there were too many restrictions on his ability to run Viljandi but it must also have been clear to him that Germany was preparing for war, Russia was preparing to take back some of its former territory and Estonia was likely to be swept aside in whatever followed. In September 1939, the Estonian government was forced to sign a Mutual Assistance Pact with the USSR, which allowed 25,000 troops to move onto Estonian soil and in June 1940, the first Soviet occupation began.

By this time, Maramaa had effectively been forced out of politics and given a teaching post at a school in Vigala near Viljandi. On Christmas Eve 1940, Maramaa's oldest son Ulö was arrested then tortured and shot for organising opposition candidates in the one-party elections earlier that year.

A couple of weeks later, in early January 1941, August Maramaa himself was driving home from Vigala, alone, when his car was stopped and he, too, was arrested. Following extensive interrogation by the NKVD in Tallinn (transcripts of which have recently been released), he was deported to a labour camp near Kirov and died there a year later in December 1941, unable to endure the harsh conditions, the heavy workload or the hunger. Two other Estonian prisoners later reported that they couldn't bury him properly because the ground was frozen but they had dug a shallow grave and covered his face with a coat.

Meanwhile, on the night of 14 June 1941, thousands of Estonians were arrested in a single purge and deported to the East. Maramaa's wife, Anna, was among them. She had just returned to the family home on Uuveski Te after saying goodbye to one of her daughters at the bus station when the soldiers arrived. It was months before her family knew what had happened to her and years before they discovered that she had died in a Siberian camp, probably in 1946.

The Russians left Estonia in 1941 and for three years the country was held under German rule. In the autumn of 1944, at the start of the second Soviet occupation, two of Maramaa's remaining children (one of them my mother) escaped to Germany and then the UK. One son, Kalev, tried to leave the country but was arrested and returned to Viljandi by the Russians. He died of tuberculosis in 1946.

Maramaa's eldest daughter, Maimu, tried to flee to Sweden with her family but they too were turned back. Her husband, Harri Haamer, was subsequently arrested by the NKVD and spent six years in Siberian labour camps, walking thousands of miles back to Estonia after the death of Stalin and the fall of Beria, Stalin's head of security, in 1953. Harri Haamer lived the rest of his life as the Lutheran minister of Mustla church near Viljandi, quietly campaigning for Estonian independence. It is part of family folklore that, on the desk in their house, he and his wife kept a bronze bust of August Maramaa made by the local artist A Vomm in 1936. The bust was hollow and, as an act of defiance, a full-sized blue, black and white Estonian flag was hidden inside the head throughout the Soviet occupation of Estonia. It was never discovered but flew from the church in Mustla again when Estonia regained its freedom in 1991.

Põltsamaa is famous for what it was and for what it never has been, rather than for what it is now. As a capital city for Ivan the Terrible's vassal state, it suffered badly in the fighting between Russia, Poland and Sweden in the 1570s. The months of June 1578 and June 1941 were equal in the terror and destruction caused. The town was at its most prosperous in the 18th century when production of porcelain and glass was started, as was a printing industry. At that time, it became the third-largest town in the Baltics, after Tallinn and Riga. The castle, with a Gothic exterior and a Rococo interior, dated from this era. A newspaper in Estonian was published for the first time here in 1766. Its aim was to teach Estonian peasants healthy living. No railway ever came to Põltsamaa so it missed possibilities for expansion in the late 19th century and in fact the population dropped at that time. However this would later mean that it also missed out on Russian factories and a Russian population moving in after World War II.

GETTING THERE AND AWAY The town, like Paide, makes an excellent stop *en route* from Tallinn to Tartu. Buses serve both cities, as well as Paide and the county capital of Jõgeva. Although Jõgeva itself is of little interest, buses go from there to Palamuse, Siimusti and Mustvee and to other tourist centres in the county. In the 1920s and 1930s Põltsamaa had several hotels and restaurants along the main road to serve transit traffic but now that this road bypasses the town, it is only seen by those who really want to come.

WHAT TO SEE AND DO The **rose garden** beside the river was a sensible alternative to redevelopment after the war. It claims to have 3,000 plants and 800 different species. Only the shell of the **castle** now remains but it hosts both classical and pop music festivals and summer markets. Beside it is the **museum** (*www. muuseum.poltsamaaturism.ee*), which surprisingly opened only in 1997. There are plenty of pictures of the castle as it used to be and much on the local hero Karl August Hermann (1851–1909), who combined songwriting with editing the local newspaper. Visitors who want to do more than look can try out the weaving looms and spinning wheels or play the harmonica. Few people in the entourage of Konstantin Päts, the pre-war president, escaped deportation and then death in Russia. Even fewer are alive and active today. In Britain famous cooks seem to last only as long as football managers. Päts's cook, Elle Reeder, began her broadcasting career when Fanny Craddock was a household name and she carries on in the Jamie Oliver era, although she was 94 in 2013. Her life, although not over yet, is covered too in the museum. The letters sent from Siberia and the lists remarkably kept from the June 1941 and the March 1949 deportations are necessary reminders in the museum of the horrors of the Soviet regime.

As a total contrast, the **Põltsamaa Food Museum**, with its wine cellar, is a welcome recent addition to the castle complex. This is the obvious town for such a museum as it produces most of the fruit juices, jams and wine for which Estonia is famous. An extra curiosity is the tubes of food for Soviet astronauts shown here. There is a small shop attached to the wine cellar, but a bigger one is in the road outside the castle, run by Felix, the company that organises most of the production in the town. Probably the best buy is Fest, a sparkling wine that certainly holds it own against prosecco and perhaps even against champagne.

The rebuilding of **St Nicholas Church** owes everything to the persistence of the pastor Herbert Kuurme who was still active, in his nineties, until his death in

2005. Although the population of the town is only 5,000, it has the largest active Lutheran congregation outside Tallinn. He manoeuvred the Soviet authorities so skilfully that restoration could start in 1947, decades before it was considered in other churches, and he was always sure of a large congregation, despite the political statement that such activity made in those days. The church had been briefly closed before, but that was in 1895 when two fat ladies from the congregation blocked the entrance to a German pastor trying to take over from an Estonian one. The 1941 damage was caused by German advances, not by Russian retreats, and the tower fell into the body of the church. The walls of both the castle and the church survived, as many are 4m thick. Several of the interior furnishings came from the University Church in Tartu, which after the war was converted into a library. The organ came from St John's Church in Viljandi, when it was deconsecrated in the 1950s, having been built in 1900 in Frankfurt an der Oder, now on the German–Polish border. It was fully restored in 2005.

PALAMUSE

GETTING THERE AND AWAY Palamuse is 5km from the railway station at Kaarepere on the Tallinn–Tartu line. **Buses** also link it to these cities as well as to Mustvee and to Põltsamaa.

WHAT TO SEE AND DO Every Estonian knows Palamuse through the children's book *Spring* by Oskar Luts (1887–1953). Like the best of such work, it gives a stability and timelessness totally absent in the real world. The school Luts attended in the 1890s, and which formed the background to his book, is now the **Parish School Museum** (*www.palmuseum.ee*), restored to how he would have known it and opened in 1987 to celebrate the centenary of his birth. (His death was hardly marked, as he died two weeks after Stalin in March 1953, at which point no other deaths could be mourned.) The book is currently not available in English so we must just take the word of Estonian commentators that the author was their Mark Twain. A picture of Tsar Nicholas II looks down on the classroom but more unexpected is the larder, a room of the same size, as pupils had to bring their food for the long winter with them. Another room is therefore the dormitory. The main punishment was detention, during which Russian poetry had to be learnt by heart. The former staff room has been converted into a museum about the Civil War in 1918, when Estonia fought to establish its independence from both the Bolsheviks and the White Russians.

St Bartholomew's Church (*www.palamusekogudus.ee*) is the oldest on Estonia's the mainland, dating from 1234, with only some on Saaremaa claiming a longer history. Most of what is seen now dates from a restoration in 1929 but the tower dates from 1800 and the altar and pulpit from 1693, much having been destroyed earlier that century in the Livonian War. The extent of the secret passages in the foundations shows how much this was a fortress as well as a place of worship.

SIIMUSTI

The ceramics factory in the centre of the village, **Siimusti Keraamika** (*www.siimustikeraamika.ee*), was founded in 1886 and took advantage of the narrow-gauge railways that linked the local clay pits to the national railway system, which in turn could provide an extensive distribution outlet. This must be one of the very few Estonian institutions that carried on unperturbed through every change in regime. Perhaps as most of their earlier work was very utilitarian no political objections could be made to it. The workforce that stood at 90 in Soviet times has inevitably been downsized to 35 but the design team must have been enlarged given the range of products and patterns now on offer. With typical Estonian modesty, the shop is not even in the same building as the factory, so there is no hard sell. The website shows what they produce and the prices charged at the factory, and also gives details of shops in Tallinn where these products can be bought. Buses link Siimusti with the neighbouring town of Jõgeva, which is on the Tallinn–Tartu railway line.

7

South and Southeast Estonia

OTEPÄÄ

When other towns in Estonia shutter up for the winter, Otepää bursts into life. It is the country's skiing and ski-jumping capital and the centre for other winter sports as well. The Estonian Olympic teams train here, as did their Soviet predecessors, often under floodlights, as all the ski- and toboggan-runs are illuminated. In midwinter, daylight can be down to six hours. The main skiing centre, Tehvandi, is on the edge of the town; there are many others a little further away.

An earlier name for the town – Nuustaku – comes from the German Nusstage, as a favourite autumn occupation was collecting nuts from the surrounding hazelnut woods. The current name means 'bear's head', which walkers in the countryside will appreciate: it is the name of the hill on which the town is built and its shape can probably justify this description. Visits in spring and summer are equally worthwhile, when both the town and the surrounding countryside are quieter. Descriptions of it in pre-war literature encouraged Jean-Paul Sartre to battle with the Soviet authorities for permission to visit Otepää and in the end he succeeded. Alexander Solzhenitsyn recovered in Otepää from his imprisonment in Siberia and wrote *The Gulag Archipelago* in the town.

GETTING THERE AND AWAY A new bus station and shopping centre opened in Otepää in 2008 and the tourist office is now in this complex. Bus tickets are not sold here but on board the **bus**; the most regular service is to Tartu, a journey time of around an hour. For other destinations a change is usually needed there, although the occasional bus goes directly to Tallinn, Valga or Võru.

WHERE TO STAY AND EAT Through much of the 1990s, Otepää benefited from the poor level of accommodation available in the nearby towns of Tartu, Valga and Võru. It was the only base for exploring southeast Estonia. These other towns have now caught up, but Otepää still excels in its sport facilities, particularly for ski-jumping, so hotels now work on keeping their guests within the town. They have successfully built up a conference business to ensure equal occupancy at weekends and during the week. The town and surrounding countryside are also full of opportunities for bed and breakfast and farm-stay accommodation. The tourist information office (*www.otepaa.ee*) has an extensive list. It also has maps of the ski-trails and walks for the summer visitor.

Bernhard Kolga (30 rooms) Kolgatec 22a; \766 9600; e hotell@bernhard.ee; www.bernhard.ee. As the Otepää area likes to present itself as 'Little Switzerland', the hotel's name is no surprise. Not only was the hotel purpose-built, but much of the surrounding

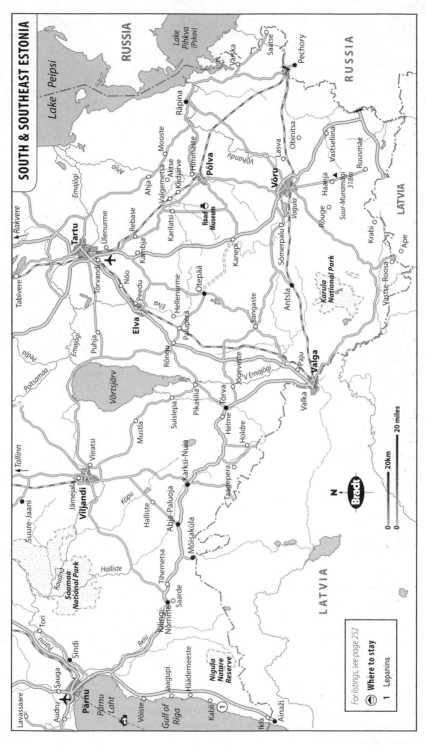

SOUTH & SOUTHEAST ESTONIA

RUSSIA

Lake Peipsi

Lake Pihkva (Pskov)

RUSSIA

RUSSIA

LATVIA

LATVIA

Värska
Saatse
Pechory

Rakvere

Ahja

Mooste
Aktse
Valgemetsa
Kiidjärve
Ahja
Põlva
Himmaste
Räpina

Rebase
Karilatsi
Road Museum
Kanepi
Sõmerpalu
Obinitsa
Lasva
Vastseliina
Ruusmäe
Haanja
Suur-Munamägi 318m

Ülenurme
Kambja
Nõo
Peedu
Tartu
Torvandi

Tabivere

Emajõgi

Otepää
Hellenurme
Palupera
Vagula
Võru
Rõuge
Krabi
Ape
Vastse-Roosa

Põlva
Võhandu

Karula National Park

Antsla
Sangaste

Elva
Elva
Rõngu
Puhja

Võrtsjärv

Emajõgi
Põltsamaa
Põltsamaa

Jõgeveste
V Emajõgi
Paju
Valga
Valka

Viratsi
Mustla
Suislepa
Pikasilla
Tõrva
Helme
Holdre
Taagepera

Jämejala
Viljandi
Kõpu
Halliste
Abja-Paluoja
Karksi-Nuia
Mõisaküla

Suure-Jaani
Raudna
Soomaa National Park
Halliste

Tihemetsa
Saarde

Lavassaare
Tori
Sindi
Sauga
Audru
Pärnu
Pärnu Laht

Kilingi-Nõmme

Reiu
Pärnu

Jaagupi
Häädemeeste
Võiste
Kabli
Ikla
Ainaži

Nigula Nature Reserve

Gulf of Riga

Tallinn

N
Brādt

20km
0
20 miles
0

For listings, see page 252
Where to stay
1 Lepanina

area was as well, & this process is continuing. An artificial lake 'opened' at the same time as the hotel in 1997, & golf courses & riding trails are now following. Unusually for Estonia, the hotel has an indoor swimming pool & in 2007 it added a spa centre. All rooms face south, over the lake, & some have kitchens for families looking for self-catering accommodation. The hotel does not only promote itself as a country retreat; the restaurant is a gallery for the local artist, Johannes Viga, who died in 1997. 2 of the suites are named after famous Estonian composers who have stayed there, Arvo Pärt & Veljo Tormis. The website shows the current restaurant menu & Estonian dishes always predominate. Expect a lot of herring, trout, ham, peas & beans. $$$

🏠 **Karupesa** (30 rooms) Tehvandi 1a; ☎ 766 1500; e karupesa@karupesa.ee; www. karupesa.ee. This hotel is run by one of Estonia's best-known skiers, Andrus Veerpalu, who has maintained the standards that were originally set when it was run by Scandic Hotels who used to operate the Palace in Tallinn. The wine list is as extensive as it always has been. It is next to the ski centre about 2km from the town centre & ski hire can be arranged. $$$

🏠 **Pühajärve** (Holy Lake) (100 rooms) ☎ 766 5500; e pipk@pipk.ee; www.pyhajarve. com. This hotel took a long time to adapt from the Soviet era to independent Estonia, but since 2001 it has rapidly converted itself into the most luxurious hotel in town, with most rooms being large & with a view over the lake. It has a number of indoor sporting facilities such as bowling which are not dependent on the weather & plenty of space outdoors to enjoy either the snow or the sun. $$$

WHAT TO SEE AND DO As with so many other towns in Estonia, the sights are mostly within walking distance of each other. It is appropriate that the town's most famous visitor since independence has been the Dalai Lama who sought solace in 1991 at **Holy Lake** (Pühajärv), situated just outside the town. A plaque commemorates his visit. This lake has been a protected area since 1929 and unholy behaviour is limited to the occasional raucous party on a long summer's evening and to one weekend in June when a rock festival takes place. The lake has the country's best inland beaches and warmest water for swimming. Walkers can follow the 16km path around the lake. The nearby rivers are well stocked with trout, pike, perch and eel.

Otepää church had an important role in Estonian history. The blue, black and white flag of the Estonian Students Union was unfurled here in 1884 and amazingly this first flag still exists and is displayed in Tallinn from time to time. In 1940 it was rescued from the National Museum in Tartu and hidden on a farm until 1991. In 1922 the design was adopted as the national flag. The interior of the church is often closed but is worth seeing if possible for the ornate wooden roof and organ. The organ was built in Tartu by Ernst Kessler, a Baltic German whose work can still be seen in several other churches in Estonia.

The Independence Memorial in front of the church is the original, and was hidden during the Soviet era. The two panels beside the entrance door that explain the history of the flag were cemented over by the Soviets, but were uncovered again in July 1989. A flag had in fact been unfurled at the church as early as October 1987 and similar daring was shown in Võru around the same time. The three still-small oak trees at the side of the church were planted after a meeting of the three Baltic presidents in 1992. The stained glass around the church is being renewed as and when funds can be raised. Services are held every Sunday during the summer only.

The **Hill Fort** behind the church dates at latest from the 7th century and evidence may well be found from earlier settlements. As many excavations around Estonia have recently proved, there was a highly sophisticated lifestyle throughout the country well before the Russian and German invasions from the 12th century. Historians from both these countries have tended to assume that serious history in Estonia only starts with their arrival. Writing implements, jewellery and weapons found here all prove the opposite and the discovery of Arab silver coins show the extent of the trading links that the Estonians established.

The **Flag Museum** is in a former vicarage. The pastor who lived there for many years in the late 19th century was Jakob Hurt, very famous in Estonia for his role in the 'National Awakening' movement. He is best remembered for his proclamation: 'Estonians will never be great in number, but we can be great through our spirit.' A room in this building is now dedicated to his memory. As well as covering the origins of the flag, and the struggles in 1918 and in the late 1980s to get it accepted, the Flag Museum shows all the efforts of the Estonian communities abroad during the Soviet occupation to keep alive knowledge of it.

The **Winter Sports Museum** used to share premises with the Flag Museum but in 2012 moved into a new building which is part of the sports centre. The earliest ski exhibited dates from 1870 but it is the clothes that will surprise visitors most; it was only in the 1950s that women gave up dresses for trousers. There is a full film display of Estonia's most famous skiers in action on the Otepää ski jump and wax models of those from the pre-video age. Before metal skis replaced wooden ones, Estonia was a major ski production centre. The ski marathon started here in 1960 and there are several film extracts of it from Soviet times. The museum is always totally up to date, so that Estonian skiing successes one winter will be reported here over the next summer. A completely new attraction from 2012 has been the **viewing platform**, which because of its recent construction is totally accessible for the disabled. This provides the most dramatic setting for a view of the ski-jumpers in action, but at other times of year the view across the woods and lakes can be enjoyed. Its height above sea level is 218m, nothing in most parts of the world, but significant in Estonia.

About twenty-five kilometres south of Otepää on the road to Valga is **Sangaste Castle** (✆ 767 9300; e info@sangasteloss.ee; www.sangasteloss.ee, **$$**), misleadingly described in most local brochures as being a 'copy' of Windsor Castle. It is in fact a wildly eccentric, red-brick, neo-Gothic manor house, which until recently had very basic accommodation with very little appeal for most tourists, let alone royalty. (The Queen and Prince Philip gave it a miss when they came to Estonia in October 2006.) In 2012 the accommodation was converted from hostel standard to that of a serious hotel but it still gives the feeling of intruding into a family home suddenly left in the 1930s. For many years in the Soviet era it served as a children's holiday home and was scarcely refurbished, but this should not put off passing visitors who can eat well here as well as staying overnight, and can try to make sense of the building, both inside and out.

The owner of the building throughout its existence as a private house was the scientist Count Magnus von Berg (1845–1938), who became famous for his work on the cultivation of rye. The high-yielding type that he grew now bears the name Sangaste and a few grains are scattered each year on his tomb in the village church. Some is grown in Canada for use in whisky. He commissioned this house in 1874 from the architect Otto Hippius, who also designed Charles Church in Tallinn and the Alexander Church in Narva, but the only link with either of these is the octagonal shape used in part of the Alexander Church, which is similar to the dining room here. Models for the design are likely to have been Minley Manor in Hampshire, Peckforton in Cheshire or Welfen near Hanover.

The large reception/meeting rooms on the ground floor exhibit hunting trophies, including sets of antlers, which presumably are from deer which the family successfully hunted, so perhaps there is a hint of the English countryside here. The first floor has a small exhibition of items and photographs linked to the family, but sadly no books from the library remain, only the oak bookcases that used to house them. However, von Berg, rather than Hippicus, must have been responsible for the total eccentricity that the building now represents. Every window is different, as are all the porches and the towers. Some minor links with Windsor Castle also can be drawn, given that von Berg probably visited the castle. Windsor has an octagonal dining room and a staircase where two sets of stairs blend into one, and the porch attached to the State Apartments is very similar to one of the designs used here. Perhaps because of his eccentricity, his wife left him in the 1880s and his sons would later do the same. Nonetheless, his daughter-in-law stayed on for many years, as did his grandson, who looked after him when he turned deaf and blind. Despite tensions during the count's lifetime, the family came together from all over the world in 1995 to celebrate the 150th anniversary of his birth. The premises were abandoned after his death and only in the 1960s did the Soviet authorities start using it as a holiday home for children.

In the park at the back of the castle is an oak tree allegedly planted by Peter the Great. This park is often also called an 'English garden' but is largely a play area for children with a wood in the background. This wood contains about 300 different species of tree.

In 2012 the village of Sangaste became a tourist centre in its own right, using rye as its theme. Vistors can learn to cook, to bake and to brew with it, which contrasts with the academic introduction given to it in the castle. It was rye bread that exiled Estonians missed more than anything else when they left in 1944 and it is now what they devour when they return. At the centre of this activity is the hotel **Rukki Maja** (*Rye Hse* \ 766 9323; e *info@rukkimaja.ee; www.rukkimaja.ee*; **$**).

TÕRVA AND HELME

The local tourist board promotes Tõrva as a centre for 'intellectual holiday-makers' and this is an apt description of what is offered. Few major events in Estonian history passed the town by, yet its lakes, forest walks and caves provide easy-going relaxation. Tar was produced here in small quantities from the late 19th century, and **tõrv** is in fact the Estonian word for tar. It was clearly profitable for the 2,000 or so people who lived there then, since they have left a remarkably diverse range of houses and gardens. More recent building has kept these high standards. In line with this intellectual tradition, it was an opera that really made the town known outside Estonia. On 29 August 1998, to commemorate the 100th anniversary of the birth of George Gershwin, his *Porgy and Bess* was performed in front of an audience of 7,000. Tõrva's two hotels were built for this event and have been able to trade on its success ever since, although Tõrva and Helme combined only have a population of 6,000.

In 2001 Tõrva signed a twinning agreement with Crowhurst in Surrey, the first such link between Estonia and Britain. It commemorated Leo Lupseck who grew up in Tõrva but came to Britain as a refugee after the war. From 1983 until his death in 2000 he served as chairman of Crowhurst Parish Council.

GETTING THERE AND AWAY There are several buses a day to Viljandi, Pärnu and Valga and these three towns provide a wide range of connections to other towns in Estonia.

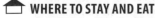 **WHERE TO STAY AND EAT**

Taagepera (32 rooms) \ 766 6390; e hotell@taageperaloss.ee; www.taageperaloss. ee. This converted manor house is in a village of the same name 18km west of Tõrva, just off the main road to Viljandi & Tallinn. South Estonia now has a country base for those wanting luxury for the same price as a standard hotel in Tallinn. Some visitors will use it as a base for walking & cycling, others for driving to & fro across the Latvian border now that EU accession has made this possible. Hunting pheasant, deer & moose is another possibility. The really self-indulgent need do nothing more than climb the tower to admire the view. The building was completed in 1912 so was hardly used as a private residence. The architect was Otto Wildau (1873–1942) who also designed the neighbouring manor houses at Peetri & Holdre. He clearly took a free-&-easy approach to his work here & it remains the building for which he is best remembered. There is a complete lack of symmetry in the outside walls, with no main façade. Some of the stonework is polished, some left rough. Perhaps foreseeing future wars, he ensured that there was minimal use of wood, that the manor was built on a hill & that the view from the 40m tower would give ample warning of the approach of hostile forces. Wildau was arrested by the Russians in 1914 & exiled to Kazan. When released in 1919 he did not return to the Baltics but took up a job with the Commerzbank in Salzemen near

Magdeburg where his work can still be seen, as it can also be in bank buildings in Gelsenkirchen & Strasbourg. **$$$**

⌂ **De Tolly** (10 rooms) Karja tn 6, Tõrva; ☏763 3349; e detolly@hot.ee; www.hotelldetolly. ee. About 1km from the bus station, set back from the road & surrounded by a private garden with a mini golf course & 2 tennis courts. Although a new building, there are hints of *Jugendstil* in some of the design, a characteristic of several large buildings in Tõrva & in neighbouring Valga. A boating lake is nearby. Until the 1870s the area was a thick forest; then clearing started for it to be developed for housing. An inn has always been on this site. The website has a picture of every room, all of which have a woman's first name rather than a number. **$$**

⌂ **Pigi Linna** (11 rooms) Valga tn 17, Tõrva; ☏766 8727; e info@pigilinna.ee; www.pigilinna. ee. Within walking distance of the bus station. It does not have a restaurant, only a café, but the enormous billiard room is considered more than ample compensation by many visitors. **$$**

WHAT TO SEE AND DO Tõrva **Church/Chamber Hall** (Kirik-Kammersal in Estonian) was built as a Russian Orthodox church in 1905 although it is hard to tell this from the largely Gothic exterior. Bombing destroyed much of the interior in 1944 and in Soviet times it was used only for concerts and art exhibitions. In 1990 the building was given to the Lutherans but, as its name suggests, it now has a dual role as the religious community is too small to support a church on its own. The interior is very plain, in keeping with Lutheran rather than Orthodox practice.

The ruined castle at the neighbouring village of Helme, 3km from Tõrva, still shows the power of the Teutonic Knights who built it at the end of the 13th century. Nearly 300 years later, it fell briefly into the hands of the Polish Empire before being seized by the Swedes. They blew it up in 1658, to prevent it falling into the hands of the Russians and Lithuanians. It was never subsequently rebuilt. The caves at the back of the ruins were originally a natural phenomenon but were then widened to provide sanctuary from the wars raging all too often round the castle. They were also extended at the end of the 18th century when the local landlord planned a grotto based on those so popular in England at the time. Amongst the more original names given to one of the caves by the local community is 'Devil's Stomach'. Helme church was bombed by the Russians in September 1944 because the tower was a German observation post. It has not been restored.

The **Barclay de Tolly Mausoleum** is near the village of Jõgeveste, about 6km from Tõrva. It commemorates one of the most famous Russian commanders who fought Napoleon in 1812 and 1813 and who culminated his triumph with a march through Paris in March 1814. His family was partially of Scottish extraction but from the 17th century had lived in what is now Latvia and Lithuania. Following the Russian conquest of Finland in 1809, he was the first governor-general there until 1812. Jõgeveste was the estate of his wife's family and his body was brought back there after his death in East Prussia in 1818. The manor house where they lived was destroyed during World War II and nothing now remains on its site. The mausoleum was completed in 1823 on the instructions of de Tolly's wife Eleanor von Smitten. She commissioned Apollon Shchedrin, a leading St Petersburg architect, to design it and its structure has remained intact since then, although the two coffins were opened during World War II. It was extensively restored in 2007, when a museum was built at the back, which describes his life and gives the background to his rivalry with Marshall Kutuzov. The exterior design suggests parallels to a Roman triumphal arch, the interior to a chapel with an altar recess where the bust of de Tolly is placed. The statue on the right is of Athena, the Greek goddess of war, trampling over Napoleonic flags and on the left the statue of a sitting woman represents the symbol of mourning. The sculpture below the monument shows de Tolly entering Montmartre, in Paris. The seven stars above symbolise his seven military victories. Younger visitors sometimes assume it is the EU symbol. Outside are the tombs of de Tolly's son and daughter-in-law and a Soviet memorial to soldiers killed in the 1944 invasion of Estonia.

PÕLVA AND THE RUSSIAN BORDERLANDS

Although rarely visited by foreigners, the county and town of Põlva are very popular as a holiday centre for Estonians. There is a simple explanation for the number of nervous, young, single Russian-speaking men to be seen in the Hotel Pesa. Their wives are in the nearby maternity hospital giving birth, not an advisable activity over the border in Pskov but well worth the €700 charged for a full service here and which would costs thousands of euros in St Petersburg. A trip by the father to the Russian consulate in Tartu provides the necessary documentation for the baby to return home. The town has therefore come to life year-round and not just through the summer.

Despite the proximity of the border, this is now more of a curiosity than a threat and, although a fence runs along the Russian side, it is hard to think of this as being NATO's frontline since April 2004. If there are guards, they are few and far between. Foreigners who do make the effort to come will find a calm pace of life, an extensive variety of architecture and scenery and many reminders of life a century or two ago. Long gone is the light industry that attracted Volga-German and Ukrainian immigrants towards the end of the Soviet era in the 1980s.

GETTING THERE AND AWAY Buses go about once an hour from Põlva to Tartu and some of these continue to Tallinn. Local buses also operate hourly to Räpina and to Värska, with less frequent services to Saatse and Koidula. Three buses a day travel from Värska via Põlva and Tartu to Tallinn. Tartu provides connections to the rest of Estonia from this area. Although there are several crossing points to Russia, no public transport operates through them.

 WHERE TO STAY AND EAT

⌂ **Värska Spa** (101 rooms) Värska; ☎799 3901; e info@spavarska.ee; www. spavarska.ee. Any potential visitor is strongly advised against looking at the website since it lists in great detail every possible illness the spa can cure. In fact most visitors are Estonians simply wanting the comfort of some spa treatment to enhance a conventional holiday. Much of this treatment is based on the mud in the nearby lake. The hotel opened in 1980, & now that it has been modernised will in due course probably try to follow the Saaremaa pattern of attracting year-round Finnish groups. They also hope to attract Russians now that Estonian visas are easier

for them to obtain. **$$$**
🛏 **Pesa Hotel** (30 rooms) Uus 5, Põlva;
📞799 8530; e broneering@kagureis.ee; www.
kagureis.ee. It is sad that this hotel is situated in
the only part of town that can be described as ugly,
but it has a well-sheltered balcony & garden where
meals are served in the summer, & the trees block
the view of surrounding blocks of flats. There are
enough rooms to cater for individuals & groups. All
rooms have showers & not baths. A surprising &

welcome extra in the hotel is a swimming pool in
the health centre accessible from the hotel. The bus
station is within walking distance. **$$**
🛏 **The Räpina Hotel** (16 rooms) Tartu mnt 2;
Põlva; 📞730 0460; e info@rapinahotell.ee;
www.rapinahotell.ee. The Räpina is just what is
needed here, being large enough for birdwatching
groups, but small enough for individuals to meet
each other in the evening to exchange experiences.
$$

WHAT TO SEE AND DO

Põlva All Estonians know **Põlva** for its dairy and most of the country's milk and cheese comes from this region. Põlv means 'knee' and the name comes from a legend about a girl allegedly interred in the church wall in a kneeling position. In 1840 the first temperance society in Estonia was founded here and in 1858 a precursor to the Tartu Song Festival took place.

The current **St Mary's Church** (*Pärna*) dates only from 1840 but the altar panelling and the picture it includes of the Last Supper date from 1650; both were restored in 2001. The painting of the Resurrection dates from 1845 and is by Ludwig von Maydell, best known for his work in St Olav's in Tallinn and for his illustrations of children's books. Several vicars here achieved national prominence. Pastor Treublut served for 65 years from 1716 to 1781, a record nobody else has surpassed, although the late Herbert Kuurme in Põltsamaa (see pages 206–7) almost equalled this feat. Jüri Kimmel was vicar from 1945 to 1982 so had to serve entirely under the Soviet regime when it was at its toughest. He fought bravely to keep what church property he could, always sure of the support of an equally tenacious congregation, which resisted efforts from the local school to prevent their children attending; one headmaster in 1969 personally tried to chase 20 children out of the church during a New Year service. Pastor Kimmel died as he was about to hold a service.

The **Põlva Peasant Museum** (*www.polvatalurahvamuuseum.ee*) is 18km northeast of Põlva, just off the road to Tartu. This former schoolroom where the museum is situated was built in 1945 when it had 76 pupils. The number dropped steadily and by 1966 it was down to 21 and the school was closed in 1972. Many furnishings date from around 1900. Look out for the panel that explains the introduction of surnames to Estonian peasants in the mid 19th century. The school was comparatively affluent, having a harmonium as well as a violin; most would have been lucky to have just a violin. The dried peas beside the oven were the basis of punishment; pupils had to kneel in great discomfort on them for 15 minutes with the intense heat at their side. The lunchboxes shown in the teachers' room were also the basis of punishment. They could be confiscated and returned only in the late afternoon.

The village shop has been rebuilt as it was in 1920–40 with a range of goods, most of which would never have been seen there between 1945 and 1990. Estonian bitterness at the wasted years of the occupation is so easy to understand here. Behind these buildings is a 'natural' map of Võru county, assembled by local children with clumps of trees for the forests, wooden tracks for the roads and a miniature railway line to link Põlva and Võru. The museum is on both sides of the road. On the western side is a history of the local clothing industry showing how flax was made into garments. There are also threshing machines imported from Britain before World War I.

South of Karilatsi and west of Põlva is the Varbuse Post Station where horses were changed in Swedish and tsarist times. In 2005 it opened as the **Road Transport Museum**, Maanteemuuseum (*www.muuseum.mnt.ee*), and it was then quite simply the best museum in Estonia, putting everything in Tallinn and Tartu to shame. Since 2011, it perhaps has to compete with the Seaplane Harbour Museum in Tallinn for this accolade. Lively teenagers, anoraks and scholars will all be happy here, and for those who know Estonia well it will be a relief to find lively presentations, space and light instead of a few drab display cases. Visitors can endure the discomforts of stagecoaches and hear the struggles of horses getting a grip on ice. The different contemporary surfaces used on roads are carefully explained to the ignorant layman. Panels, films and slides show how roads were used for the postal service, by the military, for agriculture and then in cartography. In the Middle Ages, they were so important that pilgrims left money in their wills for future maintenance.

The 20th century is easier to bring to life, whether in showing how a bridge is rebuilt in wartime or how a motorway is laid in peacetime. It would be German prisoners in the late 1940s who laid the concrete slabs that became the foundation of the Tallinn–Narva highway, whereas centuries earlier roads had been logs lain across swamps. It is hard to believe that Estonia had only 50km of asphalted roads in 1940, but then it makes sense that there were only 3,500 cars in the whole country. This figure dropped to 1,300 in 1950, but climbed to 116,000 in 1980, to 464,000 in 2000, and then reached 530,000 in 2009 – a car for every two adults in the country: a figure that had changed little by 2013.

The stables used to house 33 horses; the building is now a **restaurant** ($$) that can feed about three times this number of people at any one time. Do not forget to go over the road to what look like hangars; this is where all the vehicles are exhibited. It includes the prototype of what might have become an Estonian car.

If the Estonian human population is still a cause for concern, the ant one certainly is not. Although nobody has actually counted them, there is little reason to doubt the figure of three million given as the population of the **Akste Ant Colony** about 12km northeast of Põlva. This reserve can only be visited with a guide and it is perhaps comforting to hear from him that community life there is as fraught as in any human one. The ants that get along with each other create hills 2m high; others concerned with privacy burrow similar distances underground.

Räpina It is rare to be frustrated at the lack of even gentle development in an Estonian town, but this used to be the feeling of many visitors to **Räpina**, 30km east of Põlva. However 2012 brought a hotel, a museum and major landscaping of the gardens. If it took most places in Estonia at most ten years to throw off their Soviet past, it took Räpina 20, but the results are now clear to see. Its first significance was in April 1242, when Alexander Nevsky marshalled his forces here before the 'Battle of the Ice' on Lake Peipsi, which would halt the eastern progress of the Teutonic Knights. For centuries afterwards, the Narva River and Lake Peipsi would be the furthest extent of first the Catholic and then the Lutheran faith. Given the constant warfare in this area in the 16th and 17th centuries, plus the fact that all the buildings were probably made of wood, nothing remains from those days or earlier.

It is for the parks, formal gardens and lakeside walks that one comes here now, as much as for the buildings. One does not expect to see vines in Estonia, but here 30 varieties of grapes are grown every year, although not to a size that warrants harvesting them. An apricot tree blooms each year and there are two cork trees that have both survived from the 1920s. The wooden pavilion from 1847 has retained its original pillars and, being beside the lake, remains the tradition spot for pledging eternal love. The parks beside the river are well maintained with the care given to the lawns creating an almost English feel to them. The landscape artist however was German, Walter von Englehardt, who soon after completing his work here in 1905 would be appointed director of the Düsseldorf Municipal Garden.

There are several mentions in this book of pastors who served their communities for as long as 60 years. Here it is of course a gardener who showed similar devotion. Adolf Vaigla was appointed as supervisor in 1935 and would hold this job for 60 years, from the first period of independence into the second, with two Soviet and one German occupations in between.

The Räpina we see now dates from the early 18th century, when Russian rule was secured and would remain so for 200 years. The paper mill produced banknotes for Catherine the Great. However, the façade of the manor house, one of the best preserved neo-Classical buildings in Estonia, dates from the late 19th century and since 1884 it has housed Estonia's best-known horticultural college and also a related museum. Of most interest here are probably the textbooks that date from Soviet times and also the radiators which date from 1938, in the first period of Estonian independence, but which are still in good working order. (If only the same could be said of what the Soviets would bequeath to Estonia in 1991.)

Värska The town of **Värska** developed around St George's Orthodox Church; the current building dates from 1904. Note the cemetery beside the church, quite a rarity in Estonia, as following the plague in the early 18th century, burial inside a church was forbidden on health grounds. Isolated sites well away from the village were chosen instead. The site of the earlier wooden church here is marked by a cross in the cemetery. At the church door is a memorial plaque for the victims of deportation to Siberia in 1941 and 1949. Indoors note the two choir stalls, one for Estonians and one for Setos (see below). Värska is proud of the fact that all its clergymen since the 18th century have been Estonian speakers.

Once mineral water was discovered here its role as a spa was assured, whatever the political regime. In fact in Soviet times, its role was more secure than it is now, given that the state used all hotel and spa facilities available, whereas since privatisation they have been exposed to ruthless market forces. In recent years tourists have been attracted by the **Seto Farm Museum** (*www.setomuuseum.ee*), which opened in 1994. 'Museum' is hardly the correct name for it, cultural centre or even theme park being more appropriate. (For a serious museum on the Seto community and background on them, see pages 219 and 224.) One room does represent life for this community in 1920–40 but otherwise there is plenty of singing and dancing, the chance to try cooking on a log fire and the temptations of what must be the largest souvenir shop in Estonia. If you are short of towels and long dresses, this is the place to come, as prices are set for Estonians rather than for foreigners. The very modern tower behind the farm serves most of Estonia's mobile phones.

In conjunction with the EU, a lot of effort has recently been put into promoting the area to visitors and in 2013 a dedicated **Seto Tourist Information Centre** was set up in Värksa at Pikk 12 in the town centre (*www.vistsetomaa.ee*). Much is made here of the **Seto Külävüü**, the Seto Village Belt, which is the name given to a route which links all the Seto villages on the Estonian side of the border. (Sadly they are now cut off from others, and from their former capital of Petsory, by the strongly guarded Russian border.) A leaflet on it is available here, as is one titled 'Local Tastes and Impressions' which shows all the activity now under way. The website is more than a tourism one, with a detailed introduction to all aspects of Seto history and culture. Before leaving Värksa, it is important for car drivers to fill up with petrol and to take any necessary money from an ATM, as neither is available further south 'along the belt'.

If it really is better to travel than to arrive, the road from Värska to Saatse certainly proves the point. The Russian border gets closer and closer and then actually crosses the road on two occasions, once for about 100m and then for about 2km. The only indication of this are signs forbidding pedestrians and not allowing traffic to stop, plus the clear presence of soldiers in watchtowers and on patrol. In 1992 the Russians, not normally conciliatory to Estonia in any way, agreed to the continuing use of this road by Estonians as it is the only link with the rest of the country for several villages. The border has no particular rationale anywhere in Põlva county, having been set in 1944 when it was only between two provinces of the USSR, not between western and eastern Europe. Until then, Estonian territory stretched several kilometres further east and south, as was agreed in the Tartu Peace Treaty signed by Estonia and the USSR in 1920. Should a border treaty ever be signed between Russia and Estonia, it is likely that with various land swaps this anomaly, called the 'Saatse boot', will be eliminated.

Saatse The town of **Saatse** has an Estonian Orthodox Church that dates from the mid 19th century, although its iconostasis is a lot earlier and several paintings have been saved from a previous church on this site. It is named after St Paraskeva, who protected crops and good health. There is also a museum which proudly boasts a collection of 20,000 objects, all nominally related to the Seto community (see page 223). These are largely tools made by men, to contrast with the women's handicrafts displayed in the museum at Obinitsa (see page 224). The museum was brought to life in 2012 with the addition of many pre-war films and a few from the Soviet period, together with music, for those who want to hear it. (Unlike in Estonian restaurants, the music is not compulsory.)

The building has had a very chequered history, even by Estonian standards. It looks like a modest private residence, but in fact was built as an officers' holiday home in 1908, then converted into a hospital. Between the wars and through the early Soviet period it was a boarding school, becoming a museum in 1963. It used the term 'local folklore' to avoid Soviet objections to honouring the Seto. However, most visitors will want to stride through the woods here for further glimpses of the incongruous border. It is easy to approach and there is no problem with photography. The Russians mark their side very clearly with fencing and often with a cleared area in front of it; the Estonians limit themselves to the occasional border post. There is a road crossing point near the village but this is only for local cyclists with, of course, visas.

VÕRU

Võru is unusual in Estonian terms in being a totally planned town that has retained its original layout of wide straight streets. Catherine II supervised its design during the 1780s and little has changed since. The surrounding county, which borders on Latvia and Russia, is the only hilly area in Estonia, so it attracts walkers and skiers. To Estonians, Võru is best known as the town where the famous 19th-century author Friedrich Reinhold Kreutzwald lived.

Võru is proud of its connection with Kreutzwald and is particularly conscious of its Estonian heritage, which it actively promotes. Neither in Soviet times, when there were no borders, nor now when there is one with both Russia and Latvia, has

Võru county been interested in either neighbour. International links elsewhere are also fewer than in other counties. It is in no hurry to Westernise or expand in any way, apart from in music festivals, so it should remain for many years a congenial, small, county town.

GETTING THERE AND AWAY Some **buses** go directly from Võru to Tallinn, Narva and Pärnu but it is normally necessary to change in Tartu or Valga for onward travel to the rest of the country. There is an extensive local network going south to Rõuge and Vastse-Roosa and east to Obinitsa and Värska. No buses cross the Russian border in this area. For travellers with a Russian visa, transfers can be arranged to the border at Koidula and then on the other side to Petseri. As Petseri is only about a kilometre from the border, it is almost possible to walk. The railway line at Võru no longer carried passengers in 2013 but with the expansion of railway services elsewhere in Estonia, this situation may change.

WHERE TO STAY

Kubija (57 rooms) Männiku 43a; 786 6000; e info@kubija.ee; www.kubija.ee. This luxury hotel has the most detailed website of any in Estonia, zooming in on any room detail a potential visitor may wish to examine. Located in a pine forest on the edge of the town, its range of sports & business facilities means few guests need to leave the complex during their stay. In 2005 it added a sleep clinic to its services & started to provide eco-rooms with clay furnishings. A complete refurbishment of the hotel was undertaken in 2012. Patients at the clinic have 28 links to the computer whilst they sleep so that all aspects of their night behaviour can be analysed. This is a field in which Estonian medicine specialises, as in 2014 it will host the European Sleep Research Society Congress. All the wood & fabrics used in the hotel are from the local area. One of the suites in the hotel is named after Erki Nool, who won a gold medal for Estonia in the decathlon at the 2000 Sydney Olympics. In fact the hotel is rapidly becoming a shrine to Erki Nool, even though he is of course still very much alive.

By 2003, a statue of him pole-vaulting had pride of place in the foyer & his collection of shoes was also displayed there. The hotel then opened a large sports centre to further link his name with them & a large spa centre followed. There is a presidential suite, distinguished by the security room provided for his guards, but if the president & the Olympic champion should arrive at the same time, there is no doubt who would receive the most attention. The Kubija has the only large restaurant in Võru which is used by local people & by those passing through – & cynics might say, by those who need to recover from a visit to Russia. $$$

Tamula (22 rooms) 4 Vee; 783 0430; e hotel@tamula.ee; www.tamula.ee. This 3-star hotel is a completely new building on the lakeshore, within walking distance of all the sites in the town. Although it only serves b/fast & snacks at reception, it is close enough to the eateries listed below. All rooms have balconies with an extensive view over the lake. A large car park & its private tennis courts separate the hotel from the town, so a quiet environment is assured. $$

WHERE TO EAT AND DRINK

Katariina Café Katariina allee 4. Located close to the Town Museum, during the day this is another eating option. $
Pub Õlle Jüri 17. Perfectly satisfactory, but with a somewhat smaller menu. $

Rānduri Pubi Juri 36b. Located in the town centre, this restaurant can be recommended for those who prefer a more casual (& cheaper) environment. $

WHAT TO SEE AND DO The **Võrumaa Museum** (*Katariina 11; www.vorumuuseum.ee*) is recommended for coverage of the 1918–20 war of independence, of the resistance to the Soviet occupation organised by the Forest Brothers in the late 1940s, and of the independence movement of the late 1980s. A model of one of the Forest Brothers' hideouts has been rebuilt. One room is devoted to Frits Suit, the mayor of Võru throughout the first independence period from 1919–40. It has been a major challenge for his successors to emulate the diversity of cultural achievements that he instigated. The three Kriisa brothers, Jakob, Juhaw and Tannil, were Estonia's most famous organ builders and the museum has reconstructed their workshop for exhibition. They were active from the 1880s until World War II. The business has continued through each generation and is now run by Tannil's great-grandchildren.

The **Catherine Church** is not named after the saint, but after the Russian empress, who found the necessary building money and who would approve of the way it still dominates the town landscape; surprisingly it is Lutheran and not Orthodox. It was built between 1788 and 1793 and mixes Baroque and Classical styles. The architect was Christoph Haberland, well known for his work in Riga, where he designed the Town Hall and what would later become the Wagner Concert Hall. The organ is of course the work of the Kriisa brothers.

Between the wars, during the first period of Estonian independence, the church served both an Estonian- and a German-speaking congregation. One bomb hit the church in 1944 but the necessary restoration was completed by 1949. The church has always had the plain interior seen today and was not imposed in Soviet times, as often happened elsewhere. The impressive altar painting dates from 1855 but nothing is known of the artist or other works of his that may still exist. The two sets of lights on each side of the altar represent St Paul and St Peter. Two of the chandeliers are from the 19th century but the more modern one dates from 1970 when a regular member of the congregation ordered it, to commemorate her son. The park at the eastern side of the church was laid out in 1961 on what had previously been church land.

The monuments to Estonian freedom fighters that were destroyed during the Soviet period were all quickly and extensively restored in this area. It was sadly necessary in 1995 to build another memorial, which is in the square beside the Catherine Church. It is to the 17 town councillors who lost their lives when the *Estonia* sank off the Finnish coast in September 1994. The sculptor is Mati Karmin, who also designed the monument to this tragedy on Hiiumaa Island, as well as, on a happier note, the *Kissing Students* in front of Tartu Town Hall.

Võru was the home town of **Friedrich Reinhold Kreutzwald** (1803–82) and his statue dominates the shoreline at the end of Katariina allee. It is by Amandus Adamson (1855–1929) (see page 45), Estonia's most famous sculptor, and copies of it can be seen in all large towns in Estonia. The **Kreutzwald Memorial Museum** (*Kreutzwaldi 31*) is in the house where he practised as a doctor for 40 years. He treated a lot of poor Estonian patients as the other doctor in the town only spoke German. They could not pay, which explains his constant financial problems and the modest furniture to be seen here. Most rooms remain largely as he would have known and used them in his practice. The stairs up to his study are very steep and it is suggested that he maintained them as such to prevent his disabled wife from disturbing him when he was writing. The house came into state hands when his spinster daughter died in 1939.

Kreutzwald is best known for his work in getting the Estonian language used in science and literature at a time when it was still seen as a language just for peasants and anything worthy of record had to be written in German. His most famous book is *Kalevipoeg*, a 20,000-verse epic on Estonia's mythical hero. Ironically it was first published in German because tsarist censorship delayed the publication of an Estonian edition. He was a campaigner on many issues, particularly temperance. Between 2000 and 2011 translations were published in English, French and German.

In 2007 the museum expanded into two other buildings belonging to the house. The former barn is now a 'Kalev' room, explaining the background to the legend and the former store displays the many translations of his works, including some that were done during his lifetime. It also houses a collection of paintings by two exiled Estonian artists, Jüri Erik Hammer and Gunnar Neeme, who both lived in Australia.

Võru has a good beach on Lake Tamula, where a music festival takes place each July. A proper promenade beside the shore will be completed in 2014.

BEYOND VÕRU

South of Võru are the two extremes of Estonia, both within the Haanja Nature Park. Twelve kilometres south on one road is **Suur Munamägi**, the highest 'mountain' in the Baltics at just over 300m, while a similar distance from Võru is the lake at Rõuge, with a depth of 38m. Surprisingly, there was never a fortress at Suur Munamägi and small wooden watchtowers only dated from the 19th century. The **tower** (www.suurmunamagi.ee) now here, a short climb from the road, was built in 1939 and added a further 30m in height. The date is significant as it was one of the last Functionalist buildings to be completed before the Soviet occupation and was sited in an area that had no links with any of the occupying powers. The glass gallery on the top was added in 1970 as the growth of the surrounding trees would otherwise have blocked the view, which extends across innumerable forests and lakes, well into Russia and Latvia. It is very different, but equally worthwhile, in all four seasons. Locals like to claim that on a clear night it is possible to see the lights of Tartu, 85km away. Some also hope that in due course two cartfuls of gold left by Charles XII of Sweden, as he hurriedly retreated from the armies of Peter the Great, may be rediscovered in the area. The lower floors of the tower house a museum on nature protection. The major extension, which includes a lift, was completed in 2005. It is worth coming down the stairs to see the photographic exhibition of the area, and also the temporary exhibitions of local art. Admission prices vary with a surcharge for taking the lift, except for pensioners who pay the same either way. Opening hours are much more extensive during the summer, and in midwinter it only opens briefly at weekends. Full details are on the website.

A settlement at **Rõuge** dates back to the 5th century and seems to have been destroyed and re-established about once every century for the next 600 years until it was finally abandoned, not being revived again until the 18th century. The settlement was excavated extensively in early Soviet times in the hope of finding evidence of a very Russian environment but nothing was found. From then, research continued at a much slower pace, but has now been revived. The scenery here is totally different from the rest of the country, as the hilly environment offers a waterfall and fast-flowing streams, which in turn gave energy to a watermill which generated electricity for the village until 1956. Construction of the church began in 1730 and continued until the 1920s as it was attacked in 1918. The organ is by the Kriisa brothers.

Another settlement only half an hour's drive further south from Rõuge has a very different origin. It is at **Vastse-Roosa** on the Latvian border and was where the Estonian and Latvian guerrilla movement, called the Forest Brothers, hid from their Soviet persecutors (see pages 26–7). Visitors who have seen the Cu Chi Tunnels in Vietnam will find many similarities. Life could continue for days underground with all evidence of exits and entries concealed. The area is of course isolated and well forested so hiding was easier than in the more open countryside further west.

Tourists can in fact stay a night in a bunker and one is named after a former prime minister of Estonia, Mart Laar, since he did precisely that. Before entering politics, he was a historian and he has written the standard book on the Forest Brothers, which is available in English.

There is now quite a holiday air in the surroundings of the bunkers and it is possible to have more conventional accommodation in the farmhouse beside them. Some might feel that a sombre memorial to the Forest Brothers would be more appropriate than the fun now on offer here. For those with no such worries, the real temptation though is Metsakohin, or 'Rustle of the Forest', which is literally the local firewater. A lit match is put to each bottle when it is opened to prove its strength to sceptical visitors. A sign in the café pleads with guests to leave sober, quite a tall order after tasting this brew, and those who cannot manage to do so are offered free accommodation for the night. To check events and facilities here, visit www.metsavennatalu.ee.

Visitors wanting to proceed south can cross the border here and television viewers may remember Michael Palin doing so in his *New Europe* series televised in 2007. Ape is the first town on the Latvian side and it is a short journey to Aluksne from there, although in Latvian it has two syllables, not one! With Latvia joining the euro in January 2014, there is no longer any need to change currency.

Eight kilometres east of Võru towards Obinitsa is the village of **Lasva**, which suddenly became famous in 2008 for the **Jaaniraotu Farm** (*www.jaaniraotu.ee*) that opened there. It combines an aviary with about 30 varieties of birds with a nursery full of shrubs. One does not expect to meet swans, peacocks and pheasants in the Estonian countryside, so they are particularly welcome. The commercial side is selling wooden houses for assembly elsewhere with father discussing this whilst mother and children play with the animals. Those who cannot afford a house, can buy a rabbit instead for €20.

Thirty kilometres east of Võru is **Obinitsa**, centre of the local Seto community. The Setos are linked ethnically and linguistically to Estonia but many of their customs have a Russian origin. Although they would attend Russian Orthodox services, they would rarely understand the language and they maintained pagan customs for centuries after these had been dropped by both Estonians and Russians. It is probably because of their adherence to the Orthodox Church that they were allowed to build one in Obinitsa in 1952, at a time when religious communities elsewhere in Estonia were suffering particularly strong persecution. The building materials were all collected by local people and they gave their labour free of charge. They often had to work at night, as they would not have been released from their work for this.

Kreutzwald was the first Estonian to make any study of their communities but serious anthropological work only began in the 20th century. The current border between Estonia and Russia cruelly divides many families, particularly as Petseri/Pechory used to be their headquarters. Estonians now admit that the Seto were neglected as a community during the first independence period, with a standard of living well below that in the rest of the country. The new Estonian government did however insist in 1920 that girls attend school, which previously they had not done. The Soviets saw little difference between them and the Estonians so Seto agriculture was collectivised in the same way. This did at least ensure that electricity finally reached the Seto community in 1962. Finnish organisations are now providing considerable support for the Seto and help publicise their cause outside Estonia. As there is no formal way of defining a Seto, estimates of the current size of the community differ, but about 1,300 is the number living in Estonia and 600 in Russia.

The **Seto Museum** in Obinitsa (*www.obinitsamuuseum.ee*) opened in 1995 and is built as a family house. It shows a 'Red Corner' with icons draped in red scarves, as this was a traditional colour of the Seto. It has nothing to do with the Soviet use of red. Children were not allowed to play there. The wooden chest was for women to store their handicrafts, an activity they could learn without formal schooling. As a dowry the bride traditionally had to provide gloves, belts, bedspreads, shawls and long dresses. They would also have become skilled in ceramics by then. The museum has an extensive display of the very elaborate costumes the Seto women used to wear, and still do on festive occasions. Women who could afford it had silver breastplates and often other accessories in silver as well. These would be buried with her. What is missing in exhibits is shown in photographs. A book donated by Lennart Meri, president in the 1990s, is displayed. His inscription asks for it to be read, not exhibited, but this wish has not been carried out. The statue of the mythical hero Kalevipoeg was allowed in Soviet times because one was also cast of Lenin. This museum contrasts with the one at Saatse (see page 219), which concentrates on tools made by Seto men. Note the roadsigns, which make the point.

About 3km north of Obinitsa are the **Piusa Caves** (*www.piusa.ee*). The sandstone here was excavated for over 40 years from 1922 to 1966 to supply Estonia's glass factories but now safer and faster opencast mines are used for this. The caves have now been taken over by a large colony of bats but they do not object to occasional tourists walking around. It is reassuring that staff are now always on duty, which was not previously the case. From Piusa, it is possible to travel north to Värska and Põlva or east into Russia at the Koidula border crossing point. From 2013 there has been a train service to Piusa from Tartu via Koidula and Põlva. No public transport crosses the Russian border so those with visas will need to walk the 2km or so to Petseri.

The remains of the fortress at **Vastseliina** (*www.vastseliina.ee*) are about 20km southeast of Võru. Hopefully, excavations will, in due course, find evidence of an earlier Estonian fortification, but at the moment it is possible to see the remains of a castle dating back to the 14th century, when the Teutonic Knights were finally able to conquer the Estonian tribes. The limestone was excavated locally, although it was previously thought to have been brought from Isborsk, now over the border in Russia. Given its current total rural environment, it is hard to think of this castle as a constant battleground for the following three centuries between the Swedes, the Poles and the Russians, but its 4.5m-thick walls were certainly needed to defend it. Peter the Great was its last conqueror, when he drove out the Swedes in 1702, but he did not bother to restore it given that the more powerful armaments by then available made it redundant.

There was some fighting around the castle in 1944 and about 100 German troops were buried here at that time. Their bodies were only taken back to Germany in 1990. The skeleton of a German sniper was found in the castle ruins as late as 1951.

A roadside inn beside the castle was converted into a museum in 2012. It covers the history of castles throughout Estonia and in particular the lives of soldiers forced to defend them. On view are models of their tents and the armour that could weigh 40kg. The 25m tapestry was inspired by the one at Bayeux in Normandy, although it takes prehistory rather than a specific battle as its theme.

VALGA

For some 200 years, the border town of Valga has, to put it mildly, had a bad press. In the 19th century travellers wrote of squalor and mental deficiency in both the Estonian and Latvian populations. In the 20th century, both during the first period of independence and very recently, travellers complained of visa and currency problems, of long delays for connecting trains and buses, or of not being able to cross the border at all. In tsarist times and earlier, it did not much matter that the town had a mixed population of Estonians and Latvians but this was crucial during the struggle for independence at the end of World War I when both wanted to claim it. Most of the town is in Estonia, although the Latvian side forms a compact town, Valka, in its own right.

There was a serious risk of war between both sides until Sir Stephen Tallents from the British Foreign Office managed to impose a border running through the town. He did not enjoy the mission and never returned, quite happy to rely for reports on its success from equally cynical observers. Tallents then went on to pioneer public relations, at first with the Post Office and then at the BBC. Tallents House, the Post Office building in Edinburgh which opened in 2001, shows how respected he still is in this field, as does a medal that carries his name, which is awarded by the Institute of Public Relations. He was the first president of the institute when it was founded in 1948.

Valga has one other link with Britain, through someone whose life took a totally different course from that of Tallents: the communist writer Salme Palme Dutt. Born in 1888, she was of the generation able to be active as the revolutionary movement spread amongst factory workers from the 1905 uprisings onwards. She suffered exile in Siberia for her activity and then moved to Finland. She came to Britain in the 1920s and remained active as a journalist in the Communist Party right up to her death in 1964.

Valga prides itself on the many pioneers who came from the town who were of Estonian ethnic origin. Mats Erdell (1792–1847) was the first Estonian to own a manor house. Johannes Martson (1868–1935) became mayor of Valga in 1901, six years before Tallinn had an Estonian in this position. Alfred Neuland (1895–1966) was the first Olympic gold medallist at the Antwerp Games in 1920. He returned to Valga and set up a flower shop. Hella Wuolijoki (1886–1954) would never have tolerated such a quiet life. She left Valga for Helsinki in 1905 and witnessed the first salvoes of the Russian Revolution there. She wrote radical plays, by then in Finnish, ran oil and timber companies and just avoided being executed as a spy by the Soviets in World War II.

The restoration of independence to Estonia and Latvia led to a firm border being re-imposed and the two towns breaking all links. Even hospital patients could not be brought across, because insurance was not valid. For the same reason most local cars could not be driven across the border. Ironically it was the British in 1999 that made the first move to bring both sides together again when the British Council established a joint English-language school. This was followed in 2001 by the opening of a joint tourist office and an exhibition of paintings by Estonian children in the Valka Museum. Sadly the Latvians moved out the following year and now have a separate office again on their side of the border. However, EU entry forced greater co-operation and put an end to the anomalies mentioned above. In 2005, EU funds provided much-needed tourist material covering both towns and a marketing campaign began under the slogan 'One city. Two states.' As part of the Schengen Agreement from late 2007 all border controls between Estonia and Latvia were removed and some further, if still reluctant, co-operation began between the two sides. Perhaps the divisions between the two countries were best shown by the lack of Estonian–Latvian dictionaries. Until around 2004, the latest one produced in Latvia dated from 1967 and in Estonia from 1959. The Soviet military presence previously made Russian the predominant language in both parts but Russian speakers now represent less than 50% of the population on both sides of the border. Although the town has a population of only around 21,000 (15,000 on the Estonian side and about 6,000 on the Latvian side), four languages are now used there, with English being the link between the three communities among younger people.

GETTING THERE AND AWAY

By bus Valga has excellent bus links to Tallinn, Tartu, Viljandi and Võru, and also services to the surrounding villages. Buses stop in the station forecourt and tickets are bought in the station. There are five or six services a day to Tallinn, a journey that takes four hours and stops *en route* in Viljandi, which is roughly halfway. Four buses a day go to Tartu, a journey of two hours with an *en route* stop at Otepää. The bus journey to Võru, which also takes two hours, is the most scenic with several *en route* stops in the Karula National Park.

By train There is a twice-daily service between Tartu and Valga, with a connection to Riga, although it is necessary to buy separate tickets for each train. The Estonian train times are on the website www.edel.ee and those for Latvia are on www.ldz.lv.

Crossing the border There is a train three times a day from Valga to Riga which stops *en route* at Cesis, Valmiera and Sigulda, useful for those wanting to continue a tour in Latvia or who plan to start a visit to Estonia in Valga. The cost to Riga is about €6.

The local bus station in Valka on the Latvian side is close to the border. There are fives buses a day to Riga and others to Smiltene and to Valmiera. The best source of information on these is the town website (*www.valka.lv*).

Most contemporary travellers do not see the town at all, as they cross at the main international border on the Tartu–Riga road about 2km from the centre. A joint border crossing, with one large building, opened in 2000 and replaced a ramshackle selection of wooden shacks that had done service for the previous ten years. This building became half-redundant when both countries joined the EU and gave up customs controls. After the Schengen Agreement, they became totally redundant, so it is a weird experience driving through a new complex that is totally deserted.

Valga is, however, worth seeing and, now that international travellers can cross in the town itself, first or last impressions of Estonia and Latvia can be much more positive. The border appears in various guises. In the countryside, since 2008, it is often unmarked; in the town, some border markers have been left but of course the barbed wire and other barriers that were erected in the 1990s have now all been removed. It will be a relief from January 2014 that the euro will be used on both sides of the border.

 WHERE TO STAY Apart from being a possible transit stop for tourists *en route* to Latvia, Valga can be considered as an alternative to Tartu or Otepää when hotels there are full or too expensive. As none of the museums in Tartu open before 10.30, it is possible to leave Valga soon after 09.00 without missing any possible visits there. The journey to Cēsis in Latvia likewise takes about 90 minutes.

⌂ **Metsis** (18 rooms) Kuperjanovi 63; ☎766 6050; e info@hotellmetsis.com; www.hotellmetsis.com. Valga needed this hotel in 1991 but finally got it in 2005. It is a conversion from a late 19th-century town house & one can easily visualise carriages drawing up in the drive. Its rooms are all large & the hunting trophies in the dining room show how former owners will have enjoyed their spare time. 'Metsis' is the Estonian word for capercaillie (wood grouse). Game is therefore of course on the menu in the restaurant but so is a wide range of fish & poultry. Do, however, remember to leave room for one of the ice creams on the sweet menu. **$$**

🏠 **Otra Elpa** (5 rooms) Vaigžnu 12; ✆472 2280; e otraelpa@inbox.lv. This modern guesthouse in Valka opened in 2003. It is conveniently situated in the town centre & close enough to the border for those who want to walk across. Its public rooms & corridors have a wide selection of photos of the town in Soviet times & during the first period of independence. Its restaurant is the best place to eat on the Latvian side. **$**

✖ WHERE TO EAT AND DRINK

✖ **Conspirator** Vabaduse 29; ✆766 1489; www. conspirator.ee. For many years there was just 1 serious restaurant in the town & this was it; the Conspirator is highly recommended for its wide menu & low charges. It's quite usual for the prices in Estonia to be 20 years 'out of date'; here they revert to the 1960s. It also does not play loud background music, a pleasant relief in comparison to most restaurants in Estonia, so plotters wanting to live up to the name of the restaurant might want to speak in hushed tones. **$$**

✖ **Lilli** Kuperjanovi 6; ✆766 3509; www.lilli. ee. The Lilli opened in 2007 in what had originally been an elegant town house built in the 1930s. It contrasts well with the other restaurants, concentrating on an Estonian menu & in the summer offering a terrace, so eating outside is now possible in Valga. **$$**

✖ **Horan** Kesk 16; ✆764 1655. In 2003 this 2nd serious restaurant opened beside St John's Church offering a great variety of Korean & Chinese food. In any town its menu & prices would be welcome; here they are even more so, given the lack of choice elsewhere & the surprise at finding them in such a small town. **$**

✖ **Voorimehe Pubi** Kuperjanovi 57; ✆767 9627. For lighter meals in a more casual environment this pub can be recommended. It was once a coaching inn & the décor looks back to the times when guests arrived on horseback rather than by car. **$**

WHAT TO SEE AND DO

Valga Valga is fortunate that a castle was never built here so it avoided the battles that repeatedly destroyed so many other Estonian towns. A number of 19th-century wooden houses have survived and others date from the 1920s and 1930s, when the industrial wealth of the town increased and led to the construction of a number of elegant private houses.

The **railway station** is a peaceful architectural anachronism where visitors may well first arrive, although this is more likely to be by bus rather than by train as it also serves as the bus terminal. The station was built by German prisoners of war in 1949 (they were allowed back to Germany only in 1955) so has all the flamboyance, space and light of Soviet buildings from that era. There must be few other towns with a population of 15,000 that can boast a station with chandeliers and a balcony. For years between 1990 and 2008, the station only came to life properly in the middle of the night, when the nightly Moscow–Riga trains passed through, as otherwise it was used only for a declining number of domestic services. The year 2008, with the implementation of the Schengen Agreement, saw the start of a service to Riga and a faster service to Tartu started in 2010 when the line had been properly repaired. Its well-maintained toilets are open all day and can be welcome after the four-hour bus journey from Tallinn. About 100m into town from the station is a restored 2-6-2 steam engine from the 1950s.

Crossing Jaama, taking Enno and then turning left into Pargi, the area is dominated by the Russian Orthodox **Issodor Church**. It dates from the 1890s when the two recently opened railways to Tartu and to Pskov brought many Russian speakers to the town and increased the congregation to around 5,000. Most of the building costs were met by the central Russian government and can be seen as part of its campaign to minimise religious and linguistic dissent in the Baltic region. Although many Russian speakers left after Estonian independence in 1920, taking all the church records with them, the congregation stayed at this number because of the support for the church amongst the Estonian Orthodox community. The building suffered badly during the Soviet era when, although it stayed open, it was not maintained or guarded so fell victim to neglect and vandalism. There are currently insufficient funds for the serious restoration that is desperately needed and with the opening of the Russian church in Valka (see pages 231–2) these are now unlikely to happen soon, if at all.

Returning to Jaama, next on the left is Valga's major employer, the food-processing plant. Turning right into Vabaduse and passing the hospital on the left, then comes the **Valga Museum**. In the 19th century this was the site of one of the early temperance societies in Estonia, but the current building dates from 1911 and was converted initially into a restaurant and then into a theatre during the first independence period. More recently it was a bank, as is clear from some of the strong doors that now guard the exhibits. The original museum collection dates from 1955 but much of the display was destroyed in a fire in 1988. Local enthusiasm and generosity meant that when it reopened here in 1999, the new collection was much more extensive than the earlier one had been and could include many items and topics that were banned in the Soviet period.

The ground-floor rooms have temporary exhibitions, usually of local painters.

OVER THE BORDER

When I visited Valk the barbed-wire entanglement which had previously marked the boundary had been taken down, but I was told at an inn on the Latvian side that special police permission was necessary to cross the dividing street, that the penalty for going without a permit was a fine or one day's imprisonment, and that the sentries would stop me if I tried to pass.

As I believe in conforming to the regulations (however tedious) of a country in which I am a visitor, I set off to find the police station. I had walked some distance through the rather uninteresting town and was just beginning to think that the police station was a long way when, looking up to see what street I was in, I saw the strange word 'tan' instead of the familiar Latvian 'iela' – street. It seemed that I was in Estonia. To make sure, I went into a shop and bought some chocolate.

The Latvian money I tendered in payment was refused. This was Estonia, the good lady told me uncompromisingly and in Estonia one paid in Estonian kroon. No she could not change my lat. I could either pay for the chocolate in the proper currency or give it back.

Then came the question of how to get back to Latvia. After what I had been told, it seemed highly probable that I might shortly find myself lodged in an Estonian (or Latvian) jail. The prospect of either was unpleasant. I retraced my footsteps until I saw ahead of me a sentry box. There seemed no life about it so I sauntered by and, glancing in as I passed, I saw that it was empty. Standing in the middle of the cobbled roadway, with one foot in Latvia and the other in Estonia, I took a photograph of that crooked street, and then hurried on, keeping to the Latvian pavement.

Extract from The New Baltic States *by Owen Rutter. The author visited Valga in 1924; Valk is the German name for the town that fell on both sides of the border.*

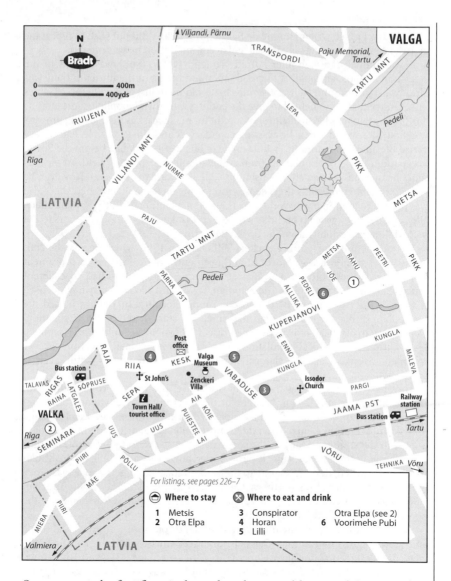

For listings, see pages 226–7

🛏 **Where to stay**		✕ **Where to eat and drink**	
1	Metsis	**3** Conspirator	Otra Elpa (see 2)
2	Otra Elpa	**4** Horan	**6** Voorimehe Pubi
		5 Lilli	

One room on the first floor is devoted to the natural history of the region and is particularly strong on fossils and skeletons. The other rooms concentrate on the urban environment and are pioneering in the use of wax models, which other Estonian museums are now following. The two most prominent ones here are of Johannes Martson, mayor shortly before World War I, and Marta Parna, headmistress of the girls' secondary school at the same time. The significance of this is that both were the first ethnic Estonians to have these posts. Elsewhere, even then, senior positions were taken by Russians or Germans. Exhibits and models show the changes in day-to-day life since the mid 19th century. The most moving section recreates the Magadani Camp in Siberia where many local residents were deported in 1941 and again in 1949. In the future the exhibits will be extended to cover the establishment of the border in 1920. One panel refers to a night spent in

Valga by the French writer Honoré de Balzac, who clearly did not wish to repeat the experience in view of the paltry food and accommodation he was offered.

A wax model of weightlifter Alfred Neuland (1895–1966) was added to the collection in 2005, although at the road junction in front of the museum there was already a statue of him. He was Estonia's first gold medallist at the Olympic Games in Antwerp in 1920 so helped to give the country worldwide publicity, just after its 'birth'. (The Latvians like to claim some credit for his success as his sporting prowess was first discovered when he was at secondary school in Riga.) He had a very varied life after this, running a whole range of businesses in Valga before the Soviet occupation, while continuing to train successors in his sporting field. At various times he opened a flower shop, a fishing-tackle shop and drove a taxi. However, he is best remembered for his dress sense, and for his impeccably polished shoes. He was moved to Tallinn after World War II and ran a lemonade bottling plant there, although he never gave up his links with the sporting world. Along the stairs to the second floor are exhibits from the Soviet period.

Behind the museum is the **Zenckeri Villa** built in 1902, which during the 20th century was to house every form of authority and political grouping prominent in Estonia. Parties both for and against pre-war president Päts had, at different times, their headquarters here. The Estonian, Soviet and Nazi military have all used it, as have the Communist Party and the Young Pioneers. In 1989, it hosted the first public display of the Estonian flag since the start of the Soviet occupation. Continuing to be ahead of its time, as early as 1996 when the building was a public library, it offered the local population their first access to email. If Estonia is ever renamed @stonia, Valga can claim the credit. It is now the town's cultural centre and a café.

Turning left into Kesk at the end of Vabaduse, the former **Town Hall** is on the left-hand side after 200m. It is one of the most impressive wooden buildings in the town and its façade is regularly painted. It now houses the helpful **Valga Tourist Information Centre** (*www.turism.valgamaa.ee*), which is open seven days a week in the summer. Many of the souvenirs they sell reflect a joint role, as they incorporate both national flags. It has a wider range of booklets in English than might be expected, devoted mainly to the work of local architects and artists. They have a lot of material on northern Latvia, also in English. The **Valka Tourism Information Bureau** at Riga iela 22 (*www.valka.lv*) is slightly further from the border on the other side, about 400m.

St John's Church, opposite the Town Hall, stands out for its unusual oval shape and was designed by the Riga Classicist architect Christoph Haberland in 1780, who also designed Catherine's Church in Võru (see page 221) and Riga Town Hall. Because of financial constraints, the building was only completed in 1816. The organ, built by the German Friedrich Ladegast in 1867, is still in excellent condition, partly because the church remained open in the Soviet period. It can be heard at Sunday services and sometimes at concerts during the week. Worship in Estonian started here in 1880; it had previously been in German. The granite monument on the side of the church facing the tourist office is a replacement for one erected in 1934 and destroyed by the Soviets in 1940. It commemorates 200 Finns who fought in the Estonian War of Independence in 1918. On the square in front of the church is a plaque to commemorate Stefan Batory, the 16th Polish king whose empire encompassed much of what is now southern Estonia. As he was of Hungarian origin, both Hungary and Poland contributed towards the cost of this plaque. He granted town rights to Valk as it was then known, which is why he is commemorated even though he came as a conqueror.

About 6km north of Valga on the road to Tartu is the **Paju Memorial**. This commemorates the battle that took place here on 31 January 1919 between the Finns and Estonians on one side and the Latvians and Bolsheviks on the other. Although he won the battle, the Estonian commander Julius Kuperjanov died of his wounds two days later. The longest street in Valga is named after him.

Valka Valka is a town dominated by death: with a population of only 7,000, its history has determined that it needs six **cemeteries**. Two are in the town centre, a short walk eastwards from the border crossing on Sepa/Seminara. One of these can be described as conventional, as in the 19th century it served the whole community. Tombstones in the four languages used in the town – Estonian, German, Latvian and Russian – could acceptably be placed side by side. Social distinctions of course remain with the Baltic-German landlords having more space and artistry than their staff, and sometimes even a private chapel of rest. The high fences around some family graves date from the first independence period when several metalworkers were active in Valka. This art did not survive World War II so more recent fences are much lower. During the 20th century vandals seized some of the metal crosses and others have fallen down but otherwise the succession of brutal occupiers largely left this cemetery alone. Only some tombs of German soldiers killed in World War I were covered over by the Soviets and these were immediately restored in the 1990s. It is fortunate that the main tomb here is to Janis Cimze (see below) who was seen as progressive by the Soviets and that the German quotations are from Schiller, the 18th-century writer who was also acceptable to them.

The Soviet cemetery is to the south of this one and the current monument, 'Mother Earth', dates from 1984, the 40th anniversary of the battle here between the Germans and the Russians, which claimed the lives of the 400 soldiers buried here. Unlike many other Soviet war memorials in the Baltics, nobody will take exception to the modest style or the location of this one and the Russian government has even provided funds for its maintenance. The sculptress, Arta Dumpe, has also produced a monument at Litene to Latvian officers killed by the NKVD in June 1941. The names of those killed are inscribed into a semicircular marble wall as not all the bodies could be found or identified.

The other four cemeteries are on the western side of the town, due south of the main border crossing used by lorries and coaches, which are not allowed across the smaller ones in the town centre. These were all restored in 2003 and show that, whilst everybody, whatever their behaviour in life, is entitled to a decent burial, enemies should still be kept apart in death. The largest one is Jewish, which reflects the size of the community before World War II. A road fortunately divides this one from the German military one, which is a general memorial since in 1944 it was impossible for them to bury their casualties as they retreated. The Latvian freedom fighters from World War I are commemorated in a statue, 'Old Latvian Warrior', which was unveiled in 1922. It was hidden on the other side of the road during the Soviet occupation and has been returned to its original site, but was deliberately not restored as a symbol of the damage caused to Latvia at that time. Another cemetery is a general one for Latvians who have died since World War II. Russians are buried separately, opposite a political monument to the uprisings of 1905, 1917 and 1919.

Between the cemetery and the town centre, a completely new **Russian Orthodox church** has been built, which opened in the summer of 2006. It is claimed that elderly Russians begging outside churches in Riga provided the necessary funds for this. Perhaps this explains the modest brick exterior and the side buildings, which used long individual logs, as is the custom in the Russian countryside. The iconostas was completed in 2007 and a school will follow. The church is open daily to visitors from 12.00 to 16.00.

On the approach to the town centre is a large artificial hill, with some concrete entrances protruding from it. These **underground bunkers** were built in the 1950s to shelter Soviet military chiefs during a crisis and to provide a command centre for them to launch attacks from the many missile sites scattered across the Baltics. Had the Cuban crisis in October 1962 developed further, it is probably from here that the Soviet military response would have been co-ordinated. Nobody of Latvian origin was allowed into this area during the Soviet regime.

The town-centre church, **St Catherine's**, is Lutheran; as a church with this name has stood on the site since 1477, the name has nothing to do with the later Russian empresses. The current building dates from 1907 but with so many alterations made since then it is impossible to describe it as being of any particular style. A series of steep steps are open to fit visitors wanting to climb the tower for a view across both towns. The sundial outside the church commemorates one murdered and two seriously injured Latvian policemen who were attacked by smugglers in 2002.

The main conventional attraction of Valka is the former **seminary** about 3km from the border on the Riga road, which carries the name of its founder, Janis Cimze (1814–81). It was opened as a museum in 1970, although the name **Local History Museum** (*www muzejs.valka.lv*) took attention away to some extent from Cimze. Returning from Germany in 1839 with a thorough university education, Cimze was to spend the rest of his life here, firstly teaching just in German, but then more and more in Latvian and Estonian. As his pupils would be largely training as primary-school teachers attached to churches, he concentrated as much on music as on language. One of the pianos here dates from his time, but the others are more recent. The collection portrays his life, shows the variety of texts and songs he used, and some of the tributes sent at the time of his death. Although his pupils were aged 17–25, he felt the need for a detention room, the 'Blue' room as it was called from the colour of its painting. 'Sentences' lasted from six to 24 hours. What is now the library was his private quarters. Since independence, the museum has been extended upstairs, where one room of the building is devoted to the military history of the 1917–20 period, when Latvians in this area were fighting Germans, Estonians, White Russians and Bolsheviks, mostly at the same time. Another reviews the first independence period.

A smaller, disused barn houses a **farming museum** and depicts former local life around the theme of the four seasons showing how the weather dictated most activity. Outside of work, it shows the production of candles in February, the painting of eggs at Easter, and the preparation of wreaths at Christmas. The long dining table would have belonged to a family rich enough to employ servants. They would eat at the same table and at the same time, but clearly divided. Some of the items displayed, such as the spinning wheel and the baker's oven, are still in regular use. On leaving the building, note Lenin's head, abandoned beside the outside wall.

8

Western Estonia and the Islands

HAAPSALU

Haapsalu has taken its time to catch up with the rest of Estonia. Its role as an air-force base restricted access until the end of the Gorbachev era and, as late as 1995, visitors were entitled to feel that it was a town looking backwards, not forwards. It had indeed much to look backwards at, with a turbulent history stretching back to its foundation in 1279. Given its strategic location, every invader over the centuries had to secure the town, no matter at what cost. Most were to rebuild it, but Peter the Great, when he arrived in 1715, decided simply to destroy it so that the Swedes, with whom he was still fighting, would have little incentive to return. It would never again be seen as a major fortress. By 1715, as a result of war and plague, Haapsalu's population had dropped to around 100 and even a century later it had only risen to 600. Its sudden rise to fame can be ascribed to one man, Dr Carl Abraham Hunnius, and to one product, mud. In 1825 Hunnius opened his first sanatorium and the popularity of the town was quickly established amongst the St Petersburg nobility.

Once the royal family showed an interest, as it soon did, the town's continuing status was assured. Tsar Nicholas I himself came in 1852 for the first time, and Alexander II, who succeeded him in 1855, made repeated visits throughout his reign and Haapsalu became a major summer resort with a regular 'season'. Tchaikovsky paid his first visit in 1867 and a wide range of his music was written in Haapsalu, including his *Songs without Words* and of course the *Souvenir de Hapsal* written in 1867. He is commemorated by a marble bench on the seafront, the marble coming from Saaremaa Island.

The sea is very shallow in the bay, which makes it warmer than elsewhere in Estonia, giving rise to the name 'Africa Beach'. The water temperature is often around 21°C (70°F) in the summer, much higher than anywhere else in the Baltic Sea. The protection of the bay makes the sea less prone to storms, so the town became one of the most popular resorts along the Baltic coast.

During the first independence period from 1920 to 1940, the town was so successful that even a Soviet history printed in 1976 had to admit that 'some achievements may be called excellent', a remarkable accolade in view of the normal presentation in such books of 'bourgeois Estonia'. Although Haapsalu was cut off from St Petersburg during this period, visitors from Sweden and Finland, together with those from around Estonia, ensured continued prosperity. Most of the buildings around the town date from these years and a stroll along its streets reflects the ambience of the town during the first independence period. The town remained a treatment centre during the Soviet period but, as foreigners were banned, it could only receive patients allocated by local trade unions. A small-scale, fish-processing

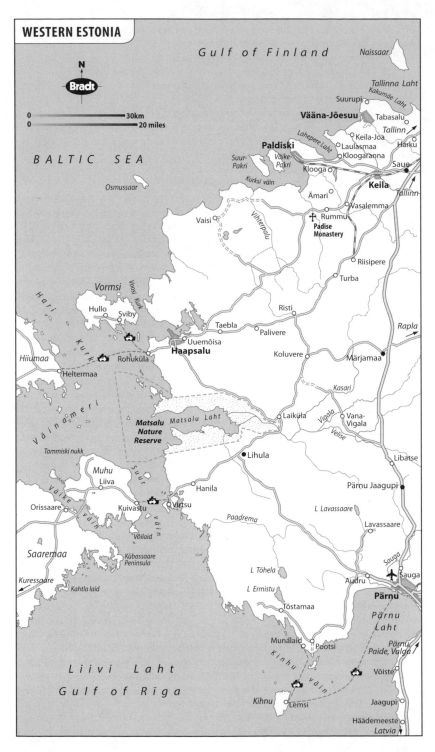

WESTERN ESTONIA

N

Bradt

0 ━━━━━ 30km
0 ━━━━━ 20 miles

BALTIC SEA

Osmussaar

Gulf of Finland Naissaar

Tallinna Laht

Suurupi *Kakumäe Laht*

Vääna-Jõesuu Tabasalu

Tallinn

Lahepere Laht Keila-Joa

Paldiski Laulasmaa Harku

Suur- Kloogaranna

Pakri *Väike-* Klooga Saue

Pakri

Kurksi väin Keila

Ämari *Tallinn*

Vasalemma

Vaisi Rummu †Padise

Vihterpalu Monastery

Riisipere

Turba

Vormsi *Voosi Kurk*

Hullo Sviby Risti

Taebla Rapla

Palivere

Hari Uemõisa

Kurk **Haapsalu** Koluvere

Hiiumaa Rohuküla Märjamaa

Heltermaa

Kasari

Väinameri Laiküla Vigala Vana-

Vigala

△ **Matsalu** *Matsalu Laht* *Velise*

Nature

Reserve

Tammiski nukk Lihula Libatse

Muhu *Suur*

Liiva Hanila Pärnu Jaagupi

Orissaare *Väike* Kuivastu Virtsu *väin* L Lavassaare

Paadrema Lavassaare

väin Võilaid

Kübassaare

Saaremaa Peninsula L Tõhela *Sauga*

Kuressaare L Ermistu Audru Sauga

Kahtla laid **Pärnu**

Tõstamaa

Pärnu

Laht

Munalaid Pootsi *Pärnu,*

Paide, Valga

Kinhu väin

Liivi Laht Võiste

Gulf of Riga Kihnu Lemsi Jaagupi

Häädemeeste

Latvia

plant was established and a former craft tradition in embroidery was continued. Fortunately the last few years have seen a turnaround and if its prestigious early role does not return in its entirety, Haapsalu will still have a serious role to play in tourism and industry. This has been shown in a totally new seafront between the Promenade Hotel and the Kuursaal, which was built between 2010 and 2012. It has certainly been reflected in the constant expansion of museums that continued unhindered by any financial problems during 2009. That summer, there was in fact only one outward sign of the credit crunch – the incomplete St Petersburg Hotel, next to the castle entrance, which was due for completion by then.

The major attractions for tourists are the castle, the railway museum and the beach walks, supplemented during the summer by an increasingly sophisticated cultural programme. It is probably best not to visit Haapsalu before 15 May or after 16 September since most of the museums are closed then, unless special arrangements are made beforehand. The castle ramparts are open all year every day from 10.00 to 19.00, and from 2006 – when extensive restoration was completed – tough walkers have had the opportunity to walk along the walls and up several towers. Wi-Fi was also installed at the same time.

GETTING THERE AND AWAY Buses, both local and long distance, leave from the railway station forecourt and tickets can be bought in advance from the office inside the station. Ironically, since the closure of the passenger line in 1995, the only tickets the station can sell are those for buses. There are hourly services to Tallinn. Express buses take 1½ hours, others about two hours. There are several services a day to Pärnu, Tartu and to Hiiumaa Island. In the summer, buses also operate to Virtsu for Saaremaa Island. For location of listings see map, page 238.

WHERE TO STAY

Baltic Hotel Promenaadi (34 rooms) Sadama 22; 473 7250; e promenaadi@ baltichotelgroup.com; www.promenaadi.ee. When the Promenaadi opened in 1999, with its exclusive location by the sea, cut off from 'hoi polloi', Haapsalu could perhaps claim to have returned to its former glory. Part of the hotel, a villa once owned by the Ungern-Sternberg family (see pages 281–2), entertained royalty 100 years ago. Most rooms have a balcony with a sea view, as of course the restaurant does. Amongst its unusual but welcome dishes is ginger & carrot soup. The Baltic Group also operates 2 very different hotels in Tallinn: the Imperial & the Vana Viru. **$$$**

Fra Mare Health Centre/Hotel (115 rooms) Ranna 3; 472 4600; e framare@framare. ee; www.framare.ee. There is no need to feel guilty being well here. While some people have a genuine complaint, most visitors like to spend some time having a conventional holiday & some time keeping fit & having a check-up. Many probably never leave the complex throughout their stay. The hotel offers something unique to Haapsalu, with ample space in the building & in

the surroundings. Stay up for sunset across the bay & do allow time for a leisurely walk to & from the town. **$$$**

Laine (95 rooms) Sadama 9; 472 4400; e info@laine.ee; www.laine.ee. By 2006 this enormous hotel had finally put its Soviet past behind it, with total renovation both inside & out. It could then compete properly with the Fra Mare here or with hotels in Pärnu or Kuressaare. Note the statue of the walking-stick breaker at the front of the hotel, who symbolises what the treatment centre here expects to achieve. It offers spa packages for long-term visitors but many just come for the day, or just for the evening to have dinner in the Blu Holm Restaurant (**$$$**). It will however be for the whole evening, given the duration of the sunset during the summer & the variety of music played. **$$$**

Kongo (21 rooms) Kalda 19; 472 4800; e kongohotel@hot.ee; www.kongohotel.ee. In taking the name of a former nightclub that was on this site in Soviet times, the Kongo is perhaps bringing some much-needed frivolity to Haapsalu. On the other hand, the nightclub was known to be rowdy & the name was linked to the civil war then under way in the Congo. Colours throughout are light, there is a garden & the kitchenettes attached to 5 of the rooms will attract families & prove that life need not begin at 50 for holidaymakers in Haapsalu. **$$**

⌂ **Päeva Villa** (20 rooms) Lai 7; ✆473 3672; e paevavilla@hot.ee; www.paevavilla.ee. This is in fact 2 newly built villas with 20 rooms between them, situated in a quiet residential area 10mins' walk from the town centre. Ideal for those who want to avoid 'entertainment' in the evening. The

restaurant is extraordinarily Russian with dark red drapes & napkins & with extensive varnish on the furniture. Portraits of 4 Russian emperors (dating from 2000!) look down on the guests, but with milder expressions than in other portrayals of them. In such surroundings, start the meal with the reasonably priced caviar pancakes & vodka. **$$**

⌂ **Hotel St Petersburg** Since 2008, this property beside the entrance to the castle has been left half-restored. Hopefully during the currency of this book the work can be financed & completed, so that it will open as Haapsalu's first 5-star hotel.

✕ WHERE TO EAT AND DRINK

✕ **Kuursaal** Promenadi 1; ✆473 5587; www.haapsalukuursaal.ee. A large restaurant overlooking the sea on the seafront. Because of its size, groups tend to eat here, in the hands of local catering students, many of whom move on later to very successful careers in this field. Having been closed for several years, 2011 saw it restored to much, if not really to all, of its former glory. The website gives details of the concerts held here during the summer. **$$$**

✕ **Dietrich** Karja 10; ✆509 4549; www.dietrich. ee. Over a century after the Dietrich family became known as the best bakers in town, their name is being revived to help restore the town's fame in this field. Judging from their first season in 2013, they should succeed, given the sensible match of price & quality. The interior looks back, but the outdoor dining on the street shows how much they aim to please summer clients in the 21st century. **$$**

✕ **Müüriääre** Karja 7; 473 7527; e kohvik@ muuriaare.ee; www.muuriaare.ee. Until 2010, there were few restaurants or even cafés in

Haapsalu outside the hotels, so the opening of Müüriääre was most welcome & others have now realised the potential market in this field. The furnishings are a complete, but deliberate, muddle. No chair matches another, nor does any work of art on the walls nor does any cushion on the sofas, which are an alternative to the tables. The cooking is however more conventional, specialising in light quiches & cakes. The owner, Epp-Maria Kokamägi (b1959) could only be an artist & indeed she is. Not only this, but she is married to Estonia's most famous contemporary painter Jaak Arro. To see more of her work, visit her gallery just around the corner from here at Kalda 2 & take a preliminary view of it on www.eppmaria.ee. Although called a café, most visitors eat a full meal here since it takes a long time to absorb all the artistic surroundings & it is in any case open every day until 22.00. Do make sure to use the toilet, whether you need to or not, since it will save a visit to an applied art museum elsewhere in Estonia. The owners are so proud of its décor that it warrants a picture on their website. **$$**

WHAT TO SEE AND DO

Haapsalu Castle The castle (*www.haapsalulinnus.ee*; ⊕ *grounds year-round 07.00–midnight; interior only in summer, usually 1 May–15 Sep*). The town centre has always played the combined role of fortress and cathedral. When first built with local limestone at the end of the 13th century, it had a far more isolated location than it does now as it was right beside the sea and could be more easily defended. The land around it has risen quite considerably in the intervening seven centuries. It has probably had the most turbulent history of any castle in Estonia, with frequent fires adding to the many attempts to conquer it. A convenient legend of the 'Lady in White', whose ghost stalks the supposedly all-male redoubt each August, has given rise to an annual festival centred on the castle with *son et lumière* performances each evening. She was alleged to have had an affair with a priest, disguising herself successfully as a pageboy for two years before being discovered. When this finally happened, her punishment was to be impaled on the castle walls. During full moon in August, her ghost can be 'seen' through the central window of the cathedral.

The ruins themselves involve tough climbs, so are not for the frail, but a walk around the outside walls, 800m in length, is not difficult. These ramparts date from the 16th to 17th century, when the Swedes built them, and consisted of seven towers and four gates. As so often with major fortifications in Estonia, they were never actually used, and were allowed to decay from the 18th century onwards. The church was restored in the 1880s and its acoustics make it an excellent venue for concerts. It is now part of the **Castle Museum** and is used as a concert hall and exhibition centre since none of the former furnishings remain. Heating was finally installed in 1991 as previously the venue could only be used in the summer. Half-hearted restoration had taken place since 1971, when the decision was finally taken that it would be used as a concert hall. Earlier in the Soviet period it had been a granary and there were even plans to convert it into an indoor swimming pool. The interior is a completely bland whitewash over all the walls. It is important not to miss the side chapel where there is a wooden statue commemorating martyred mothers. It was commissioned in 1991 by a local doctor, Heino Noor, who had been active in the resistance against the Soviet occupation. The unveiling took place on 24 April 1992, his birthday, but more importantly it was the 50th anniversary of the murder of his mother in a Siberian prison camp. Given the close links between Sweden and Haapsalu, the Swedish queen Silvia attended this ceremony. The museum has an extensive collection of 15th- and 16th-century weapons and armour. It was closed for a year in 2005 for restoration so is now spaciously displayed and well labelled in English. Photographers should climb the watchtower, despite the narrow, winding steps, for the street and town views that can be enjoyed there. Midday is a good time to be around to hear the bells which were restored in 2008.

That was also the year when the cellars were opened to visitors. They exhibit weapons from the 14th century, during the transition from crossbows to guns. It is easy to forget how long it took for guns to be more accurate, so it was only in the 16th century that crossbows could be completely abandoned. These weapons, together with ammunition and suits of armour, were only discovered in 1989 and it is assumed that they were hidden at sometime during the Livonian Wars at the end of the 16th century. Some cellars were empty and open; they were used for rubbish or storage in Soviet times. As with the watchtower, access is down steep steps so is only for the really able-bodied.

Museums The **Läänemaa Museum** (*www.muuseum.haapsalu.ee*) at Kooli 2 has taken great trouble to bring to life all of Haapsalu's history and every year it seems to expand its collection. It is also one of very few in Estonia that has set up wheelchair access. There are models of boats used in the harbour as well as Arabic coins to show the extent of early trade links. The archaeological collections have been put into one large case with a shelf for each century from the 13th onwards. A wax model of Hans Alver, Haapsalu's most famous pre-war mayor, seated at his desk, forms the centre of a display showing the town at that time. Sadly he was deported to Siberia where he died. Smuggling was very profitable then, with Finland being under prohibition, and displays show how even wooden legs were used to bring spirits into Finland. There are several paintings by Oskar Kallis (1892–1917) who, despite dying so young, had already during his short life become one of Estonia's most famous artists, probably because of his daring use of colour. A large comparative photograph collection was introduced into the museum in 2009. It contrasts the current scene with pictures from 50 to 100 years ago.

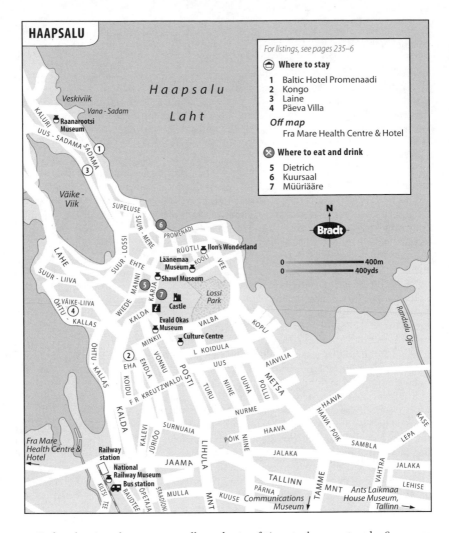

HAAPSALU

Haapsalu Laht

Veskiviik
Vana - Sadam
Raanarootsi Museum
KALURI
UUS - SADAMA
SADAMA
SADAMA

Väike - Viik

SUPELUSE
SUUR - MERE
PROMENAADI
RÜÜTLI ▲ Ilon's Wonderland
Läänemaa Museum ▲
KOOLI
SUUR - LOSSI
EHTE
VEE
Shawl Museum
Lossi Park
LAHE
SUUR - LIIVA
WIEDE MANNI
KALDA
KARJA
Castle
VÄIKE-LIIVA
OHTU
KALLAS
Evald Okas Museum
VALBA
Culture Centre
KOPLI
MINKII
L KOIDULA
OHTU - KALLAS
EHA
ENDLA
VONNU
KOIDU
POSTI
UUS
AIAVILIA
METSA
PÕLLU
F R KREUTZWALDI
TURU
NIINE
UUHA
NURME
HAAVA
KALDA
KALEVI
JÜRIOO
SURNUAIA
PÕIK
NIINE
HAAVA
HAAVA - POIK
SAMBLA
LEPA
KASE
JALAKA
Fra Mare Health Centre & Hotel
Railway station
JAAMA
LIHULA
National Railway Museum
Bus station
KIUTSI TEE
RAUDTEE
OPETAJA
STADIONI
MULLA
JAAMA
MNT
MNT
KUUSE
PÄRNA
TALLINN
TAMME
MNT
Communications Museum
Ants Laikmaa House Museum, Tallinn →
VAHTRA
JALAKA
LEHISE

For listings, see pages 235–6

🏠 **Where to stay**
1 Baltic Hotel Promenaadi
2 Kongo
3 Laine
4 Päeva Villa

Off map
Fra Mare Health Centre & Hotel

✖ **Where to eat and drink**
5 Dietrich
6 Kuursaal
7 Müüriääre

N

Bradt

0 ———————— 400m
0 ———————— 400yds

Randsalu Oja

Before leaving the museum, allow plenty of time to buy postcards. Some are irreverent, some are historic, some are works of art and many combine all three characteristics. They are very cheap.

Ilon's Wonderland (*Kooli 5; www.ilon.ee*) opened at the back of the museum building in summer 2006, in what had previously been a children's library. Like all the other museums in Haapsalu it extends every year. Ilon Wikland spent her childhood in Haapsalu before fleeing to Sweden in 1944 at the age of 14. She then became famous as the illustrator of the many children's books written by Astrid Lindgren. After Estonia became independent, she renewed her links with Haapsalu and decided to donate her collection of 800 original illustrations for her books to the town. About 100 are shown at any one time, and mostly at a child's eye level rather than at a height geared to adults. In the summer of 2009 a fully equipped children's centre opened here with open classes in face painting, spinning, cooking and paper cutting all in the context of Astrid Lindren's stories. The garden also opened at that time. Haapsalu has really done her proud.

On the wall of the building is a plaque to Anna Hedwig Bull (1887–1981) who saved several thousand Armenian children in Turkey during World War I and then worked for 40 years in welfare camps in Syria amongst the displaced Armenian community there.

The statue of the German writer Friedrich Schiller (1759–1805), which stands in front of the museum, is one of several originally commissioned by Baltic Germans in the 19th century soon after his death. Most, including this one, were frequently vandalised during the different military campaigns that afflicted Estonia. The restoration dates from 1957, as Schiller was seen in the Soviet Union as a very progressive writer.

The **Shawl Museum** (*Ehte 4*) is one room in a large handicrafts centre on the corner of Ehte, Karja and Kooli, about 100m from the castle entrance. Second to mud, Haapsalu shawls are what has made it famous. The Russian royal family bought them in the 19th century, the Swedish one in the 1920s and 1930s and then they started to do so again in the 1990s. In the communist era, if favours were needed from powerful women in Moscow, a Haapsalu shawl often worked wonders. It had the same effect as a bottle of Vana Tallinn did on powerful men. Greta Garbo helped to spread their fame from Sweden to New York in the 1930s. The shawls are always square and in two parts, with the edge being woven separately. It has to be fine enough to pull through a ring.

A stay in Haapsalu, particularly out of the main summer season, should always include a visit to the **Haapsalu Kultuurikeskus** (Culture Centre) (*www.galerii. kultuurimaja.ee*) on the corner of Valba and Posti. The austere Soviet exterior is not inviting but the interior is the complete reverse. Few days or evenings pass without a performance or two taking place here, not to mention the range of paintings always exhibited. It also has a library with many English books and an internet centre. Check the website for details of current events.

The **National Railway Museum** (*www.jaam.ee*) is housed in the former station, which dates from the building of the railway in 1905. St Petersburg had been linked to Tallinn and Paldiski from 1870 but it took determined lobbying from Haapsalu for the line to be finally extended. Once it was, the royal family made extensive use of it, and the station had to be built accordingly. The passenger service between Risipere and Haapsalu closed in 1995 and is now a cycle track, although trains still run from Risipere to Tallinn. The platform is covered for a distance of over 200m as there could be no risk of the royal family getting wet, and the museum is now housed in what was the imperial reception room. It displays uniforms, models of the different steam engines used during the 90-year history of the line, some refurbished engines, tickets (including one for the route London–Tallinn) and snow-clearing equipment. (Items used on Estonia's narrow-gauge railways are at a separate museum in Lavassaare, near Pärnu – see pages 254–5.)

The **Evald Okas Museum** (*www.evaldokasemuuseum.ee*) on Karja 24, opened in 2003, commemorating this painter who was born in 1915 and was still active when he celebrated his 90th birthday in 2005 and in fact for several years afterwards as he only died in 2011. The building is a former private residence, which had been abandoned for years, so the pictures hang on bare walls and the museum can only open in the summer as the building is not heated. (In the winter, look at the website which shows a wide range of his work.) The artistic tradition continues with the next generations, as Okas's three children are respectively a painter, architect and glass designer and several of his grandchildren have followed suit. To some, his current reputation is tarnished by his very close involvement with the Soviet regime and with his willingness to retreat with them to Yaroslavl during the war. The chances given to him for extensive foreign travel gave rise to considerable suspicion and envy amongst his many colleagues who were forbidden ever to leave the USSR. Soviet books refer to his 'significant contribution to Leniniana', given the number of portraits he painted of Soviet leaders. However, many people have always respected his non-political work and it is a sign of the times that his work can be displayed in public again. Many of his paintings were of nude women, even those produced during the Soviet retreat in 1941. A number of nudes are shown here and none of the others have any political slant. His political work can, however, always be seen in the Soviet section of KUMU in Tallinn (see pages 118–19) and at the Maarjamäe Palace (see pages 121–2) just outside Tallinn. The museum holds a hot glass symposium every August and family activities are arranged in the garden at the back.

The **Rannarootsi Museum** (*www.aiboland.ee*) on Sadama 31 covers the centuries of links between Estonia and Sweden and the history of the Swedish communities that were settled on the mainland and on the islands until 1944, when they mostly fled ahead of the Russian invasion. Before the war, 8,000 Swedish speakers had lived in Estonia, largely along the coast north of Haapsalu and on the islands of Ruhnu and Vormsi. They had their own secondary school in Haapsalu and sent an MP to parliament. It is known that about 5,000 people lived in this area as early as the 16th century, but what remains uncertain is when they first arrived. It may have been as early as the 11th century. The upstairs room is set out as a Vormsi farmhouse.

The **Communications Museum** (*www.sidemuuseum.ee*) at Tamme 2a concentrates mainly on telephones and telephone exchanges, though it also covers radio sets, televisions and loudspeakers, plus what probably ought to be called adding machines rather than calculators. Considering that the museum dates from Soviet times, a remarkable number of the exhibits come from America and Germany. The sequence from manual through semi-automatic to fully automatic is shown with well-preserved equipment from each era, and space is also given to the many systems that failed. Specialists in this field may want to compare the 200 different forms of cable shown.

The **Ants Laikmaa House Museum** (*www.laikma.eu*) is 12km from Haapsalu, shortly before the village of Taebla and a 1km walk from the road to Tallinn. The bus stop is at the end of the side road leading to the house. The artist Ants Laikmaa (1866–1942) in fact spent only the last ten years of his life here; his furniture and decorations reflect the travelling he was able to do, particularly to Germany and to Russia. Having such a long life, and not working under any restrictions, he was able to produce a wide range of landscapes and portraits, a selection of which have been assembled here. He is often compared to Augustus John, both for his painting and for his private life. However, this is more than a studio and memorial to him. It is a botanical garden too, with several trees and flowers dedicated to famous artistic contemporaries. It was his wish to be buried in the garden, as he did not want to leave it, even in death.

Visitors *en route* to the port of Rohuküla for ferries to Hiiumaa or to Vormsi will notice soon after leaving Haapsalu an abandoned manor house on the left-hand side of the road. Its name was Lindenhof and the first building here dated from 1523. Work started on the current one in 1898 and was completed in 1908 for a former mayor of Haapsalu, Ewald von Ungern-Sternberg. In 1909, he spent one night there, but was already dead on this occasion as his body was being brought back from St Petersburg to be buried with his family on Hiiumaa. The building has never been used since.

Behind the manor house is the abandoned Soviet airfield of Kiltsi with a runway of over 2km and 28 hangars. With advance permission, it is possible to drive along the runway, which is otherwise now used for car trials.

PÄRNU

Admitted to the Hanseatic League in 1346, the port for many centuries rivalled Tallinn and Riga, but since the 19th century has been better known as a health centre and seaside resort, as well as for its yachting harbour, so it competed more with Haapsalu. As a health centre, it was less successful than Haapsalu, but it more than made up for this with its success as a resort. Estonia's most famous man, pre-war president Konstantin Päts, and Estonia's most famous woman, the 19th-century poet Lydia Koidula, both went to school in Pärnu. Koidula's school is now a museum about her life and a statue in her memory was unveiled in the park in 1929.

The town council granted permission for the building of the first bathing centre in 1837 but support was so poor that in 1857 public bathing on the beach was banned in the hope that this policy would force more people to use it. The council took complete control of the centre in 1889 and in 1904 installed electric lighting; the centre burnt down in 1915 and only in 1927 was a new building opened. Fortunately the council realised at the turn of the century that Pärnu needed to cater for the healthy as well as for the sick. The park was laid out, the yacht club established in 1906, and between the wars it attracted many foreign visitors. By 1938, over half of the 6,500 summer tourists were from abroad, Finns and Swedes replacing the Russians as there was a ferry service each summer between Stockholm and Pärnu. The yacht club closed during the Soviet period but is now thriving again. In other fields, the town council has been active in broadening the economic base of Pärnu. Small- and medium-size firms have been established in foodstuffs, textiles and timber, many with foreign backing; companies from 30 different countries now invest here. Yet tourism is likely to remain the backbone

PÄRNU IN THE 1930S

Pärnu is delightful, gay and attractive to thousands of summer visitors, among whom are many Swedish people. It is a 'cure resort' well known since the middle of the last century; and in its fine white bathing establishment one can order any or every brand of assorted bath. But in Estonia one takes one's cure more gaily than in England: this wide, sunny beach, the long *allées* which run from the town down to the water's edge, a happy mixture of birch and maple, oak and pine, the brilliant flower-beds, the dazzling white sand, the happy little villas and brightly painted balconies. All make up a summer picture which is calculated to raise the spirits of even the most weary. You can be as gay as you please in Pärnu, dance or sun-bathe, swim or sail, dine well in amusing little cafés or restaurants, play good tennis or try your hands at water sports. There are any amount of excellent pensions where for the modest sum of two guineas a week you can be fed like the proverbial fighting-cock, or you may even try the new de luxe Beach Hotel, which is the last word in terraces and balconies, sun-bathing, verandas and beach cafés. Here for most reasonable prices, moderate even in Estonian eyes, you may live right on the sea-front, stepping straight onto the silver sand, the splash of the water for ever in your ears. Patches of tall reeds along the beach give shade and shelter for sun-bathing; one of these is known locally as the 'Woman's Paradise'.

From A Wayfarer in Estonia, Latvia and Lithuania *by E C Davies, published in 1937.*

Western Estonia and the Islands **PÄRNU**

8

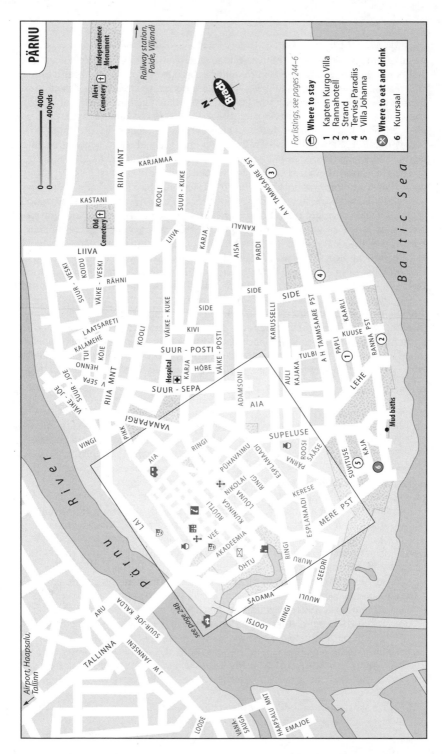

PÄRNU

0 ─── 400m
0 ─── 400yds

Railway station,
Paide, Viljandi

Independence
Monument

Alevi
Cemetery

Railway station,
Paide, Viljandi

see page 238

For listings, see pages 244–6

Where to stay
1 Kapten Kurgo Villa
2 Rannahotell
3 Strand
4 Tervise Paradiis
5 Villa Johanna

Where to eat and drink
6 Kuursaal

Baltic Sea

Pärnu River

RIIA MNT
KARJAMAA
KASTANI
Old Cemetery
KOOLI
SUUR - KUKE
LIIVA
SUUR - VESKI
KOIDU
VÄIKE - VESKI
RÄHNI
LAATSARETI
KALAMEHE
KÖIE
TUI
HENNO
V SEPA
RIIA MNT
SUUR - JOE
VÄIKE - JOE
VINGI
PIKK
VANAPARGI
LIIVA
KARJA
AISA
PARDI
KAANLI
A H TAMMSAARE PST
SIDE
SIDE
SIDE
VÄIKE - KUKE
KIVI
KOOLI
SUUR - POSTI
Hospital
KARJA
HÕBE
VÄIKE - POSTI
SUUR - SEPA
KARUSSELLI
PAPLI
KAARLI
KUUSE
RANNA PST
A H TAMMSAARE PST
TULBI
KAJAKA
AULI
LEHE
ADAMSONI
AIA
AIA
RINGI
SUPELUSE
PÜHAVAIMU
NIKOLAI
LOUNA
RINGI
KUNINGA
RÜÜTLI
VEE
AKADEEMIA
ÕHTU
ESPLANAADI
PÄRNA
ROOSI
SÄÄSE
SUVITUSE
KAJA
KERESE
MERE PST
ESPLANAADI
RINGI
MURU
SEEDRI
MUULI
SADAMA
LOOTSI
RINGI
LAI
ARU
SUUR-JOE KALDA
TALLINNA
J W JANNSENI
VANA-
SAUGA
LOODE
HAAPSALU MNT
EMAJOE

Mud baths

Airport, Haapsalu,
Tallinn

Suur-Joe

of the economy for the next few years, as the number of visitors each year climbs rapidly towards 100,000. Most still come in the summer when music lovers can enjoy a jazz festival, a zither festival and classical music concerts. Film shows, art exhibitions and opera, combined with much lower hotel prices, make visits at other times equally worthwhile. Spa hotels have their regular guests from Sweden and Finland year-round. Dates of all these events are on the website of the local tourist board, www.parnu.ee; prebooking of hotels during most of them is essential.

GETTING THERE, AWAY AND AROUND

By bus The **bus** station is beside the Pärnu Hotel (see page 245) and within walking distance of several others. There are several departures each day to Tallinn, about two hours away, and to Tartu, around three hours. Buses to Valga stop at Kilingi-Nomme, from where local connections are available to the Nigula Nature Reserve. Buses to Tõstamaa stop *en route* at the port of Manilaid, which serves Kihnu Island. This bleak port has no proper indoor waiting facilities and no catering so it is fortunate that only a wait of 15 minutes or so is necessary before the departure of the boat. Buses south to Ikla serve Häädemeeste and Kabli.

Ecolines (*www.ecolines.net*) and **Luxexpress** (*www.luxexpress.eu*) have between them about 12 services a day to Riga, the journey taking about 2½ hours. Fares vary greatly according to the level of comfort offered on the bus.

There is an extensive local bus network within the town and around the county. A bus map is available free of charge from the tourist office and the website www.bussipark.ee gives all the timetables. If bought on the bus, an individual ticket costs €1, but if bought at a kiosk, the cost is €0.64. Good value is the day ticket for €2 and a ten-day one for €7.67. These have to be bought at kiosks as they are not sold by the drivers.

By air Flights operate from Pärnu to the islands of Kihnu, Ruhnu and Saaremaa but as these services are dependent on fluctuating government subsidies, and often only run once or twice a week, they are unlikely to be of use to foreign visitors. Sometimes it is possible to fly to Ruhnu for the day in the summer, when a flight leaves Pärnu in the morning, continues to Saaremaa and then returns in the afternoon. The websites of the local airport (*www.parnu-airport.ee*) and of Kuressaare airport (*www.kuressaare-airport.ee*) on Saaremaa Island both give current schedules and fares. Visitors needing travel arrangements in the Pärnu area and to the islands can book these through **Reiser Travel** (*Adamsoni 1;* ✆ *447 1480;* e *viivika@reiser.ee; www.reiser.ee*).

By rail The railway station was moved in 1970 well out of town and now only offers one train a day to Tallinn but the embedding of a few metres of track into the pavement opposite the former station recalls the time when trains came to this point. The steam engine placed here was brought from the Lavassaare Museum (see pages 254–5) in November 2006. It dates from 1911 and was used until the 1960s at a cement works. It is probably the oldest surviving steam engine in the Baltics.

TOURIST INFORMATION

The **Pärnu Visitor Centre** (*www.visitparnu.com*) in the Old Town Hall at Uus 4 organises day trips in the county from June to the end of August.

⌂ **WHERE TO STAY** Hotel prices in Pärnu are about 30% higher in the summer season (June–August) than they are at other times. This does not prevent hotels from being fully booked then, so it is essential to make reservations well in advance. No large hotels have opened since 2007, but the demand increases each year as more Russians return to resorts they knew well in Soviet times. Some hotels will insist on a minimum stay of three nights. Visitors arriving without bookings during the peak season or during a music festival are usually presented with the choice of driving either to Tallinn or to Riga, given that the few hotels *en route* are also likely to be full on such occasions. For location of listings see maps, pages 242 and 248.

🏠 **Ammende Villa** (23 rooms) Mere pst 7; 📞 447 3888; e sale@ammende.ee; www.ammende.ee. In commissioning this building as a wedding present for his daughter in 1905, local merchant Herman Ammende made sure he would never be forgotten in Pärnu. It is probably the largest private house in the town, & certainly the most eccentric. The bricks are in no fewer than 4 different colours – yellow, red, green & white – & the timbers vary equally from very dark to totally pale. Polite critics claim it as an example of *Jugendstil* but visitors just arrived from Riga will hardly find any similarities with what they will have recently seen on Albert iela. The wrought-iron railings around the whole estate & the restrictions on parking in the street to hotel guests reinforce the exclusivity that becomes immediately apparent on entering the building. Only some broken cornices & the occasional chipped stone step will detract from this feeling. Nowhere is space lacking. The library, the sitting room & the restaurant could each absorb all the staff & guests without being crowded. All the bedrooms could host a party. The décor throughout has been deliberately assembled from the early 20th century. Pretend that World War I never took place & leave the modern world firmly beyond the railings. Certainly try to forget that in Soviet times the building was a dental clinic. Do not skimp by staying in the annex. Either fully indulge here or stay elsewhere. It is always possible just to come for a concert or to have coffee. The concert programmes can be checked on the hotel's website. Weather permitting, they take place in the gardens, otherwise indoors. **$$$$**

🏠 **Rannahotell** (62 rooms) Ranna pst 5; 📞 443 2950; e reception@rannahotell.ee; www. rannahotell.ee. This hotel is an architectural monument to Estonian Functionalism as well as being the most luxurious hotel in the town. It was built in 1937 by one of Estonia's most famous pre-war architects, Olev Siinmaa, who won a competition organised by the town council to commemorate the 100th anniversary of the

town's establishment as a health resort. Several restorations on, it is still a period piece & worth at least a stop for a meal to get the flavour of pre-war Pärnu. **$$$$**

🏠 **Koidula Park** (39 rooms) Kuninga 38; 📞 447 7030; e reception@koidulaparkhotell.ee; www.koidulaparkhotell.ee. When the hotel opened in 2003, it certainly offered a contrast to its competitors in the town centre. It was built entirely of wood, originally in 1904, & if only 1 room still has the original floorboards, at least the overall design has not changed. All rooms are small & with the showers not divided from the rest of the bathroom, but the quiet central location is more than adequate compensation. The hotel closes Oct–Mar. **$$$**

🏠 **St Peterburg** (53 rooms) Hospidali 6 (but note entrance is in Malmo not Hospidali); 📞 443 0555; e info@stpeterburg.ee; www. stpeterburg.ee. This hotel opened in 2003 in Pärnu's oldest building, an almshouse dating from 1653 but with some wood from the 13th century in the foundations. It is probably the first hotel in Estonia to dare to put up a portrait of Peter the Great in reception. Perhaps the aim is to attract nostalgic Russians as with 53 rooms it is big enough to cater easily for groups. Russians, like the British & Japanese, would enjoy the space in the public areas but would feel short-changed by the lack of pictures in the bedrooms & the absence of baths. **$$$**

🏠 **Strand** (187 rooms) Tammsaare 27; 📞 447 5370; e sales@strand.ee; www.strand. ee. This hotel seems to expand in line with the Estonian economy. 50 rooms in the late 1990s had become over 150 by 2004. Many regulars still insist on the traditional rooms with a lounge downstairs & a spiral staircase up to the bedroom. It used to matter that there was a 500m walk to the beach. Now the hotel feels very self-contained, given all the spa facilities that it offers. **$$$**

🏠 **Tervise Paradiis** (122 rooms) Side 14; 📞 445 1600; e sales@spa.ee; www.terviseparadiis. ee. When this health complex opened in 2004, it immediately became the most talked-about hotel in Estonia. Although other spa hotels in the town have far more rooms, none has a waterpark, or an outdoor pool heated year-round to 30°C. The saunas run on infrared power, which is quicker at raising heat than the traditional coal. 60% of the clientele are retired Finns so there is little risk of having a noisy neighbour. As these residents might be allergic to carpets, no rooms have them. 3 floors are taken up entirely with treatment centres, leaving the 5 higher floors for rooms, all of which have sea views. The higher they are, the higher the price. **$$$**

⌂ **Alex Maja** (10 rooms) Kuninga 20; ☎446 1866; e info@alexmaja.ee; www.alexmaja.ee. After the passion shown in Pärnu for building new spa hotels in 2004–05, it was good to see a return in 2006 to restoration in the town centre, which has since continued. The hotel has only 10 rooms, but with its location, any facilities it cannot offer directly are available on the neighbouring Rüütli Street which parallels Kuninga. Rooms are surprisingly large for a town-centre location. Do not forget to try the restaurant, particularly for its calm surroundings in midsummer when excessive life tends to dominate many others. **$$**

⌂ **Kapten Kurgo Villa** (6 suites & 5 rooms) Papli 13; ☎442 5736; e kapten@kurgovilla.ee; www.kurgovilla.ee. This is an original villa in that it has been totally adapted for family use, consisting of just 6 suites, each with 2 bedrooms, a kitchen & a bathroom, & 5 twin rooms. There is a 2nd building, called the Seamen's House, with naturally simpler accommodation than in the Captain's. It has 5 rooms with 2 tiers, beds on top & a sitting room below. The villa also has a restaurant that is open to non-residents. **$$**

⌂ **Pärnu** (80 rooms) Rüütli 44; ☎447 8911; e info@hotelparnu.com; www.hotelparnu.com. When the first foreigners turned up at this hotel in the late 1980s, they were faced with a mammoth but empty entrance hall, spartan rooms & a drab restaurant. The contrast now could not be greater; as the first hotel in the town with email & a website, it clearly aimed to take over the mantle of the Victoria which used to be the obvious 1st choice for both business & leisure travellers

wanting a central location. Its rooms are all regularly modernised & both the bar & restaurant attract considerable local business. There is wheelchair access. **$$**

⌂ **Victoria** (23 rooms) Kuninga 25; ☎444 3412; e info@victoriahotel.ee; www.victoriahotel. ee. For several years after independence this was the only good hotel in central Pärnu &, as it has only 23 rooms, may well appeal to individuals. Building started in 1920 but shortage of funds prevented completion until 1927. In Soviet times it was given the name 'Voit' (Victory). Some discreet refurbishment & a more inviting reception area would not go amiss. It could then rightly take on again its pre-war name, 'The Grand', which in fact is the name of the restaurant again, as it was given a 1920s look during a refurbishment in 2001. **$$**

⌂ **Villa Artis** (10 rooms) Adamsoni 1; ☎447 1480; e artis@reiser.ee; www.reiser.ee. This guesthouse opened in 2003 & offers the prices of suburbia but the convenience & comfort of a true town house. It is situated just far enough from both the beach & the town centre for quiet to be assured & wisely only serves b/fast so it is also spared bar noise. Stay long enough at b/fast to appreciate the art displayed there & if you come early in the autumn, pick your own apples & pears in the orchard at the back. Its novelty is a resident osteopath. It is totally non-smoking. **$$**

⌂ **Villa Johanna** (13 rooms) Suvituse 6; ☎443 8370; e info@villa-johanna.ee; www.villa-johanna.ee. There are many villas converted to small hotels in Pärnu, but this was probably the first to impose a total no-smoking policy. It combines the space & views of a villa with the convenience of a central location. 4 rooms have balconies & it is well worth paying the slightly higher price for these. **$$**

⌂ **Villa Wesset** (24 rooms) Supeluse 26; ☎697 2500; e info@wesset.ee; www.wesset.ee. This hotel, which opened in 2007, was originally built as a private house in the late 1920s for Pärnu's best chocolate producer, so it is just about small enough to keep a family feel. Rooms are large & many have balconies, but the soundproofing is poor. Fortunately the area is quiet, just far enough from the beach to avoid hearing the festivities taking place there. **$$**

✗ **WHERE TO EAT AND DRINK** Early editions of this book did not have a separate entry for this section as the best food was usually served only in the listed hotels.

8

In 2004–05 there was a turnaround with several restaurants of merit opening, and the trend has continued ever since, with restaurants here being largely recession-proof, but there are many new openings each year. Recent ones include an Armenian and a Latvian restaurant and two branches of an Italian ice cream parlour. This may well result from the Swedish and Finnish spa tourists now in Pärnu year-round and also from the increasing number of music festivals and concerts held away from the peak summer season.

✕ **Asian Village** Rüütli 51; ☎ 442 9488; www.goldendragon.ee. Throughout Europe, the arrival of a Chinese restaurant normally signals the need for varied food, & Pärnu was no exception to this. It was the first restaurant in Pärnu to quote prices in euros & to translate the menu into Russian. To prevent possible competition from Indian & Thai restaurants, dishes from both these cuisines are offered here too & Indian music is usually played in the background. $$

✕ **Kuursaal** Mere pst 22; ☎ 442 0368; www.kuur.ee. This restaurant seats 400 so not surprisingly does not take bookings from individuals. Given the length of the wooden tables, it probably makes sense to come as a party here, or in the hope of being drawn into one. Do not expect haute cuisine from any of the dishes listed on the never-ending menu but see local people enjoying themselves both in summer & in winter, particularly when the live music is played. For those with specific musical likes & dislikes, the bands playing can be checked on the restaurant's website. When live music is not being played, go outside to see the statue of the composer Raimond Valgre (1913–49). Sit on the bench & listen to the recordings of his songs which play when you do so. $$

✕ **Lemon Grass** Superluse 23a; ☎ 447 6200. The menu here is probably the longest in town as it covers almost every east Asian dish known to man, or at least to Western man. It has an intimate feel through much of the year, with tables close together, but in the summer it expands on to an enormous terrace. It is well worth the 10min walk from the beach. $$

✕ **Margarita** Akadeemia 5; ☎ 666 7669; www.margarita.ee. A Mexican restaurant is perhaps surprising here, but in winter is most welcome. Enter when the temperature outside is −10°C, absorb the tropical décor, drink a number of rum cocktails & fool yourself you are in the tropics. Portions are sensible so it is possible to

have more than 1 course in a meal. $$

✕ **Kaks Paari** (Two Pairs) Suur Sepa 13; ☎ 447 4711; www.2paari.ee. There is drink of course in this bar & it is very cheap, being a few hundred metres off the tourist beat. There is plenty of food too, but the real reason for coming here is to play poker. The website suggests coming as a team of 4, which must include at least 1 woman. No rules are given about stakes. Board games are available too, as is snooker, for those not able to control their facial expressions. $

✕ **Pärnu Muuseum** Aia 3; ☎ 443 3488; www.parnumuuseum.ee. In 1988 London's Victoria & Albert Museum achieved instant fame by advertising itself as 'an ace café with quite a nice museum attached'. Visitors here will appreciate the same scenario, as in the summer of 2013, with catering both indoors & outdoors, the café was certainly the busiest part of the building. The cakes, in quality just as much as in size, could only be rivalled in Haapsalu or in Võru, certainly not in Tallinn, & their prices were 20th rather than 21st century. $

✕ **Raehoovi Kohvik** (Townhall Courtyard Café) Nikolai 3; ☎ 449 2922. Lively restaurants appeal to many, but it is good that 1 courageous owner in 2013 realised the potential for a restaurant with minimal music in the background & a location with the crucial necessary distance from a noisy neighbour. The space in the courtyard is generous so conversations which elsewhere would reach dozens of others in the crowded peak season, are certain to remain private here. $

✕ **Vana Pootsman** (The Old Boatman) Akadeemia 5; ☎ 444 0403. With the opening of this pub in 2013, Pärnu has beaten Tallinn for the first Latvian restaurant in Estonia. Expect dishes to be heavier than elsewhere in Estonia, to be flavoured with poppy seeds & the vegetable to be peas or any variety of bean. Come dessert time, it will be hard to tell whether you are eating Estonian or Latvian food. $$

WHAT TO SEE AND DO

A walking tour All the traditional sights of interest to tourists are conveniently located within the town centre, which is still partially surrounded by medieval ramparts. However, a walk should include the Chaplin Centre and the mud baths. One main shopping street, Rüütli, runs through the town and a walking tour can conveniently **start** at the top end, **close to the bus station**. A wide range of architectural styles will be noted both in this street and in those that run off it. The old Bristol Hotel is one of the few brick buildings in Pärnu and dates from the turn of the century. Straight opposite the hotel, on the corner of Hommiku and Rüütli, is a former chemist's shop; the exterior is hardly of note, but the interior has been restored to its original 1931 décor. Work on the exterior started in summer 2004 and finished in 2007. Next door, on the corner of Rüütli and Ringi, is a building that has seen many uses since its construction in 1867. It began as the exclusive White Girls School and more recently was the Soviet military headquarters. It has now rebelled into a casino/nightclub.

Ringli used to be the terminus for the railway, with the station now being the booking office for bus tickets. The 1911 steam engine on the other side of the road was installed there in 2006 to commemorate the 110th anniversary of the opening of the railway between Pärnu and Valga in 1896. It leads into the area of Pärnu which has been undergoing continual rebuilding since at least 2000, and which now boasts the Port Arthur and Pärnu Centre shopping malls. The former is best for cheese at **Juustu Pood** and the latter for ice cream at **Mama Tõnis**. In 2012, the open area between the two centres was given the name Martens Square, to commemorate the Russian international lawyer Friedrich Martens (1845–1909) who was born in Pärnu.

Where Rüütli and Ringi meet is now **Rüütli Square** but the 40 years of its previous life as Lenin Square needed to be obliterated. The building on the left side of the square, now shared between several banks, was the last in Pärnu to be completed in 1940 before the Soviet invasion. From the end of the war until 1967, the first floor served as a temporary theatre. Straight ahead is a monument unveiled in 2009 to commemorate the first signing of the declaration of independence, which took place in Pärnu at the Endla Theatre on 23 February 1918, a day before it did in Tallinn. The monument displays the full text. To the right of the Pärnu Hotel, on the corner of Rüütli and Aia, note the model of the former Endla Theatre which stood on this site before the war. Built in 1911, it had been the best example of *Jugendstil* in Pärnu, and could have been restored after bombing but was totally destroyed by the Russians because of its association with the founding of Estonia.

Leave Rüütli Square on Aia and turn right into Kuninga, so named after King Gustav II of Sweden. This street used to link the Riga Gate, now totally destroyed, with the Tallinn Gate (see page 250) at the other end of the Old Town. Many of the neighbouring large buildings date from the late 19th century and have been schools and colleges for most of the time since then.

Equally impressive are the many open spaces visible from Kuninga; these distinguish Pärnu from other Estonian towns and are the hallmark of **Oskar Brackmann** (1841–1927), who was mayor on many occasions from 1871. The last was in 1918 when the Germans occupied Pärnu and deposed an ethnic Estonian mayor in his favour. Inevitably he in turn was deposed when the Estonians won the town back in November 1918. As a German he had in the meantime suffered deportation to Irkutsk during World War I. His statue here is therefore a modern one by Mati Karmin whose public work can be seen throughout Estonia. The park, bordered by Kuninga, Ringi and Louna, is named after **Lydia Koidula** (1843–86),

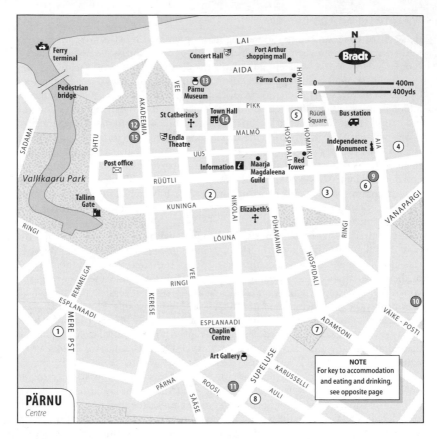

PÄRNU
Centre

Estonia's best-known woman writer. The statue of her made in 1929 was the last work of sculptor Amandus Adamson who died that year. The park has been restored to exactly as it was then, with the import of granite from Finland and bronze from Italy. On the far side of the park is the boys' school attended both by Konstantin Päts, Estonia's leader between the wars during the first independence period, and by Paul Keres (1916–75), Estonia's most famous chess player.

Return to Rüütli along Hommiku and cross it, keeping the pharmacy on your right. On the left is the 15th-century **Red Tower**, all that now remains of the medieval fortifications. Walk along Rüütli into the Old Town taking the second road on the left, Nikolai, and the Baroque façade of **Elizabeth's Church** comes into view. It was built between 1744 and 1747 and is named after the Russian empress on the throne at that time. It has two links with Riga: the spire was designed by the architect Johann Heinrich Wilbern, who designed the spire of St Peter's, and the organ, installed in 1929, is the work of Riga's most famous organ builder of that time, Herbert Kolbe. It was restored in 2013. Returning to Rüütli, note house 21/23 on the left-hand side of the street. This house has entertained two royal visitors, Karl XII of Sweden in 1700 when *en route* to fight Peter the Great at Narva, and then in 1764 Catherine the Great of Russia spent a few nights here on one of her inspection tours around her empire. The house was built in 1681 but the classical façade dates from the early 19th century. The horseshoe displayed on the front is supposed to date from Karl XII's visit. Crossing Rüütli back into Nikolai, you come to the **Town Hall**, which also has a link with Riga. The original Classicist design dates from 1797 when it was built as a private house. It then became first the governor's residence and in 1838 the Town Hall. When it returned into private hands again early in the 20th century, the *Jugendstil* north wing was added, having been designed by Wilhelm Bockslaff, Riga's most famous architect in this field. From 2010, the tourist office has been based in this building. Opposite the Town Hall, on the corner of Uus and Nikolai, is a sadly empty space. This was the site of Pärnu's oldest church, **St Nicholas**, built in Gothic red brick in the 13th century. It was seriously damaged by fire in 1944 but could have been restored. Sadly it was torn down by the Russians, probably because it had been the church of the German community. In 1989, so two years before Estonian independence was restored, a plaque was erected here by the descendants of this community. For some gentle retail therapy, the Maarja Magdaleena Guild at Uus 5 can be recommended for its range of craft shops, particularly for small articles in coloured glass. Workshops are held here for those with artistic ambitions.

St Catherine's Church, close to the Town Hall, was also named after the empress on the throne at the time. It was built between 1764 and 1768 and provided a model for most subsequent Orthodox churches in Estonia. Opening hours for the church are erratic but, if closed, it is worth returning on another occasion to see the bronze, silver and gold filigree pictures and the portrait of Catherine the Great.

On the other side of the road from the church is the 'new' **Endla Theatre** built in 1967 to replace the one destroyed at the end of the war. To the left of the theatre, in the park opposite the post office, is a memorial to the playwright and essayist August Jakobson (1904–70) who fled to Russia in 1941 with the Red Army and was closely linked to the Soviet regime until his death. He even joined a Soviet censorship committee in August 1940 to control the work of his former colleagues. His work in the 1930s had been respected, as he was always keen to expose poor working conditions in factories. Had he been less close to the Soviet regime, he would have had a reputation similar to that of Emile Zola in France. His work was described in the 1960s as 'ideologically militant' so it is not surprising that he is now hardly read in Estonia.

To the right of the theatre, overlooking the river on Aida, is Pärnu's pride and joy, the **concert hall** (*www.concert.ee/parnu*), which opened in the autumn of 2002. Although famous for the music that is offered year-round, Pärnu has never before had a suitable venue for orchestral music and opera. For the €5.75 million it cost it is a real bargain, and, as it is a circular glass building, Estonians can see both by day and by night what activities their taxes are generating. Had the world-famous conductor Neemi Järvi not lobbied and given constant support to the project, it might never have gone ahead. The main auditorium seats a thousand and can be easily adapted for choral or theatre performances; it can equally be turned into a private ballroom. The higher floors are a music school. Neemi Järvi's extended family is as musical as the Bachs and many of them participate in the annual David

Oistrakh Festival (*www.oistfest.ee*) in Pärnu each July. Future programmes at the concert hall can be seen on the website. The entrance and first floor are often used for art exhibitions, pending the building of a proper art gallery in the town.

The red-brick warehouse at Aida 3, opposite the concert hall, has since 2012 been home to the **Pärnu Museum** (*www.parnumuuseum.ee*), which for decades previously was in a totally inadequate concrete box on the corner of Aia and Rüütli Square. It prides itself on covering 11,000 years of Pärnu history, but it is the last 200 of those that will be of most interest, apart from the entrance which is a glass cover over remnants of a former town gate. Film, graphics, music and a considerable range of exhibits bring the varying regimes of these two centuries to life.

Retrace your steps along Vee to Rüütli. Rüütli ends with the house that the Functionalist architect, Olev Siinmaa, built for himself in 1933. He lived here until 1944, when he fled to Sweden. The house is now in private hands, so not open to visitors, but it was previously a medical centre in Soviet times and fortunately was kept in good condition. Many similar houses of his can be seen around the town, although without doubt he kept the best example of his work for his own use. Yet this is a very modest house considering his fame. Turning left at the end of Rüütli leads to the **Tallinn Gate**, now a unique example in the Baltics of a 17th-century town-wall gate. Those in other cities, such as Narva, have been subsequently destroyed. It was originally called Carl Gustav Gate, after the Swedish king, but this was changed after the defeat of the Swedes by the Russians. It was restored between 1977 and 1980, in Soviet times.

Beyond the gate is **Vallikääru Park**, based around the former bastions. These were built by the Swedes in the 17th century, like those in Narva and Tallinn, but were never used, either by them or by the Tsarist Empire, which defeated the Swedes in the early 18th century. Being of no further use, they were handed over to the town in 1835 and by mid-1865 a public park had been created here. Badly neglected in the Soviet era, by 2013 it had mostly been re-landscaped and includes a small harbour and effective lighting so that the area can be enjoyed after dark.

Continuing along Mere and then turning left into Esplanaadi, on the corner with Nikolai is the **Chaplin Centre** (*www.chaplin.ee*). The official name for the building is the Pärnu Uue Kunsti Muuseum (Pärnu Contemporary Art Museum). Charlie Chaplin would probably have approved of the fact that an institution named after him has taken over the former Communist Party headquarters.

Chaplin's name was used to suggest diversity and hope, although the centre concentrates as much on art as on films. It maintains a permanent collection of modern Estonian art, based entirely on donations, and often has temporary exhibitions as well. Much of the display will appeal only to those totally unaffected by obscenity and blasphemy. For instance, in a portrayal of the Last Supper, the disciples have been replaced by nearly naked women, all of course smoking and drinking to excess. A less provocative picture consists of a toilet roll stuck to a block of wood. More sensitive visitors should limit themselves to the website, which shows some of the thousand pictures donated since the opening in 1992, many from abroad.

The centre is open seven days a week, 12 hours a day, and has 15,000 visitors a year so is the complete opposite to a normal Estonian museum, which is either deserted or closed. The centre has diversified over the last few years; catering has already moved outdoors during the summer and a spice shop has opened next to the internet centre, perhaps to show the contrast with the blandness of what was produced in communist days. A more conventional art centre, **Kunstnike Maja**, at Nicholas 27, is next to the Chaplin Centre. It is used largely for sculpture exhibitions.

A five-minute walk along Mere pst ends appropriately at the **mud baths** backed by the sandy beach. These mud baths are also by Olev Siinmaa. Following suitable invigoration, a ten-minute walk back into town completes the tour. Enthusiasts for functional architecture on a grand scale will want to continue along the beach to see the Rannahotell (see page 244).

A walk of about 30 minutes, or a short bus ride south along Riia mnt, is needed to reach Pärnu's two cemeteries, the Old and then the Alevi. The **Old Cemetery** has a remarkably modest Soviet memorial of two tall slabs rather than the bombastic statuary that is normally associated with such structures. They carry the names of Soviet soldiers who died in 1944 whilst fighting in the area, Russians in the Cyrillic alphabet and Estonians in the Western one. This monument fits in with the plain iron crosses and simple gravestones that are behind it.

About 500m further south on the same side of the road is the **Alevi Cemetery** where all the great and the good from Pärnu are buried, but what is surprising is how simple all their tombs are, and very few have statues with them. Oskar Brackmann's has a line from a Goethe poem *Über allen Gipfeln ist Ruhe* (Beyond the peaks, there is calm) famously set to music by Franz Liszt, amongst many others. The Ammande family who built the hotel that carries their name (see page 244) are buried together but there is no hint of the exuberance here that characterises the hotel. Amandus Adamson lies behind the **Independence Monument** he built for the cemetery and which of course was destroyed in the Soviet period. It had to be rebuilt from his designs and photographs that fortunately remained. The monument is now surrounded again by tombs of those who fought for Estonian freedom in both world wars.

After a macabre walk here, respite on the other side of the road is deserved in the pub named after Carl Friedrich Hahn, whose modest tomb is also in the Alevi Cemetery. A landscape gardener, he was a contemporary of Oskar Brackmann and the two would often be seen walking together through the Pärnu parks and gardens for which they could both claim credit. Hahn would always be smoking a cigar, and Brackmann would carry a pointed umbrella, with which he could pick up the few items of rubbish that local residents dared to leave. Hahn lived in this building and behind it is still the arboretum where he tried out new shrubs before planting them in the town centre.

AROUND PÄRNU

Through the summer, the **tourist information centre** (*Uus tn 4* \ *447 3000*; e *parnu@visitestonia.com; www.visitparnu.eu*) in Pärnu's Old Town Hall runs excursions to many of the places listed below.

HÄÄDEMEESTE Visitors who race from Riga to Tallinn, with perhaps just a brief stop in Pärnu, miss a peaceful and elegant section of the Estonian coastline. Häädemeeste and the villages to the south are now able and happy to reveal their international role in the 19th century and their popularity in Estonia as a holiday resort during the first independence period. The construction of the highway a few kilometres inland has spared the coastline the through traffic it used to take, so even in midsummer travel here is congenial. Inevitably in the immediate aftermath of independence, Estonians who could afford to do so travelled abroad but Häädemeeste is now benefiting from an increased interest in taking holidays at home.

8

Getting there and around Buses run every 60–90 minutes along the coast from Pärnu to Ikla, stopping at all the towns and villages *en route*. No local buses cross the border at Ikla, which is about 1km from the bus station at Ainaži. However some of the Tallinn–Riga buses which stop at Pärnu also stop at Ainaži.

🏠 Where to stay

🏠 **Lepanina** (70 rooms) Kabli 86002; 🤙 443 7368; e lepanina@lepanina.ee; www. lepanina.ee. Like several other hotels in Estonia, the Lepanina transformed itself in the late 1990s from barely 2-star to clearly 4-star. That it needs only a postcode for the address shows its current stature. It is in fact set back from the main road & stretches along the coast so that all 70 rooms have a balcony & a sea view. The use of brick for all the outside walls is unusual enough; stranger still is its use indoors. Some of the suites have a private staircase to the beach. Furniture, carpets & linen throughout the hotel are of Estonian production. It is encouraging that Estonian hoteliers no longer feel the need to import such goods. The dining room is built as a ship, giving the impression of being surrounded by water &, for visitors only passing through, offers an excellent 1st or last meal to those combining a tour of Estonia & Latvia. A bonus of an evening visit in low season with the shorter days is to eat seemingly under a starlit sky. A pier was built in 2002 to facilitate boating trips & also to give swimmers direct access to sand, as the beach right beside the hotel is pebbly. The storm that raged along the coast here in Jan 2005 forced some alterations to the structure of the hotel & the beach will now be left wild. Local buses between Häädemeeste & Ikla do not pull into the hotel, but stop along the road nearby. $$$

What to see and do Baltic Germans first mention the village in 1560, but its strategic importance was only realised when the Russians replaced the Swedes as the occupation power around 1700. The gentle beaches that stretch from here well into Latvia made all too easy an invasion from the sea. Although none was ever to be attempted, contemporary visitors can still see the architectural remains of the defences established by the tsarist and Soviet regimes. Economically, Häädemeeste and two villages further south, Kabli and Treimani, would live from the sea. Their large mansions flaunt the profits that many boatbuilders and captains could draw from this activity. Those who broke the British and French blockades of this Russian coast during the Crimean War became particularly rich. Salt was the mainstay of this business.

St Michael's Lutheran Church in the town centre at Häädemeeste shows that not all the money made from shipping was consumed personally. It was built with private funds in the 1870s to attempt to draw back the local population from the Orthodox church, about 1km to the south, which was built, like many others in Estonia at the time, to try to keep them loyal to the tsarist regime. (The Orthodox churches also used the promise of land and education to bring in support.) The architect of the Lutheran church was Johann von Holtz, famous for the number of houses he designed in Riga and for the former Grand Hotel on the Alexanderplatz in Berlin.

The first village south of Häädemeeste is Jaagupi, where the sumptuous villas once housed Soviet cosmonauts during their summer holidays. **Kabli** is now best known as a birdwatching centre (*www.rannatee.ee*), which was founded in 1969 and, together with a similar one at Vilsandi National Park on Saaremaa Island, tracks the migrating flocks each May and October. The ringing centre is beside the beach and visitors can climb the watchtowers. Every autumn about 12,000 birds are ringed at this centre.

The **Jakob Markson Museum** (🤙 *449 8442; no website;* ⊕ *by appointment only*), 3km south of Kabli, is in the house of this clearly very successful captain who spent most of his long life (1840–1930) here when not at sea. This spanned the most affluent era along the coast, which came to an end firstly with the worldwide economic slump and then with the Soviet occupation after World War II. The museum, opened for the first time in 1968, houses a collection shrewdly and assiduously collected from all over Europe. The dolls, the radios, the Bristol blue glass, his home organ and his Stanfords 1890 Map of the World are likely to be of most interest. Note the two china dolls in the window facing the street; whenever Markson returned home, they would be returned to the mantelpiece. The sitting room has been 'updated' into a Soviet style so it shows the furniture most Estonian families would have had in the 1960s. The outhouses are becoming an increasingly important part of the museum and exhibit agricultural machinery from the 19th century. The house has never left the ownership of the family; Jakob Markson's great-granddaughter lives there and is the curator.

Ikla is the village on the Latvian border. The grocery store comes straight from the 1950s with every item being individually weighed and wrapped. Many of the customers are Latvian, given the lower prices in Estonia for most basic items. Until 2007, only local residents could walk across or take their bicycles, as concrete boulders plus border guards prevented any other traffic. Now it is completely open so a visit to **Ainaži** in Latvia makes an obvious extension to travel in this area. Latvia now uses the euro so no currency exchange will be necessary.

AINAŽI (*www.ainazi.lv*) Entering what is now little more than a village, it is hard to believe that in the late 19th century Ainaži was a major centre for naval education, shipbuilding and seafaring. It is about 1km from the border to the **Naval Academy Museum** (Jürskolas Muzejs). This academy served both what is now Estonia and Latvia in tsarist times. The classroom is preserved and so are the teaching materials, which include a British textbook called *Wrinkles in Practical Navigation* and several rubbers (in the British, not American, sense of the word!) from South Shields.

Continuing into the centre of the town, the bus station and tourist office are on the right-hand side of the road. At the time of writing in late 2013, the town website, with information about the museums, is only in Latvian. The **Firefighters Museum** (Ugunsdzēsības Muzejs), which is about 300m from the naval one and on the same side of the road, was founded in 1991 by enthusiastic volunteers and this passion clearly remains. Firefighting in smaller communities was a voluntary activity even in Soviet times so records of their achievements have been carefully maintained and there is also a general history of the town here. The collection is expanding into a shed next door, which houses several fire engines from Soviet times and Dutch ones used later. The Dutch always take fire engines out of service after 20 years, but the new Latvian regime in the 1990s was very grateful for them.

The most famous resident of Ainaži in the Soviet period was the former prime minister of Estonia, Otto Tief, who formed a government in September 1944 for four days between the retreat of the Germans and the arrival of Soviet forces who of course arrested him. Banished first to Siberia, then allowed to live in Ukraine, he was by the 1960s allowed to live just over the border of what was then Soviet Estonia but not actually in it. Only shortly before his death in 1976 was he allowed to return home.

HALLISTE, SAARDE AND MÕISAKÜLA A visit to these three places can be done as a day trip from Pärnu or they make sensible stops *en route* to Viljandi or Valga. Saarde is 25km east of Pärnu, Mõisaküla a further 12km east, and then Halliste another 12km, taking the Viljandi and not the Valga road.

The church at **Halliste**, a hamlet rather than a village, stands out for miles around. It suffered as so many did during both the Livonian War, in which the Swedes drove out the Russians in the late 16th century, and then a hundred years later when the reverse process took place during the Northern War. However, when wars stopped fires started and what one has to hope will be the last one was in 1959. It followed earlier fires in the 19th century. The church was a ruin between 1959 and 1989 but the determination of the local community during the Soviet perestroika period got it rebuilt and the first service was held at Christmas in 1991. The community was undoubtedly galvanised by their pastor, Kalev Raave (1926–2004), who had a career as a communist journalist and a collective farm director before turning to the Church. These earlier roles gave him the local contacts he needed for materials and money and then perestroika enabled him to raise funds abroad, well ahead of other churches which only established contacts after re-independence. His spirit clearly lives on in the enthusiastic and widespread congregation that now attends the church.

The exterior follows the Gothic designs of the 19th-century building, which replaced the one destroyed by lightning in 1863. An altarpiece by Jüri Arrak, Estonia's most famous contemporary artist, inevitably dominates the whole interior. The church seats 800, and often does for concerts, even though it is situated in the heart of the countryside. Hopefully other works of art will soon cover its plain walls.

Saarde church has fortunately had none of the problems suffered in Halliste and Mõisaküla. The current building dates from 1859, although it incorporates certain elements, such as the wall behind the altar, from an earlier late 17th-century one. Other earlier items include the memorial plaque to King Charles XI of Sweden and the bell in the tower. The most famous painting here is not the current altarpiece but is *Christ in Gethsemane*, displayed on the left-hand side of the church. It is by Ludwig von Maydell, the 19th-century painter best known for his work in St Olav's Church in Tallinn and also for the altarpiece in the church at Põlva (see page 216). Improvements continue all the time. It is hoped to replace the dull 1920s furnishings with the more exuberant style of woodwork that was here in the 19th century and to replace the mottled glass in the windows. It is unclear why a Gothic interior was chosen, yet the windows are clearly Romanesque. The church stayed open in Soviet times although the orthodox one in the village was closed then.

Mõisaküla had its heyday in the 1920s and 1930s when two narrow-gauge railway lines operated through the town, and the railway workshops here served the whole country. In their early days, they even repaired the Tsar's trains. Carriages, but not engines, were made here. The Soviets closed all these lines during the 1970s although some, including the line from Pärnu to Riga which passes through Mõisaküla, were upgraded to the wider standard gauge and trains served this route until 1996. Sadly with the tracks now uprooted in several places, this service cannot be revived and the town has not really been able to find a new role since then. Railway enthusiasts should see the museum here, located in the Town Hall, as so much has been saved from earlier times and the extensive range of photographs displayed supplements the collection. The most valuable item on display is probably an ashtray from the imperial train of Nicholas II.

In 2014 the Lutheran church here should again be open. It dates from 1934 and was destroyed by fire, perhaps an arson attack, in 1983. Restoration started in 2005.

LAVASSAARE Fifteen kilometres to the northwest of Pärnu is the **Lavassaare Railway Museum** (*www.museumrailway.ee*). Out of 630km of narrow-gauge railway that ran across Estonia until the late 1960s, the only 2km left in action are located here and the line is operated by volunteers as it has no commercial potential. The network had been built up between 1900 and 1940 and was initially maintained under the Soviet regime but, in the early 1970s, tracks were either widened to the standard gauge or closed. The museum brochure refers to this as 'liquidation as the structure of the narrow-gauge railways was a threat to Soviet ideology'. Fortunately the threat cannot have been that great, otherwise the wider range of memorabilia now to be seen in the museum building would not have been kept. It in fact opened in 1987, when the Soviet era still had four years to run. Bus 44 runs from Pärnu to Lavassaare. The museum is open only in the summer, and on Saturdays the train runs about every hour. Two plans are being considered for the future. One is to move the museum to Türi in central Estonia, as this town is the railway centre of Estonia. The other is to bring the engines and the collection to Pärnu railway station and to use some of the currently abandoned track to Mõisaküla. For current opening times and an update on future plans, check the website.

LIHULA, HANILA AND VIRTSU Many tourists driving from Pärnu to continue their holiday on Saaremaa Island completely ignore three places which deserve a stop *en route*.

Lihula The history of Lihula over the last 800 years is a story of sudden dramas interspersed with centuries of peace. It was clearly a major fortress in the early 13th century, before the Teutonic Knights seized it from local Estonians and fighters from Saaremaa. Evidence is gradually being found of settlements going back a further thousand years or more and this has given rise to its being called 'Estonia's Pompeii'. The knights understood its strategic location and completed a new castle in 1242. The excavations that have taken place over the last 35 years have now revealed the layout of the castle as it must have been then. It survived until the Livonian War between Sweden and Russia at the end of the 16th century when it was largely destroyed and the local community looted much of the stonework.

The manor house in front of these excavations dates from 1840 and the interior still suffers from its 40 years as the headquarters of a collective farm. It now houses **Lihula Museum** (*www.visitestonia.com/en/lihula-museum*) with a strange mixture of themes. Plans of the old castle are to be expected, as are the archaeological trophies displayed there. What is totally unexpected is the space given to Soviet communications, such as telex machines, telephones, radios and television sets.

At the other end of the town is a small sign to the **town cemetery**. Most visitors go to see what is not there rather than what is, and are surprised to hear that one object brought down an Estonian government in 2004, because it was removed under pressure from many international groups. The object was a statue of an Estonian soldier in German uniform, although without the swastika. At the same time, references to the Soviet Union were removed from an earlier monument. A plaque with an explanation is now the only record of this incident. How to commemorate Estonians forced to fight either for the Germans or for the Russians (and in a few cases for both on different occasions) during World War II is clearly going to remain a contentious issue for many years to come. At the end of the Soviet era, Estonia inherited a large number of monuments recording its 'liberation' from the Nazis in 1944 but, in the eyes of most Estonians, what followed was just as bad as what it replaced. In April 2007 there would be the *Bronze Soldier* controversy in Tallinn (see page 45) when the government removed a Soviet monument, which proved the continuing tension to which this issue gives rise.

Hanila The town of Hanila is just off the main road from Lihula to Virtsu but is clearly signed. Its **church** will in a way be a good introduction to those on Saaremaa as it dates from the late 13th century and could well have been built by the same architects. However, it was largely destroyed in the Livonian Wars so what is now worth seeing is the elaborate Baroque pulpit originally dating from 1707 and made from a range of local softwoods. The columns are based on the story of John the Baptist. It suffered badly from neglect in the Soviet period, particularly after the church was closed in 1970 but it was properly restored around 2000. The nearby local museum is, as so often in Estonia, the collection of one local person devoted to a specific theme, in this case clothing, textile design and fabrics. The **August Tampärgi Museum** (❨ 477 2260; www.hanila.ee/muuseum) carries his name. The stress is on winter clothes, rather than summer ones. His life spanned the entire 20th century, as he died in his nineties, so the collection reflects this.

Virtsu The small port of Virtsu serves the boats to Saaremaa Island. Tourists usually only have cause to stay here if they have missed their boat or failed to prebook for a busy ferry on a summer Friday but the **Oldtimer Museum** (Vanasõidukite Virtsu Talumuuseum) (www.missestonia.ee/unicsenior) should provide ample solice for those with a sense of humour and strong necks, who should factor into their schedules half an hour or so for a visit here. The museum is at the entrance to the town, about 2km from the port. On the ground are, as would be expected from the museum's name, a range of old cars, some extremely elegant. There are also 19th-century bicycles and carriages. It is, however, the museum's website that reveals its further appeal. The ceiling is covered with pictures of winners of the annual Miss Estonia competition.

SINDI AND TORI These small towns make a congenial day trip from Pärnu either by bus or car; alternatively they can be visited *en route* to Türi (see pages 150–1) and Paide (see pages 151–2) for those continuing a tour to central Estonia. **Sindi** is on the railway line from Pärnu to Tallinn, but as at present (2013) there are only two trains a day on this route they are unlikely to be of use to tourists. Hopefully, as it has already done elsewhere in Estonia, the train service will soon improve.

Sindi owes what fame it has to the textile industry and to the drive of the man who founded the factory here, Johann Christoph Wöhrmann (1784–1843). The **museum** in the small wooden building at Pärnu mnt 26a describes his life and the history of the textile industry in the town right up to the present day, but also finds space to cover leisure activities in the town, largely music and lacemaking. Wöhrmann is best known outside Estonia for the gardens (Vērmanes in Latvian transliteration) in central Riga which carry his name, but most of his life was devoted to the textile industry and to the business which he established here in 1830, having fled from Poland because of the popular unrest there at the time. Production started in 1834 and by 1840 the company was allowed to use the imperial eagle on its labels as formal recognition of the quality of its goods. His company really then ran the town until the Soviet occupation in 1940, paying for the railway, schools and medical insurance. It introduced a consumer association in 1902, based on a British model. Sindi was probably the first town in Estonia to have softened water. The company even printed its own money in 1919, which was regarded as much safer than any printed by the various armies fighting in Estonia at that time. Sadly most of the red-brick houses the company built for its workers were removed in 1983.

The business was nationalised in the Soviet era when production continued with about 1,200 workers involved. In 1958 its products were exhibited in the Soviet pavilion at the Brussels World Fair. In the 1980s it was privileged to be given the foreign currency to buy machinery from West Germany and Japan. It could not adapt quickly enough after independence, so went bankrupt in 1992, although was soon revived under new ownership, but now employs only 100 workers.

It is hardly known that Sindi was the birthplace of the American painter Andrew Winter (1892–1958) who fitted in a career in both the British and the US navy before settling down in Maine to paint seascapes and landscapes. The town hopes in due course to be able to acquire a few of his pictures to exhibit here.

The **Tori Stud Farm** (*www.torihobune.ee*), easily visible on the eastern side of the main road running through the village, has had as long and an even more successful history than the textile plant in Sindi. It celebrated its 150th anniversary in 2006 and the tougher economic conditions of 2009–10 seem to have had little effect on its expansion and appeal. Perhaps being 3km from the railway station was always a stimulus to proving the role horses can play in both work and pleasure. About 100 horses are regularly based here, with ten to 20 foals born each year. It is their names that are recorded on plaques, not those of mere humans. The museum here displays carriages dating back into the 19th century, together with sledges which of course were important for transportation then, given the length of Estonian winters. The wheels were all removed and hidden during the Soviet occupation to prevent the carriages from being taken to museums in Russia. That a horse features on the town coat of arms shows how important the farm has been.

A little to the north, on the western side of the main road is **Tori Church**, sometimes known as the **Estonian Memorial Church to Soldiers**, as it commemorates all Estonians who fell in battle, no matter what their cause. Most of course were killed on both sides during World War II but it is now sadly necessary to remember those who have died in Iraq and Afghanistan, where Estonian forces have taken part in NATO action. The original church dated from 1854 but was badly damaged when the Germans were retreating in 1944 and blew up the neighbouring bridge across the river. The initial Soviet plan was to take down what remained of the structure and to use the stones in road building, but it was then decided to use it as a shooting range instead. Reconstruction started at the end of the Soviet era when, under perestroika, Moscow no longer blocked free religious observance. Money then came entirely from abroad, but as soon as Estonia had its own currency, many private individuals contributed.

The organ and benches are from Sweden, the red granite from Finland. The church was sufficiently complete in 2001 for it to be reconsecrated that year. Note the altar of three millstones with pieces of iron in between, a symbol of Estonia being crushed by two enemies at once. The altar is the work of Mati Karmin (sculptor of the *Kissing Students* in Tartu, and the *Estonia* memorial in Hiiumaa, amongst many others) as is the equestrian statue outside – of St George and the dragon – which was unveiled on 20 August 2003. This date is the anniversary of the day in 1991 when Estonia re-established independence.

KIHNU ISLAND

A visitor to the island of Kihnu immediately becomes a member of the community. A tour will visit the church, the museum and the lighthouse but it could also include delivering the potatoes for the school lunch, stopping at the daily clothes market and having conversations with passers-by. As the population is around 600, the guide will know everyone. He or she will know the exact population too and could probably predict fluctuations at least six months ahead. A drop would be unusual since Kihnu families remain large, unlike in the rest of Estonia.

Fishing is again the lifeblood of the island. Visitors in the summer will see the nets stretched out across the fields, waiting to be mended. In the spring they are used to catch Baltic herring, and in the autumn perch, pike and eel. The tougher fishermen then turn to rods in midsummer and again in midwinter, having dug a hole in the ice. The nets cannot be used in the summer because of the frequent attacks by seals.

The traditional division of roles between men and women continues on the island. The local brochure writes of the support given by local women to their husbands, and of their knitting, cooking and baking. The women stay at home, bringing up their large families and the men undertake the arduous tasks needed to earn a living either on the barren land or out at sea. Previous generations of men were engaged in shipbuilding and served in local and foreign merchant navies. The men are proud to have broken the Crimean War blockade in the 1850s to get salt and iron from Gotland. Boatbuilding began here in the following decade when the war was over, with the traffic mainly being in transporting stone to Riga. Nobody made a fortune on the island so there are no grand houses. By 1914 the population had reached 1,200 and there were 68 boats. Boatbuilding obviously came to an end in the Soviet period and has not been revived. The islands take their current social cohesion very seriously and divorce remains rare. As wedding parties last three days, perhaps this is the explanation.

Transport is usually by motorbike with a sidecar for the children. There is uncertainty about opening a petrol station which might encourage more cars. Travelling in those that are based on the island, seatbelts are rarely worn. Doors are always left unlocked, except for those on the toilets in the community centre!

Unlike several other islands such as Ruhnu or Vormsi the population here has always been largely Estonian. The appeal of individual landholdings, offered by the Russian Orthodox Church in the mid 19th century, converted many from their previous Lutheran inclinations. Just before World War II, the population had again grown to 1,200 but this could not be sustained and many were unemployed or reluctantly had to leave the island to find work. About 25% fled in 1944. In March 1949, floating ice spared the island the evacuations that the Soviet authorities imposed elsewhere in Estonia and perhaps the collective approach to work islanders had always adopted also helped. The islanders were not pleased in 1971 when their collective was incorporated into one based at Pärnu and quickly took advantage of independence in 1991 to go their own way. In 1995 they were pleased at the international coverage given to them, when skirts they had donated were used in the 'Mother Tree' montage that was given by Estonia to the United Nations.

The island is now serious about promoting tourism. Estonians come for long stays at the campsites or in the farmhouses. Finns and Swedes may soon follow suit. Some may want to see the birds, in particular the goldeneyes and the cormorants. All will like the complete lack of commercialism. Other foreigners usually come for the day from Pärnu, taking the morning boat out and the evening boat back, having arranged to hire a car and a guide beforehand. As the island is 7km long and 3km wide, it is, however, just about possible to walk everywhere.

GETTING THERE AND AWAY
By boat During the summer, boats operate at least twice a day from the port at Munalaid, about 40km from Pärnu. Buses from Pärnu to Tõstamaa connect with each sailing. The bus journey takes about an hour, and the boat 45 minutes. Taking a boat from Munalaid around 09.00 and one back at 16.30 allows enough time to see most of the island. (Munalaid should not be confused with Manilaid, a small

island just off the coast to which ferries also operate from here.) There is also a boat directly from Pärnu to Kihnu, which takes two hours in each direction and allows for four hours on the island. Schedules and fares for all these boats are on the website www.veeteed.com.

By air In the winter, and sometimes in the summer too, occasional flights operate from Pärnu to Kihnu and when the ice is thick enough it is possible to drive to Kihnu from the mainland. The website of Pärnu airport (*www.parnu-airport.ee/ eng*) gives current schedules. Visitors who have not made travel arrangements to Kihnu prior to their arrival in Pärnu can arrange this through **Reiser Travel** (*Adamsoni 1;* \ *447 1480;* e *reiser@reiser.ee*). Groups can also charter boats and planes for private journeys from Pärnu.

WHAT TO SEE AND DO The centre of the island brings together the market, the largest shop (there are four others), a café, the church, the museum, the school and a cemetery. The café turns into a nightclub every evening during the summer and on Friday and Saturday during the winter. Kihnu people do not forget their dead, particularly if the person concerned died young and tragically. Some visit the cemetery every day, and the quantity of fresh flowers and candles left there bears witness to this. The community centre, completed in 2002, is large enough to accommodate the whole population under one roof. The island suffered no damage during the war and no Soviet building was added afterwards so many views are identical to those seen in the 1930s. The Soviets were so unconcerned with Kihnu that they left the airport with a grassy runway and did not tarmac the gravel roads. The **church** was built in 1715 but was extended in 1858 when it became Russian Orthodox. As a concession to its earlier use, benches are provided for the congregation, where it is normal practice to stand during Orthodox services. The cemetery has many iron crosses from a hundred years ago and then some recent additions: families who fled in 1944 are bringing back the remains of their dead for reburial in their true home and the church tries to find room for them here rather than in the general cemetery. Perhaps the most famous grave is that of Enn Uuetoa (1848–1913), better known by his nickname Kihnu Jõnn, a reckless seafarer who took to sea after only three days of training. He died on his boat *Rock City*, which is not surprising. What is surprising is that he lived as long as he did. His remains were brought back from Denmark in 1992.

    Kihnu Museum, on the other side of the road, took over the former schoolhouse in 1974. It displays the range of tools and nets used in the fishing industry. Note the family marks on the tools to identify them. It also has some signs from the collective farm that covered the entire island. The pictures are mainly by local sailors, and many were composers too. There are several pictures donated by the family of **Jaan Oad** (1899–1984), who was born in Kihnu but who made his name in Canada. He worked in Kihnu as a carpenter and sailor and continued his woodworking when he fled to Canada in 1944. Painting was always his hobby and under other circumstances he could have become professional. His main subject, shown in the paintings here, is the small boats that were built on the island during his childhood. The colour of the sky reflects the mood of the picture. Those depicting a wreck, or one which shows the flogging inflicted on sailors who took part in the 1905 uprisings, have an appropriately dark sky. Other paintings displayed here, with a similarly nautical theme, are by Georg Vidrik (1904–42) who died in the siege of Leningrad. There are plans to restore Jaan Oad's house and his paintings may then be exhibited there.

8

The current school, situated behind the old building, was completely rebuilt in 1998. Any parent will envy the small class sizes, the impeccable cleanliness and the variety of facilities offered. Eight teachers are provided for about 70 pupils and the prospectus gives the assurance that, in addition to studying the national curriculum, girls will be taught local handicraft skills.

Britain has made its mark at the southern tip of the island, since all the parts of the **lighthouse** built there in 1864 came from the Tividale Company in Tipton, Staffordshire. It is 29m high and, as the highest natural point on the island is only 8m, it gives the impression of being much taller than it really is.

SAAREMAA ISLAND

Estonians are often characterised as 'reserved', yet the mention of Saaremaa, the country's largest island, always evokes a passionate response, both from those who now live abroad and from those who have remained in Estonia.

Most families have both tragic and happy memories linked to Saaremaa. In 1944, thousands fled to exile in Sweden rather than face a renewed Soviet occupation of the island. Until 1989, Saaremaa was classified as a frontier zone so travel was severely restricted, even for local people, while visitors from outside the Soviet Union were banned completely.

The year 1989 would turn out to be remarkable for Saaremaa. The capital Kuressaare got its name back, having been called Kingisepp since 1952, after a local revolutionary, Viktor Kingisepp. His statue, which had only been erected in 1988 to celebrate the 100th anniversary of his birth, came down a year later. A delegation came from Gotland in January, and from the Saaremaa Islanders Association in Toronto during the summer. This association had 2,000 members, and after 45 years of no contact, few can have ever expected to see their homeland and their relatives again. One of the most famous returnees was Professor Paul Saagpakk (1911–96) who combined academic work in English literature with the compilation of an Estonian–English dictionary which will undoubtedly remain a standard work for decades to come.

Memories of the status of Saaremaa in the 1930s as a major health resort, when its fame was such that it warranted guidebooks in English and German, meant that this popularity was instantly restored when travel restrictions were lifted. The 1930s and the 21st century now blend together remarkably well. The island's sole major transport link, an hourly ferry to the mainland, ensures that only discerning and determined tourists make the effort to come. Both horses and windmills maintain their role in local agriculture, and traffic lights and cat's eyes are still unnecessary. The décor in several restaurants is specifically pre-war, while mud baths and concerts are major attractions for long-stay tourists. Between 2002 and 2004 three enormous spa hotels were built in the capital Kuressaare, but elsewhere 'large' hotels have 15 rooms, yet have satellite television, and the reception desk will accept credit cards. Although Kuressaare has a population of only 15,000, there are now two 24-hour shops, three ATMs, parking meters and an Irish pub.

HISTORY Estonia's troubled history has always hit Saaremaa particularly hard. Twice the Danes unsuccessfully attacked the island in the early 13th century. However, in January 1227 the Teutonic Knights brought an army of 20,000 across the frozen sea and established German rule, which would last, despite frequent rebellions, until 1559. The next 90 years would see five different conquerors, first the Danes, then the Swedes to be followed by another Danish invasion, then the

Russians and finally the Swedes again in 1645, following their victory in the Thirty Years War. The Swedes lost all their Baltic possessions to the Russians in 1710. The British navy under Sir Charles Napier blockaded the island in 1854 to prevent supplies reaching Russia during the Crimean War, and occupied it for one day. As the Russians had already fled to Pärnu and the castle at Kuressaare no longer had any military significance, there was no need to stay. The year 1875 saw the first regular passenger and cargo boats to Riga. The Tsarist Empire came to an end in 1917, but Saaremaa was immediately re-occupied by German troops who only finally left in November 1918.

The devastation of World War II, the deportations to Germany and Russia and the 'boat exodus' to Sweden led to a reduction in the population of more than 30% from 60,000 in 1939 to 40,000 in 1945; it stayed around this level during the Soviet occupation but by 2013 had dropped to 35,000. The sudden departure of the Soviet military after re-independence reduced the percentage of Russian speakers from 30% to 3%. Cemeteries and memorials to all those killed on Saaremaa during the two world wars have now been restored or rebuilt. Estonians, Germans and Russians lie beside each other in equally dignified surroundings, together with members of the Forest Brothers, the guerrilla movement that fought the Soviet occupation in the late 1940s. There were about 40 brothers on the island and their struggle lasted until 1950, when their leader Elmar Ilp was killed.

The late 19th century saw a major growth in the links between Saaremaa, the Russian mainland and other Baltic states. For the first time in its history, the island prospered as its agricultural products reached ever-wider markets. Small-scale industries linked with fishing developed, but the lack of minerals prevented the establishment of large factories. As a health resort, Kuressaare developed as rapidly as Pärnu and Haapsalu, benefiting during the Crimean War from the number of soldiers sent here to convalesce. The end of the war in 1858 saw the start of a steamer service from Riga, which ensured a constant stream of visitors every summer. Such prosperity returned quickly after World War I, as the health facilities were again needed by invalid soldiers. Meticulous statistics were kept at the sanatorium: we know, for instance, that 1,178 visitors stayed in 1924 and that between them they enjoyed 23,371 mud baths.

The local airport reached its heyday in the late 1940s when ten to 14 flights a day linked Saaremaa with the mainland. About 2,500 passengers a week used it then, although it would only be in 1958 that electricity would come to the airport, replacing candles, gaslights and radio batteries.

One coherent policy links the tsarist era, the first independence period, the Soviet occupation and contemporary Estonia – an interest in, and commitment to, the Vilsandi National Park (see page 274) which is situated along the west coast of Saaremaa and includes 160 islands. Now, as in the past, human activity has to be compatible with the needs of migrating birds and 500 species of plants. This was not difficult during the Soviet era as the ban on small-scale fishing and the use of pleasure boats in a frontier zone left the reserve totally undisturbed, but pressure on the park is growing. Inland from the west coast, at Viiudumäe, a second reserve was founded in 1957. Travel agents (see page 54) can book specialist English-speaking guides in both reserves.

Kuressaare, with a population of around 156,000, was fortunately spared much damage during most of the wars that raged elsewhere on the island. Here, at least, the succession of conquerors left a worthy heritage of Baroque, Gothic and Classicist architecture and the town is too small to have suffered industrial pollution and urban sprawl in more modern times.

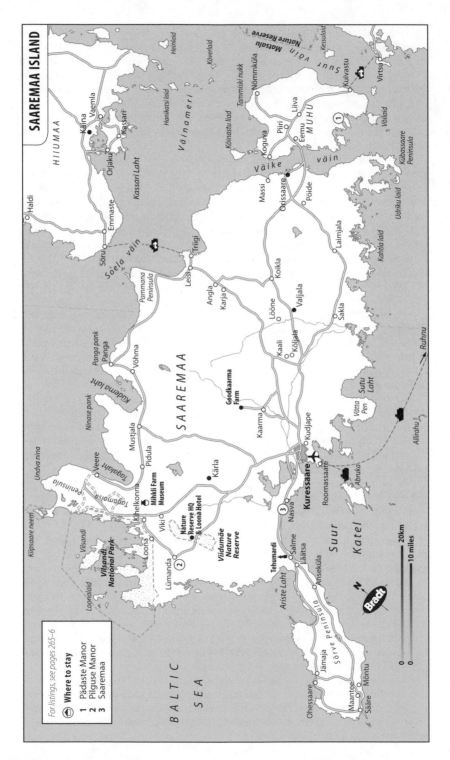

SAAREMAA ISLAND

HIIUMAA

BALTIC SEA

For listings, see pages 265–6
⊙ **Where to stay**
1 Pädaste Manor
2 Pilguse Manor
3 Saaremaa

MATSALU Nature Reserve

Suur väin

MUHU

Väike väin

SAAREMAA

Vilsandi National Park

Viidumäe Nature Reserve

Sõrve Peninsula

Suur Katel

Kuressaare

Goodkaarma Farm

Mihkli Farm Museum

Nature Reserve HQ & Loona Hotel

0   20km
0   10 miles

N Bradt

GETTING THERE AND AWAY

By boat The car and passenger **ferry** from the mainland port of Virtsu operates hourly to Kuivastu in the summer. Kuivastu is on the island of Muhu which is linked by a causeway to Saaremaa (June–September) from 06.00 to 21.00 and every two hours during the rest of the year. Icebreakers are used in winter to ensure the maintenance of the service but it is often possible in January and February to drive across the ice to both Saaremaa and Hiiumaa. Exact schedules for the ferry can be checked on the Saaremaa Shipping Company Ltd website (*www.tuulelaevad.ee*). The journey takes about half an hour. It is essential to prebook car spaces at peak times such as Friday afternoons to the island and Sunday evenings back to the mainland. This can be done by travel agents abroad (see pages 53–4) in conjunction with hotel and car-hire bookings. However, it is much more economical to take the bus from Tallinn to Kuressaare and to prebook car hire on Saaremaa as prices there are much lower than on the mainland. The bus travels on the ferry and its place is guaranteed; the fare from Tallinn to Kuressaare is about €15 each way and the service operates every two hours, the total journey time being four hours. As on other routes, pensioners can get a 50% midweek reduction on the buses operated by SEBE. There are twice-daily services to Pärnu and Tartu. A car and passenger ferry service operates three times a day from Triigi to Sõru on Hiiumaa Island and local buses connect with these services on both islands. Details of this ferry service are also on the website www.tuulelaevad.ee.

By air Flights operate twice daily between Kuressaare and Tallinn and, as they are heavily subsidised by the Estonian government, are an attractive way to travel. If booked reasonably far ahead, the fares are the same as the bus fares quoted above. Full details of these services are on the website of Kuressaare airport (*www.kuressaare-airport.ee*).

GETTING AROUND

There is a network of buses across Saaremaa and Muhu islands, apart from those which link them to the mainland and which can be used for local travel as well. The tourist office in Kuressaare has timetables for all these buses, as well as for ferries and flights.

TOURIST INFORMATION

For visitors who need to make arrangements on arrival or who wish to book additional services such as car hire, boat hire and guides, there is an office of **Arensburg Travel** in the bus station.

WHERE TO STAY

In Kuressaare Hotels in the town are mainly small, three-star locations, converted from private properties. They are all heavily booked during the tourist season from May to September, with many rooms pre-sold to Estonian in-bound tour operators. It is essential to book well in advance. During the peak summer season, which is roughly from mid-June to mid-August (although each hotel defines it differently), prices are about 20% higher. Lower prices are offered during the winter, from November to April. For location of listings see maps, pages 262 and 270.

Arensburg (46 rooms) Lossi 15; ⧠ 452 4700; e arensburg@arensburg.ee; www.arensburg.ee. The main building facing the street dates from the late 18th century & during much of the 19th was the town house of the von Nolckens, prominent on the island in law, administration & as landowners. However the last member of the family to live here, early in the 20th century, was a linguist

8

& theologian. Because of his reduced financial circumstances, he let out much of the building as an officers' club. It became a bank in the 1920s & then a court in Soviet times, both of which roles explain the strong double doors at the street entrance. Diners in the old restaurant will find it hard to believe that this was where local residents could be sentenced to years in Siberia & that the wine bar in the basement is where they awaited their trial. Fortunately tragedy & horror is now in the past & pleasure is the sole aim of its new role as a hotel. It opened as a hotel in 2002 but soon saw the scope for a spa in the town centre rather than in the outskirts where the competition then was. Rooms are divided half & half between the old & the new sections, but all prices include use of the swimming pool. Most have baths & all are much larger than might be expected in a former town house. However, it is worth considering one of the suites, either the *Opera* in the new building with its signed pictures of all the major performers at the Saaremaa annual opera festival or the *Arensburg* which has a balcony overlooking the town. The website will facilitate any decision. **$$$**

🏠 **Georg Ots** (90 rooms) Tori 2; ☎ 455 0000; e info@gospa.ee; www.gospa.ee. One of 3 enormous spa hotels that have opened beside the port since 2000 (the others are the Meri & the Rüütli). All present themselves as health & family centres, with guests not needing to venture outside the complexes. They are not targeting the ill, but the fit who want to stay that way & those who think they are showing their age, even if they do not feel it yet. They are mostly booked for at least a week at a time by regular tourist groups from Scandinavia. **$$$**

🏠 **Grand Rose Spa** (55 rooms) Tallinna 15; ☎ 666 7000; e info@grandrose.ee; www.grandrose.ee. Within the space of a year (2006), a modest hotel in the town centre was transformed into a large resort, one that not only has a swimming pool but one filled with seawater. This is, of course, in addition to all the spa facilities. A terrace and outdoor dining has been added since. **$$$**

🏠 **Linna** (18 rooms) Lasteaia 7; ☎ 453 1888; e linnahotell@kontaktid.ee; www.linnahotell.ee. The reception area may be small but where space really matters, in the rooms, it is granted in abundance, & many rooms have balconies too. The location down a side street ensures peace & quiet

& the 5min walk into the town centre is hardly a burden. The hotel does not have a restaurant open to individuals, although group meals can always be provided. **$$$**

🏠 **Arabella** (51 rooms) Torni 12; ☎ 455 5885; e hotell@arabella.ee; www.arabella.ee. Few entering the hotel now could imagine its many years as a student hostel. Not being in the town centre gives it the advantage of guaranteed quiet & plenty of parking space for coaches, cars & bicycles. Sports groups like to stay here & are a stimulus to other guests to keep fit whilst in their company. **$$**

🏠 **Johan Spa** (47 rooms) Kauba 13; ☎ 454 0000. Unlike most family hotels in Kuressaare that have stayed small, this one has greatly expanded, & now includes an outdoor but heated swimming pool & a rooftop jaccuzzi. The new block has an excess of concrete, but this does not affect the comfort of the rooms. Its location 100m away from the main street ensures a peaceful environment. **$$**

🏠 **Kuursaal** (6 rooms) Lossipark 1; ☎ 453 9749; e info@kuressaarekuursaal.ee; www.kuressaarekuursaal.ee. Being beside the moat & overlooking the castle, it is hard to imagine a better location in Kuressaare than here. Understandably the rooms are only available in the summer, but the restaurant below, with its international menu, is open year-round. International too are the artists invited to perform at the regular concerts held here. **$$**

🏠 **Repo** (14 rooms) Vallimaa1a; ☎ 453 3510; e repo@saaremaa.ee; www.saaremaa.ee/repo. A large family house, tastefully converted into a modern hotel. It attracts many regular clients, perhaps as much for the flowers outside as for the rooms inside. The b/fast room is decorated with copies of drawings by Eduard Wiiralt, a prominent Estonian artist of the first period of independence who fled to Sweden & then Paris after the war. He died in Paris in 1954. **$$**

🏠 **Vanalinna** (12 rooms) Kauba 8; ☎ 455 5309; e info@vanalinna.ee; www.vanalinna.ee. This was one of the 1st guesthouses to open on the island when tourism again became possible after a gap of 50 years. Those early visitors are happy to return here & do so regularly; if its small rooms remain more simply furnished than elsewhere, the family atmosphere is valued highly. No other café can match the variety of cakes served & no other restaurant manages the variety of sauces for pike-perch. **$$**

Georg Ots (1920–75) was Estonia's most famous singer, who will always be linked with the country's most famous song 'Saaremaa Waltz'. He did join the Communist Party, but protected many artists who would not and ensured that Estonian songs reached both Finnish and Russian audiences. Those who remember him still treasure his memory and mourn his early death from cancer. The ferry that linked Tallinn and Helsinki in Soviet times was named after him, as is a Saaremaa cheese. Being abstemious, although not in any way teetotal, he made it clear that he did not want any alcoholic drink named after him.

'Meri' means 'sea' in Estonian so is an obvious name for a hotel in this location and 'Rüütli' means 'knights', a street name used all over the country. However, Lennart Meri was the first president of Estonia after the re-establishment of independence, and Arnold Rüütel was the second so the choice of names must have been made with that ironic background in mind, given the animosity between them. It is perhaps surprising that the hotels are run by the same and not by competitive companies, but they are at least on opposite sides of the road and not side by side.

Outside Kuressaare

⌂ **Pädaste Manor** (25 rooms) Muhu Island; ☏ 454 8800; e info@padaste.ee; www.padaste. ee. Many Estonians have talked about converting a country estate into a luxury hotel. Few actually get round to doing so, & even fewer make a success of it, but that is what has happened here. Imre Sooäär, who now styles himself 'Lord Imre', has combined a flair for both architecture & public relations to ensure that his hotel has received more worldwide publicity than all other hotels in Estonia put together. The hotel refuses to publish a brochure, on the grounds that all potential clients will have access to their website. 2008 saw a welcome expansion when the manor house opened as part of the hotel; previously accommodation was restricted to the former outhouses. Note its modest design compared with those on the mainland. The mixed use of granite & limestone, a light stone alternating with a dark one, is characteristic of Muhu from that time & this manor house was probably the first building to use it. Having last been properly restored in 1890, a great deal needed to be done, whilst respecting what remained & the use that could be made of local materials, some abandoned elsewhere. Hence the 100-year-old oak beams. The restaurant is a glass terrace carefully built into former woodland beside the house. The orange trees grown inside are of course from elsewhere but give a pleasant

summer feel to the centre, whatever the outside weather. The base of the terrace is built from 150kg blocks of granite. It is hard to believe the building & its surroundings, by then an old peoples' home, was abandoned in 1980 & then left derelict for nearly 20 years. The hotel encourages guests to experience the immediate nature. This can be just in the herb garden to check that there really are 16 varieties of basil growing there or it can be on more serious birdwatching or botanical ventures. (Saaremaa boasts 23 species of orchid). However, the rooms in the main manor house all have an electronic environment that could keep guests occupied throughout their stay, including access to 20,000 different pieces of music. The room with a poetry library must be unique too. **$$$$$**

⌂ **Loona** (11 rooms) Vilsandi Nature Reserve (about 30km from Kuressaare); ☏ 454 6510; e info@loonamanor.ee; www.loonamanor.ee. This hotel, a former manor house dating from the early 19th century, was opened in Nov 1997 & forms part of the reserve's HQ. It has an exhibition centre to show the reserve as it now is, & a fossil collection to show its past. It caters for small birdwatching groups or individuals keen to be based in the reserve. The website provides an introduction to the reserve, as well as to the hotel. Heritage Tours (*www.heritagetours.ee*), who are based in the hotel, offer specialist visits in Vilsandi

& can hire bicycles, by far the best way to travel around the reserve. **$$**

🏠 **Pilguse Manor** (25 rooms) ☎454 5445; e info@pilguse.ee; www.pilguse.ee. This manor is in the village of Jõgela near Lümanda, about 35km from Kuressaare. It was built in the 18th century & is the birth place of Fabian von Bellinghausen (1778–1852) who, despite his name, was in fact Russian. He led the first Russian expedition to Antarctica in 1820 – the next one was not until 1946. Accommodation here is simple & geared to families wanting a country base with

ample facilities for children. **$$**

🏠 **Saaremaa Hotel** (40 rooms) Mandjala (13km from Kuressaare towards the Sõrve Peninsula); ☎454 4100; e saarehotell@saaremaa.ee; www. saarehotell.ee. Previous visitors to Saaremaa will remember this hotel as the Mannikabi. It continues to be modernised every few years. Situated in a pine forest close to the sea, this is an ideal location for visitors with a car wishing to combine sightseeing & relaxation. The hotel likes to point out to guests that the only noise likely to disturb them is that of the birds singing. **$$**

✖ **WHERE TO EAT AND DRINK** Restaurant and café prices leapt up between 2005 and 2007 on Saaremaa more than anywhere else in Estonia, almost reaching Tallinn levels in some cases. Fortunately the situation is now very different and restaurants that survived 2009, as with hotels, are those that went back to their 2004 prices and so could cater for a local market during the winter. The number of restaurants and cafés has changed little in Kuressaare, the capital, although more are opening elsewhere. Hopefully, as Saaremaa extends its season beyond the traditional July and August, this trend will continue.

Places listed below, except for the Jurna Turismitalu, are all in central Kuressaare (see map, page 270).

✖ **Chameleon** Kauba 2; ☎668 2212; www. chameleon.ee. By day the attention is on children's activities, particularly face painting, outdoors if possible. When the paints are put away, out come the cocktails, the clientele ages by 15 years or so & the action moves indoors. Listen to the website to see if the evening music is likely to appeal. **$$$**

✖ **Lavendel** (Lavender) Tallinna 9; ☎455 4902. This restaurant opened in 2012 with the aim of using as many local products in its menu as practical. This certainly has not limited the menu, given the range of meat, fish, herbs & vegetables available on the island. The décor is that of a traditional farmhouse, & its small size therefore gives it a family air. **$$$**

♀ **JK Pub** Kauba 5; ☎455 5045. The passion at this pub has to be for football (soccer) as match schedules always dictate what is shown on TV. **$$**

♀ **John Bull** Lossipargi 4; ☎453 9988. This riotous pub has no closing time & brings together anyone under 30 with a passion for both rock music & motorbikes, be they local, Estonian or foreign. **$$**

✖ **Jurna Turismitalu** Kaarma village, 6km from Kuressaare; ☎452 1919; e jurna@neti.ee; www. saaremaa.ee/jurna. Roasts & grills, both of fish & meat, are the mainstay of meals here. The website has the full current menu. Otherwise, an

ideal centre for a long evening, both in summer & winter. Outdoor log fires burn year-round. **$$**

✖ **Kohvik Classic** Lossi 9; ☎455 4786. Situated almost next door to the Arensburg Hotel, it serves lighter main meals but more lavish teas. **$$**

✖ **La Perla** Lossi 3; ☎453 6910; www.laperla. ee. When it opened in 2004, it was immediately dubbed Saaremaa's 1st real restaurant & it is not hard to see why. It is 100% Italian & makes no attempt to pander to local taste. Do not ask for potatoes or rice here, & while they will serve beer, the food really does only deserve wine as an accompaniment! **$$**

✖ **Veski** Pärna 19; ☎453 3776; www.veskitrahter. eu. In a windmill behind the Town Hall, which has perhaps been rather over-restored, but the folk music & local dishes make for a congenial, 1960s- or 1970s-revival experience. It did in fact open as a restaurant in 1974, having stopped grinding in 1941. With its 4 floors & 150 places, it should always be possible to secure a table, even in midsummer. **$$**

✖ **Mamsils Pirukapood** Turu 2; ☎5660 9447. Anywhere in Estonia, walking a few metres away from the main street will always result in a pleasant surprise, & this is the reward for so doing in Kuressaare. This is a café, not a restaurant but many are the tourists who buy their pies here for a picnic or to eat elsewhere later in the evening.

'Pirukapood' translates as 'pie shop. The building is shared with the oldest chemist's on the island. $

A WALK AROUND KURESSAARE Without doubt, a tour of the capital must start at the **castle** (*www.saaremaamuuseum.ee*), the best-preserved medieval fortress in Estonia, which for many centuries combined the role of episcopal residence, prison and sanctuary. The basic quadrangular structure took 40 years to build between 1340 and 1380 and the massive walls were added in the 15th century. The Germans, Danes, Swedes and Russians all maintained the original structure but the Russians withdrew their garrison in 1836 and from then the castle no longer had any military significance so escaped damage in later wars. It was therefore not attacked by the British during the Crimean War. Vestments and weaponry from each of these periods survives and is on display. Not even bishops could live flamboyantly on Saaremaa in the Middle Ages. Austerity and simplicity are the impressions that remain. The original heating system still functions. Fortunately an early penal system does not – those sentenced to death in the second-floor Hall of Justice were allegedly thrown down a 20m shaft to be devoured by the animals waiting eagerly below.

There is an extensive exhibition of the history of Saaremaa up to 1940. The later period is of most interest to visitors; a wide range of memorabilia from the first independence period was hidden during the Soviet occupation but is now on view and is described in English. This section could do with a redesign but at least the exhibition that opened in 2006 makes up for this. It covers the German and Soviet occupations, concentrating in particular on the World War II period. It is 'hosted' by a wax model of Konstantin Päts, Estonia's pre-war president whose last major tour outside Tallinn was to Saaremaa on 20 and 21 August 1939. Films and recordings bring that tour back to life and show the genuine enthusiasm with which he was welcomed. On 23 August, his subsequent fate was determined by Germany and the USSR in the Molotov–Ribbentrop agreement. A year later he would be in prison in Russia, as would be most of his cabinet colleagues, and many would soon be dead, although Päts himself was not in fact executed by the Soviet authorities and lived on in prison until 1956. For all Estonian visitors, the message is very clear. The 50 years between 1940 and 1990 were a mixture of horror and waste.

The year 1988 was the year of absurdity as the exhibition makes clear. On 28 January, the leadership of the Estonian Soviet Socialist Republic banned displays of flags and emblems of 'countries that had exisited earlier'. On 23 June the same people would officially declare that blue, black and white were again the Estonian national colours.

It is easy to miss the natural history gallery, housed in a basement close to the entrance. Apart from displaying every animal and plant that can be seen on Saaremaa, it has a special section devoted to juniper wood, on which the island's economy will doubtless continue to be based. It is a very flexible material for furniture and the berries are a basis for gin.

During the summer, there is a full programme of concerts inside the castle; the surrounding park often hosts song festivals and carnivals. The castle stays open in theory till 19.00 every night during the summer but be ready to do battle with recalcitrant staff if you want to stay after 18.45 as they are determined to slam the doors on visitors as early as possible. From the photographic point of view, the best shots of it are to be had from the port during early evening.

The landscaping of the park dates from 1836, the date mentioned above when the garrison was withdrawn from the castle. Work proceded slowly, and the final

I was born during the first period of Estonian independence 1918–40 in Saaremaa, a large beautiful rural island with many meadows, fields, some lakes as well as birch and juniper trees. On our farm we did not have electricity. Therefore, we had to rely on oil lamps and candles. Water was brought up from the farm's well. There was of course no running water, so we had to use an outside toilet which was cold to use in winter: we had then to be careful so that our bottoms did not get stuck to the toilet seat.

During the harvest time, wheat was collected from the fields. A large threshing machine that separated the wheat from the stems and from the tares would arrive. After the machine had done its work, there was celebration, plenty of food and drink was available. I remember jumping over bodies on the floor, for the men and women had been exhausted by work and play and had fallen into deep sleep.

In 1940 Estonia was invaded by Stalin's armies and things changed dramatically. Large pictures of Lenin and Stalin had to be put on our windows, blocking the valuable outside light. Bicycles, radios and the Bible were confiscated and, if found, severe punishment was meted out. Once a Russian armed with a rifle at whose end a bayonet was stuck entered our house in order to check whether we still had any prohibited goods. It was very frightening. Some evil men had denounced my father to the Russians claiming that he had been in contact with German parachute soldiers. He was asked to tell the Russians where they were hiding. Of course, he had no idea. Nonetheless he was arrested, interrogated and only released after a few days. Fortunately he was not tortured, which was the fate of most prisoners who often were killed and thrown into the well of Kuressaare Castle.

Before the outbreak of the war between Germany and Russia, Estonian men, including my father, were conscripted by the Russians. An uncle, my mother's elder brother, too, had to fight in the Russian army. When the Germans invaded Estonia, his younger brother was conscripted by the Germans. It meant that the two brothers were fighting each other, an appalling fate, but one that was to afflict many Estonian families.

The Germans started to bomb Estonia in 1941 and destroyed quite a few farms in Saaremaa. One day we had a fortunate escape. One aeroplane just missed our farm and crashed in a nearby wood. My father, together with another man, managed to escape from the Russian army. They hid in a farmhouse where the farmer gave them his clothes to wear in exchange for the Russian uniforms, which were made of very strong material. The two men hid under mattresses when they heard Russian soldiers come. The Russians ate most of the food and fell asleep.

When the Russians began to reoccupy Estonia in 1944, my parents decided to

layout that we now see dates from 1890. The 1861 memorial is to a graveyard that was cleared as part of this landscaping. Before walking into town, take a look on the seafront at the statue in front of the spa hotels of Estonia's mythical giant hero Suur Toll and his wife Piret, bringing in a catch of fish. This dates from 2002 and is by Tauno Kangro (see page 46).

Kuressaare owes its architectural affluence to Balthasar von Campenhausen, a deputy governor of the tsarist province of Livonia, who lived there for 15 years from 1783 to 1797. A plague devastated the town in 1710 and by the 1760s fewer than a hundred buildings, mainly thatched wooden cottages, were occupied. In their places were to come large, stone, Classicist houses with red-tiled roofs. Many had leave the country. Early one morning my father and my grandfather cycled to Atla village. My grandfather knew that a boat would sail from there to Sweden. They went with a rowing boat to a small island. They intended to spend the night in a small farm or barn. However, in the evening they heard a boat and then the sound of men coming to the house. Assuming that they were Germans, they hid under mattresses. But to their surprise Estonian was spoken. They discovered that the men were Estonians who came from Sweden to pick up clergymen and some important people and take them to Sweden. But they had lost their way and found themselves in dangerous waters at the bottom of Vilsandi lighthouse between large rocks and close to the German coastguards. A local young man told them that there was another smaller island, Salava Island, nearby, which was surrounded by deep water. With the young man's help they reached that island safely. In the morning the young man cycled to Koimla village and told us to go to Salava Island. My uncle, who had escaped from the German army, came with us. Our horse pulled the wagon, which was partly filled with hay. I was with my mother and sister as well as with my aunt and her mother. Since my uncle wore his German army uniform, we were prepared to hide him under the hay in case the Gestapo came to ask us where we were going. If they found us, we intended to say that we were going fishing. Fortunately we reached Salava Island without any difficulty. It was a clear night. My uncle burnt his German uniform. We were not able to take anything with us, but I did manage to pick up some family photographs. Unfortunately, there was not enough space on the boat for my aunt, her mother and my uncle to come with us.

I remember being very seasick on the boat, but when we reached Gotland Island in Sweden early in the morning we were escorted to a large room where my father and grandfather, who had gone ahead, met us. There was also hot chocolate and biscuits to greet us, a most wonderful sight that I had not seen for a long time. But soon I felt sad because the other members of the family had had to stay behind. We had our own flat and I went to school there. Understandably my grandfather was very unhappy to be without his wife and daughter and decided to go back to Estonia. However happy he was to be reunited with his wife and daughter, everything else was terrible for him. Because my aunt was not able to tell me the truth since all letters were censored, I discovered it only when I came to Estonia in 1993, for the first time after an absence of 49 years. The Russians did not believe his story but were convinced that he was a spy and imprisoned him for three years. After his release he was so harassed that finally he was unable to bear it any more and hanged himself one night in the attic.

courtyards, stone walls and decorative gateposts. Leaving the castle grounds, return towards the town centre along **Lossi** where houses number 12 and 15, almost opposite each other, stand out as examples from this period, despite the imitation Gothic portal added to number 15 in the 19th century. (Number 15 is now the Arensburg Hotel so this building is described on pages 263–4.)

Next on the left is **St Nicolaus Church**, built in 1790. The frieze and the hanging kerchiefs show the dedication to Classicism at that time. As we approach the Town Hall Square, houses become appropriately grander. Note numbers 6 and 7 with their stone window frames, pilasters and wide cornices. Number 7 was the police station, but no new tenant had taken over the building by 2013. Number 1 has

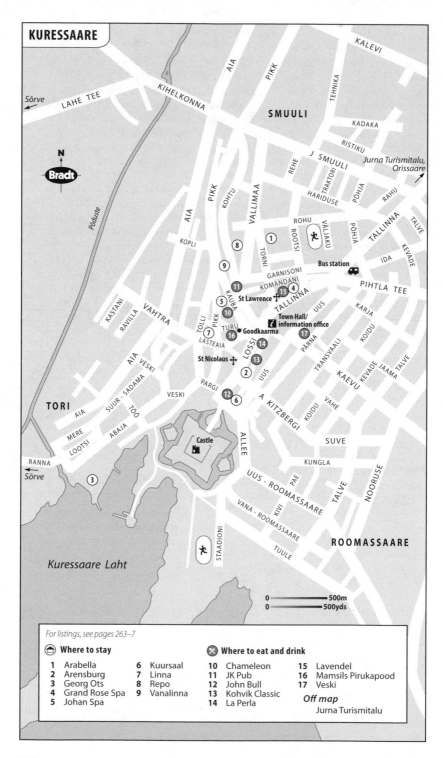

KURESSAARE

Sõrve

LAHE TEE

KIHELKONNA

AIA · PIKK · KALEVI

SMUULI

KADAKA

RISTIKU

Jurna Turismitalu,
Orissaare

REHE · J SMUULI · TRAKTORI · PÕHJA · RAHU

HARIDUSE

PIKK · KOHTU · VALLIMAA · ROHU · VALJAKU · TALLINNA · TALVE

AIA · KOPLI

ⓘ

⑧

⑨

TORNI · ROOTSI · PÕHJA · IDA · KEVADE

Bus station

GARNISONI
KOMANDANI

PIHTLA TEE

KASTANI · RAVILLA · VAHTRA

⑪ ⑮ ④
St Lawrence
⑤
⑩

TALLINNA · UUS · KARJA · KOIDU

TOLLI · PIKK · KAUBA

TURU
⑦ ⑯ · Goodkaarma

Town Hall/
ℹ information office

⑰

LASTEAIA

LOSSI · ⑭

PÄRNA · TRANSVAALI

KAEVU · KEVADE · JAAMA · TALVE

AIA · VESKI

St Nicolaus ✝

② · UUS

⑬

KOIDU · VAHE

SUUR · SADAMA · TÖÖ

VESKI

PARGI

⑫ ⑥

A · KITZBERGI

TORI

AIA · MERE · ABAJA · LOOTSI

Castle

ALLEE

SUVE

KUNGLA

NOORUSE

RANNA
Sõrve

③

UUS · ROOMASSAARE

PAE · TALVE

STAADIONI

VANA · ROOMASSAARE

KIVI

ROOMASSAARE

TUULE

Kuressaare Laht

0 ———— 500m
0 ———— 500yds

N
Bradt

Põduste

For listings, see pages 263–7

always been the seat of county government so has been well maintained under all political regimes. Opposite the police station is the **monument** to Estonians killed in the 1918 War of Independence against the Germans and the Russians. The original, by Amandus Adamson (see page 45), was destroyed, not just once, but twice by the Soviets since the Germans allowed it to be rebuilt during their occupation. This was the site for just one year of the statue of Viktor Kingisepp (see page 260) erected in 1988 on the 100th anniversary of his birth but which was pulled down the next year as part of the re-indepence campaign.

Entering the square, the **Town Hall** is on the right. It dates originally from 1654 but only the 'guardian lions' at the entrance are part of the original structure. Fortunately the Classicist and Baroque features that were added during frequent restorations blend well. The most recent restoration was in the 1960s, which included the dolomite stairs at the front of the building. As a typical concession to modern, commercial Estonia, one room in the main building is let out as an art gallery, and the basement has been discreetly converted into a restaurant. The Town Hall also houses the **tourist information office**. This is the best place to buy postcards and books on Saaremaa, since it is much cheaper than most shops or hotels, and they have a wide choice. The office is open every day during the summer. They also keep all the local bus timetables for travel around the island and to other parts of Estonia. Behind the Town Hall is one of the island's largest windmills, no longer in use as such but restored and converted into the Veski restaurant (see page 266).

Just off the square at Kauba 3, **Goodkaarma** (*www.goodkaarma.com*) opened a shop in 2009 for products from their farm (see pages 275–6). Their website gives full details of what they produce, but their specialisation, unique to them on the island, is organic soap. Opposite the Town Hall is a small market with tasteful souvenirs, including salad spoons, beer mugs and butter dishes carved from the local juniper wood. The array of woollen goods sold throughout the summer is a reminder of the weather Estonia has to endure for much of the winter. Prices here are a little lower than in Tallinn as the goods are all locally produced; this work provides useful employment out of the tourist season.

Coming out of the market back into the square, turn right into **Turu** and then right again into **Kauba**. Here the whole architectural history of Kuressaare is represented, with the first buildings of the 21st century already planned for this street. Numbers 5 and 11 are careful restorations of 17th-century, single-storey, Baroque residences whereas numbers 7 and 10 are again Classicist buildings with broader windows, cornices and decorative carvings. Number 10 is the café of the Vanalinna Hotel.

Return to the square and turn left past the market into **Tallinna**. Number 9 is one of the few wooden houses to retain some of its original façade, although the stone columns were restored in the 1980s. It is currently shared between the local newspaper and the Lavendel restaurant. Number 11, probably Kuressaare's largest private residence until World War II, has retained much of its 18th-century stonework, as has number 19, which has always housed various governmental offices. It is now the customs office. St Lawrence Church, on the corner of Torni and Tallinna, dates from the 1830s, although a church has been on this site since the 17th century. In August 2003 the 13 stained-glass windows, totally paid for by private donations, were unveiled. The artist is Urmo Raus who now lives in Holland. (It was because he lived abroad that his work was not accepted in Tartu.) Whilst working here he had to wear a gas mask as protection against the gold vapour. The abstract designs represent St Lawrence who distributed the emperor's treasure amongst the poor.

On the other side of the road, number 20 has maintained the original design of its Classicist façade but has had to be frequently restored. It was a theatre in the 1930s and it is hoped that funds can be raised for it to be reopened on this basis. Currently it is an art gallery.

Turn left into **Rootsi** and then left again into **Komandandi**. Just before the junction with Torni, on the right-hand side of the road, is the surprisingly modest single-storey house that belonged to Balthasar von Campenhausen during the 15 years that he lived in Kuressaare. It is now a music school.

The walk can end here, but for those interested in late 19th-century buildings, it is worthwhile returning to the castle grounds to visit the **Kuursaal**, which after several years of uncertainty was reopened in its original style in 2012. Outside it has added an open-air cinema that can function regularly given Saaremaa's dependable summer climate.

On the other side of the road, note Pargi 5a. During the Soviet period this building had great significance, as it had been the childhood home of the Estonian communist **Viktor Kingissepp** who was executed in 1922. He lived there until 1906 and returned once more in 1913 but, as he was subsequently involved in clandestine work, the next nine years of his life were spent largely in hiding in Tallinn. To prepare to commemorate the 100th anniversary of his birth in 1988, the house was turned into an extensive memorial to his life.

In the early 1990s the museum removed most references to him and focused on his conventional father Eduard Kingissepp (1856–1926) and called itself the Citizen's Museum. It finally closed in 2004 and the building is now a college. In 1955 the name of the town was changed from Kuressaare to Kingissepp but ironically, in 1988, which was still in the Soviet period, it reverted to Kuressaare under the pressures of the burgeoning independence movement. The streets that compulsorily bore Kingissepp's name in every Estonian town were immediately given back their pre-war names. (There is still a town with his name in Russia, between Narva and St Petersburg, but Kingissepp is now completely forgotten in Estonia.)

Visitors in May and June should continue the walk by taking the road beside the college, called Veski, along to the Saaremaa Valss Hotel/Spa Centre. This is when all the gardens in this part of the town can be enjoyed. A number of different small roads lead back to the town centre, all of which have similarly worthwhile gardens.

THE SÕRVE PENINSULA Before World War II, about 6,000 people lived on the peninsula, mostly engaged in boatbuilding and fishing. Bitter fighting took place here in 1944 between the retreating Germans and the advancing Russians. By 1945 the population was down to about 1,500 following German and Russian deportations and the exodus to Sweden. Most of the area became a military base, although fishing was slowly revived in the 1980s when a daily flight took eel, perch and herring to expensive Moscow restaurants. A visit now is a surreal experience, seeing what was abandoned by the different armies that fought there and speculating on how the area could recover from 50 years of neglect. A day is needed to drive or cycle along this 95km itinerary. Whilst it follows a bus route, the service is not sufficiently frequent to allow stops at all the sights mentioned, although a shortened tour could nonetheless be done this way. Take a picnic and, if driving, fill up in Kuressaare as at the time of writing there are no petrol stations on the peninsula.

Kuressaare must be one of the smallest towns in the world with a bypass; the Sõrve road is the southern sector of it. Leave town on Kihelkonna and turn left at the roundabout where it meets the bypass (Ringtee). After 8km, pass the village of **Nasva**, now best known for its yacht club, based at a hotel built at the end of a pier. For those unable to reach Sõrve, this is the best place to enjoy late sunsets or dramatic storms. After a further 8km, note the obelisk on the left, which is the **Soviet War Memorial** at **Tehumardi**. Local dolomite is blended into the concrete that always dominates such monuments.

Beside the road are the renovated graves of several German soldiers. No German graves or memorials were allowed during the Soviet period but current government policy is to commemorate all fighters during the many wars that raged across Estonia. Tehumardi was the site of one of the worst battles during the German retreat in autumn 1944. About 300 Germans and 200 Russians were killed during the one night of 9/10 October. In all, about 10,000 troops on each side would be killed before the Soviet army could conquer the whole island. Fourteen villages were largely destroyed, as was much of the forest.

Three kilometres south of Tehumardi is **Läätsa** with a small, smoked-eel processing plant. It produces only two to three tons a year now compared with 200–300 tons before the war, but it is planning to expand. After a further 3km is **Anseküla**. Its lighthouse has been rebuilt but beside it are the foundations of the church destroyed in 1944. Note the cross erected here in 1990 to commemorate the church. After 16km is perhaps the saddest village on the peninsula, **Mõntu**, with a ruined manor house and former fishing village turned into an oil refinery. Remains of its barbed-wire entanglements show its crucial role in the Soviet defence system. However, after the war, it was used for shipping potatoes to Riga. In 2005 a summer ferry service to Ventspils in Latvia started to operate from here and it certainly helped to revive the local community.

Two kilometres further on, turn right to **Maantee**, a completely deserted Soviet rocket station. Poles are left but no wires, rows of empty squares represent former windows, and weeds are slowly beginning to grow again in the soil polluted by leaking oil. There are many other smaller, similar sites throughout the Baltic republics; it is a pity that the Russians chose not to leave with more dignity and consideration. After a further 3km comes the end of the peninsula and **Sääre Lighthouse**, now a meteorological observation post. The current building dates from 1960 although the first one was built in 1770. The tsarist armies set up a defence station here during World War I, but it never saw action. It is not usually possible to climb the lighthouse although ample views towards the Latvian coast can be enjoyed from the ground. In 2013 a visitor centre with a lighthouse museum opened here (*www.sorvekeskus.ee*).

On the beach there was for several years a shipwreck that dated from Christmas 1995 when 80 Kurds landed, they assumed, in Sweden. They were in due course returned to Latvia but only after they had been fêted by the islanders.

Continuing along the west coast, look out immediately for a clump of houses, one with a garden full of military memorabilia. There is a small private museum here, the **Sõrve Military Museum**, which opened in 2008. It does not have a website, but it shows much of the weaponry used by both sides in World War II. What captions there are have been written in Estonian, so note the word *saksa* which means German and *vene* which means Russian, in order to distinguish who used what. After 2km, turn left to **Stebeli Commando**, a gunnery point built by the Soviets in 1939 under a military agreement imposed on the Estonians that autumn. Like its tsarist predecessor at Sääre, it was never used. It has four underground storeys, which have not yet been excavated. Soon the scenery becomes Estonian again. There is a windmill at Ohessaare and at **Jämaja** is a church that survived the war intact. It was built in 1864 and although the Germans used it for stabling horses it was, surprisingly, reopened as a church by the Soviets. The cemetery has a metal cairn memorial to the *Moero*, which was sunk by the Soviet air force on 22 September 1944. It had 3,000 refugees on board, of whom only 650 survived. This tragedy was of course never reported in Soviet times and subsequently has been overshadowed by all the books and films about the sinking of the *Gustloff* in January 1945, which claimed 9,000 lives. The second memorial is to a boat that sank in 1908 while carrying rails to Tallinn. Keeping along the coast road, after a few kilometres another shipwreck used to be visible here. This was a Greek oil tanker that capsized in 1980, to the delight of the Soviet border guards and the local Estonian population who, in an unusual display of co-operation, completely looted it and had their first taste of Western consumer goods ten years before anyone else on the island. The wreck broke up in the mid-1990s. From Salme (where there is a petrol station), return to Kuressaare through Nasva, leaving the horrors of the 1940s behind.

TOURING SAAREMAA AND MUHU ISLANDS Most churches, museums and other attractions are open daily from early June until the end of August. At other times, guides can usually arrange an opening, obviously with advance warning. Saaremaa has a team of dedicated tour guides who are well worth using to amplify the itineraries described here. During the summer, tour operators book them well in advance for individuals and for groups and this is advisable too at other times of year. Museums have fixed admission charges but most churches now 'suggest' a donation of €1–2 per person to help their high maintenance costs.

Day one Leave Kuressaare on the Kihelkonna road and after 12km turn left towards Lümanda. In the hamlet of Viidu, turn right and after 3km a sign indicates a right turning which leads after about 200m to the headquarters of **Viidumäe Nature Reserve**. This building was a leper colony until the turn of the century when it was converted into a scientific research centre. The whole reserve is only 16km², and consists entirely of forest or swamp; yet it is home to 700 different species of butterflies and 200 species of moths. There is also a unique spring fen that grows here, now called Saaremaa Rattle, which was found for the first time in 1933. Returning to the main road, an observation tower comes into view. Built on the highest point of Saaremaa, which is 60m, the tower adds a further 23m so gives a good view over the reserve and the neighbouring villages. It is an 8km drive to the next town of **Lümanda**. Although not on the coast, it was traditionally a boatbuilding centre and this work is now being revived. Four hundred residents escaped in 1944 on the boats they hurriedly built for this purpose. Turn right towards **Kihelkonna**, and **Vilsandi National Park** is reached after about 5km. Turn left on entering the reserve for the headquarters at the hamlet of Loona. The hotel here (see pages 265–6) was built in 1997 and is an ideal base for birdwatching enthusiasts.

The park includes 160 islands and is named Vilsandi after the largest. It is situated halfway between the hibernation areas of central Europe and the breeding grounds in the Arctic for about a million birds, although only a few hundred birds reside permanently on the reserve. No building is allowed within 200m of the sea in order to protect them. With its maritime climate, the reserve is warmer than other parts of Estonia in winter with no more than 60 days of snow a year, half of what is normal on the mainland. As a result, a larger range of plants grows here than is possible elsewhere in the country.

Returning to the main road, Kihelkonna is a further 4–5km. The **church** dates originally from the 13th century when the town had far greater importance as a harbour than it does now. The altarpiece, carved in 1591, has survived remarkably well. The picture of the Last Supper and the didactic texts in Latin and German are characteristic of that period. Bell towers built beside the church rather than as part of it were common in the 17th century but this is now the only one remaining on Saaremaa. The tower was added in 1899 to a height of 60m and it is possible to climb it for a view over the island. It is in fact the highest point in Saaremaa and has therefore also served as a lighthouse. The organ dates from 1805 and is probably the oldest functioning organ in Estonia. There were frequent minor alterations carried out in the middle of the 19th century, but the basic structure has been retained. The stained glass dates from the 1980s, the end of the Soviet period. In either very good or very bad weather a detour can be taken at this point to the leaning lighthouse at **Kiipsaare**, on the south of the Tagamõisa Peninsula. It was built in 1930 and a storm in 1992 washed away the extensive sandy beach that used to surround it. The final 2km are accessible only on foot, but the long summer sunsets visible from here make the walk worthwhile. Otherwise leave Kihelkonna on the Kuressaare road for a short detour and, after about a kilometre, stop at the **Mihkli Farm Museum** which is on the right-hand side of the road in the village of Viki. Such museums are common throughout Estonia but this one has particular items to note such as the high stone walls and the long chimney hood which suggest a Latvian model rather than an Estonian one. It also has its own windmill. The tools and furnishings are all from this site; nothing has been brought from elsewhere. Return to Kihelkonna and continue to the **Tagamõisa Peninsula**, an area of wild scenery for walking and relaxing amongst the lakes, cliffs and beaches. Boats from Sweden and cruises use the small harbour at Veere. There are several routes back to Kuressaare; a leisurely drive will take about 45 minutes.

Day two Leave Kuressaare on Tallinna, cross the ring road and take the next turn left after 3km. Turn left again after a further 3km and continue for 5km to **Kaarma**, famous for its dolomite mine. This stone was used not only for the castle at Kuressaare but also in buildings as far away as Tallinn and St Petersburg. Some has even been used on the Moscow metro. It is fortunate that stone rather than wood was always the main building material on Saaremaa so more early churches have survived here than on the mainland. **St Peter's Church** at Kaarma dates originally from 1270 and was probably built by the Germans as proof of their successful conquest of the island. Ironically, the inscription beside the portal giving the final completion date as 1407 is the earliest written in Estonian. Inside, two stone carvings should be noted, the figures of Peter and Paul on the central pillar and the animal carvings on the base of several pillars. The dogs and lions represent good while deer, pigs and wolves depict evil. Some of the 16th-century wooden altarpiece remains, but the stone and wooden pulpit is the best-preserved interior piece. The stone reliefs portray scenes from the life of Christ and are modelled on those on the pulpit at Lübeck Cathedral. The village of Kaarma is important to the British Estonian community as it is the birthplace of Oskar Kallas, who was Estonian ambassador in London during the first independence period, between 1922 and 1934.

A slight detour should be made from Kaarma to the **Goodkaarma farm** at the village of Kuke. Signs with the GK logo point out the route. Set up only in 2007, it has now become one of Saaremaa's best-known businesses and tourist attractions. Its main product is organic soap and the website (*www.goodkaarma.ee*) gives full details of each variety. The production process can be seen, but do ring first before coming (the English-language phone number is ⟍ 5348 4006) or book on the website. Some soaps, such as Kaali and Saaremaa Honey, have local names; others such as Je t'aime and Wall Street clearly do not. However, the main point is that visitors now have a completely different possible outlet for genuine local souvenirs, as a contrast to juniper kitchenware or vodka. Soya candles bought here can easily be saved until Christmas, for those who prefer candles to electric lights on their trees. The café here offers as many local products as possible and is one of very few outside Kuressaare that warrant a special journey.

Twelve kilometres from Kaarma are the **Kaali Craters**, for years the subject of speculation and legend. Lennart Meri, former president of Estonia, joined the debate in 1976 with his book, *Silverwhite*. The truth is in fact straightforward, if dramatic. The craters were formed by a meteorite that fell probably around 3,000 years ago, though it could have been earlier. The largest lake is over 100m wide and gives the impression of being completely undisturbed since its violent origin. A new visitor centre opened here in 2005, which provides all the geological background to the meteor and a survey of the different uses to which dolomite can be put. The souvenir sellers outside have shown considerable imagination in how it can be carved into a statue or candle-holder light enough to take home by air. It is easy to miss the schoolhouse next door but it is now a centre for exhibiting and selling local lace. Note the coat of arms that was fortunately hidden during Soviet times. The inscription is in German: 'Das Wort Gottes Bleibt Ewig' (The word of God is everlasting).

Take the road north towards Leisi for 18km to reach **Karja**. There, **St Catherine's Church**, the smallest on Saaremaa, can be found, but nonetheless containing rooms for refugees and travellers. Note the symbols that form part of the wall murals, probably of pagan origin. The carvings on the pillars show how international the island had become during the 15th century. Masons trained in Germany, Sweden and probably France all contributed to their diverse themes and designs. Note also St Catherine clasping a book as the patron saint of scholars, and St Nicholas, the patron saint of sailors, with a monk kneeling beside him holding a boat. Just to the north of Karja are the five **Angla Windmills**, the symbol of Saaremaa. They are almost the only ones remaining on the island; in the mid 19th century, there were about 800 in active use.

Valjala is a 16km drive south from Angla, passing through Parsama and Koikla. **St Martin's Church** here could equally well be described as a fortress. The original building dated, as did Kaarma and Karja, from the 13th century but following its destruction in 1343 it was rebuilt from massive hewn blocks similar to those used in the castle at Kuressaare. The interior is far simpler than in other churches but the modern stained glass adds welcome colour to it.

Valjala is a 30km drive from the causeway that links Saaremaa with **Muhu Island**. Before leaving Saaremaa, take a short detour to **Maasi** to see the remains of the fortress, and also to enjoy the sea view across to Muhu. The fortress was blown up in 1576 by the Danes in an attempt to forestall the Swedish invasion and nothing was done for the next 300 years. In 2000, serious excavation started and by 2004 electricity had been installed so it is no longer necessary to take a torch to explore the vaults. At the neighbouring port of **Orissaare**, a 16th-century wreck of a cargo boat used to be exhibited. It was only brought to the surface in 1987, but is now in the Seaplane Harbour Museum in Tallinn (see pages 114–15). The nearby café, with its extensive view, is a good place to break for a meal or snack. As Kuivastu, the port for ferries to the mainland is on Muhu, tourists who bring their own cars can visit Muhu on arrival or departure. Shortly after the end of the causeway, at **Eemu** on the right side of the road, is one of the few working windmills left on either island. Turning left after a mile, the road leads to the **Muhu Museum** (*www.muhumuuseum.ee*) formerly the Koguva Village Museum, a great contrast to the Mihkli Farm Museum on Saaremaa. Here most of the buildings are from the early 20th century and the lifestyle depicted could almost be described as affluent. The author **Juhan Smuul** (1922–71) lived in one of the houses. Although he wrote entirely during the Soviet period, his work is still read in contemporary Estonia (a small statue of him stands on the Writers House in Tallinn, see page 107). Sadly, the few translations that were published of his books during his lifetime are now out of print. Amongst the equipment displayed is that for home brewing and baking bread. Most coastal areas of Estonia have a history of smuggling and Muhu is no exception. The brandy vats on show were used in the early 19th century for runs to the German port of Memel, now the Lithuanian port of Klaipeda.

The statue of Smuul unveiled in the village here in summer 2006 has had a very mixed history. It went up first in Kadriorg Park in Tallinn in 1990, but neglect and vandalism, some of it political, led to its being removed for several years. It seemed inappropriate to have what might be seen as a 'Soviet' monument so close to the Presidential Palace. The next idea was to move it to the very Russian suburb of Lasnamäe, where a road was being named after him. The sculptor turned down this idea, not wanting his work to be downgraded, which such a move would have suggested. In the end it was sold to Koguva for one kroon and its future is clearly assured amongst a population who still greatly respect their most famous inhabitant.

Drive east for 8km to **Piiri** and turn left into the woodland. After about 1km the clear remains of a Soviet rocket store can be made out. All that is left of the surrounding military base is what could not be dragged or flown back home in 1994, so is largely shells of the barracks where the troops lived, well cut off from the local population.

Right in the centre of Muhu Island, on the main road to Kuivatsu, is the village of **Liiva**, dominated by **Muhu church**. It dates from the late 13th century, early in the rule of the Teutonic Knights. The base of the altar dates from that time, as does the circular window in the west wall. The mural paintings are probably from a hundred or so years later. They were only rediscovered in 1913, having been concealed under plaster since the Reformation. It is thought that the artist might have come from Gotland since there are similarities with work in churches there. A tombstone for 'Johannes from Gotland' might in fact be that of the artist. Fires destroyed most of the woodwork in 1640 and again in 1710, but the 17th-century pulpit does survive and is similar to the one in Karja church. The thickness of the western wall, with its staircases and in-built rooms, shows how often the church must have been used as a hiding place. The roof was badly damaged in a German bombing raid in 1941 and was only replaced in 1958, after which the building was used as a granary. It was only returned to the church in 1989. With considerable financial support from Sweden, the church was rebuilt after independence and reconsecrated in May 1994. The year 2008 saw the opening of a café/restaurant in Liiva called **Kalakohvik** (Fish and Coffee) on the south side of the main road through the village. This is of course not the only combination they offer, but perhaps it shows their diversity, most welcome on Muhu, since otherwise there is nothing between very basic cafés and the luxury of Padaste.

Return to Saaremaa along the causeway and after 6km turn left. If there is time, stop after a further kilometre at the ruined church at **Pöide**. Before the war it was as splendid as the others already described but its use as a military depot by the Soviet army and the destruction of the tower by lightning in 1940 have ruined the

8

interior. Reconstruction has begun and part of the flooring is of glass to reveal the archaeological discoveries below. The village of Sakla, 18km further on, was the location of Estonia's first collective farm, founded in 1947 and called Kingissepp, after the communist leader executed in Tallinn in 1922. Kuressaare is a further 25km drive. Just before the ring road, turn left into **Kudjape Cemetery**. Several of the chapels are in the Classicist style noted already in the town. This was the site of a ten-day battle in September 1941, before the Germans defeated the Russians. A year earlier German troops had seized Paris with relative ease; Saaremaa proved much tougher. Their cemetery was turned into a farm after the war but it has now been reconsecrated. Here Saaremaa can finally come to terms with its suffering during the middle of the 20th century. Apart from the main area for the local Estonian population, there are now separate cemeteries for the Jewish community, the German soldiers and the Soviet occupiers. One Briton is buried here, too: a Captain Brown who died in 1917 during the invasion of Riga harbour. In the German cemetery, individual graves are provided for those who died in 1941 as the Germans advanced toward Leningrad. The battles here were the first serious Soviet resistance they faced. For those who died in 1944 during their retreat, only an all-purpose granite memorial can be provided as the Russians made no effort to identify individual German corpses. In the Estonian section, note the memorials for the deportees to Siberia and for the ten local residents who died in the Estonia tragedy in 1994. Between them is a memorial to the Kitt family whose suffering during the 20th century is probably paralleled by that of all too many Saaremaa families. One member died *en route* to Siberia and four others out there. Two drowned trying to escape across the Baltic Sea in 1944. Others who succeeded in escaping died in due course of natural causes in England, Finland and the United States, but none died of natural causes at home on Saaremaa.

ABRUKA ISLAND

The island of Abruka is situated 6km off the coast of Saaremaa, due south of Kuressaare. A local joke runs: there are three species on Abruka, fishermen, writers and sheep. Visitors who make the effort to reach the island will soon appreciate the origin of such an opinion. Abruka has certainly made no effort to attract tourists in large numbers and is perfectly happy to receive a handful of largely local visitors each day in the summer. A small boat from Roomassaare harbour serves Abruka. During the summer it is normally possible to take a morning boat out and an afternoon one back. The tourist office in Kuressaare will have schedules and costs. The more active can kayak from Saaremaa and then take a nature trail of 5km or so.

In 2013 there was no catering available on the island but snacks and drinks were available at the port on arrival. This should be checked before departure and, if necessary, a picnic taken from Saaremaa. Small groups may want to consider hiring their own boat to give flexibility to the length of stay. In winter, it is possible to walk or drive over the ice to Abruka.

The island currently has a population of about 30 year-round residents compared with the 170 or so through much of the Soviet era. A far larger number spend summer on the island; both Finns and Estonians are now upgrading former farmhouses to serve this purpose.

Much of the land is forested, mainly with elms, mountain ash and oak trees. Orchids grow extensively and a wide variety of moths and butterflies can be seen. The main building is the former **Sibaabaa Centre**. From its design it could only be a collective-farm headquarters and this is indeed the role it served, in the 1950s for fishing and then for the increasing number of sheep and cows brought to graze on the island. There are plans to convert it into a hostel, but a kinder solution would be to remove it. A farm was renovated in 2001–04 to house the island's **museum** which is largely a photographic collection. It not only covers the history of the island over the last 150 years, but two other sections cover Estonian lighthouses and life underwater off the Estonia coast. The **cemetery**, as so often in contemporary Estonia, gives a vignette of the struggles fought around it. The Russians and the Lutherans not only required a divided cemetery, but also separate entry gates. Burials in the Soviet period lack any link with religion. The most famous tombs are those of two cousins whose bodies were returned from Sweden to Abruka for burial. Johannes Aavik (1880–1973) was Estonia's most famous linguist and Joosep Aavik (1899–1989) was equally well known as a conductor, organist and teacher. As in many other communities near the sea, a memorial has been built to commemorate the sinking of the *Estonia* on 28 September 1994. Four islanders were killed in this disaster, over 10% of the population.

RUHNU ISLAND

Ruhnu (*www.ruhnu.ee*) has always been an anachronism in Estonian history. It has both benefited and suffered as a result of its isolated location. Events that would be forgotten elsewhere within weeks are still chronicled centuries later. A major event in the 18th century, for instance, was a peasant arriving drunk to church in 1729 and being put in the stocks for four consecutive Sundays. The only civilian murder on the island took place in 1738. A prison with two cells operated throughout the 19th century but it was closed in 1894 through lack of use. There would be bitter fighting between the Russians and the Germans in summer 1941 as resistance from Soviet forces slowly began. From 1944 until 1989 Ruhnu was particularly isolated on the pretext of military sensitivity.

In 1919, as the Russian and German empires collapsed, Estonia, Latvia and Sweden all expected Ruhnu to fall into their hands. On 17 January of that year, the provisional government of Estonia proclaimed the island of Ruhnu as part of Estonia but inhabitants only found this out in May when the first boat of the summer was able to get there. Realising that it would be necessary to speak Swedish and to barter (money would only come to Ruhnu about 20 years later), government representatives from Tallinn arrived with flour, spirits, salt, leatherwear and gun cartridges. They accepted 20,000kg of seal blubber in return, which in due course went rancid as there were insufficient preservation facilities in Tallinn at the time. The new Estonian government therefore had a political but not an economic victory over its neighbours and Ruhnu has been Estonian ever since. Families received surnames in 1927 and the land that had previously been farmed collectively was divided into private plots in 1930.

In order to escape the return of the Russians, all but two families left for Sweden in 1944, abandoning not only their houses but also 200 cows, 300 sheep, 150 horses and 300 hens. For at least the previous 600 years, the population had been Swedish speaking and had fluctuated in numbers between 200 and 300. Only around 1710 did it drop to about 100 when the troops of Peter the Great brought the plague with them as they conquered all of Estonia from the Swedes. Peter did, however, leave the Swedish legal system intact, and the Germans nominally restored it during their three-year rule from 1941 to 1944. Although there were always Soviet military garrisons on the island, the permanent population would never even reach 100 again and it is now around 60, of whom eight serve on the village council.

8

The Soviets replaced the Swedish population with residents of Saaremaa who were forced to leave what would become military bases. They tried to find oil but after digging down 400m found only hot springs. They set up a collective farm for potatoes in 1949, brought in electricity in 1958 and telephones only in 1988. Yet in 1966, there were 30 motorbikes – one for every seven members of the population. Perhaps because of this quantity of traffic, the lane to the harbour was renamed 'Prospekt Gagarin' after the first man in space. The fish collective, with equal pretentiousness, was called 'Beacon of Communism'. The Soviet commander was the last Russian to leave the island, with his family, on 23 December 1994, six months after Soviet troops had left the mainland. They did not, however, take all their vehicles and some of those they abandoned can still be seen, now largely covered in weeds.

Since the restoration of Estonian independence, logging has begun again and fishing expanded. Tourism has been generated on a small scale, with about 3,000 visitors a year coming to enjoy total peace and quiet. Half of these are Estonian, a quarter are Latvian and most of the rest are Swedes.

Within a day tourists can visit the village museum, the two churches and the lighthouse. A minibus meets the plane and drives the couple of kilometres into

ARRIVAL ON RUHNU ISLAND

And then slowly wandering towards us, knocking off the heads of the mushrooms with his stick came man indeed, the Governor-General of the Island, a short, lame elderly man, the keeper of the lighthouse to whom the men of Ruhnu come for a casting vote in all debates. He has no official authority; no laws confer power on him or limit it but he is the Keeper of the Light, the guardian of the one piece of civilisation imposed on Ruhnu by the mainland, the representative of those who do not live on islands and I suppose tradition invests him with a sort of dignity. In the old days he was sent by a Tsar of Russia to keep the light on this little island in a sea surrounded on all sides by Russian territory. The men of Ruhnu are Swedes, and a Tsar of Russia had driven their race from the mainland. Nowadays the sea of which Ruhnu is, as it were, the central pool is no longer Russian. Its coasts are Latvian and Estonian. The Tsar is no more.

The lighthouse-keeper greeted us. He had heard our fog-horn, and since the people were busy with their harvesting on the other side of the island, he had himself come down to meet us, and to warn us that the wind was changing and that we must soon look to our ship. He knew a few words of English, but more willingly spoke Russian, which he knew well, besides, of course, Estonian and Swedish. He was surprised to see us so late in the year and on learning my nationality, asked with the embarrassing curiosity of foreigners, to whom this bit of our mingled foreign and domestic affairs is always hard to explain, 'Well, Mister and how is it with Ireland?' This was the first of several disappointments, for I had hoped in voyaging among these remote islands to be quit of politics for once. But I hid my feelings and told him that the Irish were settling their affairs in the Irish way and then got him to talk of his own country.

Extract from Racundra's First Cruise *by Arthur Ransome, written in 1922. Ransome spent much of 1921 and 1922 in the Baltics.*

the village. The **museum** has a comprehensive collection of artefacts for every occupation. The two **churches** are side by side but only the modern stone one, which dates from 1912, has services. Over-optimistically, it was built to seat 400. A church service is held daily, rather than once a year at Christmas, which was the Soviet practice. As there are only 22 practising Christians on the island, the pastor sometimes conducts this service without a congregation. However, he assures those who query this practice that 'the angels are always there'. The church is still lit by candles in the chandeliers and on the windowsills. The wooden church, St Magdalena, dates from 1643 and is named after the first girl to be baptised there. It is the oldest wooden church in Estonia and was renovated in 1851. The stained glass is a modern (1990) copy of what was taken to Sweden in 1944. Much of the stone for the later church came from Sweden, as did the crucifix, which was presented by the Swedish navy in 1924. The organ was likewise a gift, in 1991, but over two decades later it still awaits a regular player to make use of it. The font is likely to have been cast in the 14th century so pre-dates even the wooden church.

The **lighthouse** is about a kilometre's walk from the village. The impressive plaque from 'Force et Chantiers de la Méditerranée' makes clear its French origin, shared by many Estonian lighthouses. It is 36m high and was built in 1875 in Le Havre. It was designed by Gustave Eiffel, who is most famous of course for his tower in Paris. It is an easy and worthwhile walk to the top, which offers a view of the whole island.

GETTING THERE AND AWAY Individuals can visit Ruhnu during the summer when, at least once a week, a morning **flight** from Pärnu to Kuressaare on Saaremaa stops there *en route*, returning in the late afternoon. These flights are heavily subsidised by the Estonian government, so schedules vary year by year according to the level of their generosity and are usually only confirmed in late April. **Tour operators** can charter boats or planes for groups from both Pärnu and Kuressaare. **Boat** services also run regularly during the summer from Kuressaare but their schedules are rarely known before May. The journey takes about two hours. The island's website has current information on flights and boats.

HIIUMAA ISLAND

Popular with Finns, Swedes and the Estonians themselves, Hiiumaa has yet to make itself known in the English-speaking world although it should be the easiest area to visit. Every major site on the island has large, descriptive signboards in English and the local tourist authority has produced a wide range of guidebooks and leaflets. Their logo is appropriately a lighthouse and it appears on road signs and at sites.

Hiiumaa makes minimal concessions to the early 21st century. Hotels have been modernised, the roads are kept in a reasonable state of repair, and a regular ferry service ensures close links with the mainland. Yet there are few restaurants, little evening entertainment and the former manor houses remain largely unrestored. It is an island for cyclists, birdwatchers and escapists. Real life on Hiiumaa has been as tough as everywhere else in Estonia, but local stories always have happy endings, appropriate for an island of peace and nature.

One name haunts the island, that of the Ungern-Sternberg family who first came to Hiiumaa in the 18th century. Some members had a particularly brutal bent: Otto Reinhold Ludwig von Ungern-Sternberg set up false lighthouses to generate shipwrecks so that he could then loot their contents. Shortly after buying the manor house at Suuremõisa in 1796, he shot one of his sea captains during a meeting there and guides like to point out a stain that they claim is this captain's blood. In 1918, Major-General Baron Roman Fyodorovich von Ungern-Sternberg began a three-year struggle to forestall the establishment of communism in Mongolia. He personally bayoneted, crucified and strangled hundreds of opponents before being shot by a firing squad formed from mutineers in his own army. Not surprisingly he is known in Mongolia as the 'Mad Baron'. Other members of the family remained on Hiiumaa as relatively benevolent landowners, industrialists and shipbuilders. Most of the tourist sites on the island are linked to this family.

The Soviet occupation after World War II was far less harsh than on Saaremaa: the military left in 1961, no building of more than four storeys was allowed and the Russian-speaking population never exceeded a few hundred. The former Communist Party headquarters in Kärdla blend easily into the current surroundings and are now an adult education centre.

GETTING THERE AND AWAY Visitors will usually arrive from the mainland at the port of Heltermaa, a 90-minute **ferry** journey from Rohuküla on the mainland. Bus services from Tallinn and Haapsalu are linked to their schedules and they serve most villages on the island. The ferry operates about five times a day. There is also a twice-daily service from Triigi on Saaremaa to Sõru on Hiiumaa, although this is sometimes suspended in winter due to bad weather. Details of both ferry services are given on www.tuulelaevad.ee. Subsidised **flights** operate twice a day from Tallinn to Kärdla and as they take about 30 minutes rather than the four hours needed with the bus, the cost of around €18 one-way, or €36 return is well worthwhile, at least in one direction. Should the subsidies be withdrawn, these prices will of course increase dramatically. The airport reached its heyday in 1987 when 34,000 people used it. This dropped to 727 in 1995 but by 2012 had risen to around 11,000.

GETTING AROUND
As on Saaremaa, it is possible to travel around the island by bus. Hiring a car, however, is certainly to be recommended and two full days would be needed to do justice to the island. Take a local guide, not so much to provide a formal background to visits, but to offer an outpouring of legends. The tourism information centre in Kärdla (*Hiiu 1; www.hiiumaa.eu;* see pages 288–9) can arrange this.

 WHERE TO STAY AND EAT
🏠 **Padu** (10 rooms & 8 apts) 22 Heltermaa mnt, Kärdla; 📞463 3037; e info@paduhotell.ee; www.paduhotell.ee. Although small, this is the main hotel in Kärdla. It is spacious with an elegant wooden interior. All rooms have a balcony. Guests have the use of the extensive garden, which makes it ideal for families with small children. Prices here include dinner. $$$

🏠 **Viinaköök** (19 rooms) Sadama 2 Körgessaare; 📞469 3337; e sales@viinakook.com; www.viinakook.com. Even by Estonian standards, this building has had a very chequered history. It opened as a distillery in 1881, was then in early 1914 converted into an artificial silk factory that was in production for just 1 month before World War I brought an end to this. Next it became a gunpowder storage depot until it was blown up in 1917. For the next 40 years or so it remained abandoned, until it opened in 1961 as a fish processing plant. This did not survive long after the downfall of the Soviet Union so the building was again abandoned. This hotel & restaurant brought it back to life in 2007, but only for a short summer season. It is open from 1 Jun–20 Aug, although the restaurant is sometimes open through Sep. Local people as much as tourists enjoy the soup buffet & the daily catch of fish that is always served both at lunch & at dinner. $$$

🏠 **Heltermaa** (18 rooms) Heltermaa harbour; 📞469 4146; e info@heltermaahotell.ee; www.heltermaahotell.ee. Opened in 1997, this modern hotel is part of the harbour complex & is ideal for individuals & groups planning to arrive late or leave early. A 2-night stay here with a full day for sightseeing would allow for many of the sights. There are several nearby walks into the juniper forests, enhanced in spring with bluebells & in autumn with mountain ash. Public buses around the island & those to the mainland all stop here so the hotel is a good base for visitors without cars. **$$**

🏠 **Liilia** (13 rooms) Hiiu 22 Kaina; 🖉463 6146; e info@liiliahotell.ee; wwwliiliahotell.ee. This hotel has 2 features unique on the island, a billiard table & a room adapted for the disabled. The staff speak good English & if any hotel on Hiiumaa joins an international chain it will be this one. It is situated in the centre of the village & each room has a separate design. **$$**

🏠 **Lōokese** (42 rooms) Kaina; 🖉463 6107; e info@lookese.ee; www.lookese.ee. Although

it's a former collective farm on the outskirts of the village, this is in fact a very pleasant place to stay. Being set off the main road, it is quiet, has been modernised & has become the largest hotel on the island. The hotel has a heated outdoor swimming pool & in 2005 started to offer spa services. To individuals it is only open in summer, May–Aug, but can open at anytime for groups. It is under the same management as the Liilia. **$$**

🏠 **Nordtooder** (9 rooms) Rookopli 20, Kärdla; 🖉463 2140; e info@nordtooder.ee; www. nordtooder.ee. When it opened in 2005, this hotel was the first one to do so on Hiiumaa for many years. It was unusual in its model of gently adapting a late 19th-century town house, rather than attempting anything more modern. **$$**

A TOUR OF HIIUMAA A drive around the coast of the island, with the occasional diversion inland, covers most places of interest. When Arthur Ransome brought the *Racundra* to Heltermaa in 1921, it could accommodate only three boats, the inn had only sacks of straw for beds and money was so rare that change was given in loaves of bread. **Heltermaa** is now a modern harbour with an indoor shopping mall, a well-furnished hotel and space for several car ferries. Six kilometres from Heltermaa is the island's oldest church at **Pühalepa**; the basic stone structure dates from the late 13th century but the interior has been frequently abandoned or deliberately damaged. It served as a granary during the Soviet period but with the help of the Finnish government was fortunately restored in 1991. Some of the late Baroque sculpture from the 17th century can still be recognised and beside the altar is the tomb of Lawrence Clayton, an admiral in the Swedish navy and one of the earliest Scots to be linked with Estonia. The stairway leading up to the attic was built so that this area could be a refuge whenever the church was attacked.

Members of the Ungern-Sternberg family are buried in the churchyard, with most of the tombstones being inscribed in German. Note the many boulders in the surrounding fields. Inevitably, a legend has arisen about these to the effect that they represent the attempts of the devil to destroy religion by throwing them at the church. A more prosaic explanation is that they were left by retreating glaciers at the end of the Ice Age. The tall, neat pile of boulders about 200m from the church, called the Contract Stones, is thought to be an attempt by the Ungern-Sternberg family to provide a model of the Egyptian pyramids, which several of them had visited.

A couple of kilometres along the road towards Käina is the manor house of **Suuremõisa**. It is easy to imagine what an impressive building it must have been when first constructed in the 18th century and when bought in 1796 by the Ungern-Sternberg family. Equally grandiose was the formal garden, the terracing and the entrance gate. Indoors, only the central oak staircase remains from that time. Since 1924 the building has been used as a school although restoration work is slowly being undertaken, both indoors and out.

Continuing towards Käina, a short stop can be made after 8km at the wool factory in the village of **Vaemla**. Some original 19th-century machines are still in use – they were produced in Bialystok in what is now Poland – and the factory produces sweaters, socks and gloves. They do of course have a shop for these goods

8

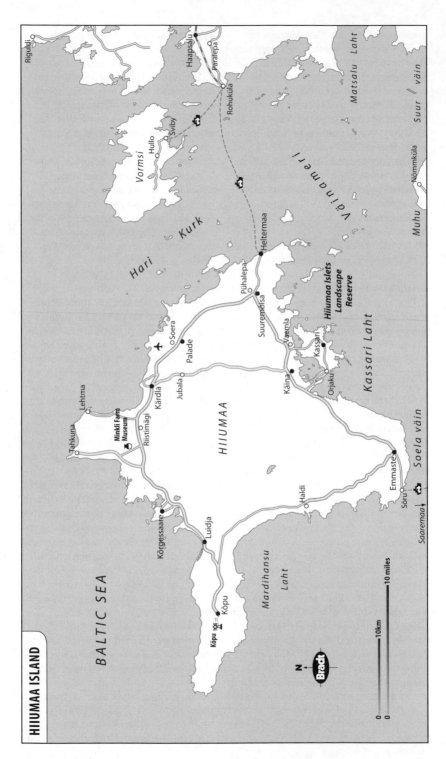

but there is no hard sell. Turning left off the road to Kärdla and Käina, head to the peninsula of **Kassari**. This is now resuming its role as the summer retreat for Estonian artists and writers. Jaan Kross, the country's best-known 20th-century writer, had his summer house here, as did Aino Kallas, who was famous in the 1930s. Locals like to recall her comment, 'God looked favourably upon me as he gave me Kassari.' (Her husband Oskar was Estonian ambassador in Britain from 1922 to 1934.)

Near the village of Kassari is a branch of the **Hiiumaa Museum** (*www.muuseum. hiiumaa.ee*). Most of the interior dates from the mid-1960s when the building was converted from a school to a museum. The former teachers' rooms have however not changed since the 1920s. Earlier it had been the servants' quarters of a nearby manor house that burnt down in 1928. The museum has an imaginatively presented collection of material covering the political and natural history of the island, both being equally violent. The damage done by storms has been as great as that resulting from warfare. Archaeology has tended to be a recent activity in Estonia as its occupiers were not keen to find out about civilisation before their arrival. Hiiumaa seems to have been an exception with the collection here having been assembled in the 1970s. Examples of the different types of wood that grow on the island are shown, as are carvings from them. The most unusual item of furniture is a double rocking chair. The Soviet era is extensively covered, with green and red being the predominant colours in the early period, switching to blue in the 1970s. Some daring pictures from that time, such as of long queues outside shops, have been brought together here. The museum was probably the first one in Estonia that offered a play area for children but others are now sensibly copying this idea. The lifeboat displayed in front of the museum is one of the few salvaged from the *Estonia* disaster in September 1994 (see page 122).

Kassari Church is unusual for its thatched roof, the only one on a functioning Estonian church. Sadly the interior was abandoned in Soviet times so there was no maintenance then and refurbishment had to start from scratch in the 1990s. The Stackelberg family (see page 88) are buried here as is the model used by Johann Köler for his portrait of Jesus Christ in the Kaarli Church in Tallinn (see pages 99–100).

The surrounding **Käina Bay** has been a bird sanctuary since 1962, although ironically it was before then a well-known area for hunting. Gulls and warblers are the most common species breeding here and it is also the site for many migrating waterbirds.

In Käina it is impossible to ignore the tragic side of Estonian history. The ruins of the church result from a German bombing raid in 1941; the original building had survived from the 16th century. The community centre was once the home of the local Baltic-German landlord, Alexander Hoyningen-Heune, who was the first islander to be sent to Siberia; during World War I he was accused of spying when a German aircraft made an emergency landing on his estate.

The bland exterior of the **Lookese Hotel** and its location outside the village show that it can only have been a collective farm during the Soviet period. Yet many small wooden houses in the village have survived all political and military turmoil and in May their gardens impress even British visitors.

About a kilometre from the village of Käina is the **Rudolf Tobias Museum**. The famous composer (1873–1918), shown on the old 50 Kroon note, lived here until he was 12 years old. Later he studied in St Petersburg under Rimsky-Korsakov. (The house and much of the furniture were built by his father, who was a joiner.) The museum was opened in 1973, on the 100th anniversary of his birth, and since then

8

concerts have taken place regularly. However, much of R Tobias's music, including his most famous work, *Jonah's Mission*, was not performed during the Soviet period because of its religious overtones. This oratorio had its first performance in Leipzig in 1909 but was 'repremiered' in Tallinn in 1989 when more liberal policies were adopted in the final years of the Soviet Union.

Leaving Käina towards the southwest, another road to Kassari is to the left after 5km, passing what is now the small port of Orjaku. It is difficult to believe that towards the end of the tsarist era, shortly before World War I, this was planned as one of the largest ports in Russia, maintaining a fleet of battleships. Some expansion as a yachting and fishing harbour is now envisaged. Boatbuilding was banned in the Soviet period but has recently begun again and provides employment in the villages of Emmaste and Nurste along the western coast.

The bell at **Emmaste church** has now become the most famous one in Estonia. Like all too many others, it stopped ringing in 1943 when the Germans started to seize metal from all possible sources to melt down for arms production. However, despite its weight of 200kg, it was dismantled by six brave villagers and hidden underground without being discovered. The secret remained throughout the Soviet era and only in the early 1990s did the two survivors from the original team of six start to search for it again. They finally succeeded in December 1994, with the help of a metal detector. The bell rang again on Christmas Eve, from its original position in the belfry, and in his address to the nation that day, President Meri said: 'Let the restored bell of Emmaste ring out as a symbol of a country whose freedom has also been restored.'

Sõru is the port used now for the ferry from Triigi on Saaremaa. The motor-assisted sailing boat being restored on the beach started life in private hands as the *Alar* in the spring of 1939. Being 30m long, it was large for the Baltic Sea. It was built from Hiiumaa pine and Saaremaa oak. It fell first into Soviet and then into German hands and the Germans used it to evacuate troops in 1944, changing its name to the *Kurland*. Being in Hamburg at the end of the war, it fell into British hands between 1945 and 1949 but was later in Sweden and Denmark. It came back to Sõru in 1998 when it was named the *Ernst Jaakson* after the 20th century's longest-serving diplomat. Jaakson started work in the Estonian consulate in San Francisco in 1928, moved to New York in 1932 and stayed there, largely serving the Estonian exile government until 1991. From 1991 to 1993 he was ambassador to the US and to the UN and continued to work part-time until 1998. His diplomatic career therefore lasted 70 years. Restoration work started on the boat in 2007 and the completion date will depend on the level of donations received. The **Sõru Museum** on the other side of the road has a model of how the restored boat will look, as well as memorabilia from the harbour as it was in 1939.

The **Kõpu Lighthouse** on the northwestern tip of Hiiumaa has been the island's most significant landmark since it was built on the orders of the Hanseatic League in 1490. Its beam of light could be seen from 40km away. Only in 1997 did it lose this role when radar from the smaller lighthouse at Ristna took over. Those fit enough to climb to the top will reach, at 100m, one of the higher spots in Estonia, with views over to Saaremaa as well as across the whole of Hiiumaa. This is best enjoyed around sunset. The interior of the lighthouse was completely renovated in 2002. Originally, wooden fires provided the light and such an enormous number of trees were felled to provide for this that, as a result, most of the Kõpu Peninsula was deforested. A team of six was on duty every night to guard the fire but it still went out during storms. Oil was used briefly in the late 19th century; the electric light installed in 1900 was exhibited in the Paris Exhibition of that year and its use finally brought to an end both shipwrecks and piracy. Several other lighthouses on Hiiumaa are of French design. Beside the Kõpu Lighthouse are the remains of a Soviet border station and a school, converted from a former Russian Orthodox church built in 1910.

The drive along the northern coast of the island from Kõpu to the capital Kärdla is about 40km. On the left-hand side of the road, 2km from Kõpu, a short stairway marks the start of the **Hiiumaa nature trail**. It is an easy walk of about 2km, clearly marked throughout, and for those unwilling to risk the climb up the lighthouse, the view from what is locally described as the 'highpoint' (all of 70m!) provides ample compensation. A varied and constantly increasing number of shrubs, flowers, mosses and trees can be seen on this short walk, and sometimes even elk or deer as well.

Before reaching the small beach resort of Luidja, the road becomes narrower, with only a gravel surface and several unnecessarily sharp bends. On the locally produced map, its colour ominously changes from red to white. Luckily this sector is only 5km long and can be driven in all weathers. Inevitably, on Hiiumaa, there is a whole range of stories to explain its original routing and the passion that allows its continuing state of neglect. It will clearly be a further few years before a modernist view prevails and the road is widened and straightened. Luidja is a popular camping site for Estonian families and has the best beach on the island for children.

Ten kilometres further on is the port of **Kõrgessaare**, which was the most important settlement on the island in the 16th century when it was the major port for trading with Sweden. The Ungern-Sternberg family hoped to revive it, building a distillery and a fish-processing plant around 1900, but World War I dashed these plans. A local brochure produced in the 1990s touchingly writes that Kõrgessaare 'is crying out for restoration'. The opening of the Viinakook restaurant and guesthouse is hopefully the beginning of this process.

About 2km from Kõrgessaare, on the left, is **Reigi church**, isolated in the countryside but once serving a largely Swedish-speaking parish of which now only a few houses remain. This church was built around 1800 to replace an earlier wooden one and little has been altered since then. Many members of the Ungern-Sternberg family are buried in the churchyard and the family coat of arms can be seen over the entrance. To show the contrast between Hiiumaa's international links in the 19th century and its isolation during much of the 20th, it is worth noting in the churchyard the gravestone of Heinrich Eduard who lived in Reigi but met his Italian wife in Cheltenham, England. The allegedly colourful private lives of early pastors in the village have provided material for a novel by Aino Kallas (see page 285), *The Pastor of Reigi*, which she wrote in her house at Kassari in 1926. In 1971 it was made into an opera by the composer Eduard Tubin who was by then living in exile in Sweden. Permission was only granted in 1979 for its performance in Estonia, even though Tubin was already a frequent traveller back to his homeland well before then.

After 4km, turn left and continue until the road stops at the **Tahkuna Lighthouse**. Like so many others in Estonia, it was built by Gustave Eiffel's engineering company and was assembled in France before being brought here in parts in 1875. This could be done because it is one of the earliest made of iron instead of stone. The forest *en route* has many abandoned military installations from both world wars and also relics of the narrow-gauge railway that used to transport goods on the island until it was abandoned in 1955. The Soviets hurriedly built a massive defence network here in 1941 on the assumption that it would be the site chosen for landing by German forces. In fact the Germans landed at Emmaste but the Russians made some attempt to defend this area, instead of simply fleeing, which is what they tended to do elsewhere in Estonia. Soviet histories claim that when their ammunition ran out, soldiers committed suicide by jumping from the top of the lighthouse rather than suffer the disgrace of imprisonment.

Whatever the weather, there are dramatic views across the Baltic from the top of the lighthouse which was opened to the public in 2006 and even from the hamlet around the lighthouse for those not able to make the climb. The lighthouse is also the site of a memorial – a crucifix and bell – to the children who died in the *Estonia* tragedy on 28 September 1994. The spot was chosen as the nearest point on land in Estonia to the position where the boat sank. The bell rings when the intensity of the wind parallels that on the fatal night.

On the return journey stop first at the **Military Museum** (*www.militaarmuuseum. ee*), about 2km south of the lighthouse. It opened in the summer of 2007 and had to be immediately fortified, such was the attraction of the weapons shown here to thieves. The collection concentrates on World War II, but material has been added from the Georgian War of 2008. It also gives the history of Soviet involvement with Hiiumaa from 1939 when 2,000 troops arrived in one day and the island became an air base for attacks on Finland during the 1939–40 Winter War. The large Soviet oil painting showing the return of their forces in October 1944 used to hang in Haapsalu Station. Collectors are now passing on material to the museum so doubtless it will quickly expand. Amongst recent gifts are an army dental chair from 1980 and German petrol tanks hidden before their retreat in 1944. The very detailed website was still only in Estonian in late 2013, except for details of opening hours which are translated into English.

Take the left turning after 4km for **Mihkli Farm Museum**. This is more interesting than many others in Estonia since it was in use until 1987 so has a livelier feel about it. All the buildings and the tools are original and it was run on co-operative rather than collective principles.

Turn left at the junction with the main road and after 2km note the sign for **Ristimägi**, the Hill of Crosses. This site commemorates the final service held here by around 1,000 Swedes before they were deported to the Ukraine in 1781, a journey that few survived. In the Soviet era, crosses were left on this isolated site as a form of religious defiance and now wedding parties often leave flowers here. First-time visitors to the island are encouraged to make a small cross from twigs and to add it to the site.

A final 5km leads to **Kärdla**, the capital. It is advertised as 'drowning in greenery' since there is no industry, and it has several parks and woods and a population of only 4,200. Because there are no blocks of flats and most houses have a garden, it gives the impression of being bigger than it really is. The local population could afford to live like this because of the success of the textile factory. Many of the wooden houses dating from the 1880s could only be sold to other workers, not to outsiders. The main square used to be dominated by the factory founded by the Ungern-Sternberg family in 1829. By 1845, around 500 workers were employed and Kärdla cloth had become famous around the Baltic. Many of the houses built for the workers are still inhabited. The factory was destroyed by the Russians as they retreated from the Germans in 1941. Only in 2000 was reconstruction completed and the building is now the Long House (Pikk Maja), which houses the **Hiiumaa Museum**. It covers the history of Kärdla, which is really the history of the factory with models of workers' houses. It shows the factory currency, which also circulated in Haapsalu and even in Tallinn when other money was thought to be less reliable. Wood was a backup to currency and was often presented as a wedding present. Skilled carvers made a lot of items from one trunk, such as boxes for candles and for bread. Moving to the other end of the social scale, some furniture belonging to the Ungern-Sternberg family is on show here. The piano was owned by Eduard Tobias and had been in his house before being brought to this museum.

Behind the Long House is the former Swedish cemetery, which was not harmed by any subsequent occupiers. The Lutheran church dates from 1863. The organ, built in 1904, was one of the last in Estonia to be ordered from Germany. Kärdla sensibly makes no concessions to tourists although they double the population to around 8,000 during the summer. Relaxation is the main ingredient of a stay here so those seeking a 'lively' holiday wisely stay away.

Returning to the ferry at Heltermaa, after 7km you will come to **Soera Farm Museum**. The turbulent history of the last 150 years has fortunately passed this farm by and the buildings remain as they were in the mid 19th century. The museum was first opened in 1979 and most of the tools and furnishings are original. The loom and spinning wheel played a major role in day-to-day life, as did the sauna. The museum brews its own beer and most ingredients used in meals come from the island. A 20km drive ends the tour back at Heltermaa.

VORMSI ISLAND

Whoever nominally controlled the Estonian mainland and its islands from the 12th century onwards, Vormsi (*www.vormsi.ee*) would always stay Swedish. No other language was spoken there and no other culture took root. Neither the Baltic Germans nor the Russians ever attempted to set up estates there. To some extent this explains the poverty prevailing until the 1920s. In the 19th century, four families often shared one large barn as living quarters and, being too poor to buy tools, they would peel potatoes with their hands. That was a very violent period too when most of the wood sent to the mainland was stolen. If there was no money for tools, there certainly was for drink. Thirteen bars served the population of 2,000. Into this bleak environment came in 1873 the Swedish Baptist missionary, Lars Österblom, who would stay for the next 15 years and almost single-handedly brought stability and hope back to Vormsi.

The 1920s brought not cars or tractors but horses. Previously the only animal transport had been bulls, but as these were killed for food during World War I, the horses replaced them. Modernisation would follow, but much more slowly than on the other islands. A journey was a memorable visit to the next village; travelling to the mainland was for many out of the question. In 1943, after 700 years, most of the community left in contempt of Nazi Germany and in fear of the Red Army. Twenty people stayed behind, and the island was repopulated with Estonians from elsewhere.

Whilst Saaremaa would have to endure a massive Soviet military presence, Vormsi, like Hiiumaa, was spared this and a collective-farm headquarters is the only architectural legacy of their 45-year occupation. Sweden has, however, left its place names, and its Lutheranism. Swedish financial support, both government and private, is now helping to restore the earlier links. Descendants of families who fled in 1943 are now returning and building summer houses. It is likely that their land will be returned to them, if they are willing to farm it again. This Swedish support during the summer, when they employ many local people in rebuilding their houses, is crucial for the local economy as are the visits by many predominantly Swedish tour groups. The Vormsi website gives 18 reasons (in English) why young families should consider settling there. With a current population of around 300, an influx would be most welcome.

8

GETTING THERE AND AROUND In the summer, Vormsi is reached by a **boat** that operates two to four times a day from Rohuküla, the harbour near Haapsalu which also serves Hiiumaa. The journey takes 45 minutes. Schedules can be checked on www.veeteed.com. **Buses** go at least hourly from Haapsalu station to Rohuküla. The boat to Vormsi takes cars. However most Vormsi residents drive around the island in old Russian Ladas, leaving their new Volvos parked on the mainland at Rohuküla harbour. In midwinter, several more glamorous ways of travel are available, on skis, by dog sleigh and, once the ice is more than 30cm thick, driving by car. A local **minibus** meets the ferry and its entire route around the island takes about an hour. A normal way of seeing the island is to take the bus into Hullo and then a later service around the island that connects with the departing ferry.

✗ **WHERE TO EAT AND DRINK** Close to the harbour is the **Krog Pub** (*www.krog.ee;* $), which opened in 2009. Being open until midnight Sunday–Thursday and until 03.00 Friday–Saturday. It soon brought Vormsi evenings to life in a way that had never been seen there before.

WHAT TO SEE Hullo is the main village on the island and is about 5km from the landing stage where the boats arrive. The first sight is that of the ruined **Russian Orthodox church**, nestling incongruously in an equally ruined collective farm. It was probably the most ineffective attempt of all those made around Estonia in the second half of the 19th century to woo the local community into a Russian environment. The congregation was reported in 1886 to be 162; by 1938 it had dropped to seven, with services having been abandoned many years previously.

On first arrival, the centre of Hullo looks as though little has changed since the 1930s. However, a big '@' sign outside the library invites customers to use the internet and the primary school next door has four online computers as well.

About a kilometre north of the village is **St Olav's Church**. A stone at the side of the west door lists the many dates when the church was rebuilt, following either specific attacks or longer-term vandalism. Records refer to a wooden church in the 13th century, with stone being gradually added from the 14th century. The structure seen today dates largely from 1929, although the interior is completely modern. The pre-war pulpit was taken to Sweden where it is now exhibited in the Stockholm Culture Museum. The one here is an exact copy, paid for like much else in the church by the Swedish-Estonian community. The church was reconsecrated on 29 July 1990, St Olav's Day, in front of a congregation of 1,500 who had come especially from Sweden, bringing with them the statue that is displayed inside the church. St Olav was the patron saint of craftsmen, which has not been forgotten in the woodwork on display. Note in this context the 'hanging' boat, a model of a 19th-century sailing ship. The collection of photographs beside the organ shows the church in 1920, 1972 and 1990. The two holes in the wall behind the altar were built to enable lepers to hear the service from outside without infecting the congregation indoors.

The circular crosses in the **cemetery** number 343, and date from 1724 to 1923. Each one has a family emblem. The large tombstone dating from 1929, which commemorates three freedom fighters who had died in 1919 during the War of Independence, is probably unique in Estonia in that it was not removed by the Soviets. The Swedish inscription *Frihetskämparna* (freedom fighters) probably saved it, as no Russian understood what it meant. Isolated to the east of the church is the tomb of Lars Österblum who, as a Baptist, could not be buried either in the church itself or even in the main cemetery.

Appendix 1

LANGUAGE   *Maila Saar*

PRONUNCIATION Words in Estonian are pronounced with the stress on the first syllable. Individual letters are pronounced as follows:

Vowels

a	as the English u in but
aa	is like a in father
e	as in bet
ee	as in the English eh or French de
i	as in pin
ü	as the German ü
o	as in off
oo	as eau in the French peau
u	as in put
uu	as the oo in food
ä	almost as in cat, but with a less open mouth
ää	is the same as ä, but with a more open mouth
ö	as the ir in girl, but with rounded lips
öö	as the oeu in the French voeu
õ	is peculiar to Estonian and is pronounced with the lips in the position of a short e while the tongue is retracted
õõ	is the same as õ, but longer
ü	is produced by pronouncing i with a protrusion of the lips and a narrow opening of the mouth
üü	is the same as ü, but longer and clearer

Consonants

b	is voiceless, almost like the p in copy
d	is voiceless as the t in city
g	is voiceless as the ck in ticket
k, p and t	are stronger and longer than the voiceless g, b, and d
h	is the same as in English, but less aspirated
j	like y in you
l	as in lily
m	is the same as in English, but shorter
n	as in English
r	is trilled
s	is voiceless and weaker than the English s

| v | as in English |
| z | as the s in was |

USEFUL WORDS AND EXPRESSIONS
Greetings and basic communication

hello	*tere*	When?	*Millal?*
good morning	*tere hommikust*	Where (is)?	*Kus (on)?*
good evening	*tere õhtut*	Excuse me, please	*Vabandage, palun*
good night	*head ööd*	Help me, please	*Aidake, palun*
yes	*jah*	More slowly, please	*Aeglasemalt, palun*
no	*ei*	Repeat it, please	*Korrake, palun*
please	*palun*	Write it down, please	*Kirjutage see üles,*
thank you	*tänan*		*palun*
less	*vähem*	I do not understand	*Ma ei saa aru*
a little (more)	*(natuke) rohkem*	I do not want	*Ma ei taha*
enough	*küllalt, aitab*	It is (too) late	*See on (liiga) hilja*
now (later)	*praegu (hiljem)*	It is bad	*See on halb*
How long?	*Kui kaua?*	It is good	*See on hea*
How much (is it)?	*Kui palju*	Silence, please	*Vaikust, palun*
	(see maksab)?	Wait	*Oodake*

Days

Monday	*esmaspäev*	Saturday	*laupäev*
Tuesday	*teisipäev*	Sunday	*pühapäev*
Wednesday	*kolmapäev*	today	*täna*
Thursday	*neljapäev*	yesterday	*eile*
Friday	*reede*	tomorrow	*homme*

Numbers

1	*üks*	8	*kaheksa*
2	*kaks*	9	*üheksa*
3	*kolm*	10	*kümme*
4	*neli*	11	*üksteist*
5	*viis*	12	*kaksteist*
6	*kuus*	20	*kakskümmend*
7	*seitse*	100	*sada*

Signs

No parking	*Parkimine*	Exit	*Väljapääs*
	keelatud	Emergency exit	*Tagavaraväljapääs*
Speed limit	*Kiiruspiirang*	Open	*Avatud*
Entrance	*Sissepääs*	Closed	*Suletud*
No entry	*Mitte siseneda*	Toilet	*WC*

Travelling

Call a taxi please	*Palun kutsuge*	My luggage is	*Minu pagas on*
	takso	missing	*kadunud*
Call an ambulance	*Kutsuge kiirabi*	passport	*pass*
I have lost my way	*Olen eksinud*	valid visa	*kehtiv viisa*
My car has broken	*Mul läks auto*	customs,	*toll, tollimaks*
down	*katki*	customs duty	

baggage room	pagasiruum	traffic accident	liiklusõnnetus
airport	lennujaam	traffic police	liikluspolitseinik
bus stop	bussipeatus	back	tagasi
coach terminal	bussijaam	forward	edasi
ferry port	reisisadam	straight ahead	otse
railway station	raudteejaam	to the north	põhja suunas
(city) centre	(kesklinn) keskus	to the south	lõuna suunas
street, square	tänav, väljak	to the east	ida suunas
traffic lights	valgusfoor	to the west	lääne suunas
car repair	autoparandus	to the left	vasakule
driving licence	juhiluba	to the right	paremale

Money

credit card	krediitkaart	free of charge	tasuta
currency exchange	rahavahetus	in cash	sularahas
exchange rate	vahetuskurss		

Accommodation

vacant room	vaba tuba	an extra bed	lisavoodi
with bath (shower)	vanniga (dushiga)	hot and cold water	soe ja külm vesi
with private toilet	oma tualettruumiga	kitchen facilities	köögi kasutamine
		Is there a lift?	Kas teil lift on?
at the front	tänava poole	Please clean this	Palun see puhastada
at the back	hoovi poole		
on a lower floor	madalamal korrusel	Please wash this	Palun see pesta
		The voltage is 220	Elektripinge on 220
reduction for children	allahindlus lastele		

Restaurants and meals

beer	õlu	brown/white bread	leib/sai
coffee (with milk)	kohv (piimaga)	fried fish	praetud kala
drinking water	joogivesi	green salad	roheline salat
juice	mahl	mutton/lamb	lambaliha/talleliha
milk	piim	roast chicken	kanapraad
mineral water	mineraalvesi	roast pork	seapraad
wine (red, white)	vein (punane, valge)	roast turkey	kalkunipraad
		salt	sool
wine list	veinikaart	seafood	mereannid
Estonian cuisine	eesti kook	sugar	suhkur
beefsteak	biifsteek	veal	loomaliha
boiled/oven-baked potatoes	keedetud/ahjus küpsetatud kartulid	vegetable soup	köögiviljasupp
		vegetarian dishes	taimetoidud

Appendix 2

FURTHER INFORMATION

BOOKSHOPS There is no specialist bookseller for new books on the Baltic states in Britain or North America. In Britain, **Stanfords** stock a wide range of guidebooks, phrasebooks and maps as well as more general background reads on the area (*29 Corn St, Bristol BS1 1HT;* ◀*0117 929 9966 & 12–14 Long Acre, London WC2E 9LP;* ◀ *020 7836 1321; www.stanfords.co.uk*). **Daunt Books** (*83–84 Marylebone High St, London W1U 4QW;* ◀*020 7224 2295; www.dauntbooks.co.uk*) has an extensive Baltic section, including political histories and fiction set in the area.

Searching under 'Estonia' on the website www.abebooks.co.uk will offer a wide choice of secondhand books.

In Tallinn, the bookshop with the widest stock in English, both of current books and secondhand ones, is **Raamatukoi** at Harju 1, which is conveniently situated in the town centre close to St Nicholas Church and Town Hall Square, but they stay closed on Sundays and over national holidays. There are several other specialist secondhand bookshops in Tallinn, which are listed in *Tallinn In Your Pocket*, including **Juhan Hammer** (*Roosikrantsi 6;* ◀*644 2633*), which has a website with the appropriate address of www.oldbooks.ee. The home page apologises for his 'pidgin Englis' but the site gives a full list of his stock and prices. An alternative is **Slothrop's** (*Pikk 34; www.slothrops.ee*), which is a good source for secondhand English-language books on all topics (see advert on page 49). A wide range of material was published in English during the Soviet period. Throughout Estonia, most bookshops have a secondhand section. Those in **Rahva Raamat** (*Pärnu mnt 10 in Tallinn*) and **Ülikooli Raamatupood** (The University Bookshop) (*Ülikooli 11 in Tartu*) are particularly extensive.

FURTHER READING

History Only one easily available book in English covers Estonia exclusively. Although titled *Estonia: Return to Independence*, Rein Taagepera's book in fact covers all of Estonia's recorded history. The author was eight years old when he left the country but writes with an accessible warm style unusual in the diaspora. The first sentence of the book consists only of two dramatic words, 'Estonia exists'; whilst this is now obvious, for 50 years the chances of being able to write such a sentence were very remote. The same author, in conjunction with Romuald Misiunas, has also written *The Baltic States: Years of Dependence 1940–1990*, a more detailed study of the German and Soviet occupations.

The standard book on the pre-war Baltics is *The Baltic States: The Years of Independence* by Georg von Rauch. Covering the entire 20th century is *The Baltic Nations and Europe* by John Hiden and Patrick Salmon. The first edition in 1991 accurately predicted independence and the 1994 edition includes an update to cover it. Specifically dealing with the establishment of the Baltic countries after World War I is *Makers of the Modern World: Piip, Meierovics and Voldemaras* by Charlotte Alston. These were the three foreign ministers involved in the Versailles negotiations. This book is part of a large series on politicians active at that time which has been published by Haus from 2010 onwards. In 2013 it was finally possible for Western readers to have access to details on fighting in World War II. Prit Buttar's *Between Giants* shows how easily the Germans drove Soviet forces out of Estonia in 1941 and how tough their resistance was in 1944.

Covering the whole of Estonian history, going back to prehistoric times, but particularly thorough on the Soviet period, is *Estonia and the Estonians* by Toivo Raun, which was published in 2001. Clare Thomson had the good fortune to travel extensively in the three Baltic states in the run-up to their independence in August 1991 and her *Singing Revolution*, published in early 1992, describes the hopes and fears of many of the inhabitants at that time.

A very moving account of the late 1980s and early 1990s is *The Baltic Revolution* by Anatol Lieven, which has sadly not been updated since 1994 but which remains the standard book covering that era in the three Baltic states. *A History of Twentieth-Century Russia* by Robert Service details tsarist, Soviet and Russian involvement in Estonia. Covering all the attempts to hinder and then to overthrow the Bolsheviks in 1917–20, much of which took place in Estonia, is Robert Service's *Spies and Commissars*. Equally cloak and dagger, but very contemporary is Edward Lucas's *Deception, Spies, Lies and How Russia Dupes the West*. Again much of the action takes place in Estonia.

Baltic Approaches by Peter Unwin has vivid descriptions of contemporary town and country life in Estonia and its neighbours, together with historical background. It is an excellent introduction for those visiting several countries around the Baltic. A similarly absorbing book is *Fifty Years of Europe: An Album* by Jan Morris, which has several vignettes of Estonia and its Baltic neighbours. A fully updated edition of *Racundra's First Cruise* by Arthur Ransome, edited by Brian Hammett, was published in 2003 to coincide with the 80th anniversary of this trip. The book describes the Estonian coast and islands in the early 1920s. There are detailed descriptions of the Estonian islands he visited, as well as of the mainland ports, together with contemporary photographs alongside those Ransome took then. A biography of Ransome, *The Last Englishman* by Roland Chambers, covers his complex life of which Estonia was only a small, but crucial part.

War in the Woods, written by Mart Laar in 1992, shortly before he became prime minister of Estonia, details the guerrilla struggle waged in the late 1940s against the Soviet authorities. *Sentence Siberia: A Story of Survival* by Ann Lehtmets is literally that. She describes her arrest in 1941 and her detention in Siberia until 1957 when she was allowed first to return to Estonia and then to join relatives in Australia. *An Estonian Childhood* by Tania Alexander describes growing up there during the 20 years of independence after World War I. A biography of her mother, Moura, by Nina Berberova, was published in English in 2006 and makes a good parallel read. Much of this is also set in Janeda, the family estate in Estonia, after World War I. Leaping to the present day, *To the Baltic with Bob* by Griff Rhys Jones quite rightly became a bestseller in 2004 as a very amusing account of a sailing trip that includes Estonia.

To readers of French can be recommended *L'Estonie* by Suzanne Champonnois, published by Karthala, which is an excellent general history of the country.

It is encouraging that Western publishers now feel the need to introduce Baltic cooking. *The Food and Cookery of Estonia, Latvia and Lithuania*, by John Silvena, is the result.

A number of secondhand books on Estonia are worth seeking out and copies of the following are not too difficult to find. Ronald Seth's *Baltic Corner: Travels in Estonia* published in 1938 describes Tallinn, Saaremaa and Narva, as well as Petseri Monastery which is now under Russian administration. *Man and Boy* by Sir Stephen Tallents covers British military involvement in the Baltics at the end of World War I and his attempts to arbitrate a fair border between Estonia and Latvia. *The New Baltic States* written by Owen Rutter in 1925 is a very detailed travelogue covering the three countries. The Estonian section concentrates on Tallinn and Tartu. *Picturesque Estonia* by Hanno Kompus published originally in 1938 but reprinted and updated in Stockholm in 1950, does not, despite its title, have very many pictures but the text is a moving introduction to Estonia as tourists found it just before World War II. *The Baltic States* published in 1938 by the Oxford University Press for the Royal Institute of International Affairs covers the political and economic development of Estonia from 1918 and includes detailed statistics. *Estonia: A Reference Book* by Villbald Raud and published in 1953 covers similar ground with additional material on the early Soviet period.

Many books published in English during the Soviet period are still sold in Estonia, some at very low prices as booksellers want to get rid of them, others at very high prices as their scarcity value becomes appreciated. Whilst the political commentaries in them will now be seen as offensive in Estonia, the confidence and sometimes arrogance of Soviet writers, even in the late 1980s, contrasts with the constant worries of Estonian ones. Brochures such as *Monuments and Decorative Sculpture of Tallinn* published in 1987 will soon be the only memory of the massive statues of Soviet heroes that used to dominate Tallinn's squares. *The Architecture of Tallinn*, published in the same year, serves as a similar record of the housing estates, sports stadia and government buildings that date from the 1960s and 1970s. Two books from the 1970s simply titled *Haapsalu* and *Viljandi* have enticing text in English from a time when there was no chance whatsoever of English-speaking visitors being allowed into either city. *The History of Tartu University 1632–1982* by Karl Siilivask has much of interest on the 19th century after the university was reopened in 1802. *The History of the Estonian SSR* by Juhan Kahk and Karl Siilivask is useful for the Soviet interpretation of Estonian history from the Middle Ages onwards. Published in 1985, it just misses the subtleties of perestroika, except on its final page, which quotes a speech from Mikhail Gorbachev in which he looked forward to 'an invigoration of the entire system of political and social institutions'. *Soviet Estonia* by V Druzhnin in 1953 is written with a fervour that would later only be associated with North Korea. After only eight years of Soviet rule his readers are assured that Estonians 'now liberated from slavery, are working with joy and look confidently forward to the future'.

Biography Harvill Press has published *Winter Sea*, an autobiography by Alan Ross, much of which is set in Tallinn. *Arvo Pärt in Conversation* describes the life of Estonia's most famous composer.

Fiction Four books by the 20th-century Estonian writer Jaan Kross have been published in English by Harvill Press. They are *The Czar's Madman*, set in the early 19th century; *Professor Martens' Departure*, set in the late 19th century; and then *The Conspiracy & Other Stories* and *Treading Air*, both published since independence so able to draw on Kross's grim personal experiences. In 2007, Norvik Press published *The Beauty of History* by Viivi Luik, which was written in 1991, but set in 1968.

In 2010 we finally saw a translation of a novel by Estonia's most famous writer in the 1930s, A H Tammsaare, *Misadventures of the New Satan*.

Sophie Oksanen's *Purge*, a novel set in two parts in Estonia, firstly in the early days of the Soviet occupation and then shortly after its end, gave her instant worldwide fame when the book appeared in English in 2010. A recent novel, covering an earlier period over both world wars, is *Forest Brothers* by Geraint Roberts, which links British naval activity with Estonia. More modern is *Between Each Breath* by Adam Thorpe, set in Hampstead, north London, and Saaremaa.

As most books on this reading list are inevitably sombre in tone, it is nice to be able to recommend a very light-hearted read, *Foreign Parts* by Sarah Grazebrook, which is based on an imaginary British theatre group travelling around Estonia.

Estonian publications Although Estonian publishers now produce many books in English, few of these are available abroad but they can be bought without difficulty on arrival. Prices are much lower than for comparable books in western Europe. *History of Estonia* by Mati Laur and Ago Pajur is comprehensive and well illustrated both with photographs and maps. The eight-page chronology is helpful for reference but, amazingly, the book has no index or bibliography. Ann Tenno's *Pictures of Estonia* is without doubt the best souvenir to bring home. Many of the pictures are taken from the air and all four seasons are well represented. *Uks Päev Rakveres/One Day in Rakvere* is the result of 13 photographers all descending unannounced on this small town on 1 July 1999. On the whole, they were welcomed by those who noticed them, but in some of the pictures, the occasional frown, or the lack of any expression at all, adds great authenticity to the book. Madli Puhvel's *Symbol of Dawn* is a biography of Estonia's most famous poetess, Lydia Koidula, but the book is also an introduction to both town and country life in the late 19th century. Ants Hein's *Ghost Manors of Estonia* charts the sad history of many manor houses abandoned by the Baltic Germans in the 1920s but the book is made hard to use for foreigners by the lack of an index and a map showing the location of the buildings described. In contrast *Manor Houses of Estonia* by Ann Tenno and Juhan Maiste covers both restored and unrestored buildings. *Birds of Estonia* by E Leibak is the definitive work for ornithologists. Similarly definitive is *Lake Peipsi: Flora and Fauna* by Ervin Pihu which also covers birds, fish and reptiles. *Cross and Iron* by Eerik Kouts and Heinz Valk describes burial crosses to be seen in rural cemeteries throughout the country. *The Guide to Tallinn 1935 and 1985* by Einar Sanden, which was published abroad, reprints a 1935 text and adds a harrowing commentary on Tallinn in 1985. Prospective tourists are given 17 embarrassing questions on the Soviet occupation with which to taunt their Intourist guides. A professor at Tartu University, Heinart Sillastu, in his *Through Rose-Coloured Glasses* explains how he was able to travel abroad in Soviet times, but also with stringent controls before departure and during the tour.

The Churches on the Island of Saaremaa by Kaur Alttoa will hopefully be a model for other Estonian travel writers to follow. The text is clear, the photographs extensive and the map is up to date. There is surprisingly no serious guidebook to Tallinn but the booklet *Architectural and Art Monuments in Tallinn* by Sulev Maevali has considerable detail on all the main churches in the Old Town. Most titles available cover just a single building or a single theme. In this later category two recent titles stand out: *20th Century Architecture in Tallinn* by Karin Hallas and *Walking Tours of Tallinn* by Karen Jagodin. *Functionalism in Estonia* by Mart Kalm covers this architectural trend of the early 20th century but the book will certainly also interest the general reader as it is well illustrated. Clear maps show the routes to buildings the casual tourist would not otherwise find.

I am happy to welcome the appearance of several guidebooks with more detail than this one could ever provide. Indrek Rohtmets courageously ignores Tallinn and Tartu in his *Cultural Guide to Estonia* to concentrate on all the churches, houses and monuments elsewhere, many of which would not even be known to local people. I have to declare an interest in Malle Salupere's *Millenary Tartu* as I edited the English-language edition. Gastronomy is not a cookbook topic one used to associate with Estonia but the appearance of *The Estonian Gourmet* by Siiri Kirikal in 2006 perhaps shows how wrong this preconception was.

German-language books Railway enthusiasts for the area have to read German, as the only, but definitive, book on this topic is *Eisenbahnen im Baltikum* by Herman Hesselink.

Readers of German are spoilt for choice in all other fields. The Baltic Germans wrote massive works whilst in Estonia and the next generations have continued the tradition from abroad. Since the restoration of independence many German scholars have worked in Estonia so art, architecture and natural history have been extensively covered. Regular catalogues for new and secondhand books on the Baltics and also for reprints are produced by Harro v Hirschheydt (*Neue Wiesen 6, D 30900 Wedemark-Elze;* \+49 5130 36758; e *contact@hirschheydt-online.de; www. hirschheydt-online.de*). The site www.amazon.de lists all current books on Estonia under 'Estland' and all instructions for ordering can be downloaded in English.

Language *The Estonian Dictionary and Phrasebook* by Ksenia Benyukh is sufficiently comprehensive for anyone brave enough to open their mouth in Estonian. For the dedicated student, the Routledge *Colloquial Estonian* book by Christopher Moseley and the accompanying audio course is essential. *Teach Yourself Estonian* by Mare Kitsnik and Leelo Kingisepp was published in 2008.

Maps and atlases At the time of writing, there are no good detailed maps of Estonia published abroad. However, Stanfords sell many of those listed below at their British shops. The *Eesti Teedeatlas* (Estonian Road Atlas) published by Regio is updated every year and is essential for tourists planning to hire a car, as many smaller roads in the countryside are not signposted. The text, which includes a summary of Estonian driving regulations, is translated into English and it also has town plans. The most recent edition was published in July 2013. Regio also publish regional maps, town plans and reprints of historical town plans from the 19th century and the previous independence period. Their head office is at Riia 24, Tartu 51010 (738 7300; e *regio@regio.ee; www.regio.ee*).

The *Eesti Linnuatlas* (Estonian Bird Atlas) has detailed maps and lists with a summary of birdwatching possibilities in English. Sailors will find invaluable *Harbours of the Baltic States* by Fay and Graham Cattell, which is updated every year on the basis of their visits to the harbours covered. It provides all the detailed information needed by yachtsmen visiting the three Baltic countries. It is available from the Cruising Association (*www.cruising.org.uk*).

Journals The British–Estonian Association (BEST) has a regular journal *Lennuk* which is sent to members. A selection of articles from Lennuk together with other information on Estonia is on the BEST website (*www.britishestonianassociation. co.uk*). Membership forms for BEST can be downloaded from this site, which is a good source of information on meetings about Estonia taking place in Britain.

Tourist information The Estonian Tourist Board is at www.visitestonia.com and their site should be the first port of call for any visitor. It has maps, practical information and leads to the websites of all their local tourist offices. More general information on any particular town can be found by keying in the town name followed by the Estonian two-letter code 'ee'. Most, but not all, of these sites are in English. Therefore, to reach Tartu, the address is www.tartu.ee. To cover the county of Tartu, rather than just the town, the address is www.tartumaa.ee. (The suffix 'maa' is the Estonian for 'county'.)

Culture The most wide-ranging cultural site is that of the Estonian Institute, which provides all its factsheets on www.einst.ee. This site also has the complete contents of the magazines *Estonian Art* and *ELM* (Estonian Literary Magazine), particularly useful as so few books cover these topics and hard copies of these magazines are hard to find in Estonian shops. Estonian embassies stock copies but they can now all be read on the institute's website.

The Tallinn concert calendar is at www.concert.ee/eng/index.html. Tartu University has a general site on its history at www.ut.ee and details of recent archaeological excavations are on the site of the Estonian Inspectorate of Antiquities, www.muinas.ee.

The *In Your Pocket* website (*www.inyourpocket.com*) and its local publications cover events in Tallinn, Tartu and Pärnu. Irreverence is guaranteed in every issue.

Red tape The Ministry of Foreign Affairs can be found at www.vm.ee/eng. This site gives full details of visa regulations, Estonian embassies and consulates and its news bulletins are a useful source on recent news from Estonia. Most Estonian embassies have their own sites. That for the Washington embassy is www.estemb.org and for the London embassy is www.estonia.gov.uk. Customs regulations are on www.customs.ee.

Appendix 2   FURTHER INFORMATION

A2

40 Years of Pioneering Publishing

Uganda 7
Philip Briggs
with Andrew Roberts

Guyana 2
Kirk Smock

52 Wildlife Weekends
A YEAR OF BRITISH WILDLIFE-WATCHING BREAKS
James Lowen

World War I Battlefields
A Travel Guide to the Western Front
Sites • Museums • Memorials

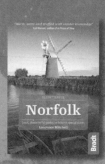
Norfolk
Laurence Mitchell

Madagascar Wildlife 4
Daniel Austin
Nick Garbutt

savannah diaries
brian jackman

PERU Highlights
Alexander Stewart

In 1974, Hilary Bradt took a road less travelled and published her first travel guide, written whilst floating down the Amazon.

40 years on and a string of awards later, Bradt has a list of 200 titles, including travel literature, Slow Travel guides and wildlife guides. And our pioneering spirit remains as strong as ever – we're happy to say there are still plenty of roads less travelled to explore!

BACKPACKING ALONG ANCIENT WAYS
IN PERU AND BOLIVIA

HILARY AND GEORGE BRADT

TRAVEL PIONEERS
FOR OVER 40 YEARS
40

Bradt ...take the road less travelled

Index

Page numbers in **bold** indicate main entries; those in *italics* indicate maps.

INDEX OF ADVERTISERS